The Rowman & Littlefield Handbook of Policing, Communication, and Society

The Rowman & Littlefield Handbook Series

This contemporary series of academic handbooks provides an authoritative guide to relevant and emerging topics across the humanities and social sciences. To encourage greater dialogue across disciplines, this series engages high-quality, original, and multidisciplinary research on topics, themes, and key debates in academia today.

- Each handbook draws together newly commissioned work to provide a comprehensive benchmark for a field or subdiscipline.
- The individual handbooks include an international team of contributors, with valuable expertise, knowledge, and perspective in their fields.
- Handbooks in this series correspond to the latest topics on courses around the world.

Each Handbook is available for purchase in both print and digital formats. For more information, see www.rowman.com.

The Rowman & Littlefield Handbook of Christianity in the Middle East
    Edited by Mark A. Lamport and Mitri Raheb
The Rowman & Littlefield Handbook of Media Management and Business
    Edited by L. Meghan Mahoney and Tang Tang
The Rowman & Littlefield Handbook of Policing, Communication, and Society
    Edited by Howard Giles, Edward R. Maguire, and Shawn L. Hill

The Rowman & Littlefield Handbook of Policing, Communication, and Society

Edited by HOWARD GILES,
EDWARD R. MAGUIRE, and SHAWN L. HILL

Foreword by
DARREL W. STEPHENS

ROWMAN & LITTLEFIELD
Lanham • Boulder • New York • London

Published by Rowman & Littlefield
An imprint of The Rowman & Littlefield Publishing Group, Inc.
4501 Forbes Boulevard, Suite 200, Lanham, Maryland 20706
www.rowman.com

6 Tinworth Street, London SE11 5AL, United Kingdom

Copyright © 2021 by The Rowman & Littlefield Publishing Group, Inc.

All rights reserved. No part of this book may be reproduced in any form or by any electronic or mechanical means, including information storage and retrieval systems, without written permission from the publisher, except by a reviewer who may quote passages in a review.

British Library Cataloguing in Publication Information Available

Library of Congress Cataloging-in-Publication Data
Names: Giles, Howard, 1946– editor.
Title: The Handbook of policing, communication, and society : an interdisciplinary approach / edited by Howard Giles, Edward R. Maguire, and Shawn Hill.
Description: Lanham : Rowman & Littlefield, 2021. | Series: The Rowman & Littlefield handbook series | Includes bibliographical references and index. | Summary: "The Rowman & Littlefield Handbook of Policing, Communication, and Society brings together well-regarded academics and experienced practitioners to explore how communication intersects with policing in areas such as cop-culture, race and ethnicity, terrorism and hate crimes, social media, police reform, crowd violence, and many more"— Provided by publisher.
Identifiers: LCCN 2020053039 (print) | LCCN 2020053040 (ebook) | ISBN 9781538132890 (cloth) | ISBN 9781538132890 (epub)
Subjects: LCSH: Police. | Police ethics. | Police-community relations. | Criminal justice, Administration of.
Classification: LCC HV7921 .H34 2021 (print) | LCC HV7921 (ebook) | DDC 363.2/3—dc23
LC record available at https://lccn.loc.gov/2020053039
LC ebook record available at https://lccn.loc.gov/2020053040

*We dedicate this book to Jane, Betty, and Alexis,
for their love, support, and patience*

Contents

Foreword by Darrel W. Stephens — ix

Introduction: Policing through the Lens of Intergroup Communication, by Howard Giles, Edward R. Maguire, and Shawn L. Hill — 1

SECTION I • COMMUNICATING *WITHIN* POLICE-RELEVANT AGENCIES

1 Police Culture: Us versus Them Communication, by *Shawn L. Hill and Howard Giles* — 17

2 Doing Organizational Justice: The Role of Police Manager Communication, by *Scott Wolfe* — 35

3 The Critical Role of Communication in the Recruitment of Police Officers, by *Charlie Scheer and Jeremy M. Wilson* — 47

4 Interagency Communication: Homicide Investigations, by *Joseph B. Kuhns and Shannon Messer* — 57

SECTION II • POLICE COMMUNICATION *WITH* DIVERSE COMMUNITIES

5 Race, Policing, and Communication: Old Problems, Twenty-First-Century Struggles, by *Travis Dixon, Marisa A. Smith, and Kristopher R. Weeks* — 75

6 Intergroup Biases: Policing and Gender, by *Cara E. Rabe-Hemp and Amie M. Schuck* — 91

7 Policing and LGBTQ+ Communities, by *Stephen Owen* — 105

8 Policing Muslim Communities: The Importance of Procedural Justice in Communication and Engagement Activities, by *Kristina Murphy* — 123

9 Law Enforcement Partnerships: Changing Communication Skills and Interventions in Response to People in Crisis, by *Ellen Scrivner* — 135

SECTION III · COMMUNICATING *ABOUT* POLICING TO AND FROM THE COMMUNITY

10 The Role of Communication Reform in Community Policing, by *Edward R. Maguire* — 153

11 Speaking Truth from Power through Strategic Police Communication, by *Michael S. Scott* — 173

12 The Role of The Police in Fostering Community Resilience: A Communication Perspective, by *J. Brian Houston, Chandrika C. Collins, and Scott E. Branton* — 187

13 "I See You": The Mediation of Complaints Can Build Understanding and Trust, by *Bernard K. Melekian* — 201

14 The Media and Our Perceptions of the Police, by *Matea Mustafaj and Jan Van den Bulck* — 213

15 Social Media and Intergroup Encounters with "Cops": Biased Samples, Echo Chambers, and Research Opportunities, by *Joseph B. Walther* — 229

16 Newsworthiness of Police: Changes In Print Media Coverage of Police Post-Ferguson, by *David H. F. Tyler and Edward R. Maguire* — 245

SECTION IV · COMMUNICATION DYNAMICS *RELATED TO* SPECIFIC TYPES OF CRIMES AND INCIDENTS

17 Language in Traffic Stop Interactions: Patterns in Language Use and Recommendations for Fostering Trust and Compliance, by *Belén Lowrey-Kinberg* — 263

18 Understanding the Communication Dynamics Inherent to Police Hostage and Crisis Negotiation, by *Amy R. Grubb* — 275

19 Improving Law Enforcement Responses to Gender-Based Violence: Domestic and International Perspectives, by *Caroline Bettinger-López and Tamar Ezer* — 297

20 Direct Communication in Focused Deterrence, by *David M. Kennedy* — 313

21 Policing Hate Crimes and Terrorism in the Digital Age, by *Brian Blakemore* — 337

22 Crowd Theory, Communication, and Policing, by *Clifford Stott, Matthew Radburn, and Leanne Savigar-Shaw* — 355

Conclusion: New Directions in Policing and Intergroup Communication, by *Howard Giles, Shawn L. Hill, Edward R. Maguire, and Daniel Angus* — 371

INDEX — 391
ABOUT THE CONTRIBUTORS — 407

Foreword

Darrel W. Stephens

Policing in America is very different today from what it was in the late 1960s when the 1967 President's Commission on Law Enforcement and the Administration of Justice made over two hundred recommendations for improving the entire criminal justice system. About half of the recommendations were directed at the police. The commission called for empirical research, higher standards for officers, diversity in the workforce, improved relationships with the community, a national emergency number, better training, and many other changes aimed at improving policing.

The police have changed. Even in light of recent tragedies, which will spark a reexamination of many parts of the profession, they are more diverse, better educated, and better equipped with modern technology; they have also become more evidence based and have improved relationships through initiatives like community- and problem-oriented policing. Despite the continuous change in policing over the past fifty years, the police continue to face enormous challenges as the pace of change in the world around them accelerates. The massive change in technology presents the police with great opportunities and an entirely new level of challenges. One of the most significant challenges for the police is communication.

The communications challenge for the police is formidable, particularly in large diverse communities. Internal communications are problematic because there is little opportunity for face-to-face contact—30 to 40 percent of the workforce in a 24/7 environment is not at work at any given time. Messages must be delivered and explained by supervisors and command personnel who may not have the same point of view as the chief. External communications are complicated by the endless options for news and information and the speed with which bad news travels. Use of the traditional news media outlets (newspapers and television) is an important option for the police, but it must be understood that their audiences are shrinking. Cable news and a wide variety of sources of information on the Internet, including social media, are significant sources of news and information for the public.

Recognizing the critical importance of communications in policing, Giles, Maguire, and Hill have assembled an impressive cadre of contributors (including themselves) to create the book they have coedited. *The Rowman & Littlefield Handbook of Policing,*

Communication, and Society is the most comprehensive volume available today that addresses communication in all aspects of policing—and the timing couldn't be more relevant. The book begins with an examination of the all-important issue of police culture. The old adage "culture eats policy for lunch" is certainly applicable to the world of policing, so the chapter provides a solid underpinning for the rest of the book.

A chapter on community policing looks at its impact on internal and external communications. This is a critically important topic in engaging officers and the community on the best approaches to creating and maintaining safe neighborhoods. The book also examines equally important topics such as realistic expectations of the police, race, bias, the media, crisis intervention, and many other critical topics.

Policing, Communication, and Society contains twenty-two chapters of important material that will serve as a valuable tool to inform practitioners at all levels of policing as well as the academic community—in many respects it could be used as a desk reference.

I have been involved in policing and local government for over fifty years. I served as a police officer, police chief for twenty-plus years of that time in four different cities, a city administrator, chief's association executive director, and a faculty member at Johns Hopkins University. In all of those roles, I would have found *Policing, Communication, and Society* a very helpful source of information to deal with the challenges I have encountered along the way.

My congratulations on an exceptional contribution to the policing literature.

Policicing through the Lens of Intergroup Communication

Howard Giles, Edward R. Maguire, and Shawn L. Hill

This book takes a valued and uniquely *interdisciplinary* perspective, by bringing together research and theory in criminology, psychology, and communication, as well as pragmatic insights from scholarly practitioners experienced in the policing world (see Engel and Whalen 2010; Glaser and Charbonneau 2018). Participating in this handbook are some of the most well-regarded academics and innovative and experienced practitioners in their respective fields, exploring topics that are impacting law enforcement and society in significant ways that enhance its scientific base (see Denault et al. 2020). This book examines how communication intersects with policing in areas such as cop culture, race and ethnicity, terrorism and hate crimes, social media, police reform, procedural justice, crowd violence, and police complaints, to name a few. Within these arenas, it also provides palpable examples of power struggles, which can be intergroup in nature (see chapter 1).

An intergroup interaction involves people communicating with one another based on their group memberships (e.g., "the police" and "those policed") rather than their own personal idiosyncrasies (Dragojevic and Giles 2014). A person would be considered communicating with another "ingroup" member when they identify *similar* and *favorable* characteristics or qualities of the other person, which allows them to differentiate themselves favorably from the "outgroup," or people who do not share what they perceive as favorable characteristics (Tajfel 1974). Social identity theorists (e.g., Tajfel and Turner 1986) would posit that, even beyond power struggles, merely categorizing someone as a member of a relevant and contrasting outgroup—however minimal these differences might be—is likely to foster discriminatory beliefs and actions toward them while, at the same time, solidifying positive attitudes toward other ingroup members, including the enhancement of self-esteem. This exploration of the evolving intergroup relationship between police officers and the public provides a platform to explore practical and theoretical pursuits.

Recently, there has been an outpouring of other handbooks on policing; yet while potent in treatises years ago (Thompson and Jenkins 1983; Womack and Finley 1986), the critical roles of *communication* phenomena and processes in understanding policing practices have received only sporadic attention.[1] This is surprising considering the emphasis on reducing police use of force and the critical role of various communication and de-escalation strategies in police training curricula and police reform more generally (Los Angeles Police Department 2016; PERF 2016; Shipley 2019; Use of Force Reporting 2019). Furthermore, such a perspective has laid fallow since the last volume devoted to this subject matter nearly twenty years ago (Giles 2002). Even when research does address communication issues in policing, it has not embraced much of an *intergroup communication* stance (see Molloy and Giles 2002), one we see as vital to understanding policing in many of its facets. In essence, the scholarly literature on intergroup communication has explored how construing oneself and others in the same encounter—primarily in terms of their memberships in contrasting social groups (e.g., races, genders, religions, nationalities, occupations, etc.)—can affect the nature and content of the communication between them (see Giles 2012; Giles and Harwood 2018; Giles and Maass 2016). Intergroup communication (see chapter 1)—an integral feature of much of this volume—is especially salient for policing in that most of the contacts between police officers and the public constitute intergroup encounters (see Boivin, Faubert, Gendron, and Poulin 2018).

This book is an expansive endeavor designed to fill much of the above void—and one that is timely for at least three reasons. First, significant societal changes (such as digital technology, including cell phones and social media) have greatly influenced the process of policing (Cutting Edge Technology 2019; Innovations in Smart Policing 2020) and public perceptions of the police (see chapters 15 and 21). Relatedly, such changes have impacted the nature of the critical roles of leadership (e.g., Pfeifer 2020) within law enforcement organizations with, ideally, internal messaging promoting officers' sense of autonomy and control (see Gillet, Becker, Lafrenière, Hart, and Fourquereau 2017; Otis and Pelletier 2005), including the necessity for forging meaningful relationships with the media (Media Relations 2019).

Second, in the last few years, the United States has witnessed the resurrection of well-publicized events portraying police as perpetrators of racial violence (Campbell, Nix, and Maguire 2018; Maguire, Nix, and Campbell 2017; Sherman 2020). In tandem, there has been a reported decline in trust in law enforcement among adolescents during this time (Fine, Kan, and Cauffman 2019). Third, there have been attempts by government (e.g., as evident in California's 2019 Stephon Clark's Law) and police-related institutions, such as the International Association of Chiefs of Police and the Police Executive Research Forum, to proactively encourage change and attempt to improve police-community relationships (see Hollywood, Goodison, Woods, Vermeer, and Jackson 2019; President's Task Force on 21st Century Policing 2015; Primicerio and Normore 2018) and collaborations (Crime Prevention Communities 2019).

After a welcome, informative, and supportive foreword by Stephens, in this introduction, we begin by examining recent high-profile events that highlight tensions between police and the communities they serve, affording attention to one of the most recent of these (the killing of George Floyd in Minnesota, 2020) in several chapters. Much talk, in general, these days in American society and politics (and elsewhere) revolves around heated notions of "us" versus "them" (see Kienzle and Soliz 2017; Maass, Arcuri, and Suitner 2014; see chapter 1). Indeed, officers' appearance (e.g., hair style),[2] uniform, armament and vehicles can make them appear militaristic to the public as an outgroup, further exemplifying the enormous power differential and legal ability to use lethal force (Balko 2013; Kraska and Kappeler 1997). Other intergroup dynamics such as race, ethnicity, gender, and sexual orientation lead to further differences between police officers and the people they encounter on the job, let alone the disparity in diversity, albeit changing, found within many police departments (see Clinkinbeard and Rief 2020; House 2018). Finally, we briefly outline the chapters in this book and summarize their contributions to our understanding of policing, communication, and society.

RECENT INTERGROUP TENSIONS AS A BACKDROP TO THIS VOLUME

On August 9, 2014, Darren Wilson, a white police officer, fatally shot an unarmed young African American man, Michael Brown, in Ferguson, Missouri (see DOJ Report 2015; Johnson 2018). In the months following the shooting, a hailstorm of media attention was devoted to the incident; protests and civil unrest occurred throughout the United States, and a contentious debate about the use of force by police officers ensued (see chapters 6, 16, and 17). Although the Bureau of Justice Statistics (2018) reports that only 2 percent of US residents who had contact with the police experienced threats of force or use of force, incidents such as this one induce many people to *feel* as though they are not uncommon (Bureau of Justice Statistics 2018) whereas given the number of contacts officers have with the public on a daily basis they are extremely uncommon. Yet why did this particular event ignite such enduring, impassioned reactions?

Simply put, this incident's cascading effect on Ferguson, and more generally the United States and nations across the globe (see chapter 16), is due to a clash of social categories: Michael Brown was an African American resident and Darren Wilson was a white police officer. The shooting of Michael Brown ignited long-standing tensions between police and African American residents in Ferguson. A later investigation by the US Department of Justice (DOJ 2015, 2) found that the Ferguson Police Department had engaged in "a pattern of unconstitutional policing" that harmed the community and undermined the perceived legitimacy of police among residents. Moreover, the investigation found that these issues were especially harmful for African American residents because the Ferguson Police Department had engaged in "intentional discrimination on the basis of race" (4). In addition to these local dynamics, the response to Michael Brown's death was also shaped by an emerging movement focusing on police treatment of marginalized community groups (especially minorities). Just twenty-three days earlier, a white New York City police officer attempted to arrest an African American man named Eric Garner for selling loose cigarettes and resisting arrest by applying a choke hold, which led to Garner's death. Both incidents facilitated the growth of Black Lives Matter (BLM), a powerful social movement focusing on racial injustice in the United States (Garcia and Sharif 2015).

In the weeks and months following the incident, individuals took to the streets in both peaceful and violent protests, allegedly chanting, "Hands up! Don't shoot!" This was a reference to Brown's alleged cry when detained by Wilson and a metaphor for protestors' opposition to police violence. Poignantly, the president of the International

Association of Chiefs of Police (IACP), Terrence Cunningham, apologized (on behalf of police) for the historic mistreatment of minorities by police, calling it a "dark side of our shared history," when addressing thousands of officers at the IACP Annual Conference on October 17, 2016. Some police union representatives criticized Cunningham's speech, noting that it could help to fuel anti-police sentiment in the United States (Mark 2016).

On the other side of the intergroup ledger, ABC News reported that a police officer was shot through the head as he sat in his patrol car on December 7, 2019, in Fayetteville, Arkansas. Wearing a uniform displaying his identity as a police officer was apparently his only "crime," and in some arenas, killing a cop earns one considerable prestige, especially in gang culture (see Decker and Pyrooz 2015). But when a police officer is murdered, other social and family identities attached to the human being wearing the uniform (e.g., son, husband, father, basketball fan, etc.) are also killed (see Violence against Police 2019). In April 2004, a police officer was killed in front of the Pomona courthouse. Chief James Lewis was reported as stating, "It's clear the motive was to kill a police officer, but not this specific police officer" (Gorman and Winton 2014).

Some suggest that in the aftermath of events in Ferguson, there is now a "War on Cops" (MacDonald 2016). Recent research finds no evidence to support this premise. Regardless of the measure of violence used—fatal assaults, nonfatal assaults with injury, or nonfatal assaults without injury—violence against police officers has not increased in recent years (Maguire et al. 2017; Shjarback and Maguire 2019). However, several high-profile ambushes of police officers in the line of duty have taken an understandable toll on the collective psyche of American police officers. In December 2014, a gunman shot and killed NYPD officers Rafael Ramos and Wenjian Liu as they sat in their patrol car in Brooklyn. In July 2016, a gunman shot fourteen police officers in Dallas during a Black Lives Matter protest, killing five of them and injuring nine. Later that same month, a gunman shot six police officers in Baton Rouge, killing three of them and injuring three. Evidence suggests that all three of these ambush-style shootings were acts of revenge against police for the recent killings of unarmed black men (Blinder 2017; Frosch and Molinski 2016; Zoroya and Hughes 2014). Thus, although there has not been a statistical increase in the number of American police officers killed or assaulted in the line of duty, there remains a strong perception among police officers of a war on cops (Kaste 2016; Nix, Wolfe, and Campbell 2018).

Not unrelatedly, FBI data reveal that there have been 277 active shooter incidents in the United States between 2000 and 2018, with 2,430 casualties (https://www.fbi.gov/about/partnerships/office-of-partner-engagement/active-shooter-incidents-graphics). Such incidents have devastating effects on first responders. Virginia Beach Police chief Jim Cervera claimed that police work naturally takes an emotional toll: "It's the death by 1,000 cuts. It's the water torture, drip by drip. It eventually has a toll on who you are as a person . . . to walk into a scene like this, it has an instantaneous effect on you. They're going to be forever changed" (see Hayes 2019). Officers are among the most vulnerable to taking their own lives compared to workers in other professions (Heyman, Dill, and Douglas 2018), with at least 167 officer suicides occurring in 2018. The number of police suicides is greater than the number of deaths that occur in the line of duty (for the roles of communication in organizational conversations about, and prevention of, suicides, see Myers 2020). Even when suicide does not occur, untreated exposure to trauma can exert a dramatic toll on officers' physical and mental health (Maguire, Somers, and Padilla 2020).

Clearly, these types of incidents we have just outlined are inherently *intergroup* and intercultural in nature (for a discussion of the distinctive histories and perspectives of these approaches, see Giles and Watson 2008). They reveal tensions between multiple, and sometimes overlapping, social identities: African American, Muslim, Hispanic, LGBTQ, and White, police and civilian, privileged and oppressed, white police and black police. In this book we draw on analyses and theories of intergroup relations and communication (along with other perspectives) that provide a deeper, more nuanced, perspective on these events and allied social movements.

In early 2020, the police worldwide faced a historic challenge in dealing with a global pandemic, COVID-19 (Law Enforcement and COVID-19 2020; see also, chapter 21). To preserve the social distancing guidelines recommended by public health authorities, police were forced to withdraw from the routine daily interactions with the public that define modern policing. The positive interpersonal policing practices that help to embrace the partnership essential to community policing and enhance public perceptions and legitimacy of police were significantly limited. Officers also drastically reduced their enforcement activities, making fewer traffic and pedestrian stops, and refraining from making arrests for nonviolent and petty offenses (see https://www.policeone.com/coronavirus-covid-19/). Police agencies struggled with depleted workforces as officers who were either infected or exposed to the virus were forced to self-isolate or quarantine. Many police officers had to enforce stay-at-home orders issued by governments, bringing them into conflict with people who view such orders as inconvenient or unnecessary, and even unconstitutional. They also had to monitor jail and prison inmates who were released into the community to prevent rampant spread of the virus in these institutions. These and other issues brought about by the pandemic represented a massive intergroup communication challenge for the police and one that received media attention across the globe (in Britain, for example, see Casciani 2020).

OVERVIEW OF THIS BOOK

While we are gratified by the scope and breadth of the topics included in the book, we were, inevitably, unable to cover every social group or communicative relationship encompassed within the complex intergroup dynamics of law enforcement (see conclusion to this book). While we have required some modest consistency in structure across chapters, we have given our authors freedom to follow their own instincts in terms of writing formats, and this particularly so, given that authors derive from different academic disciplinary backgrounds (of communication, criminology and criminal justice, law, sociology, and psychology), while others are police practitioners. Hence, the reader will see variable ways of crafting chapter titles, introductory, and concluding sections, and whether and where they feel confident in formulating and conveying future research agendas. We contend that these and other forms of diversity enhance stylistic liveliness for readers.

The main body of this book is divided into four sections that, while having their own distinctive foci, are not mutually exclusive. While some chapters could have been included in more than one section, a major aim of the conclusion to this book is to underscore how the processes inherent in the four parts are fundamentally interdependent. Understanding the interplay between these various processes provides a more comprehensive and sophisticated understanding of the role of communication and intergroup dynamics in policing.

The first section addresses issues concerning communication within law enforcement agencies and between them and other relevant units and institutions. In chapter 1, Hill and Giles open up the substantive contributions to this book by examining the emergence, maintenance, and implications of "us" versus "them" mentalities, a dynamic that manifests all too often in police–community relations. After providing a brief history of intergroup communication, they explore the complex ways in which this "us" mentality *within* the police organization is developed from the recruitment process, within police academy training, and throughout an officer's career.

Chapter 2 by Wolfe focuses on managerial philosophies within police departments, arguing that officers will accommodate their agency's ethos and norms more readily when they feel they are being treated fairly by their supervisors, managers, and administrators. He contends that leaders would benefit from training (that is subsequently monitored and evaluated for its effectiveness) not only in terms of embracing the ideals of organizational justice but also in communicating that goal in ways that benefit the welfare of officers on the front line. Chapter 3 by Scheer and Wilson continues the theme of workforce management within police agencies at a time when both recruitment and retention of officers are challenging prospects, especially when appealing to millennials and Generation Z (see Francis 2020). They provide a catalogue of compelling communicative recommendations to overcome current problems in hiring quality personnel and enhancing prospects for retaining them over the long term, including the messaging of the department's criteria for selection and promotion.

The final chapter in this section is chapter 4 by Kuhns and Messer. It examines how various units within police agencies can work more cohesively together but also, inevitably, how they work in tandem with colleagues in *other* professional agencies, such as social workers, mental health workers, district attorneys, medics, and others. While such interagency communication is widespread across a variety of social problems, these authors focus specifically on the investigation and prosecution of homicide cases, emphasizing the need to build collaborative tactics of sharing information, aligning common goals, and communicating empathically with victims' families with a view to solving a murder. Section I, in sum, highlights the need for engaging research on, and developing a more sophisticated theoretical understanding of, fostering effective communication both *within* police organizations, and between police organizations and the communities and institutions that comprise their external environments.

Section II examines communication and policing in five diverse types of communities. In chapter 5, Dixon, Smith, and Weeks reengage the initial topic of this introduction, namely, recent intergroup tensions. They provide an understanding of racial disparities in encounters between police and the public, such as in traffic stops and stop-and-frisk occasions as well as officer-involved shootings. The authors discuss possible reasons for the alleged differences in policing members of various racial and ethnic groups as well as the public consequences for these actions. Chapter 6, by Rabe-Hemp and

Schuck, examines the intergroup processes and theories that lead to the perpetuation of women being marginalized in law enforcement. They discuss the kinds of social threats to their identity, culture, and values that certain male officers might experience when communicating with their female counterparts. Their reactions to these threats provide the foundation for dissatisfactory and unproductive gender barriers and they suggest the fostering of a superordinate police identity as a response for combatting and ameliorating gender tensions and boundaries. In chapter 7, Owen examines the policing of LGBTQ+ groups and discusses ways in which microaggressions (e.g., slurs and other forms of derogatory language) against LGBTQ+, especially in law enforcement climates that promote heterosexuality as the normal or preferred sexual orientation, can sully relations between these groups. Owen proposes a "tool kit" of communicative remedies, including a greater willingness to contact LGBTQ+ individuals and organizations and to promote institutional liaisons between police and these entities.

In chapter 8, Murphy also examines phobias—this time Islamophobia—that stigmatize and marginalize Muslim communities. Procedural justice in community-oriented policing is argued to be a significant way of building trust among, as well giving a voice to, the latter, thereby increasing their likelihood of avoiding radicalization and working with law enforcement in countering terrorism. However, for this to be accomplished effectively, Murphy calls for the need for strong messages of societal unity to be regularly propounded. This section ends with chapter 9 by Scrivner, who examines the police response to people who are homeless and/or mentally challenged. These vulnerable communities deserve to be treated with empathy by police and other representatives of the state. Moreover, police are often able to refer people in these communities to shelters and treatment facilities, rather than relying on more traditional law enforcement approaches. This chapter, like others in section II, adopts a historical perspective and examines the lessons we can learn from crisis intervention models and police teams (with allied agencies) that can problem-solve and work collaboratively and transparently to meet the needs of these at-risk communities.

The chapters in section II underscore the need for a more profound understanding of, and compassion for, the diverse values, distinctive needs, and cultures of the many different kinds of communities law enforcement serves. They lay bare a wide variety of unfortunate (and sometimes hostile) incidents of intergroup communication and expressed prejudice arising from many groups in society (see Kende and McGarty 2019). There is, however, a shared appreciation that responsible and collaborate partnerships engaging in high quality and tolerant contact are keys for enhancing police-community climates (see Verkuyten and Yogeeswaran 2017).

The seven chapters in section III revolve around how and why law enforcement communicates about policing to the communities it serves and how the latter responds to and communicates about being policed. Chapter 10 by Maguire discusses the role of communication reform in the community policing movement. Community policing is widely considered one of the most influential reform movements in policing in recent decades. This chapter examines the research evidence on the extent to which community policing has influenced internal communications within police organizations and external communications between police and communities. In chapter 11, Scott picks up the theme of police reform by examining unrealistic expectations the public have for, and communicate to, law enforcement to which, ironically, the latter can accommodate. He argues for an alternative, more strategic and pragmatic communication model that forges a *dialogue* with society that is balanced in terms of maintaining law, order, and security without unnerving individuals' ability to act with free will. Houston, Collins, and Branton, in chapter 12, implicitly take up this dialogic approach by revealing the value for communities of being empowered by law enforcement to be resilient and feel safe in the face and wake of crises. They contend, however, that such a communicative approach can really only be maximally effective once officers and departments, in turn, feel resilient in terms of managing their own ordeals and challenges of safety and public scrutiny.

In chapter 13, Melekian examines the ways in which law enforcement has historically managed public complaints against their officers' actions and expressed attitudes. Traditional (and even technological) ways of doing business such as lawsuits and internal affairs investigations by police departments often leave members of the public feeling marginalized and without a proper voice. These mechanisms also leave officers feeling overly and unnecessarily scrutinized. Melekian endorses the use of mediation processes that allow both sides to communicate their accounts of what occurred, their feelings, and their intentions in ways that are more likely to result in a successful resolution of the complaint.

The above intergroup expectations and feelings are influenced by decades of media attention to police institutions and to encounters between police and the public. The last three chapters in this section focus on this topic. In chapter 14, Mustafaj and Van den Bulck document the allure the public has for depictions of crime and law enforcement and how the messages and images across different genres of the media impact our understanding of social reality and the social stereotypes created and maintained by them. These scholars look at how criminals, victims, and law enforcement are depicted and psychologically processed by readers and viewers as well as the journalistic values and other factors that elevate stories to media attention and place them on the public agenda. Chapter 15 by Walther also looks at new media depictions of exchanges between police and the public on YouTube videos and the attending user-generated comments. He invokes the so-called "echo chamber effect" to comment on how watching—perhaps by accident—one video depicting police overreactions can lead to social media accounts providing the viewer with further (and algorithmically curated) depictions of similar scenarios. Thus, social media algorithms, by regulating what types of content viewers see, can have a powerful effect on undermining public perceptions of police legitimacy.

In chapter 16, the final chapter in this section, Tyler and Maguire examine the influence of a single incident—the police shooting of Michael Brown in Ferguson, Missouri—on national media coverage of the police in the *New York Times*. The authors demonstrate how the Ferguson incident had a powerful effect on the volume of news coverage about police in the United States. Unlike some of the other controversial police shootings and deaths in police custody they examine, the Ferguson incident had a singular influence on media coverage of the police in one national newspaper of record. The authors discuss why Ferguson had such powerful effects on media coverage of the police, and more generally how the agenda setting roles of major media outlets help shape public discussion and debate, and indeed public opinion, about the police.

In sum, the diverse chapters in section III underscore a couple of key themes. First, there is a widespread lack of trust—and even mistrust—for law enforcement in many communities (particularly in the United States) that is accompanied by the police feeling undervalued by society. Second, and relatedly, the communication pathways between these two social collectives are fraught with misattributions and misunderstandings (see Coupland, Wiemann, and Giles's [1991] miscommunication model). Third, and consequently, both groups have to move beyond existing modes of intergroup communication. Relatedly, Ellis (2006) proposed two ways of ameliorating intractable conflicts. First, both parties must communicate a willingness to *jointly* redefine and rewrite histories and narratives, thereby empowering both parties. Second, the ingroup must listen to and empathize with the outgroup, while also being prepared to be self/ingroup critical (see Nagda's [2006] notion of "dialogic listening").

Finally, section IV examines communication processes in the policing of six specific types of violations, crimes, and incidents. Chapter 17, by Lowrey-Kinberg, focuses on language use by officers and drivers during traffic stops, an occasion when the public interact first or most often with law enforcement officials. She demonstrates that officers who are most procedurally just and communicatively accommodative in terms of being respectful and oriented to drivers' concerns incur more positive outcomes and cooperation than officers who rely less on these communicative practices. The relevance of these findings to more tangible communication training for policing on the street encounters with the public is emphasized.

Chapter 18 by Grubb examines the verbal and behavioral tactics officers draw upon in hostage and crisis negotiation situations. Police negotiators are characterized as expert communicators who invoke a panoply of communicative techniques to de-escalate and attempt to resolve such scenarios. The chapter examines a variety of theoretical models and a range of different quantitative and qualitative methods to investigate these communicatively challenging and dangerous situations in moving to best practices for success.

Chapter 19 by Bettinger-López and Ezer focuses on a globally endemic crime—gender-based violence (GBV)—and the role of gender bias in the policing response to it. The chapter examines communicative strategies involved in interviewing trauma victims and survivors and encouraging them to provide highly sensitive details and information. It also examines strategies for interviewing suspects. The authors explore the intricacies in the reporting of investigations of domestic abuse as well as complexities inherent in managing important and diverse community agencies that can provide to support to victims. We contend that Bettinger-López and Ezer's examination of the fraught relationships between survivors (especially of marginalized groups) and law enforcement are intergroup in nature. Therefore, solutions to disrupt the biases in recognizing and investigating GBV and to improve responses from law enforcement (such as the COURAGE project) can benefit significantly from research on improving intergroup communication.

Chapter 20 by Kennedy focuses on communicative features of policing group-involved violence, particularly as it relates to inner city gangs. His interventions focus on group dynamics rather than focusing, like most interventions, on individual offenders. Kennedy is one of the architects of "focused deterrence," a recasting of deterrence theory with significant implications for reducing group-involved violence. Structured intergroup communication between gangs and coalitions of community groups (including representatives from law enforcement, social services, education, and the faith community) is a core element of violence reduction strategies that Kennedy and his team rely on. In this chapter, Kennedy reflects on the communication aspects of focused deterrence theory and its application in communities around the world.

Chapter 21 by Blakemore looks at the policing of extremism and terrorism as well as hate crimes that are targeted against an array of social groups albeit manifest in different forms in the digital age. After examining variable definitions of hate crimes in different nations, the chapter emphasizes that these particular crimes are not only violent acts, but also pernicious forms of communication. The communication aspects of hate crime merit further examination and may provide opportunities for intervention. The intricate balance between affording individuals and groups on the Internet free speech and the need to prevent and address offensive and subversive messaging is discussed. The final contribution to this section, chapter 22 by Stott, Radburn, and Savigar, analyzes the communicative dynamics of policing crowd behavior. The chapter begins by taking a historical focus on how crowd behavior had been understood and explained as irrational and how it could be interpreted similarly by police. Stott notes that police tend to embrace these historically inaccurate perspectives on crowds. As a result, they often rely on overly coercive public order and crowd policing strategies that not only raise civil rights concerns but also tend to escalate conflict rather than de-escalating it. Drawing upon studies on managing social protests, sporting events, and mass emergencies, the chapter explores the implications of intergroup relations theory and allied empirical support for the policing of crowds

In sum, the chapters that make up section IV underscore the idea that police can benefit in numerous ways when they choose to engage in communicative practices that are consistent with intergroup communication theory and related research evidence. Such practices lead to healthier organizational cultures, more effective investigative outcomes, improved community partnerships, reduced levels of conflict, and a variety of other prosocial benefits. Included among these communicative tools are interpersonal and intergroup accommodations, the application of procedural justice, the de-escalation of intergroup conflict, the avoidance of unnecessary and often inflammatory coercion, the genuine expression of empathy for victims and their traumatic experiences, and finding common ground between social groups.

The readers of this book will encounter a variety of topics and communication pathways, and much, much more. In the conclusion to this volume, the editors attempt to make cohesive sense of this complex landscape by means of integrative visualizations and a heuristic model that also locates the preceding chapters within its conceptual spaces. This is then invoked as an interpretive tool for understanding a particular set of intergroup tensions involving race issues and a dramatic public outcry. Finally, in this book's conclusion, this and other issues provide us with a template for outlining research challenges and practical recommendations for police-community communications in the future.

One of this book's aims is to be a comprehensive textual resource that has wide international relevance and will be intriguing enough for police practitioners to invest further in more sophisticated communication training based on theory, enabling them to reach out more effectively to a range of relevant social groups. In tandem, another of our aims is to engender interest in developing the topic of law enforcement and the processes of policing within both the fields of communication and intergroup relations as being a critical, understudied *societal* topic having considerable applied potential. Furthermore, this cannot be driven by a silo-like insular academic approach but one that needs to be fermented in active interdisciplinary cooperation and theory.

NOTES

1. Not only have handbooks on policing emerged in the United States in the last ten years (e.g., Bradford, Jauregui, Loader, and Steinber 2016; Bryant and Bryant 2019; Reisig and Kane 2014; Lave and Miller 2019; Steverson 2008) but, also, elsewhere in the world (e.g., Mesko, Fields, Lobniker, and Sotlar 2013; Newburn 2012). With respect to modest attention to communication processes and practices in these volumes, it is important to recognize previous work that has highlighted these aspects (Gundersen and Hopper 1984; Kidd and Braziel 1999; Womack and Finley 1986; see also, Parish and Cambria 2019).

2. For research on the significance of appearance and clothing for intergroup relations on the one hand and for perceptions of police on the other, see Kebulsek, Giles, and Maass 2017 and Simpson 2018, respectively.

REFERENCES

Balko, Radley. 2013. *The Rise of the Warrior Cop: The Militarization of America's Police Forces.* New York: PublicAffairs.

Blinder, Alan. 2017. "Gunman Called Police Shootings a 'Necessary Evil' in a Suicide Note." *New York Times*, June 30. Retrieved from https://www.nytimes.com/2017/06/30/us/gavin-long-suicide-note-baton-rouge.html .

Boivin, Rémi, Camille Faubert, Annie Gendron, and Bruno Poulin. 2018. "The 'Us vs Them' Mentality: A Comparison of Police Cadets at Different Stages of Their Training." *Police Practice and Research* 21 (1): 49–61.

Bradford, Ben, Beatrice Jauregui, Ian Loader, and Jonny Steinber. 2016. *The SAGE Handbook of Global Policing*. Thousand Oaks: Sage.

Bryant, Robin, and Sarah Bryant, eds. 2019. *Blackstone's Handbook of Policing Students* (thirteenth edition). New York: Oxford University Press.

Bureau of Justice Statistics. 2018. *Contacts between the Police and Public, 2015*. Washington DC: Department of Justice.

Campbell, Bradley A., Justin Nix, and Edward R. Maguire. 2018. "Is the Number of Citizens Killed by Police Increasing? A Pre/post Ferguson Analysis." *Crime and Delinquency* 64 (3): 398–420.

Casciani, Dominic. 2020, April 20. "Coronavirus: What Powers Do the Police Have?" BBC News Online. Retrieved from http://www.bbc.com/news/explainers-52106843.

Clinkinbeard, Samantha S., and Rachel M. Rief. 2020. "Four Steps to Bring More Women into Policing." *Police Chief* 87 (4): 40–45.

Coupland, Nikolas, John M. Wiemann, and Howard Giles. 1991. "Talk as 'Problem' and Communication as 'Miscommunication': An Integrative Analysis." In *"Miscommunication" and Problematic Talk*, edited by Nikolas Coupland, Howard Giles, and John M. Wiemann, 1–17. Newbury Park: Sage.

"Crime Prevention Communities." 2019. [Special section]. *Police Chief* 86 (10): 30–68.

"Cutting Edge Technology." 2019. [Special section]. *Police Chief* 88 (4): 26–52.

Decker, Scott H., and David C. Pyrooz, eds. 2015. *The Handbook of Gangs*. New York: Wiley Blackwell.

Denault, Vincent, Pierrich Plusquellec, Louise M. Jupe, Michel St-Yves, Norah E. Dunbar . . . Peter J. van Koppen. 2020. "The Analysis of Nonverbal Communication: The Dangers of Pseudoscience in Security and Justice Contexts." *Anuario de Psicología Jurídica [Yearbook of Psychology]* 30: 1–12. Retrieved from https://doi.10.5093/apj2019a9. [This article is a translation of the French article "L' analyse de la communication non verbale : Les dangers de la pseudoscience en contextes de sécurité et de justice" published with the authorization of the French journal *Revue Internationale de Criminologie et de Police Technique et Scientifique*.]

DOJ: U.S. Department of Justice Report. 2015. *Report Regarding the Criminal Investigation into the Shooting Death of Michael Brown by Ferguson, Missouri Police Officer Darren Wilson*. Washington DC: Department of Justice. Retrieved from https://www.justice.gov/sites/default/files/opa/press-releases/attachments/2015/03/04/doj_report_on_shooting_of_michael_brown_1.pdf .

Dragojevic, Marko, and Howard Giles. 2014. "Language and Interpersonal Communication: Their Intergroup Dynamics." In *Handbook of Interpersonal Communication*, edited by Charles R. Berger, 29–51. Berlin: De Gruyter Mouton.

Ellis, Donald G. 2006. *Transforming Conflict: Communication and Ethnopolitical Conflict*. Lanham: Rowman & Littlefield.

Engel, Robin S., and James L. Whalen. 2010. Police-Academic Partnerships: Ending the Dialogue of the Deaf, the Cincinnati Experience." *Police Practice and Research* 11 (2): 105–16.

Fine, Adam D., Emily Kan, and Elizabeth Cauffman. 2019. "Adolescents' Confidence in Institutions: Do America's Youth Differentiate between Legal and Social Institutions?" *Developmental Psychology* 55 (8): 1758–67.

Francis, Joselyn. 2020. "Creating a Culture of Success." *Police Chief* 87 (4): 46–53.

Frosch, Dan, and Dan Molinksi. 2016. "Bomb Materials, Guns, Ammo Found in Dallas Shooter's Home." *Wall Street Journal*, November 23. Retrieved from https://www.wsj.com/articles/dallas-shooting-suspect-targeted-white-officers-was-killed-when-officials-detonated-bomb-1467982329.

Garcia, Jennifer J-L., and Mienah Z. Sharif. 2015. "Black Lives Matter: A Commentary on Racism and Public Health." *American Journal of Public Health* 105 (8): e27–30.

Giles, Howard, ed. 2002. *Law Enforcement, Communication, and Community*. Amsterdam: John Benjamins.

Giles, Howard, ed. 2012. *The Handbook of Intergroup Communication*. New York: Routledge.

Giles, Howard, and Jake Harwood, eds. 2018. *The Oxford Encyclopedia of Intergroup Communication* (Vols. 1 & 2). New York: Oxford University Press.

Giles, Howard, and Anne Maass, eds. 2016. *Advances in Intergroup Communication*. New York: Peter Lang.

Giles, Howard, and Bernadette M. Watson. 2008. "Intercultural and Intergroup Parameters of Communication." In *International Encyclopedia of Communication*, edited by Wolfgang Donsbach, Vol. 6, 2237–48. Blackwell: Oxford.

Gillet, Nicolas, Caroline Becker, Marc-André Lafrenière, Isabelle Hart, and Evelyne Fouquereau. 2017. "Organizational Support, Job Resources, Soldiers' Motivation Profiles, Work Engagement, and Affect. *Military Psychology* 29 (5): 418–33.

Glaser, Jack, and Amanda Charbonneau. 2018. "Law Enforcement: Finding Common Purpose." In *Making Research Matter: A Psychologist's Guide to Public Engagement*, edited by Linda R. Tropp, 104–21. Washington DC: American Psychological Association.

Gorman, Ann, and Richard Winton. 2014. "Boy Says He Gunned Down a CHP officer." *Los Angeles Times*, April 23. Retrieved from https://www.latimes.com/archives/la-xpm-2004-apr-23-me-shot23-story.html .

Gundersen, Dennis F., and Robert Hopper. 1984. *Communication and Law Enforcement*. New York: Harper & Row.

Hayes, Christal. 2019, June 3. How Cops Cope with Shooting Trauma: 'They're Going to be Forever Changed.'" *USA Today* Online. Retrieved from https://www.usatoday.com/story/news/nation/2019/06/03/virginia-beach-mass-shooting-how-cops-cope-trauma/1321462001/.

Heyman, Miriam, Jeff Dill, and Robert Douglas. 2018. *The Ruderman White Paper on Mental Health and Suicide of First Responders.* Retrieved from http://dir.nv.gov/uploadedFiles/dirnvgov/content/WCS/TrainingDocs/First%20Responder%20White%20Paper_Final%20(2).pdf .

Hollywood, John S., Sean E. Goodison, Dulani Woods, Michael J. D. Vermeer, and Brian A. Jackson. 2019. *Fostering Innovation to Respond to Top Challenges in Law Enforcement.* Santa Monica: Rand Corporation.

House, Cathryn H. 2018. "The Changing Role of Women in Law Enforcement." *The Police Chief* 85 (10): 60–66.

"Innovations in Smart Policing." 2020. [Special section]. *Police Chief* 87 (3): 32–55.

Johnson, Ron (with Alan Eisenstock). 2018. *Thirteen Days in Ferguson.* Carol Stream: Tyndale House.

Kaste, Martin. (2016). "How the Perceived 'War on Cops' Plays into Politics and Policing." *National Public Radio* (December 29).

Keblusek, Lauren, Howard Giles, and Anne Maass. 2017. "Language and Intergroup Communication." *Group Processes and Intergroup Relations* 20 (5): 632–43.

Kende, Anna, and Craig McGarty. 2019. "A Model for Predicting Prejudice and Stigma Expression by Understanding Target Perceptions: The Effects of Visibility, Politicization, Responsibility, and Entativity." *European Journal of Social Psychology* 49 (5): 839–56.

Kidd, Virginia, and Rick Braziel. 1999. *Cop Talk: Essential Communication Skills for Community Policing.* San Francisco: Acada Books.

Kienzle, Jennifer, and Jordan Soliz. 2017. "Intergroup Communication." In *Intercultural Communication*, edited by Ling. Chen, 369–88. Boston: de Gruyter Mouton.

Kraska, Peter B., and Victor E. Kappeler. 1997. "Militarizing American Police: The Rise and Normalization of Police Paramilitary Units." *Social Problems* 44 (1): 1–18.

Lave, Tamara Rice, and Eric J. Miller, eds. 2019. *The Cambridge Handbook of Policing in the United States.* Cambridge: Cambridge University Press.

Law Enforcement and COVID-19. 2020. *Police Chief* 87 (5). Online Supplement: https://www.cdc.gov/coronavirus/2019-ncov/downloads/COVID19-symptoms.pdf .

Los Angeles Police Department. 2016. *Categorical Use of Force 2016.* Retrieved from http://www.lapdonline.org/categorical_use_of_force_2016.

Maass, Anne, Luciano Arcuri, and Caterina Suitner. 2014. "Shaping Intergroup Relations through Language." In *The Oxford Handbook of Language and Social Psychology*, edited by Tom Holtgraves, 157–76. New York: Oxford University Press.

MacDonald, H. 2016. *The War on Cops: How the New Attack on Law and Order Makes Everyone Less Safe.* New York: Encounter Books

Maguire, Edward R., Justin Nix, and Bradley A. Campbell. 2017. "A War on Cops? The Effects of Ferguson on the Number of U.S. Police Officers Murdered in the Line of Duty." *Justice Quarterly* 34 (5): 739–58.

Maguire, Edward R., Logan J. Somers, and Kathleen E. Padilla. 2020. "Promoting Officer Health and Wellness." In *Transforming the Police: 13 Key Reforms*, edited by Charles M. Katz and Edward R. Maguire. Long Grove: Waveland Press.

Mark, Michelle. 2016. "A Police Chief Apologized for the Historic Mistreatment of Minorities—and Not Everyone Is Happy." *Business Insider* (October 18). https://www.businessinsider.com/police-chief-faces-criticism-for-apologizing-for-historic-mistreatment-of-minorities-2016-10.

"Media Relations." 2019. [Special section]. *Police Chief* 86 (8): 22–54.

Mesko, Gorazd, Charles B. Fields, Branko Lobniker, and Andrej Sotlar, eds. 2013. *Handbook on Policing in Central and Eastern Europe.* New York: Springer.

Molloy, Jennifer, and Howard Giles. 2002. "Communication, Language, and Law Enforcement: An Intergroup Communication Approach." In *Excavating the Taken-for-Granted: Essays in Social Interaction*, edited by Phillip J. Glenn, Curtis D. LeBaron, and Jenny S. Mandelbaum, 327–40. Mahwah: Lawrence Erlbaum.

Myers, Jennifer. 2020. "Key Strategies to Prevent Suicide among Law Enforcement." *Police Chief* 87 (5): 26–31.

Nagda, Biren A. 2006. "Breaking Barriers, Crossing Borders, Building Bridges: Communication Processes in Intergroup Dialogues." *Journal of Social Issues* 62 (3): 553–76.

Newburn, Tim, ed. 2012. *The Handbook of Policing.* London: Routledge. Online: eBook ISBN: 9780203118238.

Nix, Justin, Scott Wolfe, and Bradley Campbell. 2018. "Command-Level Police Officers' Perceptions of the 'War on Cops' and De-policing." *Justice Quarterly* 35 (1): 33–54.

Otis, Nancy, and Luc G. Pelletier. 2005. "A Motivational Model of Daily Hassles, Physical Symptoms, and Future Work Intentions among Police Officers." *Journal of Applied Social Psychology* 35 (10): 2193–214.

Parish, Rachel, and Jack Cambria. 2019. *The Other Side of the Door: The Art of Compassion in Policing.* St. Paul: DRI Press.

PERF: Police Executive Research Forum. 2016. *Critical Issues in Policing-Integrating Communications, Assessment, and Tactics.* 2020. Retrieved from https://www.policeforum.org/training guide.

Pfeifer, Michael. A. 2020. "Embracing the Opportunity for Change." *Police Chief* 87 (1), 26–29.

President's Task Force on 21st Century Policing. 2015. *Final Report of the President's Task Force on 21st Century Policing.* Washington DC: Office of Community Oriented Policing Services.

Primicerio, Jarod, and Anthony Normore. 2018. "Transformation of Community-Police Relations through History." *The Police Chief* 10 (85): 52–58.

Reisig, Michael D., and Robert J. Kane, eds. 2014. *The Oxford Handbook of Police and Policing.* New York: Oxford University Press.

Sherman, Lawrence W. 2020. "Targeting American Policing: Rogue Cops or Rogue Cultures?" *Cambridge Journal of Evidence-Based Policing.* Advance Online: https://doi.org/10.1007/s41887-020-00046-z.

Shipley, Peter. 2019. "Connecting Research, Decision-Making, and Police Training." *Police Chief* 86: 28–35.

Shjarback, John, and Edward R. Maguire. 2019. "Extending Research on the 'War on Cops': The Effects of Ferguson on Non-Fatal Assaults against U.S. Police Officers." *Crime and Delinquency.* Advance Online: https://doi.org/10.1177/0011128719890266.

Simpson, Rylan. 2018. "Officer Appearance and Perceptions of Police: Accoutrements as Signals of Intent." *Policing: A Journal of Policy and Practice* 14 (1): 243–57.

Steverson, Leonard A. (2008). *Policing in America: A Reference Handbook.* Santa Barbara: ABC-CLIO Publications.

Tajfel, Henri. 1974. "Social Identity and Intergroup Behavior." *Social Science Information* 13 (2): 65–93.

Tajfel, Henri, and John C. Turner. 1986. "The Social Psychology of Intergroup Behavior." In *Psychology of Intergroup Relations,* edited by Stephen Worchel and William G. Austin, 7–24. Chicago: Nelson-Hall.

Thompson, George J., and Jerry B. Jenkins. 2013. *Verbal Judo: The Gentle Art of Persuasion.* New York: William Morrow.

"Use of Force Reporting." 2019. [Special section]. *Police Chief* 86 (6): 24–51.

Verkuyten, Matkel, and Kumar Yogeeswaran. 2017. "The Social Psychology of Intergroup Toleration: A Roadmap for Theory and Research." *Personality and Social Psychology Review* 21 (1): 72–96.

"Violence against Police." 2019. [Special section]. *Police Chief* 86 (2) 26–44.

Womack, Morris M., and Hayden H. Finley. 1986. *Communication: A Unique Significance for Law Enforcement.* Springfield: Charles C. Thomas.

Zoroya, Gregg, and Trevor Hughes. 2014. "Social Media Post Threatened 'Pigs.'" *USA Today* (December 21).

SECTION I
COMMUNICATING *WITHIN* POLICE-RELEVANT AGENCIES

CHAPTER 1

Police Culture

Us versus Them Communication

Shawn L. Hill and Howard Giles

Police professional subculture (so-called *cop culture*) exists in a state of evolution in law enforcement as generations of officers and policing eras have changed since the inception of modern policing. Manning (1977) contends many variations of police subculture can exist within departments. However, the *"us versus them"* mentality, also depicted by Skolnick (1966) as the *police working personality*, has proved recalcitrant and, according to many, has remained pervasive (Myhill and Bradford 2013). The presence of the *us versus them* orientation within the police culture, despite its hindrance on realizing the community policing philosophy sought by the nation's law enforcement executives, implores an examination of the various modes of communication (and absence thereof) that allows such a condition to exist and, arguably, flourish. From police selection processes (see Kappeler, Sluder, and Alpert 1998), police academy training, informal rank and file socialization, law enforcement policy, and the social norms and ingroup bias transmitted through media (see Vezzali, Hewstone, Capozza, Giovannini, and Wolfer 2014), police officers, and the public alike, are constantly subjected to the contrasting nature of their (intergroup) existence.

The relationship between "the police" and "those policed" is *intergroup* in nature (see the introduction). Intergroup situations are such that people are relating to one another based on their social category membership rather than on their own personal idiosyncratic temperaments (see Dragojevic and Giles 2014). Recognizing that *communication* is one of the primary ways for law enforcement to meet the fundamental challenges faced by the profession (Sklansky 2011), there is a growing need, due in part to mass public absorption of media, to explore and understand the importance and influence of communication, both direct and indirect, between and about police and the people in the communities they serve[1] (see chapter 14). McIntyre, Paolini, and Hewstone

(2016) suggest that indirect and vicarious forms of contact (non-face-to-face contact) via social media and digital communication are increasing to an unprecedented level, which is evident by the significant research interest in phenomena (e.g., White, Turner, Verrelli, Harvey, and Hann 2019).

To many, even the very use of the terms "police" and "community" have drastically different connotations, most often distinguishing the identities of the two groups as separate (see chapter 10). The power differential between the two groups is perhaps the most significant distinguishing characteristic. Police are gifted with a unique authority (in the United States, and often abroad) that provides a legal vessel for sanctioned violence and coercion, whereas other members of society have legal sanctions preventing the same (Gaines and Kappeler 2015). Policing history has demonstrated that sanctioned violence has been the cause for intergroup anxieties.

The basis for intergroup anxieties between police and citizens can be attributed to the role police play in society, coupled with their unique position of influence. Police have the legal power to arrest citizens and use physical coercion to achieve their objectives. Also central to anxieties from marginalized community groups is that most everyone, even those historically (or currently) marginalized, will likely need to call upon and depend on the police for assistance at some point. Therefore, although police powers are necessary to protect the civil liberties of some, police misconduct can represent one of the biggest threats to civil liberties of others (Kappeler et al. 1998). Perhaps most poignant are the intergroup anxieties that exist between police and African Americans (see examples in the introduction and chapter 5). Evidence of this can be seen in the confidence gap in police between White and African Americans in the United States. According to a 2015 Gallop Report, only 30 percent of African Americans expressed confidence in their local police in contrast to 57 percent of White Americans. Considering the origins and evolution of policing in the United States, these gaps could stem from, among other events, the use of police as slave patrols beginning in the 1700s (Reichel 1988). The more recent actions of angry protesters and looters demanding the "defunding" of the police in the United States after the police killing of George Floyd, an unarmed African American man in police custody, would suggest that the confidence level has fallen even more significantly (see the conclusion to this book). These events highlight the increasing state of the *us versus them* relationship between police and the public which, we argue, is intergroup in nature, and perpetuated by the occupational character produced, in part, by the socialization of police officers.

This chapter intends to provide a theoretical and practical framework for understanding, arguably, one of the most salient intergroup relationships existing, namely, *us versus them* mentalities in communication. Additionally, we contend that although police–citizen use of force encounters draw much media attention and, thereby, broad viewership (see chapters 14 and 15), the majority of police–citizen encounters do not involve such force. However, we posit that the majority of police–citizen encounters do involve *communication*, which is a foundational component of the socialization, training, and culture of police departments. The communication within police subculture impacts the police worldview and, subsequently, how police relate to and communicate with the community. For example, Kappeler et al. (1998) explain how, although law enforcement work is recognized as a dangerous occupation, police are often trained in a way that "resembles preparation for being dropped behind enemy lines." Relatedly, and emphasizing its integral role in policing, communication is also often used as a primary tenet for de-escalation of force by police in nationally recognized police training programs (ICAT 2016).

In what follows, we first introduce the field of, and selected theory in, the study of intergroup relationships and communication that spells out the origins of such *us versus them* mentalities. We then explore the cultural foundations that necessitate and perpetuate such processes by examining police training as a means of instilling recruits with a unique and comprehensive view (or philosophy) of life and the world (hereafter referred to as a "police worldview"). In this way, we highlight some direction for police executives and academics to provide pathways forward to mitigate the harm resulting from potent intergroup anxieties, dilemmas, and conflicts.

INTERGROUP RELATIONS, COMMUNICATION, AND WORLDVIEWS

While *us versus them* mentalities and actions have doubtlessly permeated many thousands of years of human existence, research and theory on this topic is more recent and gained momentum in the mid-twentieth century (e.g., Allport 1954; Sherif, Harvey, White, Hood, and Sherif 1961). Much of this was triggered by the events in World War II and the Holocaust, with social scientists seeking to understand more clearly why humans could do such horrific things to each other. Of relevance here was figuring out why many of us so quickly attribute enduring social characteristics to particular *individuals* based only on their membership in a particular group (ethnicity, sexual orientation, profession, etc.). Social scientists also struggled to figure out how people can experience such intense emotions (e.g., pity, anger, disgust) associated with these membership categorizations. Put differently, how and why does social stereotyping emerge (e.g., see Cuddy, Fiske, and Glick 2008)?

Many important theories abound and continue to be invoked in the field of intergroup relations (see Taylor and Moghaddam 1994), but, arguably, the most predominant framework driving most of this research worldwide has been social identity theory (SIT; Tajfel and Turner 1986; Turner and Giles 1981). The essence of the theory is that when individuals define themselves mainly in terms of their group identity (whether it be race, religion, occupation, organization, or whatever) and perceive themselves and others as members of ingroups and outgroups, certain processes unfold that are unique and distinct from those integral to interpersonal encounters. The latter is construed in terms of people dealing with each other predominantly in terms of their individual behaviors—their personal, idiosyncratic qualities and temperaments (Dragojevic and Giles 2014). Intergroup dynamics occur when people view each other not just as individuals but as members of a group, whether an ingroup (a group that you belong to) or an outgroup (a relevant contrasting group of which you are not a member).

The late Henri Tajfel used to claim, when talking about his theory with others, that 70 percent of social interactions between unfamiliar, and even closely related, others were intergroup in nature. Interestingly, Swann et al. (2014) showed that priming core values and increasing psychological arousal among those who shared a powerful—almost visceral—identification with their social group induced them to feel strong family-like ties with like members, as well as endorse extreme sacrifices for the ingroup (i.e., fight and even die for the group). These researchers identified this bond as "intergroup fusion." Intergroup fusion provides some explanation for the strong bonds that can form between police officers, especially those in special teams such as SWAT (special weapons and tactics). Relatedly, it is almost axiomatic that when fellow police officers support each other emotionally and socially, such ties engender greater well-being and collective resilience (Biggs, Brough, and Barbour 2014; Hill and Giles 2019). Compellingly, it has been found that officers who do indeed provide peer support, and especially at professionally challenging times, also benefit transactionally by bolstering their *own* engagement in their work (Zeijen, Petrou, Bakker, and Van Gelderen 2020).

These bonds can produce desired commitment and interdependence to one another, as well as potentially undesirable cultural norms, such as what is often referred to as "the blue code of silence." The blue code of silence (also blue wall or blue curtain) refers to an element of police subculture that promotes an internal solidarity (the "us") within law enforcement that, in part, discourages officers from reporting a range of police misconduct by their peers (Westmarland and Rowe 2018; see also *ethos of secrecy*, Kappeler et al. 1998). Relatedly, some researchers have argued previous attempts to change undesirable aspects of police culture are a result of flawed interventionist strategies and have observed successful change under the right conditions (Ganapathy and Cheong 2016).

An important element of SIT is that it recognizes even the most minimalist ways of dividing up or categorizing people—even classmates—into two groups arbitrarily, according to criteria such as eye color or wearing a colored badge, could provoke the groups into discriminating against each other and distilling negative feelings (Tajfel, Billig, Bundy, and Flament 1971). Many cognitive and behavioral biases follow because of these kinds of social categorizations (see chapter 6), such as evaluating other ingroup members and their characteristics and products more favorably than those of contrasting outgroup members (Hewstone, Rubin, and Willis 2002). Likewise, the well-cited "linguistic intergroup bias" (e.g., Maass, Salvi, Acuri, and Semin 1989) indicates that desirable ingroup and undesirable outgroup behaviors are described to others in abstract language (for example, generous and hateful, respectively). In contrast, ingroup undesirable and outgroup desirable behaviors are described in language that more concretely specifies the particular actions targeted (e.g., and correspondingly, forgetting money is owed someone and giving money to charity; see Sutton and Douglas 2008). This tacitly conveys that the former are more typical traits, while the latter are more atypical, thereby revealing a positive image of the ingroup. In parallel, group members can stereotype *themselves* by taking on the attributes and values they and their peers believe characterize their own group (Turner, Hogg, Oakes, Reicher, and Wetherell 1987). In this way, ingroup members are able to communicate easier with other ingroup members because they have taken the same perspective, and perhaps even more important in a police culture context, they (police) are more likely to be *open* to their partner's perspective, and motivated to engage with their partner's messaging, than the outgroup, or in this case, the public (Greenway, Peters, Haslam, and Bingley 2016).

Socialization and Police Culture

New law enforcement hires are most often socialized in a paramilitary environment (for an intergroup perspective, see Wilson and Chernichky 2016). In this sense, Boivin, Faubert, Gendron, and Poulin (2018) suggest that pre-entry experiences, such as perhaps watching agency recruitment videos (Balko 2014) and cop shows (Perlmutter 2000), begin to shape a prospective police applicant's worldview. Hence, they can even enter the selection process with attitudes that may already differ from others. Chappell and Lanza-Kaduce (2010) found that even with attempts to introduce new community-oriented curriculum in a police academy, the *us versus them* mentality and paramilitary structure was the most salient learning environment in the police recruits, training. Researchers have found that by the end of academy training, police recruit attitudes were substantially changed, representing a more conservative and diminished empathetic perspective (Christie, Petrie, and Timmins 1996; Stradling, Crowe and Tuohy 1993). Addressing the police selection process, Kappeler et al. (1998, 91) contend that it produces an applicant that shares a conformist view of the world based on "ideology, appearance, and conduct." As such, applicants may enter the profession with a difficulty in identifying with marginalized community members who do not share their ideologies. This ideological contrast is further established by eliminating police recruits from the academy who do not conform to the paramilitary training environment.

Law enforcement has long embraced the warrior ethos, which emphasizes honor, duty, and the willingness to engage in sanctioned violence. Traditionally, police academies are grounds upon which the warrior ethos is drilled into recruits and begins to forge their worldview. This ethos shapes how police perceive their role in society and how they interact with community (Stoughton 2016). The constructing of the police worldview, in part, by law enforcement academies and subsequent socialization through agency culture appear to stand in contrast with, arguably, increasing community expectations of the police as guardians. This contradiction perpetuates the *us versus them* mentality that impedes successful immersion and acceptance of officers in their respective communities. By the time new officers don their uniform and badge for the first time, they have begun to see the world differently. Stoughton (2016) posits the police warrior worldview decreases the officer's perception of the importance of public trust and, therefore, the motivation to act in a way that increases that trust. Additionally, in survey data from two US police departments, McLean et al. (2019) found that officers who embraced the guardian mindset placed greater priority on communication during a police–citizen encounter. Officers see people outside of their profession as the "outgroup" and view them with suspicion (Kappeler et al. 1998). This "outgroup" view and suspicion, reinforced through various modes of communication within police culture, is contradictory to the philosophy of community policing, the model of policing that dominates discussions of police reform across the United States (see chapter 10).

Thereafter, police training academies, many of which are paramilitary "stress academies," and exposure on the job are the grounds upon which a police occupational personality is forged (Skolnick 1966; for an intergroup perspective on organizational acculturation, see Woo and Myers 2016). In this way, police subcultures generally incorporate strong elements of *us versus them* views concerning themselves vis-a-vis certain other sectors of society (Boivin et al. 2018). They also forge a consistent police mentality allied with established ingroup norms among new recruits and seasoned officers alike (see Hogg 2018). Furthermore, these norms are manifest in the kinds of talk, topics, and views condoned by them under many circumstances as well as in the underlying reasons for their expression (Hogg and Giles 2012). Not unrelatedly, Waddington (1999) suggested that police culture can also be explained as an adaptation that "gives purpose" to what sometimes can be a difficult and inherently traumatic occupational experience.

Consider, also, new graduates of police academies, who after a difficult and tenuous academy program, often attend graduation ceremonies where community leaders offer inspirational speeches. These messages often highlight the significant changes in the officers' lives now that they have become a "sworn" law enforcement officer. In a sheriff's academy graduation ceremony, the guest speaker, a rabbi, stated,

> Today our deputies are truly warriors for peace. They fight the war against crime. They fight the war against drugs. They fight the war against terror . . . guide them as they prepare themselves both morally and physically to fight the righteous battle of good against evil. . . . In order to conquer evil we must prepare to battle against it. (LASD 2014)

While we recognize the dangers and complex mission of law enforcement (and support the concept of the warrior ethos as a *sometimes called upon* component of the guardian mindset), in the context of intergroup communication, the message to the graduates further sets them apart from the public and, arguably, sets the stage for the officers to seek to "conquer" those in the community who they identify as "at war" with law enforcement. Professional policing, a predominant model of policing in the United States from the 1950s to the 1970s, prioritized crime suppression and holding the "thin blue line." However, the warrior mindset as a principal characteristic of culture is reminiscent of military missions and, arguably, at odds with the current *community policing* model of today's law enforcement agencies, which highlights a "coproduction" of public safety in partnership with the community (see chapter 10).

Police are subjected to other forms of communication or messages reinforcing their intergroup existence, and promoting the *us versus them* mentality, throughout their career. As an example, police-related magazine advertisements are often designed to emphasize the police mission to "hunt" for criminals. In one instance, an advertisement from a police magazine poses the question "What are *they* hiding . . . weapons?" reinforcing the we/they intergroup relationship between police and the public with an emphasis on the dangers the public poses to police.[2] We suggest that the types of influences listed above, in part, routinely expose officers to the *us versus them* mentality throughout their career. This routine exposure to one's social identity (see self-categorization theory: Turner et al. 1987) causes a person's social category (i.e., police officer) to become even more salient in intergroup communications (Dragojevic and Giles 2014). In other words, the more police officers are exposed to how "different" they are and how different they appear to others, the more they will identify as being *apart* from the public.

Police organizational culture can have significant impacts on how an agency's model of policing is delivered. White (2001), in observing the influence of police executives on deadly force encounters, found that personal philosophies of those executives can outweigh formal policy when it comes to officers' discretion, supporting the notion that officers' interactions with the public can be significantly influenced by the organizational culture. Relatedly, Nix, Wolfe, and Campbell (2018) found that command-level officers who perceived the "war on cops" as legitimate were more likely to believe de-policing is common. These researchers suggest that command level officers who hold these beliefs (that the war on cops and de-policing are real) are more likely to allow or encourage de-policing behavior in their department.

In looking at changing police culture through police recruitment and training, Chan (1997) highlights how police executives are often enthusiastic about organizational reform, but those efforts are stymied by an internal conflict of management culture and street cop culture (Reuss-Ianni 1983). Research also suggests that the benefits of training programs in law enforcement can be undermined by the police occupational subculture (Brogden, Jefferson, and Walklate 1988, 57). For long-term change in police culture, training and education must be "relevant to police operations and pitched at a practical rather than abstract level."

Intergroup Communication

In line with the foregoing, when people define themselves in terms of their own group identity, they strive to make themselves as distinct as possible from other socially relevant groups, communities, or organizations on valued dimensions (Tajfel and Turner 1986). A pervasive way of doing this is through one's language and communicative styles as ingroup members (e.g., adolescents, gang members, academics), creating inclusive new forms of slang, colloquialisms, and jargon that can exclude others, while diverging and accentuating their accents, discourse, and nonverbal cues from outgroup speakers in social interaction (Palomares, Giles, Soliz, and Gallois 2016). In common with members of other organizations whose norms instill in them the need to develop their own within-group communication patterns (Poole 2011), "cop talk" is ubiquitous in law enforcement (Pacanowsky and Anderson 2009; Trujillo and Dionisopoulos 1987; see also "the talk," chapter 5).

Tajfel and his colleagues were clearly concerned with issues of language and communication from the earliest days of intergroup theory development in the 1970s (e.g., Bourhis, Giles, Leyens, and Tajfel 1979; Giles 1977, 1978) and this took on considerable momentum in subsequent decades through journal special issues (e.g., Clément 1996; Reid and Giles 2005), edited books (e.g., Gudykunst 1986; Giles and Maass 2016), and a handbook and two-volume encyclopedia (Giles 2012a; Giles and Harwood 2018). Research and theory arising from this tradition—which has almost tripled in the last ten years (Keblusek, Giles, Maass, and Gardikiotis 2018)—has been manifest in diverse ways. These include studies showing that television viewers tend to select TV channels that only portray their own ingroups favorably and avoid, or not select, shows that portray them in a more negative light (e.g., Reid, Giles, and Abrams 2004; see also

Harwood and Roy 2005). Another is evident from work suggesting that immigrants' failure to acquire their host's dominant language to the level of native-like proficiency is not due—as is often interpreted—to a lack of aptitude or motivation to acculturate but, arguably, to them energetically protecting their valued ways of talking (e.g., Giles and Byrne 1982). These studies help us to understand why language in subcultures, such as cop culture, is slow to evolve in part because it is intertwined with the social identity of the police officer.

One important theory of interpersonal communication—communication accommodation theory (CAT; Giles 2016)—that has spawned much work across cultures, languages, disciplines and social contexts (Soliz and Giles 2014) draws heavily on these intergroup dynamics. It explores how the adjustments we make to accommodate each other communicatively are fundamental to successful interaction (Giles and Gasiorek 2013). CAT helps explain how our intergroup histories inform our communicative adjustments and attitudes. These adjustments, however, can also be *nonaccommodative*, hindering communication and creating social distance in intergroup exchanges (Gasiorek 2018). For example, while an officer's perception of an interaction may be that it was professional and courteous ("Move along, nothing to see here"), the other involved party may feel quite differently.

CAT allows for the circumstances where one party (police) feels it appropriately adjusted their communication, whereas the other party (civilian) does not feel the communication was accommodating. In this way, CAT proposes that one person's *subjective* accommodation does not necessarily translate into *objective* accommodation (Gasiorek 2016). Relatedly, this proposition of CAT begins to explain why a large portion of complaints against police officers are attitudinal in nature (see chapter 13). During informal interactions, the result of a poor police–citizen interaction may seem inconsequential, but considering the complexity of the relationship between police and citizens, the result of nonaccommodation by police or civilian can be tremendously angstful or worse. A nonaccommodative police officer can engage in poorly received interaction with a citizen during a detention or arrest, even when the officer operates well within policy and law. What is interpreted as a procedurally just set of behaviors by the public will be contingent, of course, on the nature of the context as well as the characteristics of the observers. In tandem, there is rapidly expanding research regarding the ways in which procedural justice shapes a citizen's perception of fairness and their willingness to cooperate with police (Reisig 2007; Sunshine and Tyler 2003). Relatedly, the *subjective* interpretation of communication accommodation also touches on the criticism some academics have highlighted with procedural justice theory (PJT). It has been suggested that PJT may be limited in some ways, such as its approach to social identity processes. For example, Radburn et al. (2018) argue that "perceptions of procedural fairness should not be viewed as independent from the identities of those making the judgements and the social context within which they occur" (3).

However, rather than outline further work having emerged from the intergroup communication tradition (for recent overviews, see Gallois, Watson, and Giles 2018; Pines, Harwood, and Giles 2018; Rakić and Maass 2019), we will, instead, succinctly convey some of the so-called and major *Principles of Intergroup Communication* proposed in this literature (see Giles 2012b) and provide modest, but explicit, examples of how these principles root themselves in police culture:

- Language and other diverse modes of communication (identifying a person as an "officer" by title) serve as markers—and sometimes are the criteria—for the multiple categories to which group members belong (e.g., Scherer and Giles 1979).
- Groups' messages about their intergroup histories (academy training) and demographics, along with other practices (police recruitment advertisements with "police chases" and "action clips"), institutionalize distinctive cultures that coexist with comparative others (e.g., Bourhis, Sachdev, Ehala, and Giles 2019).
- The communicative practices and boundaries (police power of arrest) that differentiate social groups can, in turn, dynamically redefine or change the very nature of the intergroup relations themselves (e.g., Abrams, O'Connor, and Giles 2002).
- Group members will strive, and sometimes be strategically encouraged to acquire (or acculturate to) the communicative practices of others (desire to assimilate into police organizational subculture, field training from senior officers). This "accommodative chase" can be prolonged and, oftentimes, ultimately abandoned because of its deleterious effect on maintaining a positive social identity (e.g., Keblusek, Giles, and Maass 2017).
- Through the establishment, negotiation, and expression of ingroup norms, individuals can foster more control over their everyday lives, enabling them also to recognize ingroup deviants and publicly discredit and marginalize such offenders (those policed). Similarly, group leaders who more prototypically manifest the values and communicative practices of the ingroup (informal rank and file leaders who perpetuate cultural norms) emerge and/or are elected over influential others (e.g., Hogg 2001, 2018).

INTERGROUP COMMUNICATION AND POLICING

In this section, we examine aspects of law enforcement-citizen communication that have been mined primarily from an intergroup communication perspective. Research shows that those with negative attitudes toward the police (ATP) have often had (or vicariously heard significant others reporting as having had) disturbing—or at least dissatisfactory—police contacts in the past. In this regard, they perceived the police as having treated them poorly, whether verbally or otherwise.

There are numerous studies addressing ATP cross-disciplinarily, although these have been conducted in very different locales over time, with varying methodologies and outcome measures and, hence somewhat inevitably, contrary findings. In general, and in the United States, older, female, urban, better educated, higher incomed, homeowners, and married respondents in lower-crime neighborhoods consistently manifest more positive ATPs than their social counterparts (see Tyler and Huo 2002). Ethnic perceptions of law enforcement in the United States have, in particular, received widespread empirical attention; Caucasians and Asians have the most favorable ATPs and trust in police, followed by Hispanics and Native Americans, and then African Americans (e.g., Taylor, Turner, Esbensen and Winfree, 2001; see chapter 5).

Given estimates that 97 percent of American police work involves interacting with the public (Thompson 1983), it is surprising that the impact of *communication* on ATP has not been systematically examined. Relatedly, Wolfe et al. (2020), in evaluating training programs for police officers, showed officers who participated in *social interaction training* placed higher priorities on *procedurally fair communication*.

Indeed, communication is regarded as "the central most important commodity that the officer has at his [or her] disposal" (Sklansky 2011; Womack and Finley 1986, 14). In three investigations using different procedures, agencies, and representative samples of various populations, Giles et al. (2006) found that in one of these studies of adults in a small city in California, perceptions of how communicatively accommodating officers[3] had been in the past was a better predictor of their evaluations of local law enforcement than their age, gender, or ethnicity. In addition, respondents spontaneously highlighted officers' *communication practices* as more important than any other factor (e.g., more officers on patrol, more minorities and women) when suggesting what improvements should be made to law enforcement services.

Underscoring further the important role of officer *non*accommodativeness (e.g., Myers, Giles, Reid, and Nabi 2008) in forging negative community attitudes is Cox and White's (1988) finding that an officer's inappropriate behavior could induce more negative attitudes than whether or not a citation was issued. In this vein, Tyler and Huo (2002) suggested that individuals are willing to defer to legal authorities only if there is some trust within the interaction, and when they feel that they are being treated in a procedurally fair and just manner (see chapters 8 and 18). What these scholars refer to as dignified, fair, and respectful treatment in the criminal justice literature can be regarded as manifestations of accommodation theory in the communication and sociolinguistic disciplines (see, for example, Giles, Willemyns, Gallois, and Anderson 2007; see also chapter 17); for a comparison of these two theoretical perspectives, see Lowrey, Maguire, and Bennett 2016).

In a series of studies from fourteen communities, having very different histories of police–citizen conflict (including Russia, the United States, Japan, and the United Arab Emirates), increased perceptions of communication accommodation led to more public compliance. Typically, the more police officers were seen to be communicatively accommodating (e.g., listening and taking drivers' perspectives into account), the more they were perceived to be trustworthy which, in turn, led members of the public to be more willing to report complying with their requests and demands (see, for example, Choi, Khadavy, Raddawi, and Giles 2019).

Intergroup Contact and Communication in the Field

The above studies have all involved surveys and self-reports and we end this section by introducing more naturalistic studies of intergroup communication and policing. Traffic stops are contact settings where citizens are most likely to encounter officers face to face (Langan, Greenfeld, Smith, Durose, and Levin, 2001; see also chapter 17). These can be emotionally charged, oftentimes involving uncertainty among citizens about a violation, and intergroup identities can be very salient (see Shon 2005). For many officers too, this contact situation can be communicatively challenging if the intent is to render a comprehensible, but non-offensive outcome for the citizen. For predictable methodological reasons, actual analyses of ongoing interactions with officers in the field are somewhat rare.

One award-winning set of studies that picks up the gauntlet here—a recipient of the National Academy of Sciences's 2018 Cozzarelli Prize for "outstanding scientific excellence and originality"—is by Voigt et al. (2017). They obtained data from officers' body cameras and examined over thirty-six thousand single adjacent utterances between officers and members of the public involved in traffic stops. They determined, by means of coders' ratings and computational analyses of the utterances' transcripts, that officers were more respectful, friendly, formal, and impartial with White than Black drivers. This emerged irrespective of the severity of the offense or outcome of the stop, with Whites being more reassured (e.g., "no big deal") while Black drivers were more often told to keep their hands on the wheel. While a step in the right direction, we see possible limitations to the study and, hence, its social implications, including only a very small set of the data set was analyzed and this being accomplished only on randomly selected, *transcribed* exchanges.[4]

Relatedly, and theoretically taking onboard an intergroup communication perspective, Dixon, Schell, Giles, and Drogos (2008) examined complete videotaped exchanges between officers and drivers in traffic stops in the city of Cleveland (see chapter 5). They were able to content analyze African American and White police officers' communications with citizens of these same racial groups with a randomly stratified sample of video-recorded traffic stops. Trained coders examined each stop for more than one hundred contextual and officer–driver variables. Among other interracial patterns noted, African American drivers were more likely than White drivers to experience what was labeled "extensive policing." Here, African American drivers were detained for an average of 2.6 minutes longer than White drivers, with typically more than one police officer present. In addition, African American drivers were between three to five times more likely than White drivers to be asked to leave the vehicle, asked if they were carrying drugs or weapons, and have themselves, their passengers, and/or their vehicles searched for illegal items (see Tillyer and Klahm IV 2015).

At the same time, African American drivers were coded as more nonaccommodative than Whites, that is, less apologetic, courteous, and respectful, and more belligerent. While each party's accommodativeness predicted the other's level, intergroup encounters were coded as more nonaccommodative than those where both driver and officer were of the same racial backgrounds. Here, the communication climate was found to be characterized by officers listening less, being more indifferent, more dismissive, and less approachable, respectful and polite than in intra-ethnic situations (for similar outcomes with Hispanic drivers in southern California, see Giles, Linz, Bonilla, and Gomez 2012).

Ironically, it seems that communication training and embracing accommodative competences are given short shrift in police academies and police culture. We are in dire need of more research and recognition of these dynamics. This handbook is one modest way of underscoring the importance of these issues and for a whole host of social groups and between—as well as within—group outcomes (e.g., mediating complaints, recruitment).

CONCLUSIONS

Research in the field of communication provides explanation and insight into the *us versus them* relationship between police and citizens. As the nation, and arguably the world, is reimagining what policing looks like in the future, evidence from intergroup communication research offers a platform to begin, and a pathway toward, a more accommodative police officer. Empirical evidence related to intergroup dialogue provides a foundation to reduce intergroup anxieties and encourage empathy between ingroups and outgroups, such as "the police" and "those policed." Relatedly, research and evidence surrounding CAT offers a path forward to reduce unnecessary conflict by providing an understanding of the dynamics that occur during a police–citizen interaction and a glimpse toward how those interactions can be adjusted for more improved outcomes (see, again, chapter 2).

Furthermore, CAT allows us to understand the communication adjustments that occur as people adapt their communicative behavior in context (Gasiorek 2016). These adjustments are dependent, in part, by group membership and affected by the experience of one's social identity such as linguistic and sociocultural backgrounds including power differentials, stereotypes, and identity conflicts (Zhang and Giles 2017). An individual's motives play a role in the communicative adjustments they make (Giles 2016). Two aspects of CAT are convergence and divergence. *Convergence* occurs when one adjusts communicative behaviors to be more similar to another, whereas *divergence* works to create social distance and recognizes conversation partners will *nonaccommodate* due to a group member's perceived identity conflict (*the police* and *those policed*). Divergence is increased in more salient identity-threatening situations (Zhang and Imamura 2018). Additionally, people have different expectations regarding the appropriate levels of adjustment for communication partners to find a reference point or common ground.

Therefore appropriate and optimal levels of communicative adjustments can be subjective, based on how one sees the world (Giles and Smith 1979). In this regard, how different groups—dominant vis à vis subordinate—may interpret the ingredients of a common ground, a shared identity, or superordinate label may differ greatly and, thereby, be potentially very contentious (see Dovidio, Gaertner, Ufkes, Saguy, and Pearson 2016). In this sense, how "the police" and "those policed" may differentially see the ingredients and implications of overarching group constructs (such as, say, "All Americans" or "citizens") *could*—and it is an intriguing empirical question to be explored—be quite dilemmatic.

The police worldview is unique, in part due to the unparalleled power differential police hold in society. Scholars of police culture suggest that a primary tenet of police culture is the belief that they are the keepers of the "thin blue line" between chaos and order. In the context of intergroup communication regarding a person's professional identity, a police officer would consider anyone outside of the profession an outgroup member. Therefore, police interactions with "those policed" *begin* in a significant identity-threatening environment. Perceptions by the police identifying sectors of the public as members of an outgroup are, arguably, forged primarily during police selection processes and police training environments, and then reinforced in police culture throughout officers' careers. Clearly, more naturalistic, observational research is necessary to unpack how *us versus them* mentalities are communicatively transmitted and sustained as well as discursively and nonverbally reacted to in each of these three domains, and with what attitudinal, affective, and behavioral effects. It would be interesting to determine whether features of these intergroup communicative climates alienate particular participants consumed by them and lead to attrition from the profession. Finally, we posit that CAT allows us to understand and predict (and, thereby, assist in *defusing*) the forms of *divergence* that occur as contacts between police and the public that quickly unravel from the onset, often leading to undesirable and sometimes violent results.

NOTES

1. The authors wish to recognize that police are part of the community and are using the term "community" in this text to represent "those-policed" for the benefit of clarity.
2. Exemplifed in Lazor Labs. 2018. "Enforcer II Tint Meter." *Police Chief* 85 (8): 3.
3. Officer accommodativeness was measured, in many of these studies, by means of the following items: How pleasant are the police officers? How accommodating are police officers? How respectful of students are police officers? How polite are police officers? How well do police officers explain things? See Giles (2016) for recent research and elaborations of CAT, which explores the antecedents and social consequences of people accommodating (and nonaccommodating) to people who represent different social groups and identities.
4. The literature does acknowledge problems with analyzing transcriptions (e.g., ten Have 2002) and also raises concerns about the work and consequences of transcribers who are not the actual investigators (Tilley 2003); we do not know the origins of this process in this case. Crucially, too, the lack of *non-*linguistic data—let alone the avowed reasons for the traffic stops—are interpretively constraining. Among many other commentators, Jones and LeBaron (2002) argued compellingly for "an integrated approach in which verbal and nonverbal messages are studied as *inseparable* phenomena when they occur together" (our italics). In addition, the lack of socially diagnostic vocal and facial cues are also problematic. Crivelli and Fridlund (2018) noted, for instance, that an "angry" face is not necessarily an indication of underlying anger, but oftentimes a sign of threat, implying "stop what you're doing!" Finally, scholars identify most gestures as part of the linguistic and not the nonverbal system, such that accompanying gestures can add to the meaning of speech (Goldin-Meadow 2003).

REFERENCES

Abrams, Jessica, Joan O'Connor, and Howard Giles. 2002. "Identity and Intergroup Communication." In *The Third Handbook of Intercultural Communication,* edited by William B. Gudykunst and Bella Mody, 225–40. Thousand Oaks: Sage.
Allport, Gordon W. 1954. *The Nature of Prejudice.* Oxford: Addison-Wesley.
Balko, Radley. 2014. *Rise of the Warrior Cop.* Philadelphia: Persus Books.
Biggs, Amanda, Paula Brough, and Jennifer Barbour. 2014. "Relationships of Individual and Organizational Support with Engagement: Examining Various Types of Causality in a Three-Wave Study." *Work & Stress* 28: 236–54.

Boivin, Rémi, Camille Faubert, Anne Gendron, and Bruno Poulin. 2018. "The 'Us Versus Them' Mentality: A Comparison of Police Cadets at Different Stages of Their Training." *Police Practice and Research.* Advance Online: https://doi.10.1080/15614263.2018.1555480 .

Bourhis, Richard Y., Howard Giles, Jacques-Paul Leyens, and Henri Tajfel. 1979. "Psycholinguistic Distinctiveness: Language Divergence in Belgium." In *Language and Social Psychology*, edited by Howard Giles and Robert N. St. Clair, 158–85. Oxford: Blackwell.

Bourhis, Richard Y., Itesh Sachdev, Martin Ehala, and Howard Giles. 2019. "Forty Years of Group Vitality Research." *Journal of Language and Social Psychology* 38 (4): 408–21.

Brogden, Mike E., Tony Jefferson, and Sandra Walklate (1988). *Introducing Policework*. London: Unwin Hyman.

Brough, Paula, Shannyn Chataway, and Amanda Biggs. 2016. "'You Don't Want People Knowing You're a Copper!' A Contemporary Assessment of Police Organizational Culture." *International Journal of Police Science & Management* 18 (1): 28–36.

Chan, Janet. 1997. *Changing Police Culture: Policing in a Multicultural Society*. Cambridge: Cambridge University Press.

Chappell, Allison T., and Lonn Lanza-Kaduce. 2010. "Police Academy Socialization: Understanding the Lessons Learned in a Paramilitary-Bureaucratic Organization." *Journal of Contemporary Ethnography* 39 (2): 187–214.

Choi, Charles W., Gholam Hassan Khadavy, Rana Raddawi, and Howard Giles. 2019. "Perceptions of Police-Civilian Encounters: Communication and Intergroup Parameters in the USA and the United Arab Emirates." *Journal of International and Intercultural Communication* 12 (1): 82–104.

Christie, Gayre, Simon Petrie, and Perri Timmins. 1996. "The Effect of Police Education, Training and Socialization on Conservative Attitudes." *Australian & New Zealand Journal of Criminology* 29: 299–314.

Clément, Richard, ed. 1996. "The Social Psychology of Intergroup Communication" [Special Issue]. *Journal of Language and Social Psychology* 15 (3): 222–392.

Cox, Terry C., and Mervin F. White. 1988. "Traffic Citations and Student Attitudes toward the Police: An Examination of Selected Interaction Dynamics." *Journal of Police Science and Administration* 16 (2): 105–21.

Crivelli, Carlos, and Alan J. Fridlund. 2018. "Facial Displays Are Tools for Social Influence." *Trends in Cognitive Science* 22 (5): P388–99.

Cuddy, Amy J., Susan T. Fiske, and Peter Glick, P. 2008. "Warmth and Competence as Universal Dimensions of Social Perception: The Stereotype Content Model and the BIAS Map." In *Advances in Experimental Social Psychology* 40, edited by Mark Zanna, 61–148. San Diego: Elsevier.

Dixon, Travis Terry L. Schell, Howard Giles, and Kristin L. Drogos. 2008. "The Influence of Race in Police-Civilian Interactions: A Content Analysis of Videotaped Interactions Taken during Cincinnati Police Traffic Stops." *Journal of Communication* 58 (3): 530–49.

Dovidio, John F., Samuel L. Gaertner, Elze G. Ufkes, Tamar Saguy, and Adam R. Pearson. 2016. "Included but Invisible? Subtle Bias, Common Identity, and the Darker Side of 'We.'" *Social Issues and Policy Review* 10 (1): 6–46.

Dragojevic, Marko, and Howard Giles. 2014. "Language and Interpersonal Communication: Their Intergroup Dynamics." In *Handbook of Interpersonal Communication*, edited by Charles R. Berger, 29–51. Berlin: De Gruyter Mouton.

Gaines, Larry, and Victor Kappeler. 2015. *Policing in America*. New York: Routledge.

Gallois, Cynthia, Bernadette M. Watson, and Howard Giles. 2018. "Intergroup Communication: Accommodation, Identity, and Effective Interactions." *Journal of Communication* 68 (2): 309–17.

Ganapathy, Narayanan, and Harry Cheong. 2016. "The 'Thinning' Blue Line: A Bourdieuian Appreciation of Police Subculture." *International Journal of Comparative and Applied Criminal Justice* 40 (4): 325–42.

Gasiorek, Jessica. 2016. "Theoretical Perspectives on Interpersonal Adjustments in Language and Communication." In *Communication Accommodation Theory: Negotiating Personal Relationships and Social Identities across Contexts*, edited by Howard Giles, 13–35. Cambridge: Cambridge University Press.

Gasiorek, Jessica. 2018. "Nonaccommodation." In *The Oxford Encyclopedia of Intergroup Communication*, edited by Howard Giles and Jake Harwood, Vol. 2, 179–92. New York: Oxford University Press.

Giles, Howard, ed. 1977. *Language, Ethnicity and Intergroup Relations*. London: Academic Press.

Giles, Howard. 1978. "Linguistic Differentiation between Ethnic Groups." In *Differentiation between Social Groups*, edited by Henri Tajfel, 361–93. London: Academic Press.

Giles, Howard, ed. 2012a. *The Handbook of Intergroup Communication*. New York: Routledge.

Giles, Howard. 2012b. "Principles of Intergroup Communication." In *The Handbook of Intergroup Communication*, edited by Howard Giles, 3–16. New York: Routledge.

Giles, Howard, ed. 2016. *Communication Accommodation Theory: Negotiating Personal and Social Identities across Contexts*. Cambridge: Cambridge University Press.

Giles, Howard, and Jane L. Byrne. 1982. "An Intergroup Model of Second Language Acquisition." *Journal of Multilingual and Multicultural Development* 3 (3): 17–40.

Giles, Howard, Jennifer Fortman, Rene Dailey, Valerie Barker, Christopher Hajek, Michelle Anderson, and Nicholas O. Rule. 2006. "Communication Accommodation: Law Enforcement and the Public." In *Applied Interpersonal Communication Matters: Family, Health, and Community Relations*, edited by Rene M. Dailey and Beth A. Le Poire, 241–69. New York: Peter Lang.

Giles, Howard, and Jessica Gasiorek. 2013. "Parameters of Non-Accommodation: Refining and Elaborating Communication Accommodation Theory." In *Social Cognition and Communication*, edited by Joseph Forgas, Orsolya Vincze, and János László, 155–72. New York: Psychology Press.

Giles, Howard, and Jake Harwood., eds. 2018. *The Oxford Encyclopedia of Intergroup Communication*, vols. 1 and 2. New York: Oxford University Press.

Giles, Howard, Dan Linz, Doug Bonilla, and Michelle Gomez. 2012. "Police Stops of and Interactions with Latino and White (Non-Latino) Drivers: Extensive Policing and Communication Accommodation." *Communication Monographs* 79 (4): 407–27.

Giles, Howard, and Anne Maass, eds. 2016. *Advances in Intergroup Communication*. New York: Peter Lang.

Giles, Howard, and Philip M. Smith. 1979. "Accommodation Theory: Optimal Levels of Convergence." In *Language and Social Psychology*, edited by Howard Giles and Robert N. St. Clair, 45–65. Oxford, Blackwell.

Giles, Howard, Michael Willemyns, Cynthia Gallois, and Michelle Anderson. 2007. "Accommodating a New Frontier: The Context of Law Enforcement." In *Social Communication*, edited by Klaus Fiedler, 129–62. New York: Psychology Press

Goldin-Meadow, Susan. 2003. *Hearing Gesture: How Our Hands Help Us Think*. Cambridge: Harvard University Press.

Greenway, Katherine, Kim Peters, S. Alexander Haslam, and William Bingley. 2016. "Shared Identity and the Intergroup Dynamics of Communication." In *Advances in Intergroup Communication*, edited by Howard Giles and Anne Maass, 19–34. New York: Peter Lang.

Gudykunst, William B., ed. 1986. *Intergroup Communication*. London: Edward Arnold.

Harwood, Jake, and Abhik Roy. 2005. "Social Identity Theory and Mass Communication Research." In *Intergroup Communication: Multiple Perspectives*, edited by Jake Harwood and Howard Giles, 189–211. New York: Peter Lang.

Hewstone, Miles, Mark Rubin, and Hazel Willis. 2002. "Intergroup Bias." *Annual Review of Psychology* 53 (1): 575–604.

Hill, Shawn, and Howard Giles. 2019. "Resilience as a Department Cultural Initiative: Sustaining Wellness." *Police Chief* Online, May 29. http://www.policechiefmagazine.org/resilience-as-a-department-cultural-initiative/?ref=29226880c75535d64987cc8172f1943f .

Hogg, Michael A. 2001. "A Social Identity Theory of Leadership." *Personality and Social Psychology Review* 5 (3): 184–200.

Hogg, Michael, A. 2018. "Self-Uncertainty, Leadership Preference, and Communication of Social Identity." *Atlantic Journal of Communication* 26 (2): 111–21.

Hogg, Michael, A., and Howard Giles. 2012. "Norm Talk and Identity in Intergroup Communication." In *The Handbook of Intergroup Communication*, edited by Howard Giles, 373–88. New York: Routledge.

ICAT: Integrated Communications, Assessment and Tactics. 2016. Retrieved from https://www.policeforum.org/assets/icattrainingguide.pdf .

Jetten, Jolanda, Catherine Haslam, and S. Alexander Haslam, eds. 2012. *The Social Cure: Identity, Health, and Well-Being.* New York: Psychology Press.

Jones, Jeffrey M. 2015. *In U.S., Confidence in Police Lowest in 22 Years.* Gallup: Politics. Retrieved from https://news.gallup.com/poll/183704/confidence-police-lowest-years.aspx .

Jones, Stanley, E., and Curtis D. LeBaron. 2002. "Research on the Relationship between Verbal and Nonverbal Communication: Emerging Integrations." *Journal of Communication* 52 (3): 499–521.

Kappeler, Victor E., Richard D. Sluder, and Geoffrey P. Alpert. 1998. *Forces of Deviance: Understanding the Dark Side of Policing.* Long Grove: Waveland Press.

Keblusek, Lauren, Howard Giles, and Anne Maass. 2017. "Language and Intergroup Communication." *Group Processes and Intergroup Relations* 20 (5): 632–43.

Keblusek, Lauren, Howard Giles, Anne Maass, Antonis Gardikiotis. 2018. "Intersections of Intergroup Communication Research." *Atlantic Journal of Communication* 26 (2): 75–85.

Langan, Patrick A., Lawrence A. Greenfeld, Steven K. Smith, Matthew R. Durose, and David J. Levin. 2001. *Contact between Police and the Public.* Washington, DC: Bureau of Justice Statistics.

LASD: Los Angeles Sheriff's Department Training Academy. Re-Dedication Ceremony Part 1 of 2. 2014. Retrieved from https://www.youtube.com/watch?v=5dPRHN7u-Io .

Lowrey, Belén, Edward R. Maguire, and Richard R. Bennett. 2016. "Testing the Effects of Procedural Justice and Overaccommodation in Traffic Stops: A Randomized Experiment." *Criminal Justice and Behavior* 43 (10): 1430–49.

Maass, Anne, Daniela Salvi, Luciano Acuri, and Gün R. Semin. 1989. "Language Use in Intergroup Contexts: The Linguistic Intergroup Bias." *Journal of Personality and Social Psychology* 57 (6): 981–93.

Manning, Peter K. 1977. *Police Work: The Social Organization of Policing.* Cambridge: MIT Press.

McIntyre, Kylie, Stefania Paolini, and Miles Hewstone. 2016. "Changing People's Views of Outgroups through Individual-to-Group Generalization: Meta-Analytic Reviews and Theoretical Considerations." *European Review of Social Psychology* 27 (1): 63–115.

McLean, Kyle, Scott E. Wolfe, Jeff Rojek, Geoffrey P. Alpert, and Michael R. Smith. 2019. "Police Officers as Warriors or Guardians: Empirical Reality or Intriguing Rhetoric." *Justice Quarterly.* Advance Online: https://doi: 10.1080/07418825.2018.1533031 .

Myers, Paul, Howard Giles, Scott A. Reid, and Robin Nabi. 2008. "Law Enforcement Encounters: The Effects of Officer Accommodativeness and Crime Severity on Interpersonal Attributions Are Mediated by Intergroup Sensitivity." *Communication Studies* 59 (4): 1–15.

Myhill, Andy, and Ben Bradford. 2013. "Overcoming Cop Culture? Organizational Justice and Police Officers' Attitudes toward the Public." *Policing: An International Journal* 36 (2): 338–56.

Nix, Justin, Scott Wolfe, and Bradley Campbell. 2018. "Command-Level Police Officers' Perceptions of the 'War on Cops' and De-policing." *Justice Quarterly* 35 (1): 33–54.

Pacanowsky, Michael E., and James A. Anderson. 2009, online. "Cop Talk and Media Use." *Journal of Broadcasting* 26 (4): 741–55.

Paessen, Heidi, Jeroen Maesschalk, and Kim Loyens. 2019. "Beyond Police Culture: A Quantitative Study of the Organizational Culture in 64 Local Police Forces in Belgium." *Policing* 24 (5): 814–31.

Palomares, Nicholas, Howard Giles, Jordan Soliz, and Cynthia Gallois. 2016. "Intergroup Accommodation, Social Categories, and Identities." In *Communication Accommodation Theory: Negotiating Personal Relationships and Social Identities across Contexts*, edited by Howard Giles, 123–51. Cambridge: Cambridge University Press.

Perlmutter, David. 2000. *Policing the Media.* Thousand Oaks: Sage.

Pines, Rachyl, Jake Harwood, and Howard Giles. 2018. "Communicating Intergroup Matters: The Encyclopedia in Context." In *The Oxford Encyclopedia of Intergroup Communication*, edited by Howard Giles and Jake Harwood, Vol. 1., xvii–xx. New York: Oxford University Press.

Pinizzotto, Anthony J., Edward F. Davis, and Charles E. Miller III. 1997. *In the Line of Fire: A Study of Selected Felonious Assaults on Law Enforcement Officers.* Washington DC: U.S. Department of Justice.

Poole, M. Scott. 2011. "Communication." In *APA Handbook of Industrial and Organization Psychology*, edited by S. Zedeck, Vol. 3: 249–70. Washington DC: APA.

Radburn, Matthew, Clifford Stott, Ben Bradford, and Mark Robinson. (2018). "When Is Policing Fair? Groups, Identity and Judgements of the Procedural Justice of Coercive Crowd Policing." *Policing and Society* 28 (6): 647–64.

Rakić, T., and Anne Maass. 2019. "Communicating Between Groups, Communicating About Groups." In *Language, Communication, and Intergroup Relations: A Celebration of the Scholarship of Howard Giles*, edited by Jake Harwood, Jessica Gasiorek, Herbert Pierson, Jon F. Nussbaum, and Cindy Gallois, 66–97. New York: Routledge.

Reichel, Philip. 1988. "Southern Slave Patrols as a Transitional Police Type." *American Journal of Police* 7 (2): 51–77.

Reid, Scott A., and Howard Giles, eds. 2005. "Intergroup Relations: Its Linguistic and Communicative Parameters" [Special Issue]. *Group Processes and Intergroup Relations* 8 (3): 211–328.

Reid, Scott A., Howard Giles, and Jessica Abrams, J. 2004. "A Social Identity Model of Media Usage and Effects." *Zeitschrift für Medienpsychologie* 16 (1): 17–25.

Reisig, Michael D. 2007. "Procedural Justice and Community Policing—What Shapes Residents' Willingness to Participate in Crime Prevention Programs?" *Policing: Journal of Policy and Practice* 1 (3): 356–69.

Reuss-Ianni, Elizabeth. 1983. *Two Cultures of Policing: Street Cops and Management Cops*. New Brunswick: Transaction Publishers.

Scherer, Klaus, and Howard Giles, eds. 1979. *Social Markers in Speech*. Cambridge: Cambridge University Press.

Sherif, Muzafer, O. J. Harvey, B. Jack White, William R. Hood, and Carolyn W. Sherif. 1961. *Intergroup Conflict and Cooperation: The Robbers Cave Experiment*. Norman: University of Oklahoma Book Exchange.

Shon, Philip C. H. 2005. "'I'd Grab the S-O-B by His Hair and Yank Him Out the Window': The Fraternal Order of Warnings and Threats in Police–Citizen Encounters." *Discourse and Society* 16 (6): 829–45.

Sklansky, David A. 2011. *The Persistent Pull of Police Professionalism*. New Perspectives in Policing (Executive Session on Policing and Public Safety), March. Harvard Kennedy School. Malcolm Wiener Center for Social Policy. Retrieved from https://www.ncjrs.gov/pdffiles1/nij/232676.pdf.

Skolnick, Jerome. 1966. *Justice without Trial: Law Enforcement in a Democratic Society*. New York: John Wiley.

Soliz, Jordan, and Howard Giles. 2014. "Relational and Identity Processes in Communication: A Contextual and Meta-Analytical Review of Communication Accommodation Theory." *Annals of the International Communication Association* 38 (1): 107–44.

Stoughton, Seth W. 2016. "Principled Policing: Warrior Cops and Guardian Officers." *Wake Forest Law Review* 51. Retrieved from https://ssrn.com/abstract=2830642.

Stradling, Stephen G., Gail Crowe, and Alan P. Tuohy. 1993. "Changes in Self-Concept during Occupational Socialization of New Recruits to the Police." *Journal of Community and Applied Social Psychology* 3 (2): 131–47.

Sunshine, J., and Tom R. Tyler. 2003. "The Role of Procedural Justice and Legitimacy in Shaping Public Support for Policing." *Law & Society Review* 37: 513–48.

Sutton, Robert M., and Karen Douglas, eds. 2008. "Celebrating Twenty Years of Linguistic Bias Research" [Special Issue]. *Journal of Language and Social Psychology* 27 (2): 105–229.

Swann Jr., William B., Ángel Gómez, Michael D. Buhrmester, Lucia López-Rodríguez, Juan Jiménez, and Alexandra Vázquez. 2014. "Contemplating the Ultimate Sacrifice: Identity Fusion Channels Pro-Group Affect, Cognition, and Moral Decision Making." *Journal of Personality and Social Psychology* 106 (5): 713–27.

Tajfel, Henri, Michael G. Billig, Robert P. Bundy, and Claude Flament. 1971. "Social Categorization and Intergroup Behavior." *European Journal of Social Psychology* 1 (2): 149–77.

Tajfel, Henri, and John C. Turner. 1986. "The Social Psychology of Intergroup Behavior." In *Psychology of Intergroup Relations*, edited by Stephen Worchel and William G. Austin, 7–24. Chicago: Nelson-Hall.

Taylor, Donald M., and Fathali M. Moghaddam. 1994. *Theories of Intergroup Relations: International Social Psychological Perspectives*, 2nd ed. Westport: Praeger.

Taylor, Terrance, K. B. Turner, Finn-Aage Esbensen, and Thomas L. Winfree. 2001. "Coppin' an Attitude: Attitudinal Differences among Juveniles toward Police." *Journal of Criminal Justice*, 29 (4): 295–305.

ten Have, Paul. 2002. "Reflections on Transcription." *Cahiers de Praxématique* 29: 21–43.

Thompson, George J. 1983. *Verbal Judo: Words for Street Survival*. Springfield: Charles C. Thomas.

Tilley, Susan A. 2003. "'Challenging Research Practices: Turning a Critical Lens on the Work of Transcription." *Qualitative Inquiry* 9 (5): 673–704.

Tillyer, Ron, and Charles F. Klahm IV. 2015. "Discretionary Searches, the Impact of Passengers, and the Implications for Police–Minority Encounters." *Criminal Justice Review* 40 (3): 378–96.

Trujillo, Nick, and George Dionisopoulos. 1987. "Cop Talk, Police Stories, and the Social Construction of Organizational Drama." *Central States Speech Journal* 38 (3–4): 196–209.

Turner, John C., and Howard Giles, eds. 1981. *Intergroup Behavior*. Oxford: Blackwell.

Turner, John C., Michael A. Hogg, Penelope Oakes, Stephen D. Reicher, and Margaret Wetherell. 1987. *Discovering the Social Group: Self-Categorization Theory*. Oxford: Blackwell.

Tyler, Tom R., and Yuen Huo. 2002. *Trust in the Law*. New York: Russell Sage.

Vezzali, Loris, Miles Hewstone, Dora Capozza, Dino Giovannini, and Ralf Wolfer. 2014. "Improving Intergroup Relations with Extended and Vicarious Forms of Indirect Contact." *European Review of Social Psychology* 25 (1): 314–89.

Voigt, Rob, Nicholas P. Camp, Vinodkumar Prabhakaran, William L. Hamilton, Rebecca C. Hetey, Camilla M. Griffiths, David Jurgens, Dan Jurafsky, and Jennifer L. Eberhardt. 2017. "Language from Police Body Camera Footage Shows Racial Disparities in Officer Respect." *Proceedings of the National Academy of Sciences* 114: 6521–26.

Waddington, P. A. J. 1999. "Police (Canteen) Subculture: An Appreciation." *The British Journal of Criminology* 39 (2): 287–309.

Westmarland, Louis, and Michael Rowe. 2018. "Police Ethics and Integrity: Can a New Code Overturn the Blue Code?" *Policing and Society* 28 (7): 854–70.

White, Fiona A., Rhiannon N. Turner, Stefano Verrelli, Lauren J. Harvey, and Jeffrey R. Hann. 2019. "Improving Intergroup Relations between Catholics and Protestants in Northern Ireland via E-contact." *European Journal of Social Psychology* 49 (2): 429–38.

White, Michael D. 2001. "Controlling Police Decision to Use Deadly Force: Reexamining the Importance of Administrative Policy." *Crime & Delinquency* 47 (1): 131–51.

Wilson, Steven R., and Skye M. Chernichky. 2016. "Intergroup Communication Perspective on Military Families and Military-Civilian Divide." In *Advances in Intergroup Communication*, edited by Howard Giles and Anne Maass, 265–82. New York: Peter Lang.

Wolfe, Scott, Jeff Rojek, Kyle McLean, and Geoffrey Alpert. 2020. "Social Interaction Training to Reduce Police Use of Force." *The Annals of the American Academy of Political and Social Science* 687 (1): 124–45.

Womack, Morris M., and Hayden H. Finley. 1986. *Communication: A Unique Significance for Law Enforcement*. Springfield: Charles C. Thomas.

Woo, Dajung, and Karen Myers. 2016. "Organizational Socialization and Intergroup Dynamics." In *Advances in Intergroup Communication*, edited by Howard Giles and Anne Maass, 227–46. New York: Peter Lang.

Zeijen, Marijnteje E. L., Paraskevas Petrou, Arnold B. Bakker, and Benjamin R. Van Gelderen. 2020. "Dyadic Support Exchange and Work Engagement: An Episodic Test and Expansion of Self-Determination Theory." *Journal of Occupation & Organization Psychology*. Advance Online: https://doi.org/10.1111/joop.12311 .

Zhang, Yan Bin, and Howard Giles. 2017. "Communication Accommodation Theory." In *The International Encyclopedia of Intercultural Communication*, edited by Young Y. Kim, 95–108. New York: Wiley Blackwell.

Zhang, Yan Bing, and Makiko Imamura. 2018. "Communication Accommodation Theory and Intergroup Communication." In *The Oxford Encyclopedia of Intergroup Communication*, edited by Howard Giles and Jake Harwood, Vol. 1, 133–50. New York: Oxford University Press.

CHAPTER 2

Doing Organizational Justice

The Role of Police Manager Communication

Scott Wolfe

Employees in all work settings expect their supervisors to treat them fairly and with respect (Lind 2001). This normative expectation of justice—being treated with fairness and respect—has been the focus of study for scholars in several disciplines over the past forty to fifty years. A majority of research on the concept of justice can be found in the organizational behavior, management, and human relations literatures. Scholars typically conceptualize justice as a multifaceted construct referred to as organizational justice that captures employees' views of the procedural, distributive, informational, and interpersonal justice of their supervisors. Research shows that employees' perceptions of supervisor organizational justice rank among the strongest predictors of work behaviors, attitudes, emotions, and job orientations. For example, employees who believe their supervisors are just or fair tend to be more committed to their organization and its goals, have greater productivity, and are less likely to violate organizational rules or policies (Cohen-Charash and Spector 2001; Colquitt et al. 2001). In short, organizational justice produces many pro-organizational behaviors and related outcomes.

Guided by this evidence, criminal justice scholars have placed considerable attention on the role of organizational justice among police employees in recent decades. Police officers who believe their supervisors have treated them with organizational justice have greater organizational commitment and job satisfaction, are more trusting of their organization, and are less likely to engage in misconduct (Mesko et al. 2017; Myhill and Bradford 2013; Wolfe and Nix 2017; Wolfe and Piquero 2011). A recent meta-analysis of the organizational justice effect revealed that the concept has a strong relationship with many work outcomes among criminal justice employees (Wolfe and Lawson 2020).

Organizational justice matters to criminal justice employees (see chapter 3). Missing from much of the criminal justice literature is a discussion of the policy implications of this research. Specifically, how can police managers put organizational justice principles into practice? The current chapter will address this issue. First, I will provide an overview of organizational justice and the outcomes it produces in criminal justice work settings. In the second section, I will discuss how police managers can "do" organizational justice in their everyday activities. Particular attention will focus on the types of management activities that can benefit from organizational justice and how police managers can use the principles of justice to more effectively communicate with their subordinates and elicit beneficial employee outcomes.

WHAT IS ORGANIZATIONAL JUSTICE?

Jason Colquitt (2012), a leading organizational justice scholar, argues that employees routinely evaluate their supervisors' behavior, decisions, and procedures because their actions can have important economic and social consequences for employees. Workers' job security, pay, promotional opportunities, and similar outcomes are all subject to the decision making of their supervisors. The uncertainty and feelings of vulnerability this creates leads employees to search for evidence or signs that their supervisors have their best interests in mind (Tyler and Lind 1992; Van den Bos 2001). The primary metric employees use to temper feelings of uncertainty or vulnerability are evaluations of the level of justice in their supervisors' actions and decisions. Just, or fair, supervisor behavior is an indication that they have their employees' best interests in mind.

Research on the role of justice within authority-subordinate relations began with Adams's (1965) equity theory. Adams argued that employees formulate evaluations of their supervisors primarily by calculating the ratio of their inputs (e.g., productivity, experience, tenure, education) to the outcomes they receive from their organization (e.g., promotions, pay increases, assignments). According to the theory, employees' supervisor justice evaluations are based on a comparison of these input-output ratios to their colleagues. Inequity will be perceived if an employee believes he or she has contributed more to the organization in comparison to what they have received from the organization, especially if the ratio is incongruent with their colleagues' ratios. This component of justice has become known as *distributive justice* and focuses on the extent to which employees believe resources are fairly allocated within their organization.

Other influential scholars built on Adams's work and advanced the study of justice in the workplace by arguing that employees' evaluations of their supervisors also focus on the perceived fairness of the processes supervisors use to arrive at decisions (Leventhal 1976, 1980; Leventhal, Karuza, and Fry 1980; Thibaut and Walker 1975). This dimension of justice is referred to as *procedural justice*. Employees perceive procedural justice when they are provided some level of control during supervisors' decision-making processes and when they believe procedures are consistently applied, free of bias, correctable, representative, accurate, and ethical (Folger and Konovsky 1989; Greenberg 1987, 1990).

Bies and Moag (1986) developed another justice dimension in the mid-1980s that they termed *interactional justice*. This concept focused on employees' perceptions of the interpersonal treatment they receive from their supervisors. For example, employees feel their supervisors are fair when they are treated with respect and provided timely information. Greenberg (1993) argued that Bies and Moag's concept of interactional justice should be separated into two dimensions—*interpersonal* and *informational justice*. Colquitt (2001) agreed with this assessment by suggesting that interpersonal justice represents employees' perceptions of the level of respect and propriety provided by supervisors, and informational justice is the extent to which supervisors communicate with their subordinates in a candid, timely, and thorough manner. He also developed a measure of *organizational justice* by integrating aspects of each of the previously mentioned justice dimensions. Through a series of sophisticated statistical models Colquitt (2001, 396) demonstrated that "organizational justice is best conceptualized as four distinct dimensions: procedural justice, distributive justice, interpersonal justice, and informational justice." For this reason, most scholars today agree that organizational justice comprises each of the four sub-dimensions of justice.

The organizational behavior and management literature dealing with the organizational justice effect on employees' work outcomes is immense. In the early 2000s, two meta-analyses revealed that employees' organizational justice evaluations of their supervisors were associated with a long list of pro-organizational behaviors and attitudes. Organizational justice appears to increase employees' productivity, organizational commitment, and job satisfaction (Ambrose and Schminke 2009; DeConinck 2010; Ferrin and Dirks 2002; McFarlin and Sweeney 1992). Furthermore, employees that feel they have received organizational justice from supervisors are more likely to engage in organizational citizenship behaviors—going above or beyond minimum job requirements—and less likely to engage in work misconduct (Bechtoldt et al. 2007; Fox, Spector, and Miles 2001).

Fairness heuristic theory helps explain why organizational justice is important to employees. The theory proposes that employees routinely face a two-sided "fundamental social dilemma" when interacting with their supervisors (Lind 2001). On the one side, employees make personal sacrifices for their organizations (e.g., time, effort, social capital) because they may benefit in the form of goal attainment (e.g., promotion, pay raise) or work efficiency (e.g., making the job easier in the long run). Additionally, making sacrifices for the organization may allow an employee to secure a self-identity that is consistent with the overarching goal of the organization. In policing, for example, officers endure long hours and willingly place themselves in harm's way because they wish to contribute to a greater good (e.g., public safety and justice). On the other side of the social dilemma, however, is the reality that such an investment creates vulnerability and increases the possibility that the organization will exploit the employee. As Lind (2001, 61) puts it, "if one links one's identity and sense of self to some larger social or organizational identity, there is always the risk that one will experience rejection by the group and an attendant loss of identity."

Fairness heuristic theory suggests that employees resolve this dilemma and decide whether to pursue their own self-interest or risk possible rejection or exploitation by judging the extent to which their supervisors are trustworthy (Van den Bos, Lind, Vermunt, and Wilke 1997). Because judging trustworthiness is difficult, employees use a mental shortcut, a heuristic, to gauge supervisor trustworthiness. Subordinates evaluate the extent to which their supervisors are organizationally fair because such treatment communicates to employees that they are valued members of their organization and their self-identity is secure. Thus, when employees perceive organizational justice they are more comfortable making sacrifices for their employer. Uncertainty management theory further explains the importance of organizational justice. Employees face uncertainty in their working environments—for example, whether they can trust their supervisors, whether they will be included in upcoming layoffs, or whether they will receive their annual bonus. To manage this uncertainty, employees gauge their supervisors' organizational justice (Lind and Van den Bos 2002; Van den Bos and Lind 2002). In this way, fairness not only serves as a proxy for trust but also as a coping mechanism for various sources of uncertainty in the workplace. Experiencing organizational justice helps reduce any uncertainty an employee may be facing. As Lind and Van den Bos (2002, 216) stated, "What appears to be happening is that people use fairness to manage their reactions to uncertainty, finding comfort in related or even unrelated fair experiences."

Organizational Justice among Criminal Justice Employees

Criminal justice agencies are similar to business organizations in that they serve a client base, have a hierarchical command structure, and must rely on individual employees to accomplish the broader goals of the organization. Subordinate-authority relations are similar in both settings in most ways. Indeed, mirroring the findings from the broader organizational behavior literature, research has shown that criminal justice employees are more likely to engage in a wide range of pro-organizational behaviors and hold favorable work attitudes when they believe their supervisors have treated them with organizational justice (Wolfe and Lawson 2020).

Police officers seem to benefit tremendously from organizational justice. Officers have greater organizational commitment and identification when they evaluate their supervisors as organizationally fair, and are less likely to hold cynical orientations toward police work or the citizens they serve when they feel fairly treated by supervisors (Bradford and Quinton 2014; Bradford et al. 2014; Donner et al. 2015; Myhill and Bradford 2013; Rosenbaum and McCarty 2017; Trinkner, Tyler, and Goff 2016). Organizational justice also appears to increase overall job satisfaction and agency trust (Donner et al. 2015; Wolfe and Nix 2017). From a behavioral standpoint, officers who believe their supervisors are fair are more likely to support the use of democratic policing (Tankebe 2014; Trinkner, Tyler, and Goff 2016; Van Craen and Skogan 2017a, b). Specifically, such officers are more likely to support the idea of treating citizens with respect and dignity and being restrained in the use of force compared to their colleagues who do not feel their supervisors use organizational justice. This supports the argument that organizational justice engenders attitudes and behaviors that benefit the organization or its goals. Indeed, organizational justice has also been shown to protect officers from engaging in misconduct (Bradford et al. 2014; Haas et al. 2015; Tyler, Callahan, and Frost 2007; Wolfe and Piquero 2011).

Consistent with fairness heuristic and uncertainty management theories (Hogg and Adelman 2013; Hogg and Belavadi 2018; Lind and Van den Bos 2002; Van den Bos 2001), a recent study by Wolfe and colleagues (2018) found that US Border Patrol agents placed more emphasis on organizational justice if they experienced more uncertainty at work. Agents that were uncertain about the future direction of the larger organization or the impact of recent negative publicity of policing on their job (see chapters 14 and 15) appeared to closely watch the extent to which their supervisors were fair. They did so as a way to cope with uncertainty. The study revealed that agents who experience either high or low levels of uncertainty were both highly satisfied with their jobs *as long as they both perceived high levels of organizational justice from their supervisors*. Conversely, agents that viewed their supervisors as unfair *and* experienced high uncertainty had the lowest levels of job satisfaction.

The coping and protective effects of organizational justice have also been observed in other studies examining the impact of negative publicity on police officers. Nix and Wolfe (2016) surveyed 510 sheriff's deputies and found a significant portion indicated they were less motivated to work in law enforcement and believe the job has gotten more dangerous in the years after Michael Brown's death in Ferguson, Missouri, and subsequent civil unrest across the United States (see chapter 16). This reduced motivation and increased feelings of danger are a manifestation of the "Ferguson Effect," which suggests that public criticism of the police has caused officers to view their jobs differently and behave in different ways when interacting with citizens (Pyrooz, Decker, Wolfe, and Shjarback 2016). However, deputies that felt they had been treated with organizational justice were significantly less likely to be impacted by this so-called "Ferguson Effect" than their colleagues who did not perceive the same level of fairness from their supervisors. Within the same sample, Wolfe and Nix (2016b) observed that deputies who reported being impacted by the negative publicity stemming from Ferguson were significantly less willing to work with community members to solve local problems. Again, however, this harmful effect was mitigated if the deputies felt their supervisors were organizationally fair. This suggests that community-policing efforts can be augmented by supervisors treating subordinates with organizational justice even in the current climate of intense public scrutiny of the police.

It is clear from this review of the organizational justice effect that police officers value fair supervisor treatment and such treatment produces a gamut of behaviors and attitudes beneficial to the success of their agencies. What often gets lost in translation within the research literature, however, is how practitioners can actually practice organizational justice. The next section will address this issue.

DOING ORGANIZATIONAL JUSTICE IN POLICE AGENCIES

What are the everyday situations in which police supervisors can integrate organizational justice into their managerial practices? This section will provide brief examples of situations police managers may face where organizational justice may be useful.

Own Organizational Justice in Your Managerial Philosophy

For starters, it is important to emphasize that organizational justice is not a technique or intervention to be used in specific situations or when problems arise. Organizational justice should be at the forefront of police supervisors' managerial philosophy for them to be effective managers. All managerial actions and decisions should be guided by fairness and transparency. Hundreds of research studies demonstrate that employees expect to be treated fairly and, when they receive fair treatment, they produce more and better outcomes for their organizations. Accordingly, police managers should keep an eye toward ensuring distributive, procedural, informational, and interpersonal justice during all their supervisory behaviors and interactions. When decisions are being made, police managers should strive to ensure outcomes are fairly distributed to all employees. Communication is key to ensuring such distributive justice. It is difficult for employees to judge whether their outcomes are fair compared to their colleagues. It is incumbent on the supervisor to communicate to his or her employees to ensure they understand why certain outcomes occurred. By doing so, a police manager can bolster both distributive and informational justice simultaneously. Managers should also ensure procedures are free from bias, can be corrected if mistakes happen, and integrate employees so they have a voice in the process. And, of course, police managers should ensure they always treat and communicate employees in an optimally accommodative manner with respect (interpersonal justice; see also Giles and Smith 1979). Degrading, condescending, and impolite treatment of a subordinate is a surefire (nonaccommodative) way to ensure that employee will *not* buy into agency goals or produce high quality work outputs (see Gasiorek 2016).

Finally, it is necessary to routinely communicate with subordinates about decisions, policy changes, organizational goals, and the like. Patrol officers are the lifeblood of a police agency. They are responsible for carrying out departmental initiatives and accomplishing goals. These officers, like any employees, are curious about why they are being told to do certain things. This is not a new phenomenon attributed to the millennial generation, as some old-timers like to argue. Rather, employees of all types, from cubicles to battlefields, want to know why their supervisor is requesting them to perform a particular task. Most of the time, employees do not expect such information from their supervisors because they feel entitled. Rather, employees want this information because they want to be committed to their own actions. Jocko Willink and Leif Babin recently wrote a widely read and easily approachable leadership book based on their experience as Navy SEAL commanders on the battlefields of Iraq (see also Hogg, Van Knippenberg, and Rast 2012; Rast, Gaffney, Hogg, and Crisp 2012; Rast, Hogg, and Van Knippenberg 2018). Their main argument resulted in the name of the book—*Extreme Ownership* (2017). Willink and Babin suggest that all leaders need to practice extreme ownership of their decisions and actions. Any team failure is directly tied to failure of the leader. They emphasize the importance of communicating the mission to one's troops (whether real troops or office employees). Subordinates need to understand the mission before they can be committed to and accomplish its directives. This is informational justice—communicating with subordinates to provide timely, accurate, and useful information. If a manager fails to adequately communicate to subordinates why they need to perform a task, employees may fail to buy into the task and, therefore, fail to accomplish its goal. This failure is the manager's problem, not the employees' problem. Battlefield missions are more successful when troops have been told what the goal is and why. The same is true in policing.

Communicating Policy Changes

Police agencies can benefit in a number of ways when organizational justice is used during specific situations that routinely occur within departments. Change is constant in policing, particularly policy change. Frontline officers often become frustrated by policy changes because they can appear, at best, arbitrary and, at worst, detrimental to the agency. When making and implementing policy changes, the goal of police managers is to gain support for the new policy from frontline officers (Wolfe and Nix 2016a). Every effort should be made to include impacted employees in the decision-making process leading to policy changes (procedural justice). This does not require that all employee concerns be integrated into the final decision. Rather, employees should be provided a voice and opportunity to communicate concerns regarding potential policy changes (Colquitt 2001). The opinions of all impacted employees should be sought rather than the voice of a select few. Hand picking only a small segment of the organization to participate in the decision-making process will only produce the opposite of the desired outcome—it will be perceived as organizational *injustice*. Having representatives from key stakeholder groups within an organization can help make such discussions efficient. Many agencies have officer advisory councils that involve an elected representative from different segments of the agency (e.g., patrol, investigations, records, etc.) speaking on behalf of their colleagues at monthly or quarterly command staff meetings. Such groups can help provide a voice of individual officers to the command staff. Other agencies will have to work with officer unions. Such a relationship should be used as a vehicle to allow officers a voice in the policy change process. Regardless of the way voice is provided, police managers must ensure they honestly listen to concerns and treat constituents with respect and dignity (interpersonal justice). A condescending demeanor from a supervisor could undermine the entire process (Nix, Wolfe, and Tregle 2018).

All policy changes should be clearly communicated to all impacted employees within a police department (informational justice). A memorandum regarding a policy change is sufficient when dealing with some mundane issues. However, most (if not all) policy changes should be implemented with a command-level officer communicating to frontline officers the reasons for the change. Command officers are busy folks but communicating about policy changes with frontline officers cannot be overlooked. A commander taking the time to visit roll calls and communicate the reasons for a policy change (even if small) to his or her officers will increase feelings of justice because it will help mitigate concerns that the change was made for arbitrary reasons. Additionally, such communication will demonstrate respect to frontline officers (interpersonal justice). Routinely changing policy and failing to communicate with officers about the changes will slowly chip away at any sense of fairness officers have regarding their command staff. Ensuring policy changes are handled in an organizationally fair manner will help engender commitment to the policy and, in turn, the desired behavioral changes the policy change targets (Rodell and Colquitt 2009).

Internal Investigations

Internal investigations are an unfortunate, but common, occurrence within police agencies (see chapter 13). Such investigations may stem from a citizen complaint, officer report, or supervisor-initiated inquiry. Regardless of their source, organizational justice management techniques should guide the investigations. For starters, clear policies should guide officer behavior and policies should be adequately trained in the academy and revisited periodically with departmental employees (informational justice). This is especially important for new officer hires who attend an academy training that is hosted by an external organization (e.g., a state police agency or local community college). These officers will not be exposed to specific agency policies until they begin working with their agency after the completion of academy training. In such situations, agencies must ensure that their policies are adequately communicated to new hires. Second, police managers should strive to make internal investigations as transparent as possible. Today's policing is characterized by public criticism and calls for greater transparency with the public. Managers must remember, however, their employees expect transparency as well. Officers that are being investigated should be integrated into the process as much as possible to improve their sense of procedural fairness. Many investigations lead to unsubstantiated claims and managers want to avoid alienating officers from the agency because of their experiences with the investigatory process.

Relatedly, police managers should keep other employees informed about internal investigations as much as policy and law permit. Accommodatively keeping officers informed about the status of an ongoing investigation can help squash concern that the process is unfair (Giles 2016). And, finally, when decisions are rendered, the results of the investigation should be communicated with agency employees (again, to the extent permitted by policy and law). Such communication can go a long way in subverting the influence of rumors and reduce uncertainty by allowing employees to understand the process and why a particular decision was made. When policy or law does not allow for truly transparent discussions of internal investigations, police managers should still communicate with their subordinates and explain why they cannot provide more information. This type of informational justice will help send the message to officers that their supervisors care about transparency and have their subordinates' best interests in mind.

Training Requirements

Another constant in policing is training. Officers are exposed to numerous types of training throughout their careers. They receive intense training in the academy on a variety of topics ranging from the use of force to report writing. Once on the street they will experience training of all types including short roll call training intended to reacquaint officers with a particular tactic or policy, extended annual recertification training focused on specific skills, and "outside expert" training on various topics led by law enforcement consultants or university researchers. Unfortunately, the quality of police training varies greatly. Moreover, many officers see training programs as redundant, unnecessary (because they believe they already perform the targeted skill well), or politically motivated (e.g., training geared toward community relations in response to an apparent legitimacy crisis). These problems can seriously undermine a training program before it even gets off the ground.

My colleagues and I recently completed an experimental evaluation of a police officer social interaction training program through a partnership with the Fayetteville (NC) and Tucson (AZ) Police Departments (Wolfe, Rojek, McLean, and Alpert 2020). One issue we explored in the evaluation was officer receptivity to the training program and how it may impact training success. We observed that officers who evaluated their supervisors as organizationally fair were more motivated to attend the training program compared to their colleagues that viewed their supervisors as unfair (McLean, Wolfe, Rojek, Alpert, and Smith, 2020; Wolfe, Rojek, McLean, and Alpert, 2020). Organizational justice also appeared to increase trainees' satisfaction with the training and the number of skills trainees believed they gained from the program. In this way, organizational justice increases training motivation and receptivity, which likely increases officers' willingness to use the trained skills on the street.

Police managers can harness the principles of organizational justice to improve training motivation and receptivity in several ways. First, when a training program is going to be implemented, police managers must communicate with frontline officers about the program's purpose and intended outcomes. Such conversations are key to gaining buy-in and support of the program and help avoid officers dismissing the training as another "useless outside expert offering an opinion." Second, police managers should seek input from their officers regarding experiences with the training. This will allow appropriate changes to be made and for officers to feel their supervisors have their best interests in mind.

CONCLUSIONS

Organizational justice is an important part of a successful police managerial philosophy. Simply put, officers that feel they have been treated fairly by their supervisors are more likely to adopt attitudes and engage in behaviors that are consistent with their agency's goals. Police managers could benefit from integrating organizational justice into all their supervisory actions including those discussed as examples in this chapter. Moving forward, we need to know more about whether police supervisors can be trained on how to use organizational justice. A police practitioner-academic researcher partnership that develops and evaluates an organizational justice training program for police managers would go a long way in determining the extent to which officers can be trained to be fair leaders and whether such training improves outcomes for officers in their agency.

REFERENCES

Adams, J. S. 1965. "Inequity in Social Exchange." In *Advances in Experimental Social Psychology* 2, edited by Leonard Berkowitz, 267–99. New York: Academic Press.

Ambrose, Maureen L., and Marshall Schminke. 2009. "The Role of Overall Justice Judgments in Organizational Justice Research: A Test of Mediation." *Journal of Applied Psychology* 94 (2): 491–500.

Bechtoldt, Myriam N., Conny Welk, Dieter Zapf, and Johannes Hartig. 2007. "Main and Moderating Effects of Self-Control, Organizational Justice, and Emotional Labour on Counterproductive Behaviour at Work." *European Journal of Work and Organizational Psychology* 16 (4): 479–500.

Bies, Robert J., and J. F. Moag. 1986. "Interactional Justice: Communication Criteria of Fairness." In *Research on Negotiations in Organizations*, edited by R. J. Lewicki, B. H. Sheppard, and M. H. Bazerman, 43–55. Greenwich: JAI Press.

Bradford, Ben, and Paul Quinton. 2014. "Self-Legitimacy, Police Culture and Support for Democratic Policing in an English Constabulary." *British Journal of Criminology* 54 (6): 1023–46.

Bradford, Ben, Paul Quinton, Andy Myhill, and Gillian Porter. 2014. "Why Do 'the Law' Comply? Procedural Justice, Group Identification and Officer Motivation in Police Organizations." *European Journal of Criminology* 11 (1): 110–31.

Cohen-Charash, Yochi, and Paul E. Spector. 2001. "The Role of Justice in Organizations: A Meta-Analysis." *Organizational Behavior and Human Decision Processes* 86 (2): 278–321.

Colquitt, Jason A. 2001. "On the Dimensionality of Organizational Justice: A Construct Validation of a Measure." *The Journal of Applied Psychology* 86 (3): 386–400.

Colquitt, Jason A. 2012. "Organizational Justice." In *The Oxford Handbook of Organizational Psychology*, edited by S. W. J. Kozlowski, Vol. 1, 526–47. New York: Oxford University Press.

Colquitt, Jason A., Donald E. Conlon, Michael J. Wesson, Christopher O. L. H. Porter, and K. Yee Ng. 2001. "Justice at the Millennium: A Meta-Analytic Review of 25 Years of Organizational Justice Research." *Journal of Applied Psychology* 86 (3): 425–45.

DeConinck, James B. 2010. "The Effect of Organizational Justice, Perceived Organizational Support, and Perceived Supervisor Support on Marketing Employees' Level of Trust." *Journal of Business Research* 63 (12): 1349–55.

Donner, Christopher, Jon Maskaly, Lorie Fridell, and Wesley G. Jennings. 2015. "Policing and Procedural Justice: A State-of-the-Art Review." *Policing* 38 (1): 153–72.

Ferrin, Donald L., and Kurt T. Dirks. 2002. "Trust in Leadership: Meta-Analytic Findings and Implications for Research and Practice." *Journal of Applied Psychology* 87 (4): 611–28.

Folger, R., and Mary A. Konovsky. 1989. "Effects of Procedural and Distributive Justice on Reactions to Pay Raise Decisions." *Academy of Management Journal* 32 (1): 115–30.

Fox, Suzy, Paul E. Spector, and Don Miles. 2001. "Counterproductive Work Behavior (CWB) in Response to Job Stressors and Organizational Justice: Some Mediator and Moderator Tests for Autonomy and Emotions." *Journal of Vocational Behavior* 59 (3): 291–309.

Gasiorek, Jessica. 2016. "The "Dark Side" of CAT: Nonaccommodation. In *Communication Accommodation Theory: Negotiating Personal Relationships and Social Identities across Contexts*, edited by Howard Giles, 105–22. Cambridge: Cambridge University Press.

Giles, Howard, ed., 2016. *Communication Accommodation Theory: Negotiating Personal Relationships and Social Identities Across Contexts*. Cambridge: Cambridge University Press.

Greenberg, Jerald. 1987. "A Taxonomy of Organizational Justice Theories." *The Academy of Management Review* 12 (1): 9–22.

Greenberg, Jerald. 1990. "Employee Theft as a Reaction to Underpayment Inequity: The Hidden Cost of Pay Cuts." *Journal of Applied Psychology* 75 (5): 561–68.

Greenberg, Jerald. 1993. "The Social Side of Fairness: Interpersonal and Informational Classes of Organizational Justice." In *Justice in the Workplace: Approaching Fairness in Human Resource Management*, edited by R. Cropanzano, 79–103. Hillsdale: Lawrence Erlbaum Associates.

Haas, Nicole E., Maarten Van Craen, Wesley G. Skogan, and Diego M. Fleitas. 2015. "Explaining Officer Compliance: The Importance of Procedural Justice and Trust Inside a Police Organization." *Criminology & Criminal Justice* 15 (4): 442–63.

Hogg, Michael A., and Janice Adelman. 2013. "Uncertainty-Identity Theory: Extreme Groups, Radical Behavior, and Authoritarian Leadership." *Journal of Social Issues* 69: 436–54.

Hogg, Michael A., and Sucharita Belavadi. 2018. "Uncertainty Management Theories." In *The Oxford Research Encyclopedia of Intergroup Communication*, edited by Howard Giles and Jake Harwood, Vol. 2, 447–61. New York: Oxford University Press.

Hogg, Michael A., Daan van Knippenberg, and David E. Rast III. 2012. "The Social Identity Theory of Leadership: Theoretical Origins, Research Findings, and Conceptual Developments." *European Review of Social Psychology* 23 (1): 258–304.

Leventhal, Gerald S. 1976. "The Distribution of Rewards and Resources in Groups and Organizations." In *Advances in Experimental Social Psychology* 9, edited by Leonard Berkowitz and Elaine Walster, 91–131. New York: Academic Press.

Leventhal, Gerald S. 1980. "What Should Be Done with Equity Theory? New Approaches to the Study of Fairness in Social Relationships." In *Social Exchange: Advances in Theory and Research*, edited by Kenneth Gergen, Martin S. Greenberg, and Richard H. Willis, 27–55. New York: Plenum.

Leventhal, Gerald S., J. Karuza, and W. R. Fry. 1980. "Beyond Fairness: A Theory of Allocation Preferences." In *Justice and Social Interaction*, edited by Gerold Mikula, 167–218. New York: Springer-Verlag.

Lind, Edgar A. 2001. "Fairness Heuristic Theory: Justice Judgements as Pivotal Cognitions in Organizational Relations." In *Advances in Organizational Justice*, edited by Jerald Greenberg and Russell Cropanzano, 56–88. Stanford: Stanford University Press.

Lind, Edgar A., and Kees Van den Bos. 2002. "When Fairness Works: Toward a General Theory of Uncertainty Management." In *Research in Organizational Behavior*, edited by Barry M. Staw and Robert M. Kramer, 181–223. Boston: Elsevier.

McFarlin, Dean B., and Paul D. Sweeney. 1992. "Distributive and Procedural Justice as Predictors of Satisfaction with Personal and Organizational Outcomes." *Academy of Management Journal* 35 (3): 626.

McLean, Kyle, Scott E. Wolfe, Jeff Rojek, Geoffrey P. Alpert, and Michael R. Smith. 2020. "Randomized controlled trial of social interaction police training." *Criminology & Public Policy* 19: 805-832.

Mesko, Gorazd, Rok Hacin, Justice Tankebe, and Chuck Fields. 2017. "Self-Legitimacy, Organisational Commitment and Commitment to Fair Treatment of Prisoners: An Empirical Study of Prison Officers in Slovenia." *European Journal of Crime, Criminal Law and Criminal Justice* 25 (1): 11–30.

Myhill, Andy, and Ben Bradford. 2013. "Overcoming Cop Culture? Organizational Justice and Police Officers' Attitudes Toward the Public." *Policing* 36 (2): 338–56.

Nix, Justin, and Scott E. Wolfe. 2016. "Sensitivity to the Ferguson Effect: The Role of Managerial Organizational Justice." *Journal of Criminal Justice* 47 (1): 12–20.

Nix, Justin, Scott E. Wolfe, and Brandon Tregle. 2018. "Police Officers' Attitudes toward Citizen Advisory Councils." *Policing: An International Journal* 41: 418–34.

Pyrooz, David C., Scott H. Decker, Scott E. Wolfe, and John A. Shjarback. 2016. "Was There a Ferguson Effect on Crime Rates in Large US Cities?" *Journal of Criminal Justice* 46: 1–8.

Rast, David E., Amber M. Gaffney, Michael A. Hogg, and Richard J. Crisp. 2012. "Leadership under Uncertainty: When Leaders Who Are Non-prototypical Group Members Can Gain Support." *Journal of Experimental Social Psychology* 48: 646–53.

Rast, David E., Michael A. Hogg, and Daan van Knippenberg. 2018. "Intergroup Leadership Across Distinct Subgroups and Identities." *Personality and Social Psychology Bulletin* 44: 1090-1103.

Rodell, Jessica B., and Jason A. Colquitt. 2009. "Looking Ahead in Times of Uncertainty: The Role of Anticipatory Justice in an Organizational Change Context." *Journal of Applied Psychology* 94: 989–1002.

Rosenbaum, Dennis P., and William P. McCarty. 2017. "Organizational Justice and Officer 'Buy in' in American Policing." *Policing* 40 (1): 71–85.

Smith, Philip M., and Howard Giles. 1979. "Accommodation Theory: Optimal Levels of Convergence." In *Language and Social Psychology*, edited by Howard Giles and Robert St. Clair, 45–65. Oxford: Blackwell.

Tankebe, Justice. 2014. "The Making of 'Democracy's Champions': Understanding Police Support for Democracy in Ghana." *Criminology & Criminal Justice* 14 (1): 25–43.

Thibaut, John, and Laurens Walker. 1975. *Procedural Justice: A Psychological Analysis*. Hillsdale: Lawrence Erlbaum Associates.

Trinkner, Rick, Tom R. Tyler, and Phillip Atiba Goff. 2016. "Justice from Within: The Relations Between a Procedurally Just Organizational Climate and Police Organizational Efficiency, Endorsement of Democratic Policing, and Officer Well-Being." *Psychology, Public Policy, and Law* 22 (2): 158–72.

Tyler, Tom. R., Patrick E. Callahan, and Jeffrey Frost. 2007. "Armed, and Dangerous (?): Motivating Rule Adherence among Agents of Social Control." *Law & Society Review* 41 (2): 457–92.

Tyler, Tom. R., and E. Allan Lind. 1992. "A Relational Model of Authority in Groups." In *Advances in Experimental Social Psychology 25*, edited by Mark P. Zanna, 115–91. San Diego: Academic Press.

Van Craen, Maarten, and Wesley G. Skogan. 2017a. "Achieving Fairness in Policing: The Link between Internal and External Procedural Justice." *Police Quarterly* 20 (1): 3–23.

Van Craen, Maarten, and Wesley G. Skogan. 2017b. "Officer Support for Use of Force Policy: The Role of Fair Supervision." *Criminal Justice and Behavior* 44 (6): 843–61.

Van den Bos, Kees. 2001. "Uncertainty Management: The Influence of Uncertainty Salience on Reactions to Perceived Procedural Fairness." *Journal of Personality and Social Psychology* 80 (6): 931–41.

Van den Bos, Kees, and E. Allan Lind. 2002. "Uncertainty Management by Means of Fairness Judgments." In *Advances in Experimental Social Psychology*, edited by Mark P. Zanna, 34:1–60. San Diego: Academic Press.

Van den Bos, Kees, E. Allan Lind, Riël Vermunt, and Henk A. M. Wilke. 1997. "How Do I Judge My Outcome When I Do Not Know the Outcome of Others? The Psychology of the Fair Process Effect." *Journal of Personality and Social Psychology* 72 (5): 1034–46.

Willink, Jocko, and Leif Babin. 2017. *Extreme Ownership*. New York: St. Martin's Press.

Wolfe, Scott E., and Spencer G. Lawson. 2019. "The Organizational Justice Effect Among Criminal Justice Employees: A Meta-Analysis." Unpublished manuscript.

Wolfe, Scott, Jeff Rojek, Kyle McLean, and Geoffrey Alpert. 2020. "Social interaction training to reduce police use of force." *The ANNALS of the American Academy of Political and Social Science* 687: 124-145.

Wolfe, Scott E., Jeff Rojek, Kyle McLean, and Geoffrey Alpert. 2019. "Advancing a Theory of Police Officer Training Motivation and Receptivity." Unpublished manuscript.

Wolfe, Scott E., and Justin Nix. 2016a. "Managing Police Departments Post-Ferguson: Officers Want Fairness and Transparency from Their Bosses." *Harvard Business Review*. September 13.

Wolfe, Scott E., and Justin Nix. 2016b. "The Alleged 'Ferguson Effect' and Police Willingness to Engage in Community Partnership." *Law and Human Behavior* 40 (1): 1–10. https://doi.org/10.1037/lhb0000164.

Wolfe, Scott E., and Justin Nix. 2017. "Police Officers' Trust in Their Agency: Does Self-Legitimacy Protect against Supervisor Procedural Injustice?" *Criminal Justice and Behavior* 44 (5): 717–32.

Wolfe, Scott E., and Alex R. Piquero. 2011. "Organizational Justice and Police Misconduct." *Criminal Justice and Behavior* 38 (4): 332–53.

Wolfe, Scott E., Jeff Rojek, Victor M. Manjarrez, and Allison Rojek. 2018. "Why Does Organizational Justice Matter? Uncertainty Management among Law Enforcement Officers." *Journal of Criminal Justice* 54 (1): 20–29.

Wolfe, Scott, Jeff Rojek, Kyle McLean, and Geoffrey Alpert. 2020. "Social Interaction Training to Reduce Police Use of Force." *ANNALS of the Academy of Political and Social Science*: 687 (1): 124–45.

CHAPTER 3

The Critical Role of Communication in the Recruitment of Police Officers

Charlie Scheer and Jeremy M. Wilson

Recruiting police officers is one of the most significant challenges facing law enforcement leaders today. In the modern police era, recruitment has remained a critical challenge even as agencies have experienced both feast and famine in terms of the public's interest in law enforcement careers. Today, there is an apparent "crisis" in police recruitment as social, economic, and political forces have transformed the contemporary global workforce (Taylor et al. 2006). A shortage of qualified applicants, a persistent difficulty in recruiting for workplace diversity, and the turnover of employees for myriad reasons imperil the very function of a police department (Farr 2018; Morison 2017; Orrick 2008). How police organizations seek officers is of urgent importance and it requires they rely upon a spectrum of communications skills to do so.

Communication is critical to the police workforce development process, from recruitment, selection and hiring to training, career progression and executive succession planning (see chapter 1). To be sure, each stage requires unique forms of communication in terms of style, form, content, purpose, and other attributes. Modestly, this chapter focuses on the first stage of recruitment. It aims to frame key aspects of the recruitment process and the importance of communication to them, highlighting roles, opportunities, and challenges for both the organization and recruit.

RECRUITS: FOR WHAT ARE POLICE AGENCIES LOOKING?

Prior to discussing the complexities of police recruitment, it helps to first consider the skills and attributes agencies are seeking in candidates. Over time, there have been various attempts to quantify the knowledge and skills needed for police work. These attributes undoubtedly have changed over time, as the expectations of police officers have grown in size and complexity with the assumption of new duties (Wilson, Dalton, Scheer, and Grammich 2010). Community demand for increased transparency, oversight of use-of-force incidents, the application of de-escalation strategies, and crisis intervention skills ensure that police officers must excel in communications (e.g., Lim, Matthies, and Keller 2012; see chapter 9). As Scrivner (2006) explains, many of these skills can be associated with a "calling" to service professions that imbues the communications skills themselves with a degree of empathy behind each public contact, which may in turn accentuate the need to develop and hone such skills. This ensures staff will draw upon their communications skills as they continue to develop them.

A recent study by the International City-County Management Association (ICMA) (2018) surveyed a national sample of police departments and organization members (such as chambers of commerce and civic groups) about the ideal characteristics that they feel would form a "model" police officer. Of the top ten characteristics identified by the respondents, six relate to the ability of persons to engage in critical forms of interpersonal communication, such as diffusing volatile situations (especially in domestic violence incidents), engaging in training, and creating feelings of trust between the police department and the community (ICMA 2018). Elsewhere, the preferred skills for police recruits identified by the respondents emphasize multiple abilities that rely on communications skills: critical and strategic thinking, relationship-building, the ability to use technology and social media, and the ability to analyze data (ICMA 2018).

Clearly, both agencies and the public maintain a complex array of expectations for recruits. It is important to observe that the expectations span multiple domains, and chief among them is communication. To be sure, potential employees with such skill sets and attributes are in high demand among many professions. The ability of the police agencies to attract such candidates is increasingly difficult as potentially more attractive employment alternatives are available elsewhere.

THE RECRUITMENT CHALLENGE

For the police manager seeking to maintain staffing levels, being able to *retain* good officers who perform well and share the department's vision, or are simply a "good fit" for the department, is just as critical (if not more so) as the ability to attract, screen, and hire the right new candidates. It is more efficient to retain an officer than it is to recruit a new one. This challenge of resiliency can consume staff at all levels of the department, from line-level officers who create a culture that reinforces the desire to apply, to personnel and training divisions who are responsible for the mechanics of personnel management, to leadership who communicate a vision of the agency's work culture and desire to continually develop employees for long careers (Everly 2011; Woo and Myers 2016; see chapter 2). What is critical about this challenge is that it persists despite many shifting social trends even as it is affected by them. For instance, earlier recruitment concerns were followed by powerful social and political changes that affected the workforce landscape: the terrorist attacks of September 11, 2001, the 2008 recession, and the subsequent economic recovery (Kaminski 1993; Morison 2017; Orrick 2008; Taylor et al. 2006; Wilson et al. 2010). The challenge has persisted despite empirical interpretations of its source, magnitude, or any promising practices which would appear designed to "resolve" it.

This dilemma has left police managers with an intriguing consequence: proactive and innovative strategies must be used to recruit and retain police officers, not because contemporary circumstances demand it temporarily, but for the organization's long-term sustainability. No longer can police departments assume unlimited qualified applicants, as may have been the case in previous eras. The contemporary demands on police and skills required to properly perform police tasks have raised the stature of the profession so that police departments are competing with other professions which may be far more experienced at recruiting and may appeal with more attractive long-term careers (Morison 2017). This dilemma has thrust recruitment to the forefront of police managerial concerns. While the results of this new landscape are still being assessed, it is clear that some police agencies are embracing the new challenge, while others are struggling at recruiting and retaining employees (Jordan, Fridell, Faggiani, and Kubu 2009; Matthies, Keller, and Lim 2012; McGreevy 2006). It is also apparent that this phenomenon is not limited to police agencies within the United States but is global in scope (NPCC/APCC 2017).

THE CRITICAL ROLE OF COMMUNICATION IN THE RECRUITMENT CHALLENGE

Police officers rely upon interpersonal communication in nearly every aspect of their daily duties, from interacting with citizens, to court testimony, to critical incident preparation among their peers. The current recruitment challenge presents itself as a paradox in this context, as one might assume these same agents could clearly communicate the exceptional nature of their agencies and the benefits of the career as a whole. Yet, recruiting remains a struggle, as evidenced by growing numbers of agencies with unfilled positions. The source of police agencies' inabilities to adequately communicate their visions and the realities of the job, and the effect this has on recruitment, is unknown due to the lack of systematic research of the efficacy of police recruitment practices.

In fact, the nature of this paradox can be further illustrated through all the early stages of the police workforce development process:

- the recruitment of candidates for entry-level positions;
- the selection of candidates for hire;
- the immersion of new recruits in multiple initial stages of training; and
- the development of new officers for career longevity.

In each of these stages of the police workforce development process, agency representatives (recruiting staff, management, and line officers alike) may use different communication approaches with overlapping goals. But there also exists a set of larger principles that reflects the organizational mission. In each of these stages of personnel development, communication is not simply a one-way activity. Recruiters, managers, and other stakeholders must create an environment for dialogue between the recruit or employee, and the organization. The department must work to create an open environment that fosters communication and mitigates barriers to it (Courtney, Kirkland, and Viguerie 1997; Everly 2011; Woo and Myers 2016).

RECRUITING QUALIFIED CANDIDATES

Recruiting candidates for police work has become a notoriously time- and resource-consuming task (Copple 2017; Scrivner 2006). In previous eras, police duties were more rigidly defined, and candidates for police positions were at times plentiful. Today, expectations of police officers have expanded such that traditional job requirements of candidates have been transformed (Wilson et al. 2010; see chapter 1). What is consistently required of contemporary candidates, and what constitutes "a qualified job candidate," has been reassessed in light of modern professional expectations. But due to the lack of data evaluating police recruitment practices, the degree to which police agencies have transformed their recruitment activities, skills, and abilities to match these growing expectations is debatable (Castaneda and Ridgeway 2010; Scheer, Rossler, and Papania 2018).

Recruiting Potential Candidates for Hire

The candidate recruitment process normally begins with a police agency's assessment of workforce needs to determine what numbers, varieties, or target candidates are needed (Lim et al. 2012; Wilson et al. 2010). Police departments perform this task in different ways with different levels of abilities and success (Wilson and Weiss 2014). Some agencies may simply settle on what specific numbers are allowed for hire based upon a host of relatively constricting standards, enforced by budgetary constraints, civil service requirements, and other structures inherent in public administration. It is here that the distinct feature of police recruiting, as opposed to the private industries that police agencies find themselves competing against in the contemporary economic landscape, is revealed. While police departments have communicated the escalating need for more skilled, competitive, qualified, and talented individuals due to contemporary demands, they struggle with overcoming these restrictions to achieve hiring success (Jensen and Graves 2013). Police agencies, for instance, typically cannot recruit for a specialized narcotics officer, shift supervisor, or detective—they are restricted by inherent structural constraints to recruit only for the entry-level, which is an immediate challenge. The recruiter, then, must communicate the immediate benefit of starting at the entry-level, and explain the career ladder, its time considerations, and its benefit to the recruit. To do so properly is to communicate an organizational brand, mission, and the breadth of career opportunities that await the candidate, as well as explaining the big-picture benefit of serving in entry-level positions. Interested applicants to police positions, then, must be made acutely aware of these requirements, and it is in the agency's long-term interest not to obscure these characteristics and not allow them to appear as restrictive, but instead advantageous and appealing.

Listening to the Candidates and Negotiating Their Expectations

It is incumbent on the police recruiter to not only communicate the advantages and uniqueness of their agency in fostering a positive career, but to listen sincerely to each candidate's unique needs, adapting their communication strategy to different candidate perspectives on the world of work, beliefs about the role of police, and work–life concerns (Giles 2016). This is a clear challenge for the police department. It can also be confusing as agencies seek to diversify their workforce profiles in accordance with community expectations and increasing demands for police legitimacy (Rossler, Scheer, and Suttmoeller 2018; see chapters 8 and 17). Notoriously uncompetitive salaries and the nature of the police entry-level position almost ensure that police cannot compete with the more attractive and financially rewarding world of private industry (Morison 2017; Orrick 2008). The police recruiter must communicate an understanding of the career as a calling and match the expectations of the recruit to the offered lifestyle, benefits, and service components and rewards of their particular brand of policing with candidate expectations.

This is not unlike the traditional "sales pitch" of the career recruiter in other professions, but it carries a host of challenges for police agencies. First, there is an undefined and almost abstract understanding in contemporary policing about the importance of good recruiting and what makes a good recruiter. Myriad anecdotes exist about the lack of success police officers, be they specialized recruiters or not, have in communicating with potential candidates in both controlled settings (such as recruitment "events") or in instantaneous interactions with the public (Cobb 2020; DeLord 2009; Haggerty 2009).

Second, while resources and strong theoretical background may exist in similar fields, little is known about the extent to which police departments take advantage of existing recruiter training and information available to recruiters to facilitate their activities (Breaugh 2009; Cobb 2020; DeLord 2009). In situations where potentially interested recruits are available, this lack of training and experience may result in missed opportunities for police departments.

Third, there is a challenge in determining which among police cohorts makes the best recruiter. Many agencies have decided against having "professional recruiters" or seasoned staff in exchange for allowing younger, more recent hires be a part of the recruiting process (Haggerty 2009). The expectation is that the communications skills of officers and representatives with a closer experiential level and compatible worldview to those of the recruit will result in heightened communication of the agency's expectations, requirements, and brand (Cobb 2020). It also asks the question of whether or not such an approach occurs out of need (as in, the agency simply cannot afford or structure a proactive, measured recruitment plan), or if the agency is making a forthright effort to match the perceived perspectives of recruits with the ideological and generational views of existing employees. It is also unclear the degree to which recruitment endeavors are police organizational priorities in the contemporary landscape. What is needed is empirical support that rigorous assessment of the nature of police recruiting techniques and potential efficacy could provide.

Scheer et al. (2018) found that deep divisions exist between the career expectations of potential recruits and the perspectives of police agencies and their recruiters. Despite the interests of many undergraduate students taking criminal justice courses in entry-level police careers, they lack an understanding of the nature of the career ladder, training specifics, and the lifestyle changes associated with the career (see chapter 1). Survey respondents stated that having a mentor show them, as well as their families, significant others, and friends, the entirety of career options, activities, and perceived exciting characteristics of the job, would have assisted in career decision making. This presents opportunities for the police recruiter. The study results demonstrate that a more proactive, measured, and personal relationship that can be constructed between the recruit and the candidate may resolve fundamental needs of the recruit in convincing influential entities such as concerned family members (especially for African American survey respondents) to embrace police careers. To do so may have implications for career longevity and employee engagement that transform the entirety of the police organization (Jordan et al. 2009; PERF 2019; Scheer et al. 2018).

Current Status and Pushing Forward

The roles that police play in recruiting interested candidates are restricted by the nature of the institution in which they operate, requiring agency representatives to "sell" the career and their agency in a proactive, professional manner that may hopefully build a lasting and trustworthy relationship. The degree to which police departments are embracing this challenge is unknown. Structural constraints such as time, budget, brand management, personnel knowledge, and perceptions of recruiting ability restrict the police department from competing with more assertive career alternatives such as private industry. It is unlikely in the coming years that police agencies will be able to compete with signing bonuses, employee perks, and career characteristics of private companies that are competing for the same interested candidates. What is needed is a systematic reevaluation of the function of recruiting, and an assessment of what must be communicated to the candidate and who among agency personnel makes the best messenger.

THE "IRONY OF POLICE RECRUITING"

Systematic research on the nature of the police recruitment challenge and the effectiveness of strategies to address it has been limited, resulting in many questions about what is needed and what works when it comes to recruitment. Shortcomings in the existence and accessibility of data contribute to this gap in knowledge. With few evidence-based lessons, agencies are faced with a challenge that is elusive and whose responses are largely untested. DeLord (2009) criticizes police departments for either being incapable or unwilling to embrace the new landscape, but in defense of police leadership, they have little empirical insight to guide their decision making (Wilson 2012).

Policing is unique among professions, but, like others, those in the profession must communicate the true nature of what they do in an appealing manner. Ask an emergency room nurse to talk to potential applicants to nursing school, and they may tell stories of extreme stress, holiday hours, and days where the rigors of the job cause them to question the decision to become a nurse at all. The nurse may contend that such "frank talk" is beneficial for the interested persons, but the audience listening may not feel the same; they may only need reinforcement of their curious interest. They may also need a mentor or "buddy" to help them navigate the career application process, and answer questions they may not feel appropriate to ask anyone (see chapter 1). This is the irony of recruiting, and personnel management as a whole, in police work: While the work itself and the career can be intrinsically rewarding, and the career may represent a true "calling" as contrasted with other human services professions, oftentimes the task of recruiting falls to individuals who, for a variety of reasons, cannot communicate its rewards and optimistic attributes due to what Crank (2004) called its grittiness.

In the case of police recruitment, the effort to communicate what is exciting, rewarding, and interesting about the career may fail for a number of reasons. It may be that the recruitment staff are not appropriately skilled in the recruitment "art," or their personality and interpersonal attributes undermine their ability to establish solid connections with candidates. In some cases, recruiting may be performed by a person who has achieved the most seniority but may not be the best to speak about the issues on the minds of the persons most targeted by the recruiting effort. Additionally, many agencies spend more time focusing on the need for recruiting as a whole, but still have little knowledge of the target audience, or they suffer a poorly defined and recognizable brand that resonates with potential applicants.

A renewed focus on communication can transform recruitment and avoid various breakdowns. One way that an agency may enhance recruiting efforts is to communicate a transparent, consistent message about procedure and brand. For example, experienced staff members may desire to leave an organizational legacy for future generations, and they can challenge others to consider ways to leverage their mission to enable stronger relationship-building with future applicants. Much in the same way this legacy can impact recruiting, it can influence persons' desires to stay, reducing voluntary turnover.

By creating an environment where personnel share their authentic experience with potential applicants, police organizations can avert the communication breakdown giving rise to the irony of recruiting. Seasoned professionals must be positioned to communicate across generational and experiential barriers. Typically, recruiters themselves have undergone similar pathways to career advancement, and they have diverse methods of communicating what attracted them, why they stay, what they view as valuable about the career, their core beliefs and perspectives about the trajectory of the organization and their role in it, and agendas in accomplishing recruiting goals. Minus a strong research-based foundation for building and maintaining workforces, police practitioners must be proactive in developing and employing communication strategies to bolster recruitment and the maintenance of staff levels.

CONCLUSIONS

Recruitment efforts are as diverse as the agencies that implement them. Many may seem to work in limited contexts but have not been systematically evaluated. Here, we offer prospects for advancing police recruitment that can help illuminate ideas for advancing police recruitment research that can help illuminate the ways in which communication among staff, potential applicants and the public can advance police recruitment. Key questions include the following:

- What is the most efficient way to communicate with recruits?
- What aspects of the selection and hiring processes are most important to communicate?
- What strategies best promote a culture of open communication and learning?
- When communicating with recruits, what is the most efficient mix of messaging content and how might it vary?
- How can the voices of the public best be brought into the recruitment processes?
- What attributes make the most effective recruiters?
- At the recruitment stage, what aspects of career progression are most important to share?
- How might police agencies create engagement opportunities to promote communication about police life and opportunities?
- What sort of professional development best benefits a recruiter and how can it be institutionalized?
- What are the greatest recruitment communication challenges and how can they be overcome?
- How can further research on the role of communication in police recruitment be facilitated?

Police recruitment is critical to the workforce development process, and communication is critical to police recruitment. Through existing police recruitment research and practice, we know of key stakeholders involved in the communication process, areas of the recruitment process where communication is paramount, and communications issues that arise when it comes to attracting candidates to the profession. However, while advances are slowly being made, important knowledge about police communication strategy and effectiveness as it relates to recruitment is largely unknown. For the good of the profession, this is an important area about which police practitioners and scholars should further "communicate."

REFERENCES

Breaugh, James A. 2009. "The Use of Biodata for Employee Selection: Past Research and Future Directions. *Human Resource Management Review* 19 (3): 219–31.

Castaneda, Laura, and Greg Ridgeway. 2010. *Today's Police and Sheriff Recruits: Insights from the Newest Members of America's Law Enforcement Community.* Santa Monica: RAND Corporation.

Cobb, Matt. 2020, January. "How to Develop a Police Recruiting Presentation That Works." *PoliceOne.* Retrieved from https://www.policeone.com/police-recruiting/articles/how-to-develop-a-police-recruiting-presentation-that-works-EsmccZZswzbTdjXi/.

Copple, James E. 2017. *Law Enforcement Recruitment in the 21st Century: Forum Proceedings.* Washington DC: Office of Community Oriented Policing Services.

Courtney, Hugh, Jane Kirkland, and Patrick Viguerie. 1997. "Strategy under Uncertainty." *Harvard Business Review*, November. Retrieved from https://hbr.org/1997/11/strategy-under-uncertainty .

Crank, John. 2004. *Understanding Police Culture*, second edition. Cincinnati: Anderson Publishing.

DeLord, Ron (Combined Law Enforcement Agencies of Texas). 2009. *From the Field Experiences Series*. June. Interview Santa Monica: RAND Corporation. Retrieved from https://www.rand.org/ise/centers/quality_policing/cops/resources/field_experiences/ron_delord.html .

Everly, George S. 2011. "Building a Resilient Organizational Culture." *Harvard Business Review*, June. Retrieved from https://hbr.org/2011/06/building-a-resilient-organizat .

Farr, Christian. 2018. "White CPD Recruits Hired More Than Minorities, Report Finds." NBC Chicago 5. Retrieved from https://www.nbcchicago.com/news/local/chicago-police-recruit-minority-hiring-469613583.html .

Giles, Howard, ed. 2016. *Communication Accommodation Theory: Negotiating Personal Relationships and Social Identities across Contexts*. Cambridge: Cambridge University Press.

Haggerty, Cathy. 2009 *From the Field Experiences Series*. July. Interview. Santa Monica: RAND Corporation. Retrieved from http://www.rand.org/ise/centers/quality_policing/cops/resources/field_experiences/catherine_haggerty.html .

International City-County Management Association (ICMA) / Vera Institute of Justice. 2018. *The Model Police Officer: Recruitment, Training and Community Engagement*. September. Washington DC: International City-County Management Association.

Jensen, Carl J., and Melissa Graves. 2013. *Leading Our Most Important Resource: Police Personnel Issues in the Year 2020*. Washington DC: Bureau of Justice Assistance, Law Enforcement Forecasting Group.

Jordan, William, Lorie Fridell, Donald Faggiani, and Bruce Kubu. 2009. "Attracting Females and Racial/Ethnic Minorities to Law Enforcement." *Journal of Criminal Justice* 37 (4): 333–41.

Kaminski, Robert J. 1993. "Police Minority Recruitment: Predicting Who Will Say Yes to an Offer for a Job as a Cop." *Journal of Criminal Justice* 21 (4): 395–409.

Lim, Nelson, Carl F. Matthies, and Kirsten M. Keller. 2012. "Workforce Development for Big City Law Enforcement Agencies." *Issues in Policing Series*. Santa Monica: RAND Corporation.

Matthies, Carl F., Kirsten M. Keller, and Nelson Lim. 2012. "Identifying Barriers to Diversity in Law Enforcement Agencies." *Issues in Policing Series*. Santa Monica: RAND Corporation.

McGreevy, Patrick. 2006. "LAPD Is Under the Gun on Recruitment." *Los Angeles Times*, July 2. Retrieved from http://articles.latimes.com/2006/jul/02/local/me-recruit2 .

Morison, Kevin P. 2017. *Hiring for the 21st Century Law Enforcement Officer: Challenges, Opportunities, and Strategies for Success*. Washington DC: Office of Community Oriented Policing Services / Police Executive Research Forum.

NPCC/APCC: National Police Chiefs' Council and Association of Police and Crime Commissioners. 2017. *Policing Vision 2025*. Coventry: College of Policing. Retrieved from http://www.npcc.police.uk/documents/policing%20vision.pdf .

Orrick, W. Dwayne. 2008. *Recruitment, Retention, and Turnover of Police Personnel: Reliable, Practical, and Effective Solutions*. Springfield: Charles C. Thomas.

PERF: Police Executive Research Forum. 2019. *The Workforce Crisis, and What Police Agencies Are Doing about It*. Washington DC: Police Executive Research Forum. Retrieved from https://www.policeforum.org/assets/WorkforceCrisis.pdf .

Rossler, Michael, Charles Scheer, and Michael Suttmoeller. 2018. "Patrol Career Interest and Perceptions of Barriers among African-American Criminal Justice Students." *Policing: An International Journal* 42 (3): 421–40.

Scheer, Charles, Michael Rossler, and Leonard Papania. 2018. *Interest in Police Patrol Careers: An Assessment of Potential Candidates' Impressions of the Police Recruitment, Selection, and Training Processes*. Hattiesburg: The University of Southern Mississippi.

Scrivner, Ellen. 2006. *Innovations in Police Recruitment and Hiring: Hiring in the Spirit of Service*. Washington DC: Office of Community Oriented Policing Services.

Taylor, Bruce, Bruce Kubu, Lorie Fridell, Carter Rees, Tom Jordan, and Jason Cheney. 2006. *Cop Crunch: Identifying Strategies for Dealing with the Recruiting and Hiring Crisis in Law Enforcement*. Washington DC: Police Executive Research Forum.

Wilson, Jeremy M. 2012. "Articulating the Dynamic Police Staffing Challenge: An Examination of Supply and Demand." *Policing: An International Journal of Police Strategies and Management* 35 (2): 327–55.

Wilson, Jeremy M., and Alexander Weiss. 2014. "Police Staffing Allocation and Managing Workload Demand: A Critical Assessment of Existing Practices." *Policing: A Journal of Policy and Practice* 8 (2): 96–108.

Wilson, Jeremy, Erin Dalton, Charles Scheer, and Clifford Grammich. 2010. *Police Recruitment and Retention for the New Millennium: The State of Knowledge*. Washington DC: Office of Community Oriented Policing Services.

Woo, DaJung, and Karen Myers. 2016. "Organizational Socialization and Intergroup Dynamics." In *Advances in Intergroup Communication,* edited by Howard Giles and Anne Maass, 227–45. New York: Peter Lang.

CHAPTER 4

Interagency Communication

Homicide Investigations

Joseph B. Kuhns and Shannon Messer

Enhancing interagency communication between criminal justice agencies is an important goal of the criminal justice system (for literature on interprofessional communication, see, for example, Cropper, Ebers, Huxham, and Ring 2008; Selsky and Parker 2005). As one example, law enforcement agencies must work collaboratively with prosecutors to move homicide cases through the criminal justice system. Most homicide cases culminate in plea bargain offers and deals, some cases are dismissed for various reasons, and occasionally a homicide case goes to trial. Some homicide investigations, of course, remain open and transition into cold cases that may be prosecuted at a much later time.

Regardless, the relationship between law enforcement agencies and prosecutor's offices, and between homicide detectives and homicide case prosecutors, can be tumultuous. Prosecutors are primarily interested in securing convictions, while homicide investigators are initially focused on arresting suspects. Prosecutors require enough evidence to prove guilt beyond a reasonable doubt, while homicide detectives merely need probable cause to secure an arrest and clear a homicide from their caseload. Therefore, the processes and evidence required to move a case from investigation to arrest to prosecution (or dismissal) requires some level of ongoing communication and collaboration between homicide detectives and prosecutors.

This chapter draws attention to the importance of ongoing and active interagency communication and collaboration between these two criminal justice entities. A case study from Charlotte, North Carolina, provides a viable model for other agencies to consider adopting. Specifically, the Charlotte Mecklenburg Police Department (CMPD) and the Mecklenburg County District Attorney's Office developed and implemented a form of direct intergroup contact referred to as the "roundtable" process. The roundtable process involves homicide detectives, homicide prosecutors and, to a lesser extent, families of victims, who work collaboratively to review homicide case evidence, consider and collaboratively determine plea bargain deals or assess the likelihood of successful conviction at a trial, and secure additional evidence for investigations that require more work. The Charlotte roundtable process has been active since 2010. CMPD defines "clearance" consistently with the Federal Bureau of Investigation (i.e., by arrest of through exceptional means; Federal Bureau of Investigation 2013) and has documented an average homicide clearance rate of 79.5 percent between 2011 and 2018, a figure well above the national average in the United States (which was 61.6 percent in 2017; Federal Bureau of Investigations 2019). Relying on feedback from a semi-structured set of face-to-face interviews with every homicide detective at CMPD, detectives reported being highly supportive and satisfied with the roundtable process. We recommend that the roundtable model be considered and replicated by other law enforcement agencies and prosecutors' offices that are interested in improving communication and collaboration when investigating and prosecuting homicide cases.

THE IMPORTANCE OF EFFECTIVE COMMUNICATION SYSTEMS WITHIN LAW ENFORCEMENT

It has been argued that the terrorist attacks on the United States on September 11, 2001, exposed the "continued fragmentation of criminal justice" (Reynolds, Griset, and Scott Jr. 2006, 3; Schnobrich-Davis and Terrill 2010). Since then, many organizations and agencies across the nation have made communication and cooperation among a growing network of criminal justice-related entities a top priority. Some of these changes have centered on technological innovations, such as computer-aided dispatch and computerized case management systems, which are designed to share data between law enforcement and other criminal justice agencies (Hough, Mccorkle, and Harper 2019; Reynolds et al. 2006). These information-sharing technologies have also proven to be invaluable to homicide detectives.

The range of criminal justice agencies involved in investigating crimes and prosecuting and housing offenders and responding to calls for service is numerous and varied. Finding ways to communicate necessary and timely information within and between criminal justice, social, media, and political organizations remains an ongoing challenge for most law enforcement agencies within and outside of the United States. This is especially true for smaller police departments, and within smaller jurisdictions, where unusual crime or public safety events such as homicide investigations, mass shootings, or natural disasters can severely stretch the limits of available resources, thereby necessitating assistance, communication, and intervention from neighboring agencies and partners (Schnobrich-Davis and Terrill 2010).

Communication processes and mechanisms within law enforcement also assume many forms (see chapters 2 and 3). For example, criminal task forces are a common method of interagency collaboration. Most, but not all, task forces are short-lived and often focused on specific mission, but some federal task force efforts in the United States may continue indefinitely (budgets permitting). Conversely, law enforcement councils

(LECs) are generally developed, maintained, and designed to endure over the course of time. LECs allow agencies to effectively pool resources and personnel to respond to changing sets of circumstances. This structure not only ensures that investigative agencies establish a stable communication foundation with one another but also that limited funds in a community do not negatively impact citizens and public safety within that community. Consortiums, like LECs, have been created within numerous states in the United States and have helped to maintain control of investigations internally while strengthening each agency individually. LECs also tend to grow, establishing specialized units and adding personnel to reinforce existing units. Training LEC members is often regulated and consistent (Schnobrich-Davis and Terrill 2010). In short, these collaborative efforts within law enforcement are generally helpful.

Intergroup Communication within the Law Enforcement Environment

Law enforcement collaborations require careful and constant communication. When bringing together agencies and entities that may have similar goals, but perhaps vastly different processes for achieving those goals, conflicts naturally arise. Effective intergroup communication (IGC) ensures that interagency collaborations remain functional and productive. IGC principles posit that when people interact with one another, it is most often their membership in notable social groups (e.g., ethnicity, gender, age), not their individual characteristics, that create the context for their communications (e.g., Jones and Watson 2013). The dynamic nature of such communication is often complicated and can put both interactants in an unstable position from the beginning. Because each interactants' prejudices, emotions, past experiences, and motivations are influencing communication, police-civilian interactions are often tenuous and a bit of a balancing act (Barker et al. 2008).

IGC also offers a basis for understanding conflict and miscommunication; particularly communication between dominant and subordinate groups such as those within criminal justice systems (Jones and Watson 2013). Gallois, Watson, and Giles (2018, 309) suggest most communications take place "between members of groups that are potentially opposed, or where there is a clear sense of 'us' versus 'them'" (see chapter 1). As a result, sometimes communications are tense or hostile (especially in the context of police–suspect interrogations) and can descend into overt discrimination, as is often seen between members of different races (Gallois et al. 2018). Further, we often "wear" our group memberships through required uniforms and dress codes, according to identity scholars (Adam and Galinsky 2012; Keblusek, Giles, and Maass 2017). What characteristics are attributed to these uniforms, however, is contextualized by past experiences, media symbolism, and influential cognitions (Adam and Galinsky 2012).

Many intergroup communication participants have negative and positive attitudes toward other groups, which influences the effectiveness of routine interactions. Within law enforcement, for example, some friction may arise when officers are interacting with members of the public. Conflict may be less likely when detectives are working with prosecutors or other criminal justice actors. Prosecutors and detectives are essentially on the same side (with some clear exceptions, as described below). However, because the threshold for arrest is lower than the threshold for conviction, and because officers are initially interested in making arrests and prosecutors are ultimately focused on securing convictions, both parties may sometimes feel as if they are on opposing sides or working against one another. Further, most communication training rests on the assumption that people are motivated to communicate well, but regardless are differentially able—or even willing—to do so (see Cargile and Giles 1996; Gallois 2003). Citizens, officers, and prosecutors would all naturally vary in their respective ability to communicate, and cultural differences, language barriers, media portrayals, power inequalities (Abeyta and Giles 2017), and historical context within local jurisdictions would also impact communications. In some rare cases, of course, the prosecutor may be prosecuting a law enforcement officer (discussed below), so communications and investigative priorities will differ substantially.

Effective Communication within the Context of Homicide Investigations

Communications and intra- and interagency interactions within the criminal justice system, and particularly within the context of homicide investigations, are rarely optimal. The criminal justice system and process are adversarial by nature, and assertions of bias and prejudice (real or perceived) are common within many criminal justice systems. Within organizations with strong subcultures (e.g., law enforcement) groupthink, the reluctance to think critically and challenge dominant theories, can further enable and exacerbate confirmation bias (see chapters 1 and 6). Groupthink can occur in highly cohesive groups that are under pressure to make important decisions (Rossmo 2016).

Decisions regarding homicide investigations and prosecutions are obviously critically important. As a result, ongoing and improved effective communication within the context of homicide investigations is particularly important. For example, continuous communication is needed during the initial processing of a crime scene(s). Efficient communication between crime scene technicians and detectives ensures that physical evidence is not contaminated, lost, or destroyed, and helps detectives move the case in one direction or another. Additional personnel who are frequently called to homicide scenes include crime scene technicians, forensic specialists, sketch artists, photographers, perhaps the district attorney, members of the media, and others. Homicide detectives must also be able to communicate effectively with other detectives, patrol officers, superiors, witnesses, suspects, crime scene technicians, prosecutors and judges, medical examiners, and the victim's family members. These communications might involve instructions, data and evidence collection, sharing evidence, communicating with other detectives who are engaged in various aspects of the investigation, and so forth.

Challenges to Effective Communication within Homicide Investigations

Communication processes within homicide investigations are difficult and may be disrupted for various reasons, and the implications of disrupted communication processes are important within this context. As a basis of context, homicide clearance rates declined substantially in the United States from 1970 to 1998 (Wellford and Cronin 2000) and recently hovered around 62 percent (Federal Bureau of Investigations 2019). The reasons for these declining clearance rates are varied, but poorly developed working relationships and communication with prosecutors, and with local and state crime labs, have been linked to lower clearance rates (Cronin et al. 2007). Close and direct communication between homicide investigators and the medical examiner's office is also critically important, such that many departments, but not all, require that their detectives attend autopsies during homicide investigations (Carter and Carter 2016).

More broadly, the quality of the initial investigation phase—which includes actions of first responders—is crucial to the ultimate success of the entire investigation. Preserving crime scenes is critical and detectives and supervisors must make patrol officers fully aware of their impact on the success of the subsequent investigation (Cronin et al. 2007; Wellford and Cronin 1999). Departments with stronger relationships between investigators and patrol officers and crime scene specialists, and that have "clear delineation of roles and responsibilities," would potentially develop more effective working relationships and ultimately have more success at solving homicides (Cronin et al. 2007, 26).

Further, during the earliest stages of homicide investigations, detectives must simultaneously and quickly communicate with numerous entities including their agency communications divisions/units or public information officers (so they can alert other agencies if a suspect remains free), media outlets, executives and superiors, initial responding officers, witnesses, and so on (Technical Working Group on Crime Scene Investigation 2000). As a result, detectives are sometimes perceived as "information managers" as much as communicators and they must manage and respond to multiple flows of information and data from a wide range of sources, and work to keep the information flowing across various channels and constituencies (Carter and Carter 2016; Joyal 2012). Evidence of "ingroup solidarity" is likely among detectives, crime scene technicians, and medical examiners, as they are working toward the same goal (Williams 1999). However, other key individuals (e.g., witnesses, the media, public information officers) may find themselves with opposing needs (Coupland, Weimann, and Giles 1991; Petronio, Ellemers, Giles, and Gallois 1998).

Mistrust between citizens, victims, victims' families, and law enforcement agencies and representatives is perhaps another communication challenge and a potential contributor to declining homicide clearance rates. Intergroup differences between civilians and police may hinder effective policing because, among other reasons, officers (and the public) have difficulty with communication accommodation (Giles, Linz, Bonilla, and Gomez 2012). A better understanding of communication accommodation theory (CAT) may assist officers in stressful police–civilian interactions; evidence suggests that communication accommodation influences an individual's willingness to comply with officer instructions and demands (e.g., Giles et al. 2006). Further, managing suspects and witnesses is a delicate process. Witnesses may have relevant descriptions of suspects, vehicles, known associates of the victim and/or suspect, information regarding the circumstances of the event (e.g., gang activity, drug sales, or prostitution practices), and other valuable, time-sensitive intelligence (Technical Working Group on Crime Scene Investigation 2000). Suspects may or may not be motivated to talk to detectives, significantly affecting the likelihood of a successful investigative outcome (Barker et al. 2008).

Further, Carter and Carter (2016) determined that in many homicide cases, witnesses (and suspects) may fear or distrust the police, particularly in neighborhoods, communities, and countries where law enforcement agencies have not invested sufficient time and energy (e.g., community policing) toward building trust and connecting to the community, or perhaps where controversial officer-involved shootings or locally publicized abuses of authority have occurred (see chapter 10). Evidence also suggests that the willingness of citizens to cooperate with police, particularly in larger urban areas and within minority communities (Rosenfeld, Jacobs, and Wright 2003), has decreased in the United States since 2005 (Kubrin 2005; Maguire, King, Johnson, and Katz 2010). This decrease temporally coincides with declining homicide clearance rates, suggesting one may influence the other (Maguire et al. 2010). As a result, it has become more difficult for police to identify alleged offenders, especially in stranger-to-stranger crimes (Wellford and Cronin 1999).

Community fear and mistrust may also impact the families of victims and suspects, limiting their willingness to cooperate with investigations or even talk to detectives at all (see chapters 17 and 19). Research has suggested that canvassing the nearby crime scene area, an important aspect of most homicide investigations, was rarely prioritized in communities with lower homicide clearance rates (Brookman, Maguire, and Maguire 2019; Maguire et al. 2010). Crime Stoppers and citizen tip lines are sometimes good sources of additional information, but these programs also tend to work better in communities where the police have a stable and healthy relationship with the community (Carter and Carter 2016).

BEST PRACTICES AMONG AGENCIES WITH HIGHER HOMICIDE CLEARANCE RATES

Within the context of criminal investigations generally, and homicide investigations more specifically, some recent research has examined "best practices" (Carter and Carter 2016; Hough et al. 2019; Keel, Jarvis, and Muirhead 2009). This research suggests some law enforcement practices are linked to higher homicide clearance rates, as well as increased probability of those homicide cases being successfully tried by prosecutors (see, for example, Brookman et al. 2019; Wellford and Cronin 1999). The importance of "best practices" research cannot be overstated as the clearance rate for homicides in the United States has dropped significantly since the 1960s (Braga and Dusseault 2018; Carter and Carter 2016; Hough et al. 2019; Keel et al. 2009). Regardless, in the United States, about half of all homicides are cleared by arrest within the first seventeen days (Regoeczi, Jarvis, and Riedel 2008). Further, 46 percent of homicides cleared by arrests are cleared within one day and 78 percent are cleared within the first week.

Many external factors are related to homicide clearance rates, some of which are not under the direct control of investigating detectives. These factors include victim demographics and demographics of the surrounding community, the number of detectives assigned to the homicide unit or case, and "political influences that may foster or hinder the clearance of homicides . . . in these jurisdictions" (Keel et al. 2009, 51; also see Brookman et al. 2019; Maguire et al. 2010; Wellford and Cronin 1999; Xu 2008).

Still, there are some investigative best practices directly within law enforcement control that, when followed consistently, are also linked to higher clearance rates. Wellford and Cronin (1999) indicate that clearance rates are higher in agencies where: (1) the homicide unit is centralized; (2) oversight for homicide investigations is highly structured; (3) the homicide unit routinely communicates timely case information with other investigative units and with patrol officers; (4) leadership meets with the homicide unit on a regular basis and conveys specific clearance goals for the unit; and (5) the homicide unit is sufficiently resourced. Caseload management is also an important predictor of higher clearance rates (Keel 2012).

Again, one of the most commonly cited investigative factors related to higher homicide clearance rates is the presence of witnesses and the ability of detectives to glean accurate information from them (Keel et al. 2009; Wellford and Cronin 1999). The importance of witness statements during a homicide investigation also draws attention to the importance for potential bystanders to feel comfortable conversing with investigating officers and detectives. Unfortunately, there is ample evidence to suggest that many homicides that take place in poorer, high-crime neighborhoods, by and against ethnic minorities, often involve witnesses who do not perceive law enforcement as trustworthy and therefore are reticent to involve themselves in investigations (Braga and Dusseault 2018; Borg and Parker 2001; Hough et al. 2019; Rosenfeld, Jacobs, and Wright 2003). Ethnic minorities are often more likely to hold negative attitudes toward the police, often perceiving police officers as being unfair and prejudiced (Hurst, Frank, and Browning 2000; Tyler and Huo 2002; Weitzer and Tuch 2005). Examination of police officers' attitudes and behavior suggests that these negative perceptions are often warranted. Indeed, studies across different Western countries have indicated that police officers receive relatively high racial prejudice scores compared to members of the general population (Colman and Gorman 1982; Pitkänen and Kouki 2002; Wortley and Homel 1995; see chapter 5). Some evidence suggests that these perceptions may also be justified based on officers' decisions during shoot–don't shoot scenarios (Correll et al. 2007). This mistrust can also negatively impact communication willingness, processes, and effectiveness during homicide investigations (Carter and Carter 2016), which may minimize willingness to "snitch" and may even increase the risk for those who are willing to cooperate (Rosenfeld, Jacobs, and Wright 2003).

Other important factors that can improve homicide clearance rates include access to sophisticated analyses of crime scene evidence, formal training of homicide detectives and other investigative partners, and the ability to pinpoint a suspect early in the investigation (the last likely a result of exemplary skill in the previous two; Brookman et al. 2019; Carter and Carter 2016; Keel et al. 2009; Wellford and Cronin 1999). Many of these factors are also relevant to prosecutors, who must consider the available evidence when deciding whether to offer a plea deal, move to a trial, or drop a case altogether. It follows that police-prosecutor relationships and communication are critically important within the context of homicide investigations.

The Importance of Police–Prosecutor Communications during Homicide Investigations

In a study of high performing homicide units across the United States, Keel (2008) determined that departments that involved prosecutors early in the investigative process had higher clearance rates. Average clearance rates were progressively lower as time elapsed between the beginning of the case and the initiation of prosecutor involvement. Departments that characterized their relationship with prosecutors as good or excellent had, on average, 6.2 percent higher clearance rates than those who characterized their relationships as fair or poor (Keel 2008). Vecchi (2009) observes that resources are often scarce within the public safety arena. For this reason, prosecutors only consider prosecuting a limited number of cases. Soliciting input earlier in the investigation allows prosecutors to offer advice on how to strengthen a case. Glazer (2001, 12) posits that prosecutors can sometimes "make connections between the many players on the street," and they are not constrained by territorial divides between local, state, and federal law enforcement agencies; she refers to it as "being at the information crossroads."

Within this context, the ways in which both law enforcement and prosecutorial misconduct and bias can influence investigations merits some attention (Davis and Leo 2017). Studies suggest that both entities consistently complain about the competence of the other (McDonald, Rossman, and Cramer 1982; McIntyre 1975; Rowe 2016). However, agencies in the United States that have established a cooperative relationship with their district attorneys' offices fare better (Carter and Carter 2016). In some cases, prosecutors directly respond to homicide crime scenes; in others, a prosecutor is assigned to a police homicide unit; in yet another model, the district attorney's office has specifically designated homicide prosecutors. In each of these models, "investigators and prosecutors maintained open, functional relationships and the results included an increase in clearances and increased successful prosecutions" (Carter and Carter 2016). Additionally, a supporting network of people and processes is crucial for ensuring that information databases are fed sufficient inputs, and that outputs (information on hits or matches) are quickly produced and disseminated to investigators (Brady and King 2017).

A CASE STUDY OF INTERAGENCY COMMUNICATION/COLLABORATION: THE CHARLOTTE ROUNDTABLE PROCESS

The authors worked with the Charlotte Mecklenburg Police Department to learn more about communication and collaboration among and between homicide detectives and prosecutors in Charlotte, North Carolina. CMPD is the largest law enforcement agency in North Carolina, with over two thousand sworn officers and a large civilian support network, and the Mecklenburg County Prosecutor's Office handles all homicide cases in the jurisdiction.

As a part of a broader project, every homicide detective and supervisor (twenty-four active detectives, two former detectives who were working in the cold case unit, four sergeants, and one lieutenant) was interviewed alone, and some were interviewed again within smaller group sessions. The homicide unit interviewing process began with a series of meetings with the lieutenant and two of the four active sergeants, who provided background information on the unit, its mission, resources and challenges, and on the Charlotte roundtable process. It was important to solicit direct input from every detective and supervisor in the homicide unit since every detective contributes to homicide investigations, each brings different levels of experience and varied work styles and communication preferences to the mission, and many detectives have different sets of skills that may facilitate investigative efficiency or inefficiency. Some of the newer detectives had not participated in the roundtable process at the time of the interview, but others had participated many times. The face-to-face interviews were conducted between February and May 2019 at the Charlotte Mecklenburg Police Department headquarters. For various reasons, the interviews were not audio-recorded; rather, systematic notes were gathered and carefully organized. The general purpose of the interviews included the following:

1. exploring the law enforcement backgrounds and investigative experiences for each detective in the unit and documenting and validating the steps required in "typical" homicide investigation;
2. outlining the range of steps that are required for investigating various forms of homicide (e.g., typical, domestic, indoor/outdoor, etc.) and estimating the average time required to complete distinct phases of "typical" homicide investigations;
3. understanding "atypical" homicides that may extend investigative time commitments for detectives and others (e.g., multiple victims/offenders, cases with multiple crime scenes, cold cases, officer-involved shootings that result in fatalities [discussed below]; and
4. understanding detective experiences with, and perceptions of, the roundtable process.

Prior to the development of the roundtable process, the CMPD and the Mecklenburg County District Attorney's Office had an unhealthy and challenging intergroup relationship. In 2009, a new chief assumed command of CMPD, and shortly thereafter he publicly criticized the former district attorney (DA) for lenient plea offers and a lack of communication and community engagement in the plea-bargaining process. In turn, the DA complained about the quality of the homicide cases that were being presented to their office. The lack of communication and collaboration was quite apparent and well-documented in local newspapers. An opportunity to solve both problems emerged through the roundtable (intergroup) process, which began when a new district attorney was appointed in 2010.

Intergroup contact theory suggests that routine contact between groups can improve intergroup attitudes when and if it takes place under optimal conditions (Allport 1954; Pettigrew 1998; see chapter 1). The contact hypothesis has been tested extensively throughout the past fifty years, across a wide range of participants and target groups, settings, and methodological designs. The results of these studies have generally been supportive (Pettigrew 1998). In a recent meta-analysis, which included samples from studies written between 1949 and 2000, Pettigrew and Tropp (2006) demonstrated that intergroup contact is also significantly associated with reduced prejudice. This is likely a result of shifting expectations regarding "accommodation" in communication, a theory that suggests individuals move toward and away from others, by changing their communicative behavior (Giles 2016).

The roundtable process offers an example of intergroup contact theory in practice that improved communication, helped develop healthy working relationships, and moved the police department and prosecutor's office forward with establishing common goals regarding homicide investigations. In addition to ensuring that a prosecutor was physically present at all homicide scenes, the new DA instituted the roundtable process. In short, the Homicide Team Roundtable is a series of group meetings that include every member of the Homicide Prosecution Team, the district attorney, and the CMPD homicide supervisors (one lieutenant and four sergeants). The group meets twice a month, every month. Each active homicide case is discussed and debated at these meetings. Case evidence is presented by lead detectives, witness testimony and evidence concerns are discussed, sentencing laws are considered and reviewed, and other relevant facts and factors are openly debated among the parties. The group deliberates the case collectively and collaboratively.

To be clear and fair, there have been occasional disagreements among the parties, but those disagreements are openly discussed and debated. Ultimately, the roundtable group attempts to reach an agreement and a decision about case dismissal or delay (for various reasons) or the specific criteria to be included with a plea offer or moving to trial. Once a decision is reached and agreed upon, homicide investigators (lead detectives) and prosecutors (sometimes) meet with the victim's family to share and discuss the recommendation and decision, solicit their input (to the extent possible), explain the rationale behind the decision, and listen to feedback. These meetings are critical communication points between the criminal justice system and the community and assist in improving trust and confidence in both the police and the prosecutor (Kuhns and Messer 2019; Stetzer 2013).

CONSIDERING THE IMPACT OF OFFICER-INVOLVED SHOOTINGS ON POLICE-PROSECUTOR COMMUNICATIONS

Officer-involved shooting (OIS) investigations, including those that involve civilian or officer fatalities, are particularly challenging investigations for both law enforcement agencies and prosecutors. There are a wide range of OIS investigative models that are used across law enforcement agencies in North America (Kuhns, Cambareri, Messer, and Stephens 2018). In Charlotte, the homicide unit investigates every officer-involved shooting within the jurisdiction. Specifically, all ten members of the "Shoot Team" (generally the most experienced homicide detectives) are dispatched to every OIS event, and those involving fatalities often include all supervisors from the homicide unit. OIS investigations therefore deploy more resources than typical homicides, which are assigned to a squad of six detectives.

OIS events that involve fatalities are simultaneously investigated by the Shoot Team (the internal criminal investigation), internal affairs (administrative investigation), the

State Medical Examiner's Office, and the district attorney (external criminal investigations). Extensive cross-unit coordination and communication is required. OIS scenes can be complicated, particularly in cases where multiple officers are involved and possibly discharging multiple weapons and/or scenes that involve more than one suspect (which is rare). Increased internal and external pressure from CMPD executives, the public, the district attorney, and the media requires CMPD homicide detectives to remain at OIS scenes for longer periods of time, interview more witnesses than usual, and focus additional attention on gathering video and forensic evidence from various sources, including from bystanders, local businesses, and others. Depending on the circumstances, civil cases may be filed by the families of victims involved in OIS events (Giles and Anderson 2003).

Further, the job of investigating and prosecuting police officers who commit crimes typically falls on local prosecutors (Chemerinsky 2000; Levine 2016), which extends preexisting concerns of bias and favoritism in jurisdictions that involve regular communication and cooperation between prosecutors and homicide detectives. Arguably, prosecutors are more critical than judges when it comes to ensuring the appearance of justice within the criminal justice system, given their unbridled level of discretion in charging and prosecuting cases and their limited external oversight (Sklansky 2016). Asking local prosecutors to become adversaries of their closest professional allies raises process-oriented and democratic legitimacy issues, particularly in communities where confidence in the criminal justice system may already be compromised. The apparent conflict of interest between local prosecutors and police–defendants is so anathema to our system of justice such that some jurisdictions are moving toward assigning special prosecutors (perhaps from other jurisdictions) to investigate OIS cases (Levine 2016) and/or external investigators for OIS events involving fatalities (Kuhns et al. 2018).

CONCLUSIONS

The Police Executive Research Forum (2018) suggests that homicide units should be composed of more than just homicide detectives, and that the flow of information and communication should be encouraged among and between prosecutors and detectives. A team approach should be emphasized, and police leaders should prioritize improving cross-agency communication and collaboration. Police departments should consider assembling a homicide investigation team that is led by a primary homicide detective (lead detective) and that includes other investigators (CMPD assigns squads of six detectives to every homicide), a crime analyst (CMPD has one assigned to the homicide unit), crime scene technicians, a specific prosecutor assigned to the case, representatives from the patrol unit, the medical examiner's office, and any other units relevant to the case. Police agency leaders should work with leaders from the local prosecutor's office to establish strong information-sharing protocols and ensure that their policies and goals are aligned, including reaching a consensus on what information is needed for charging decisions, whether and when prosecutors will respond to crime scenes, how prosecutors will be involved in interviews and interrogations, and ongoing communication protocols between detectives and prosecutors. To promote better relationships with the community, police leaders should continue to expand their efforts to implement strong outreach programs and community-wide initiatives. Homicide units should take an organized, comprehensive approach to respond to victims' families; for example, by having a social worker or victim's advocate located within the homicide unit (the lead detectives serve this role in Charlotte).

Many of these recommended practices generally describe how homicide investigations occur in Charlotte, North Carolina, a city with an impressively high homicide clearance rate of almost 80 percent (Kuhns and Messer 2019), which is well above the national average (Federal Bureau of Investigation 2019). The roundtable process enables effective intergroup communication and ensures that police-prosecutor-community communication channels remain open and active.

Evidence suggests that homicide clearance rates have improved in other large cities (e.g., Boston, MA) following the implementation of recommended best practices (Braga and Dusseault 2018). Effective communication during homicide investigations, within and between law enforcement and other criminal justice agencies/actors and the public, is one of the critical best practices (Carter and Carter 2016; Wellford and Cronin 1999). However, McDermott and Hulse (2012) observe that there is no universal comprehensive communication training within law enforcement that focuses on active listening, problem-solving, persuasion, and conflict management. Given the importance of intergroup communication within the context of homicide investigations, law enforcement agencies and prosecutor's offices should consider sending their personnel to this type of training, and perhaps consider developing and adopting a roundtable process (Kuhns and Messer 2019). Within this context, prosecutors could regularly train detectives on case preparation protocols to improve investigative quality and, ultimately, achieve higher homicide clearance rates. Recognizing that when the occasional OIS case is investigated, these already established communication processes and preexisting relationships may allow those rare, but highly controversial, events to be transparently and independently investigated (Kuhns et al. 2018), which may help to achieve justice and improve trust in law enforcement and the prosecution of offenders.

REFERENCES

Abeyta, Audrey, and Howard Giles. 2017. "Intergroup Communication, Overview." In *The International Encyclopedia of Intercultural Communication*, edited by Young Y. Kim, 1147–60. New York: Wiley/Blackwell.

Adam, Hajo, and Adam Galinsky. 2012. "Enclothed Cognition." *Journal of Experimental Social Psychology* 48 (4): 918–25.

Allport, Gordon W. 1954. *The Nature of Prejudice.* Reading: Addison-Wesley.

Barker, Valerie, Howard Giles, Chris Hajek, Hiroshi Ota, Kim Noels, Tae-Seop Lim, and LinlnaBeth Somera. 2008. "Police-Civilian Interaction, Compliance, Accommodation, and Trust in an Intergroup Context: International Data." *Journal of International and Intercultural Communication* 1 (2): 93–112.

Borg, Marion J., and Karen F. Parker. 2001. "Mobilizing Law in Urban Areas: The Social Structure of Homicide Clearance Rates." *Law and Society Review* 35 (2): 435–66.

Brady, Patrick Q., and William R. King. 2017. "Technology and Homicide Investigation." In *The Handbook of Homicide*, edited by Fiona Brookman, Edward R. Maguire, and Mike Maguire, 517–532. Chichester: Wiley Blackwell.

Braga, Anthony A., and Desiree Dusseault. 2018. "Can Homicide Detectives Improve Homicide Clearance Rates?" *Crime and Delinquency* 64 (30): 283–315.

Brookman, Fiona, Edward R. Maguire, and Mike Maguire. 2019. "What Factors Influence Whether Homicide Cases Are Solved? Insights from Qualitative Research with Detectives in Great Britain and the United States." *Homicide Studies* 23 (2): 145–174.

Cargile, Aaron, and Howard Giles. 1996. "Intercultural Communication Training: Review, Critique, and a New Theoretical Framework." *Annals of the International Communication Association* 19 (1), 385–404.

Carter, David L., and Jeremy G. Carter. 2016. "Effective Police Homicide Investigations: Evidence from Seven Cities with High Clearance Rates." *Homicide Studies* 20 (2): 150–76.

Chemerinsky, Erwin. 2000. "The Role of Prosecutors in Dealing with Police Abuse: The Lessons of Los Angeles." *Virginia Journal of Social Policy & the Law* 8: 305–28.

Colman, Andrew M., and L. Paul Gorman. 1982. "Conservatism, Dogmatism, and Authoritarianism in British Police Officers." *Sociology* 16 (1): 1–11.

Correll, Joshua, Bernadette Park, Charles M. Judd, Bernd Wittenbrink, Melody S. Sadler, and Tracie Keesee. 2007. "Across the Thin Blue Line: Police Officers and Racial Bias in the Decision to Shoot." *Journal of Personality and Social Psychology* 92 (6): 1006–23.

Coupland, Nikolas, John M. Wiemann, and Howard Giles. 1991. "Talk as 'Problem' and Communication as 'Miscommunication': An Integrative Analysis." In *"Miscommunication" and Problematic Talk*, edited by Nikolas Coupland, Howard Giles, and John M. Wiemann, 1–17, Newbury Park: Sage.

Cronin, James M., Gerard R. Murphy, Lisa L. Spahr, Jessica I. Toliver, and Richard E. Weger. 2007. *Promoting Effective Homicide Investigations*. Washington, DC: Office of Community Oriented Policing Services, U.S. Department of Justice.

Cropper, Steve, Mark Ebers, Chris Huxham, and Peter S. Ring. 2008. *The Oxford Handbook of Inter-Organization Relations*. Oxford: Oxford University Press.

Davis, Deborah, and Richard A. Leo. 2017. "A Damning Cascade of Investigative Errors: Flaws in Homicide Investigation in the USA." In *The Handbook of Homicide*, edited by Fiona Brookman, Edward R. Maguire, and Mike Maguire, 578–98. Chichester: Wiley/Blackwell.

Federal Bureau of Investigation. 2013. *Uniform Crime Reports; Clearances*. Washington DC: Government Printing Office.

Federal Bureau of Investigation. 2019. *Uniform Crime Reports; Homicide Clearance Rate*. Washington DC: Government Printing Office.

Gallois, Cynthia. 2003. "Reconciliation through Communication in Intercultural Encounters: Potential or Peril?" *Journal of Communication* 53 (1): 5–15.

Gallois, Cynthia, Bernadette M. Watson, and Howard Giles. 2018. "Intergroup Communication: Identities and Effective Interactions." *Journal of Communication* 68 (2): 309–17.

Giles, Howard, ed. 2016. *Communication Accommodation Theory: Negotiating Personal Relationships and Social Identities across Contexts*. Cambridge: Cambridge University Press.

Giles, Howard, and Michelle L. Anderson. 2003. Review of *Liability, Stress, and Community: Communicative Issues in Policing*. *Journal of Communication* 53 (3): 545–50.

Giles, Howard, Jennifer Fortman, Rene Dailey, Valerie Barker, Chris Hajek, Michelle L. Anderson, and Nicholas O. Rule. 2006. "Communication Accommodation: Law Enforcement and the Public." In *Applied Interpersonal Communication Matters: Family, Health, and Community Relations*, edited by Rene Dailey and Beth A. Le Poire, 241–69. New York: Peter Lang.

Giles, Howard, Dan Linz, Doug Bonilla, Michelle L. Gomez. 2012. "Police Stops of and Interactions with Latino and White (Non-Latino) Drivers: Extensive Policing and Communication Accommodation." *Communication Monographs* 79 (4): 407–27.

Glazer, Elizabeth. 2001. "Crime Busting and Crime Prevention: Dual Role for Prosecutors." *Criminal Justice,* 15 (4): 10–15.

Hough, Richard, Kimberly D. Mccorkle, and Sarah Harper. 2019. "An Examination of Investigative Practices of Homicide Units in Florida." *Homicide Studies,* 23 (2): 175–94.

Hurst, Yolander G., James Frank, and Sandra Lee Browning. 2000. "The Attitudes of Juveniles toward the Police: A Comparison of Black and White Youth." *Policing: An International Journal of Police Strategies & Management* 23 (1): 37–53.

Jones, Liz, and Bernadette Watson. 2013. "Intergroup Communication." *Communication*, edited by Patricia Moy, 1–1. Oxford: Oxford University Press.

Joyal, Renee Graphia. 2012. "How Far Have We Come? Information Sharing, Interagency Collaboration, and Trust within the Law Enforcement Community." *Criminal Justice Studies* 25 (4): 357–70.

Keblusek, Lauren, Howard Giles, and Anne Maass. 2017. "Communication and Group Life: How Language and Symbols Shape Intergroup Relations." *Group Processes and Intergroup Relations* 20 (5): 632–43.

Keel, Timothy. 2008. "Homicide Investigations: Identifying Best Practices." *FBI Law Enforcement Bulletin* 77 (2): 1–9.

Keel, Timothy. 2012. *Detecting Clues in Homicide Management: A Homicide "Best Practices" Research Project*. Washington DC: Federal Bureau of Investigation, US Department of Justice.

Keel, Timothy G., John P. Jarvis, and Yvonne E. Muirhead. 2009. "An Exploratory Analysis of Factors Affecting Homicide Investigations: Examining the Dynamics of Murder Clearance Rates." *Homicide Studies* 13 (1): 50–68.

Kubrin, Charis E. 2005. "Gangstas, Thugs, and Hustlas: Identity and the Code of the Street in Rap Music." *Social Problems* 52 (3): 360–78.

Kuhns, Joseph B., and Shannon Messer. 2019. *Charlotte Mecklenburg Police Department Homicide Unit Workload Assessment*. Charlotte: K4 Associates, Inc.

Kuhns, Joseph B., Josie Cambareri, Shannon Messer, and Darrel Stephens. 2018. *Independent Investigations of Officer-Involved Shootings: Current Practices and Recommendations from Law Enforcement Leaders in the United States and Canada*. Retrieved from Major Cities Chiefs Association, https://www.majorcitieschiefs.com/pdf/news/ois_fiinal_report_9_27_18.pdf.

Levine, Kate. 2016. "Who Shouldn't Prosecute the Police." *Iowa Law Review* 101 (4): 1447–96.

Maguire, Edward R., William R. King, Devon Johnson, and Charles M. Katz. 2010. "Why Homicide Clearance Rates Decrease: Evidence from the Caribbean." *Policing & Society* 20 (4): 373–400.

McDermott, Peter J., and Diana Hulse. 2012. "Interpersonal Skills Training in Police Academy Curriculum." *FBI Law Enforcement Bulletin* 81 (2): 16–20.

McDonald, William F., Henry H. Rossman, and James A. Cramer. 1982. *Police-Prosecutor Relations in the United States: Final Report*. Washington DC: National Institute of Justice.

McIntyre, D. M. 1975. "Impediments to Effective Police Prosecution Relationships." *American Criminal Law Review* 13 (2): 201–31.

Petronio, Sandra, Naomi Ellemers, Howard Giles, and Cynthis Gallois. 1998. "(Mis)communication across Boundaries: Interpersonal and Intergroup Considerations." *Communication Research* 25 (6): 571–95.

Pettigrew, Thomas F. 1998. "Intergroup Contact Theory." *Annual Review of Psychology* 49 (1): 65–85.

Pettigrew, Thomas F., and Linda R. Tropp. 2006. "A Meta-Analytic Test of Intergroup Contact Theory." *Journal of Personality and Social Psychology* 90 (5): 751.

Pitkänen, Pirkko, and Satu Kouki. 2002. "Meeting Foreign Cultures: A Survey of the Attitudes of Finnish Authorities towards Immigrants and Immigration." *Journal of Ethnic and Migration Studies* 28 (1): 103–118.

Police Executive Research Forum (PERF). 2018. *Promising Strategies for Strengthening Homicide Investigations: Findings and Recommendations from the Bureau of Justice Assistance's Homicide Investigations Enhancement Training and Technical Assistance Project*. US Bureau of Justice Assistance. Retrieved from https://www.bja.gov/Publications/promising-strategies-for-strengthening-homicide-investigations.pdf.

Regoeczi, Wendy C., John Jarvis, and Marc Riedel. 2008. "Clearing Murders: Is It about Time?" *Journal of Research in Crime and Delinquency* 45 (2): 142–62.

Reynolds, K. Michael, Pamela L. Griset, and Ernest Scott, Jr. 2006. Law Enforcement Information Sharing: A Florida Case Study. *American Journal of Criminal Justice* 31 (1): 1–17.

Rosenfeld, Richard, Bruce A. Jacobs, and Richard Wright. 2003. "Snitching and the Code of the Street." *The British Journal of Criminology* 43 (2): 291–309.

Rossmo, D. Kim. 2016. "Case Rethinking: A Protocol for Reviewing Criminal Investigations." *Police Practice and Research*, 17 (3): 212–28.

Rowe, Brenda I. 2016. "Predictors of Texas Police Chiefs' Satisfaction with Police–Prosecutor Relationships." *American Journal of Criminal Justice* 41 (4): 663–85.

Schnobrich-Davis, Julie, and William Terrill. 2010. "Interagency Collaboration: An Administrative and Operational Assessment of the Metro-LEC Approach." *Policing* 33 (3): 506–30.

Selsky, John W., and Barbara Parker. 2005. "Cross-Sector Partnerships to Address Social Issues: Challenges to Theory and Practice." *Journal of Management* 31 (6): 849–73.

Sklansky, David A. 2016. "The Nature and Function of Prosecutorial Power." *Journal of Criminal Law & Criminology* 106 (3): 473–520.

Stetzer, William T. 2013. *A Collaborative Approach to Plea Offers*. Charlotte: Mecklenburg County Prosecutor's Office.

Technical Working Group on Crime Scene Investigation. 2000. *Crime Scene Investigation: A Guide for Law Enforcement*. Washington DC: Bureau of Justice Assistance, US Department of Justice, National Institute of Justice

Tyler, Tom R., and Yuen J. Huo. 2002. *Trust in the Law: Encouraging Public Cooperation with the Police and Courts*. New York: Russell Sage Foundation.

Vecchi, Gregory M. (2009). "Principles and Approaches to Criminal Investigation, Part 1." *Forensic Examiner* 18 (2): 8–13.

Weitzer, Ronald, and Steven A. Tuch. 2005. "Racially Biased Policing: Determinants of Citizen Perceptions." *Social Forces* 83 (3): 1009–30.

Wellford, Charles, and James Cronin. 1999. *An Analysis of Variables Affecting the Clearance of Homicides: A Multi-State Study*. Washington DC: Justice Research and Statistics Association.

Wellford, Charles, and James Cronin. 2000. "Clearing Up Homicide Clearance Rates." *National Institute of Justice Journal* 243: 1–7.

Williams, Angie. 1999. "Communication Accommodation Theory and Miscommunication: Issues of Awareness and Communication Dilemmas." *International Journal of Applied Linguistics* 9 (2): 151–65.

Wortley, Richard K., and Ross. J. Homel. 1995. "Police Prejudice as a Function of Training and Outgroup Contact." *Law and Human Behavior* 19 (3): 305–17.

Xu, Yili. 2008. "Characteristics of Homicide Events and the Decline in Homicide Clearance: A Longitudinal Approach to the Dynamic Relationship, Chicago 1966–1995." *Criminal Justice Review* 33 (4): 453–79.

SECTION II

POLICE COMMUNICATION *WITH* DIVERSE COMMUNITIES

CHAPTER 5

Race, Policing, and Communication

Old Problems, Twenty-First-Century Struggles

Travis Dixon, Marisa A. Smith, and Kristopher R. Weeks

Over the last few years, concerns regarding racial inequity during police interactions have remained at the forefront of political and policy discussions. Media coverage, political debates, videos disseminated via social media, and public protests highlight apparent police mistreatment of minorities (see the introduction and the conclusion to this book). Public outcry following officer-involved shootings, such as the 2014 shooting of Michael Brown, or the more recent deaths of Breonna Taylor (Oppel 2020) and George Floyd (Hill et al. 2020), sparks debate about fatal officer encounters (see chapter 16 and the this book's conclusion). Spurred by social media, viral recordings of traffic and pedestrian stops by police regularly instigate dialogue about police-community relations. We argue that interpersonal interactions and mediated vicarious experiences with police officers shape people's trust of law enforcement (see chapter 8). A lack of trust between citizens and law enforcement can erode the ability of officers to reduce crime in partnership with the community (Barker et al. 2008). Communication scholarship elucidates key aspects of interpersonal and mediated encounters that can create trust or mistrust between police and citizens. In this chapter, we discuss theories and behaviors highlighted by communication scholars that explain the racial divide in perceptions of the police, manifesting in a lack of trust by communities of color.

ROUTINE TRAFFIC STOPS, COMMUNICATION ACCOMMODATION, AND PERCEPTIONS OF POLICE BIAS

There are two kinds of experiences that the public likely have with the police—direct and vicarious. The most common direct experience would be the common traffic stop (Barker et al. 2008; Dixon, Schell, Giles, and Drogos 2008). Two theories stand out when we consider these direct experiences: communication accommodation theory (CAT) and social identity theory (SIT).

CAT provides a wide-ranging framework designed to predict and explain the adjustments interactants (e.g., officer and citizen) make to create, maintain, or decrease social distance (Giles 2016). Social distance does not refer to the physical distancing related to the COVID-19 pandemic. Instead, social distance in this context refers to a person's immediate (and often unconscious) communicative adjustment to be more similar or dissimilar toward another person (Dragovic, Gasiorek, and Giles 2016). It proposes that communication can be influenced by the immediate situation and sociohistorical context in which it is imbedded. Sociohistorical context includes the history of relations between police and community members (Giles, Willemyns, Gallois, and Anderson 2007; see also this book's conclusion). For example, disproportionate investigatory stops (Epp, Maynard-Moody, and Haider-Markel 2017), especially prevalent in African American communities during the Reagan era "War on Drugs" (Alexander 2010), provide sociohistorical context for greatly deflated levels of trust during routine traffic stops (see chapter 16). SIT further elucidates that our personal identities become linked with our perception of our own group in relationship to other groups (see chapters 1, 6, and 22). Therefore, interactants (e.g., White officer, Black citizen) often act as members of their respective groups rather than as individuals. This leads them to preference ingroup members (e.g., fellow White people, including officers) rather than outgroup members (e.g., dissimilar Black people). Some of those ingroup preferences lead interactants to communicate their kinship or closer social distance as predicted by CAT. Thus, ingroup members reflect more kindness, consideration, and similar language style to reflect a type of social "closeness."

CAT says that people use communication to demonstrate their attitudes toward one another—an indicator of the social distance between them. It highlights the process of convergence, a strategy whereby one adapts their communicative behaviors (e.g., verbal and nonverbal patterns) to become more similar to their interactant's behavior. Convergence represents attempts to decrease social distance (e.g., between officers and interactants) and spur cooperation, while divergence represents an attempt to reestablish social boundaries (Barker et al. 2008; Giles, Willemyns, Gallois, and Anderson 2007).

CAT and the Routine Traffic Stop

CAT suggests that understanding communication between officers and the public requires looking at interactants, their motivations, and how their communicative strategy may be perceived. Therefore, it may be illustrative to consider the routine traffic stop from both the position of the officer and public interactants. Many Black people have been given the "talk." The talk remains a series of strategies passed down from African

American parents to their children to encourage the use of accommodative statements and stances when undergoing a routine traffic stop. Black children are encouraged to deploy convergent behavior designed to discourage officers from arresting, beating, or killing them (Brunson 2007). However, despite these efforts, Black people often encounter harsh treatment by the police, which may lead them to engage in divergent communication during traffic stops.

However, officers, having received less accommodative behavior from Black people, may deploy more divergent communicative behaviors during routine traffic stops with African Americans. In fact, Dixon et al. (2008) investigated each of these possibilities by content analyzing over three hundred dash cam video interactions between Black and White officers and drivers in Cincinnati. In line with SIT and CAT, they found that officers and drivers exhibited more accommodative behaviors (e.g., speaking with more respect and politeness) when officers and drivers were from the same race. However, Black drivers performed more divergent communication (e.g., less courteous and apologetic) compared to White drivers overall. Moreover, officers engaged in more divergent behavior when interacting with drivers from different races.

Limits of Accommodation and Racial Disparity

The more divergent communication exhibited by Black drivers might be linked to the fact that they do not receive the same treatment once detained by police, and this may influence their accommodative behaviors. For example, Dixon et al. (2008) found that Black drivers were subject to more extensive policing than White drivers. This included stops that lasted for a longer duration for Black than White drivers; more officers present during the traffic stop for Black versus White drivers; and a higher likelihood that a Black rather than White occupant was searched during stops. Moreover, these scholars found that Black drivers became more belligerent the longer they were detained. Ultimately, these kinds of personal adverse encounters with police officers can drive a decreased trust in the police (e.g., Lai and Zhao 2010) and increase the belief that police perform illegitimate actions (e.g., Gau and Brunson 2012). This also illustrates the limits of convergence. Black drivers may have difficulty remaining accommodative when White officers engage in divergence and extensively police them. At the same time, White officers encountering less accommodative behavior from Black drivers might view the harsher actions of fellow officers toward Black drivers as justified behavior. We should note that such interactions are interdependent with divergence from either officer or member of the public more likely to engender even more divergence over time (Dixon et al. 2008). All of this may perpetuate a lack of trust between officers (particularly White officers) and African Americans.

For an illustration of the deterioration of this trust, surveys have highlighted a disconnect between public and police perceptions of fatal officer-involved shootings of African American citizens. A Pew Research Center study surveyed 7,917 police officers from 54 police agencies, as well as 4,500 public respondents. According to the survey, 67 percent of police officers view fatal police encounters with African Americans as isolated incidents, as opposed to a sign of a broader problem. The public, however, reports that these incidents are indicative of larger issues. Sixty-eight percent of police officers report that protests against law enforcement are primarily motivated by anti-police bias, while only 10 percent of officers believe these protests occur out of a genuine desire for officer accountability (Morin, Parker, Stepler, and Mercer 2017). Furthermore, the public increasingly views policing policies, like the New York City Police Department's stop-and-frisk program, as the cause of racially inequitable citizen stops (Chang and Poston 2019). We should note here that some of these officer opinions and their comfort level with over-policing Black people might be driven by implicit bias. We explore these processes more below and then extend them to mediated contexts.

COGNITIVE ASSOCIATION, IMPLICIT BIAS, RACE, AND POLICING

An obvious disconnect can be seen in the paragraph above. Police believe that bad behavior by law enforcement occurs rarely, while the public sees this as more regular and systematic. This makes sense from the officer's perspective because policing is supposed to be a service occupation. This disconnect can be partially explained through implicit and explicit biases developed through media consumption (Eberhardt, Goff, Purdie, and Davies 2004).

According to Spencer, Charbonneau, and Glaser (2016), implicit biases operate outside of conscious awareness but, nonetheless, shape our behaviors. These biases derive from cognitive associations or stereotypes that link specific groups with certain behaviors or traits (e.g., Black people are criminals or Black people are violent). Such implicit biases influence judgments that lead to biased policing through a process of misattribution and disambiguation. Implicit bias and priming have also been used by communication scholars to understand how people process mediated and interpersonal messages. Our minds rely on various cognitive associations that lead to fast judgments about various social categories (e.g., Blacks are most likely up to no good). This is sometimes called heuristic processing (Dixon 2020). Our cultural context (including media, which is discussed below), socialization, and intergroup experiences (e.g., a White person who grew up in an overtly racist family) influence the accessibility of these cognitive links.

Heuristic processing and implicit bias explain why African American off-duty officers remain much more likely to be killed by fellow officers compared to White off-duty officers (Charbonneau, Spencer, and Glaser 2017). Moreover, uncertainty exacerbates the influence of racial bias during officer decision making. Therefore, certain driver behaviors during traffic stops (e.g., reaching for a wallet sometimes looks like reaching for a gun) can contribute to disproportionate violence against Black drivers (Glaser, Spencer, and Charbonneau 2014). Finally, it should be noted that besides the obvious death and injury that result from bias, racial profiling itself often leads to negative consequences. Hackney and Glaser (2013) found that profiling of Black confederates in a laboratory study encouraged more cheating among White participants. This again shows how this heuristic processing can lead to poor outcomes regarding policing. This study has real-world implications as reporting indicates that White people who are stopped and searched by the police tend to have contraband more often than Black people who are searched (Chang and Poston 2019).

Psychologists, criminologists, and communication scholars have for decades studied the mechanism and outcomes associated with the implicit bias illustrated in the studies above. Many of them point to cultural information and social interaction that form implicit cognitive linkages between social groups and stereotypes. Mediated messages in the form of television or news media form cultural information that facilitates implicit bias (see chapter 10). Furthermore, mediated messages contribute to explicit endorsements of racial stereotypes associated with African Americans (e.g., African Americans are culpable; Dixon 2006, 2008) or other groups of color (e.g., Figueroa-Caballero and Mastro 2018). Therefore, information that Black and White non-officers and officers receive via the media might facilitate vicarious intergroup interactions that deepen mistrust. We turn to the role of mediated messages in furthering mistrust and perpetuating stereotypes below.

MEDIA CONTENT, EFFECTS, AND POLICE–PUBLIC MISTRUST

Media might also be a source of vicarious experiences by officers and citizens that encourages negative intergroup dynamics and promotes stereotyping (see chapter 15). Media reinforce messages about groups that shape attitudes and behaviors, particularly regarding race and the police (Dixon and Azocar 2007). For example, traditional entertainment media consistently portrays officers as successful at clearing cases, yet as also hypermasculine and overly aggressive (Dowler and Zawilski 2007; Oliver 1994; Scharrer 2001). Research has found that media consumption of these distorted images increases the belief that police engage in misconduct (see chapter 15). However, at the same time, they tend to be depicted as extremely proficient at solving crimes. Moreover, news media consistently overrepresent officers as being White and heroic (Dixon 2017a; Dixon, Azocar, and Casas 2003; Dixon and Linz 2000). This leads news consumers to assume that unidentified officers are White and to think more positively about these officers as a result (Dixon 2007).

The depiction of African American people remains stark in comparison to White officers. As we have noted elsewhere, research has found that African Americans have been overrepresented as criminal suspects in news programming compared to official crime reports (Dixon and Linz 2000). In entertainment programming, particularly in gaming, Blacks tend to consistently be depicted as aggressive and resistant to pain (Dixon, Weeks, and Smith 2019). Moreover, the news overrepresents Black families as poor and criminal (Dixon 2017b). These mediated depictions shape the conceptions of Black people among media consumers. Scholars have found that news consumers exposed to these stereotypes support the death penalty for Black suspects and believe Black criminals to be incorrigible (Dixon 2008).

There are three potential implications of these effects for our current discussion. First, officers, especially White officers, who consume traditional entertainment and news media, will develop strong cognitive associations between African American people and criminality. This consumption would then lead to greater implicit bias when the police interact with Black people and hence reduce trust between Black persons and

White officers. Second, Black people will be more suspicious of officers because of their media portrayal as hypermasculine rulebreakers. Third, citizens, especially White citizens, will be slower to embrace police reform and quicker to support punitive stances against people of color (further contributing to systemic discrimination in the criminal justice system; see Dixon and Azocar 2007). These conclusions can be buttressed by a number of theoretical perspectives that we mention below.

Cultivation and Traditional Media Effects

As we note above, implicit bias, cognitive accessibility, and priming help explain the communication dynamics and behaviors in the interactions between officers and members of the public, particularly when they do not share the same racial background. Communication scholars have utilized these same theories to explain the effects of stereotypical media consumption. In addition, they have also developed a framework, known as media cultivation, that incorporates the theoretical notions of accessibility and implicit bias (Dixon 2020). Cultivation implies that our view of the real world starts to look like the media world the more we consume said media content. In other words, *cultivation* refers to the long-term shaping of social reality from repeated prior media exposure.

Therefore, a White officer who encounters an individual cognitively related to a previously viewed media stereotype (e.g., Black poor person) might make a quick (and possibly inaccurate) judgment about them based on repeated exposure to this stereotypical depiction over time (e.g., they must be a criminal). This suggests that heavy traditional news and entertainment media might reinforce the negative conception of Black people in the mind of officers. Cultivation has a number of underlying constructs. One of them is resonance. Resonance refers to when a mediated encounter matches an interpersonal encounter, making previous mediated encounters more powerful in shaping perceived reality (Busselle and Van den Bulck 2020). For example, if I have seen numerous Black criminals in the movies and have just been robbed by a Black criminal, I am much more likely to embrace the mediated "reality" of Black criminality. Resonance has implications for when Blacks face mistreatment and verbal aggression at the hands of police. For them, the prior media depictions of over-aggression match the divergent communication behaviors of officers they may encounter during stops, making a lack of trust much more likely.

EMERGING MEDIA, POLICE–COMMUNITY RELATIONS, AND THE SOCIALLY MEDIATED STEREOTYPING MODEL

However, we increasingly receive our news via social media and other online technologies (Dixon 2017c) rather than analog television or newspapers (see chapters 10 and 21). These emerging technologies allow us to curate our own news and to follow "sources" that tend to reinforce our group identity as predicted by SIT. Therefore, officers might consume news media that upholds their own group identity and disparages other groups (e.g., Black people who may be assumed to be criminals or provocateurs).

Similarly, Black digital media consumers might encounter "news" that includes the sharing of videos and other content that shows police abuse (Anderson and Hitlin 2016; Bigman, Smith, Williamson, Planey, and McNeil Smith 2019). These behaviors can be explained by the socially mediated stereotyping model (SMSM; Dixon, 2017c). The SMSM contends that most digital media consumers remain susceptible to unconscious bias reinforcement through algorithms and selection preferences. This bias strengthens when digital consumers seek stereotype confirmation (e.g., officers are abusive or Black people are criminals).

SMSM may partly explain why 75 percent of officers report that interactions between police and African Americans have become tenser after recent high-profile incidents that have likely been shared over social media (Morin et al. 2017). Moreover, African Americans and Latinos who fear their group identity will cause them to be racially stereotyped report lower trust in the police (Kahn, Lee, Renauer, Henning, and Stewart 2016). These people of color have vicariously experienced the mistreatment of African Americans by officers through social media and may have also directly experienced resonance from the divergent communication behaviors of officers who have detained them. They may be experiencing the self-reinforcing principles described in SMSM.

Traffic and Pedestrian Stops: Racialized Treatment in Tone and Searches

We should note that there remains ample evidence that African Americans often receive poor service from law enforcement. These apparent racial disparities in policing remain the most significant limitation to convergent communication strategies designed to encourage cooperation and trust. We highlight a few examples here and then place summaries in table 6.1. Traffic stops, in particular, substantially influence drivers' trust in law enforcement (Barker et al. 2008). Research suggests that racially disproportionate traffic stops and differential experiences *during* traffic stops indicate racial disparities (Tillyer and Engel 2013). African Americans are consistently subjected to more intensive policing experiences during routine traffic stops, such as being detained for a longer period of time, as well as having passengers and their vehicles searched (Dixon et al. 2008; Poston and Chang 2019).

African American and Latino pedestrians are also disproportionately targeted for *frisks*, that is, the search of an individual through a pat down of their outer garments for weapons or drugs (Legewie 2016). For example, Gelman, Fagan, and Kiss (2007) examined the New York City Police Department's "Stop and Frisk" policy to determine whether there was any racial bias in undertaking this effort at curbing crime. They found that even after controlling for a number of factors, including arrest rate and neighborhood factors, that African Americans and Latinos were more frequently stopped than Whites. Similarly, Ridgeway (2007) analyzed NYPD pedestrian stop data and found that Black suspects were slightly more likely to have been frisked than White suspects. In fact, a great deal of research highlights problematic racial disparities connected to pedestrian, passenger, and vehicle searches. Pre-textual stops are not conducted to enforce traffic or pedestrian regulations but, instead, allow officers to temporarily detain pedestrians and drivers viewed as reasonably suspicious. While

TABLE 5.1. Racial Disparities

Race	Source	% of Population	% of Stops	Use of Force	% of Searches	Likelihood of Being Searched	% Contraband Found	Likelihood of Deadly Force
Black	Legewie 2016—peer reviewed	25	54	22	—	—	—	—
White	Legewie 2016—peer reviewed	45	10	16	—	—	—	—
Latino	Legewie 2016—peer reviewed	28	32	24	—	—	—	—
Black	Epp, Maynard-Moody, and Haider-Markel 2017—peer reviewed	—	—	—	—	5 times as likely as Whites	—	—
Black	Ryan (2015)—peer reviewed	—	—	—	—	2.5 times as likely as Whites	—	—
Black	Chang and Poston (2019)—periodical	31	65	—	—	—	—	—
Black	Poston and Chang (2019)—periodical	9	27	—	24	—	17	—
Latino	Poston and Chang (2019)—periodical	—	—	—	16	—	16	—
White	Poston and Chang (2019)—periodical	—	—	—	6	—	20	—
Black	Johnson et al. (2019)—peer reviewed	—	—	—	—	—	—	6.67 times more likely to be Black than white
Latino	Johnson et al. (2019)—peer reviewed	—	—	—	—	—	—	3.33 times more likely to be Latino than White

police departments across the United States utilize investigatory stops to prevent crime, investigatory stops disproportionately target African Americans (Epp et al. 2017). Once stopped, African American drivers tend to be subject to more searches of their person and vehicles (Ryan 2015).

An analysis in Los Angeles found similar disparities in the proportion of African Americans involved in police stops. The *Los Angeles Times* examined stops conducted by the Los Angeles Police Department's specialized metropolitan division from 2015 through 2018 (Chang and Poston 2019). The data demonstrates that African American drivers are stopped at rates double their representation in the Los Angeles population (Poston and Chang 2019). Even though laws prohibit investigatory searches on the basis of race, African Americans are searched at rates higher than Whites. When considering the race of the officer, Rojek, Rosenfeld, and Decker (2012) found that searches during stops involving a White officer and African American driver (8.22 percent) were more common than searches of African American drivers by African American officers (3.89 percent). The racial composition of the neighborhood also influenced the rate of searches experienced by White and African American drivers. In communities with a low percentage of African American residents, searches occurred most often when they involved White officers and African American drivers. However, when the community was predominantly African American, searches of White drivers by White officers were most common. The authors suggest that these diverging rates of stops within communities of differing African American populations potentially represents "out-of-place" policing. African Americans in predominantly White neighborhoods may be met with suspicion and, therefore, have the police called on them by White residents. In addition, officers might stop these drivers because their presence violates the officers' expectations and, subsequently, they must be "up to no good" (Rojek et al. 2012).

The disparate application of searches during traffic stops is not justified by the amount of contraband produced by these searches. Research demonstrates that officers find weapons or drugs through searches in a greater percentage after stopping White drivers, even though African American drivers are stopped at a disproportionately higher rate than White drivers (Poston and Chang 2019).

Police Use of Force

Not only are African Americans subjected to a disproportionate amount of stops and searches, they also may encounter greater use of force (Kramer and Remster 2018). In New York City, African Americans and Latinos are not only stopped at proportions greater than their representations in the populations, they also experience a higher rate of physical force by police officers than White people (Legewie 2016). Kramer and Remster (2018) found that Black suspects are particularly more likely to experience potential lethal force when police uncover criminal activity, and this disparity is greatest for Black youth compared to White youth. Similarly, Willits and Makin (2017) found that officer body-worn-camera footage revealed less time before deploying force against African American suspects compared to White suspects.

In addition, Cesario, Johnson, and Terrill (2019) looked for potential racial disparities in police shootings by comparing the amount of African American and White

Americans killed by police based on the category of their criminal activity (i.e., murder, violent crime, weapons violations). When using violent crime rates as a benchmark, these researchers found no evidence of racial disparities in officer-involved shootings, including shooting of unarmed citizens and shootings due to misidentified objects. However, Johnson, Tress, Burkel, Taylor, and Cesario (2019) did find that African Americans are disproportionately involved in officer-involved shootings compared to Whites.

While those citing these works would conclude that racial disparities in officer-involved shootings are nonexistent, the analytical methods used by the researchers pose concerns. Skeptics posit that researchers must determine whether African Americans are over- or underrepresented in officer-involved shootings relative to their encounters with police (Knox and Mummolo 2020) or relative to their representation in the population (Menifield, Shin, and Strother 2019).

Nix, Campbell, Byers, and Alpert (2017) used this approach when examining 990 fatal officer-involved shootings in 2015. Specifically, the researchers examined the representation of unarmed and aggressive African Americans and other racial groups among those fatally shot by police. When examining the racial makeup of suspects attacking the police officer(s) or other people killed by police, African Americans and other racial/ethnic groups were less likely to have been an aggressor than White Americans. Additionally, among unarmed persons killed by police during this same period, African Americans outnumbered Whites.

THE COMMUNICATION AND INTERGROUP CONSEQUENCES OF RACIAL DISPARITIES ON TRUST

Thus far, we have described a significant amount of disparity that would lead to communication divergence rather than convergence during both pedestrian and vehicle stops by the police. Such negative interactions might be facilitated by a combination of implicit bias, stereotyping, and media consumption and, therefore, lead to distrust of the police. Such distrust would then lead to less cooperation and involvement in community-oriented policing (Barker et al. 2008; see chapter 10). For example, a survey of 756 residents in the Houston metropolitan area found that African Americans report more negative attitudes and less trust in the Houston Police Department than White residents (Lai and Zhao 2010). The researchers also examined relationships between personal experience and perceptions of the police. They found that satisfaction with the police's work in the residents' neighborhood was significantly related to attitudes toward and trust in the Houston Police Department. Residents who reported lower satisfaction with police work in their neighborhood, including interaction with citizens and crime prevention efforts, reported lower levels of attitudes and trust (Lai and Zhao 2010).

Police behavior during traffic stops also impacts public perception. Police departments often use searches during traffic stops as a crime prevention mechanism. However, when motorists receive requests from officers to search their vehicles, drivers' report decreased perceptions of the stop's legitimacy (Gau and Brunson 2012). Racial identification also impacts perceptions of stop legitimacy with African Americans reporting the greatest level of stop illegitimacy. Given that African Americans are disproportionately subjected to vehicular searches during traffic stops (Epp et al. 2017), these relationships help explain African American perceptions of the police. Specifically, these authors found that vehicle searches during traffic stops damage trust in police, more so than the officer's language (e.g., level of respect).

CONCLUSIONS

This chapter discussed how interpersonal interactions and media content may influence relationships between the police and African Americans. We have offered communication accommodation, social identity theory, implicit bias/cognitive accessibility, SMSM, and cultivation to explain the possible opportunities and pitfalls to trust between Black people and police officers (particularly White officers). We discussed the role of CAT and SIT in defining how communication messages during police–public interactions can either increase or decrease social distance, leading to either more or less trust. However, we also discussed how processes associated with implicit bias/cognitive accessibility, cultivation, and SMSM reinforce stereotyping that leads to racially biased policing. We then detailed some of these disparities as seen in stops, searches, and use of force. Furthermore, we reviewed the negative outcomes these disparities pose for the public's trust in the police, especially those from Black and Latino communities. This review assists our understanding of fragmented opinions about policing held by the public and officers, but it can also aid in answering an integral question. How can police departments remedy the negative physical, cognitive, and attitudinal effects of policing procedures during encounters with African American and Latino populations?

Research demonstrates that merely increasing the amount of African American officers does not change institutional regulation and practices (Nicholson-Crotty, Nicholson-Crotty, and Fernandez 2017). Instead, we believe that police departments should first acknowledge the factors underlying racial differences in policing. Police departments must recognize and alter their institutional cultures and incentives, such as their reliance on disproportionate pedestrian and traffic stops. Institutional practices, such as the utilization of investigatory stops for crime prevention, open the door for racial disparities in the application of these procedures (Rojek et al. 2012). Although intended for positive outcomes, drivers may find such stops illegitimate (Gau and Brunson 2012).

Overreliance on investigatory stops can decrease trust in policing institutions and depress attitudes toward police officers (Epp et al. 2017; Gau and Brunson 2012). Consequently, the assessment of practices adopted by police departments and the recognition of any inadvertent consequences these practices present is integral for the equitable treatment of Americans during police interactions. We would argue that both departments and officers can begin to fix the wounds of mistrust by focusing on the nature of the routine traffic stop (Dixon et al. 2008). Two issues should be addressed: the extent to which the officer in question provides less accommodative and positive communicative interaction with African American and Latino drivers; and the extent to which these stops involve additional scrutiny (duration, searches) that may not be warranted by the circumstances (see chapter 16). In addition, there needs to be a recognition that these adjustments in training and intervention are more likely to be successful if they incorporate the understanding that biased policing occurs in the absence of explicitly "racist" thoughts. Instead, they often occur because of well-documented, pernicious stereotypes that operate largely outside of conscious awareness and control (Spencer et al. 2016). One strategy being taught in some policing academies that needs to continue is the notion of mindfulness. Mindfulness encourages moving judgments from a below conscious to conscious level that greatly diminishes the influence of stereotypes. It is the process of making distinctions (Barker et al. 2008). Such distinctions separating people of color from perceived inherent criminality needs to be facilitated so that service and cooperation with these communities can thrive.

REFERENCES

Alexander, Michelle. 2010. *The New Jim Crow: Mass Incarceration in the Age of Colorblindness*. New York: The New Press.

Anderson, Monica, and Paul Hitlin. 2016. "Social Media Conversations about Race: How Social Media Users See, Share and Discuss Race and the Rise of Hashtags Like #BlackLivesMatter." *Pew Research Center*. http://www.pewinternet.org/wp-content/uploads/sites/9/2016/08/PI_2016.08.15_Race-and-Social-Media_FINAL.pdf .

Barker, Valerie, Howard Giles, Christopher Hajek, Hiroshi Ota, Kimberly Noels, Tae-Seop Lim, and LilnaBeth Somera. 2008. "Police-Civilian Interaction, Compliance, Accommodation, and Trust in an Intergroup Context: International Data." *Journal of International and Intercultural Communication* 1 (2): 93–112.

Bigman, Cabral A., Marisa A. Smith, Lillie D. Williamson, Arianna M. Planey, and Shardé McNeil Smith. 2019. "Selective Sharing on Social Media: Examining the Effects of Disparate Racial Impact Frames on Intentions to Retransmit News Stories Among U.S. College Students." *New Media & Society* 21 (11–12): 2691–709.

Brunson, Rod K. 2007. "Police Don't Like Black People: African-American Young Men's Accumulated Police Experiences." *Criminology & Public Policy* 6 (1): 71–101.

Busselle, Rick, and Jan Van den Bulck. 2020. "Cultivation Theory, Media, Stories, Processes and Reality." In *Media Effects: Advances in Theory and Research*, edited by Mary B. Oliver, Art Rainey, and Jennings Bryant, 69–82. New York: Routledge.

Cesario, Joseph, David J. Johnson, and William Terrill. 2019. "Is There Evidence of Racial Disparity in Police Use of Deadly Force? Analyses of Officer-Involved Fatal Shootings in 2015–2016." *Social Psychological and Personality Science* 10 (5): 586–95.

Chang, Cindy, and Ben Poston. 2019. "'Stop-and Frisk in a Car:' Elite LAPD Unit Disproportionately Stopped Black Drivers, Data Show." *The Los Angeles Times*. https://www.latimes.com/local/lanow/la-me-lapd-traffic-stops-20190124-story.html .

Charbonneau, Amanda, Katherine Spencer, and Jack Glaser. 2017. "Understanding Racial Disparities in Police Use of Lethal Force: Lessons from Fatal Police-on-Police Shootings." *Journal of Social Issues* 73 (4): 744–67.

Dixon, Travis L. 2006. "Psychological Reactions to Crime News Portrayals of Black Criminals: Understanding the Moderating Roles of Prior News Viewing and Stereotype Endorsement." *Communication Monographs* 73 (2): 162–87.

Dixon, Travis L. 2007. "Black Criminals and White Officers: The Effects of Racially Misrepresenting Law Breakers and Law Defenders on Television News." *Media Psychology* 10 (2): 270–91.

Dixon, Travis L. 2008. "Crime News and Racialized Beliefs: Understanding the Relationship Between Local News Viewing and Perceptions of African Americans and Crime." *Journal of Communication* 58: 106–25.

Dixon, Travis L. 2017a. "Good Guys Are Still Always in White?: Positive Change and Continued Misrepresentation of Race and Crime on Local Television News." *Communication Research* 44 (6): 775–92.

Dixon, Travis L. 2017b. "A Dangerous Distortion of Our Families: Representations of Families, by Race, in News and Opinion Media." Family Story and Color of Change. https://colorofchange.org/dangerousdistortion/.

Dixon, Travis L. 2017c. "How the Internet and Social Media Accelerate Racial Stereotyping and Social Division: The Socially Mediated Stereotyping Model." In *Race and Gender in Electronic Media: Challenges and Opportunities*, edited by Rebecca A. Lind, 161–178. New York: Routledge.

Dixon, Travis L. 2020. "Media Stereotypes: Content, Effects, and Theory." In *Media Effects: Advances in Theory and Research*, edited by Mary B. Oliver, Art Rainey and Jennings Bryant, 243–57. New York: Routledge.

Dixon, Travis L., and Cristina Azocar. 2007. "Priming Crime and Activating Blackness: Understanding the Psychological Impact of the Overrepresentation of African Americans as Lawbreakers on Television News." *Journal of Communication* 57 (2): 229–53.

Dixon, Travis L., Cristina Azocar, and Michael Casas. 2003. "The Portrayal of Race and Crime on Television Network News." *Journal of Broadcasting & Electronic Media* 47 (4): 495–520.

Dixon, Travis L., and Daniel G. Linz. 2000. "Overrepresentation and Underrepresentation of African Americans and Latinos as Lawbreakers on Television News." *Journal of Communication* 50 (2): 131–54.

Dixon, Travis L., Terri Schell, Howard Giles, and Kristin Drogos. 2008. "The Influence of Race in Police-Civilian Interactions: A Content Analysis of Videotaped Interactions Taken during Routine Cincinnati Police Traffic Stops." *Journal of Communication* 58 (3): 530–49.

Dixon, Travis L., Kristopher Weeks, and Marisa Smith. 2019. "Media Constructions of Culture, Race, and Ethnicity." *Oxford Research Encyclopedia of Communication*. https://doi.org/10.1093/acrefore/9780190228613.013.502.

Dowler, Kenneth, and Valerie Zawilski. 2007. "Public Perceptions of Police Misconduct and Discrimination: Examining the Impact of Media Consumption." *Journal of Criminal Justice* 35 (2): 193–203.

Dragojevic, Marko, Jessica Gasiorek, and Howard Giles. 2016. "Accommodative Strategies as Core of the Theory." In *Communication Accommodation Theory: Negotiating Personal Relationships and Social Identities across Contexts*, edited by Howard Giles, 36–57. Cambridge: Cambridge University Press.

Eberhardt, Jennifer L., Phillip A. Goff, Valerie J. Purdie, and Paul G. Davies. 2004. "Seeing Black: Race, Crime and Visual Processing." *Journal of Personality and Social Psychology* 87 (6): 876–93.

Epp, Charles R., Steven Maynard-Moody, and Donald Haider-Markel. 2017. "Beyond Profiling: The Institutional Sources of Racial Disparities in Policing." *Public Administration Review* 77 (2): 168–78.

Figueroa-Caballero, Andrea, and Dana Mastro. 2018. "Examining the Effects of News Coverage Linking Undocumented Immigrants with Criminality: Policy and Punitive Implications." *Communication Monographs* 86 (1): 46–67.

Gau, Jacinta M., and Rod K. Brunson. 2012. "One Question Before You Get Gone . . .": Consent Search Requests as a Threat to Perceived Stop Legitimacy." *Race and Justice* 2 (4): 250–73.

Gelman, Andrew, Jeffrey Fagan, and Alex Kiss. 2007. "An Analysis of the New York City Police Department's 'Stop-and-Frisk' Policy in the Context of Claims of Racial Bias." *Journal of the American Statistical Association* 102 (479): 813–23.

Giles, Howard. 2016. *Communication Accommodation Theory: Negotiating Personal Relationships and Social Identities across Contexts*. Cambridge: Cambridge University Press.

Giles, Howard, Michael Willemyns, Cindy Gallois, and Michelle Chernikoff Anderson. 2007. "Accommodating a New Frontier: The Context of Law Enforcement." In *Social Communication*, edited by Klaus Fiedler, 129–62. New York: Psychology Press.

Glaser, Jack, Katherine Spencer, and Amanda Charbonneau. 2014. "Racial Bias and Public Policy." *Policy Insights from the Behavioral and Brain Sciences* 1 (1): 88–94.

Hackney, Amy A., and Jack Glaser. 2013. "Reverse Deterrence in Racial Profiling: Increased Transgressions by Nonprofiled Whites." *Law and Human Behavior* 37 (6): 348–53.

Hill, Evan, Ainara Tiefenthäler, Christiaan Triebert, Drew Jordan, Haley Willis, and Robin Stein. 2020. "8 Minutes and 46 Seconds: How George Floyd Was Killed in Police Custody." Retrieved from: https://www.nytimes.com/2020/05/31/us/george-floyd-investigation.html .

Jetelina, Katelyn K., Wesley G. Jennings, Stephen A. Bishopp, Alex R. Piquero, and Jennifer M. Reingle Gonzalez. 2017. "Dissecting the Complexities of the Relationship between Police Officer–Civilian Race/Ethnicity Dyads and Less-Than-Lethal Use of Force." *American Journal of Public Health* 107 (7): 1164–70.

Johnson, David J., Trevor Tress, Nicole Burkel, Carley Taylor, and Joseph Cesario. 2019. "Officer Characteristics and Racial Disparities in Fatal Officer-Involved Shootings." *Proceedings of the National Academy of Sciences* 116 (32): 15877–82.

Kahn, Kimberly B., J. Katherine Lee, Brian Renauer, Kris R. Henning, and Greg Stewart. 2016. "The Effects of Perceived Phenotypic Racial Stereotypicality and Social Identity Threat on Racial Minorities' Attitudes about Police." *The Journal of Social Psychology* 157 (4): 416–28.

Klinger, David, Richard Rosenfeld, Daniel Isom, and Michael Deckard. 2016. "Race, Crime, and the Micro-Ecology of Deadly Force." *Criminology and Public Policy* 15 (1): 193–222.

Knox, Dean, and Jonathan Mummolo. 2020. "Making Inferences about Racial Disparities in Police Violence." *Proceedings of the National Academy of Sciences* 117 (3): 1261–62.

Kramer, Rory, and Brianna Remster. 2018. "Stop, Frisk, and Assault? Racial Disparities in Police Use of Force during Investigatory Stops." *Law & Society Review* 52 (4): 960–93.

Lai, Yung-Lien, and Jihong Solomon Zhao. 2010. "The Impact of Race/Ethnicity, Neighborhood Context, and Police/Citizen Interaction on Residents' Attitudes toward the Police." *Journal of Criminal Justice* 38 (4): 685–92.

Legewie, Joscha. 2016. "Racial Profiling and Use of Force in Police Stops: How Local Events Trigger Periods of Increased Discrimination." *American Journal of Sociology* 122 (2): 379–424.

Menifield, Charles E., Geiguen Shin, and Logan Strother. 2019. "Do White Law Enforcement Officers Target Minority Suspects?" *Public Administration Review* 79 (1): 56–68.

Morin, Rich, Kim Parker, Renee Stepler, and Andrew Mercer. 2017. "Behind the Badge: Amid Protests and Calls for Reform, How Police View Their Jobs, Key Issues and Recent Fatal Encounters between Blacks and Police." The Pew Research Center. Retrieved from https://www.pewsocialtrends.org/wp-content/uploads/sites/3/2017/01/Police-Report_FINAL_web.pdf .

Nicholson-Crotty, Sean, Jill Nicholson-Crotty, and Sergio Fernandez. 2017. "Will More Black Cops Matter? Officer Race and Police-Involved Homicides of Black Citizens." *Public Administration Review* 77 (2): 206–16.

Nix, Justin, Bradley A. Campbell, Edward H. Byers, and Geoffrey P. Alpert. 2017. "A Bird's Eye View of Civilians Killed by Police in 2015: Further Evidence of Implicit Bias." *Criminology & Public Policy* 16 (1): 309–40.

Oliver, Mary B. 1994. "Portrayals of Crime, Race, and Aggression in 'Reality-Based' Police Shows: A Content Analysis." *Journal of Broadcasting & Electronic Media* 38 (2): 179–92.

Oppel Jr., Richard A. 2020. "Here's What You Need to Know about Breonna Taylor's Death." *New York Times*. https://www.nytimes.com/article/breonna-taylor-police.html .

Poston, Ben, and Cindy Chang. 2019. "LAPD Searches Blacks and Latinos More. But They're Less Likely to Have Contraband than Whites." https://www.latimes.com/local/lanow/la-me-lapd-searches-20190605-story.html .

Ridgeway, Greg. 2007. "Analysis of Racial Disparities in the New York Police Department's Stop, Question, and Frisk Practices." RAND Corporation. Retrieved from https://www.rand.org/pubs/technical_reports/TR534.html .

Rojek, Jeff, Richard Rosenfeld, and Scott Decker. 2012. "Policing Race: The Racial Stratification of Searches in Police Traffic Stops." *Criminology* 50 (4): 993–1024.

Ross, Cody T. 2015. "A Multi-Level Bayesian Analysis of Racial Bias in Police Shootings at the County-Level in the United States, 2011–2014." *PLOS ONE* 10 (11): 1–35.

Ryan, Matt E. 2015. "Frisky Business: Race, Gender and Police Activity during Traffic Stops." *European Journal of Law and Economics* 41 (1): 65–83.

Saleh, Amam Z., Paul S. Appelbaum, Xiaoyu Liu, T. Scott Stroup, and Melanie Wall. 2018. "Deaths of People with Mental Illness during Interactions with Law Enforcement." *International Journal of Law and Psychiatry* 58 (May–June): 110–16.

Scharrer, Erica. 2001. "Tough Guys: The Portrayal of Hypermasculinity and Aggression in Televised Police Dramas." *Journal of Broadcasting & Electronic Media* 45 (4): 615–34.

Spencer, Katherine B., Amanda K. Charbonneau, and Jack Glaser. 2016. "Implicit Bias and Policing." *Social and Personality Psychology Compass* 10 (1): 50–63.

Swaine, Jon, Oliver Laughland, Jamiles Lartey, and Ciara McCarthy. 2016. "The Counted: People Killed by Police in the US." https://www.theguardian.com/us-news/ng-interactive/2015/jun/01/the-counted-police-killings-us-database .

Tate, Julie, Jennifer Jenkins, and Steven Rich. 2019. "2019 Police Shootings Database." Retrieved from https://www.washingtonpost.com/graphics/2019/national/police-shootings-2019/ .

Tillyer, Rob, and Robin S. Engel. 2013. "The Impact of Drivers' Race, Gender, and Age during Traffic Stops: Assessing Interaction Terms and the Social Conditioning Model." *Crime & Delinquency* 59 (3): 369–95.

Weitzer, Ronald, and Steven A. Tuch. 2004. "Race and Perceptions of Police Misconduct." *Social Problems* 51 (3): 305–25.

Willits, Dale W., and David A. Makin. 2017. "Show Me What Happened: Analyzing Use of Force through Analysis of Body-Worn Camera Footage." *Journal of Research in Crime & Delinquency* 55 (1): 51–77.

Worden, Robert E., and Sarah J. McLean. 2017. *Mirage of Police Reform: Procedural Justice and Police Legitimacy.*" Berkeley: University of California Press.

CHAPTER 6

Intergroup Biases

Policing and Gender

Cara E. Rabe-Hemp and Amie M. Schuck

The purpose of this chapter is to discuss how the intergroup dynamics of women in policing in the United States affect the values and practices of law enforcement agencies and the interactions between officers and the public. According to the social identity approach (SIA), social identities are developed and made visible through communication, including language (vocabulary, domain-specific jargon, and labels) and nonverbal cues (uniforms, badges, and hair; Dragojevic and Giles 2014; Reicher, Spears, and Haslam 2010). Important consequences of the SIA process include the depersonalization of one's self and of others, the formation of stereotypes, and intergroup bias, which is the propensity to systematically evaluate representatives of one's own membership group (the ingroup) more positively than representatives of a non-membership group (the outgroup; Hewstone, Rubin, and Willis 2002). Although the SIA framework is often used to explain why dominant groups discriminate, it can also be used to identify resistance by marginalized groups and highlight possibilities for change (see this book's conclusion).

In this chapter, we focus on four specific areas regarding intergroup dynamics and women in policing. First, we outline important conceptual and measurement issues. This includes an overview of the status of women in policing in the United States and a presentation of relevant concepts about police culture. Second, we describe prominent theories within the SIA framework with an eye toward understanding the fundamentals of intergroup dynamics and explaining why women remain underrepresented and marginalized in policing. Third, we discuss how intergroup dynamics affect police-public relations in the United States. In particular, we describe how intergroup dynamics may affect organizational structures and institutional policies, as well as officer decision making when facing potential use of force situations. Finally, the chapter concludes with some recommendations for reducing the negative consequences of intergroup dynamics in policing.

CONCEPTUAL AND MEASUREMENT CONSIDERATIONS

Current Status of Women in Policing in the United States

In the United States, women are underrepresented in policing and the problem of underrepresentation grows at each administrative stratum. Today, women make up about 12.5 percent of sworn full-time police officers (US Department of Justice 2013). In 2013, 7.3 percent of first-line supervisors were women, 6.9 percent of intermediate supervisors were women, and 2.7 percent of chief executives were women (US Department of Justice 2013). Even more concerning, data suggests that the growth rate for women in policing has plateaued for the first time since women were given patrol powers. Curtis Crooke, from the Office of Community Oriented Policing Services, summarized that "gender inequity is still a defining aspect of law enforcement, even in today's world of slowly increasing employment fairness" (Crooke 2013, 1). Despite the obstacles and challenges facing women in policing, female officers continue to make progress, breaking down barriers (Rabe-Hemp 2018; Schuck 2019). For example, twelve of the largest one hundred police departments in the United States are led by women (Reaves 2015).

POLICE CULTURE

The concept of police culture originated from ethnographic studies, which discovered a layer of informal occupational values functioning under the rigid hierarchical structure of police organizations (Paoline 2003). While a comprehensive overview of police culture is beyond the scope of this chapter, several elements are important to the current topic. First, the negative elements of the traditional police culture (isolation, internal solidarity, cynicism, suspiciousness, physical dominance, and a crime-fighting mentality) have been linked to a negative working personality for officers, higher rates of harassment and discrimination against women and minority officers, and the obstruction of meaningful police reform (Brown, Silvestri, Linton, and Gouseti 2019; Chan 1997). Second, the socialization process of the police culture is especially powerful, leading to a strong "us versus them" mentality (see chapter 1). The "us versus them mentality" suggests that all police, regardless of gender, color, ethnicity, or sexuality, "bleed blue," meaning that their personal identities are subverted by a strong workgroup identity. Recently, scholars have questioned the uniformity of the police culture (Ingram, Paoline, and Terril 2013; Mazerolle and Terrill 2018). Some argue that women officers are more resistant to assimilating negative elements of the police culture into their own working personality because of their outgroup status; and as a consequence, they may be less likely to be involved in negative police–public encounters, and they may be associated with more successful reform efforts (Barnes, Beaulieu, and Saxton 2018; Schuck 2014, 2018; Schuck and Rabe-Hemp 2016).

MEASUREMENT ISSUES

Scholars have used a range of measures to capture intergroup bias including those related to negative stereotypes, such as badge bunny, dyke, station queen, and estrogen mafia. Scholars have used a range of measures to capture intergroup bias including those related to negative stereotypes, such as badge bunny, dyke, station queen, pansy police, and estrogen mafia; prejudicial attitudes, including beliefs that women are less capable than men in terms of the physical and emotional aspects of the occupation; discrimination and inequality, which are associated with lower retention rates and fewer career opportunities for women officers; and harassment, both sexual and nonsexual. Measures can focus on explicit mechanisms (those that are intentional or conscious) or implicit ones (those that are automatic, unintentional, or subconscious). Measures are also used to delineate the difference between ingroup favoritism (positive benefits for group members) and outgroup negativity (blaming or punishing outgroup members, which is also sometimes called outgroup denigration). Special attention has been given to measuring the psychological consequences of intergroup bias within the context of tokenism. This includes measuring the negative outcomes associated with enhanced visibility and social isolation, such as low job satisfaction, pressure to perform, feelings of role entrapment (having to choose between alternative female stereotypes), and women-on-women workplace hostility (Kringen and Novich 2018; Rabe-Hemp 2008a, 2009; Shelley, Morabito, and Tobin-Gurley 2011; US Department of Justice 2018).

FIRST- AND SECOND-GENERATION BIAS

The biases for women in policing are generally framed as first- or second-generation biases (Steffens and Viladot 2015). First-generation biases refer to explicit mechanisms of injustice based on discrimination. In general, this is more likely to be associated with outgroup negativity or denigration than with ingroup favoritism. In the United States, overt sex discrimination is much less common because of passing of laws that prohibit sex discrimination, such as the Civil Rights Act of 1964 and the Equal Employment Opportunity Act, as well as settlements from lawsuits brought against law enforcement agencies by women officers (Lonsway and Alipio 2008). Second-generation patterns of bias involve structural, relational, and situational patterns that produce differential access, opportunities, and outcomes for women over time (Sturm 2001). Second-generation inequalities are more likely to be the result of unconscious bias than of deliberate exclusion.

THEORETICAL OVERVIEW

The Social Identity Approach

The complementary theories of social identity theory (SIT) and self-categorization theory (SCT) comprise the SIA, which is designed to explain the group-level behavior arising from the complex interplay between the psychological self and social identity (Tajfel 1978; Tajfel and Turner 1986; see chapter 1 and 22). The SIA has four general parts: (1) the social-psychological component, which describes the cognitive processes that make identity salient and connect self-evaluation to group membership, along with the motivational processes that drive group assessments; (2) the systems component, which identifies the conditions under which social competition occurs including the strength of the boundaries between groups, as well as the stability and legitimacy of the intergroup system; (3) the social component, which is characterized by the larger social, political, and cultural context that defines groups and the status systems by which they operate (Rubin and Hewstone 2004); and (4) the communication component that defines how these biases are expressed and transmitted in discourse and behavior (Menegatti and Rubini 2018; Wingate and Palomares 2018). The SIA suggests that the processes of categorization, identification, and comparison are normal and associated with positive outcomes for individuals, such as status, esteem, resources, and social capital. The approach also helps to explain prejudice because once groups are identified as rivals, they are forced to compete in order to maintain their status.

The creation, maintenance, and dissolution of group boundaries is important. If the group membership is salient and of value to an individual, he or she will identify with the group, but what if the social identity is negative? Research suggests that individuals have three alternatives when dealing with a negative social identity: (1) social mobility, in which the group members assimilate into higher-status groups; (2) reframing a negative social identity into a more positive one by changing the ingroup-outgroup comparisons; and (3) improving the group status through competition (Tajfel and Turner, 1997). Good examples of the second and third alternatives are officers turning the negative slur "pig" into "pride-integrity-guts" and officers promoting the slogans "all lives matter" or "blue lives matter" in response to the Black Lives Matter movement (Anderson, Knutson, Giles, and Arroyo 2002).

SOCIAL CATEGORIZATION AND LINGUISTIC INTERGROUP BIAS

Stereotypes are an important part of the SIA. People define themselves and others into categories that are "prototypes," or a "set of features that best defines a category" (Giles, Reid, and Harwood 2010, 246). SCT theorists view categorization as a fundamental cognitive process and consider stereotyping as functional (Rosch and Lloyd 1978). Prototypes also play a role, in how we see others, through a process called depersonalization, which leads to perceiving all members of the group as interchangeable (Turner, Hogg, Oakes, Reicher, and Wetherell 1987). Prejudice and stereotypes are learned and propagated through communication and by watching other's behavior (Aboud and Doyle 1996; Brown 1995). Linguistic intergroup bias shows us that it takes very little motivation to maintain a stereotype because information that confirms the stereotype is more likely to be noticed and remembered than contradictory data, and because individuals have a cognitive tendency to describe behaviors and beliefs that are consistent with the stereotype in ways that can be observed and validated (Fyock and Stangor 1994; Maass, Ceccarelli, and Rudin 1996).

IMPROVING INTERGROUP RELATIONS

One of the most effective methods to improve intergroup relations is to simultaneously promote the common superordinate identity while at the same time maintaining the integrity of important subgroup identities. Most intergroup bias reduction strategies are grounded in Gordon Allport's research on prejudice reduction, which suggests that contact between group members reduces negative stereotypes and results in less prejudice toward outgroup members (Allport 1954). The common ingroup identity model (CIIM) suggests that contact between group members improves group relations by changing an individual's representation of the situation from two groups (us and them) to one superordinate group (we) (Gaertner, Dovidio and Bachman 1996). Advocates of the mutual intergroup differentiation model (MIDM) suggest that contact between groups should be structured in a way that does not threaten group identities (Hewstone 1996). Rather than trying to eliminate status differences, MIDM suggests that contact should be structured in a way that both preserves the salience of the groups and recognizes each group's strengths with equal value. Underpinning both CIIM and MIDM is the idea that in the simultaneous activation of the superordinate and subordinate identities, the categorizations are crossed, and the perceived differences between the groups are decreased.

EXPLAINING INTERGROUP BIAS IN WOMEN IN POLICING

Social Dominance Theory and Integrated Threat Theory

Social dominance theory and integrated threat theory shed light on why policing continues to be exclusionary to women. Social dominance theory explores group-based social hierarchies and how "processes at different levels of social organization, from cultural ideologies and institutional discrimination to gender roles and psychology of prejudice, work together to produce stable group-based inequality" (Pratto and Stewart 2011, 1). Applied to policing, we see that social hierarchies are maintained by isolating female officers, emphasizing differences rather than similarities between women and men, and stigmatizing non-gender-conforming behaviors. Through these mechanisms male officers reinforce the status quo, while at the same time, ensuring they maintain power to define what is valued and rewarded in the workplace. Integrated threat theory suggests that prejudice and negative attitudes toward female officers can be explained by the perceived threats that male officers feel as a result of the presence of women. According to Walter G. Stephan, who coined the theory in 2000, there are four types of threats: *realistic, symbolic, negative stereotype,* and *intergroup anxiety* (Stephan and Stephan 2000). *Realistic* threats refer to the physical well-being and to the economic and political power of the ingroup. *Symbolic* threats denote the differences in values and morals between the ingroup and outgroup. *Negative stereotypes* define how the groups "see" one another. Finally, *intergroup anxiety* is experienced by the ingroup as a result of interactions with outgroup members. In sum, increasing female representation may be threatening to the dominant group in terms of increased (actual and/or perceived potential) power and social influence (Bourhis, Sachdev, Ehala, and Giles 2019).

TOKENISM

The groundbreaking feminist and organizational theory of tokenism written by Rosabeth Moss Kanter in her book, *Men and Women in Corporations*, identified a number of discriminatory social processes that are characteristic of dominant groups and proposed that the numeric increase of tokens groups (comprising less than 15 percent of the organization) would undermine these processes (Kanter 1977). Applied to women in policing, the theory held that if the representation of female officers in an agency increased beyond 15 percent, their visibility would decrease, the differences between men and women would no longer be apparent, and women would integrate. In sum, Kanter believed that sheer numbers would break down the walls of inequality. There have been a few empirical tests of tokenism in policing, and from this research, we know that overcoming inequality is more complicated than increasing numerical representation (Archbold and Schulz 2008; Gustafson 2008; Stichman, Hassell, and Archbold 2010). Kanter's work fails to consider the power of sexism, the influence of larger social-structural systems, and the conflicting and sometimes counterintuitive identity women construct to be successful in the workplace. Most important, Kanter's framework does not take into account the idea that women in male-dominated professions may experience discrimination, sexual harassment, and segregation not because of a lack of numeric representation but because they are simply women; and as such, their mere presence in the workplace violates gender norms regarding work.

INEQUALITY REGIMES

Joann Acker's inequality regimes framework helps us understand why numbers are not enough to eliminate gender inequality (Acker 2006). According to her, inequality regimes are "loosely interrelated practices, processes, actions, and meanings that result in and maintain class, gender and racial inequalities" (443). In Acker's framework, inequality regimes are the by-product of the conflict over who gets to define how work is structured, including what is valued and rewarded, as well as how employees are treated. Through this lens, we see that the legitimacy of women's voices is reduced, resulting in female officers' social exclusion from decision-making processes (Reskin 2003; Ridgeway 1997). Currently, within the law enforcement occupation, women make up fewer than 3 percent of the police chiefs nationwide (Reaves 2015). The lack of legitimacy of female voices in these crucial decision points reproduces gender inequality by reinforcing the masculinist vision of policing, which in turn serves as a justification for why few women choose to pursue a career in law enforcement.

OPTIMAL DISTINCTIVENESS THEORY

Optimal distinctiveness theory, which posits that social identities derive from a fundamental tension between the need for inclusion and uniqueness, illustrates why some female officers, in addition to male officers, participate in defining an occupational value system that socially excludes other women. Coined by Marilynn B. Brewer, *optimal distinctiveness theory* contends that maintaining a social identity with both distinctiveness and inclusivity is a balancing act (Brewer 1991; Leonardelli, Pickett, and Brewer

2010). For example, when a group's boundaries become too inclusive, it threatens an individual's need for distinctiveness. In turn, these threats to distinctiveness may be met with greater attempts to be exclusive or with more exclusive criteria for multiple ingroup membership (Brown and Hewstone 2005; Dovidio, Gaertner, and Saguy 2009; Schmid and Hewstone 2011).

This theory also explains why some female officers adapt to police cultures in ways that are not beneficial to other women, through the strategies of othering and defeminizing to become "just one of the guys" (Harrington 2002; Martin 1980). These techniques help individual female officers gain acceptance in the larger police cultures, but do not positively affect their image, limiting their impact on and access to the power structure of the organizations (Archbold and Schulz 2008; Rabe-Hemp 2009). While this fact would seem counter to what we know about social identity, namely, that we perceive our ingroups more favorably than our outgroups, we should keep in mind that mere inclusion into a group does not always elicit ingroup favoring behaviors.

POLICE-PUBLIC RELATIONS

Over the past decade, a series of high-profile, violent altercations between officers and young men of color, sparked a national debate about police use of deadly force (President's Task Force on 21st Century Policing 2015). The use of force is by far the most controversial aspect of the authority of the police. The police are a "mechanism of the distribution of situationally justified force in society" (Bittner 1980, 129). In other words, to maintain the democratic process, society gives the police the exclusive power to use force in order to achieve democratic ends.

The processes involved in intergroup bias may help explain the disproportional use of force against non-White citizens. For example, scholars argue that stereotypes about young Black men (capable of committing crimes, acutely violent, and having superhuman strength) and the ingroup dynamics of the police (a strong ingroup orientation, unique values, and skewed experiences with outgroup members) help to explain why the police are more likely to use of force against young Black men than any other group (Hall, Hall, and Perry 2016). On the bases of the CIIM and MIDM models, the logical conclusion of these hypotheses is that more Black officers are associated with less police use of force. However, in general, the research is not supportive of this proposition, either at the individual level (Black officer behavior) or the organizational one (the percentage of Black officers; Edwards, Esposito, and Lee 2018; Johnson, Tress, Burkel, Taylor, and Cesario 2019).

Research, however, is supportive of the idea that women officers are associated with less police use of force and less excessive use of force (Rabe-Hemp 2008b; Schuck and Rabe-Hemp 2007). How do the concepts and theories related to intergroup dynamics help to explain this relationship? The first set of potential explanations focuses on how women officers' outgroup status affects the occupational socialization process. For example, women officers may use less force than men officers do because they are less likely to adopt a hypermasculine identity (a working personality in which physical domination is strongly valued) and follow the principles of the culture of honor posture (where noncompliance threatens one's identity; Harris 2000).

The second set of explanations focuses on how women officers' outgroup status affects changes in the organization. From a social categorization perspective, the increased representation of women in policing may bring about problems within police workgroups, such as disrupted communication, decreased cooperation, relational conflicts, and less group cohesion (Chattopadhyay, Tluchowska, and George 2004). While these characteristics are typically defined as problems to be avoided, in organizational reform movements, such as the current situation in policing, these are important precursors necessary for meaningful change (Warner, Steel, and Lovrich 1989). In our own research, we have explored diversity as a successful strategy for building justice-centered organizations that are more responsive to the public. We found that departments with less diversity were more likely to use order maintenance arrests, especially in communities of color, as a key strategy for maintaining public safety than agencies with greater diversity. Our research suggests that high levels of workforce inequality grounded in polarized intergroup dynamics are mirrored in the department's policing strategies in the community. We argue that increasing the representation of women in policing will result in agencies becoming less reliant on large-scale arrest-driven order maintenance strategies because greater equality in the organization is associated with more inclusive decision making, the development of alternative policing strategies, and the diversification of metrics that define good policing (Schuck and Rabe-Hemp 2019).

This may be because diversity is an important source of information that brings about change in how an organization delivers its "product." Applied to policing, one argument is that women "do" policing differently. In other words, their socialization differences and insights may lead to different solutions in policing. Some empirical evidence shows that increasing the representation of women in policing affects the social control mechanisms that citizens experience by (a) shifting the policing philosophy to more community-centered approaches, (b) reducing the police use of force and the number incidents involving excessive use of force, and (c) providing better services to victims of crime (Meier and Nicholson-Crotty 2006; Pew Research Center 2017; Rabe-Hemp 2008b; Schuck 2017; Schuck and Rabe-Hemp 2007). In their narratives, female police officers discuss utilizing a communication style that is less reliant on force and more reliant on problem-solving, thus gaining compliance without the need for physical force (Rabe-Hemp 2018). However, we express caution in stereotyping and essentializing women's performance in policing.

The final set of perspectives focuses on how women's outgroup status affects the attitudes and behaviors of the public. Symbolic representation suggests that the public's attitudes and behaviors may be affected by their perceptions of police agencies. Symbolic representation works as follows: More women in policing is associated with public perceptions of normative legitimacy. These perceptions of legitimacy translate to greater support for the agency, as well as to the police officers who represent the agency. These ideas were recently explored in a randomized controlled experiment, and the results suggest that citizens believed that increasing women's participation in policing would reduce police corruption, because women are seen as outsiders to policing and are more risk averse than male officers (Barnes, Beaulieu, and Saxton 2018).

CONCLUSIONS

The intergroup dynamics of women in policing, including self-categorization, depersonalization, stereotyping, and intergroup bias, creates, reinforces, and replicates the exclusion of women as agents of formal social control and, as a consequence, impacts American policing both in principle and in practice. Theories like social dominance and integrated threat help to explain the continued exclusion of women, while theories such as tokenism, inequality regimes, and optimal distinctiveness help us to understand women's experiences and how to overcome barriers preventing more women from participating in the profession. Moving forward, more research is needed to better elucidate the mechanisms involved in the continued exclusion of women. For example, what are the realistic, symbolic, intergroup, and negative stereotyping threats regarding women in policing? Which threat has the largest effect on male officer's attitudes and behaviors, and which threat has the largest effect on community member's beliefs and actions? How do law enforcement leaders modify feelings of threat, and what specific techniques can be used to improve relations between women and men officers? In a more simplistic discussion about sexism, men would be the ingroup, women would be the outgroup, and recategorization strategies drawn from the CIIM and MIDM models—such as contact and salient superordinate identity—would reduce intergroup bias by changing the "women vs. men" mentality to a "we are all police" perspective. However, because women in policing are often associated with reform movements, the intergroup dynamics are more complicated. Women officers need to simultaneously assimilate values of police culture into their identity and take on the working personality of an officer, while at the same time push back against a culture almost exclusively defined by men to value systems of masculinity. More research is needed to understand this paradox and how leaders can successfully integrate the values that come with sex diversity into their organization. One important question is whether and through what processes the presence of the subgroup identity of women disrupts the social unity of the male-dominant ingroup and alters the superordinate identity of the police officer.

Currently, there is a significant amount of research on how prejudice and discrimination produce formal and informal barriers to the recruitment and advancement of women in policing (Rabe-Hemp, 2018). Partnerships between researchers and law enforcement agencies are necessary to garner insight as well as tools that will help to mitigate the negative consequence of unproductive and detrimental intergroup dynamics. Future research needs to be interdisciplinary, collaborative, and transformative to fully understand the impact of intergroup dynamics between women and men on the American policing system.

REFERENCES

Aboud, Frances E., and Anna-Beth Doyle. 1996. "Parental and Peer Influences on Children's Racial Attitudes." *International Journal of Intercultural Relations* 20 (3–4): 371–84.

Acker, Joan. 2006. "Inequality Regimes Gender, Class, and Race in Organizations." *Gender and Society* 20 (4): 441–64.

Allport, Gordon W. 1954. *The Nature of Prejudice*. Reading: Addison-Wesley.

Anderson, Michelle Chernikoff, Thomas J. Knutson, Howard Giles, and MaryLinda Arroyo. 2002. "Revoking Our Right to Remain Silent: Law Enforcement Communication in the 21st Century." In *Law Enforcement, Communication, and Community*, edited by Howard Giles, 1–32. Amsterdam: John Benjamins.

Archbold, Carol, and Dorothy Moses Schulz. 2008. "Making Rank: The Lingering Effects of Tokenism on Female Police Officers' Promotion Aspirations." *Police Quarterly* 11 (1): 50–73.

Barnes, Tiffany D., Emily Beaulieu, and Gregory W. Saxton. 2018. "Restoring Trust in the Police: Why Female Officers Reduce Suspicions of Corruption." *Governance* 31 (1): 143–61.

Bittner, Egon. 1980. *The Functions of the Police in Modern Society: A Review of Background Factors, Current Practices and Possible Role Models*. Cambridge: Oelschlaeger, Gunn Hain.

Bourhis, Richard, Itesh Sachdev, Martin Ehala, and Howard Giles. 2019. "Assessing 40 Years of Group Vitality Research and Future Directions." *Journal of Language and Social Psychology* 38 (4): 409–22.

Brewer, Marilynn B. 1991. "The Social Self: On Being the Same and Different at the Same Time." *Personality and Social Psychology Bulletin* 17 (5): 475–82.

Brown, Jennifer, Marisa Silvestri, Kenisha Linton, and Ioanna Gouseti. 2019. "Implications of Police Occupational Culture in Discriminatory Experiences of Senior Women in Police Forces in England and Wales." *Policing and Society* 29 (2): 121–36.

Brown, Rupert. 1995. *Prejudice: Its Social Psychology*. Oxford: Blackwell.

Brown, Rupert, and Miles Hewstone. 2005. "An Integrative Theory of Intergroup Contact." In *Advances in Experimental Social Psychology* 37, edited by Mark Zanna, 255–343. San Diego: Academic Press.

Chan, Janet. 1997. *Changing Police Culture: Policing in a Multicultural Society*. Cambridge: Cambridge University Press.

Chattopadhyay, Prithviraj, Malgorzata Tluchowska, and Elizabeth George. 2004. "Identifying the Ingroup: A Closer Look at the Influence of Demographic Dissimilarity on Employee Social Identity." *Academy of Management Review* 29 (2): 180–202.

Crooke, Curtis. 2013. "Women in Law Enforcement." *Community Policing Dispatch*, 6, Retrieved from https://cops.usdoj.gov/html/dispatch/07-2013/women_in_law_enforcement.asp .

Dovidio, John F., Samuel L. Gaertner, and Tamar Saguy. 2009. "Commonality and the Complexity of 'We': Social Attitudes and Social Change." *Personality and Social Psychology Review* 13 (1): 3–20.

Dragojevic, Marko, and Howard Giles. 2014. "Language and Interpersonal Communication: Their Intergroup Dynamics." In *Handbook of Interpersonal Communication*, edited by Charles R. Berger, 29–51. Berlin: Walter de Gruyter.

Edwards, Frank, Michael H. Esposito, and Hedwig Lee. 2018. "Risk of Police-Involved Death by Race/Ethnicity and Place, United States, 2012–2018." *American Journal of Public Health* 108 (9): 1241–48.

Fyock, Jack, and Charles Stangor. 1994. "The Role of Memory Biases in Stereotype Maintenance." *British Journal of Social Psychology* 33 (3): 331–43.

Gaertner, Samuel L., John F. Dovidio, and Betty A. Bachman. 1996. "Revisiting the Contact Hypothesis: The Induction of a Common Ingroup Identity." *International Journal of Intercultural Relations* 20 (3–4): 271–90.

Giles, Howard, Scott Reid, and Jake Harwood, eds. 2010. *The Dynamics of Intergroup Communication*. New York: Peter Lang.

Gustafson, Joseph L. 2008. "Tokenism in Policing: An Empirical Test of Kanter's Hypothesis," *Journal of Criminal Justice* 36 (1): 1–10.

Hall, Alison V., Erika V. Hall, and Jamie L. Perry. 2016. "Black and Blue: Exploring Racial Bias and Law Enforcement in the Killings of Unarmed Black Male Civilians." *American Psychologist* 71 (3): 175–86.

Harrington, Penny E. 2002. "Advice to Women Beginning a Career in Policing." *Women and Criminal Justice* 14 (1): 1–14.

Harris, Angela P. 2000. "Gender, Violence, Race, and Criminal Justice." *Stanford Law Review* 52 (4): 777–807.

Hewstone, Miles. 1996. "Contact and Categorization: Social Psychological Interventions to Change Intergroup Relations." In *Stereotypes and Stereotyping*, edited by C. Neil Macrae, Charles Stangor, and Miles Hewstone, 323–68. London: Guilford.

Hewstone, Miles, Mark Rubin, and Hazel Willis. 2002. "Intergroup Bias." *Annual Review of Psychology* 53 (1): 575–604.

Ingram, Jason. R., Eugene Paoline, and William Terrill. 2013. "Multilevel Framework for Understanding Police Culture: The Role of the Workgroup." *Criminology* 51 (2): 365–97.

Johnson, David J., Trevor Tress, Nicole Burkel, Carley Taylor, and Joseph Cesario. 2019. "Officer Characteristics and Racial Disparities in Fatal Officer-Involved Shootings." *Proceedings of the National Academy of Sciences* 116 (32): 15877–82.

Kanter, Rosabeth M. 1977. *Men and Women of the Corporation*. New York: Basic Books.

Kringen, Anne Li, and Madeleine Novich. 2018. "Is It 'Just Hair' Or Is It 'Everything'? Embodiment and Gender Repression in Policing." *Gender, Work and Organization* 25 (2): 195–213.

Leonardelli, Geoffrey J., Cynthia L. Pickett, and Marilynn B. Brewer. 2010. "Optimal Distinctiveness Theory: A Framework for Social Identity, Social Cognition, and Intergroup Relations." In *Advances in Experimental Social Psychology* 43, edited by Mark Zanna and James Olson, 63–113. New York: Elsevier.

Lonsway, Kimberly A., and Angela M. Alipio. 2008. "Sex Discrimination Lawsuits in Law Enforcement: A Case Study of Thirteen Female Officers Who Sued Their Agencies." *Women and Criminal Justice* 18 (4): 63–103.

Maass, Anne, Roberta Ceccarelli, and Samantha Rudin. 1996. "Linguistic Intergroup Bias: Evidence for In-Group-Protective Motivation." *Journal of Personality and Social Psychology* 71 (3): 512–26.

Martin, Susan. 1980. *Breaking and Entering: Policewomen on Patrol*. Berkeley: University of California Press.

Mazerolle, Lorraine, and William Terrill. 2018. "Making Every Police-Citizen Interaction Count." *Criminology and Public Policy* 17 (1): 89–96.

Meier, Kenneth J., and Jill Nicholson-Crotty. 2006. "Gender, Representative Bureaucracy, and Law Enforcement: The Case of Sexual Assault." *Public Administration Review* 66 (6): 850–60. Retrieved from http://www.jstor.org/stable/4096602 .

Menegatti, Michela, and Monica Rubini, M. 2018. "Gender Bias and Sexism in Language." In *The Oxford Encyclopedia of Intergroup Communication*, edited by Howard Giles and Jake Harwood, Vol. 1, 451–68. New York: Oxford University Press.

Paoline, Eugene A. III. 2003. "Taking Stock: Toward a Richer Understanding of Police Culture." *Journal of Criminal Justice* 31 (3): 199–214.

Pew Research Center. 2017. *Behind the Badge*. Pew Research Center: Washington DC. Retrieved from http://www.pewsocialtrends.org/2017/01/11/behind-the-badge/ .

Pratto, F. and Stewart, A.L. 2011. *Social Dominance Theory. In the Encyclopedia of Peace Psychology*, D.J. Christie (Ed.). Retreived on line: https://doi.org/10.1002/9780470672532.wbepp253 .

President's Task Force on 21st Century Policing. 2015. *Final Report of the President's Task Force on 21st Century Policing*. Washington DC: Office of Community Oriented Policing Services.

Rabe-Hemp, Cara E. 2008a. "Survival, in an 'All Boys Club': Policewomen and Their Fight for Acceptance." *Policing* 31 (2): 251–70.

Rabe-Hemp, Cara E. 2008b. "Female Officers and the Ethic of Care: Does Officer Gender Impact Police Behaviors?" *Journal of Criminal Justice* 36 (5): 426–34.

Rabe-Hemp, Cara E., 2009. "Policewomen or Policewomen? Doing Gender and Police Work." *Feminist Criminology* 4 (2): 114–29.

Rabe-Hemp, Cara E. 2018. *Thriving in an All-Boys Club: Female Police and Their Fight for Equality*. Lanham: Rowman & Littlefield.

Reaves, Brian. 2015. *Local Police Departments, 2013: Personnel, Policies, and Practices*. Washington DC: Bureau of Justice Statistics.

Reicher, Stephen, Russell Spears, and S. Alexander Haslam. 2010. "The Social Identity Approach in Social Psychology," In *The Sage Handbook of Identities*, edited by Margaret Wetherell and Chandra Talpade Mohanty, 45–62. Thousand Oaks: Sage.

Reskin, Barbara F. 2003. "Motives and Mechanisms in Modeling Inequality." *American Sociological Review* 68 (1): 1–21.

Ridgeway, Cecelia L. 1997. "Interaction and the Conservation of Gender Inequality: Considering Employment." *American Sociological Review* 62 (2): 218–35.

Rosch, Eleanor, and Barbara B. Lloyd. 1978. *Cognition and Categorization*. Hillsdale: Lawrence Erlbaum.

Rubin, Mark, and Miles Hewstone. 2004. "Social Identity, System Justification, and Social Dominance: Commentary on Reicher, Jost et al., and Sidanius et al." *Political Psychology* 25 (6): 823–44.

Schmid, Katharina, and Miles Hewstone. 2011 "Social Identity Complexity: Theoretical Implications of the Social Psychology of Intergroup Relations." In *Social Cognition, Social Identity, and Intergroup Relations: A Festschrift in Honor of Marilynn B. Brewer*, edited by Roderick M. Kramer, Geoffrey J. Leonardelli, and Robert W. Livingston, 77–102. New York: Psychology Press.

Schuck, Amie M. 2014. "Gender Differences in Policing: Testing Hypotheses from the Performance and Disruption Perspectives." *Feminist Criminology* 9 (2): 160–85.

Schuck, Amie M. 2017. "Female Officers and Community Policing: Examining the Connection between Gender Diversity and Organizational Change." *Women and Criminal Justice* 27 (5): 341–62.

Schuck, Amie M. 2018. "Women in Policing and the Response to Rape: Representative Bureaucracy and Organizational Change." *Feminist Criminology* 13 (3): 237–59.

Schuck, Amie M. 2019. "Women Policing in the US: Post-Gender Institutions?" In *Women Policing across the Globe: Shared Challenges and Successes in the Integration of Women Police Worldwide*, edited by Cara E. Rabe-Hemp and Venessa Garcia, 31–48. Lanham: Rowman & Littlefield.

Schuck, Amie M., and Cara Rabe-Hemp. 2007. "Women Police: The Use of Force by and Against Female Officers." *Women and Criminal Justice* 16 (4): 91–117.

Schuck, Amie M., and Cara Rabe-Hemp. 2016. "Citizen Complaints and Gender Diversity in Police Organizations." *Policing and Society: An International Journal of Research and Policy* 26 (8): 859–74.

Schuck, Amie M., and Cara Rabe-Hemp. 2019. "Inequalities Regimes in Policing: Examining the Connection between Social Exclusion and Order Maintenance Strategies." *Race and Justice* 9 (3): 228–50.

Shelley, Tara O'Connor, Melissa Schaefer Morabito, and Jennifer Tobin-Gurley. 2011. "Gendered Institutions and Gender Roles: Understanding the Experiences of Women in Policing." *Criminal Justice Studies* 24 (4): 351–67.

Steffens, Melanie C., and Maria Angels Viladot. 2015. *Gender at Work: A Social Psychological Approach*. New York: Peter Lang

Stephan, Walter G., and Cookie White Stephan. 2000. "An Integrated Threat Theory of Prejudice." In *Reducing Prejudice and Discrimination*, edited by Stuart Oskamp, 23–46. Mahwah: Lawrence Erlbaum.

Stichman, Amy J., Kimberly D. Hassell, and Carol A. Archbold. 2010. "Strength in Numbers? A Test of Kanter's Theory of Tokenism." *Journal of Criminal Justice* 38 (4): 633–39.

Sturm, Susan. 2001. "Second Generation Employment Discrimination: A Structural Approach." *Columbia Law Review* 101 (1): 458–568.

Tajfel, Henri, ed. 1978. *Differentiation between Social Groups: Studies in the Social Psychology of Intergroup Relations*. London: Academic Press.

Tajfel, Henri, and John C. Turner. 1986. "The Social Identity Theory of Intergroup Behavior." In *Psychology of Intergroup Relation*, edited by Stephen Worchel and William G. Austin, 7–24. Chicago: Hall Publishers.

Tajfel, Henri, and John Turner. 1997. "An Integrative Theory of Intergroup Conflict." In *Organizational Identity*, edited by Mary Jo Hatch and Majken Schultz, 56–65. Oxford: Oxford University Press.

Turner, John C., Michael Hogg, Penelope J. Oakes, Stephen D. Reicher, and Margaret Wetherell. 1987. *Rediscovering the Social Group: A Self-Categorization Theory*. Oxford: Basil Blackwell.

Turner, John, Penelope Oakes, S. Alexander Haslam, and Craig McGarty. 1994. "Self and Collective: Cognition and Social Context." *Personality and Social Psychology Bulletin* 20 (5): 454–63.

US Department of Justice, Office of Justice Programs, Bureau of Justice Statistics. 2013. *Law Enforcement Management and Administrative Statistics* (LEMAS). Ann Arbor, Inter-university Consortium for Political and Social Research [distributor]. Retrieved from https://doi.org/10.3886/ICPSR36164.v2 .

US Department of Justice. Office of the Inspector General (OIG). 2018. *Review of Gender Equality in Department's Law Enforcement Components.* Retrieved from https://oig.justice.gov/reports/2018/e1803.pdf .

Warner, Rebecca L., Brent S. Steel, and Nicholas P. Lovrich. 1989. "Conditions Associated with the Advent of Representative Bureaucracy: The Case of Women in Policing." *Social Science Quarterly* 70 (3): 562–78.

Wingate, V. Skye, and Nicholas A. Palomares. 2018. "Gender Issues in Intergroup Communication." In *The Oxford Encyclopedia of Intergroup Communication*, edited by Howard Giles and Jake Harwood, Vol. 1, 468–86. New York: Oxford University Press

CHAPTER 7

Policing and LGBTQ+ Communities

Stephen Owen

Police relationships with lesbian, gay, bisexual, transgender, queer (see GLAAD 2016), and allied (LGBTQ+) communities have long been troubled, ranging from distrust to tension to outright antagonism (for definitions and a thorough discussion of sexualities, see Englert and Dinkins 2016; for a discussion of the use of the plural term, "communities," see Owen et al. 2018, footnote 1). While progress has been made, recent studies suggest that LGBTQ+ communities continue to feel a lack of trust in law enforcement. The purpose of this chapter is to explore the relationship between police and LGBTQ+ communities, contextualized when possible through a lens of communication (see Fasoli 2018; Hajek 2018). The balance of existing research in this area focuses largely on two themes: How the police perceive LGBTQ+ communities, including LGTBQ+ officers who are their colleagues, and how LGBTQ+ communities (i.e., civilians) perceive the police. Much less research has focused on the specific communicative dynamics that shape these perceptions, but one key conclusion of this chapter is that the topic remains a rich opportunity for future work.

The discussion here will focus primarily on law enforcement and LGBTQ+ communities in the United States. The institution of law enforcement varies significantly across countries, in terms of history, function, organization, norms, laws, and more (Haberfeld and Cerrah 2008). And, LGBTQ+ communities likewise vary, in terms of their histories, levels of social acceptance, legal statuses, cultures, and more (Chiang 2019). Because the relationship between policing and sexuality is so grounded in each nation's experience, a focus on one country's experience is illustrative; however, readers are encouraged to seek the fine scholarship that can provide cross-cultural comparisons (e.g., Miles-Johnson 2018; Williams and Robinson 2004).

The chapter will begin with theoretical and historical perspectives, both of which shape perceptions of the police. From there, discussion will turn to the informal dynamics of police organizations and research findings about LGBTQ+ perceptions of the police, including a focus on the role of language and communication.

HETERONORMATIVITY AND INTERSECTIONALITY

The theories of heteronormativity and intersectionality offer lenses that can help understand the relationship between the public and the police as mediated by sexuality (see chapter 19). Heteronormativity is a perspective that values heterosexual relationships and sexualities over others, whether by explicit choice (e.g., bias against sexual minorities) or by institutional structure (e.g., privileging heterosexual marriage over same-sex relationships, prior to the 2015 Supreme Court case *Obergefell v. Hodges*, or by privileging religious belief over requirements for businesses to serve sexual minorities, as permitted by the 2018 Supreme Court case *Masterpiece Cakeshop v. Colorado Civil Rights Commission*). Prior studies have identified law enforcement as a heteronormative agent (e.g., Dwyer 2011, 2015), which will be further illustrated through the police practices documented below. The mere perception that heteronormativity exists—even if unintentionally communicated by otherwise well-meaning officers and agencies—can be detrimental to relations with LGBTQ+ communities.

Intersectionality is the simple but important concept that individuals may identify with multiple social categories, the cumulative effect of which is "not merely additive but intersectional and multiplicative" (Peterson and Panfil 2014, 4). As a theory, intersectionality is focused on the concept of social justice, as one means of understanding and overcoming societal oppressions. The intersections that lend the theory its name may be conceptualized as "interlocking systematic oppressions . . . across time and geography," positing that individuals have multiple identifiers, each of which may carry its own oppressive burdens, the cumulative effects of which may be more than the sum of their parts (Few-Demo and Allen 2020; this is also consistent with Giles and Ogay 2007, who note that communication involves negotiating status as related to "salient social category memberships," 294). Individuals defy simplistic categorizations, and each individual may be shaped by multiple perspectives, including not only their sexuality but also their racial and ethnic backgrounds, socioeconomic status, occupational identifiers, region or urban/rural split, and more. As such, it is an incomplete conceptualization to identify individuals as, for instance, "gay" or "lesbian" and to presume that comprises the holistic entirety of their worldview (see Barnett et al. 2019).

Intersectionality can magnify differences between police and community when persons identify with multiple groups who have experienced difficulties with—or oppressions by—law enforcement, whether an individual has experienced actual discrimination or victimization, or has experienced it vicariously through the experiences of others (Nadal et al. 2015; Walker 1997). Research has documented numerous groups that have experienced poor relations with law enforcement (see chapters 5, 6, and 8). They are sometimes labeled the "dangerous classes" (Shelden 2001, 16–19) due to the perception—grounded in bias rather than a reality—that they are dangerous or threaten hegemonic social order, leading them to be aggressively targeted by legislative or police actions. This has been historically true for racial minorities (see Peck 2015; Williams and

Murphy 1990; see chapter 5), and as will be documented below has also been true for sexual minorities. Further research is needed to fully understand the significant intersectionalities between sexual orientation, race, and gender that may shape perceptions of the police (Owen et al. 2018).

Intersectionality can also help to explain why the term LGBTQ+ *communities*, rather than community, was used earlier in this chapter. It is a misnomer to suggest that sexuality can be conveyed as *simply* as identifying as "homosexual" versus "heterosexual" (e.g., Gebhard and Johnson 1979). Even the notion of a continuum is overly simplified, as there are many identifiers that persons may feel best represent their sexuality. In so observing, it is important to avoid "presuming that there is a single or comprehensive community identifier" (Owen et al. 2018, 669) pertaining to sexuality. As such, sexuality itself is intersectional.

Taken together, this suggests that there are a multitude of perspectives that can shape public perceptions of the police vis-à-vis sexuality, requiring multifaceted analyses to capture the nuances of intersectional public opinion. Yet, underlying any discussion must be the heteronormativity that has been endemic within society.

HISTORICAL PERSPECTIVES ON POLICE HETERONORMATIVITY

Heteronormativity has a long history in the United States (see Marchia and Sommer 2019), and that history has overlapped with the history of law enforcement practices. Prior to the Supreme Court case of *Lawrence v. Texas*, decided in 2003, sodomy (i.e., oral and/or anal sex, sometimes described in legal codes as "crimes against nature") was illegal. In some states, the law prohibited both same-sex and opposite-sex sodomy, but in other states, only same-sex sodomy was criminal; regardless of the codes, the reality was that the law was a prime example of heteronormativity, focused on controlling sexual minorities—and, most specifically, gay men (on sodomy laws, see Eskridge 2008).

One early high-profile scandal related to law enforcement efforts to control sexual minorities—and which ultimately involved entrapment—focused on gay sailors in Newport, Rhode Island, and was an effort of the Navy and the Newport Police Department, overseen by Assistant Secretary of the Navy Franklin D. Roosevelt. The 1919 Newport scandal prompted public outrage not because the power of law was used to entrap gay men but, rather, due to the techniques that were used to do so; undercover operatives engaged in sexual acts with men suspected to be gay in order to prove the allegations of homosexuality (Zane 2018). In the mid-twentieth century, interviews with gay men who cruised (i.e., searched for sexual activity) in public parks also revealed concerns about entrapment, through the actions of police officers posing as gay men seeking assignations (Humphreys 1975).

Even law enforcement agencies in what are now regarded as LGBTQ+-friendly cities have had legacies of less-than-friendly contacts with LGBTQ+ communities. Provincetown, Massachusetts, experienced clashes between the police and LGBTQ+ activists in the late 1980s and early 1990s, focused on arrests that were viewed as homophobic and a perceived lack of attention by the district attorney to hate crimes (Faiman-Silva

2004). From the 1950s through the 1980s, the Philadelphia Police acquired the reputation of over-enforcing the law against LGBTQ+ communities, under-enforcing it against those who victimized them, and engaging in shakedowns and corrupt practices against LGBTQ+ establishments (Bailey 1999). From the 1940s through the 1960s, the San Francisco Police were criticized for accepting payoffs to reduce enforcement at some LGBTQ+ establishments, and engaging in raids at others (Boyd 2003). And the list could go on.

In the 1960s, a nascent gay rights movement emerged, sparked in the United States by the 1969 raid on the Stonewall Inn (a bar, not a hotel) in New York City. That it was a police action that prompted an awareness and advocacy for gay rights should not go unnoticed; the patrons of the bar actively resisted arrest, no doubt weary of the regularity with which the police department undertook raids of LGBTQ+ establishments. As described by D'Emilio and Freedman (1988, 319), "Rioting continued far into the night, as crowds of angry homosexuals battled the police up and down the streets of Greenwich Village. The following day, graffiti proclaiming 'Gay Power' was scribbled on walls and pavements in the area. The rioting that lasted throughout the weekend signaled the start of a major social movement." Across the Atlantic in the United Kingdom, it was a government commission that began the path toward change; over forty years before the *Lawrence v. Texas* case in the United States, the Crown's Committee on Homosexual Offenses and Prostitution (1963, 187) recommended "that homosexual behavior between consenting adults in private be no longer a criminal offense."

Clearly, change was in the offing. Some may argue that these earlier types of police practices reflected the laws or social norms of the time. However, heteronormativity has continued to manifest itself through declarations of homosexuality as a mental illness that, while repealed by the American Psychiatric Association in 1974 (D'Emilio and Freedman 1988), has continued in debates about so-called conversion therapies that seek to convert sexual minorities to heterosexual behavior (see Waidzunas 2015). Sodomy laws, while ruled unconstitutional by the Supreme Court, still remain unredacted in some legal codes, which has in some instances resulted in police harassment of sexual minorities (Associated Press 2014). Survivors of same-sex domestic violence indicate a lack of confidence in law enforcement response which, in turn, might lead them to not call the police to report their victimization (Burke, Jordan, and Owen 2002). Officers have been held accountable in lawsuits for failing to protect transgender persons (see *Brandon v. County of Richardson* 2001) and for unlawfully violating privacy rights by disclosing another's sexual orientation (see *Sterling v. Minersville* 2000; see also Owen and Burke 2003).

One of the most thoroughly documented reviews of modern police practice as it pertains to LGBTQ+ communities was compiled by the New York City Civilian Complaint Review Board (2016, 4), an agency separate from the New York Police Department but which is charged with reviewing complaints that are filed against officers. A study of complaints based on sexuality received from 2010 to 2015 found that the board "received 466 distinct complaints (with 1,969 allegations) related to or from members of the LGBTQ community." While only a small number (74 allegations) were upheld after investigation, these numbers, and only from one city, are enough to give pause when considering how detrimental the perception—and reality—of bias must be for LGBTQ+ communities.

POLICING ORGANIZATIONS

Over eighty years ago, Barnard (1938) observed that informal forces within organizations were instrumental in communicating organizational values that shape practice. Subsequent academic discussion has focused on the concept of organizational culture (see Meek 1988 for an overview) and how it can "give to the organization a distinctive way of seeing and responding to the world" (Wilson 1989, 93). While some debate surrounds the notion of organizational cultures, their benefit is in explaining potential links to action—that is, how informal organizational values or beliefs shape organizational behavior (Morgan 1986). Indeed, variations in organizational cultures have been found to affect police organizations and how they approach the practice of law enforcement in federal (Wilson 1989) and local agencies (Wilson 1968).

For this reason, it is important to explore how heteronormativity is manifest within police agencies and among students of criminal justice (many of whom will enter the law enforcement profession). Homophobia has been documented within police organizations. One study of a mid-sized local law enforcement agency compared the perspectives of supervisors and officers:

> Supervisors held significantly more positive attitudes toward gay men, were significantly more supportive of lesbian and gay civil liberties, were less accepting of negative stereotypes . . . and were less likely to discriminate. . . . Line-level officers are significantly more likely to discriminate and apparently do so regardless of their personal feelings toward lesbian and gay men, again supporting the idea that discrimination is related as much to contextual factors as to individual attitudes. (Bernstein and Kostelac 2002, 322)

Later work found that homophobia among police officers was associated not only with an acceptance of anti-LGBTQ+ stereotypes, but also with perceived status—namely, viewing LGBTQ+ persons with lower status or ability (Bernstein 2004). Of course, homophobia within law enforcement ranks is a concern for fear that it could lead to differential treatment based on a person's sexuality (Lyons et al. 2005).

This extends to include difficulties that LGBTQ+ officers sometimes experience within their own agencies. This is an area in need of further research, but several findings are worth noting. A study of police chiefs in Texas indicated that some found homosexuality to be "morally distasteful" (Lyons, DeValve, and Garner 2008, 115). At the same time, a comprehensive case study of a California police department found that openly gay or lesbian officers have been accepted. In that case, "a quiet but remarkable process of normalization . . . developed that has reduced much of the emotional and moral charge that the prospect of serving with gay colleagues generated originally" (Belkin and McNichol 2002, 89).

Turning to the role of language, consider this result from a study of organizational climate conducted at a midwestern agency: "With regard to sexual orientation, gay, lesbian, and bisexual officers report significantly more negative workplace experiences than heterosexual officers on only one dimension: perceptions of vulgar language" (Hassell and Brandl 2009, 419–20). This is consistent with the results of a survey administered to lesbian and gay police officers from multiple agencies, which identified "homophobic comments as the common and most frequent attitudinal barrier" reported in the workplace (Colvin 2009, 95). The interpretation of this finding illustrates the power of language: "As a population that may not be visible to others, these officers may very well have been exposed to the most honest attitudes of other officers; their language used to reinforce established or entrenched police department cultural norms" (Colvin 2009, 96).

As an important disclaimer, with over fifteen thousand local police departments in the United States, not counting state and federal agencies (Hyland and Davis 2019), it is not unreasonable to suppose that there will be significant variation across agencies in terms of their manifest heteronormativity. While some agencies will demonstrate more acceptance of, and support for, LGBTQ+ communities than others, heteronormativity remains an issue that agencies must honestly address when exploring how to provide strengthened outreach to LGBTQ+ communities.

Heteronormative bias demonstrated by criminal justice students is likewise important to study, as they ostensibly will be a reasonable proportion of candidates to enter the sworn police ranks. Again, results have been mixed. Some studies have detected higher levels of anti-LGBTQ+ bias among criminal justice students (Cannon 2005; Miller and Kim 2012; Olivero and Murataya 2001; Tucker et al. 2019), while one recent study found no difference between students in criminal justice and other majors (Olson 2017). In another example of intersectionality, this research has also found that, in addition to major, students who are male are more likely to hold negative attitudes, students who have gay friends are more likely to hold positive attitudes, and students reporting higher levels of religiosity are more likely to hold negative attitudes (see Cannon 2005; Miller and Kim 2012; Olson 2017; Tucker et al. 2019). In fact, one study found that, while there were differences based on major, male gender was ultimately the driving force in predicting homophobia among students (Tucker et al. 2019).

With the above, it is incumbent upon both police agencies and post-secondary institutions providing criminal justice education to consider how to mitigate heteronormativity and to build inclusion that promotes diversity, inclusion, and the legitimacy that is critically important for building public trust in the police (see Hawdon 2008). One means for doing so is a focus on language.

THE ROLE OF LANGUAGE IN LGBTQ+ PERCEPTIONS OF THE POLICE

Language and communication play a powerful role in all human interaction, but particularly in understanding the relationship between the police and the public (e.g., Choi and Giles 2012). Sir Robert Peel, widely credited with establishing the London Metropolitan Police as the first modern police agency in 1829, is reputed to have written, "the police are the public and the public are the police" (*New York Times* 2014); this sentiment is consistent with his goal for policing to not only have legitimacy, but also to be community focused (see Radalet and Carter 1994). However, literature related to the police personality and police subculture has been more likely to find it marked by cynicism, distrust of the public, and a code of silence to outsiders (summarized in Owen et al. 2020). This, in turn, has the potential to shape communications that reify status differentials between police and non-police, and between police and communities that have been labeled as "dangerous classes"—including those of LGBTQ+ persons.

Communication accommodation theory (CAT) suggests that communication is shaped "by the socio-historic context in which the interaction is embedded," and that it may "signal [persons'] attitudes towards each other and their respective social groups" (Giles and Ogay 2007, 294). Of particular interest are processes of convergence and divergence, the former being a set of communicative tools to build connection between parties, and the latter being a set of tools used to identify or heighten differences. Consider the already tense circumstances involving interactions with LGBTQ+ communities; heteronormativity has long prevailed, generating the sociohistoric context described above that must be bridged to improve LGBTQ+ relations with the police. This is manifest even today through communication choices in which officers engage in divergent communication rather than attempting to find common ground. Sometimes this is intentional; at others times, it is inadvertent, but it speaks to the need to identify effective and respectful communication pathways.

While not specific to LGBTQ+ populations, Giles and colleagues (2006, 260) reported a series of studies that demonstrated the power of communication, noting that it can sometimes be "a larger predictor than trust . . . [and] socio-demographic variables" in determining how the public views the police. Subsequent work has found that trust in the police may in fact mediate the relationship between communication strategies and positive views of the police (Choi et al. 2019). This a powerful coupling pertaining to LGBTQ+ communities, as it suggests that legacies of heteronormativity—which diminish trust—can impair relationships with the police even when communication is strong; conversely, it also suggests that poor communication and inappropriate uses of language can erode relationships even if heteronormativity has been proactively addressed in a way that promotes trust.

Most problematic, certainly, is language that is intentionally used—or which a reasonable person would understand as having negative connotations—which, in turn, can negatively influence interactions. Whether or not this is done to deliberately elevate status at the expense of others (for a perspective on status dynamics, see Johnstone 1981), or due to a lack of awareness of the likelihood to offend, it has the same deleterious effect. The New York City Civilian Complaint Review Board (2016), for instance, documented 856 complaints against New York City police officers from 2010 to 2016, based on language officers were alleged to have used. The most frequently cited term, perhaps not surprisingly given its negative emotive value, was "faggot" (266 complaints); others included "homo" (67 complaints), "dyke" (19 complaints), and "tranny" or other language offensive to transgender persons (33 complaints). The board noted the difficulty of investigating such allegations, as proof was difficult to establish.

King (2016) conceptualizes some language as a form of violence against LGBTQ+ communities due to the harms it can pose. For instance, the use of language directed toward males that includes "the use of words like 'fag,' 'pussy,' 'gay,' and 'girl'. . . both explicitly and implicitly encourages sexism and homophobia" (18). Misgendering transgender persons, in which they are identified by other than their desired pronouns or gender labels, is likewise harmful, as it "invalidates their identity" (see Heinz 2018, 21). This becomes an area of potential complexity for persons unfamiliar with transgender communities and the corresponding language etiquette (for a law enforcement context, see Burke, Owen, and Few-Demo 2015), and is an instance in which an inadvertent comment may be perceived as hurtful by its recipient—that is, an unintended divergent communication.

Also pernicious are microaggressions, defined by Nadal (2014, para. 4) as "everyday encounters of subtle discrimination that people of various marginalized groups experience throughout their lives." One classic example, also referenced by Nadal, is the slang phrase, "that's so gay." While it does not necessarily refer to sexuality, having taken on its own meaning as labeling something as undesirable, the impact felt by LGBTQ+ communities is as an attack on their identity. Indeed, microaggressions carry negative psychological impacts to their recipients, even when unintended (Nadal 2014; for a recent and comprehensive meta-analysis documenting negative effects of microaggressions, see Lui and Quezada 2019). Again, this becomes an unintended divergent communication—and in the case of microaggressions, these communications frequently trace their origins toward the powerful sociohistoric contexts that espoused narratives hostile toward, or dismissive, of LGBTQ+ communities.

Surprisingly, there has been little research conducted on LGBTQ+ perceptions of the police, and even less—generally only tangential—on how police use of language influences those perceptions. This is an area in need of further research, not only on divergent communications, but also on instances in which convergent communications help to build community relations.

DOCUMENTING THE LGBTQ+ PERCEPTIONS OF THE POLICE

As of this writing, there are seven known studies that have explicitly sought to analyze contemporary LGBTQ+ perceptions of the police in the United States. The above context—heteronormativity, intersectionality, history, organizational dynamics, and language—no doubt has been the primary driver of the results, which generally suggest that LGBTQ+ communities do not have strong, positive perceptions of law enforcement. To convey the flavor of prior research, each study will be presented individually, chronologically in the order of publication, as each has its own unique context and implications. This helps to best summarize what is known about the relationship between LGBTQ+ communities and the police.

Walker (1997) conducted a series of focus groups to study how members of the public thought that police misconduct should be addressed, and how that corresponded to their expectations of law enforcement. Discussion centered on a hypothetical case study. One of the focus groups comprised gay and lesbian participants (the *n* was not reported, and there was no reference to inclusion of bisexual or transgender persons). Some participants in the focus group expressed concern that persons may be targeted if officers perceived them to be gay or lesbian, such as through identifiers placed on a vehicle. Interestingly, Walker (1997, 217) found that "members of the gay and lesbian group . . . expressed the most intense personal response" to the hypothetical incident, finding the (again, hypothetical) officer's misconduct to be a personal affront; they were also "the most likely to want some form of personal encounter with the officer, mainly so they could express themselves directly to the officer" (Walker 1997, 218). This speaks to the significance of communication, and potentially toward a restorative justice model (see Cullen and Jonson 2012) to allow members of the community, themselves, to bridge a communication divergence through deliberative discussion.

Gillespie (2008) administered a survey to attendees (n=179) at a Pride festival, asking participants to rate policing services that were delivered at the festival, itself. Overall levels of satisfaction were rated very highly, with a substantial majority indicating that they were satisfied with police services and that the police did a good job. This may appear to run counter to the earlier statement that research has generally detected a poor relationship between the police and LGBTQ+ communities. However, it merits consideration that the survey was specific to policing at the Pride event, and that the department—the Atlanta Police Department—had recently appointed a liaison officer for the LGBTQ+ community. Gillespie (2008, 642) notes that "although this study was not an evaluation of Atlanta's Gay and Lesbian Liaison Unit, it seems likely that the efforts of the Atlanta Police Department had not gone unnoticed by the GLBT communities." This illustrates the importance of convergence, as the police department specifically found opportunities to build relationships that could have the effect of repairing sociohistoric heteronormativity and strengthening communication. Regarding intersectionality, the only differences based on sample demographics were that younger and more affluent respondents viewed the police more positively than those who were older and less affluent.

Nadal, Quintanilla, Goswick, and Sriken (2015) conducted a series of three focus groups (n=16 participants) addressing perceptions not just of law enforcement, but also of the legal system, more broadly. Participants were lesbian, gay, bisexual, and queer (LGBQ; no transgender persons were included in this sample). The results yield important insights about the dynamics of the relationship between LGBQ communities and the police, with a particular emphasis on communication. All participants raised concerns about the sensitivity of the police and how they interact with LGBQ persons, as further illustrated by numerous accounts of microaggressions. Respondents also indicated that they engaged in "passing" (Nadal et al. 2015, 467) behaviors when interacting with the criminal justice system, in which they changed their usual presentation of self to correspond or converge to gender norm stereotypes. Significant intersectionality was also present, as summarized by one respondent's impression of stop and frisk policies: "[LGBTQ] people of color, I think, are just, like, even doubly marginalized by that situation" (Nadal et al. 2015, 470). Taken together, Nadal and colleagues' work found a lack of trust in the legal system, and the dynamics are clear and consistent with communication accommodation theory (Giles 2016)—namely, that LGBQ persons accommodate their communication (viewed here as the constellation of activities surrounding a holistic presentation of self) toward societal stereotypes, fearing that a failure to do so will potentially heighten the already divergent communication experienced in the form of insensitive or microaggressive messages.

Serpe and Nadal (2017) administered a survey to a sample (n=266) that included both transgender (identified as trans* in the study, reflecting a broad range of gender identifications or non-identifications) and cisgender persons; participants identified as a range of sexual orientations, including heterosexual, gay, lesbian, bisexual, asexual, pansexual, and questioning. Participants completed the Perceptions of Police Scale, previously developed by Nadal and Davidoff (2015), and the Comfort with Police Self-Report Measure, developed for the research. Persons identifying as trans* "experienced significantly less positive perceptions of police" and "less comfort interacting with police" (Serpe and Nadal 2017, 292) than persons identifying as cisgender. Serpe and Nadal (2017, 293) hypothesize that these results "may be grounded in direct or secondary experiences with police bias, victimization, or generally poor experiences." There was little evidence of intersectionality, beyond a finding that Black cisgender females held lower perceptions of the police than White cisgender females.

Owen, Burke, Few-Demo, and Natwick (2018) sought to test whether lesbian, gay, bisexual, and transgender persons have different perceptions of the police than heterosexuals. Their sample (n=787) completed three scales developed for the project: the Policing Qualities Scale; Policing Outcomes Scale; and LGBT Policing Scale. On each scale, lesbian, gay, bisexual, and transgender (LGBT) respondents reported lower levels of satisfaction with the police. Results also indicated that lesbian, gay, and bisexual persons were less likely than heterosexual persons to believe that the police treat LGBT communities fairly. Because the sample included persons who had served as police officers, the authors also tested differences between persons with and without law enforcement experience. Those with police experience were more likely to believe that LGBT persons were treated fairly, suggesting a potential disconnect between the perceptions held by law enforcement and the perceptions held by the communities they serve. While intersectionalities between sexual orientation and race and sexual orientation and gender were tested, no intersectional relationships were detected.

Satuluri and Nadal (2018) surveyed LGTBQ (n=41) and heterosexual (n=47) persons to test not only for differences in perceptions of the police, but also for how those perceptions are related to mental health. Utilizing the Perceptions of Police Scale and the previously validated Mental Health Inventory (Veit and Ware 1983), the authors found that LGBTQ persons have more negative perceptions of law enforcement, and that lower perceptions of the police were associated with anxiety, depression, and behavioral control. While cautioning that results regarding mental health are "purely correlational and not causal in nature," the authors observe that "if LGBTQ people hold negative perceptions of police due to experiences of being discriminated against or abused, such experiences could have an adverse effect on their mental well-being" (Satuluri and Nadal 2018, 52).

Finally, Dario, Fradella, Verhagen, and Parry (in press) studied the relationship between procedural justice and police legitimacy (see chapters 8 and 17). Surveys (n=428) were distributed to attendees at the Phoenix Rainbows Festival, an event for LGBTQ+ communities. Procedural justice, fairness, and legitimacy were measured with a scale developed for the project. Results found that "procedural justice is a significant predictor of police legitimacy" (Dario et al. in press) and that LGBT respondents provided lower legitimacy scores. Interestingly, further analysis revealed that gay men and heterosexual women, collectively, perceived higher levels of police legitimacy than lesbian women and heterosexual men, collectively. In exploring age and race, intersectionality was not prevalent, although the study did note that "Hispanic respondents [reported] greater perceptions of police legitimacy when compared to non-Hispanic respondents" (Dario et al. in press). The authors conclude on an optimistic note, namely that perceptions of the police have improved in the locale where the survey was conducted, but that there remain avenues for continued growth.

There are several observations that can be drawn from this discussion. The first is that, unless law enforcement agencies have taken specific steps to connect with LGBTQ+ communities, the perceptions of the police skew negative. The second is that additional research is necessary; extant studies utilize different methods, samples, and goals, and while pointing in the same direction, additional data would help to understand what underlies perceptions and how they may be addressed. Finally, it is prudent to understand LGBTQ+ perceptions of the police as being rooted in *communication* transactions. Fundamentally, these perceptions relate to whether the police and public can accommodate one another's communication needs, understanding the often negative sociohistoric context in which they are set, and ideally with a goal of striving to converge toward understanding, empathy, and problem-solving rather than to diverge toward labeling, microaggressions, and diminished status.

THE LIMITS OF DATA ABOUT LANGUAGE

To date, there is little research on the frequency with which inappropriate language is utilized by law enforcement toward LGBTQ+ communities. Bernstein and Kostelac (2002, 317) found that, in one agency, "19% [of officers] admitted to calling a homosexual man or woman an insulting name [and] 11% admitted to making negative comments or asking insulting questions about someone's sexuality or personal life." Previously reported results, above, indicate that this language also is sometimes used against other officers, as well.

Owen, Burke, Few-Demo, and Natwick (2018, 677) included the following item on their LGBT Policing Scale: "The police use derogatory language against members of the LGBT community." On a Likert scale of 1 (strongly disagree) to 4 (strongly agree), the mean score reported in the initial LGBT Policing Scale administration was 2.69, suggesting that the issue is more than anecdotal.

Clearly, given the importance of communication and the impacts that it can have, more research is necessary—ideally coupling communication theories with research on police perceptions grounded in criminal justice frameworks (e.g., Giles et al. 2006). One underlying theme throughout this chapter is the impact that communication—whether verbal, nonverbal, attitudinal, formal, or informal—can have in framing police-related interactions that impact LGBTQ+ communities; and this, in turn, may go far in shaping how LGBTQ+ communities perceive the institutions of law enforcement.

CONCLUSIONS

This chapter demonstrates that there is room for improvement in police relationships with LGBTQ+ communities. The question remaining is how to effect this change, for which there are no simple answers. Indeed, a full text could be devoted to combatting homophobia and heteronormativity in society.

Communication must play a central role, and more specifically, working to build convergent communication between the police and LGBTQ+ communities in order to enhance trust and promote police legitimacy. This may include the use of the "teachable moment" to challenge microaggressions, to address current issues pertinent to LGBTQ+ communities, or to address issues of concern as they emerge (Fradella, Owen, and Burke 2009, 139). This can—and should—also include helping officers learn the most appropriate language to avoid unintentional offense (e.g., Burke, Owen, and Few-Demo 2015).

The potential for this approach was illustrated particularly through Gillespie's (2008) study conducted at the Atlanta Pride festival, as the positive perceptions of police were at least partially attributed to outreach efforts that had been made by the Atlanta Police Department. This suggests that efforts to connect to LGBTQ+ communities (see also Salonga, 2017, for other examples) may provide benefits. Some departments have adopted liaison programs, in which one or more officers are designated as official contacts with LGBTQ+ communities and as a resource within the police department for addressing LGBTQ+ issues, which can help to promote convergent communications both internal and external to the agency. However, as Dwyer and Ball (2012) concluded in an Australian study, there is almost no extant research about these programs; studies of the implementation and outcomes of such programs has the potential to advance the field considerably.

Related to communication, law enforcement agencies must also recognize that one key starting point is understanding how officers currently perceive their work in policing LGBTQ+ communities. While research has studied general police attitudes toward heteronormativity and LGBTQ+ communities' perceptions of the police, the linkage between the two—that is, how police officers perceive their own work—is lacking. Owen, Burke, Few-Demo, and Natwick (2018) approached this, in noting that current or former police officers were more likely than non-officers to feel that LGBTQ+ persons were treated fairly by the police. Miles-Johnson and Death (2019) conducted a study with Australian police officers, and found lesbian, gay, and bisexual officers fared higher on some aspects of LGBTQ+ policing, while heterosexual officers fared higher on others. As has been a constant theme throughout this chapter, their findings reify the notion that perceptions and police practices should not be viewed as unidimensional. Work of this sort can help provide a baseline to understand what types of trainings or interventions are most appropriate to combat heteronormativity in law enforcement agencies.

Within police agencies, research (Israel et al. 2017) has found that during training designed to challenge police heteronormativity, there are indicators that can be observed to signal how receptive officers are to the instruction. A sense of self-awareness, appreciation for empathy, a willingness to communicate with LGBTQ+ communities while recognizing the oppressions that they have faced, among others, signal a willingness to engage. With this, it takes well-prepared and attentive trainers to not only design sessions, but to implement them with an eye for these signals and the ability to quickly adjust the delivery based on their observations. Of course, organizational change can be challenging, especially if agencies are grappling with manifest homophobia. Lessons may be drawn from research on educational institutions and their change efforts (Steck and Perry 2018), which highlight the importance of proactive leadership in recognizing—and being willing to challenge—heteronormativity, as well as a careful examination of organizational policy and practice. Some existing policies may, intentionally or unintentionally, promote heteronormativity, and these need to be revised; conversely, there may be opportunities to develop other policies that challenge heteronormativity, while potentially also building positive convergent communications.

Much of the above discussion focuses on one of two approaches: changing individual attitudes or revising institutional and organizational structures, all with the aim of repairing relationships between law enforcement and LGBTQ+ communities. However, Herz and Johansson (2015) argue that neither is sufficient, the former being "too idealistic" and the latter with the potential to inadvertently "contribute to reinforcing heteronormative structures in society" (1018). Instead, they propose an approach that begins at a middle point, arguing that "people's everyday life, agency, and social practices in where they act need to be the starting point of analysis" (1019). This would call for a context-driven (e.g., space, time, culture) and intersectional approach to understanding the unique power dynamics that shape, in this case, police-public heteronormativity, and moving forward from there to consider the "subjects and structures" (1019) that impact or are impacted by it.

The search for a one-size-fits-all solution to the historical and current challenges of police relationships with LGBTQ+ communities is elusive because it likely doesn't exist—at least, not under the sensible approach articulated by Herz and Johansson (2015). As such, perhaps recommendations, including those offered here, are best viewed as a "tool kit" for approaching the issue as it uniquely manifests for each law enforcement agency and the population it serves. And, to return to the theme posited throughout this analysis, *communication* must be the inexorable organizing theme, for it is only through effective communication that a convergent, respectful, empathetic, and meaningful dialog and pattern of interactions may be structured, helping to heal and to advance police relationships with LGBTQ+ communities.

REFERENCES

Associated Press. 2014. 12 States Still Ban Sodomy a Decade after Court Ruling. *USA Today*, April 21.

Bailey, Robert W. 1999. *Gay Politics, Urban Politics: Identity and Economics in the Urban Setting*. New York: Columbia University Press.

Barnard, Chester I. 1938. *The Functions of the Executive*. Cambridge: Harvard University Press.

Barnett, Andrew P., Ana M. del Río-González, Benjamin Parchem, Veronica Pinho, Rodrigo Aguayo-Romero, Nadine Nakamura, Sarah K. Calabrese, Paul J. Poppen, and Maria C. Zea. 2019. "Content Analysis of Psychological Research with Lesbian, Gay, Bisexual, and Transgender People of Color in the United States: 1969–2018." *American Psychologist* 74 (8): 898–911.

Belkin, Aaron, and Jason McNichol. 2002. "Pink and Blue: Outcomes Associated with the Integration of Open Gay and Lesbian Personnel in the San Diego Police Department." *Police Quarterly* 5 (1): 63–95.

Bernstein, Mary. 2004. "Paths to Homophobia." *Sexuality Research and Social Policy* 1 (2): 41–55.

Bernstein, Mary, and Constance Kostelac. 2002. "Lavender and Blue: Attitudes about Homosexuality and Behavior toward Lesbians and Gay Men among Police Officers." *Journal of Contemporary Criminal Justice* 18 (3): 302–28.

Boyd, Nan Alamilla. 2003. *Wide Open Town: A History of Queer San Francisco to 1965*. Berkeley: University of California Press.

Brandon v. County of Richardson, 624 N.W.2d 604 (Neb. 2001).

Burke, Tod, Michael L. Jordan, and Stephen S. Owen. 2002. "A Cross-National Comparison of Gay and Lesbian Domestic Violence." *Journal of Contemporary Criminal Justice* 18 (3): 231–257.

Burke, Tod W., Stephen S. Owen, and April Few-Demo. 2015. "Law Enforcement and Transgender Communities." *FBI Law Enforcement Bulletin*, June 11.

Cannon, Kevin D. 2005. "'Ain't No Faggot Gonna Rob Me!': Anti-Gay Attitudes of Criminal Justice Undergraduate Majors." *Journal of Criminal Justice Education* 16 (2): 226–43.

Chiang, Howard, ed. 2019. *The Global Encyclopedia of Lesbian, Gay, Bisexual, Transgender, and Queer (LGBTQ) History*. Farmington Hills: Charles Scribner's Sons.

Choi, Charles, and Howard Giles. 2012. "Intergroup Messages in Policing the Community." In *The Handbook of Intergroup Communication*, edited by Howard Giles, 264–77. New York: Routledge.

Choi, Charles W., Gholam H. Khajavy, Rana Raddawi, and Howard Giles. 2019. "Perceptions of Police-Civilian Encounters: Intergroup and Communication Dimensions in the United Arab Emirates and the USA." *Journal of International and Intercultural Communication* 12 (1): 82–104.

Civilian Complaint Review Board. 2016. *Pride, Prejudice and Policing: An Evaluation of LGBTQ-Related Complaints from January 2010 through December 2015*. New York: Civilian Complaint Review Board.

Colvin, Roddrick. 2009. "Shared Perceptions among Lesbian and Gay Police Officers: Barriers and Opportunities in the Law Enforcement Work Environment." *Police Quarterly* 12 (1): 86–101.

Committee on Homosexual Offenses and Prostitution. 1963. *The Wolfenden Report: Report of the Committee on Homosexual Offenses and Prostitution*. New York: Stein and Day.

Cullen, Francis T., and Cheryl Lero Jonson. 2012. *Correctional Theory: Context and Consequences*. Thousand Oaks: Sage.

Dario, Lisa M., Henry F. Fradella, Megan Verhagen, and Megan M. Parry. In press. "Assessing LGBT People's Perceptions of Police Legitimacy." *Journal of Homosexuality*.

D'Emilio, John, and Estelle B. Freedman. 1988. *Intimate Matters: A History of Sexuality in America*. New York: Harper & Row.

Dwyer, Angela. 2011. "'It's Not Like We're Going to Jump Them': How Transgressing Heteronormativity Shapes Police Interactions with LGBT Young People." *Young Justice* 11 (3): 203–220.

Dwyer, Angela. 2015. "Teaching Young Queers a Lesson: How Police Teach Lessons about Non-Heteronormativity in Public Spaces." *Sexuality and Culture* 19 (3): 493–512.

Dwyer, Angela E., and Matthew J. Ball. 2012. "GLBTI Police Liaison Services: A Critical Analysis of Existing Literature." In *Proceedings of the Australian and New Zealand Critical Criminology Conference*, edited by Isabelle Bartkowiak-Theron and Max Travers, 11–18. Hobart: University of Tasmania.

Englert, Patrick, and Elizabeth G. Dinkins. 2016. "An Overview of Sex, Gender, and Sexuality." In *Sex, Sexuality, Law, and (In)Justice*, edited by Henry F. Fradella and Jennifer M. Sumner, 1–30. New York: Routledge.

Eskridge, William N., Jr. 2008. *Dishonorable Passions: Sodomy Laws in America, 1861–2003*. New York: Viking.

Faiman-Silva, Sandra L. 2004. *The Courage to Connect: Sexuality, Citizenship, and Community in Provincetown*. Urbana: University of Illinois Press.

Fasoli, Fabio. 2018. "Gay Straight Communication." In *The Oxford Encyclopedia of Intergroup Communication*, edited by Howard Giles and Jake Harwood, Vol. 1, 436–51. New York: Oxford University Press.

Few-Demo, April L., and Katherine R. Allen. 2020. "Gender, Feminist, and Intersectional Perspectives on Families: A Decade in Review." *Journal of Marriage and Family* 82 (1): 326-345.

Fradella, Henry F., Stephen S. Owen, and Tod W. Burke. 2009. "Integrating Gay, Lesbian, Bisexual, and Transgender Issues into the Undergraduate Criminal Justice Curriculum." *Journal of Criminal Justice Education* 20 (2): 127–156.

Gebhard, Paul H., and Alan B. Johnson. 1979. *The Kinsey Data: Marginal Tabulations of the 1938–1963 Interviews Conducted by the Institute for Sex Research*. Bloomington: Indiana University Press.

Giles, Howard, ed. 2016. *Communication Accommodation Theory: Negotiating Personal Relationships and Social Identities across Contexts*. Cambridge: Cambridge University Press.

Giles, Howard, Jennifer Fortman, René M. Dailey, Valerie Barker, Christopher Hajek, Michelle Chernikoff Anderson, and Nicholas O. Rule. 2006. "Communication Accommodation: Law Enforcement and the Public." In *Applied Interpersonal Communication Matters: Family, Health, and Community Relations*, edited by René M. Dailey and Beth A. Le Poire, 241–69. New York: Peter Lang.

Giles, Howard, and Tania Ogay. 2007. "Communication Accommodation Theory." In *Explaining Communication: Contemporary Theories and Exemplars*, edited by Bryan B. Whaley and Wendy Samter, 293–310. Mahwah: Lawrence Erlbaum.

Gillespie, Wayne. 2008. "Thirty-Five Years After Stonewall: An Exploratory Study of Satisfaction with Police among Gay, Lesbian, and Bisexual Persons at the 34th Annual Atlanta Pride Festival." *Journal of Homosexuality* 55 (4): 619–47.

GLAAD. 2016. *GLAAD Media Reference Guide* (tenth edition). New York: GLAAD.

Haberfeld, M. R., and Ibrahim Cerrah, eds. 2008. *Comparative Policing: The Struggle for Democratization*. Thousand Oaks: Sage.

Hajek. Christopher. 2018. "Gay Male Culture and Intergroup Communication. In *The Oxford Encyclopedia of Intergroup Communication*, edited by Howard Giles and Jake Harwood, Vol. 1, 422–36. New York: Oxford University Press.

Hassell, Kimberly D., and Steven G. Brandl. 2009. "An Examination of the Workplace Experiences of Police Patrol Officers: The Role of Race, Sex, and Sexual Orientation." *Police Quarterly* 12 (4): 408–30.

Hawdon, James. 2008. "Legitimacy, Trust, Social Capital, and Policing Styles: A Theoretical Statement." *Police Quarterly* 11 (2): 182–201.

Heinz, Matthew. 2018. "Communicating while Transgender: Apprehension, Loneliness, and Willingness to Communicate in a Canadian Sample." *SAGE Open Online* 8 (2): Retrieved from https://doi.org/10.1177/2158244018777780 .

Herz, Marcus, and Thomas Johansson. 2015. "The Normativity of the Concept of Heteronormativity." *Journal of Homosexuality* 62 (8): 1009–20.

Humphreys, Laud. 1975. *Tearoom Trade: Impersonal Sex in Public Places*. New York: Aldine de Gruyter.

Hyland, Shelly S., and Elizabeth Davis. 2019. *Local Police Departments, 2016: Personnel*. Washington DC: Bureau of Justice Statistics.

Israel, Tania, Jay N. Bettergarcia, Kevin Delucio, Todd Raymond Avellar, Audrey Harkness, and Joshua A. Goodman. 2017. "Reactions of Law Enforcement to LGBTQ Diversity Training." *Human Resource Development Quarterly* 28 (2): 197–226.

Johnstone, Keith. 1981. *Impro: Improvisation and the Theatre*. New York: Routledge.

King, Jessica. 2016. "The Violence of Heteronormative Language towards the Queer Community." *Aisthesis* 7: 17–22.

Lui, P. Priscilla, and Lucia Quezada. 2019. "Associations between Microaggression and Adjustment Outcomes: A Meta-Analytic and Narrative Review." *Psychological Bulletin* 145 (1): 45–78.

Lyons, Phillip M., Jr., and Christine M. Anthony, Karen M. Davis, Krissie Fernandez, Angela N. Torres, and David K. Marcus. 2005. "Police Judgments of Culpability and Homophobia." *Applied Psychology in Criminal Justice* 1 (1): 1–14.

Lyons, Phillip M., Jr., Michael J. DeValve, and Randall L. Garner. 2008. "Texas Police Chiefs' Attitudes toward Gay and Lesbian Police Officers." *Police Quarterly* 11 (1): 102–17.

Marchia, Joseph, and Jamie M. Sommer. 2019. "(Re)defining Heteronormativity." *Sexualities* 22 (3): 267–95.

Masterpiece Cakeshop v. Colorado Civil Rights Commission, 584 U.S. ___ (2018).

Meek, V. Lynn. 1988. "Organizational Culture: Origins and Weaknesses." *Organization Studies* 9 (4): 453–73.

Miles-Johnson, Toby. 2018. "Confidence and Trust in Police: How Sexual Identity Difference Shapes Perceptions of Police." *Current Issues in Criminal Justice* 25 (2): 685–702.

Miles-Johnson, Toby, and Jodi Death. (2019). "Compensating for Sexual Identity: How LGB and Heterosexual Australian Police Officers Perceive Policing of LGBTQ+ People." *Journal of Contemporary Criminal Justice*. Advance Online: https://doi.org/10.1177/1043986219894431 .

Miller, Holly A., and Bitna Kim. 2012. "Curriculum Implications of Anti-Gay Attitudes among Undergraduate Criminal Justice Majors." *Journal of Criminal Justice Education* 23 (2): 148–73.

Morgan, Gareth. 1986. *Images of Organization*. Newbury Park: Sage.

Nadal, Kevin L. 2014. "Stop Saying 'That's So Gay!': 6 Types of Microaggressions that Harm LGBTQ People." *Psychology Benefits Society*. Retrieved from https://psychologybenefits.org/2014/02/07/anti-lgbt-microaggressions/ .

Nadal, Kevin L., and Kristin C. Davidoff. 2015. "Perceptions of Police Scale (POPS): Measuring Attitudes towards Law Enforcement and Beliefs about Police Bias." *Journal of Psychology and Behavioral Science* 3 (2): 1–9.

Nadal, Kevin L., Amalia Quintanilla, Ariana Goswick, and Julie Sriken. 2015. "Lesbian, Gay, Bisexual, and Queer People's Perceptions of the Criminal Justice System: Implications for Social Services." *Journal of Gay and Lesbian Social Services* 27 (4): 457–81.

New York Times. 2014. "Sir Robert Peel's Nine Principles of Policing," April 16. Retrieved from https://www.nytimes.com/2014/04/16/nyregion/sir-robert-peels-nine-principles-of-policing.html .

Obergefell v. Hodges, 576 U.S. ___ (2015).

Olivero, J. Michael, and Rodrigo Murataya. 2001. "Homophobia and University Law Enforcement Students." *Journal of Criminal Justice Education* 12 (2): 271–81.

Olson, Lisa M. 2017. "Criminal Justice Students and Sexual Prejudice." *Journal of Criminal Justice Education* 28 (3): 428–40.

Owen, Stephen, and Tod Burke. 2003. "The Court of Appeals Made the Correct Decision." *Campbell Law Observer*, February.

Owen, Stephen S., Tod W. Burke, April L. Few-Demo, and Jameson Natwick. 2018. "Perceptions of Police by LGBT Communities." *American Journal of Criminal Justice* 43 (3): 668–93.

Owen, Stephen S., Henry F. Fradella, Tod W. Burke, and Jerry W. Joplin. 2020. *Foundations of Criminal Justice* (third edition). New York: Oxford University Press.

Peck, Jennifer H. 2015. "Minority Perceptions of the Police: A State-of-the-Art Review." *Policing: An International Journal* 38 (1): 173–203.

Peterson, Dana, and Vanessa R. Panfil. 2014. "Introduction: Reducing the Invisibility of Sexual and Gender Identities in Criminology and Criminal Justice." In *Handbook of LGBT Communities, Crime, and Justice*, edited by Dana Peterson and Venessa R. Panfil, 3–14. New York: Springer.

Radalet, Louis A., and David L. Carter. 1994. *The Police and the Community* (fifth edition). New York: Macmillan College Publishing Company.

Salonga, Robert. 2017. "San Jose Police Launch Vigorous LGBT Recruitment, Outreach." *The Mercury News*, August 24.

Satuluri, Sriya, and Kevin Nadal. 2018. "LGBTQ Perceptions of the Police: Implications for Mental Health and Public Policy." *LGBTQ Policy Journal* 8: 43–55.

Serpe, Christine R., and Kevin L. Nadal. 2017. "Perceptions of Police: Experiences in the Trans* Community." *Journal of Gay and Lesbian Social Services* 29 (3): 280–99.

Shelden, Randall G. 2001. *Controlling the Dangerous Classes: A Critical Introduction to the History of Criminal Justice*. Boston: Allyn & Bacon.

Steck, Andy K., and David Perry. 2018. "Challenging Heteronormativity: Creating a Safe and Inclusive Environment for LGBTQ Students." *Journal of School Violence* 17 (2): 227–43.

Sterling v. Minersville, 232 F.3d 190 (2000).

Tucker, Jane M., Mary P. Brewster, Shannon T. Grugan, Lisa M. Miller, and Sadeiah M. Mapp-Matthews. 2019. "Criminal Justice Students' Attitudes toward LGBTQ Individuals and LGBTQ Police Officers." *Journal of Criminal Justice Education* 30 (2): 165–92.

Veit, Clairice T., and John E. Ware. 1983. "The Structure of Psychological Distress and Well-Being in General Populations." *Journal of Consulting and Clinical Psychology* 51 (5): 730–42.

Waidzunas, Tom. 2015. *The Straight Line: How the Fringe Science of Ex-Gay Therapy Reoriented Sexuality*. Minneapolis: University of Minnesota Press.

Walker, Samuel. 1997. "Complaints against the Police: A Focus Group Study of Citizen Perceptions, Goals, and Expectations." *Criminal Justice Review* 22 (2): 207–26.

Williams, Hubert, and Patrick V. Murphy. 1990. "The Evolving Strategy of Policing: A Minority View." *Perspectives on Policing* 13 (1): 1–16.

Williams, Matthew L., and Amanda L. Robinson. 2004. "Problems and Prospects with Policing the Lesbian, Gay and Bisexual Community in Wales." *Policing and Society: An International Journal of Research and Policy* 14 (3): 219–32.

Wilson, James Q. 1968. *Varieties of Police Behavior: The Management of Law and Order in Eight Communities.* Cambridge: Harvard University Press.

Wilson, James Q. 1989. *Bureaucracy: What Government Agencies Do and Why They Do It.* New York: Basic Books.

Zane, Sherry. 2018. "'I Did It for the Uplift of Humanity and the Navy': Same-Sex Acts and the Origins of the National Security State, 1919–1921." *New England Quarterly* 91 (2): 279–306.

CHAPTER 8

Policing Muslim Communities

The Importance of Procedural Justice in Communication and Engagement Activities

Kristina Murphy

In recent decades, many countries around the world have faced an increase in "home-grown" terrorism.[1] While home-grown terrorist acts can be perpetrated by anyone, in countries like the United States, Canada, Australia, and throughout Europe, the term "home-grown terrorism" has typically come to denote acts of violence perpetrated by Muslim immigrants acting in the name of Islam (Vermeulen 2014). Despite such acts being perpetrated by only a small minority of the Muslim community, Vermeulen notes that authorities can often perceive the threat of violent extremism as coming from the entire Muslim community and argues that this can lead to the construction of Muslims as a "suspect community."

The construction of Muslims as a suspect community communicates a strong message to Muslims that they are distrusted and a group to be feared. Hillyard (1993) cautions against treating a whole community as suspicious, because it can have detrimental social and psychological effects on that community. For Muslims who feel constantly under suspicion by authorities, their neighbors, and the media, this can fuel feelings of stigmatization, and can lead to an "us" versus "them" mentality (Blackwood, Hopkins, and Reicher 2013; Murphy, Madon, and Cherney 2020; see chapter 1). This serves to marginalize Muslims from the rest of society, reduces Muslims' trust in people outside their own community, and reduces Muslims' willingness to work with authorities to counter terrorist threats in their own community (Cherney and Murphy 2016).

This chapter specifically highlights the importance of building Muslims' *trust in police*. Muslims' trust in police is crucial because authorities rely heavily on the Muslim community to report radicalization and terror threats occurring in their community. In a 2018 interview Australian Prime Minister Scott Morrison stated that "law enforcement authorities already get "good cooperation" from [Muslim] community leaders" and that this had "helped thwart 14 terror attacks" in Australia. But he also stated "more needs to happen" (Karp, 2018).

Drawing on empirical findings from the literature, this chapter demonstrates that the effective implementation of *procedural justice in community-based policing* is crucial for building Muslims' trust in police, and their subsequent willingness to work in partnership with police to counter terrorism. Community-based policing emphasizes procedural justice through police–public engagement (see chapter 10), consultation and partnerships, and effective and respectful communication between police and Muslim communities. Importantly, this approach serves to promote information exchange, and it generates intelligence (Innes 2006). Community policing in counterterrorism is not without its challenges, however. Hence, this chapter also acknowledges some of the key challenges that police face when engaging with Muslim communities in the counterterrorism context. Before doing so, the following section first begins by summarizing how governments have attempted to curb home-grown terrorism and how this has led to the securitization of Muslims.

THE INCREASING SECURITIZATION OF MUSLIM COMMUNITIES

Hillyard (1993) contends that when whole communities are viewed with suspicion, this often results in increasingly intrusive, heavy-handed laws and policing techniques being used against that community. We have seen this occur in the context of counterterrorism policing of Muslim communities. In response to the September 11, 2001, attacks on the World Trade Center in New York, governments around the world moved to introduce a suite of punitive laws aimed at preventing future terrorist attacks. In Australia alone, sixty-four new anti-terror laws were introduced between 2002 and 2014 in the wake of the 2002 Bali bombings (Lynch, McGarrity, and Williams 2015). These new laws gave authorities expanded powers and the ability to detain terrorist suspects with no trial, to cancel citizenship for those found guilty of terrorism offenses, to target groups perceived as security threats, and to intercept, collect, and store people's personal information. Some of these laws afforded authorities exclusive and unprecedented powers to surveil, detain, and interrogate individuals without reasonable proof of criminal intent. The unintended consequence of these laws is that they disproportionately affected Muslim communities, and perpetuated anti-Muslim racist stereotypes among the broader population (Choudhury and Fenwick 2011; Khader 2015).

Police, as enforcers of these laws, often take the lead in any strategies designed to detect or counter terrorism (Spalek 2010). While "hard power" approaches to countering terrorism like those mentioned above are certainly needed in some circumstances, they do risk fueling Muslims' distrust of police. Of particular concern for Muslim communities are laws that enable police to stop Muslims on the street even when no law has been broken, increase surveillance of Muslim communities, perform targeted searches at airports, and undertake public raids and arrests of Muslims (e.g., Blackwood et al. 2013; Cherney and Murphy 2016; Hasisi, Margalioth, and Orgad 2012). Muslims have also reported resentment toward counterterrorism police trying to gather intelligence from members of their community and from their Muslim leaders in particular (Cherney and Murphy 2016). Muslims' distrust of police has served to reduce some Muslims' willingness to work collaboratively with police to report radicalization and terrorist activity taking place in their community (Cherney and Murphy 2016). As highlighted earlier, this is concerning because police rely heavily on community members to come forward with pertinent information that can help them prevent terrorism. Without the support of the Muslim community, even the most well-resourced counterterrorism agenda will not be fully effective. This points to the importance of police developing open and respectful lines of communication with the Muslim community to enhance Muslims' trust in police and their willingness to work collaboratively with police.

THE IMPORTANCE OF EFFECTIVE COMMUNICATION BETWEEN POLICE AND MUSLIMS: A ROLE FOR PROCEDURAL JUSTICE

Muslim communities are being increasingly recognized by authorities as critical partners in counterterrorism. As Thomas, Grossman, Miah, and Christmann (2017, 6) note, "the first people to suspect or know about someone becoming involved in planning acts of violent extremism will often be those closest to them: their friends, family and community insiders" (see also Awan and Guru 2017; Williams, Horgan, and Evans 2016). Hence, there is an increasing expectation by the police that Muslim communities work with police to reduce the risk of Islamic-inspired terrorism (Spalek and Lambert 2008). We know from previous research, however, that many Muslims avoid contact with police because they view them with suspicion (e.g., Cherney and Murphy 2016). How police overcome Muslims' distrust of police is therefore an ongoing challenge.

Community-based policing models are increasingly being drawn upon to develop effective police–Muslim partnerships (Innes 2006; Spalek 2010; Spalek and Lambert 2010; see also chapter 10). For example, community-based police cultural liaison officers are used to build relationships with the Muslim community; these officers are distinct from counterterrorism investigators (see Cherney and Hartley 2017). Spalek (2010) argues that community policing is crucial to countering terrorism because it builds trust between police and Muslim communities. A major aim of community policing is to try to link the police more closely to a community in "partnership" arrangements. These engagement and partnership arrangements can involve "joint activities to coproduce services and achieve desired outcomes, giving the community a greater say in what the police do, or simply engaging each other to produce a greater sense of police-community compatibility" (Mastrofski 2006, 46). While there is not space in the current chapter to cover the numerous successful community policing programs with Muslim communities, one common feature underlying successful approaches is that they adopt the tenets of *procedural justice*. This means they pay close attention to the way that police *communicate* their power in a procedurally just manner when meeting with Muslim communities.

Procedural justice in policing involves four key tenets: (1) displays by police of their *trustworthiness*, (2) *respectful and courteous treatment* of members of the public, (3) the provision of *voice* to individuals in decision making; and (4) *neutral* treatment of members of the public (Tyler 2011; see chapters 17 and 22). If police convey trustworthy motives to the Muslim community, if they communicate with Muslims in a polite and respectful manner, if they consult with Muslims and provide them with an opportunity to voice concerns or share ideas before decisions are made about how their community is policed, and if they are neutral in their dealings with Muslim communities, then they will likely be perceived as acting with procedural justice. Tyler (2011) argues that people are strongly influenced by their judgements about the fairness of the interpersonal treatment they receive from authorities and the fairness of the procedures those authorities use to make decisions. This is because unjust treatment from authorities can communicate symbolic information about a person's identity, belonging, and position in society (Bradford, Murphy, and Jackson 2014); procedurally just treatment signals inclusion and solidarity with others, while procedurally unjust treatment signals exclusion.

Scholars suggest that exclusion from valued social groups ranks as one of the most aversive of human experiences (Murphy and Cherney 2018). Research also consistently reveals that when people feel more connected to a group, they will be more motivated to act in that group's best interests as a way of bolstering their identity with that group (Tyler 2011). In the counterterrorism context, this suggests that Muslims should feel a greater obligation to report terrorism threats to authorities to benefit all others in society if they feel they belong in society. If Muslims feel excluded, then they may feel reluctant to act in the best interests of others in society. Police use of procedural justice is key to building trust and signaling to Muslims that they are valued and respected members of society who have an important and valued role to play in the fight against terrorism.

The policing literature is full of empirical studies that demonstrate the value of procedural justice in policing. Research consistently reveals that police use of procedural justice can enhance people's satisfaction with police encounters (Hinds and Murphy 2007), can enhance people's views regarding the legitimacy of police (Sunshine and Tyler 2003; Tyler 2011), and can increase people's trust in the police (Murphy, Mazerolle, and Bennett 2014; Tyler and Huo 2002). Importantly, studies reveal that people's willingness to report suspicious behavior to police, or to report crime and/or victimization, is also associated with their assessments of police being procedurally just (e.g., Murphy and Barkworth 2014).

A small but growing collection of studies using different methodologies also shows that procedural justice might have beneficial effects when used with Muslim communities. These studies show that procedural justice policing can enhance Muslims' intentions to report terrorism-related information to police. Specifically, Cherney and Murphy (2016) conducted focus groups with 104 Muslim-Australians. Muslims reported that they were unlikely to want to work collaboratively with police in counterterrorism activities if they viewed counterterrorism police as behaving in a procedurally unjust manner toward the Muslim community (see also Cherney and Murphy 2017). Using survey data from Muslims in the United States and United Kingdom,

Tyler and his colleagues also revealed that Muslims were more likely to say they would report terrorism-related intelligence to police if they perceived police as procedurally just (Huq, Tyler, and Schulhofer 2011a, b; Tyler, Schulhofer, and Huq 2010; Schulhofer, Tyler, and Huq 2011). Survey studies in Australia report similar findings. In their survey research with eight hundred Australian Muslims, Murphy and her colleagues confirmed that when police are viewed as acting in a procedurally just manner, this enhances Muslims' willingness to work with police to prevent terrorism (e.g., Madon, Murphy, and Cherney 2016; Murphy, Cherney, and Teston 2018; Murphy, Madon, and Cherney 2020). This beneficial effect occurred even for those Muslims who strongly questioned the legitimacy of Australia's "hard power" counterterrorism laws (Murphy, Madon, and Cherney 2017), and for those Muslims who felt most stigmatized (Murphy, Madon, and Cherney 2020).

Notwithstanding this empirical evidence, it should be highlighted that there have been critiques of the procedural justice literature. Most notably, some scholars question whether the conclusions drawn from procedural justice survey-based studies reflect how people actually think and behave in real-life situations. It has been rightly suggested that survey-based methodologies (of which most procedural justice studies employ) can muddy the causal relationships between studied variables (see Nagin and Telep 2017; Radburn and Stott 2019). Radburn and Stott (2019, 421) argue that "contemporary research is in danger of conveying a misreading of [procedural justice theory] by portraying a reified social world divorced from the social psychological dynamics of [actual] encounters between the police and policed." While acknowledging this critique of existing procedural justice research, local-level engagement programs between police and Muslim communities have shown that procedural justice builds trust between police and Muslims. Murphy (2017), for example, surveyed Muslim participants both before and after completing an eight-week police-led engagement program. Murphy found that Muslim participants' trust in police improved after the program, and this was linked to their perceptions of police being procedurally just during the program.

COMMUNICATING PROCEDURAL JUSTICE IN COUNTERTERRORISM POLICING: EXAMPLES AND CHALLENGES

Trust is clearly an important precondition to any community intelligence exercise (Hillyard 1993). Nowhere is this more important than in the context of counterterrorism policing. This section highlights some of the challenges police face in engaging with the Muslim community as well as discusses how police can effectively communicate each of the four tenets of procedural justice in their engagement efforts.

Trustworthiness

For a partnership to work effectively in a sensitive context like counterterrorism, Spalek (2010, 789) suggests that police need to focus "initially upon building contingent-based trust by using activities that demonstrate *trustworthiness*." Contingent-based trust is trust that is built when a person demonstrates their trustworthiness and is a precursor to developing long-term implicit trusting relationships. For example, if a police officer acts in a way that puts the needs of another person or group first (i.e., the Muslim community), then this conveys that they have trustworthy motives (cf. Choi, Khajavy, Raddawi, and Giles 2019).

Trustworthiness can be demonstrated by police when they prioritize trust building over intelligence gathering. It is commonly acknowledged that many Muslims view police engagement and outreach efforts with suspicion, often believing them to be a front for intelligence gathering (Bullock and Johnson 2018). Police cultural liaison officers in Cherney and Hartley's (2017) study stated that it was important in their liaison roles to act openly and with integrity by not directly seeking intelligence from Muslim community members. They emphasized the importance of maintaining separation between their engagement role and the collection of community intelligence on terror threats, and they expressed a reluctance to collect intelligence if requested by counterterrorism investigators. The same police officers noted that the long-term outcome of this was that community members would feel more comfortable approaching them in the future with information that could be passed on to investigators. Hence, the *voluntary* provision of intelligence was viewed as one positive outcome of demonstrating trustworthiness in community engagement efforts.

Another good example of police attempts to build contingent-based trust with the Muslim community was cited in Cherney and Hartley (2017). They noted that in 2015, state and federal police convened a meeting with Muslim community leaders in Sydney, Australia, to inform them that arrests of two Muslim males were to occur that day. One of the Imams who attended that meeting expressed to Cherney and Hartley that this action showed a great level of goodwill from the police. The Imam, therefore, recognized the risk that police were taking by sharing this information with the Muslim community. However, these scholars also noted that these types of actions can generate risk because such acts of goodwill can backfire. Cherney and Hartley noted there was the risk that the Muslims who were to be arrested could have been tipped off and this could have had consequences for the safety of police and the community. At the same time, the Imam noted that police had informed him that the two Muslim men had been under surveillance for more than twelve months. Hence, while acknowledging the police officers' goodwill in consulting with Muslim community leaders, the Imam noted that police could have highlighted their concerns about the Muslim men much earlier so that the Muslim community leaders could have intervened in their path to radicalization.

Cherney and Hartley (2017) noted further challenges police face in building trustworthiness when holding public information sessions with the Muslim community after prominent terrorist raids. On the one hand, such sessions can give police and Muslims the opportunity to express concerns and issues associated with the raids; but, on the other hand, the sessions can fall short when particulars about the raids need to be kept confidential. Often police are unable to share as much information as they want to, and this can leave Muslims feeling that the police are withholding crucial details. This can result in further suspicion, hostility, and anger directed at police.

Respect

Police can display procedural justice in interactions with Muslims by communicating and behaving in a *respectful and courteous* manner (see also Choi et al. 2019). Respectful treatment entails not being rude or condescending to members of the Muslim community; respect can be demonstrated (1) by genuinely listening to Muslims' concerns; or (2) by respecting Muslims' customs and traditions (e.g., police removing their shoes when entering a Mosque or using a common Muslim greeting when entering an individual's house). These actions were also reiterated as important by police officers who were interviewed by Cherney and Hartley (2017). The officers saw it as important in their role as community-based police liaison officers to develop cultural awareness about the Islamic community and to have an open mind about genuinely absorbing the culture. Some interviewees also viewed listening to Muslim community members as one of the most important features of good engagement.

Voice

One important aim of community policing activities is to build trust through methods of consultation that help to enhance the perceived legitimacy of counterterrorism efforts. Research with Muslims reveals that the provision of *voice* is an extremely important feature that Muslims value in interactions with police (e.g., Cherney and Murphy 2016). A major criticism that Muslims have of most police engagement efforts is that police do little in the way of consulting or involving them in genuine discussions about how the Muslim community should be policed. For example, in their survey of eight hundred Australian Muslims, Murphy, Cherney, and Barkworth (2015) revealed that 43 percent of respondents felt that police "never" or "rarely" considered their community's views when making decisions about how to address terrorism. Further, 46 percent of the respondents also felt police "never" or "rarely" considered the Muslim community's views when trying to deal with radicalization in the community. Fewer than 14 percent of respondents felt police consulted them "often" or "always" (see also Cherney and Murphy 2016).

Failing to consult and consider the Muslim community's voice in counterterrorism policing can have dire consequences for the police. It can reduce Muslims' support for police and their willingness to collaborate with police in terrorism prevention. This can be illustrated by the following study. Glasford (2016) studied the motivation of Muslim communities to support authorities in counterterrorism. He varied the type of communication frame that the community was provided by authorities. Respondents in the study were asked to read a letter and were advised that the authorities would be visiting their neighborhood to conduct outreach activities and to gain their support of their counterterrorism activities. One letter framed the authorities as knowing what was best for the community and that they would be advising the community of their activities ("paternalistic condition"). The second letter suggested that both the authorities and community knew what was best in tackling terrorism and it included language suggesting the authorities and community were "on the same team"; this letter was designed to foster a common ingroup identity ("commonality condition"). The third letter suggested that the Muslim community would know what was best for Muslims and that they would be in the position of power when meeting with authorities to discuss how to tackle terrorism ("respect condition"). Glasford revealed that the "commonality" communication frame is the most commonly used approach by authorities in the United States, followed by the "paternalistic" and then the "respect" communication frames. This study revealed that participants in the "respect" condition were the most likely to express an expectation of fair treatment in the future from authorities when compared to participants in the paternalistic or commonality communication conditions. Those in the "respect" condition were also more likely to express trust in the authorities and were more likely to support the authority's counterterrorism approach.

Glasford's findings demonstrate the importance of authorities providing *instrumental voice* to communities. Instrumental voice occurs when people are invited to participate and provide suggestions to authorities before the authority decides how to act on an issue. Here, a group can influence an outcome that brings instrumental rewards to their group. Noninstrumental voice, in contrast, occurs when authorities invite people to speak out after a decision has already been made about how to act on an issue. In this way, groups have no influence over the outcome. Research reveals that instrumental voice is crucial for promoting a sense of procedural justice because being given voice validates individuals and communicates to them that their views are worthy of being considered (Lind, Kanfer, and Earley 1990). The challenge for police is to engage in genuine consultation at the right time during an investigation or before deciding how they will tackle an issue of concern in the Muslim community.

Neutrality

Neutrality is the final tenet of procedural justice that is important in community-based policing. There are two aspects of neutrality to consider in the context of counter terrorism: (1) how police deal with Muslims compared to non-Muslims; and (2) how police deal with *different* Muslim groups within the Muslim community. Muslims consistently argue that they are disproportionately targeted by "hard power" counterterrorism laws and police. For example, Muslims argue that they are more likely to be surveilled and are more likely to experience targeted stops at airports when compared to other groups in the population (e.g., Blackwood et al. 2015). Interestingly, efforts to engage Muslims in community-based policing are also criticized as further evidence of the securitization of Muslim communities (Awan and Guru 2017). These criticisms are valid and can result in Muslims becoming defensive about the perceived lack of neutrality in counterterrorism efforts. However, as argued by Cherney (2018, 61), such "strategies of securitization are in some cases necessary." While not all terrorist acts are perpetrated by Muslims, Islamic terrorism has dramatically increased in OECD countries since 2014. Since 2014, eighteen of the thirty-three OECD countries have experienced Islamic State–directed or inspired attacks, and these have accounted for three quarters of all terrorism-related deaths in these countries (Global Terrorism Index 2017). It would be naïve, therefore, to suggest that police should display neutrality by halting all activities that place attention on Muslim communities. However, such targeted activities must be done in a more intelligent way, where police focus on those Muslims most likely to be high risk. Such an intelligence-led policing approach (Ratcliffe 2011) steers police away from viewing and treating an entire Muslim community as a risk to be controlled. If done in a respectful manner, this approach may serve to reduce the perception among Muslims that their entire community is under suspicion.

Where individual police officers can also have some influence over neutrality in counterterrorism relates to how police engage *within* the Muslim community. In Australia, like in many other Western nations, the Muslim community is very heterogeneous. In counterterrorism policing, it is important to ensure that there is no perception of favoritism of one Muslim group over another (e.g., Shiites and Sunnies). In considering Muslim communities' views about how authorities should police and handle radicalization and terrorism, police must ensure that the individuals and groups being engaged are representative of the various Muslim groups in the country. Cherney (2018) highlighted, however, many of these groups often do not see eye to eye. As such, considering and consolidating the views of these various groups is not always possible and can be difficult to achieve.

Outreach with Muslim youth and Muslim women can also be a challenge for police. Muslim youth feel specifically targeted by counterterrorism police and are often the most distrusting of police of all Muslims (Cherney 2018); but Muslim youth can be the first to become aware of friends who are at risk of becoming radicalized (Williams et al. 2016). Efforts of police to engage with Muslim youth and build their trust are, therefore, particularly important when dealing with the issue of radicalization. To ensure neutral treatment *within* the Muslim population, police must therefore ensure they also build trust in young Muslims and engage with young Muslims' views as much as they would adult Muslims' views. Finally, in my personal conversations with police, some have indicated the challenges they face in navigating the cultural sensitivities of engaging with Muslim women. Often, male family members are required to be present when police enter a Muslim's house. Muslim women can also sometimes be reluctant to contact police in times of need without the expressed permission of their husbands or sons (cf. chapter 6). This is where learning about the Islamic culture is so important. When police have a genuine interest in learning about the Islamic culture and the expectations of police when dealing with Muslim women, this demonstrates to Muslims that police have trustworthy motives. Such actions will enable more effective engagement and consultation with a broad and representative cross-section of the Muslim population (for the importance and ways of learning about other cultures, see Liu, Volčič and Gallois 2019).

CONCLUSIONS

The policing of Muslim communities is a complex issue, particularly as it relates to counterterrorism policing. This chapter highlights that effectively engaging with Muslim communities is crucial in the fight against terrorism. Community-based policing that pays close attention to the tenets of procedural justice is most likely to promote Muslims' trust in police. The value of such an approach is that it is more likely to result in the voluntary provision of key terrorism-related intelligence than more interventionist approaches that stigmatize and marginalize Muslim communities. While implementing procedural justice in community-based policing can be a challenge, it is important because procedural justice also communicates to Muslim communities that they are respected partners in the fight against terrorism; it conveys that they are valued and respected members of society.

While this chapter discussed a number of ways in which police officers might adopt procedural justice into their engagement efforts, it is important that wider operational and policy changes are also made within police agencies. For example, employing more officers from diverse backgrounds (including Muslim police officers) will demonstrate to the community that police are representative of those they serve. However, broader societal changes also need to be made. In particular, the use of anti-Muslim rhetoric by conservative politicians and media outlets worldwide needs to stop. Messaging that associates violent extremism solely with Islam can be both stigmatizing to Muslim communities and can lead to Islamophobia in the wider community (Choudhury and Fenwick 2011). Khader (2015) notes that it can make Muslims vulnerable to extremist movements. Prime Minister Jacinda Ardern's widely praised response to the 2019 Christchurch massacre of fifty-one Muslims, in contrast, demonstrated compassion for Muslims while at the same time highlighted how leaders should communicate messages of solidarity. Prime Minister Ardern's message was simple. It highlighted that we are all part of one community, regardless of our race or religion. Her message was so important because without unity at the societal level, the fight against terrorism will never be won despite how procedurally just police may be with Muslim communities.

NOTE

1. I would like to acknowledge the funding support of the Australian Research Council (Grant No: FT180100139).

REFERENCES

Awan, Imran, and Surinder Guru. 2017. "Parents of Foreign 'Terrorist' Fighters in Syria: Will They Report Their Young?" *Ethnic and Racial Studies* 40 (1): 24–42.
Blackwood, Leda, Nick Hopkins, and Steve Reicher. 2013. "I Know Who I Am, But Who Do They Think I Am? Muslim Perspectives on Encounters with Airport Authorities." *Ethnic and Racial Studies* 36 (6): 1090–108.
Bradford, Ben, Kristina Murphy, and Jonathan Jackson. 2014. "Officers as Mirrors: Policing, Procedural Justice and the (Re)production of Social Identity." *British Journal of Criminology* 54 (4): 527–50.
Bullock, Karen, and Paul Johnson. 2018. "Police Engagement with Muslim Communities: Breaking Out, Breaking In, and Breaking Through." *Policing and Society* 28 (8): 879–97.
Cherney, Adrian. 2018. "Police Community Engagement and Outreach in a Counterterrorism Context." *Journal of Policing, Intelligence and Counter Terrorism* 13 (1): 60–79.
Cherney, Adrian, and Jason Hartley. 2017. "Community Engagement to Tackle Terrorism and Violent Extremism: Challenges, Tensions and Pitfalls." *Policing and Society* 27 (7): 750–63.
Cherney, Adrian, and Kristina Murphy. 2016. "Being a Suspect Community in a Post 9/11 World: The Impact of the War on Terror on Muslim Communities in Australia." *Australian and New Zealand Journal of Criminology* 49 (4): 480–96.

Cherney, Adrian, and Kristina Murphy. 2017. "Police and Community Cooperation in Counter Terrorism: Evidence and Insights from Australia." *Studies in Conflict and Terrorism* 40 (12): 1023–37.

Choi, Charles, Gholam Khajavy, Rana Raddawi, and Howard Giles. 2019. "Perceptions of Police-Civilian Encounters: Intergroup and Communication Dimensions in the United Arab Emirates and the USA." *Journal of International and Intercultural Communication* 12 (1): 82–104.

Choudhury, Tufyal, and Helen Fenwick. 2011. "The Impact of Counter-Terrorism Measures on Muslim Communities." *International Review of Law, Computers and Technology* 25 (3): 151–81.

Glasford, Demis. 2016. "Understanding Community Responses to Authority/Law Enforcement Minority-Outreach Intergroup Communication Frames." *START Research Brief*. The National Consortium for the Study of Terrorism and Responses to Terrorism: University of Maryland.

Global Terrorism Index 2017. *Measuring and Understanding the Impact of Terrorism*. Sydney: Institute for Economics and Peace. Retrieved from http://visionofhumanity.org/app/uploads/2017/11/Global-Terrorism-Index-2017.pdf .

Hasisi, Badi, Yorum Margalioth, and Liav Orgad. 2012. "Ethnic Profiling in Airport Screening: Lessons from Israel, 1968–2010." *American Law and Economics Review* 14 (2): 517–60.

Hillyard, Paddy. 1993. *Suspect Community: People's Experience of the Prevention of Terrorism Acts in Britain*. London: Pluto Press.

Hinds, Lyn, and Kristina Murphy. 2007. "Public Satisfaction with Police: Using Procedural Justice to Improve Police Legitimacy." *The Australian and New Zealand Journal of Criminology* 40 (1): 27–42.

Huq, Aziz, Tom R. Tyler, and Stephen Schulhofer. 2011a. "Mechanisms for Eliciting Cooperation in Counterterrorism Policing: Evidence from the United Kingdom." *Journal of Empirical Legal Studies,* 8 (4): 728–61.

Huq, Aziz, Tom R. Tyler, and Stephen Schulhofer. 2011b. "Why Does the Public Cooperate with Law Enforcement? The Influence of the Purposes and Targets of Policing." *Psychology, Public Policy, and Law* 17 (3): 419–50.

Innes, Martin. 2006. "Policing Uncertainty: Countering Terror through Community Intelligence and Democratic Policing." *Annals of the American Academy of Political and Social Science* 605 (1): 222–41.

Karp, Paul. 2018. "Morrison Urges Muslim Community to Be More 'Proactive' in Tackling Terrorism." *The Guardian*, November 12. Retrieved from https://www.theguardian.com/australia-news/2018/nov/12/morrison-urges-muslim-community-to-be-more-proactive-in-tackling-terrorism .

Khader, Jamil. 2015. "Repeating Fundamentalism and the Politics of the Commons: The *Charlie Hebdo* Tragedy and the Contradiction of Global Capitalism." *Islamophobia Studies Journal* 3 (1): 12–28.

Lind, E. Allan, Ruth Kanfer, and P. Christopher Earley. 1990. "Voice, Control, and Procedural Justice: Instrumental and Noninstrumental Concerns in Fairness Judgements." *Journal of Personality and Social Psychology* 59 (5): 952–59.

Liu, Shuang, Zala Volčič, and Cindy Gallois. 2019. *Introducing Intercultural Communication: Global Cultures and Contexts*. Thousand Oaks: Sage.

Lynch, Andrew, Nicola McGarrity, and George Williams. 2015. *Inside Australia's Anti-Terrorism Laws and Trials*. Sydney: NewSouth Books.

Madon, Natasha, Kristina Murphy, and Adrian Cherney. 2016. "Promoting Community Collaboration in Counter-Terrorism: Do Social Identities and Perceptions of Legitimacy Mediate Reactions to Procedural Justice Policing?" *British Journal of Criminology* 57 (5): 1144–64.

Mastrofski, Stephen. 2006. "Community Policing: A Skeptical View." In *Police Innovation: Contrasting Perspectives*, edited by David Weisburd and Anthony Braga, 45–68. Cambridge: Cambridge University Press.

Murphy, Kristina. 2017. *The QPS Connected Women's Program Evaluation Report: Pre- and Post-Program Survey Findings*. Brisbane: Griffith University.

Murphy, Kristina, and Julie Barkworth. 2014. "Victim Willingness to Report Crime to Police: Does Procedural Justice or Outcome Matter Most?" *Victims and Offenders* 9 (2): 178–204.

Murphy, Kristina, and Adrian Cherney. 2018. "Policing Marginalized Groups in a Diverse Society: Using Procedural Justice to Promote Group Belongingness and Trust in Police." In *Police-Citizen*

Relations across the World, edited by Dietrich Oberwittler and Sebastian Roche, 153–74. New York: Routledge.

Murphy, Kristina, Adrian Cherney, and Julie Barkworth. 2015. *Avoiding Community Backlash in the Fight against Terrorism*. Australian Research Council Report, University of Queensland and Griffith University.

Murphy, Kristina, Adrian Cherney, and Marcus Teston. 2018. "Promoting Muslims' Willingness to Report Terror Threats to Police: Testing Competing Theories of Procedural Justice." *Justice Quarterly* 36 (4): 594–619.

Murphy, Kristina, Natasha Madon, and Adrian Cherney. 2017. "Promoting Muslims' Cooperation with Police in Counter Terrorism: The Interaction between Procedural Justice, Police Legitimacy and Law Legitimacy." *Policing: An International Journal* 40 (3): 544–59.

Murphy, Kristina, Natasha Madon, and Adrian Cherney. 2020. "Reporting Threats of Terrorism: Stigmatization, Procedural Justice and Policing Muslims in Australia." *Policing and Society* 20 (4): 361–377.

Murphy, Kristina, Lorraine Mazerolle, and Sarah Bennett. 2014. "Promoting Trust in Police: Findings from a Randomized Experimental Field Trial of Procedural Justice Policing." *Policing and Society* 24 (4): 405–24.

Nagin, Daniel, and Cody Telep. 2017. "Procedural Justice and Legal Compliance." *Annual Review of Law and Social Science* 13 (5): 5–28.

Radburn, Matthew, and Clifford Stott. 2019. "The Social Psychological Processes of 'Procedural Justice': Concepts, Critiques and Opportunities." *Criminology and Criminal Justice* 19 (4): 421–38.

Ratcliffe, Jerry. 2011. "Intelligence-led Policing." In *Environmental Criminology and Crime Analysis*, edited by Richard Wortley and Lorraine Mazerolle, 263–80. New York: Routledge.

Schulhofer, Stephen, Tom R. Tyler, and Aziz Huq. 2011. "American Policing at the Crossroads: Unsustainable Policies and the Procedural Justice Alternative." *Journal of Criminal Law and Criminology* 101 (2): 335–74.

Spalek, Basia. 2010. "Community Policing, Trust and Muslim Communities in Relation to the 'New Terrorism.'" *Politics and Policy* 38 (4): 789–815.

Spalek, Basia, and Robert Lambert. 2008. "Muslim Communities, Counter Terrorism and De-Radicalization: A Reflective Approach to Engagement." *International Journal of Law, Crime and Justice* 36 (4): 257–70.

Spalek, Basia, and Robert Lambert. 2010. "Policing within a Counter Terrorism Context Post 7/7: The Importance of Partnership, Dialogue and Support When Engaging with Muslim Communities." In *The "New" Extremism in 21st Century Britain*, edited by Roger Eatwell and Matthew Goodwin, 103–22. London: Taylor and Francis.

Sunshine, Jason, and Tom R. Tyler. 2003. "The Role of Procedural Justice and Legitimacy in Shaping Public Support for Policing." *Law and Society Review* 37 (3): 513–47.

Thomas, Paul, Michelle Grossman, Samim Miah, and Kris Christmann. 2017. *Community Reporting Thresholds: Sharing Information with Authorities concerning Violent Extremist Activity and Involvement in Foreign Conflict*. CREST Report 17-018-01, Lancaster University, UK.

Tyler, Tom R. 2011. *Why People Cooperate*. Princeton: Princeton University Press.

Tyler, Tom R., and Yuen Huo. 2002. *Trust in the Law: Encouraging Public Cooperation with the Police and Courts*. New York: Russel Sage Foundation.

Tyler, Tom R., Stephen Schulhofer, and Aziz Huq. 2010. "Legitimacy and Deterrence Effects in Counterterrorism Policing: A Study of Muslim Americans." *Law and Society Review* 44 (22): 365–402.

Vermeulen, Florence. 2014. "Suspect Communities—Targeting Violent Extremism at the Local Level: Policies of Engagement in Amsterdam, Berlin, and London." *Terrorism and Political Violence* 26 (2): 286–306.

Williams, Michael, John Hogan, and William Evans. 2016. "The Critical Role of Friends in Networks for Countering Violent Extremism: Toward a Theory of Vicarious Help-Seeking." *Behavioral Sciences of Terrorism and Political Aggression* 8 (1): 45–65.

CHAPTER 9

Law Enforcement Partnerships

Changing Communication Skills and Interventions in Response to People in Crisis

Ellen Scrivner

Police leaders across the country have been facing challenges responding to the growing needs of people with behavioral health issues, which can include a range of mental health crises such as mental illness, developmental disabilities, substance abuse disorders, homelessness, or reactions to varied stressors that are experienced as overwhelming. These challenges initially emerged when state mental hospitals and community mental health resources began to lose funding and were forced to shut down. Law enforcement then had to step in and respond to those with mental health crises and eventually became the initial point of contact for many individuals in the community who needed help in dealing with their crises and who faced serious threats of incarceration. Consequently, law enforcement found a need to adopt changes in communication skills and intervention strategies. Many of the skills and strategies involved intergroup relations that were based on research directed at building trust and empathy (Hill and Giles 2018). These findings were helpful to local law enforcement, particularly as they began to collaborate with mental health practitioners and behavioral specialists. Accordingly, these partnerships and the changes in communication were instrumental in developing processes to ensure that individuals in crises could receive the assistance they needed and be diverted from incarceration (see chapter 4).

This chapter highlights how improvement in the police response to crisis situations evolved and how crisis intervention programs and crisis intervention teams (CIT) have become significant initiatives in the law enforcement community since police respond to many different types of crises. In this chapter, the terms *crisis* and *crises* refer to situations that may not be criminal, but where subjects demonstrate behaviors that raise concerns both for their own safety and for that of others. These types of crises are generally related to behavioral and mental health conditions where a different type of patrol response is needed that focuses on de-escalation. They also require a change in communication skills, which contrast to what first responders use when responding to criminal incidents. Within this context, informed discussions on crisis intervention approaches suggest that they have been instrumental in resolving these situations by getting help for affected individuals and ensuring their safety, as well as the safety of the police officers who respond.

Despite the growing popularity of CIT, a recent meta-analysis conducted by Taheri (2016) suggests that the research evidence on its effects varies. Hence, this chapter will review the varied research findings on how CIT works to determine what we really know about CIT in terms of research evidence and what are the research gaps. Moreover, in addition to changes in crisis-communication skills and related research findings, the chapter will also address the training and the formation of new partnerships that are essential to the development of the skills needed to respond to these situations. Successful programs, however, also need to be based on policies that address these complex situations, as well as changes in supervisory and management responses. As such, the chapter will discuss crisis response models that incorporate these strategies and techniques and that use the intergroup contact processes to focus on developing collaborative partnerships with the mental health community and behavior specialists, a critical factor in successful programs. Further, what is known as the Memphis Model will be explored since it has become the prototype model for law enforcement organizations across the United States.

Finally, the chapter will address how the change in the traditional police mindsets embedded throughout law enforcement history are changing. Within that context, mindsets are evolving that incorporate broader roles for public safety initiatives and for collaborative community problem-solving (see chapter 12). These broader roles may become even more dominant should community crises, such as national emergencies, continue to evolve. These broader roles may also play a key role in addressing the unfortunate and troubling increase in officer suicides, which are themselves viewed as part of the crisis spectrum. Accordingly, officers trained in crisis intervention could be called upon to help their colleagues should concerns arise about suicidal or other self-destructive tendencies. As such, the development of evidence-based programs that will provide both the individual in crisis and the responding officers with the best tools available to get the needed help and to keep everyone safe will remain a priority.

HISTORICAL PERSPECTIVE

Over the years, law enforcement adapted a communication style frequently described as *command and control* or more often referred to colloquially as the *"we-they"* approach (see chapter 1). While this type of communication was connected to what was then called the *professional model of policing* (Kelling and Moore 1988), even at that time many viewed it as a form of scapegoat thinking. However, going back to the 1970s, the policing culture had started to evolve as some police leaders became more progressive and started to experiment with what was then called "team policing" (Sherman 1973). As law enforcement's commitment to testing new policing strategies became more apparent, they began to lay the groundwork for substantive change (Walker 1993).

Given these trends, it still took time for traditional approaches to policing to begin changing. Strategic innovations were not always welcomed by first responders and were not viewed as maintaining standards, an important element of an officer's career life. Consequently, while many in law enforcement were receptive to the ideal of developing new on-scene skills, others did not agree with proposed changes in the communication skillset. Further, it is somewhat surprising that an element of this mindset persists today as evidenced in a review of current training schedules and academy curricula, where even modern law enforcement training remains focused more on firearms training and defensive tactics. For example, as of 2016, in training schedules reviewed by the Police Executive Research Forum (PERF), there was little emphasis on communication or the crisis intervention and de-escalation skills that are needed to address crisis situations (PERF 2016). In addition to the need for training about how to respond to situations using strategies other than aggressive command and control, agencies also need policies specifically related to these types of incidents. They also need trained supervisors who can select an approach that matches the needs of the situation, whether a traditional command and control approach or a more nuanced approach that is appropriate for certain types of crisis situations.

Many of the needed changes in policy, training, and supervision are clearly linked to the community policing philosophy and its associated practices (see chapter 10). These have been implemented by law enforcement leadership across the country and incorporate the collaborative engagement and problem-solving partnerships needed for resolving community problems, including intervening in mental health crises. Although community policing began to evolve through initiatives by progressive police chiefs going back to the 1950s, it clearly came into its own with the passage of the Violent Crime Control and Law Enforcement Act of 1994 (US Congress 1994). This included grant funding for one hundred thousand community policing officers and the establishment of the Office of Community Oriented Policing Services in the US Department of Justice. These grants were supported by a nationwide training program known as the Regional Community Policing Institutes (RCPI).

These training institutes helped police departments across the country implement the community policing philosophy and related problem-solving practices and changed how police responded to local issues while collaborating with the community to solve crime problems. As such, this was no longer a situation where some progressive police chiefs were willing to take a chance on making innovative change. Rather, chiefs across the country were engaging in organizational strategies to address public safety issues including preventing crime and eliminating the fear it creates; earning the trust of the community by creating very different community relationships; and supporting community members as stakeholders in solving issues related to crime. The latter also required a much broader range of communication skills, in contrast to relying primarily on command and control (see Hollywood, Goodison, Woods, Vermeer, and Jackson 2019). As such, community policing helped to change law enforcement communication styles and broadened intergroup contact activity through the development of the collaborative partnerships that were designed to build trust and respect while also fostering transparent community engagement (Community Oriented Policing Services 2014).

While the crisis intervention model was not developed as a direct result of the community policing philosophy, both did seem to come together as law enforcement was becoming more progressive and willing to try more creative approaches to problem-solving. Accordingly, both use similar forms of collaborative problem-solving communication and establish important partnerships to do so. The building of these partnerships required changes in styles, particularly when those partnerships included mental health service providers and behavioral health specialists who support jail diversion for mentally ill people who are not engaged in criminal activities. This process is another example of the value of research on intergroup contact theory, which lays the groundwork for creating successful intergroup outcomes where trust building can be strengthened (Hill and Giles 2018).

These collaborative partnerships are key to achieving an effective response and can take different forms, many of which are dependent upon state law or city/county ordinances. Yet, there is a growing trend for law enforcement to develop these partnerships to create and maintain an effective and much needed professional crisis response. As such, we have seen the development of an innovative first responder model of police-based crisis intervention with communication, health care, and advocacy partnerships. While first developed in Memphis, Tennessee, it has now spread throughout the country; what has become known as the *Memphis Model* has become the exemplar for other cities and/or law enforcement agencies.

Memphis Crisis Intervention Model

With few exceptions, modern CIT efforts are generally built upon the Memphis Model, one of the earliest crisis intervention team responses to mental health crises. Although other related approaches are being tested throughout the country, the Memphis Model is generally recognized as the prototype. It was developed by the Memphis Police Department in 1988, following the fatal shooting of a mentally ill person who also had a substance abuse problem. Under the guidance of a prominent professional psychologist, Dr. Randolph Dupont, and police Major Sam Cochran, in addition to the local chapter of the National Alliance for the Mentally Ill (NAMI), the police department and its partners created a specialized police-based program to improve how Memphis officers interacted with individuals with mental illness. The goal was to improve the safety of all involved and, when possible, engage in pre-booking jail diversion (DuPont and Cochran 2000).

The CIT program that they created is a specialized police-based response program. It is designed to provide training for self-selected officers who receive forty hours of classroom and experiential training, as well as yearly eight-hour refresher courses. The training focuses on de-escalation and defusing as well as the communication skills needed to deal with people in crises. These officers are then dispatched to crisis incidents and serve as the specialized first responders who work with treatment services in a collaborative manner to ensure diversion from jail terms, when possible, and provide access to appropriate mental health treatment for the individual(s) involved.

Bringing together the police and mental health specialists was a major factor in their success in that they engaged in collaborative problem-solving that subsequently addressed system change, accessibility to the community, and protection of people in crisis. Further, through this complex level of collaboration, the CIT officers enhanced their interactions with individuals with mental illness and with their local NAMI chapter.

In addition to helping the mentally ill receive treatment instead of incarceration and jail terms, the CIT process also purported to reduce use of force and enhance the safety of both the mentally ill and of the police officers who volunteered to become part of the crisis intervention team. This program has provided a popular model for police departments across the country and, though it continues to develop and expand, there is only limited research available to support the expansion. Hence, there is a need for a much stronger research base than what currently exists.

Research Findings

As the Memphis Model gained recognition by police professionals, Compton, Bahora, Watson, and Oliva (2008) reported that it had been replicated by law enforcement agencies across the United States (see Compton et al. 2011). Many felt it had decreased the use of force in crisis situations and helped officers feel more prepared to respond and link subjects to appropriate care. Many of these assessments were based on interviews or surveys with officers, but evaluations or outcome studies were more limited. Thus, even though it continues to receive positive reviews, with the exception of a meta-analysis conducted by Taheri (2016), the research findings on crisis intervention remain limited and somewhat confusing.

Initially, most of the early research on crisis intervention used the Memphis Model and was conducted by social science professionals who had a strong interest in programs that brought the social sciences and law enforcement together. However, Deane, Steadman, Borum, Veysey, and Morrissey (1999) had concerns that law enforcement might have mixed success in responding to situations involving the mentally ill and that people could be incarcerated inappropriately, or that the situation could end up in a use-of-force problem (see Steadman, Morrisey, Deane, and Borum 2002). Given their concerns, they examined the effectiveness of three sites with different type of programs designed to keep people with mental illness out of jail. These sites included Birmingham, Alabama (in-house mental health specialists); Memphis, Tennessee (CIT Program); and Knoxville, Tennessee (Mobile Mental Health Crisis Response Team). Their findings suggested that specialized programs such as innovative "pre-booking" diversion programs can provide police with alternatives to arrests. Further, they could help keep people with mental illness out of jail and facilitate access to treatment. Deane et al. (1999) also reported that in these samples, just over 6 percent of encounters ended up resulting in arrest among the three sites and that the Memphis CIT Program received the most positive ratings from nonspecialized officers on the force. Deane et al. (1999) attributed these findings to the fact that the program is police-based and that the city has a "police-friendly" mental health system that provides a drop-off site with a no-refusal policy. As such, they related CIT program success to two main factors: the psychiatric triage, or drop-off center, and community partnerships.

As the Memphis Model gained recognition by police professionals, Compton, Bahora, Watson, and Oliva (2008) also reported that it had been replicated by law enforcement agencies across the United States and was viewed as having decreased the use of force in crisis situations. However, their continuing and extensive review of the research on CIT programs showed different results. In that case, they ended up finding only twelve studies that could be defined as empirical research conducted in sites where the Memphis Model was in place, and their findings were quite different from those of Deane et al. (1999). Compton et al. (2008) concluded that after twenty years, very little could be said with confidence about the effectiveness of CITs. While they did cite CIT training as positively affecting officers' ability to accurately identify and respond to the mentally ill, few of the studies they reviewed had data on arrests or interactions with the police, and they could not say that it reduced the use of force.

While different from SWAT (special weapons and tactics) and hostage negotiations, which are common responses to very different types of police crisis situations, the Memphis Model could be applied to other types of crises such as those affecting the homeless, veterans with PTSD, or other incidents that require de-escalation to keep people safe during community emergencies. However, there is still a need for a stronger research base to get a better picture of how CIT results are supported by research evidence. While crisis intervention, and particularly the Memphis Model, continue to receive positive reviews despite variable research findings, more recent questions have evolved, such as those raised by Watson, Compton, and Draine (2017) who provide a more recent summary of research findings. Their results led them to question if CIT can be defined as an evidence-based practice. Further, results from the meta-analysis conducted by Taheri (2016) promote questions about the capacity of the Memphis Model for crisis intervention teams to reduce arrests and improve officer safety. While her analysis is the most comprehensive to date, only eight studies met the inclusion criteria. She concluded that the Memphis Model remains a prototype but that the use of CIT did not reduce arrests or use of force. Further, it did not increase feelings of security among officers. While the meta-analysis data are very important, the differences in program design across the sample agencies suggest that more intensive research on programs with similar designs is needed.

Clearly, the questions raised by these studies suggest that more rigorous analyses of CIT programs are necessary. This research is particularly important since the CIT model has been a key component of several US Department of Justice (DOJ) consent decrees mandating reform among local police agencies with a pattern or practice of misconduct. Lawrence and Cole (2019) examined twenty-one jurisdictions with consent decrees in place across a twenty-year timeframe (1997–2017). The most common targets of police reform agencies included use of force; stops, searches, and arrests; and bias-free policing (see chapter 5). Their report addressed the implementation of crisis intervention teams and the use of CIT-trained officers in instances where a subject may be experiencing mental health issues. As such, the CIT model could be viewed more as a de-escalation strategy that is part of a substantive crisis intervention program, which has a significant place in many DOJ consent decrees.

Such is also consistent with the findings from the Patterns and Practices Assessment of Law Enforcement Agencies' Delivery of Police Services (1994 Violent Crime Control and Law Enforcement Act, Section 14141), which provides the initial evaluation as to how the foundations of constitutional policing are being enacted without violating the rights of community members. If the assessment of police practices and behaviors raises questions as to constitutional concerns within DOJ, they may lead to the development of a consent decree. Their assessments highlight how communication is intricately related to appropriate crisis management, as well as constitutional policing, and how it clearly affects the response of people in crisis should they be treated with disrespect.

Given these issues, it is not unusual that other models for crisis intervention for law enforcement may develop, although many seem to continue the efforts of the 1988 Memphis Model, which still continues to evolve. Further, data-based estimates from Gahens (2018) show that between 7 and 10 percent of police–citizen encounters involve citizens with mental health conditions. Hence, the probability of law enforcement continuing to implement crisis intervention models retains a level of importance. Gahens's data also add additional support to the growing trends for law enforcement to implement crisis intervention models despite some of the earlier questions from referenced research that questions its effectiveness. These questions need continuous exploration.

DATA ON THE CRISIS INTERVENTION MODEL

Accordingly, the crisis intervention model represents a collaborative effort of police, mental health professionals, and community advocates who join together as partners to ensure that a police response protocol will improve outcomes and prioritize safety for all parties involved. The data from different sources support the premise that the crisis intervention model has clearly gained recognition over the years. That recognition comes from providing unique partnerships that benefit the whole community and not just the individual in crisis and their families, though all may not have families. The level of collaboration required involves more than just designating an on-site team approach. Rather, most engage in regular meetings and, in many of the teams, the police and a mental health professional respond to a call together or meet and confer at the hospital or at a designated service center. These partnerships clearly have a range of benefits aside from keeping the mentally ill out of jail and include the following (Gahens 2018):

- Reduced injuries of individuals in crisis
- Better access to treatment for individuals in crisis
- Reduced involvement with the justice system for low-level offenders
- More efficient disposition of mental health calls for service
- Fewer officer injuries
- Fewer repeat calls for service

- Families can call police during a crisis with less fear of arrest or injury
- Victims are at a reduced likelihood of repeat victimization
- Society, due to increased awareness, can combat stigma surrounding mental health

Crisis Intervention Teams

Central to the crisis intervention model are the CITs composed of officers, usually self-selected, because of their interest and ability to work with people in crises situations. They are specially trained in crisis intervention and work in collaboration with behavioral health specialists to respond to varied crises. These situations can be characterized by mental illness conditions that impair an individual's cognitive, emotional, or behavioral functions, and which may be caused by social, psychological, biochemical, genetic, or other factors. As a result, their training helps them to develop a greater understanding of mental illness and how to respond to someone who is experiencing conditions that can range from severe depression to outright psychotic behavior.

These specialized CIT officers work in teams with behavioral health specialists, such as the mental health professionals, and in some instances the CIT officers and mental health professionals may train together. This training approach can help to reduce other communication issues that can emerge due to the differences in the professional communication styles of law enforcement and mental health specialists and the different operational styles of their respective agencies. Further, they learn how to negotiate these different systems. In many instances, community advocates may also play a part in ensuring that the CIT officers are trained and utilized appropriately.

CIT training, which is usually conducted over forty hours, exposes the officers to simulated crisis situations and helps them de-escalate situations by improving communication with the individual in crisis; it also focuses on treating them with respect and dignity and establishing rapport. Within this context, they are trained to move slowly; speak in a calm, non-threatening voice with non-intimidating body language; change body language by engaging with the individual through eye contact, non-threatening voice and body language; elicit information rather than issuing orders; and paraphrase what the individual is saying to keep them focused while demonstrating empathy and concern. They are trained not to rush the scene but to try and stabilize it and to prepare for lengthy interactions in contrast to writing a ticket and getting back in service.

These are one-on-one situations, and they need to be aware that distractions such as disruptive citizens in the background can be an upsetting influence and need to be avoided. However, CIT training is not just focused on "skills." It also increases awareness of the variety of community facilities designated to help people in crisis as well as the roles that people in the community can play. This awareness extends to the homeless population, as well, since in many areas, groups like the National Alliance to End Homelessness work with the police to provide relocation and links to support systems that can create a path to stability for those who are homeless.

While the CIT laid the groundwork for patrol officer crisis communication training, some of the techniques that have been employed in use-of-force training are also useful when responding to a crisis. De-escalation skills are particularly important, and PERF has developed a communication model called Integrating Communication, Assessment, and Tactics (ICAT). While not developed specifically as a model for responding to mental health crises, the ICAT model proposes to go beyond crisis intervention teams in order to enhance the first responder's response, skills, and tactics to defuse a range of critical issues and situations that they encounter on patrol. While ICAT is still relatively new, a comprehensive training guide has been pilot tested and released (PERF 2016). It reflects a strong focus on reducing use of force in a wide variety of crises situations and involves critical thinking and variable communication skills when defusing crises.

Prior to the development of ICAT, PERF (2012) convened a summit focused on promising de-escalation strategies. This explored techniques to minimize use of force and included discussions on promising practices and strategies used to de-escalate encounters and minimize using force against people who are in crisis, be it a mental illness, a medical crisis, or a range of crises that first responders encounter. Through their discussion on promising practices, some of the participants highlighted their CIT teams and crisis response models as promising practices. They identified processes with a focus on crises intervention communication, and those agencies included the following:

- Philadelphia PD: A Bridge between Two Worlds, where police get the de-escalation and awareness training and also connect to the mental health industry through a mental health coordinator who helps get people in need into the system so they can get the help they need.
- Chicago PD: Their goal is to have CIT-trained officers on all three watches throughout the city. To ensure that they can readily respond to a crisis, the on-call roster of CIT officers is available in their operations command center so that dispatchers are able to see that a CIT officer is sent immediately to the scene of an identified crisis.
- Albuquerque PD: Believing that CIT alone was not the answer, they developed a different format called COAST (Crisis Outreach and Support Team), which is a multilayered civilian resource available to field officers. COAST helps in bridging the gap between people who are risking incarceration when trying to deal with problems on their own ineffectively and the availability of professionally trained long-term service providers. The civilian teams comprise trained professionals, and the department feels this type of program has been successful as a support process for the community as well as their officers.
- Houston PD: All officers are required to receive forty hours of training and return every other year for an eight-hour refresher course. Advanced CIT training allows for at least eight officers per day to ride with mental health clinicians. Their partnership with the county mental health agency was developed as a chronic consumer stabilization initiative (CCSI) and is designed to keep people from continuing to experience crises. In that respect, it is somewhat different from the other programs, but it does provide officers with information about people in the system so that they know what type of de-escalation to use when they come on the scene of an incident,
- Dallas and Indianapolis PDs were also included in the discussion, but their approach does not highlight crisis communication skills. In contrast, they focus on keeping

the individual physically safe and free from harm, and the on-scene patrol officers engage in a physical containment process designed to meet this goal.

In addition to the programs identified in the PERF (2012) Summit Report, other departments have been identified as having programs that pair officers with mental health workers. They include the Los Angeles Police Department and the New York Police Department, both of which have opted for their own protocols that differ somewhat from the Memphis Model:

- LAPD has a specialized mental evaluation unit with a staff of sixty that includes thirty mental health clinicians who engage as internal team members with the thirty trained officers and they respond to mental health crises as a unified team.
- NYPD has an emergency services unit whose officers have specialized training in emergency services that apply to responding to the needs of emotionally disturbed persons (EDPs). NYPD also trains all officers in basic training to handle crises calls but typically they will call in the specialized unit when they recognize that a crisis is evolving.

This PERF Summit reinforced the need for crisis communications skills for police officers across the country. People with mental health problems who encounter the police due to minor crimes can pose a risk of a volatile situation developing unless they are defused. To address these challenges, many departments are using some variation of the Memphis Model, which is crafted to fit the local needs of their agency and community. Most importantly, the summit also identified how a strong partnership with NAMI has developed and how NAMI is taking on a more prominent role in their work with law enforcement.

Ron Honberg, director of Policy and Legal Affairs, represented NAMI at the 2012 PERF Summit and credited police with making things much better than they were twenty years ago in that CIT now operates all around the country. He acknowledged that where CIT really works is when the mental health system is on board and when there is a true partnership with the police. In other venues, he has stated that once people get to the point of crisis that it is a difficult time to start treatment. Thus, officers responding to early signs of emotional turbulence and helping mental health professionals intervene earlier is the preferred NAMI approach. These situations are some of the most uncertain, and challenging normative conversational rules may not apply to many psychotics who are encountered. Clearly, not everyone in crisis is psychotic, but the type of communication skills needed to defuse crises situations is similar despite the condition of the individual. Typically, the skills are linked to defusing activities that address potentially volatile situations but which treat the individual with dignity and respect.

What we have learned from the previously referenced PERF meetings is that crisis communication is highly significant for defusing crisis situations but that there is also a need for strong collaborative partnerships with behavioral health services and community advocates that support crisis communication as a way of helping, rather than harming, individuals. Most of the partnerships and training that have been discussed highlight a response to people who require services that involve mental health intervention in contrast to jail time. However, to get to that point collaborative partnerships and open communication with behavioral or mental health system personnel are critical. Further, many also referenced how dispatchers and paramedics also need to be trained to recognize these types of calls at the outset.

LAW ENFORCEMENT COLLABORATIVE PARTNERSHIPS

The development of significant partnerships between law enforcement and mental health clearly supports crisis communication. These partnerships are critical to the success of any crisis intervention program. These partnerships can evolve through training together, but at the core of their effectiveness is their capacity to bring law enforcement and mental health/behavior specialists together in a problem-solving mode, both in the field and at regular roundtable meetings. In fact, some police departments, such as the Seattle PD, have appointed an in-house crisis intervention team coordinator who manages these meetings on a regular basis. As such, law enforcement agencies need to engage with other service providers and form a process for all to come together and meet not only to discuss individual crises responses but also to discuss potential resolutions to community problems. Within that context, it is important for community advocates to be included in these problem-solving discussions.

Beyond Crisis Intervention: Programs Focused on Communication to Affect Crime Control

Historically, as questions started to emerge regarding the effectiveness of command and control tactics as the best response for all police incidents, police strategies began expanding and started to focus on communication in general. Beyond CIT programs, many departments started to engage with the Bureau of Justice Assistance Comprehensive Communities Program (BJA-CCP), which examined new solutions for solving crime problems (Kelling et al. 1998). This program was designed to improve the delivery of multiple services, both simultaneously and collaboratively, and community collaboration was emphasized by giving some degree of program control and responsibility to residents of target neighborhoods. While not addressing the mentally ill, the community collaboration for problem-solving started to lay the groundwork for other types of programs to be developed that addressed other types of problems. For example, Boston's Operation Ceasefire targeted reducing gun violence and gang activity across the city and was developed as a problem-oriented policing initiative specifically aimed at reducing youth gun violence in 1995. It used community collaboration and partnerships with other agencies to ensure that services were provided to juvenile and young adult offenders. Rather than utilizing crisis intervention specifically, both the Ceasefire program and the BJA-CCP used collaborative communication to focus on deterrence with gangs across the city (see chapter 20).

Subsequently, the Boston program became an example of crime control and prevention strategies that relied on partnership building and collaboration with the community.

Many of these strategies eventually were recognized as related to the problem-solving pillar of the community policing philosophy as it started to develop across the country following the passage of the 1994 Crime Act. They clearly accentuated the role of collaborative problem-solving between the police and the community, and this level of community engagement was a real change in direction. Unfortunately, the 1994 Crime Act is also blamed for an increase in incarceration, which has damaged its reputation and distracted attention away from the spread of community policing, which is an important outcome of the Act (Sabol and Johnson 2019).

While crisis communication may have played a significant role in some of the public health approaches to public safety, frequently these programs were focused on others beyond the mentally ill such as youth or gang members involved in crimes (see chapter 20). Therefore, defusing crises may not have seemed like a priority. However, any public health emergency poses challenges to all officers and while the city may have the broader governing power, the police have unique roles in that they are charged with responding to everyday service demands while also managing crowds, protecting health facilities, and more recently responding to the growing number of "active shooters." As the crisis continuum evolves and multiplies, protecting the community and maintaining public order, while also protecting officers, become major priorities; and any group of skills that enhance this capacity is welcomed. Within that context, more departments are now also providing crisis intervention training in their recruit and in-service classes, in addition to maintaining very strong CITs.

Use of Technology

Police use of technology such as GIS mapping and data-driven Compstat laid the groundwork for the expanding use of technology by law enforcement, including the development of computer technology for records management, in-car computers, department websites, and social media account. These changes have helped meet the needs for modern means of communication which are no longer just an option for law enforcement; they are the new reality.

Given the growing role of technology in law enforcement, one might question if there are specific technologies that can help with crisis intervention. Within that context, technology that is helpful to crisis responses include body-worn cameras, in-car videos, smartphones, and other mobile devices that provide real-time data, clarify the changing situation, and maximize situational awareness. As the crisis continuum continues to expand beyond dealing just with individuals in crisis, other technologies may become more dominant in the field. As of now, the referenced devices are becoming standard law enforcement tools that also increase officer accountability and enhance the safety of all concerned, particularly those in crisis situations.

Beyond crisis communication, information technology continues to grow in other ways in law enforcement, such as crime forecasting via crime data and precinct-level crime forecasting centers. Also, in today's world, department websites and social media accounts are well-established information tools that can enhance the flow of information to the community and enhance police marketing efforts for purposes such as public relations and recruiting. While not all information options are relevant to crisis intervention, it may only be a matter of time before we see technologies specifically identified to work with CIT. The CIT Center at the University of Memphis as well as he International CIT Center are both examples of what can happen to not only enhance the spread of best practices but also expand the flow of information by incorporating technology sites.

When it comes to crisis communication, however, there is a need to make sure that information is getting to the right people in mental health and that privacy is not violated or information revealed that is considered confidential. Further, there is a need to make sure that the use of social media does not expand a crisis situation, since words can travel as the situation evolves and more people become involved. In those cases, CIT officers could then be in a difficult situation in having to use crowd management techniques while they are trying to defuse the individual crisis. As social media continues to expand and rapid dissemination of information increases, it will be important to determine strategies that need to be considered to mitigate the exacerbation of dynamic and unfolding crises.

Impact on Officers

All programs previously referenced can have an impact on a police officer but the involvement in crisis intervention can also impact an officer's personal life. Given their training and ongoing responses to calls, changes in their communications skills and propensity for in-depth analysis of problems, their capacity to interact appropriately with people who are upset, and changes in demeanor that supports respectful interactions with others, in contrast to command and control, all go home with the officer. As a result, they may start to seem different to family and friends as they start to engage differently with the people around them. Some of those differences may be viewed as positive by those in their personal lives, and their collaboration with those in mental health or the behavioral specialists can add new information to their problem-solving approach. However, we know very little about how CIT officers would respond should they encounter their own personal or interpersonal crises. While they may be more responsive to seeking help through resources provided by their departments, it is not clear if involvement with CIT removes the identified stigma that frequently keeps officers from seeking help. One might assume that it would, given their regular interactions with those in the mental health fields, but the reality is that we do not know.

We also do not know how their CIT role and communication skills impact their responsiveness to colleagues in crisis, particularly those who may be suicidal. What looks like a growing trend in the first responder community, police officer suicide seems to be on the verge of becoming a national issue and is having a very negative impact on all of law enforcement. While no federal agency tracks the numbers of police suicides, according to BLUE H.E.L.P. (2018), a Massachusetts nonprofit group dedicated to helping officers with PTSD and other mental health issues, at least 167 police officers took their lives in 2018, and by September 2019, 142 had died by suicide. From the chiefs on down, police are struggling with how to respond to this problem.

Clearly, CIT officers are not trained in police suicide prevention; but given their role on their squads and their training in communication skills, they may recognize when a colleague is considering a self-destructive approach to their problems before it is too late. Further, they also have more information about getting help through their agency EAPs, professional psychologists or social workers who may be on staff or contracted by their departments, or peer support programs. Helping a colleague get the help they need before it is too late could be a real asset and would certainly help remove the stigma associated with seeking mental health assistance, as well as give voice to what has become something of a silent crisis in law enforcement.

CONCLUSIONS

Crisis intervention and related crisis communication skills are clearly reflective of how law enforcement has changed over the years moving from the "professional/we-they" model to what we are seeing today that includes a process that integrates community policing, problem-solving policing, collaboration, and transparency.

Accordingly, law enforcement's approach to crises has changed and continues to evolve from what has been described as the Memphis Model, which primarily deals with defusing situations with the mentally ill and ensuring that they are diverted from jail and receive appropriate treatment. This model continues to dominate the field and remains the most well-defined mode of collaboration to improve the police response to mental health crises. It is also important to note that as new types of crises are emerging, some of which do not involve mentally ill people—such as variations in the homeless population—crisis communications become more of a priority for all officers and not just specially trained CIT officers. However, the partnership focus of CIT will remain a critical distinction.

Police often must work with specialists in other agencies who may have very different communication skills that they use in problem resolution, as do many of the community advocates who are involved in these partnerships. Given that these groups are helping to advance law enforcement despite any differences in communication, it is important that these groups meet with the police on a regular basis to continue to advance the collaborative solutions that have been developed in a transparent manner.

This chapter has highlighted key issues that reflect how the development of the crisis intervention process and related communication skills introduced important changes into law enforcement. Clearly law enforcement partnerships and related changes in communication with those in crisis, have changed dramatically. Involvement of the community in the strategic problem-solving process has introduced new ideas for problem solutions from the partnerships developed between the community and law enforcement, and law enforcement appears open to this type of problem-solving. In contrast to prior years, more than just the command staff are involved in introducing change throughout the department; and, within this context, we now see more than field personnel involved in responding to change. We also see non-law enforcement personnel included, since they, too, have a role in improving policing and problem-solving (see chapter 4).

Clearly, a stronger research base is needed to establish CIT as an evidence-based practice or to determine if other intervention models work better to resolve different types of problems. As such, the research needs to be more formalized, rigorous, and outcome-oriented; and solid evidence is needed to learn what works best in diverse jurisdictions. Consequently, we need to continue to learn about other partnerships and other tools or processes available that can enhance communication during these situations, system reforms and benefits. Further, we also need to know a lot more about how, and/or *if*, technology holds any answers to making the control of crisis situations better. In essence, while we know a great deal, we must continue to explore new options and continue with research in order to help maintain stability and community safety in neighborhoods across the country. This exploration becomes particularly important as the types of crises encountered by police continue to grow, but also could be expanding to include dangerous community situations where the police may be the point of contact as well as the means to resolution.

REFERENCES

Blue H.E.L.P. 2018. https://bluehelp.org .

Community Oriented Policing Services. 2014. *The COPS Office: 20 Years of Community Policing*. Washington DC: US Department of Justice.

Compton, Michael T., Masuma Bahora, Amy Watson, and Janet R. Oliva. 2008. "A Comprehensive Review of Extant Research on Crisis Intervention Team (CIT) Programs." *Journal of the American Academy of Psychiatry and the Law* 36 (1): 47–55.

Compton, Michael T., Beth Broussad, Mark Munetz, Janet Oliva, and Amy Watson. 2011. *The Crisis Intervention Team (CIT) Model of Collaboration between Law Enforcement and Mental Health*. Hauppauge: Nova Science.

Deane, Martha W., Henry J. Steadman, Randy Borum, Bonita M. Veysey, and Joseph P. Morrissey. 1999. "Emerging Partnerships between Mental Health and Law Enforcement." *Psychiatric Services* 50 (1): 99–101.

Dupont, Randolph, and Sam Cochran. 2000. "Police Response to Mental Health Emergencies-Barriers to Change." *Journal of the American Academy of Psychiatry and the Law* 28 (3): 338–44.

Gahens, Alyson. 2018. *Responding to Individuals Experiencing Mental Health Crises: Police-Involved Programs*. Chicago: Illinois Criminal Justice Information Authority.

Hill, Shawn, and Howard Giles. 2018. "Using Research to Build Trust and Empathy: Meaningful Change through Intergroup Contact." *Police Chief* 85 (8): 48–53.

Hollywood, John S., Sean E. Goodison, Dulani Woods, Michael J. D. Vermeer, and Brian A. Jackson. 2019. "Fostering Innovation to Respond to Top Challenges in Law Enforcement: Proceedings of the National Institute of Justice's 2018 Chiefs' Panel on Priority Law Enforcement Issues and Needs." Santa Monica: RAND Corporation. Retrieved from https://www.rand.org/pubs/research_reports/RR2930.html .

Kelling, George L., and Michael Moore. 1988. "The Evolving Strategy of Policing." In *Perspectives on Policing,* #4. Washington DC: US Department of Justice. Retrieved from https://pdfs.semanticscholar.org/a614/21a27a6c4fa0e25962ef30e95a22371c1b9c.pdf .

Kelling, George L., Mona Hochberg, Sandra Lee Kaminska, Ann Marie Rocheleau, Dennis Rosenbaum, Jeffrey A. Roth, and Wesley Skogan. 1998. *The Bureau of Justice Assistance Comprehensive Communities Program: A Preliminary Report*. Washington DC: US Department of Justice.

Lawrence, Sara, and Christine Cole. 2019. *Building Capacity: How Police Departments Can Drive Positive Change without Federal Intervention*. Boston: Crime and Justice Institute.

PERF. Police Executive Research Forum. 2012. "An Integrated Approach to De-escalation and Minimizing Use of Force." Washington DC: Police Executive Research Forum.

PERF. Police Executive Research Forum. 2016. *Guiding Principles on Use of Force*. Washington DC: Police Executive Research Forum.

Sabol, William J., and Thaddeus L. Johnson. 2019. "The 1994 Crime Bill: Legacy and Lessons—Impacts on Prison Populations." *Federal Sentencing Reporter* 32 (3): 153–56.

Sherman, Lawrence W. 1973. *Team Policing: Seven Case Studies.* Washington DC: Police Foundation.

Steadman, Henry J., Joseph Morrisey, Martha W. Deane, and Randy Borum. 2002. *Police Response to Emotionally Disturbed Persons: Analyzing New Models of Police Interactions with the Mental Health System.* Final Report #179984. Washington DC: US Department of Justice. Retrieved from https://www.ncjrs.gov/pdffiles1/nij/grants/179984.pdf.

Taheri, Sema A. 2016. "Do Crisis Intervention Teams Reduce Arrests and Improve Officer Safety? A Systematic Review and Meta-Analysis." *Criminal Justice Policy Review* 27 (1): 76–96.

US Congress. 1994. "HR 3355: Violent Crime Control and Law Enforcement of 1994." *Violent Crime Control and Law Enforcement Act of 1994*, H.R. 3355, Pub. L. 103–322.

Walker, Samuel. 1993. "Does Anyone Remember Team Policing? Lessons of the Team Policing Experience for Community Policing." *American Journal of Police* 12 (1): 33–55.

Watson, Amy C., Michael Compton, and Jeffrey N. Draine. 2017. "The Crisis Intervention Team Model (CIT): An Evidence-Based Policing Practice?" *Behavioral Science & the Law* 35 (5–6): 431–41.

SECTION III
COMMUNICATING *ABOUT* POLICING TO AND FROM THE COMMUNITY

CHAPTER 10

The Role of Communication Reform in Community Policing

Edward R. Maguire

The community policing movement represented the most significant era in police organizational change since the introduction of the telephone, automobile, and two-way radio (Reiss 1992). In the United States and elsewhere, community policing has influenced the way police, scholars, policymakers, and the public think about the role of police in society. While community policing is a complex movement comprising many strategies and activities, implicit in much of the reform rhetoric is the need to improve *communications* in the internal and external environments of police organizations (see chapters 2 and 3). This chapter begins by briefly introducing the community policing movement. Next, it outlines the implicit and explicit roles of communication in community policing. It then assesses the available evidence on the influence of community policing on internal and external communication patterns in police organizations. The chapter concludes by reflecting on how police agencies have incorporated communication reform as part of their efforts to enact the internal and external aspects of community policing.

A BRIEF HISTORY OF COMMUNITY POLICING

The roots of the community policing movement extend throughout the history of policing (Greene 2000; Walker 1980), but most analysts attribute its birth to the convergence of several prominent social forces in the United States during the 1960s (Greene 2000). Police historians have noted that until the early 1960s, American policing was a "closed" institution. The average American citizen probably had little knowledge of what police work entailed. Courts devoted little energy toward scrutiny of the police. Policing was largely closed off to the public and their representatives (Walker 1980). Several circumstances in the 1960s converged to expose American policing to the attention and scrutiny of external audiences. The civil rights movement, discontent over the Vietnam War, and other social forces, led a generation of youth to rebel against mainstream society (Barlow and Barlow 2000; Walker 1980). Police are the gatekeepers of mainstream society, and much of the civil unrest during this period brought police into contact with people engaged in various forms of protest, from peaceful civil disobedience to violent rebellion (Maguire 2015; Walker 1980; see chapter 16 and this book's conclusion).

Police use of force and mistreatment of minority citizens became a prominent theme during the 1960s (see chapters 5 and 7). Research conducted during that period showed that many police officers held racist attitudes toward minorities (Bayley and Mendelsohn 1969; Reiss 1971; Westley 1970; see also, chapter 8). Several of the riots that engulfed American cities occurred in the aftermath of police actions such as shootings, traffic stops, or raids occurring in minority neighborhoods (Stark 1972; Walker 1980). The National Advisory Commission on Civil Disorders (1968, 157) found that "deep hostility between police and ghetto communities" was a primary determinant of the urban riots that it studied. The growth of television news meant that many of these encounters between police and citizens were now broadcast to millions of homes on the evening news (Walker 1980). Shocking images of the police beating citizens emerged out of civil rights marches in Birmingham and Selma, Alabama, outside of the 1968 Democratic National Convention in Chicago, and in numerous other cities (Barlow and Barlow 2000; Greene 2000; Walker 1980). For the first time, many Americans began to see news coverage of the police beating people who looked very much like themselves and their loved ones.

Several other factors also led to increased scrutiny of the police. The US Supreme Court, under Chief Justice Earl Warren, began to consider the legality of traditional police procedures. In several landmark cases, the court restricted the powers of the police to conduct searches, obtain confessions, and prevent detainees from consulting with an attorney (Kamisar 2005). While civil libertarians praised this "due process revolution," a vigorous debate emerged about whether these new rules hampered the ability of the police to fight crime (Cassell and Fowles 1998, 2017; Leo 1996). Rising crime rates during the 1960s began to cast doubts on the effectiveness of the police. From 1960 to 1970, violent crime rates more than doubled, increasing from approximately 1.6 to 3.6 violent crimes per thousand population (James 2018). Thus, Americans began to question both the fairness *and* effectiveness of the police (Hindelang 1974, 105–7). Taken together, these factors led to a significant legitimacy crisis for US police.

From 1968 to 1971, three national commissions recommended sweeping reforms in American policing to improve the relationships between police and communities, especially minority communities.[1] For instance, the President's Commission on Law Enforcement and Administration of Justice (1967) recommended that police agencies establish community relations units and citizen advisory committees, improve training on community relations, expand the recruitment of minorities, increase training and education opportunities, enact policies limiting the use of firearms by officers, and adopt dozens of other suggestions intended to improve relationships between police and communities. While it is difficult to pinpoint the precise birth of the community policing movement in the United States, most police scholars start with the crises of the 1960s and the resulting recommendations made by several presidential commissions.[2]

Implicit in many of those recommendations was the need for communication reform in police organizations, both internally and externally.

The Emergence and Growth of Community Policing

Police began to test precursors to the community policing movement in the late 1960s and early 1970s (Walker 1993). These involved efforts to improve the relationships between police and communities and to solve enduring community problems. For instance, several communities instituted "team policing" strategies in which police officers were assigned expanded responsibility for improving conditions in certain impoverished and socially disorganized areas with high crime rates. Although the programs varied by city, they shared three features: a team assigned to a specific geographic area, improved communication and cooperation among team members, and improved communication between the team and the community (Bloch and Specht 1973; Sherman, Milton, and Kelly 1973). These efforts failed to meet their goals for several reasons that were instructive for later community policing reform efforts (Sherman, Milton, and Kelly 1973; Walker 1993).

Many agencies also created community relations units to improve relationships between police and communities. The work of these units was largely symbolic and decoupled from day-to-day encounters between police and the public (Ahern 1972; Bittner 1975; Bordua and Tifft 1971; for an intergroup perspective, see chapter 1). These efforts failed for some of the same reasons that team policing failed. Officers in the units were ridiculed by their peers for not doing "real" police work. Assigning community relations to specialized units isolated it, thus relieving others of the responsibility for this important function. Finally, the units were often unable to share the information they collected from the community with others inside the agency (Moore 1992). Although team policing and community relations units were not successful, they provided a useful foundation for the emerging community policing movement.

Throughout the 1970s, police agencies and researchers continued to institute reforms designed to improve the legitimacy and effectiveness of the police. In 1979, Herman Goldstein sketched the foundation for a new theory of police effectiveness which he called "problem-oriented policing." Goldstein recommended that police agencies stop treating "incidents" as their primary unit of work. Since incidents are often symptoms of one or more underlying problems, Goldstein argued that police should work together with citizens to identify and solve chronic problems rather than merely responding to each specific incident. Goldstein emphasized that police need to address more than just crime; they also need to address disorder and other persistent community problems that promote fear and reduce quality of life. Moreover, police need to be proactive in addressing community problems, not simply reactive. Team policing, community relations units, and problem-oriented policing represented some of the key early building blocks of the community policing movement in the 1970s and 1980s.

By the early 1990s, community policing was becoming widely recognized within policing. It occupied a major role in President Clinton's 1992 election campaign. As part of the 1994 Crime Act, the US government established the Office of Community

Oriented Policing Services (COPS) within the Department of Justice to help disseminate community policing throughout the nation (Zhao, Scheider, and Thurman 2002). As the community policing movement continued to grow, it began to encapsulate other reforms, including problem-oriented policing. Scheider, Chapman, and Schapiro (2009, 694) argued that other popular police reforms were "wholly compatible with the community policing philosophy" and should be conceptualized as falling within community policing rather than as separate innovations.

Treating community policing as a unified reform movement results in a broad definition like the one used by COPS: "Community policing is a philosophy that promotes organizational strategies that support the systematic use of partnerships and problem-solving techniques to proactively address the immediate conditions that give rise to public safety issues such as crime, social disorder, and fear of crime" (Office of Community Oriented Policing Services 2014, 3). According to COPS, community policing has three dimensions: community partnerships, problem-solving, and organizational transformation. Some scholars have adopted similar definitions of community policing that contain three dimensions: community partnerships, problem-solving, and organizational adaptation (Maguire, Kuhns, Uchida, and Cox 1997; Maguire and Wells 2002; Wells and Maguire 2009). All of these definitions have two external dimensions and one internal dimension. The external dimensions (community partnerships and problem-solving) focus on police activities that occur in, and in partnership with, the community. The internal dimension, whether called organizational transformation or adaptation, concentrates on the "alignment of organizational management, structure, personnel, and information systems to support community partnerships and proactive problem solving" (Office of Community Oriented Policing Services 2014, 3; also see Wells and Maguire 2009; Zhao 1996).

Communication reform—especially *intergroup communication*—is an important, though often implicit, element of all three dimensions of community policing. Almost all efforts to improve community partnerships involve intergroup communication, whether asking officers to "stop and talk" to residents and business owners, participate in community meetings and citizen advisory councils, or engage in procedurally just dialogue with people they encounter on the job (Choi and Giles 2012; Hill and Giles 2018). Similarly, social media campaigns involve efforts to improve intergroup relationships between police and the public (see, again, chapter 1). Communication between police and the public is one of the central features of problem-solving. Police must work with the public to identify the problems that deserve attention and to develop appropriate solutions (Goldstein 1979, 1990). Communication also plays a central role in organizational adaptation, from the adoption of management innovations like decentralization or total quality management, to efforts to improve perceptions of organizational justice within the workplace (see chapter 2).

This chapter examines the role of communication reform in the community policing movement. Just as community policing involves both externally and internally focused reforms, communication can also be conceptualized as having external and internal dimensions. External communications are those between representatives of the police organization and its various external constituents, from citizens and business owners to representatives of other agencies. Internal communications involve all of the various attempts that police leaders employ to improve communication within the organization: between officers, civilian employees, supervisors, mid-level managers, and administrators.

EXTERNAL COMMUNICATION REFORM

Police organizations, like other public service bureaucracies, engage in a great deal of boundary spanning behavior (Aldrich and Reiss 1971; Maguire 2003). The nature of this boundary-spanning behavior differs according to an employee's rank and assignment. Line-level police officers are among a class of workers that Lipsky (1980) terms *street-level bureaucrats*. Such workers spend much of their time involved in intergroup communication with constituents or clients outside of the organization. For police officers, these transactions often involve order-maintenance or enforcement activity that occurs in low visibility settings with minimal supervision (Goldstein 1960). For higher ranking officers, boundary-spanning behavior involves strategic communication with a variety of constituents. For instance, although police chiefs must engage in leadership *within* the organization, much of their work consists of communicating with politicians, community leaders, journalists, and other influential people *outside* of the organization (Mastrofski 2002; see chapter 12). Intergroup communication in policing occurs at multiple levels with varying degrees of complexity and formality, from individual-level communications between police officers and the public, to higher-level strategic communications undertaken by police leaders and public relations staff (see chapter 11).

External communication plays a central role in community policing. A useful theoretical framework for understanding external communication can be found in public relations, a field concerned with "the management of communication between an organization and its publics" (Grunig and Hunt 1984, 7).[3] Public relations theory is useful for thinking about how to establish and sustain "mutually beneficial relationships between an organization and the publics on whom its success or failure depends" (Cutlip, Center, and Broom 1994, 6). Establishing and sustaining these relationships is different than simply manipulating public opinion (Bruning and Ledingham 1999). Strong relationships between organizations and their publics involve mutual respect and provide benefits to all parties involved (Ledingham and Bruning 1998). Effective public relations strategies promote communication, acceptance, and cooperation between organizations and their publics—factors essential to an organization's legitimacy and survival (Bruning and Ledingham 1999). Because police officers serve in boundary-spanning roles that involve frequent interactions with the public, they are implicit agents of public relations.

Grunig and Hunt (1984) delineated four models of public relations that provide a useful framework for understanding external organizational communications. The four approaches are formed by cross-classifying the direction (one-way vs. two-way) and the degree of symmetry (symmetric vs. asymmetric) in the communication. One-way communication disseminates information like a monologue, from sender to receiver, while two-way communication involves information exchange, more like a dialogue. Two-way communication provides opportunities for mutual change to occur, while one-way communication allows an organization to control and dominate its publics.

	Direction	
Symmetry	One-Way Asymmetric	Two-Way Asymmetric
	One-Way Symmetric	Two-Way Symmetric

FIGURE 10.1. Public Relations Models

The symmetry of communication is also important because it concerns the degree to which an organization adapts to or cooperates with its environment (Grunig 1984). The goal of asymmetrical communication is to change the environment while leaving the organization unchanged. The purpose of symmetrical communication, however, is to modify the relationship between an organization and its environment. With symmetrical communication, publics can change organizations and organizations can change publics. This creates "a sense of openness, trust, and understanding between the organization and the key public, as well as a willingness to negotiate, collaborate, and mediate solutions to issues of concern to both the organization and critical publics" (Bruning and Ledingham 1999, 158). The concept of symmetrical communication overlaps heavily with the goals of community policing (see figure 10.1).

Two-way symmetrical communication is often prescribed as the most effective model of external communication because both the organization and its publics benefit. The purpose of this model is to establish mutual understandings between an organization and its environment. Communication takes the form of a dialogue with the possibility that both the organization and its publics will change. Using dialogue, the organization can enhance its legitimacy and autonomy through interactions with its publics, including those that pose both threats and opportunities to the organization (Sutcliffe 2001). The language used by public relations theorists to describe two-way symmetrical communication is strikingly similar to the rhetoric used by community policing reformers. Mutual recognition and dialogue are key components of community policing. For instance, according to Skolnick and Bayley (1986, 212), "police-community reciprocity means that police must genuinely feel, and genuinely communicate a feeling, that the public they are serving has something to contribute to the enterprise of policing."

Community policing is based on the premise that the community will be interested in forming a relationship with its police.[4] Similarly, the two-way symmetrical model of communication assumes that members of the public, or interest groups to which they belong, want to engage in dialogue with an organization. Police officers are sometimes frustrated when they are unable to solicit the input and participation of citizens in crime prevention and other community policing activities (Glaser and Denhardt 2010). In public relations theory, such people are referred to as "inactive publics." Hallahan (2000) argues that public relations theory has tended to ignore groups who, despite their importance to the organization, possess a low degree of knowledge about or involvement in organizations and their services. These inactive publics might lack the motivation, ability, or opportunity to engage in activities that affect the organization. Hallahan (2000) claims that members of the public who possess this knowledge, ability, and motivation are the most likely to engage in collaborative relationships with an organization. Recognizing that publics vary in terms of their motivation and ability forces organizations to tailor their communication strategies accordingly. Organizations, including the police, must identify and locate inactive publics in order to establish positive relationships. The burden to engage in this communication process often falls on the organization (Hallahan 2000).

Grunig and Grunig (1992) conclude that most organizations do not practice the communication model that would best serve them (see also Grunig 1984). Symmetrical communications are risky because they expose an organization to the turbulence of the external environment (Maguire 1997, 2003). As organization theorists have known for decades, a classic organizational response to a turbulent environment is to seal off its technical core where most of the work is done. Under such conditions, organizations often implement symbolic reforms that do not disrupt routine operations (Maguire 2014). Given the nature of their work, police organizations often operate in highly turbulent environments, therefore making it more challenging to embrace two-way symmetrical communications (Thacher 2001). Some police organizations may only implement symbolic community policing reforms to ensure a consistent flow of resources, or to confer legitimacy on the organization for "doing the right things" (Maguire and Mastrofski 2000). Structures, programs, and policies have symbolic value, and managing those symbols to send a message or convey meaning to those inside or outside the organization is a potent form of symbolic communication (Meyer 1979; Sutcliffe 2001).

Other police organizations may implement community policing based on a heartfelt concern with improving service delivery and transparency. Agencies interested in the genuine technical value of community policing would probably select a different model of external communications than those interested in merely capitalizing on its symbolic value for conferring legitimacy. The former might adopt the two-way symmetrical approach, while the latter might select one of the other approaches in which the communication is either one-way, asymmetrical, or both. The parallels between two-way symmetrical communications and community policing are substantial. Building strong and mutually beneficial relationships with community members and community groups is a core element of community policing. Two-way symmetrical communication can facilitate genuine community policing in which police organizations and their publics, both active and inactive, engage in meaningful dialogue and change.

Research Evidence on External Communication Reform

Much of the early scholarship on community policing offered a pessimistic appraisal of its impact on external communication by the police. Many policing scholars viewed community policing as a symbolic gesture intended primarily to enhance the legitimacy and power of the police. For example, according to Manning (1992, 135), external communication by police is intended to persuade publics about "the legitimate authority, credibility, and power of the police organization." Manning (1992) argued that police agencies actively use public relations to improve or maintain their public image rather than to engage in mutually beneficial dialogue with their constituents. Similarly, Klockars (1988, 240) viewed community policing as "the latest in a fairly long tradition of circumlocutions whose purpose is to conceal, mystify, and legitimate police distribution of non-negotiable coercive force." Bayley (1994, 100) cautioned that "police must not be allowed to make performance a 'con game' of appearance management."

If these early scholarly assessments of the community policing movement are accurate, then police may not have adopted the kinds of coproduction relationships or two-way symmetrical external communications called for by reformers. If communication flows in one direction from the police organization to the community to manage or manipulate public opinion of police rather than to facilitate more genuine partnerships, then community policing may be more rhetoric than reality (Gianakis and Davis 1998; Greene and Mastrofski 1988; Mastrofski 1998). Community policing may simply be a presentational strategy in which the police implement symbolic reform gestures to enhance their public image (Manning 1992). What does the research evidence say about these issues?

Most US police agencies report that they engage in community policing, especially those serving large populations (Reaves 2015). The important question is what specific reforms are implemented when agencies claim to do community policing. One way to answer that question is to examine research evidence from case studies in police agencies. For example, two different studies of the implementation of community policing in Seattle found evidence to support the types of critiques raised by Manning and other scholars. Lyons (1999, 185) found that Seattle's implementation of community policing in the late 1980s and early 1990s was focused primarily on "enhancing the power of the police to punish individuals and communities." Similarly, Reed (1999, 30) found that Seattle's implementation represented "a bastardized version of the philosophy of true community policing."

Research evidence from Chicago is more mixed. Beat meetings, which were well attended, provided a forum for police and citizens to share information, discuss problems, and establish relationships. In a little less than a third of the beat meetings observed by researchers, citizens and police demonstrated a "balanced and cooperative" relationship or "acted as partners" (Skogan and Hartnett 1997, 133–34). However, researchers found that the meetings did not result in widespread problem-solving, primarily because officers viewed it as "too much like social work" and therefore outside the scope of their responsibilities (Skogan et al. 1999, 231). Another study in Chicago found that officers considered community policing "a waste of time and did not embrace community policing values" (Graziano, Rosenbaum, and Schuck 2013, 97).

In Los Angeles, researchers found that police tended to dominate community meetings, often rejecting feedback offered by residents. Although the agency embraced the rhetoric of cooperation with the public, there was little evidence of genuine partnerships (Roussell and Gascón 2014). A separate study commended the Los Angeles Police Department for its various community policing efforts but found that the agency's culture impeded the implementation of authentic community policing. The researchers concluded that Los Angeles police officers had "an 'us versus them' mentality that inhibits collaboration between police and the community" (Glenn et al. 2003, 101).

Space limitations preclude a more thorough review of the many case studies of community policing implementation. The research shows that in some communities, police leaders sought to implement genuine community partnerships and problem-solving; whereas, in others, the reform efforts were shallower and more symbolic. Evidence from a large-scale national study of community policing found that "true" community partnerships that involve sharing power and decision making were rare, though the researchers viewed the modest progress they observed as an important breakthrough in police-community relations (Roth and Ryan 2000, 17). A more recent reflection concluded that community policing "has usually been police-centered, with minimal success in truly engaging the community and little evidence of real police-citizen co-production of public safety" (Cordner 2014, 160).

Why have police organizations faced so much difficulty in implementing community partnerships and problem-solving? One commonly cited reason is culture, whether occupational or organizational. For some officers, community policing may seem antithetical to what they perceive as the real job of the police. In a nationwide survey of police officers, 56 percent of respondents indicated a belief that "an aggressive rather than courteous approach is more effective in certain neighborhoods" (Pew Research Center 2017, 6). Moreover, culture is imprinted upon police officers early. One study found that although a Florida police academy had introduced a community policing module, other aspects of the recruit training reinforced the "paramilitary structure and culture" and an "us versus them" mentality (Chappell and Lanza-Kaduce 2010, 187). Another study in an Arizona police academy revealed that positive attitudes toward community policing and problem-solving began to dissipate as recruits entered field training and became more exposed to the department's culture (Haarr 2001).

From a community policing perspective, police officers cannot build partnerships and solve community problems effectively unless they work with the community. However, residents in some communities view police as unhelpful and often blame officers for the community's problems. Instead of seeking to collaborate with police to address these problems, sometimes they just want police to solve them (Brainard and Derrick-Mills 2011). In some communities, police officers view residents as unwilling to engage in partnerships and problem-solving, and residents believe officers do not want them involved (Graziano et al. 2013). Part of the difficulty in establishing positive working relationships may stem from differences in values and attitudes between police officers and residents (Thacher 2001). For instance, Glaser and Denhardt (2010, 322) found that most police officers believe they are able to "rise above self-interest" and make sacrifices to improve community well-being, but they question whether residents are willing to help. These differences may be more pronounced in minority communities, especially those with long-standing conflict between police and the public (Anderson 1999). For instance, a national survey found that 92 percent of White police officers believe our country has made the changes needed to give Blacks and Whites equal rights. This belief was shared by only 57 percent of White citizens and 12 percent of Black citizens (Pew Research Center 2017). Bridging such large attitudinal gaps will require more than symbolic reform.

Although the research evidence is pessimistic about the depth of community policing reform in the United States, there is still room for optimism. A systematic review of the research evidence on community policing found that it has been effective in improving citizen satisfaction with police (Gill, Weisburd, Telep, Vitter, and Bennett 2014). This is a curious finding given research evidence documenting the shallow and uneven implementation of community policing. One possibility may be that even when police efforts to implement the external components of community policing fall short of the ideal, they may still be better than traditional policing practices in sustaining and improving public perceptions of police. Research must continue to explore ways to improve relationships between police and communities. Much more research on intergroup communication between police and the community is sorely needed (see Choi and Giles 2012; Hewstone, Hopkins, and Routh 1992; and Hill and Giles 2018). Such research could provide theoretically informed and policy-relevant scientific evidence to help police leaders adopt practical solutions for bridging the gaps between police and communities.

INTERNAL COMMUNICATION REFORM

The previous section focused on the external dimensions of community policing: community partnerships and problem-solving. These dimensions constitute the core elements of the community policing movement. However, drawing on earlier lessons from team policing and community relations units, reformers realized that simply grafting these community policing activities onto existing police operations was insufficient. Instead, police agencies would need to adopt a variety of internal reforms that have been referred to as organizational transformation or adaptation (Office of Community Oriented Policing Services 2014; Wells and Maguire 2009). The internal elements of community policing are less focused on external service delivery and more focused on ensuring that police organizations have the proper structures, management and supervision styles, human resource practices, cultures, and other internal features to support community partnerships and problem-solving (Greene, Bergman, and McLaughlin 1994; Mastrofski 1998). Implicit in much of the community policing reform literature is that many of these changes are intended to improve internal *communication* within the organization (Maguire and Wells 2002). In this section, I provide a brief review of the relationship between community policing and internal communication reform and the research evidence on the extent to which these reforms have been adopted by police agencies.

Organizations are composed of a coordinated and structured set of linkages among people working to achieve a goal or set of goals within an identifiable boundary (Hall 1999). An organization is defined, in part, by its structure, which establishes the formal working relationships between its members. The structure of an organization also represents a framework within which communication occurs. Understanding the formal channels through which internal communication flows within organizations is vital. An organization's structure has numerous dimensions, among them vertical, functional, spatial, and occupational (Blau 1970; Langworthy 1986; Maguire 2003). These dimensions interact to structure the internal assignments, roles, and communications within an organization. The formal structure of an organization does not dictate the content and meaning of its communications, but it does play a key role in formalizing, constraining, and providing the context within which communication occurs (Hage, Aiken, and Marrett 1971; Johnson 1993; Lunenburg 2010).

While the formal structures of organizations are important for understanding patterns of internal communication, informal social structures such as organizational and occupational cultures and social networks also have a powerful influence on communication within police organizations. The existence of a police subculture has been discussed by observers of the police for decades (Crank 1998). This culture is characterized by such features as bravery, adventure, and a code of silence that views the police as a "thin blue line" protecting the rest of society from chaos or anarchy (see chapter 1). In addition to this *occupational* culture, police are also exposed to unique *organizational* cultures (Cordner 2017). Furthermore, depending on other factors such as race, gender, rank, assignment, and special interests, police officers may also belong to other subcultures within the occupation and the organization (Paoline 2003). Even though police officers work within a formal organizational structure and are regulated by rules, policies, standards, and procedures, their immersion in various subcultures and social networks also has powerful effects on the nature and content of their communication within the organization.

Community policing reformers have urged police leaders to adopt a variety of internal changes within police agencies to provide an appropriate framework that supports community partnerships and problem-solving (Greene et al. 1994; Mastrofski 1998). Some of the proposed changes focus on the formal aspects of the organization, such as structures, rules, policies, and procedures. Critics have argued that the paramilitary structures of police organizations are dysfunctional because they promote rigidity and formality in an industry where flexibility and the ability to craft customized solutions to unique local problems is essential (Angell 1971; Guyot 1979; Redlinger 1994; Wadman 1998). Other proposed changes focus on the informal aspects of the organization, such as organizational and occupational cultures. Critics allege that these cultures embrace traditional approaches to policing and resist innovation (Rosenbaum, Yeh, and Wilkinson 1994; Skolnick and Bayley 1986; Sparrow, Moore, and Kennedy 1990). Community policing is intended to reorient the traditional culture of police away from a primary focus on crime control, toward a broader mandate that includes community partnerships and problem-solving. Although we have separated the formal and informal aspects of organizations, they are inextricably linked. As Crank (1998, 27) notes, "police culture is embedded in and bounded by organizational structure." Community policing reformers have urged police departments to implement changes in both the formal and informal elements of organizations to facilitate community partnerships and problem-solving and to improve internal communication.

Research Evidence on Internal Communication Reform

Researchers have found that community policing did not result in substantial changes in the formal organizational structures of US police agencies. For instance, Maguire's (1997, 547–576) national study of large municipal police agencies found that community policing had resulted in "only minimal changes in organizational structure." A study of Florida police agencies found that the "organizational impacts of community policing have been minimal" (Gianakis and Davis 1998, 496). Similarly, Wadman (1998, 68) concluded that "no substantive changes have been made in the organization of America's police departments to facilitate the implementation of community policing." A national study by Maguire et al. (2003) found that police agencies had implemented some structural changes requested by community policing reformers, but not others, with some changes occurring in the opposite direction of what reformers encouraged. Another national study by Zhao, Ren, and Lovrich (2010, 224) found little evidence indicating that "the changes in organizational structures proclaimed to be important for the successful operation of [community policing] ever took place" in municipal police agencies. The structural reforms that were intended to improve internal communication in police agencies (among other benefits) do not appear to have been widely implemented in American policing.

While the community policing reform literature emphasizes the importance of changing organizational and occupational cultures in policing, empirical studies of such changes are rare. Zhao, He, and Lovrich (1998) argued that individual values and culture are linked, with each affecting the other. Their research showed that the value orientations of police officers had remained stable over the previous two decades. In a later study, Zhao, He, and Lovrich (1999) surveyed police officers from an agency with a national reputation for community policing. They found that from 1993 to 1996, officers' value orientations changed significantly. Values reflecting individual happiness, comfort, and security increased over the three-year period, while ratings for more social or collective values decreased. The social value experiencing the greatest decrease in importance among the officers was "equality." Zhao and his colleagues (1999) concluded that the value changes in their sample of officers were antithetical to the basic shifts in culture expected under community policing.

Research on police officers' attitudes might also be useful for drawing inferences about the effects of community policing on organizational and occupational culture. For instance, several studies examining attitudes about community policing have found a lack of understanding and/or acceptance among police officers (Kratcoski and Noonan 1995; Lurigio and Skogan 1994; Sadd and Grinc 1994). Greene and Decker (1989) found that a classroom program in Philadelphia designed to improve relations between police officers and residents actually resulted in poorer officer attitudes toward the community. A study of community policing in Albuquerque found that changes in organizational culture were difficult to achieve in the face of the traditional police culture (Wood, Rouse, and Davis 1999). Despite these frequent negative findings, some research has found that police agencies can change officers' attitudes. For instance, a longitudinal study in Joliet, Illinois, found that while "the absence of change was the norm rather than the exception," many officers showed favorable changes in attitudes toward and knowledge of community policing (Rosenbaum, Yeh, and Wilkinson 1994, 349). Other studies have also found evidence of positive changes in police officers' attitudes (Correia and Jenks 2011; McElroy, Cosgrove, and Sadd 1993; Wycoff and Skogan 1994).

In summary, the research evidence suggests that community policing reformers were not successful in encouraging widespread changes in the formal organizational structures of US police agencies. Some agencies made such changes, but others either did not change or implemented changes in the opposite direction of what reformers urged. With regard to changes in the informal elements of police organizations, such as attitudes, values, and cultures, the evidence is mixed. There is certainly no evidence of widespread change in the way US police officers think about community partnerships and problem-solving. However, there are success stories in individual police agencies, suggesting that such changes are indeed possible under the right conditions. Internal communication challenges associated with both structural and cultural impediments to change have played a key role in many community policing implementation failures (Wood and Davis 2002).

CONCLUSIONS

Communication reform is both implicit and explicit in the community policing reform literature. Community policing continues to be viewed by many observers as a solution to a variety of chronic problems within police organizations and in their external environments. Internally, the adoption of various organizational change strategies is designed to produce more flexible, adaptable, and responsive police agencies. Externally, the development of community partnerships and the use of collaborative problem-solving strategies is intended to produce safer, less fearful, more orderly communities in which residents view the police as fair and legitimate. Weaving together concepts and theories from multiple scientific disciplines, this chapter has provided a framework useful for conceptualizing the role of communication reform in the community policing movement. This framework raises important and policy-relevant questions about the current status of both community policing and communication reform. Research has answered some of these questions but not others.

How can researchers begin to address some of the unanswered questions about community policing and communication reform? To learn more about external communications, researchers could examine the nature and content of intergroup communications between police and communities. Such analyses could provide insights about both the symmetry and direction of communications, crucial elements of the public relations models covered earlier and the community policing movement more generally. To learn more about patterns of internal communications, research could examine the nature and flow of information within a police agency. This type of research could focus on both formal and informal communications and reveal key findings about organizational culture, organizational justice, and other issues that characterize employees' experiences within a police organization (see chapter 2).

Community policing has been described as a revolution in police service delivery. Although most police agencies in the United States claim to practice community policing, they continue to face major legitimacy crises associated with use of force, race relations, accountability, and related issues. Video footage of George Floyd's slow-motion death under a Minneapolis police officer's knee on May 25, 2020, triggered a massive wave of protests and riots across the nation. The killing of Rayshard Brooks by Atlanta police on June 12, 2020, fueled further protests associated with the #BlackLivesMatter movement. For many observers, the heavily militarized police response to the protests that occurred in the summer of 2020 provided clear evidence of the need for police reform. Federal judges in several US cities issued temporary restraining orders or injunctions to stop police from violating the constitutional rights of peaceful protesters. These issues fueled the growth of the Defund the Police movement, leading local governments to look closely at police budgets. As this book goes to press in the summer of 2020, it would be difficult to view recent events as evidence that the community policing movement is currently thriving in the United States.

Some police agencies have invested heavily in community policing out of a genuine desire to improve service quality, accountability, and legitimacy. For other agencies, community policing is a thin veneer intended to confer legitimacy without a genuine investment in police reform. Similarly, some agencies have embraced the need for communication reform both within the police organization and in its interactions with the community. For others, not much has changed during the community policing era. Current events reveal that much remains to be done in improving policing in the United States and elsewhere. Improving communication will continue to play a key role in moving police closer to the community policing ideal.

NOTES

1. These included the National Advisory Commission on Civil Disorders, the National Advisory Commission on Criminal Justice Standards and Goals, and the President's Commission on Law Enforcement and the Administration of Justice.

2. Several other developments helped lay the groundwork for the emergence of community policing. Evaluation research began to cast doubt on the three core strategies of policing: random preventive patrol, retrospective criminal investigations, and rapid response to calls for service from citizens (Bayley 1994; Skogan and Frydl 2004). A police research industry was born, with researchers beginning to specialize in research and evaluation of police practices, behaviors, and performance (Maguire and Katz 2020). Foundational studies began to examine core practices in policing, including random preventive patrol and criminal investigation (Bayley 1994; Skogan and Frydl 2004). Some of the most prominent reforms during the 1970s included college education programs for police officers and an increased emphasis on hiring females and minorities (Maguire and Katz 2020).

3. Organizational theorists use the singular term "environment" to refer to everything outside its boundaries impacted by or having an impact on the organization. Public relations theorists use the plural term "publics" to refer to the various constituencies served by an organization. I use these terms interchangeably in this chapter. An organization's environment is heterogeneous, consisting of numerous publics, in addition to other elements.

4. Just as public relations theorists use the plural term "publics" rather than the singular term "public" to describe an organization's multiple constituencies, some critics have noted that community policing reformers mistakenly view the police as serving a single or homogeneous community (Correia 2000; Lyons 1999; Reed 1999).

REFERENCES

Ahern, James F. 1972. *Police in Trouble: Our Frightening Crisis in Law Enforcement*. New York: Hawthorn Books.

Aldrich, Howard, and Albert J. Reiss, Jr. 1971. "Police Officers as Boundary Personnel." In *Police in Urban Society*, edited by Harlan Hahn, 193–208, Beverly Hills: Sage.

Anderson, Elijah. 1999. *Code of the Street: Decency, Violence, and the Moral Life of the Inner City*. New York: W.W. Norton.

Angell, John E. 1971. "Toward an Alternative to the Classic Police Organizational Arrangements: A Democratic Model." *Criminology* 9 (2–3): 185–206.

Barlow, David E., and Melissa H. Barlow. 2000. *Police in a Multicultural Society: An American Story*. Prospect Heights: Waveland.

Bayley, David H. 1994. *Police for the Future*. New York: Oxford University Press.

Bayley, David H., and Harold Mendelsohn. 1969. *Minorities and the Police: Confrontation in America*. New York: The Free Press.

Bittner, Egon. 1975. "The Impact of Police-Community Relations on the Police System." In *Community Relations and the Administration of Justice*, edited by David P. Geary, 369–89. New York: Wiley.

Blau, Peter. 1970. "A Formal Theory of Differentiation in Organizations." *American Sociological Review* 35 (2): 201–18.

Bloch, Peter B., and David Specht. 1973. *Neighborhood Team Policing*. Washington, DC: National Institute of Law Enforcement and Criminal Justice.

Bordua, David J., and Larry L. Tifft. 1971. "Citizen Interviews, Organizational Feedback, and Police Community Relations Decisions." *Law and Society Review* 6 (2): 155–82.

Brainard, Lori A., and Teresa Derrick-Mills. 2011. "Electronic Commons, Community Policing, and Communication." *Administrative Theory & Praxis* 33 (3): 383–410.

Bruning, Stephen D., and John A. Ledingham. 1999. "Relationships between Organizations and Publics: Development of a Multi-Dimensional Organization-Public-Relationship Scale." *Public Relations Review* 25 (2): 157–66.

Cassell, Paul G., and Richard Fowles. 1998. "Handcuffing the Cops? A Thirty-Year Perspective on Miranda's Harmful Effects on Law Enforcement." *Stanford Law Review* 50 (4):1055–145.

Cassell, Paul G., and Richard Fowles. 2017. "Still Handcuffing the Cops? A Review of Fifty Years of Empirical Evidence of Miranda's Harmful Effects on Law Enforcement." *Boston University Law Review* 97: 685–848.

Chappell, Allison T., and Lonn Lanza-Kaduce. 2010. "Police Academy Socialization: Understanding the Lessons Learned in a Paramilitary-Bureaucratic Organization." *Journal of Contemporary Ethnography* 39 (2), 187–214.

Choi, Charles W., and Howard Giles. 2012. "Intergroup Messages in Policing the Community." In *The Handbook of Intergroup Communication*, edited by Howard Giles, 264–77. New York: Routledge.

Cordner, Gary W. 2014. "Community Policing." In *The Oxford Handbook of Police and Policing*, edited by Michael D. Reisig and Robert J. Kane, 148–71. Oxford: Oxford University Press.

Cordner, Gary W. 2017. "Police Culture: Individual and Organizational Differences in Police Officer Perspectives." *Policing: An International Journal* 40 (1): 11–25.

Correia, Mark E. 2000. "The Conceptual Ambiguity of Community in Community Policing: Filtering the Muddy Waters." *Policing* 23 (2): 218–32.

Correia, Mark E., and David A. Jenks. 2011. "Expectations of Change: The Congruency between Beat Officers and Supervisors and its Impact on Programmatic Change." *Police Practice and Research* 12 (1): 16–34.

Crank, John P. 1998. *Understanding Police Culture*. Cincinnati: Anderson.

Cutlip, Scott M., Allen H. Center, and Glen M. Broom. 1994. *Effective Public Relations* (seventh edition). Upper Saddle River: Prentice Hall.

Gianakis, Gerasimos A., and G. John Davis, III. 1998. "Reinventing or Repackaging Public Services? The Case of Community-Oriented Policing." *Public Administration Review* 58 (6): 485–98.

Gill, Charlotte, David Weisburd, Cody W. Telep, Zoe Vitter, and Trevor Bennett. 2014. "Community-Oriented Policing to Reduce Crime, Disorder and Fear and Increase Satisfaction and Legitimacy among Citizens: A Systematic Review." *Journal of Experimental Criminology* 10: 399–428.

Glaser, Mark A., and Janet Denhardt. 2010. "Community Policing and Community Building: A Case Study of Officer Perceptions." *The American Review of Public Administration* 40 (3): 309–25.

Glenn, Russell W., Barbara R. Panitch, Dionne Barnes-Proby, Elizabeth Williams, John Christian, Matthew W. Lewis, Scott Gerwehr, and David W. Brannan. 2003. *Training the 21st Century Police Officer: Redefining Police Professionalism for the Los Angeles Police Department*. Santa Monica: RAND Corporation.

Goldstein, Herman. 1979. "Improving Policing: A Problem-Oriented Approach." *Crime and Delinquency* 25 (2): 236–58.

Goldstein, Herman. 1990. *Problem-Oriented Policing*. New York: McGraw-Hill.

Goldstein, Joseph. 1960. "Police Discretion Not to Invoke the Criminal Process: Low Visibility Decisions in the Administration of Justice." *Yale Law Journal* 69 (4): 543–94.

Graziano, Lisa M., Dennis P. Rosenbaum, and Amie M. Schuck. 2013. "Building Group Capacity for Problem-Solving and Police-Community Partnerships through Survey Feedback and Training: A Randomized Control Trial within Chicago's Community Policing Program." *Journal of Experimental Criminology* 10 (1): 79–103.

Greene, Jack R. 2000. "Community Policing in America: Changing the Nature, Structure, and Function of the Police." In *Criminal Justice 2000, Volume 3: Policies, Processes, and Decisions of the Criminal Justice System*, edited by Julie Horney, 299–370. Washington, DC: National Institute of Justice.

Greene, Jack R., William T. Bergman, and Edward J. McLaughlin. 1994. "Implementing Community Policing: Cultural and Structural Change in Police Organizations." In *The Challenge of Community Policing*, edited by Dennis P. Rosenbaum, 92–109. Thousand Oaks: Sage.

Greene, Jack R., and Scott H. Decker. 1989. "Police and Community Perceptions of the Community Role in Policing: The Philadelphia Experience." *The Howard Journal*, 28 (2): 105–23.

Greene, Jack R., and Stephen D. Mastrofski (eds.). 1988. *Community Policing: Rhetoric or Reality*. New York: Praeger.

Grunig, James E. 1984. "Organizations, Environments, and Models of Public Relations." *Public Relations Research and Education* 1 (1): 6–29.

Grunig, James E., and Larissa A. Grunig. 1992. "Models of Public Relations and Communication." In *Excellence in Public Relations and Communication Management*, edited by James E. Grunig, 285–325. Hillsdale: Lawrence Erlbaum.

Grunig, James E., and Todd Hunt. 1984. *Managing Public Relations*. New York: Holt, Rinehart & Winston.

Guyot, Dorothy. 1979. "Bending Granite: Attempts to Change the Rank Structure of American Police Departments." *Journal of Police Science and Administration* 7 (3): 253–84.

Haarr, Robin. 2001. "The Making of a Community Policing Officer: The Impact of Basic Training and Occupational Socialization on Police Recruits." *Police Quarterly* 4 (4): 402–33.

Hage, Jerald, Michael Aiken, and Cora B. Marrett. 1971. "Organization Structure and Communications." *American Sociological Review* 36 (5): 860–71.

Hall, Richard H. 1999. *Organizations: Structures, Processes, and Outcomes*. Upper Saddle River: Prentice Hall.

Hallahan, Kirk. 2000. "Inactive Publics in Public Relations." *Public Relations Review* 26 (4): 499–515.

Hewstone, Miles, Nicholas Hopkins, and David A. Routh. 1992. "Cognitive Models of Stereotype Change: 1. Generalization and Subtyping in Young People's Views of the Police." *European Journal of Social Psychology* 22 (3): 219–34.

Hill, Shawn, and Howard Giles. 2018. "Using Research to Build Trust and Empathy: Meaningful Change through Intergroup Contact." *Police Chief* 85 (8): 48–53.

Hindelang, Michael J. 1974. "Public Opinion Regarding Crime, Criminal Justice, and Related Topics." *Journal of Research in Crime and Delinquency* 11 (2): 101–16.

James, Nathan. 2018. *Recent Violent Crime Trends in the United States*. Washington, DC: Congressional Research Service.

Johnson, J. David. 1993. *Organizational Communication Structure*. Norwood: Ablex.

Kamisar, Yale. 2005. "How Earl Warren's Twenty-Two Years in Law Enforcement Affected His Work as Chief Justice." *Ohio State Journal of Criminal Law* 3 (1): 11–32.

Klockars, Carl B. 1988. "The Rhetoric of Community Policing." In *Community Policing: Rhetoric or Reality*, edited by Jack Greene and Stephen D. Mastrofski, 239–58. New York: Praeger.

Kratcoski, Peter C., and Susan B. Noonan. 1995. "An Assessment of Police Officers Acceptance of Community Policing." In *Issues in Community Policing*, edited by Peter C. Kratcoski and Duane Dukes, 169–186. Cincinnati: Anderson.

Langworthy, Robert H. 1986. *The Structure of Police Organizations*. New York: Praeger.

Ledingham, John A., and Stephen D. Bruning. 1998. "Relationship Management in Public Relations: Dimensions of an Organization-Public Relationship." *Public Relations Review* 24 (1): 55–65.

Leo, Richard A. 1996. "The Impact of Miranda Revisited." *Journal of Criminal Law and Criminology* 86 (3): 621–92.

Lipsky, Michael. 1980. *Street-Level Bureaucracy: Dilemmas of the Individual in Public Services*. New York: Russell Sage Foundation.

Lunenburg, Fred C. 2010. "Formal Communication Channels: Upward, Downward, Horizontal, and External." *FOCUS on Colleges, Universities, and Schools* 4 (1): 1–7.

Lurigio, Arthur J., and Wesley G. Skogan. 1994. "Winning the Hearts and Minds of Police Officers: An Assessment of Staff Perceptions of Community Policing in Chicago." *Crime & Delinquency* 40 (3): 315–30.

Lyons, William T. 1999. *The Politics of Community Policing: Rearranging the Power to Punish*. Ann Arbor: University of Michigan.

Maguire, Edward R. 1997. "Structural Change in Large Municipal Police Organizations during the Community Policing Era." *Justice Quarterly* 14 (3): 701–30.

Maguire, Edward R. 2003. *Organizational Structure in American Police Agencies: Context, Complexity, and Control*. Albany: State University of New York Press.

Maguire, Edward R. 2014. "Police Organizations and the Iron Cage of Rationality." In *The Oxford Handbook of Police and Policing*, edited by Michael D. Reisig and Robert J. Kane, 68–98. Oxford: Oxford University Press.

Maguire, Edward R. 2015. "New Directions in Protest Policing." *St. Louis University Public Law Review* 35 (1): 67–108.

Maguire, Edward R., and Charles M. Katz. 2020. "Introduction." In *Transforming the Police: Thirteen Key Reforms*, edited by Charles M. Katz and Edward R. Maguire, 1–8. Long Grove, IL: Waveland Press.

Maguire, Edward R., Joseph B. Kuhns, Craig D. Uchida, and Stephen M. Cox. 1997. "Patterns of Community Policing in Non-Urban America." *Journal of Research in Crime and Delinquency* 34 (3): 368–94.

Maguire, Edward R., and Stephen D. Mastrofski. 2000. "Patterns of Community Policing in the United States." *Police Quarterly* 3 (1): 4–45.

Maguire, Edward R., Yeunhee Shin, Jihong Zhao, and Kimberly D. Hassell. 2003. "Structural Change in Large Police Agencies During the 1990s." *Policing: An International Journal of Police Strategies and Management* 26 (2): 251–75.

Maguire, Edward R., and Craig D. Uchida. 2000. "Measurement and Explanation in the Comparative Study of American Police Organizations." In *Criminal Justice 2000, Volume 4: Measurement and Analysis of Crime and Justice*, edited by David Duffee, 491–557. Washington, DC: National Institute of Justice.

Maguire, Edward R., and William Wells. 2002. "Community Policing as Communication Reform." In *Law Enforcement, Communication, and Community*, edited by Howard Giles, 33–66. Philadelphia: John Benjamins.

Manning, Peter K. 1992. *Organizational Communication*. New York: Aldine de Gruyter.

Mastrofski, Stephen D. 1998. "Community Policing and Police Organization Structure." In *How to Recognize Good Policing: Problems and Issues*, edited by Jean-Paul Brodeur, 161–92. Thousand Oaks: Sage.

Mastrofski, Stephen D. 2002. "The Romance of Police Leadership." In *Advances in Criminological Theory, Volume 10: Crime and Social Organization*, edited by Elin Waring and David Weisburd, 153–196. New Brunswick: Transaction.

McElroy, Jerome E., Colleen A. Cosgrove, and Susan Sadd. 1993. *Community Policing: The CPOP in New York*. Newbury Park: Sage.

Meyer, Marshall W. 1979. "Organizational Structure as Signaling." *Pacific Sociological Review* 22 (4): 481–500.

Moore, Mark H. 1992. "Problem Solving and Community Policing." In *Modern Policing*, edited by Michael Tonry and Norval Morris, 99–158. Chicago: University of Chicago Press.

National Advisory Commission on Civil Disorders. 1968. *Report of the National Advisory Commission on Civil Disorders*. New York: Bantam Books.

Office of Community Oriented Policing Services. 2014. *Community Policing Defined*. Washington, DC.

Paoline, Eugene, III. 2003. "Taking Stock: Toward a Richer Understanding of Police Culture." *Journal of Criminal Justice* 31 (3): 199–214.

Pew Research Center. 2017. *Behind the Badge: Amid Protests and Calls for Reform, How Police View Their Jobs, Key Issues and Recent Fatal Encounters Between Blacks and Police*. Washington, DC: Pew Research Center.

President's Commission on Law Enforcement and Administration of Justice. 1967. *The Challenge of Crime in a Free Society*. Washington, DC: US Government Printing Office.

Reaves, Brian. 2015. *Local Police Departments, 2013: Personnel, Policies, and Practices*. Washington, DC: Bureau of Justice Statistics, US Department of Justice.

Redlinger, Lawrence J. 1994. "Community Policing and Changes in the Organizational Structure." *Journal of Contemporary Criminal Justice* 10 (1): 36–58.

Reed, Wilson Edward. 1999. *The Politics of Community Policing: The Case of Seattle*. New York: Garland.

Reiss, Albert J., Jr. 1971. *The Police and the Public*. New Haven: Yale University Press.

Reiss, Albert J., Jr. 1992. "Police Organization in the Twentieth Century." In *Modern Policing*, edited by Michael Tonry and Norval Morris, 51–97. Chicago: University of Chicago.

Reiss, Albert J., Jr., and David J. Bordua. 1967. "Environment and Organization: A Perspective on the Police." In ,*The Police: Six Sociological Essays*, edited by David J. Bordua, 25–55. New York: Wiley.

Rosenbaum, Dennis P., Sandy Yeh, and Deanna L. Wilkinson. 1994. "Impact of Community Policing on Police Personnel: A Quasi-Experimental Test." *Crime & Delinquency* 40 (3): 331–53.

Roth, Jeffrey A., and Thomas Ryan. 2000. "The COPS Program after Four Years—National Evaluation." *National Institute of Justice Research in Brief* (August): 1–23.

Roussell, Aaron, and Luis D. Gascón. 2014. "Defining 'Policeability': Cooperation, Control, and Resistance in South Los Angeles Community-Police Meetings." *Social Problems* 61 (2): 237–58.

Sadd, Susan, and Randolph Grinc. 1994. "Innovative Neighborhood Oriented Policing: An Evaluation of Community Policing Programs in Eight Cities." In *The Challenge of Community Policing: Testing the Promises*, edited by Dennis P. Rosenbaum, 27–52. Thousand Oaks: Sage.

Scheider, Matthew C., Robert Chapman, and Amie Schapiro. 2009. "Towards the Unification of Policing Innovations under Community Policing." *Policing: An International Journal* 32 (4): 694–718.

Sherman, Lawrence W., Catherine H. Milton, and Thomas V. Kelly. 1973. *Team Policing: Seven Case Studies*. Washington, DC: Police Foundation.

Skogan, Wesley G., and Kathleen Frydl. 2004. *Fairness and Effectiveness in Policing: The Evidence*. Washington, DC: National Academies Press.

Skogan, Wesley G., and Susan M. Hartnett. 1997. *Community Policing, Chicago Style*. New York: Oxford.

Skogan, Wesley G., Susan M. Hartnett, Jill DuBois, Jennifer T. Comey, Marianne Kaiser, and Justine H. Lovig. 1999. *On the Beat: Police and Community Problem Solving*. Boulder: Westview Press.

Skolnick, Jerome H., and David H. Bayley. 1986. *The New Blue Line: Police Innovation in Six American Cities*. New York: The Free Press.

Sparrow, Malcolm K., Mark H. Moore, and David M. Kennedy. 1990. *Beyond 911: A New Era for Policing*. New York: Basic Books.

Stark, Rodney 1972. *Police Riots: Collective Violence and Law Enforcement*. Belmont: Wadsworth.

Sutcliffe, Kathleen M. 2001. "Organizational Environments and Organizational Information Processing." In *The New Handbook of Organizational Communication: Advances in Theory, Research, and Methods*, edited by Fredric M. Jablin and Linda L. Putnam, 198–230. Thousand Oaks: Sage.

Thacher, David. 2001. "Conflicting Values in Community Policing." *Law and Society Review* 35 (4): 765–98.

Wadman, Robert C. 1998. *Organizing for the Prevention of Crime*. Doctoral dissertation, Idaho State University.

Walker, Samuel E. 1980. *Popular Justice*. New York: Oxford University Press.

Walker, Samuel E. 1993. "Does Anyone Remember Team Policing? Lessons of the Team Policing Experience for Community Policing." *American Journal of Police* 12 (1): 33–55.

Wells, William, and Edward R. Maguire. 2009. "Introduction: Making Sense of Community Policing." In *Implementing Community Policing: Lessons from 12 Agencies*, edited by Edward R. Maguire and William Wells, xv–xxiii. Washington, DC: Office of Community Oriented Policing Services.

Westley, William A. 1970. *Violence and the Police: A Sociological Study of Law, Custom, and Morality*. Boston: Massachusetts Institute of Technology.

Wood, Richard L., and Mariah C. Davis. 2002. Rethinking Organizational Change in Policing. Final Report to the National Institute of Justice. Retrieved from https://www.ncjrs.gov/pdffiles1/nij/grants/193418.pdf .

Wood, Richard L., Amelia Rouse, and Mariah C. Davis. 1999. *Policing in Transition: Creating a Culture of Community Policing*. Final Report to the National Institute of Justice. Retrieved from https://www.ncjrs.gov/pdffiles1/nij/grants/181043.pdf .

Wycoff, Mary Ann, and Wesley G. Skogan. 1994. "The Effect of a Community Policing Management Style on Officers' Attitudes." *Crime & Delinquency* 40 (3): 371–83.

Zhao, Jihong. 1996. *Why Police Organizations Change: A Study of Community Oriented Policing*. Washington, DC: Police Executive Research Forum.

Zhao, Jihong, Ni He, and Nicholas Lovrich. 1998. "Individual Value Preferences among American Police Officers: The Rokeach Theory of Human Values Revisited." *Policing: An International Journal of Police Strategies and Management* 21 (1): 22–37.

Zhao, Jihong, Ni He, and Nicholas Lovrich. 1999. "Value Change among Police Officers at a Time of Organizational Change: A Follow-up Study using Rokeach Values." *Policing: An International Journal of Police Strategies and Management* 22 (2): 152–70.

Zhao, Jihong, Ling Ren, and Nicholas Lovrich. 2010. "Police Organizational Structures during the 1990s: An Application of Contingency Theory." *Police Quarterly* 13 (2): 209–32.

Zhao, Jihong, Matthew C. Scheider, and Quint Thurman. 2002. "Funding Community Policing to Reduce Crime: Have COPS Grants Made a Difference?" *Criminology and Public Policy* 2 (1): 7–32.

CHAPTER 11

Speaking Truth from Power through Strategic Police Communication

Michael S. Scott

As is the case for most public-service occupations—indeed with most private ones as well—communication is a central concern of the police. This is nearly self-evident: Wherever people have to interact, communication is of paramount importance. And policing is intrinsically about personal and group interactions[1], often in the context of conflict. In the police field, some aspects of communication are well recognized and regularly attended to; others far less so. This chapter first maps the broad realm of police communications and then explores in greater depth one particular aspect of it: strategic police communication. Defined more fully below, strategic police communication is that which is aimed at communicating the overarching mission, objectives, and methods of a police organization so as to better position the organization for success.

A CONCEPTUAL MAP OF THE POLICE COMMUNICATIONS REALM

Conceptual maps of the police communications realm can take various forms, depending on the organizing principle. Possible organizing principles are *actors*, *medium*, *purpose*, and the *level of abstraction* of a communications plan.

Actors

A conceptual map of police communications based on the communication *actors* as the organizing principle—who is communicating with whom—might look like figure 11.1.

```
┌─────────────────────────┐  ┌─────────────────────────┐  ┌─────────────────────────┐
│ Police-public           │  │ Police-police           │  │ Police-community-partner│
│ communication           │  │ communication           │  │ organization communication│
└─────────────────────────┘  └─────────────────────────┘  └─────────────────────────┘
```

FIGURE 11.1. Police Communications by Actor

Police–public communications encompass such issues as the following:

- how the public communicates its needs and desires for police service to the police, both in individual and group contexts;
- how the police communicate to the public what services they are prepared to provide, and in what manner;
- police solicitations of information from the public, principally information that can help police detect and resolve crime and disorder; and
- police informing the public about either specific incidents or trends that affect the public's safety.

Police–police communications encompass such issues as the following:

- technology by which police officers can communicate with one another, as well as with other emergency-service providers;
- technology and procedures by which police dispatchers communicate with police officers in the field;
- the organizational systems and expectations for sharing information among police officials working in different organizational units (within and across police agencies);
- the utility of police communications jargon (e.g., 10-codes and signals, slang, acronyms) for accurately conveying critical information among officers; and
- communications between superior and subordinate police officers, both up and down the chain of command.

Police-community-partner communications encompass issues relating to how police and the non-police organizations with whom police regularly work and on whom they rely for processing their work understand one another's professional perspectives, orientations, terminology, occupational cultures, and organizational missions. Such non-police-partner organizations include those that provide victim assistance, drug and alcohol treatment, mental health treatment, child and family welfare monitoring and assistance, animal protection, and myriad others (see chapter 4). These organizational relationships typically present far greater communications and collaboration challenges than do intragovernmental or police agency-to-police agency relationships.

Medium

Another conceptual map could be based on the communication *medium* as the organizing principle: *how* police communicate with others. This might look like figure 11.2.

```
┌─────────────────────┐   ┌─────────────────────┐
│   Interpersonal verbal  │   │ Group verbal communication │
│    communication         │   │                          │
└─────────────────────┘   └─────────────────────┘

┌──────────────┐  ┌──────────────────┐  ┌──────────────────────┐
│ Data sharing │  │ Symbolic communication │  │ Mass media communication │
└──────────────┘  └──────────────────┘  └──────────────────────┘
```

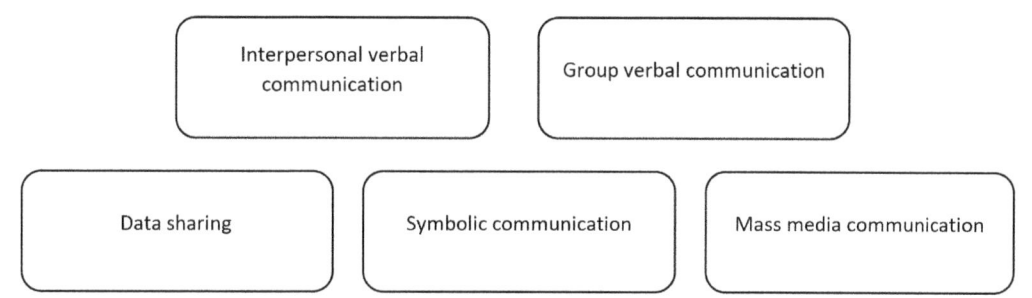

FIGURE 11.2. Police Communications by Medium

Interpersonal verbal communications encompass how police officers communicate verbally with different types of members of the public, and in what context. Distinctions might be drawn as to the appropriate language and tone police officials use in communicating with criminal suspects, crime victims, complainants, witnesses, and other types of civilians, including children and people with intellectual or developmental impairments. It also encompasses police communications across languages, with non-speaking verbal communication (e.g., sign language, TTY communication), and with people who are in various states of mental or emotional crisis or temporary impairment from drugs or alcohol (see chapter 9).

Group verbal communications encompass how police communicate during in-person meetings with groups of citizens—block watches, neighborhood associations, political activist organizations (see chapter 22), student assemblies, and others. It requires police to be sensitive to group dynamics and to the challenges of both conveying information to people with differing individual interests and information needs, and to inferring consensus among the often-disparate views of individuals within a group (see chapter 1).

Data sharing encompasses issues pertaining to whether and how police allow non-police (whether the general public, the mass media, or non-police partner organizations) to access information files gathered in the course of official police business, such as crime and incident reports.

Symbolic communications encompass issues such as what style uniforms police wear, what police weaponry is displayed openly, the types and markings of police vehicles (Simpson 2019, 2020), and the imagery conveyed by the names given to police units and ranks. Each of these symbols can alternatively convey intimidation or approachability.

Mass media communications encompasses issues pertaining to both traditional media outlets like newspapers and television and radio programs, and to modern mass media like social networks, podcasts, YouTube, and blogs. It pertains both to how police initiate communication with media outlets and to how police respond to communication requests from journalists and reporters (see chapter 14 and 15).

Purpose

Yet another map could be based on the *purpose* of communication as the organizing principle: what objectives the communication is seeking to achieve. This might look like figure 11.3.

To secure resources and authority for the police	To secure compliance with police requests/orders	To inform citizens how to comply with the law and protect themselves
To inform the public about the services that police do and do not provide	To gather intelligence to solve and prevent crimes	To justify police action

FIGURE 11.3. Police Communications by Purpose

Securing police resources encompasses justifying annual budget requests and proposals to grant police more authority, or to protect the authority they currently have, made to legislatures.

Securing compliance with police requests and orders encompasses how police officers use tone of voice, deflection, and other rhetorical devices to persuade people to do certain things without resort to physical coercion.

Informing citizens how to comply with the law and protect themselves encompasses announcing new laws, clarifying or strictly enforcing existing laws, and providing crime-prevention and safety advice, whether in the context of a single incident or individual or in the context of a larger threat to public safety affecting an entire community.

Informing the public about police services encompasses such issues as promoting the proper use of 911 for emergencies or 311 for non-emergencies and having police dispatchers directly refer complainants to appropriate service providers.

Gathering intelligence to solve and prevent crimes encompasses such issues as the following:

- recruiting, cultivating, and compensating confidential informants;
- interviewing suspects (Alison et al. 2013; Dando and Bull 2011);
- promoting anonymous tip lines for reporting crime and turning in criminals;
- negotiating plea agreements in exchange for crime intelligence; and
- canvassing neighborhoods for witnesses to crimes.

Justifying police actions encompasses such issues as the following:

- teaching police officers to properly articulate the facts and inferences in support of their decisions to detain and arrest individuals; and
- explaining to the public the rationale for certain police department policies and procedures.

Level of Abstraction

Lastly, a conceptual map of police communications could be one that distinguishes the *level of abstraction* of a communications plan as between *tactical* and *strategic* communications, a notoriously fuzzy but important distinction and one that overlaps these other three conceptual maps (see figure 11.4).

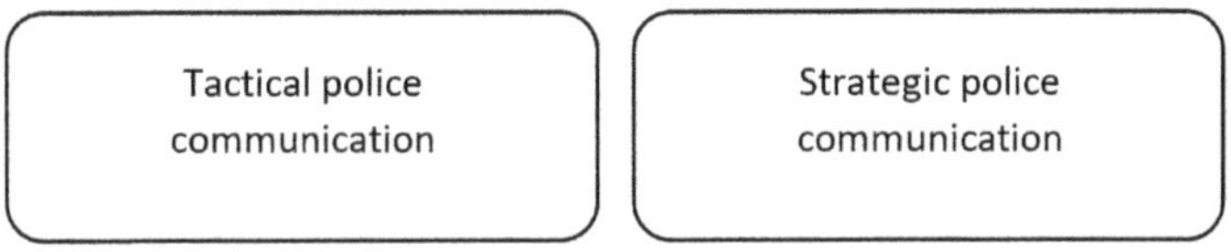

```
┌─────────────────┐  ┌─────────────────┐
│ Tactical police │  │ Strategic police│
│ communication   │  │ communication   │
└─────────────────┘  └─────────────────┘
```

FIGURE 11.4. Police Communications by Level of Abstraction

Little has been published on the distinction between tactical and strategic police communications: While some of the better texts on police administration acknowledge the important distinction between police tactics and strategies (e.g., Cordner 2016, 384–417), most do not explicitly distinguish between tactical and strategic police communication.

Tactical police communication encompasses the actors, media, and purposes described above at the level of the actual delivery or receipt of the communications. It is concerned with the mechanics, timing, tone, and specific content of communications involving police officials.

As a term of art in policing, however, tactical communication refers most commonly to how police officers use language to gain compliance from suspects and offenders in the field (see chapter 17). As a typical illustration, an announcement for a police training course in tactical communications reads as follows:

> Tactical communications is a disciplined study of verbal communication that will help officer [*sic*] stay calm and professional under verbal assault and generate voluntary compliance from even the most difficult people. This course will increase the officer's awareness of warning signs/verbiage which will enhance their safety. This course also teaches officers to identify when their words have failed and how to transition, through tactics, into the escalation of force. The ability to communicate effectively is an officer's greatest asset. This will enhance officer safety and promote public confidence in law enforcement.[2]

In contemporary policing, an increasing amount of public and police attention is being paid to the manner in which police officers speak to citizens, particularly those whom the officer suspects of some wrongdoing (Terrill 2003). The rise in concern about this aspect of police communications tracks closely with the advent of three technologies: cell-phone cameras, police body-worn cameras, and video-sharing media such as YouTube (see chapter 14). These technologies have exponentially increased public visibility of daily encounters between police officers and citizens, encounters that heretofore were witnessed only by the police officer, the citizen interacting with the officer, and a few nearby onlookers. Today, a routine police–citizen encounter could readily be witnessed by millions, if not billions, of people if recorded and uploaded to the Internet. Indeed, as I write this, one of the top-trending YouTube videos (seen about two million times) features just such a police–citizen encounter.

The episodic spikes in public and police concern about how police officers speak to citizens typically occur in the wake of police–citizen encounters that are widely deemed to reflect egregious police conduct. Among the most notorious of these encounters in recent decades in the United States were the police beating of Rodney King in Los

Angeles; the police shooting of Michael Brown in Ferguson, Missouri; the police shooting of Philando Castile in Minnesota; and the police killing of George Floyd in Minneapolis that sparked nationwide protests and looting, but there are many others, coming from communities across the entire country. Largely due to the quick and widespread publicity these encounters engender, particularly when they have been video-recorded, not only do police in the jurisdiction involved need to give fresh consideration to how their officers communicate tactically, but so too do police across the nation, and even abroad.

The heightened concern about police use of language, which is often accompanied by dubious use of physical coercion, has spurred the development and delivery of a variety of purported improvements in tactical communications. Among the most widely recognized and adopted are verbal judo[3] and more recent iterations built around the latest buzzword, de-escalation.[4]

Strategic police communication, by definition, must differ from tactical police communication, but the term and the concept are not widely used or recognized in police management circles. A few notable and commendable exceptions can be found in recent years. One is a publication titled *Strategic Communications Practices: A Toolkit for Police Executives* (Stephens, Greenberg, and Hill 2011).

Strategic communication is defined as "[an organization] communicating purposefully to advance its mission" (Hallahan et al. 2007, 4) or as "communication aligned with the [organization's] overall strategy, to enhance its strategic positioning" (Argenti, Howell, and Beck 2005, 61).

Changing an organizational mission—rather than advancing an existing one—is yet more complex and for which strategic communication is even more vital. As one police executive change agent said, "Communication is a skill that is particularly important for a change manager. Whilst this is important in operational leadership, there is just a lot more of it in change—it is all about communication" (quoted in Smith 2019, 6).

Advancing or changing an organizational mission requires attention to several essential issues, each of which requires effective communication: (1) defining the organizational mission/function(s), (2) building consensus among key constituencies for that mission, (3) articulating the overarching strategy for achieving the mission, (4) securing resources necessary to the carrying out of the mission, (5) articulating the core values by which the organization will operate, and (6) clarifying where the organization can succeed through its own resources and where it requires external resources for its success. Below I consider the application of these essential aspects of strategic communications to the police industry and to police agencies. More particularly, I consider the application of these issues to two archetypal policing models: a standard model and an alternative model.

STRATEGIC COMMUNICATION FOR TWO POLICING MODELS

The Standard Policing Model

Over much of the last one hundred years of history police have defined their function principally in terms of criminal law enforcement. Prior to then—from the inception of modern American police in the mid-nineteenth century to the end of that century—the police function was understood as being one of order maintenance and peacekeeping, and tightly aligned with the interests of the political regime in power, rather than one of criminal law enforcement (Moore and Kelling 1983). Beginning with the Progressive Movement reforms of the early twentieth century and continuing through at least the 1970s, police redefined their core mission in terms of crime control, criminal investigation, and law enforcement. Indeed, they came to describe their profession as "law enforcement" and to their members as "law enforcement officers," the latter term intended to unify those who are disparately called "police officers," "deputy sheriffs," "troopers," and "agents." This lexical shift from "police" to "law enforcement" was embedded in the movement to professionalize the police, a major objective of which was to establish an image of the police as apolitical, neutral (and thereby fair), and grounded in law rather than policy. Two major understandings of the police needed to change in order to bring about this transformation: First, governance of the police needed to be decoupled from partisan politics. And second, the police needed to extricate themselves from the time-consuming and messy business of attending to the public's social welfare needs, thereby leaving them free to concentrate their time and attention on battling serious crime.

At the federal level, FBI director J. Edgar Hoover led the charge in urging a new understanding of the role of the police on these two counts. Few actors in the history of American political life have surpassed Hoover's knack for strategic communication. Through books, radio programs, Hollywood movies, academic articles (Hoover 1953, 1964), and official communications, Hoover shaped the public's, Congress's, and his own agents' understanding of what the FBI existed to do and what it stood for (Ungar 1976). In the early 1930s, the national Wickersham Commission also advanced this cause through its investigation of and report on the state of policing (National Commission on Law Observance and Enforcement 1931). At the municipal level, first August Vollmer and then his protégé O.W. Wilson, led a similar charge, both publishing and speaking publicly extensively (Vollmer 1936; Wilson 1951, 1953) on the need for professionalizing the police, although both men also possessed a sophisticated understanding of the multiplicity of police duties and the need for police to attend to more than just crime, even if crime control were deemed their principal purpose.

Using the basic proposition that the police principally exist to control crime and enforce the law (the standard model), a corresponding strategic communications plan that addresses the six essential issues identified above could well look something like the following.

Toward *defining the police organizational mission/function(s)*, the term "law enforcement" would be preferred over "police," in part to remind the public that calling the police is appropriate for all suspected criminal activity but not appropriate for non-criminal activity.

Toward *building consensus among key constituencies for this mission*, it would be necessary to persuade local elected officials and the general public that crime poses a continuous and serious threat to the community; that the police are capable of and competent in controlling crime; and that distracting police from attending to criminal matters undermines the public's safety.

Toward *articulating an overarching strategy for achieving this mission*, heavy emphasis would be placed on vigorously investigating all crimes; minimizing the extent to which civil liberties frustrate criminal investigations; and favoring proactive policing methods to detect lawbreakers, all drawing predominantly on the logic of deterring crime through the credible threat of punishment.

Toward *securing resources necessary to the carrying out of this mission*, a sufficient number of police officers and detectives would be called for in order to ensure that all reported crimes are thoroughly investigated and proactive enforcement operations can regularly be mounted; that adequate resources are allocated for prosecutors, courts, and correctional facilities to process arrested violators; and that adequate resources are allocated to non-police government and nongovernment organizations to respond to the non-criminal matters for which the public seeks assistance.

Toward *articulating the core values by which it will operate*, emphasis would be placed on *relentlessness* in pursuing law violators and on *secrecy* for maintaining the integrity of criminal investigations and proactive enforcement operations.

And toward *clarifying where the organization can succeed through its own resources and where it requires external resources for its success*, emphasis would be placed on reminding the citizenry of its obligations to report crimes and bear witness against violators; and on the importance of a robust criminal justice system for prosecuting, convicting, confining, and monitoring criminal offenders.

To a considerable degree, whether or not it was coherent and comprehensive, most of the above characterization of a strategic policing communication plan has been in effect for much of the police industry over the better part of the past century. Its essential message is that crime control is the primary function of the police and law enforcement is the primary means for effecting it.

The standard policing model is, in many respects, an appealing one—to the police and the public alike. Among its perceived virtues to the public is that it implies considerable restraint on the power of the police: that their authority to act is limited to enforcing specific criminal statutes and that enforcement is strictly governed by the rules of criminal procedure that are overseen carefully by the courts. This further implies that police will stay out of people's business so long as they aren't committing crimes. Among its perceived virtues to the police themselves is that police work entails only highly important and exciting work—catching bad guys.

An Alternative Policing Model

In reality, however, the standard policing model has failed on several terms. It has failed in that public expectations of police have always transcended matters that are criminal in nature, extending to all manner of social ills and disorder about which the public wants something done, and soon. Indeed, not more than one-quarter of public requests for police service pertain to criminal matters. The other three-quarters pertain to such matters as controlling traffic, responding to information requests, resolving disputes, abating nuisances, and assisting vulnerable people. It has failed in that the deterrence-based tactics of the police—preventive patrol, rapid response to calls, and follow-up criminal investigation—have proved far less effective than anyone expected (Goldstein 1990). It has failed in that prosecutors, courts, and corrections agencies have had far less capacity to process all police arrests or adequately deal with the convicted offenders (Stuntz 2011). It has failed in that the criminological theories on which police relied so heavily—namely, deterrence theory—did not suffice to provide police with a theoretical basis on which to build an effective operational strategy and tactics (Kennedy 2009; see chapter 20). And, perhaps most profoundly, it failed because it left police shouldering an unrealistically heavy burden in the effort to control crime, let alone address all those other matters which the public expected government to address.

But police, being eager to satisfy public expectations, still too often accept the mandate to address a wide array of problems through the framework of the criminal law. They both try to define their role in terms of the criminal law (if it's criminal, it's police business; if it's civil, it's not) and in terms of how they respond to problems (if police accept responsibility for the problem, then they apply a criminal law enforcement response to it). All too often, both the terms on which police accept responsibility for dealing with problems and the terms on which they seek to respond to them lead to failed or otherwise bad outcomes. As illustrations, police efforts to respond to problems relating to illegal drug sales and use; homelessness and mental illness; alcohol abuse and disorder; unlawful immigration; and community fear rooted in racial or ethnic bias fail to satisfy public expectations and, particularly when law enforcement is the dominant response, exacerbate public dissatisfaction with police.

The failure of the standard policing model left police in great need of rethinking the nature of their function and then developing and implementing a strategic communications plan that would advance an alternative policing model among those who shape the expectations of the police, to include residents, elected officials, other government and nongovernment organizations, and the press.

To a significant extent, the American police (joined by their British and Canadian counterparts) did undertake a major effort, beginning in roughly the 1980s, to propose an alternative to the standard policing model. The alternative went by various names, with "community policing" being the most widely used and publicly recognized. A more coherent, comprehensive, and cogent alternative model, initially proposed in 1979, was "problem-oriented policing" (Goldstein 1979).

Using the problem-oriented approach to policing model, a corresponding strategic communications plan that addresses the six essential issues identified above could well look something like the following.

Toward *defining the police organizational mission/function(s)*, the term "law enforcement" would be discarded in favor of "police," primarily to remind the public that police attend to many matters that threaten public safety and security, both criminal and non-criminal, and to avoid the suggestion that enforcement of the law is the only—or even the principal—means available to the police to achieve their objectives. The function of the police would be defined in broad, although not unlimited terms. At the serious risk of oversimplification, their function might be described as something like this: "assisting the community and the rest of government in maintaining a safe, secure and free society."

Toward *building consensus among key constituencies for this mission*, police would encourage prosecutors to likewise recognize the broader scope of their function—a function presently referred to as "community prosecution"—and to join with police in addressing public-safety problems more holistically than by mere criminal law enforcement. The public would be educated as to the value of developing sustained, close-working relationships with the individual police officers assigned to their community as opposed to receiving quick but cursory service from the next available police officer. Other local government agencies such as those that handle economic and community development, zoning, code enforcement, parks and recreation, emergency medical services, substance abuse and mental health treatment, schooling, and so on, would be made to better appreciate the interconnectedness of their work and police work. Journalists would come to better understand the complexity and breadth of the police function and how public safety is influenced by many factors outside the direct control of the police. Elected officials would be made to better understand the limitations of merely hiring more police officers without giving careful consideration to what those officers do and, more importantly, how they are able or unable to collaborate effectively with others to satisfactorily address public-safety problems.

Toward *articulating an overarching strategy for achieving this mission*, police leaders would communicate a strategy that both responds to the relatively rare but critical emergencies for which swift and decisive action is required and the far more common incidents that are part of a pattern of incidents that, properly understood, constitute a chronic public-safety problem for which an analytical, deliberative, and consultative approach is required to reach a satisfactory resolution.

Toward *securing resources necessary to the carrying out of this mission*, police would communicate that while the resources necessary to carry out emergency operations— the firearms and other weapons, 911 systems, forensic investigation tools, and so forth— remain essential, so too are the resources needed to support information analysis and the building of effective community and interagency working relationships (information technology, training and education, research and analysis capacities, time for officers to meet with citizens and officials in other organizations and government agencies, etc.).

Toward *articulating the core values by which it will operate*, the strategic communications plan will emphasize such values as using well-analyzed data to inform decision making; close and effective external working relationships; consulting relevant stakeholders, both internally and externally; making decisions ethically and not just expeditiously; and shared responsibility for public safety among police, the community, and the entire government.

And toward *clarifying where the organization can succeed through its own resources and where it requires external resources for its success*, the strategic communications plan will acknowledge that police need more than the resources directly allocated to their organization; they also need access to resources controlled by others, whether community groups, nongovernmental organizations, other government agencies, the press, universities and research organizations, or the citizenry at large. It will reinforce the understanding that those who control the conditions and conduct that cause or facilitate crime and disorder bear some responsibility for taking actions to remedy those conditions or conduct.

CONCLUSIONS

The police are perhaps a democratic society's strongest symbol of power. And, consistent with the principles of a democratic and free society, there will forever be a need for the citizenry to be willing and able to "speak truth to power," to tell the police when they are deviating from the people's expectations as to how they wish to be policed. Also consistent with the principles of a democratic and free society is the need for the police to speak to the policed, to "speak truth from power," as it were. These communications between police and the citizenry work best as dialogues rather than as monologues or diatribes.

Many of the troubles with policing in free societies emanate from fundamental conflicts between what citizens expect of their police and what police can reasonably deliver (Goldstein 1977). Echoing Goldstein's view, Rumbaut and Bittner (1979, 284) concluded that "the most hopeful prospect for substantive police reform is the influence an informed public can exert on the direction of change in police agencies." And it is through strategic communication that the police inform the public—not as the sole voice, but as an important one—as to the challenges and realities of policing a free society. To a great degree, citizens have wholly unrealistic expectations of their police: that police will maintain law and order without disturbing citizens' freedom to do as they please. And to a great degree, police have, perhaps grudgingly, accepted the unrealistic mandate and, not unexpectedly, consistently failed to carry it out to the full satisfaction of all.

Much of what is proposed in strategic police communication for an alternative policing model is intended toward twin critical objectives. The first objective is to disabuse the public of many myths about what police are able to do and to achieve under the standard policing model by openly acknowledging that model's limitations and fallacies, many of which police themselves have perpetuated over the years. The second objective is to replace the mythology with a truthful, frank, and pragmatic policing model, one that acknowledges the delicate balances in reconciling freedom and order and the critical need police have for the public's engagement and assistance in striking the right balances. This is an inherently messy and tricky business, but it is clear that police do themselves and the public no good service in communicating a fanciful and fundamentally flawed model of policing.

An emerging body of research indicates that the alternative model of policing herein described—a problem-oriented approach—better enables the police to carry out their duties effectively, efficiently and equitably (National Research Council 2004; Scott and Clarke 2020; Weisburd, Telep, Hinkle, and Eck 2008). For purposes of this chapter, the outstanding empirical question is whether a coherent strategic police communications plan built upon this alternative model can facilitate and accelerate the thus far gradual and uneven shift from the largely discredited standard model and toward one better suited for modern, complex, and heterogeneous democratic societies.

NOTES

1. For purposes of this chapter, personal versus group interactions between police officers and civilians refers merely to whether one or more police officers are interacting with one or

more civilians during an encounter. Other communications scholars have described distinctions between interpersonal and intergroup interactions in terms of whether the people interacting identify themselves and those with whom they are interacting as individuals or as members/representatives of a group (see Dragojevic and Giles 2014). With regard to this distinction, this chapter assumes that most official police communications are more intergroup than interpersonal in nature: That is, police officials are usually communicating as representatives of their group (the police) and in so doing, typically identify their audience as members of groups (e.g., offenders, victims, witnesses, complainants, other officials), rather than from the perspective of one individual communicating with other individuals.

2. Pennsylvania State Police website, retrieved from https://www.psp.pa.gov/law-enforcement-services/Pages/Training%20Courses/Tactical-Communications.aspx.

3. Verbal judo was developed and taught by former Los Angeles police officer George Thompson (Thompson and Jenkins 1993).

4. There are many de-escalation training courses offered. One such is the Integrating Communications, Assessment and Tactics (ICAT) model, developed by the Police Executive Research Forum (2016).

REFERENCES

Alison, Laurence J., Emily Alison, Geraldine Noone, Stamatis Elntib, and Paul Christiansen. 2013. "Why Tough Tactics Fail and Rapport Gets Results: Observing Rapport-Based Interpersonal Techniques (ORBIT) to Generate Useful Information from Terrorists." *Psychology, Public Policy & Law* 19 (4): 411–31.

Argenti, Paul A., Robert A. Howell, and Karen A. Beck. 2005. "The Strategic Communication Imperative." *MIT Sloan Management Review* 46 (3). Retrieved from https://sloanreview.mit.edu/article/the-strategic-communication-imperative.

Cordner, Gary. 2016. *Police Administration* (ninth edition). New York: Routledge.

Dando, Coral J., and Ray Bull. 2011. "Maximizing Opportunities to Detect Verbal Deception: Training Police Officers to Interview Tactically." *Journal of Investigative Psychology and Offender Profiling* 8 (2): 189–202.

Dragojevic, Marko, and Howard Giles. 2014. "Language and Interpersonal Communication: Their Intergroup Dynamics." In *Handbook of Interpersonal Communication*, edited by Charles R. Berger, 29–51. Berlin: De Gruyter Mouton.

Goldstein, Herman. 1977. *Policing a Free Society*. Cambridge: Ballinger.

Goldstein, Herman. 1979. "Improving Policing: A Problem-Oriented Approach." *Crime & Delinquency* 25 (2): 236–58.

Goldstein, Herman. 1990. *Problem-Oriented Policing*. New York: McGraw Hill.

Hallahan, Kirk, Derina Holtzhausen, Betteke van Ruler, Dejan Verčič, and Krishnamurthy Sriramesh. 2007. "Defining Strategic Communication" *International Journal of Strategic Communication* 1 (1): 3–35.

Hoover, Chris. 2010. "The Strategic Communication Plan." *FBI Law Enforcement Bulletin* 79 (8): 16–21.

Hoover, J. Edgar. 1953. "Juvenile Delinquency." *Syracuse Law Review* 4 (2): 179–204.

Hoover, J. Edgar. 1964. "Combating Merchants of Filth: The Role of the FBI." *University of Pittsburgh Law Review* 25 (3): 469–78.

Kennedy, David M. 2009. *Deterrence and Crime Prevention: Reconsidering the Prospect of Sanction*. London: Routledge.

Moore, Mark H., and George L. Kelling. 1983. "To Serve and Protect: Learning from Police History." *The Public Interest* 7 (Winter): 54–57.

National Commission on Law Observance and Enforcement. 1931. *Report on Police*. Washington DC: US Government Printing Office.

National Research Council. 2004. *Fairness and Effectiveness in Policing: The Evidence*. Washington, DC: National Academies of Sciences Press.

Police Executive Research Forum. 2016. *Integrating Communications, Assessment and Tactics: A Training Guide for Defusing Critical Incidents.* Washington, DC: Police Executive Research Forum.

Rumbaut, Rubén G., and Egon Bittner. 1979. "Changing Conceptions of the Police Role: A Sociological Review." *Crime and Justice* 1: 239–288.

Scott, Michael S., and Ronald V. Clarke. 2020. *Problem-Oriented Policing: Successful Case Studies.* New York: Routledge.

Simpson, Rylan. 2019. "Police Vehicles as Symbols of Legitimacy." *Journal of Experimental Criminology* 15 (1): 87–101.

Simpson, Rylan. 2020. "Officer Appearance and Perceptions of Police: Accoutrements as Signals of Intent." *Policing: A Journal of Policy and Practice* 14 (1): 243–57.

Smith, Richard. 2019. "The 'Police Change Manager': Exploring a New Leadership Paradigm for Policing." *International Journal of Police Science & Management.* Advance Online: https://doi:10.1177/1461355719854104 .

Stephens, Darrel W., Sheldon Greenberg, and Julia Hill. 2011. *Strategic Communications Practices: A Toolkit for Police Executives.* Washington, DC: US Department of Justice, Office of Community Oriented Policing Services.

Stuntz, William J. 2011. *The Collapse of American Criminal Justice.* Cambridge: Harvard University Press.

Terrill, William. 2003. "Police Use of Force and Suspect Resistance: The Micro Process of the Police-Suspect Encounter." *Police Quarterly* 6 (1): 51–83.

Thompson, George, and Jerry B. Jenkins. 1993. *Verbal Judo: The Gentle Art of Persuasion.* Colorado Springs: Alive Communications.

Ungar, Sanford J. 1976. *FBI.* Boston: Little, Brown and Company.

Vollmer, August. 1936. *The Police and Modern Society.* Berkeley: University of California Press.

Weisburd, David, Cody W. Telep, Joshua C. Hinkle, and John E. Eck. 2008. *The Effects of Problem-Oriented Policing on Crime and Disorder.* Campbell Systematic Reviews. Campbell Collaboration. Retrieved from https://doi:10.4073/csr.2008.14 .

Wilson, O. W. 1950. *Police Administration.* New York: McGraw-Hill.

Wilson, O. W. 1951. "Progress in Police Administration." *Journal of Criminal Law, Criminology & Police Science* 42 (2): 141–54.

CHAPTER 12

The Role of Police in Fostering Community Resilience

A Communication Perspective

J. Brian Houston, Chandrika C. Collins, and Scott E. Branton

Communities that are resilient are able to experience a crisis and recover. For example, a resilient community might experience a disaster such as a hurricane and, after a time of emergency response and rebuilding, return to a state of well-being and functionality similar to what existed before the event. Specifically, this means that following a disaster, people in the community who are injured would heal, damaged and destroyed buildings would be repaired and rebuilt, economic losses would be regained, and community members would experience safety and opportunity. A community needs a variety of effective systems and sectors to be resilient. Examples of important community resilience sectors include health care, education, emergency management, media, and more. Another important sector in fostering community resilience is the police. Police are important to community resilience because they are responsible for ensuring public safety and assisting with the response to disasters and crises in a community (see chapter 9). However, the role of police in fostering community resilience is understudied. To address this gap, we examine the role of police in fostering community resilience in this chapter. Effective communication is essential to community resilience, and thus we specifically explore how police can use communication to help communities cope with and recover from disasters and crises.

To begin understanding the role of police in fostering community resilience, this chapter first examines popular definitions and models of community resilience and then considers the role of communication in fostering community resilience. After this overview, we use Houston, Spialek, Cox, Greenwood, and First's (2015) model to consider ways that police can contribute to community resilience. Overall, we identify and discuss several different areas where police have opportunities to strengthen a community's capacity to deal with a crisis. To begin, we review definitions of community resilience.

COMMUNITY RESILIENCE

Definition

Resilient communities are able to "bounce forward" following a crisis (Houston 2015; Manyena, O'Brien, O'Keefe, and Rose 2011). Bouncing forward means that, after a crisis, a community is able to return (bounce) to some pre-crisis level of functioning, but it does so at a later time (forward) and is thus likely to be changed as a result. Community resilience can be considered relative to a variety of crises, but the most common events studied in the community resilience literature are collective disasters resulting from natural hazards (e.g., tornado, hurricane) or human causes (e.g., terrorist attack, chemical spill; Houston et al. 2015). Therefore, for example, if a community experiences a disruption like an earthquake and subsequently uses internal and external resources to rebuild infrastructure, restart community programs and institutions (e.g., schools), and recover collective functioning, then it could be judged to be resilient. This resilience might be exhibited by data that illustrates a return to pre-event levels of collective economic productivity, educational achievement, or mental health and well-being after the event. Following an event, the community (including individuals, families, and organizations) is changed, but eventually returns to functioning at a level that is comparable with the functioning that occurred before the crisis. Additionally, beyond coping with events, resilient communities may be better equipped to identify issues that can cause crises and then intervene to prevent those events from occurring (Acosta, Chandra, and Madrigano 2017). For example, resilient communities may be able to identify the threat of violent extremism and work together to prevent this threat from resulting in acts of violence that negatively affect the community (Ellis and Abdi 2017; see chapter 21).

Communities include individuals, families, organizations, institutions, and neighborhoods. As such, community resilience requires dynamic and robust interconnections among these people and groups (Acosta, Chandra, and Madrigano 2017). Community resilience is inherently a *collective* activity that requires the participation of people and groups across the community (Pfefferbaum and Klomp 2013). A resilient community is not merely a community of resilient individuals; it is a collective in which communication is central to the collaborative action among members of the community (Houston 2018).

Community Resilience Models

A variety of community resilience models have been proposed (see table 12.1 for an overview of all models discussed in this chapter). Norris, Stevens, Pfefferbaum, Wyche, and Pfefferbaum (2008) posited a community resilience model that includes four core adaptive capacities: community competence, economic development, information and

TABLE 12.1. Components of Four Popular Community Resilience Models

Norris et al. (2008)	Pfefferbaum et al (2015)	Patel et al. (2017)	Houston et al. (2015)
Information/Communication • Narratives • Responsible media • Skills and infrastructure • Trusted info sources Community Competence • Community action • Critical reflection and problem-solving skills • Flexibility and creativity • Collective efficacy empowerment • Political partnerships Social Capital • Social support • Social embeddedness • Organizational linkages and cooperation • Citizen participation • Sense of community • Attachment to place Economic Development • Fairness of risk • Economic resources • Equity of resource distribution	Connection and Caring Resources Transformative Potential Disaster Management Information and Communication	Local Knowledge Community Network and Relationships Communication Health Governance and Leadership Resources Economic Investment Preparedness Mental Outlook	Communication Systems and Resources • Media • Official sources of information • Communication infrastructure • Citizens and organizations Community Relationships • Social support • Social capital • Citizen engagement • Sense of community • Attachment to place • Organizational linkages • Public–private partnerships • Political partnerships • Media relations Community Attributes • Flexibility, creativity, and efficacy • Diversity and equality • Social justice • Economic resources Strategic Communication Processes • Community competence • Community narratives • Disaster and risk processes • Community/economic development

Note: Models are listed by authors' names. Subcomponents, when included in a model, are listed with bullets.

communication, and social capital. Each of these adaptive capacities, in turn, includes multiple resources. For example, the information and communication adaptive capacity includes community narratives, responsible media, skills and infrastructures, and trusted sources of information. For Norris et al. (2008), these adaptive capacities (and the included resources) facilitate a community's recovery following an adverse event. As such, resilience is a *process* enabled through these capacities, as opposed to a static end-state.

Pfefferbaum, Pfefferbaum, Nitiéma, Houston, and Van Horn (2015) provide another community resilience model that includes five domains: connection and caring, community resources, transformative potential, disaster management, and information and communication. Overall, this model is similar to the Norris et al. (2008) approach to community resilience, though this framework includes a domain specifically focused on disaster management. Additionally, Patel, Rogers, Amlot, and Rubin (2017) conducted a systematic review of the community resilience literature and identified nine constituent elements of community resilience: local knowledge, community networks and relationships, communication, health, governance and leadership, resources, economic investment, preparedness, and mental outlook.

Communication and Community Resilience

One important component identified in all community resilience models is communication. As noted above, Norris et al. (2008) identify information and communication as one of four community resilience adaptive capacities, Pfefferbaum et al. (2015) also include information and communication in their five-domain model, and Patel et al. (2017) identify communication as one of nine community resilience constituent elements. Together, communication is a core community resilience component in each of these approaches. Moreover, other community resilience components in these models prominently feature communication. For example, Norris et al. (2008) include a social capital adaptive capacity, which requires connections and communication among community members, and a community competence adaptive capacity, which necessitates community deliberation and dialogue. Additionally, Patel et al. (2017) identify two constituent elements of community resilience for which communication is important: local knowledge, which is shared among community members via communication; and community networks and relationships, which are established and maintained through communication. Overall then, communication is a standalone component of community resilience and is also central to facilitating a variety of other community resilience capacities.

Given the importance of communication in understanding and fostering community resilience, Houston et al. (2015) developed a community resilience model based on communication and media perspectives, utilizing communication ecology, public relations, and strategic communication perspectives. The authors identified four main community resilience components: communication systems and resources, community relationships, strategic communication processes, and community attributes. The *communication systems and resources* component includes local and national media (traditional and social), community communication infrastructure (e.g., emergency sirens, cellular networks), official sources of information (e.g., government agencies, emergency responders), and citizens[1] and organizations in the community. The *community relationships* component includes a variety of communication connections and interactions, such as social capital, citizen engagement with the community, public–private partnerships, and political partnerships. The *strategic communication processes* component includes four main subcomponents: community competence, community narratives, disaster and risk processes, and community and economic development. *Community competence* involves community collective and deliberative activities such as community planning, community action, and community problem-solving. *Community narratives* include community storytelling and visioning. *Disaster and risk processes* include disaster and risk education, preparedness, and planning; disaster response coordination; and community resilience awareness building. *Community and economic development* involves the discussion and planning of community economic development and critical examinations of community economic inequities. Finally, *community attributes*, or the characteristics of a community, include the community's creativity, diversity, equality, and available economic resources.

POLICING AND COMMUNITY RESILIENCE

In this chapter, we utilize Houston et al.'s (2015) communication and community resilience model to examine the role of police in fostering community resilience. Varieties of systems and sectors have been identified as being necessary for community resilience. For example, Gurwitch Pfefferbaum, Montgomery, Klomp, and Reissman (2007) discuss business, community leadership, cultural and faith-based groups and organizations, first responders, health care, media, mental health, public health, and school and childcare settings as sectors relevant to a community's overall community resilience. Longstaff, Armstrong, Perrin, Parker, and Hidek (2010) identify several subsystems that are relevant for community resilience, including ecological, economic, physical infrastructure, civil society, and governance. While approaches such as these include sectors that may include police (e.g., first responders), existing community resilience scholarship has yet to consider the role of police in facilitating community resilience. This omission is surprising given the responsibility of police in ensuring public safety and responding to disasters and crises. Thus, we address this gap and propose that police are an integral community organization/institution that can help foster community resilience. We consider the ways that police can affect a community's resilience using a communication perspective to understanding community resilience. We primarily examine resilience relative to disasters and community crises resulting from natural hazards (e.g., tornado, earthquake) and human causes (e.g., terrorist attack, mass shooting). Identified and discussed below are opportunities for police to foster community resilience in each of Houston et al.'s (2015) four community resilience components (see figure 12.1).

Police as an Official Source of Information

Communication systems and resources are a necessary component of resilient communities. These systems and resources can include numerous communication media,

FIGURE 12.1. Overview of the Roles of Police in Fostering Community Resilience

technologies, and sources. For example, one communication system is local television news, which includes both a communication medium (television) and an information source (local news organization). Local television news may disseminate information about a disaster before, during, or after an event to facilitate resilience (Houston et al. 2019).

Within the ecology of communication systems and resources, official sources of information are important for community resilience. Official sources of information typically include governmental or organizational sources that can provide the most comprehensive and best-analyzed assessment of the situation. For example, in the United States, when the National Weather Service releases a tornado warning for a community (https://www.weather.gov/safety/tornado-ww), this constitutes the most advanced and accurate source of information that an area is in danger related to a natural hazard and that individuals need to take protective actions.

In a community, the police function as an official source of information that may be able to communicate information to community members that can help foster resilience related to an event. As first responders, police are among the first professionals on the scene following a disaster (Adams and Anderson 2019). Thus, police can provide situational updates to other responders; they can also facilitate safety and resilience by disseminating information to the public. As an example, police responding to events might inform the public about areas in a community to avoid following a disaster or could let citizens know where members of the public can provide help for those affected. The police might provide this information through press conferences, via interviews with local journalists, or directly through social media. Increasingly, social media are the mechanisms by which disaster information can be quickly shared by official sources with audiences, and police are continuing to engage social media as part of many aspects of their work (Perez 2017). In fact, Dai, He, Tian, Giraldi, and Gu (2017) found that strong community engagement with police departments was often predicated on active and intentional social media use. In all, police can function as an essential official source of information in a community that can help foster resilience related to community disasters and crises.

Police and Community Member Relationships

Another central component of a resilient community includes the community relationships that can contribute to recovery following a challenging event. Varieties of possible meaningful relationships were identified by Houston et al. (2015), including public–private partnerships, social capital, and organizational linkages. However, one missing relationship in this original model is police and community member relationships.

Police constitute an arm of the government established to promote public safety, in part, through the use of force intended to decrease crime. The power to use force against citizens requires the consent of the governed, because the establishment of the police means that some individual liberties are sacrificed in return for the protection provided (Taylor and Auerhahn 2015). Citizens are more likely to provide consent for government entities that are perceived to be legitimate, and citizen perceptions of police legitimacy can influence overall police effectiveness (Tyler 2006). Individual perceptions of police legitimacy are based on the belief that police appropriately intervene with community members regarding public conduct (Meares and Kahan 1998). Community perceptions of police legitimacy may be the result of community members believing that the police make decisions fairly and treat people appropriately (National Academies of Sciences, Engineering, and Medicine [NASEM] 2018). Fair police decision making is neutral (not biased) and considers the citizens' point of view and experience; police treating people appropriately occurs when police show respect toward citizens and act trustworthily (i.e., police "act in good faith"; NASEM 2018, 230). Ultimately, positive police and community interactions can result in healthy relationships where the role of the police is acknowledged and supported by citizens because the police are perceived to act fairly toward citizens in the service of public safety. Citizens who perceive the police to be legitimate are more likely to assist and support the police in their public safety efforts (Mazerolle, Antrobus, Bennett, and Tyler, 2013; see chapters 8 and 22).

From a community resilience perspective, strong police and citizen relationships are one form of connection that can strengthen a community's ability to cope with and recover from a crisis. For example, if the police function as an official source of information during a disaster as described previously, then citizens who trust the police will be more likely to pay attention to and use that information. Conversely, community members who are distrustful of the police may ignore or not believe this information. Additionally, if police are dispatched to a disaster scene to help ensure safety following the event, the community members who trust the police are more likely to embrace and utilize that assistance.

Unfortunately, in many US communities, there exist problematic relationships between police and underrepresented groups (see chapters 5–8). Minority group members report less trust of and engagement with the police compared to White community members (Braga, Brunson, and Drakulich 2019; Kahn et al. 2017). A lack of trust in police among underrepresented groups may stem from direct interactions with police officers (Hagan et al. 2005) and indirect exposure to police interactions via friends and family (Brunson 2007). As Braga, Brunson and Drakulich (2019, 540) explain,

> Communities of color likely view the police through a combination of lenses, including their historical functions supporting slavery, lynchings, and discrimination; their role combatting civil rights protests; a series of highly visible incidents of police abuses of black citizens, both past and present; and the personal and vicarious experiences of interactions with the police.

If police and community member relationships are necessary for community resilience, then situations where some groups in a community do not trust the police inevitably reduces the resilience of the overall community. The distrust of police among marginalized community groups represents a barrier to community resilience that has not been considered in previous community resilience literature. Thus when examining community resilience in general, and the role of police and community resilience in particular, inequalities must be considered. Relatedly, the incorporation of social justice values can more fully calibrate community resilience analysis and action (see Acosta, Chandra, and Madrigano 2017). A community justice model of policing is one approach to integrate social justice aspects into police work. In this approach, citizens communicate their priorities to inform police work (Tayler and Auerhahn 2014). This means that community perceptions and needs guide law enforcement efforts. Over time, community justice policing that incorporates and respects marginalized citizens' priorities could begin to improve relationships with police and contribute to greater community resilience.

More generally, different approaches to policing may influence trust of the police among community members. Proactive policing strategies are those that seek to prevent or reduce crime, compared to reactive policing strategies that emphasize investigating or responding to crimes that have already occurred (NASEM 2018). Proactive policing strategies can include place-based, person-focused, problem-solving, and community-based approaches (see chapter 10). Place-based policing focuses law enforcement efforts on crime "hot spots" and seeks to intervene in these areas to reduce future crime in places where it is apparently more likely to occur. Place-based policing has been found to not positively or negatively affect the community's trust of police (NASEM 2018). Person-focused policing focuses on individuals (or groups) who are thought to be more likely to commit a crime, including individuals who have committed crimes in the past.

Problem-solving policing seeks to identify problems in a community that contribute to crime and then develops solutions to address those issues. This process can potentially occur with community engagement. For example, community engagement is enhanced when police departments do more than simply distribute crime-related information but, instead, also provide information and suggestions that facilitate problem-solving (Dai et al. 2017). Problem-solving approaches have been found to strengthen community satisfaction in the police, at least in the short-term (NASEM 2018). Community-based policing attempts to engage with the community to capitalize on community resources to prevent and reduce crime. These efforts inherently involve police consultation and collaboration with community members. Like problem-solving policing, community-based policing has been found to be related to community satisfaction with the police (Gill, Weisburd, Telep, Vitter, and Bennett 2014; NASEM 2018).

Police and Strategic Communication Processes

Another community resilience component includes strategic communication processes. This component includes four subcomponents: community competence, community narratives, disaster and risk processes, and community and economic development. Police are most likely to have roles in community competence and disaster and risk processes.

Community competence efforts include activities such as community planning and action, community critical reflection, and community problem-solving. Problem-solving and community-based policing, as previously described, are proactive policing models that connect well with these community competence activities. Thus, police problem-solving and community problem-solving could be connected to and integrated with other community competence activities. That is, community efforts to develop plans and actions related to a variety of issues that might foster resilience could be integrated with police efforts to do the same in the area of public safety. This police and community deliberation, communication, and planning could occur via community meetings (Houston 2019), citizen advisory groups working with police, and police interaction with citizens in neighborhood and community spaces. Ideally, police and the broader community would have a shared understanding of problems and have mutually agreed-upon potential solutions for these issues. Some solutions might fall under the purview of the police, others may be largely community-based, and still others may be fully shared by the police and community members.

A robust approach to police and community problem-solving may align with a community-based approach to policing. Community-based policing fully considers the resources available in the community to foster public safety and, as such, requires active citizen input and participation (see, again, chapter 10). These policing processes are communicative as police and citizen interaction, discussion, and deliberation are the mechanisms that make them possible. Thus, they share many characteristics of the community competence processes included in Houston et al.'s (2015) community resilience model. NASEM (2018) notes that community-based policing may increase community efficacy, but we would posit that such a policing process done well would also bolster community resilience. Regarding community competency efforts, the police would be an essential partner in any work to solve community problems and take effective community action related to preparing for and responding to community crises. As Braga, Welsh, and Schnell (2015) discuss, an ideal approach to police and community relationships is the development of a *coproduction* model, where police and community work together to identify problems and develop solutions for the challenges identified by the community. This coproduction would require police engagement with different groups and community stakeholders across the community.

In addition to participating in community competence efforts, police also have a critical role to play in disaster and risk processes in a community. These processes can include disaster and risk planning, response coordination, and community resilience awareness building. Given the police's role in ensuring public safety and serving as first responders to community emergencies, it is imperative that police are engaged in any community discussions and planning around disasters. Community understanding of threats from natural hazards or human causes (e.g., violent extremism; Ellis and Abdi 2017) can be improved from the expert perspective of police. Additionally, police awareness and understanding of threats can be strengthened from community member insights. Community resilience efforts require the participation of all the key systems in a community, which includes police. Ongoing interaction between police and citizens about disaster risk issues may occur via meetings and social media (Sherman 2011) allowing communicative engagement to continue over time scaling up and down as needed based on events.

Finally, police have a fundamental role to play in keeping communities safe so that citizens can interact, deliberate, and connect with each other (Houston et al. 2013). Even in communities where distrust of police is high, residents routinely seek crime prevention and protection from the police (Hagan et al. 2018) because there are few other mechanisms available to help keep individuals and families safe. As such, if a community is to exhibit the high levels of social capital, community connections, and collective dialogue and planning necessary to be resilient, it will require a level of safety and cohesion that is likely supported by effective and just police (Platts-Fowler and Robinson 2016).

Police Engagement with Community Attributes

The final component of community resilience includes community attributes. This component captures the community characteristics and resources that can contribute to resilience. For example, community resources (e.g., wealth, industry, organizations) may provide capacities that help a community better cope with and recover from a disaster. Additionally, communities that are flexible, efficacious, creative, and diverse may also be more resilient compared to communities that are less so. For a community to be resilient, police will equitably serve and protect all citizens, without providing preferential treatment to some citizens over others based on race, gender, class, or other factors. Ultimately, community resilience is about the adaptive capacity of the *entire community*. If some portions of a community do not have access to resources (such as police protection), then this inequity reduces the overall level of community resilience. Moreover, the most substantial community resilience contribution that police can likely make is assisting vulnerable members of a community (Poolman, Wilshaw, and Grace 2019). Assisting individuals with the fewest resources or the most exposure to hazards will ultimately benefit the adaptive capacity of the entire community and should be a priority for police.

In addition, police should know and respect the community they serve, and part of this includes a respectful awareness of the community attributes. Engagement with a community's flexibility, creativity, diversity, and efficacy are crucial to community resilience. Police should recognize and respect a community's diverse attributes in an effort to reduce biases and strengthen relationships (Braga, Brunson, and Drakulich 2019). This engagement can occur through police and community member interactions and communication. Additionally, a community attribute not included in Houston et al.'s (2015) original model is the safety of a community. As previously discussed, a safe community will have more opportunities for the connections, interactions, and communication that can foster resilience. Additionally, a safer community is more likely to be resilient because it will likely have fewer challenges and crises to manage. The negative impacts of disasters, crises, and trauma can accrue so that the more adversity individuals and communities experience, the more difficult it is to recover due to resource depletion. In many ways, a safer community exhibits a stronger capacity for resilience.

CONCLUSIONS

In this chapter, we have provided an overview of how police can foster community resilience. We posit that police have an indispensable role in and significant capacity for helping a community prevent, prepare for, cope with, and recover from community crises. However, implicit in our previous discussion are the many ways that bad policing can harm community resilience. For example, policing that disproportionately cites, arrests, or uses force against certain groups in a community (e.g., African Americans; US Department of Justice 2015) not only harms police–citizen relations that can reduce community resilience, but may also constitute race-based traumatic stress that harms members of the community (Bryant-Davis 2007; see chapters 5 and 16). Many community systems may be capable of making a community more or less resilient; however, the particular capacity for police to be a community resilience resource or a community resilience threat is clear.

In addition to adopting policing approaches that engage community members (e.g., problem-solving or community-based policing as described previously), a key to ensuring that police have a positive impact in a community is to foster the well-being and resilience of police officers and police departments (Hill and Giles 2019). Police officers may face a variety of stressors related to their work (e.g., threats to safety, exposure to potentially traumatic events, and public scrutiny of performance) that can affect job performance and well-being. Workplace interventions and programs to support police officers and foster health coping skills and resilience may result in better police performance, contributing to more community resilience. Therefore, community investments in supporting police constitute an investment in a healthier and more adaptive community.

Understanding the role that police have in promoting resilience in a community during incidents of community crisis and disaster is the first step in developing research and practice that will yield applied methods in the future. Given the limited existing scholarship that examines the role of police in facilitating community resilience, this is the first area of future research that needs attention. Future research should identify more nuanced aspects of law enforcement's role as an official source of information for community members. One possibility is to examine how trust of police influences community members' engagement with police and use of police information. Researchers could also develop and evaluate strategies to build trust and mutual respect among police and community members. Intergroup contact theory (e.g., Harwood 2018) and communication accommodation theory (e.g., Giles 2016) are two areas of scholarship that can be utilized to develop such strategies.

Future research should also examine how police officers understand their role relative to fostering community resilience. The current chapter has described several specific ways that police can contribute to community resilience; however, it is unknown whether any of these suggestions align with the ways that police approach their work. Additionally, police officers might identify other ways their efforts can increase a community's resilience that were not identified here. Lastly, this chapter has identified the importance of safety (facilitated by the police) for community resilience. Future research should more fully engage the ways that safety fosters community resilience, with a particular focus on how community justice approaches to policing might facilitate increases in safety among vulnerable members of a community that could greatly improve the resilience of the community.

NOTE

1. Throughout this chapter we use the term "citizen" as shorthand to mean a community member. That is, we mean anyone living in a community, regardless of legal citizen status.

REFERENCES

Acosta, Joi, Anita Chandra, and Jaime Madrigano. 2017. *An Agenda to Advance Integrative Resilience Research and Practice: Key Themes from a Resilience Roundtable*. Retrieved from https://www.rand.org/pubs/research_reports/RR1683.html .

Adams, Terri M., and Leigh R. Anderson. 2019. *Policing in Natural Disasters: Stress, Resilience, and the Challenges of Emergency Management*. Philadelphia: Temple University Press.

Braga, Anthony A., Rod K. Brunson, and Kevin M. Drakulich. 2019. "Race, Place, and Effective Policing." *Annual Review of Sociology* 45 (1): 535–55.

Braga, Anthony A., Brandon C. Welsh, and Cory Schnell. 2015. "Can Policing Disorder Reduce Crime? A Systematic Review and Meta-Analysis." *Journal of Research in Crime and Delinquency* 52 (4): 567–88.

Brunson, Rod K. 2007. "'Police Don't Like Black People': African-American Young Men's Accumulated Police Experiences." *Criminology & Public Policy* 6 (1): 71–101.

Bryant-Davis, Thema. 2007. "Healing Requires Recognition: The Case for Race-Based Traumatic Stress." *The Counseling Psychologist* 35 (1): 135–43.

Dai, Mengyan, Wu He, Xin Tian, Ashley Giraldi, and Feng Gu. 2017. "Working with Communities on Social Media: Varieties in the Use of Facebook and Twitter by Local Police." *Online Information Review* 41 (6): 782–96.

Ellis, B. Heidi, and Saida Abdi. 2017. "Building Community Resilience to Violent Extremism through Genuine Partnerships." *American Psychologist* 72 (3): 289–300.

Giles, Howard, ed. 2016. *Communication Accommodation Theory: Negotiating Personal Relationships and Social Identities across Contexts*. Cambridge: Cambridge University Press.

Gill, Charlotte, David Weisburd, Cody W. Telep, Zoe Vitter, and Trevor Bennett. 2014. "Community-Oriented Policing to Reduce Crime, Disorder and Fear and Increase Satisfaction and Legitimacy among Citizens: A Systematic Review." *Journal of Experimental Criminology* 10: 399–428.

Gurwitch, Robin H., Betty Pfefferbaum, Juliann M. Montgomery, Richard W. Klomp, and Dori B. Reissman. 2007. *Building Community Resilience for Children and Families*. Oklahoma City: Terrorism and Disaster Center at the University of Oklahoma Health Sciences Center.

Hagan, John, Bill McCarthy, Daniel Herda, and Andrea Cann Chandrasekher. 2018. "Dual-Process Theory of Racial Isolation, Legal Cynicism, and Reported Crime." *Proceedings of the National Academy of Sciences* 115 (28): 7190–99.

Hagan, John, Carla Shedd, and Monique R. Payne. 2005. "Race, Ethnicity, and Youth Perceptions of Criminal Injustice." *American Sociological Review* 70 (3): 381–407.

Harwood, Jake. 2018. "Intergroup Contact." In *The Oxford Encyclopedia of Intergroup Communication*, edited by Howard Giles and Jake Harwood, Vol. 1, 765–77. New York: Oxford University Press.

Hill, Shawn, and Howard Giles. 2019. "Resilience as a Department Cultural Initiative." *Police Chief Online*. Retrieved from https://www.policechiefmagazine.org/resilience-as-a-department-cultural-initiative/ .

Houston, J. Brian. 2015. "Bouncing Forward: Assessing Advances in Community Resilience Assessment, Intervention, and Theory to Guide Future Work." *American Behavioral Scientist* 59 (2): 175–80.

Houston, J. Brian. 2018. "Community Resilience and Communication: Dynamic Interconnections Between and among Individuals, Families, and Organizations." *Journal of Applied Communication Research* 46 (1): 19–22.

Houston, J. Brian. 2019. "Community Resilience and Social Media." In *New Media in Times of Crisis*, edited by Keri K. Stephens, 177–92. New York: Routledge.

Houston, J. Brian, Megan K. Schraedley, Mary E. Worley, Katherine Reed, and Janet Saidi. 2019. "Disaster Journalism: Fostering Citizen and Community Disaster Mitigation, Preparedness, Response, Recovery, and Resilience across the Disaster Cycle." *Disasters* 43 (3): 591–611.

Houston, J. Brian, Hyunjn Seo, Leigh Anne Taylor Knight, Emily J. Kennedy, Joshua Hawthorne, and Sara L. Trask. 2013. "Urban Youth's Perspectives on Flash Mobs." *Journal of Applied Communication Research* 41 (3): 236–52.

Houston, J. Brian, Matthew L. Spialek, Joy Cox, Molly M. Greenwood, and Jennifer First. 2015. "The Centrality of Communication and Media in Fostering Community Resilience: A Framework for Assessment and Intervention." *American Behavioral Scientist* 59 (2): 270–83.

Kahn, Kimberly Barsamian, J. Katherine Lee, Brian Renauer, Kris R. Henning, and Greg Stewart. 2017. "The Effects of Perceived Phenotypic Racial Stereotypical and Social Identity Threat on Racial Minorities Attitudes about Police." *The Journal of Social Psychology* 157 (4): 416–28.

Longstaff, Patricia, Nicholas Armstrong, Keli Perrin, Whitney Parker, and Matthew Hidek. 2010. "Building Resilient Communities: A Preliminary Framework for Assessment." *Homeland Security Affairs* 6 (3): 1–23.

Manyena, Siambabala Bernard, Geoff O'Brien, Phil O'Keefe, and Joanne Rose. 2011. "Disaster Resilience: A Bounce Back or Bounce Forward Ability?" *Local Environment* 16 (5): 417–24.

Mazerolle, Lorraine, Emma Antrobus, Sarah Bennett, and Tom R. Tyler. 2013. "Shaping Citizen Perceptions of Police Legitimacy: A Randomized Field Trial of Procedural Justice." *Criminology* 51 (1): 33–63.

Meares, Tracey L., and Dan M. Kahan. 1998. "Law and (Norms of) Order in the Inner City." *Law & Society Review* 32 (4): 805–38.

National Academies of Sciences, Engineering, and Medicine (NASEM). 2018. *Proactive Policing: Effects on Crime and Communities*. Washington DC: The National Academies Press.

Norris, Fran, Susan Stevens, Betty Pfefferbaum, Karen Wyche, and Rose L. Pfefferbaum. 2008. "Community Resilience as a Metaphor, Theory, Set of Capacities, and Strategy for Disaster Readiness." *American Journal of Community Psychology* 41 (1): 127–50.

Patel, Sonny S., M. Brooke Rogers, Richard Amlot, and G. James Rubin. 2017. "What Do We Mean by 'Community Resilience'? A Systematic Literature Review of How It Is Defined in the Literature." *PLoS Currents Disasters* 9 (Feburary 1). Retrieved from https://doi:10.1371/currents.dis.db775aff25efc5ac4f0660ad9c9f7db2 .

Perez, Kaitlyn. 2017 (June 30). "Social Media Has Become a Critical Part of Law Enforcement." *International Police Foundation*. Retrieved from https://www.policefoundation.org/social-media-has-become-a-critical-part-of-law-enforcement/ .

Pfefferbaum, Rose L., and Richard W. Klomp. 2013. "Community Resilience, Disasters, and the Public's Health." In *Community Engagement, Organization, and Development for Public Health Practice*, edited by Frederick G. Murphy, 275–98. New York: Springer.

Pfefferbaum, Rose L., Betty Pfefferbaum, Pascal Nitiéma, J. Brian Houston, and Richard L. Van Horn. 2015. "Assessing Community Resilience: An Application of the Expanded CART Survey Instrument with Affiliated Volunteer Responders." *American Behavioral Scientist* 59 (2): 181–99.

Platts-Fowler, Deborah, and David Robinson. 2016. "Community Resilience: A Policy Tool for Local Government?" *Local Government Studies* 42 (5): 762–84.

Poolman, Sarah, Richard Wilshaw, and Jamie Grace. 2019. "Human Rights in Policing: The Past, Present and Future." *The Political Quarterly* 90 (3): 449–56.

Sherman, Aliza. 2011 (August 31). "How Law Enforcement Agencies Are Using Social Media to Better Serve the Public." *Mashable*. Retrieved from https://mashable.com/2011/08/31/law-enforcement-social-media-use/ .

Taylor, Caitlin J., and Kathleen Auerhahn. 2014. "Community Justice and Public Safety: Assessing Criminal Justice Policy through the Lens of the Social Contract." *Criminology & Criminal Justice* 15 (3): 300–320.

Tyler, Tom R. 2006. *Why People Obey the Law* (second edition). Princeton: Princeton University Press.

US Department of Justice. 2015. *Department of Justice Report Regarding the Criminal Investigation into the Shooting Death of Michael Brown by Ferguson, Missouri Police Officer Darren Wilson*. Retrieved from https://www.justice.gov/sites/default/files/opa/press-releases/attachments/2015/03/04/doj_report_on_shooting_of_michael_brown_1.pdf .

CHAPTER 13

"I See You"

The Mediation of Complaints Can Build Understanding and Trust

Bernard K. Melekian

During my forty-five-year tenure in law enforcement, including thirteen years as a police chief, one of my greatest sources of frustration, both personal and professional, arose from attempting to resolve civilian complaints related to officer conduct. The stated objective of the complaint process is to resolve the complaint in a manner that is fair, is just, and satisfies all of the involved parties. Unfortunately, all too often, the process produced the opposite effect. The search for a better system led me to consider mediation, which though not perfect, went a long way toward achieving the desired outcome.

The law enforcement disciplinary process is intended to demonstrate both transparency and accountability with respect to the law enforcement officer's relationship with the public. Stated another way, the process should ensure that the officer's conduct reflects the stated values of both the jurisdiction employing the officer and the law enforcement profession. The achievement of these objectives relies on a formal legalistic system that generally fails to achieve these stated ends. In this chapter, I will argue that the use of mediation to resolve complaints can provide both transparency and accountability for the majority of complaints.

SOCIAL NORMS IN POLICE AND PUBLIC INTERACTIONS

Groups in conflict-affected societies develop social rules and norms to define how they will interact with other groups as well as with the group with whom they identify

(Ginty 2014). An officer's relationship with the public is transactional; that is, it generally occurs under a predetermined set of circumstances and is defined by role expectations and preconceived perceptions on the part of both the public and the officers. The tensions between the police and the communities they serve arise, in today's society, from both a lack of trust in and a misperception of the motivations of the "other" (Kastoryano 2010). If an interaction with an officer goes so badly that the civilian—the non-law enforcement person interacting with the officer—feels compelled to file a formal complaint, the traditional process that follows mirrors a criminal investigation. Specifically, interviews are conducted, evidence is gathered, and a trier of fact makes a determination as to the guilt or innocence of the accused officer. In the alternative, mediation offers a means by which the two parties can arrive at place of understanding as to the actions and motivations of the other (Walker, Archbold, and Herbst 2002).

One key to understanding both the complaint process and the role that mediation can play in facilitating that process, is to acknowledge the critical aspect of social roles and expectations. In my experience, the majority of complaints against officers do not involve illegal conduct such as brutality or corruption. Often, they are not even violations of policy. Rather they are attitudinal; that is, they tend to stem from perceptions of rudeness or dismissive or condescending attitudes on the part of the officer (Giles, Willemyns, Gallois, and Anderson 2007) or a belief that the officer's actions are motivated by bias or prejudice toward the involved party. At a macro level, such preconceptions may already be present prior to the contact between the officer and the civilian (see the introduction). These preconceptions may arise from shared experiences within the civilian's group, media reports (see chapters 14 and 15), or prior personal experience (Hasisi 2008). At the micro level, that is at the moment of interaction, these preconceptions may be reinforced by the officer's body language, tone of voice, or subtle actions such as eye-rolling or failing to acknowledge the citizen's statements (see Tyler 2006).

Law enforcement officers, particularly those working in a uniformed patrol function, are expected to conform to the role expectations of the job. Thus, the individual civilian interacting with a law enforcement officer approaches that interaction with definite expectations as to how the officer will conduct himself or herself. It is not critical, or perhaps even relevant, that such expectations be factually based. It is equally important to realize that the officer also approaches the interaction with a definitive expectation as to how the civilian should conduct *themselves*. However, this interaction does not involve two equal players. The power in this transaction lies with the officer and both parties are aware of that fact. I have defined this reality as transactional inequality, and the consequence is that both parties, but particularly the citizen, are expected to conform to a socially proscribed set of behaviors. Communication accommodation theory suggests that these predefined role-behaviors limit the ability for the involved individuals to connect on a more personal level. Rather they ensure that the communication remains a more socially scripted syntax (e.g., Gasiorek and Giles 2015).

The interaction occasioned by the issuance of a traffic citation offers a good example of an intergroup encounter (i.e., between the officer and the civilian). Each party approaches the interaction with different motivations and expectations. These expectations are defined from both an individual and a community perspective. Calling upon expectancy violation theory, dissatisfaction with the process arises when one or both parties deviate from these social expectations (Burgoon 1993).

The interaction begins with the driver being pulled over by an officer, usually by means of activating lights and sirens to gain the driver's attention (see chapter 17). Upon approaching the driver's vehicle, often cautiously and with their hand on their weapon, the officer's first words will be to ask for the violator's license and registration. An equally common response on the part of the driver will be to ask the reason for being stopped. Should the officer choose to repeat the demand for the license and registration prior to answering question, the interaction is already moving—and divergently so—in a negative direction (see Gasiorek 2016).

Even if the driver complies, he or she will likely ask again about the reason for the stop. Regardless of whether the officer answers and offers an explanation (e.g., "you went through the stop sign without stopping"), the driver will likely want to debate the validity of the officer's assertion. It is quite likely that the tone and manner of the driver will contribute significantly to the ultimate outcome of this interaction, such as whether the driver receives a citation or a warning. Conversely, research shows that the tone and manner of the officer will have a strong influence on how the driver perceives not only this specific officer but the police more generally (e.g., Maguire, Lowrey, and Johnson 2017).

Each party has entered into this interaction with very different expectations. The officer seeks first and foremost to ensure his or her own physical safety. As a necessary part of that analysis, the officer seeks to determine both the identity and the attitude of the person being contacted. As part of that analysis, the officer seeks to ensure that the driver complies with all instructions and/or expected norms (see the introduction and chapter 17). In other words, the officer wants to know who he or she is dealing with and whether or not this interaction is likely to result in an altercation, whether verbal or physical.

Conversely, the driver's attitude is highly dependent on his or her perception about the reason for the stop combined with any preconceived views of the police. It is likely that there will be a high level of anxiety as the officer approaches the vehicle. This anxiety is likely to be heightened if the driver identifies with a group which has been historically (or currently) marginalized by law enforcement (e.g., a Black driver being stopped in a predominantly white neighborhood; see chapter 5) or if the driver is concerned about personal issues that, if known to the officer, will have potentially negative consequences (e.g., a warrant for unpaid tickets).

As it pertains to communication accommodation theory, this example is illustrative (see Gasiorek 2015). This interaction, even though well scripted (i.e., everyone generally understands what is expected of them), does not prevent all of the involved parties from playing out this dynamic solely from their own point of view. Generally, from the onset of the encounter until the two parties go their separate ways, the interaction plays out according to social norms. The officer, in his or her role as a representative of the government replete with uniform and the corresponding tools of authority, makes a legally appropriate request (e.g., may I see your driver's license and registration).

The driver, exercising his or her individual rights, inquires as to the reason for the stop and may well debate the validity of the officer's stated purpose for the stop.

Whether or not this interaction results in a citation, a written warning, or a verbal warning is almost immaterial. Indeed, procedural justice research (see chapter 8) suggests that the outcome of this interaction is far less important than the level of empathy and human connection (Tyler 2006). This is due in no small part to the resentment engendered by the powerlessness that drivers often feel in these types of interactions (see Overbeck, Tiedens, and Brion 2006).

Of critical importance is the fact that the responsibility for setting the tone and level of connectedness rests with the officer, as the power equation in this human interaction is not balanced. The officer controls the time and place of the stop. The officer determines the level of physical control he or she will exert (e.g., determining whether or not the driver should get out of the car). In short, the officer provides direction to the civilian and expects to receive compliance. The manner in which this direction is provided, and the degree of compliance received, are the X factors in this transaction (Melekian 2012).

Communication accommodation theory suggests that dialogue geared toward understanding of the "other's" motivation can help to bridge the described divide (e.g., Gasiorek and Giles 2015). Unfortunately, the street at the point of interaction with respect to this traffic ticket limits the opportunity for such interaction. As previously mentioned, both parties have anxiety around issues, which may not be readily apparent to the other party.

Traditionally, the method by which the public expresses dissatisfaction with the conduct of an officer is through the formal complaint process. Until approximately the last twenty years or so, the complaint process was often opaque and presented significant obstacles to a complainant who felt mistreated by law enforcement. While the effort to ensure public access to the complaint process has improved, there has been a corresponding increase in emphasizing the rights of individual officers. The conflict between officer rights and transparency to the public persists to this day.

THE TRADITIONAL COMPLAINT PROCESS

The traditional complaint process is based on a legalistic model, sometimes referred to as the "Criminal Trial Model," and is designed to gather objective facts (Roach 1999). With respect to allegations of excessive force, for example, it is highly probable that a thorough investigation will be able to establish whether such a complaint is factual at its core and what, if any, mitigating circumstances may be relevant.

However, the complaint process is not as effective in resolving issues that are more subjective, such as those complaints of which the core issue must be resolved by determining what the officer's attitude or motivation may have been at the point of interaction with the complaining party. These types of complaints arise as much from nonverbal cues, such as tone of voice, facial expressions, and body language in general, as from what the officer may have actually said.

The perceived intention to such nonverbal cues can be a function of the officer's delivery, the recipient's perception based on historical personal experience, or a combination of both. Regardless, determining motivation and intent under such circumstances is difficult at best. Technological tools, such as body cameras or car-based cameras, were developed with the thought that they might help to establish more clearly what happened at the point of contact. However, even the presence of video has not been shown to have a significant impact on either the public's trust in resolving complaints or on changes in officer conduct (Police Executive Research Forum 2018).

The traditional complaint process often begins at the front desk of a police station, which can be an intimidating environment under the best of circumstances. While other means of filing complaints are emerging, such as online reporting, these changes primarily apply to the point of entry, but have not resulted in overall systemic change. The complainant, either by phone or in person, must approach an officer indicating that they wish to file a complaint. Generally, the complaining party is either given a form or referred to a ranking officer who conducts a preliminary interview. In the past, it was not uncommon for the interviewing officer to greet the complainant with calculated indifference, if not with outright hostility. A more enlightened officer, usually a supervisor or watch commander, might offer to counsel the involved officer through the informal disciplinary process. Regardless of the behavior exhibited by the officer, generally the desired outcome was for the complaining party to leave without having filed a formal complaint.

Should a formal complaint be filed, it is then forwarded through the department's internal investigative process, usually referred to as internal affairs or professional standards. The speed by which the complainant will be contacted by the investigator is often a function of the seriousness of the allegations, the degree of external pressure, and the investigator's caseload. The complainant is generally the first person to be interviewed by the investigator. The interview is generally formal in nature and is often recorded, either by audio or video. After that interview is completed, the investigator moves on to speak with any relevant witnesses and ultimately the involved officer(s).

As was the case at the time of the stop, there is seldom any opportunity for an open, back-and-forth dialogue. The complainant's perceptions about the officer, the officer's perception of the complainant, and any background issues on either side are seldom explored. Even if they are, such subjective perceptions, particularly on the part of the complainant, have little bearing on the ultimate determination with respect to what sanctions, if any, will be imposed.

Once the interviews are complete, the investigator's report and any supporting evidence are forwarded through the department's review process, generally a review by the officer's chain of command. The final outcome is generally classified into one of the following categories:

- *Sustained*, meaning that the alleged policy violation occurred;
- *Not Sustained*, meaning that the allegations could not be proved or disproved; or
- *Unfounded*, meaning that the alleged violations did not occur.

In addition, some agencies have added a fourth category of *Exonerated/Justified*, meaning that the alleged actions occurred but were warranted under the circumstances.

Sustained complaints can take even longer to resolve, depending on whether the officer chooses to file an appeal. Depending on the jurisdiction and its respective labor agreements, this process can be extraordinarily complex and time consuming. Even in those states (e.g., California) that mandate that most complaints must be adjudicated within one year, it is not unusual for a complicated case to consume the entire permitted period.

Regardless of the outcome, the complainant will generally receive a letter that indicates only a disposition category (e.g., *Sustained*, *Not Sustained*, etc.). There is seldom any explanation as to how the decision was arrived at or what facts led to the decision. If the complaint is found to be *Not Sustained* or *Unfounded*, as is the case with an overwhelming number of complaints, the complainant's skepticism about the entire process has likely been reinforced.

Even in those cases where the complaint is ruled as *Sustained*, the complainant is seldom informed as to what, if any, discipline was imposed on the offending officer. The complainant will generally still not have a sense of having been heard, which research suggests is what most complainants actually want from the process. Absent this, the outcome is likely to be perceived as unsatisfactory from the complainant's perspective (Walker and Archbold 2000). If the allegation is serious (e.g., excessive force, false arrest), the complainant has the option of pursuing civil litigation. However, with those complaints that are attitudinal in nature, this option is seldom viable.

Similarly, the officer will receive a disposition memo that also indicates the final outcome. From the officer's perspective, especially if the officer believes that he or she did nothing wrong, there may be only a sense of having participated in a legal kabuki dance. If the complaint is ultimately found to be *Sustained*, the officer now has a disciplinary incident on record and may be left with the sense that the system is neither fair nor caring about the complexity of decisions required in the field. Conversely, if the complaint is *Unfounded* or *Not Sustained*, the officer may feel a sense of resentment for having been forced to endure a legalistic process for no apparent reason.

Thus, regardless of the outcome, neither party is likely to be satisfied. The stated goals of ensuring adherence to both legal standards, and the law enforcement agency's stated values, as well as demonstrating public accountability have likely not been achieved. Perhaps worse, if there was an opportunity for learning, understanding, or personal growth, it has likely been squandered.

Over the years, some effort has been made to move the investigative process outside of the law enforcement agency. Police review boards, civilian complaint panels, and civilian-run investigative processes such as Seattle's Office of Police Accountability (OPA) are all efforts to increase both the perception and the reality of objectivity in the investigative process (see Dailey, Reid, Anderson, and Giles 2006). However, all these alternative models maintain the legalistically based approach of fact-gathering, formal interviews, and strict adherence to due process. Consequently, the attainment of understanding and human connection remains out of reach.

THE MEDIATION PROCESS

As a result of the limitations in both the traditional investigative process, those housed within the law enforcement agency and those handled by various forms of outside oversight, there have been numerous attempts to find a less formal and less legalistic manner of resolving attitudinal complaints. Mediation is part of the larger alternative dispute resolution movement (Walker, Archbold, and Herbst 2002). It is used in a number of life's arenas, including divorces, business disputes, and so on (e.g., Burrell, Donohue, and Allen 1990; Donohue, Allen, and Burrell 1985; Eisenkopf and Bächtiger 2013). Regardless of the circumstance, the goal is always essentially the same—to create an environment where each party feels as though they have been heard, which in turn is more likely to achieve a sense of resolution for everyone involved.

Although the process may vary among jurisdictions, the essence of the mediation process is straightforward. The agency establishes guidelines for those complaints that qualify for mediation. Generally, these are the attitudinal complaints; that is, those complaints that are a product of perception and thus not likely to be resolved by a fact-finding model. The complaint moves through the normal process except that at some designated point, it is identified as being suitable for mediation.

It must be stressed that cases in which one or both parties have a high level of emotional investment in the outcome or who are deeply angry are likely not suitable for mediation. Where racial bias is alleged, this analysis is even more critical. There is a deep scholarly divide as to whether racially based issues, much like use of force allegations, are ever suitable for mediation.[1] This is a consequence of both historical experience and the inherent power imbalance. Consequently, it is critically important that both parties be screened to determine their suitability (i.e., openness to the mediation process) for participation in the process.

Generally, the structure of the mediation process must be outlined in advanced. While individuals may be willing to participate in this process, their representative groups may be less inclined. For instance, police unions have been historically opposed to the mediation process out of concern that their officers will be trapped into making incriminating statements. Displaying an equal level of distrust, community advocacy groups often feel quite strongly that mediation is a backdoor attempt to avoid holding officers accountable for their behavior.

Both parties enter the complaint process from a win/lose perspective. Neither may realize that the ultimate goal of mediation is to achieve greater understanding, not to win. Not everyone is emotionally equipped, whether due to their own personality or the specific circumstances of the matter, to accept mediation's outcome. If the complainant and the involved officer are willing to participate in the mediation process, they will meet at a neutral location under the auspices of a trained and experienced mediator. In Pasadena, California, the Los Angeles County Bar Association provided the facilitator/mediator. In Minneapolis, the Civilian Review Authority, the oversight body for the Minneapolis Police Department, utilized the services of the Minnesota Mediation Center.

The facilitator talks with each party individually to explain what to expect from the process, how each of them will be given the opportunity to tell their story, and, perhaps most importantly, that each party is expected to listen to the other. Under the guidelines that are established in advance, most of which require confidentiality, the complainant and the officer each tell their version of what occurred. The facilitator may assist by asking clarifying questions, articulating the desired outcomes, and ensuring that both parties have the opportunity to present their point of view and to ensure that their point of view has been heard. Again, the desired outcome is understanding, not victory.

At the end of the session, if both parties agree that the process was satisfactory and that they are satisfied with the outcome, then the matter is considered resolved. The process is considered to be a success if both parties feel that they had a chance to tell their story and, most importantly, that they were heard and understood. In the end, the complainant will receive a letter documenting that the mediation process took place and that the outcome was satisfactory. The officer will still have a record in his or her personnel file that a complaint was made, but it will only indicate the matter was resolved by mediation.

Conversely, if the complainant does not feel the matter was successfully resolved, then the complainant can return the process to the traditional legalistic model. Part of the initial agreement is that, should this eventuality occur, none of the statements made in the mediation process may be used in subsequent internal affairs interviews. The percentage of cases in which mediation is perceived to have failed is very low, although admittedly mediation is still not widely used (Greenwald and Beck 2018).

PROCESS DISTINCTIONS

There are two key differences between the use of mediation and the use of the traditional investigative process for the resolution of complaints. In the formal complaint process, the actions of all parties are scripted. That is, they are narrowly defined along legalistic and procedural grounds. While there may be a thorough recitation as to the facts of the matter, there is very little opportunity for either party, but particularly the complainant, to feel as if the system is listening to them. Put another way, mediation offers an opportunity for a successful direct intergroup contact facilitated by an appropriate third party (Fisher 1983).

The traditional complaint model, with its emphasis on fact-gathering, does not facilitate the resolution of complaints that are attitudinally based. These types of complaints, which often arise from a perception that the officer's actions reflected an inappropriate attitude (e.g., subtle contempt or condescension) or bias can generally not be resolved by a recitation of the facts of what occurred. Fact-gathering is seldom useful in determining the officer's motivation, especially when one or both parties possess strongly held preconceptions as to the motivations of the other party.

Attitudinal complaints often result from a failure of communication, that is, a failure to connect on a personal level (or underaccommodate; see Gasiorek 2016) combined with the power inequality between the two parties at the time of the interaction. The traditional manner of investigation previously described will not significantly reduce intergroup barriers in order to allow the parties to see beyond us versus them (see chapter 1). Most of the limiting factors that were present during the traffic stop remain in place. Everything about the complaint process is scripted and formulaic. The forms used, the questions asked, and so forth, are focused on gathering the facts in a legally acceptable manner.

Indeed, one of the reasons for the scripting lays with the underlying recognition that every complaint may ultimately result in litigation. If the complainant is formally interviewed, the interview is likely recorded (audio and sometimes video), and the questions are focused solely on the facts of the matter (e.g., What exactly did the officer say? Did you believe that you committed a traffic violation? etc.). If there is some external validation source nearby (e.g., a dash camera in the police vehicle), the investigator may be able to verify the basic facts as to what occurred. However, it will not do anything to convey the officer's reason for the stop in a manner acceptable to the complainant.

Conversely, if the driver was hostile or abusive to the officer at the time of the stop, there is nothing in the dash-cam video that will explain any underlying stressors that may have influenced the driver. This is especially true if the complainant believes that the officer's primary reason for the stop was racially motivated or if the complainant believed that the officer's body language, facial expressions, and the like conveyed the officer's inherent bias or contempt.

Mediation, however, takes both the complainant and the officer out of their socially defined roles. One of the more interesting areas of discussion with respect to mediation revolves around whether the officer should participate while wearing a uniform. There are strong feelings on both sides of this argument. Research suggests that creating environments where power neutrality exists between ingroups and outgroups (i.e., removing the uniform, which is representative of authority) is more likely to allow intergroup barriers to be reduced (Giles et al. 2007). Regardless of what is worn, the officer and the complainant are facing each other on a more equal footing than the traditional investigative process allows.

It has been my experience that two key factors need to be present to ensure that the mediation process will be successful. First is a structure that has been designed and agreed upon in advance by both the community, usually through their advocacy groups, and the police unions. Second is the selection of a mutually agreed-upon third party who has credibility and the respect of both parties.

One of the most significant barriers to the successful implementation of a successful mediation program is a lack of trust on both sides of the social divide. Law enforcement officers and their unions are often opposed to the use of mediation because they feel that they may be tricked into making an incriminating statement. Additionally, it can be emotionally challenging for officers to step outside of their established role and interact with someone with whom they have engaged in enforcement activities (e.g., issued a citation, written a field interview card, etc.).

Conversely, many individuals, particularly those who have had negative interactions with the police, often have a high degree of distrust with respect to law enforcement procedures, including complaint resolution. If the individuals involved believe that law enforcement officers have historically never been held to account, they are unlikely to believe that mediation is a serious step toward accountability.

These distrustful paradigms are firmly entrenched with both officers and community members (see chapter 1). Overcoming this distrust is a significant challenge. A reflection of this fact is that there is no national database around the use of complaint mediation. The 2002 Office of Community Oriented Policing Services (COPS) report highlighted only sixteen programs nationwide and two of those were not operational (Walker, Archbold, and Herbst 2002).

CONCLUSIONS

We live in a time of significant social polarization. There is a loss of faith in government and institutions, and this loss manifests itself very notably in terms of relationships between the police and the communities they serve. This lack of trust in law enforcement has become painfully evident in the aftermath of the police killing of George Floyd. Communities, particularly marginalized communities, have made it clear that they feel unheard and irrelevant (see chapters 8 and 16). All too often their perceptions are correct. Simultaneously, law enforcement officers are frustrated, as they often find that any action that they take, regardless of their intention or the attendant circumstances, is analyzed, criticized, and held up for public scrutiny. From the officer's perspective, this scrutiny does not include any attempt to understand the reality the officer faced at the moment of interaction. Both sides of this divide are strongly wedded to their perspective and often view the "other" from a highly suspicious and distrusting perspective. This distrust extends to the complaint resolution systems that are designed to bridge that divide.

The search for a technological solution that would display the truth of what occurred at the moment when the officer and the civilian interacted with absolute clarity has been underway for some time. Video technology, both in vehicles and on the person of the officer, have not provided the hoped-for resolution. This may be due to the expectation, however inarticulately defined, that the video camera could and would provide insight into the motivations of all the parties involved. Instead, while it may provide a clearer view of what occurred, it cannot offer a clearer view of the underlying perceptions and motivations of either party.

Ultimately, the traditional complaint process, with its legally based structure, is inadequate for resolving such complaints, particularly when most of those complaints arise from misunderstandings, misperceptions, or simply the predictable response to an involuntary interaction with authority. In spite of that fact, it is the legalistic paradigm—whether through the legal system (i.e., a lawsuit) or a legalistically based investigative model (i.e., the internal affairs process)—that is most often utilized to resolve citizen complaints.

During the interaction in the street, each party comports themselves through a socially proscribed set of behaviors. The complaint process continues this social dance, since it is based on the criminal trial model, which is focused on the identification and punishment of wrongdoers. Consequently, the process assigns specific roles and expected behaviors to each of the parties. At no time, either during the interaction or during the subsequent complaint process, is either party free to be heard and understood in the way the human psyche demands.

Mediation, if properly implemented, can give each party the opportunity to tell their story in the way that they wish to tell it. Perhaps most importantly, they can describe their perception of what occurred as well as the emotional impact of the interaction. It is this focus on perceptions (i.e., feelings), rather than just the facts, that is both the promise and the challenge with respect to the use of mediation in the resolution of complaints against law enforcement officers.

NOTE

1. Interview with Dr. Samuel Walker, July 9, 2019. My thanks to Dr. Walker for giving so freely of his time.

REFERENCES

Burgoon, Judee K. 1993. "Interpersonal Expectations, Expectancy Violations, and Emotional Communication." *Journal of Language and Social Psychology* 12 (1–2): 30–48.

Burrell, Nancy A., William A. Donohue, and Mike Allen. 1990. "The Impact of Disputants' Expectations on Mediation: Testing an Interventionist Model." *Human Communication Research* 17 (1): 104–13.

Dailey, Rene, Scott A. Reid, Michelle C. Anderson, and Howard Giles. 2006. "Community Review of Police Conduct: An Intergroup Perspective." *Social Psychological Review* 8 (2): 20–34.

Donohue, William, Mike Allen, and Nancy Burrell. 1985. "Communication Strategies in Mediation." *Mediation Quarterly* 10 (4): 75–89.

Eisenkopf, Gerald, and André Bächtiger. 2013. "Mediation and Conflict Prevention." *Journal of Conflict Resolution* 57 (4): 570–97.

Fisher, Ronald J. 1983. "Third Party Consultation as a Method of Intergroup Conflict Resolution: A Review of Studies." *The Journal of Conflict Resolution* 27 (2): 301–34.

Gasiorek, Jessica. 2015. "Perspective-Taking, Inferred Motive, and Perceived Accommodation in Nonaccommodative Conversations." *Journal of Language and Social Psychology* 34 (5): 577–86.

Gasiorek, Jessica. 2016. "The 'Dark Side' of CAT: Nonaccommodation." In *Communication Accommodation Theory: Negotiating Personal Relationships and Social Identities across Contexts*, edited by Howard Giles, 85–104. Cambridge: Cambridge University Press.

Gasiorek, Jessica, and Howard Giles. 2015. "The Role of Inferred Motive in Processing and Evaluating Non-Accommodation." *Western Journal of Communication* 79 (4): 456–71.

Giles, Howard, Michael Willemyns, Cindy Gallois, and Michelle C. Anderson. 2007. "Accommodating a New Frontier: The Context of Law Enforcement. In *Social Communication*, edited by Klaus Fiedler, 129–62. New York: Psychology Press.

Ginty, Roger Mac. 2014. "Everyday Peace: Bottom-up and Local Agency in Conflict-Affected Societies." *Security Dialogue* 45 (6): 548–64.

Greenwald, Howard, and Charlie Beck. 2018. "Bringing Sides Together: Community-Based Complaint Mediation." *Police Chief* 85 (8): 36–42.

Hasisi, Badi. 2008. "Police, Politics, and Culture in a Deeply Divided Society." *Journal of Criminal Law and Criminology* 98 (3): 1119–45.

Kastoryano, Riva. 2010. "Codes of Otherness." *Social Research* 77 (1): 79–100.

MacDonald, Heather. 2017. *The War on Cops; How the Attack on Law and Order Makes Everyone Less Safe*. New York: Encounter Books.

Maguire, Edward R., Belén V. Lowrey, and Devon Johnson. 2017. "Evaluating the Relative Impact of Positive and Negative Encounters with Police: A Randomized Experiment." *Journal of Experimental Criminology* 13 (3): 367–91.

Melekian, Bernard. 2012. *The Police Disciplinary Process*. Ann Arbor: ProQuest Dissertations, LLC.

Overbeck, Jennifer, Larissa Z. Tiedens, and Sebastien Brion. 2006. "The Powerful Want to, the Powerless Have to: Perceived Constraint Moderates Causal Attributions." *European Journal of Social Psychology* 36 (4): 479–96.

Police Executive Research Forum. 2018. *Cost and Benefits of Body-Worn Camera Deployments*. Washington DC: Police Executive Research Forum.

Roach, Kent. 1999. "Four Models of the Criminal Process." *Journal of Criminal Law and Criminology* 89 (2): 671–716.

Tyler, Tom R. 2006. *Why People Obey the Law*. Princeton: Princeton University Press.

Walker, Samuel E., and Carol Archbold. 2000. "Mediating Citizen Complaints against the Police: An Exploratory Study." *Journal of Dispute Resolution* 11 (2), 231–44.

Walker, Samuel, Carol Archbold, and Leigh Herbst. 2002. *Mediating Police Complaints*. Washington DC: Office of Community Oriented Policing Services.

CHAPTER 14

The Media and Our Perceptions of the Police

Matea Mustafaj and Jan Van den Bulck

In most populations, most people have either no or very limited contact with the police (Bureau of Justice Statistics 2011). They do, however, have explicit and implicit knowledge and beliefs about the nature of police work and the outlook, attitudes, behaviors, and beliefs of law enforcement officers. Where direct experience is largely missing, indirect experience fills the gap. For most people, most knowledge of policing will come from the media rather than personal experience (Surette 2007; Williams and Fedorowicz 2019). This chapter explores how policing is portrayed in both the news and the entertainment media and what effects have been charted of such portrayals on beliefs, attitudes, and behaviors of the media audience. Many of the oldest theories in media research were initiated by concerns about the perceived omnipresence of violence narratives in both fiction and nonfiction media. Hence, there is a long history for some of these findings.

We start by examining depictions of law enforcement in both traditional and contemporary sources of news and consider some implications of these representations. We then move on to discuss law enforcement depictions in fiction. Both news and fiction focus on violent crime, but they differ in the ways they tend to portray police officers. We discuss these differences and the various impacts media representations may have on attitudes toward law enforcement, public fear of crime, criminal proceedings, and perceptions of police legitimacy. We conclude with a discussion of new media and some challenges and opportunities that the new media environment presents for law enforcement.

LAW ENFORCEMENT IN THE NEWS

Media attention to crime is about as old as the popular media (e.g., Mason 2003). While the first newspapers focused on what would now be called international news, by the second half of the nineteenth century, certain newspapers began to discover that crime news interested their readers. King (2009) has shown that all reporting has not stayed equal across the centuries. An analysis of reporting on court cases in England in the eighteenth century showed that violence and murder were not the best predictor of newspaper coverage, but the severity of sentencing was. This shows that from the earliest start of high-volume crime reporting, questions of fairness in reporting and in representation were valid concerns, as would have been the worry that a skewed selection of events to report (e.g., toward events that lead to harsher sentencing) might influence the public's perceptions of, and opinions about, the criminal justice system. Dryer (2007), who studied trials and newspaper reporting in the period between 1898 and 1902, suggests that the attention given by the murder section of the *New York Times* to certain criminal trials influenced when and how those trials were conducted. The question whether news reporting can influence the legal justice system and policing has, therefore, been a valid one from the start.

Ever since the early days of crime reporting, the world of criminal justice has remained a mainstay of news reporting (see chapter 16). A comparative study spanning thirty years between 1960 and 1989, and fourteen countries from three different continents, suggested that crime reporting across the globe looked remarkably similar, regardless of the sociopolitical climate and judicial tradition of each studied country (Marsh 1991). The Internet revolution has led to a proliferation of platforms and channels that purport to bring mainstream or alternative news, while shifts in revenue have led to challenges to the traditional news disseminators (Starr 2012). It therefore remains to be seen whether Marsh's finding still hold in the current era. The news is not just a clinical overview of all the phenomena that happened in the hours before the news was made public, ranked by order of importance, given that no such ranking exists or would even be possible. News is always a selection made by a particular person or group of persons. As early as 1964, White (1950), based on a study of newsrooms in the 1950s, discovered the importance of what was coined the gatekeeper function of certain members of news organizations in deciding what made it into the news and what was left out. While news selection and news dissemination is increasingly influenced or even performed by algorithms (see Diakopoulos and Koliska 2017), this does not change the fact that news remains a selection.

Marsh (1991) identified a number of selective processes influencing which crime and law enforcement stories received more attention. One of the most important factors is the nature of crimes and transgressions that receive the most coverage. Marsh noted an overrepresentation of violent crimes (and, consequently, an underrepresentation of property crime) compared to reality in as far as that can be expressed in official crime statistics (Bottomley and Pease 1986). Other researchers have also found this pattern (e.g., Dixon, Azocar, and Casas 2003). Indeed, news coverage about crime is mostly unrelated to real-world rates of crime. For example, Gilliam and Iyengar (2000) found that, in their sample of local television news in Los Angeles, 83 percent of news stories were about violent crime. In addition, there were about as many stories about murder as there were about nonviolent crime (even though murder accounts for less than 1 percent of all crime in Los Angeles).

The focus on violent crime is driven, in part, by journalistic values of newsworthiness that favor stories that are dramatic and personalized (Bennett 2016; Martin 2018; see chapter 16). Media consumers tend to be more interested in stories that involve something shocking or unusual (Gekoski, Gray, and Adler 2012). Murder is not nearly as prevalent in the real world as it is in the news, but it captures the attention of the audience, so reporters are incentivized to cover it. Traditional media has seen a reduction in advertising revenue over time as companies increasingly move their advertisements to digital spaces where it is cheaper and can be more precisely targeted (Starr 2012). This leads to increased competition among news outlets for viewers' attention.

The need to capture audience attention along with space limits for news outlets often leads to more dramatic, personal, and fragmented story lines that emphasize chaos and disorder (Bennett 2016). These types of storylines likely contribute to the overrepresentation of violence in the news and come at the expense of covering the complexities of the issues related to the incident being covered. There does appear to be a difference in this respect between television news and newspapers. Television news reports tend to focus on the incident in this episodic frame—they are more likely to be reported in a way that elicits emotion in order to attract the attention of the viewer. Newspapers tend to report events with more context, including data like crime trends, relationships to other social problems, and statistical analyses (Druckman 2005; Iyengar 1991).

Studies looking at the depiction of police officers in the media have found contradictory results, with some finding that police are portrayed positively in the media, and others finding they are generally portrayed negatively (Surette 2007). Some have suggested that the police and the media have a kind of symbiotic relationship, with the media relying on police to provide quick and reliable crime information and the police using the media to strategically manage their image (Ericson, Baranek, and Chan 1987; Fishman 1981). However, researchers have found that, while entertainment media tend to portray police officers in a positive light, news media often portray them more negatively. Indeed, some content analyses indicate an increase in negative coverage over time (Reiner, Livingstone, and Allen 2000). Studies have found that news media characterize police as ineffective and incompetent (Ericson, Baranek, and Chan 1991; Surette 2007). Since the 1960s, the number of articles describing a crime as being solved has dropped significantly (Reiner, Livingstone, and Allen 2003).

As coverage emphasizing police effectiveness has, arguably, decreased, the number of articles about police misconduct has increased. Use of force incidents have sometimes been normalized in the news and presented as necessary to keep crime levels under control (Lawrence 2000). While use of force has generally been acknowledged as a defining characteristic of law enforcement as a profession, excessive police use of force is ambiguous and efforts to define it have been volatile. The fear of crime that is often generated through the media can increase punitive attitudes and grant police leniency in defining what a necessary use of force entails in crime fighting. Research has shown that media tends to increase public fear of crime and that fear of crime is associated with more punitive criminal justice attitudes, higher aggression toward perpetrators, and less aggression toward law defenders (e.g., Dowler 2003; Reith 1999).

While there has been more reporting of police misconduct, many of these accounts have historically avoided implicating police as an institution. On television news, these use of force incidents are often presented as the result of problematic behavior of one individual police officer, and not as an issue with the criminal justice system or police as an institution (e.g., Reiner 2007; Surette 2007). Though in general there has been a long standing debate about the power dynamics in the media–police relationship (Leishman and Mason 2012), historically, the news media have relied heavily on official accounts from the police which allowed the institution to shape how incidents of misconduct were presented to the public (Lawrence 2000). Often news stories on these events are centered on the brief and episodic statements of police spokespersons and politicians. They are typically presented as issues of a particular individual and distanced from the institution as a whole (Lawrence 2000; Reiner, Livingstone, and Allen 2003).

Lawrence (2000) contends that unplanned dramatic events, such as police use of force incidents, have opened the door to a more diverse set of voices. This is aided by new media and the ability of citizens and activists to share videos and shape the narrative before officials are able to do so. In recent years, we have seen a surge in coverage of alleged police brutality in minority neighborhoods, especially in predominantly Black neighborhoods. According to McLaughlin (2015), the videos captured of some of these incidents may lend credibility to the stories of minority victims and wear down the skepticism of the public that police officers would act so violently. For example, Lawrence (2000) argues that part of what made the Rodney King beating so significant is that the incident itself was captured on video. More recently, there has been news coverage of a string of use of force incidents involving unarmed Black men. The shooting of teenager Michael Brown in Ferguson and of the twelve-year-old Tamir Rice in Cleveland are just a few examples in a string of high-profile police shootings of Black men that have garnered increased media attention (see, again, chapter 16). Coverage of these types of events may be more likely to call into question police as an institution or culture (see chapter 1). These incidents undermine public trust in law enforcement and create a rift between police and the communities they are meant to serve (e.g., Weitzer 2002).

In the modern media environment, people get much of their news and information outside of traditional television or print news platforms. Instead, they are turning to newer media for this information like the Internet and social media (e.g., Perrin and Duggan 2015). Little is known about how the content of online news may be similar to or different from more traditional news sources; very few studies have considered the impact of this growing new media consumption on attitudes toward police. In one recent study, Intravia, Wolff, and Piquero (2018) found that people who viewed news online tended to have more negative attitudes toward police legitimacy than television news or entertainment media consumption. This suggests that Internet sources may be likely to portray law enforcement more negatively (see chapter 15). This is not surprising when we consider social movements like Black Lives Matter and similar influential hashtags that are aimed at exposing instances of police brutality and calling for a change in policing culture.

LAW ENFORCEMENT IN FICTION

There is a second narrative. From the earliest examples of the modern entertainment media, law enforcement, its officers, and the lawbreakers they deal with, have been a central focus of stories, both serious and comedic. Although it seems intuitive to think of news coverage when thinking about how media shapes perceptions of crime and law enforcement, fiction may be an even larger contributor to that mediated knowledge. The average person in the United States tends to spend more time with entertainment than with news programs—up to twice as much per day (Donovan and Klahm 2015; Prior 2005). It is likely that a portion of this time is spent watching crime-based fiction. Crime has been a popular topic in entertainment media for a long time. Phillips and Frost (2010) found that a third of the top forty shows in 2004–2005 were crime dramas. Indeed, crime fiction appears to be a staple of mainstream television in most countries (Dirikx, Van den Bulck, and Parmentier 2012; Phillips and Frost 2010), and tends to be among the most watched programs in the United States (Donovan and Klahm 2015).

Hence, it is conceivable that some of the knowledge that citizens hold about law enforcement, particularly when they have had no experience with it themselves, might come from entertainment programming. Studies have demonstrated that viewers often view crime dramas as a veridical source of real-world law enforcement proceedings. Indeed, Dowler and Zawilski (2007) found that over 40 percent of Americans believe that crime shows are somewhat or very accurate. This suggests that viewers of crime dramas could learn about real-world crime proceedings from these programs. Two major questions for media researchers, then, are what are they learning from these fictional portrayals, and how accurate is it?

Crime shows and other violent media content have been a focus of academic concern for a long time. Like news media, entertainment media contains a disproportionately high representation of violence. In his early work, Gerbner et al. (1980) documented an overwhelming amount of violence across media content. Crime on entertainment television was found to be more violent, random, and dangerous than crime in real life. These depictions are not only prevalent in crime shows or television shows in general, but also movies, video games, music videos, and cartoons (Anderson et al. 2003). Some have estimated that a typical child in the United States will have seen more than one hundred thousand murders before they finish elementary school (Huston et al. 1992). Although this estimate is from more than two decades ago, it is not likely to have decreased. Indeed, Signorielli, Morgan, and Shanahan (2019) found that, by most of their measures, violence on television reached historically high levels in the 2010s, and it continues to be a dominant theme in media programming.

As above, murder has historically been the primary crime in most movies, and property crimes have generally been underrepresented (Greer and Reiner 2015; Reiner, Livingstone, and Allen 2000). Likewise, content analyses have found that the crimes depicted in fictional crime shows tend to be violent, focusing heavily on murder (e.g., Brown 2001; Cavender and Deutsch 2007; Deutsch and Cavender 2008; Rhineberger-Dunn, Rader, and Williams 2008). Although violence has been a staple of entertainment for decades, it has become increasingly graphic since the 1970s. After the 1960s, we began to see more sex- and drug-related crimes as central aspects of storylines, and crime was increasingly represented as a ubiquitous threat (Greer and Reiner 2015). Not only is the frequency at which crimes occur vastly different from real-world statistics, the circumstances under which they occur are also not true to official reports of the types of crimes depicted. Most murders in fiction are planned and often motivated by greed (Allen, Livingstone, and Reiner 1998), and sex crimes are usually committed by strangers who often submit their victims to extreme brutality, and often end in murder (Greer and Reiner 2015). In reality, most murders occur as part of a fight or domestic dispute (Dorling 2004), and sex crimes are often committed by people that are known to the victim (Greer 2003).

When it comes to depictions of law enforcement, fictional crime shows tend to depict it as an exciting, fast-paced job filled with crime fighting—little attention is given to the more mundane parts of the job, such as paperwork (Culver 1978; Perlmutter 2000; Van den Bulck 2002). Police officers are often romanticized and portrayed as heroic crime fighters (Surette 1998) sometimes working outside of the confines of the law in the name of justice. Some scholars have argued that this kind of "rule-bending" is often depicted as a necessary part of effective policing (Dirikx, Van den Bulck, and Parmentier 2012; Eschholz, Mallard, and Flynn 2004; Van den Bulck 2002). Indeed, studies have found that many crime dramas depict police officers violating civil liberties, but this is usually portrayed in a positive way (e.g., Britto, Hughes, Saltzman, and Stroh 2007). For instance, officers are depicted as effective avengers of a victim's suffering, or defenders of victims against violence and serious harm (Greer and Reiner 2015). Although there are increasing depictions of less-than-honest police officers in fiction, these patterns of depicting police officers' actions as noble and justified are still overwhelmingly present.

In contrast to crime news, crime fiction overrepresents the extent to which police officers effectively solve crimes and make arrests. The majority of crimes in fiction are solved and criminals are caught (Estep and MacDonald 1984; Kooistra, Mahoney, and Westervelt 1998; Zillman and Wakshlag 1985). A content analysis of the television show *Law and Order: Special Victims Unit* by Britto and colleagues (2007) found that 100 percent of the crimes on the show lead to an arrest—double the actual rate in New York City at the time (Donovan and Klahm 2015). This has historically been a pattern in films as well. No movie before 1952 depicted criminals escaping capture, though this has happened with greater frequency in films and television shows since then (Greer and Reiner 2015; Lichter, Lichter, and Rothman 1994; Reiner, Livingstone, and Allen 2000). Crime-based reality shows also exaggerate how often police officers make arrests (e.g., Oliver 1994; Cavender and Fishman 1998), displaying perhaps the most positive portrayals of law enforcement. Although they tend to portray police officers acting aggressively toward suspects, this behavior is typically framed as justified and necessary to contain dangerous offenders.

The portrayals and effectiveness of law enforcement in fiction has led to what is called the "CSI effect." This refers to the impact that CSI and other crime-related shows has on actual legal proceedings. These shows tend to portray forensic science as "high-tech magic, solving crimes quickly and unerringly" (Schweitzer and Saks 2007, 358). These representations are exaggerated and not necessarily reflective of reality, but they can have very real consequences for the perceptions of juries who have likely not had any other direct experience with such proceedings. Trial-related effects have generally been hypothesized to increase the burden on both the prosecution and the defense. In particular, some have argued that these shows have raised juror's expectations of what kind of evidence should be offered at trials, generally encouraging the expectation that the somewhat flashy forensic science that is displayed on TV will be presented to them as real-life jurors. This can lead to a higher acquittal rate among jurors who feel they have not seen enough solid evidence to pronounce the defendant guilty (Podlas 2006; Schweitzer and Saks 2007). Alternatively, some have argued that CSI and other shows have overstated the power of forensic evidence and thus lead to a false sense of how conclusive this type of evidence can be among jurors (Podlas 2006). These effects are not mutually exclusive—both can be true. In any case, this is a very real and consequential impact of crime television. The expectations that the public has for what constitutes evidence and what is possible in court may be tied to their perceptions of the effectiveness of law enforcement officers as well as the guilt of perpetrators that they have arrested. This can introduce more complications to the criminal justice process as a whole.

CULTIVATING PERCEPTIONS OF LAW ENFORCEMENT

Evidence suggests that the images we see on television have implications for how we construct our social reality. This proposed relationship is called cultivation theory in the communication literature (Gerber et al. 1980). Although cultivation theory has garnered much criticism since its inception (e.g., Potter 2014), it remains an influential theory in media effects. In his early work, Gerber et al. (1980) found that people who were heavy as opposed to light television viewers tended to hold beliefs about the real world that were more consistent with what was portrayed on television. This was demonstrated across a variety of domains including violent crime estimates, perceptions of social groups, and estimations of the effectiveness of police officers, and so forth (Morgan 2012).

This is especially true for those that have had little or no direct contact with the content being displayed—media sources are more influential in these cases (e.g., Liska and Baccaglini 1990; Skogan and Maxfield 1981). If a viewer has, in real life, been the victim or perpetrator of a crime or has experienced other parts of the justice system, it is not as likely that media sources will be at the root of their beliefs and attitudes about law enforcement. However, evidence suggests that a considerable proportion of public knowledge about crime is derived from media sources (Roberts and Doob 1990; Surette 1998).

Given that representations of law enforcement vary across genres, researchers have found varying effects of television viewing on perceptions of law enforcement. The effect of entertainment media consumption on attitudes toward law enforcement is understudied; very few papers exist examining this relationship. One of the few papers that investigates this relationship finds that viewers of crime dramas tend to perceive police officers as being effective at managing crime and believe that police officers only use force when necessary (Donovan and Klahm 2015). This is not surprising given the generally positive representations of police that exist in entertainment media.

In regard to news, some have claimed that the public has had a favorable view of police as an institution in part due to its ability to strategically manage news media coverage, emphasizing the effectiveness of police solving crime (Christensen, Schmidt, and Henderson 1982). These positive portrayals can reinforce support for harsher penalties, as well as increasing police presence and power (Sacco 1995). However, some scholars have claimed that the news media portray police as ineffective and incompetent, but that this actually may result in support for more police, more prisons, and more criminal justice funding (Surette 1998). Some research has found that exposure to television news and crime-based reality programs is associated with higher confidence for White research participants, but not necessarily for Black or Latino participants. The same study found that, in cases where a viewer has had first-hand experiences with crime, their crime-related media consumption may not have much of an influence on their perceptions of law enforcement (Callanan and Rosenberger 2011). However, it may be a different story for news coverage of police misconduct. For example, Lasley (1994) found that positive opinions of police significantly dropped after coverage of the Rodney King beating and arrest. Other studies have found a similar relationship between police misconduct and a decrease in positive perceptions of law enforcement (e.g., Weitzer 2002).

Although this work is enlightening, very little recent work continues this focus on the impact of media consumptions on attitudes toward and perceptions of the police (Callanan and Rosenberger 2011). This is surprising given the implications that these effects could have for law enforcement. For example, it has been argued that these public perceptions and attitudes are important for the public's perceptions of legitimacy of law enforcement and, as a result, the extent to which citizens are willing to comply with them (e.g., Mazerolle, Antrobus, Bennett, and Tyler 2013; Tyler 1990, 2004).

MEAN WORLD SYNDROME

Although much of the research regarding representation of violence on television has centered around how it may foster aggression (Anderson and Carnagey 2014; Anderson et al. 2003), its ability to cultivate fear is potentially more widespread. Overrepresentations of violent crime in the media paint a frightening and dangerous picture of reality. Heavy television viewers, especially those who have not had direct experience with crime, are likely to perceive the world in accordance with what is being portrayed. Indeed, Gerbner and his colleagues (1980) demonstrated that those who were heavy television viewers had lower trust in others and feared being victimized, an outcome that he referred to as the *mean world syndrome* (Morgan 2012). Heavy viewers believed crime was more prevalent than real-world statistics indicate and were more likely to take precautions against crime. Studies since then have supported this theory, demonstrating a relationship between exposure to traditional news media and greater fear of victimization (e.g., Kort-Butler and Sittner Hartshorn 2011). Scholars have found a difference in effects of exposure to television news and newspapers, due to their tendency to frame events differently. Interestingly, the more emotional, episodic framing of television news tends to produce more fear about crime than does the more contextual framing in newspapers (Chiricos, Eschholz, and Gertz 1997; Romer, Jamieson, and DeCoteau 1998).

Similarly, those who heavily watch crime reality and drama programs tend to have a greater fear of crime (e.g., Chiricos et al. 1997; Dowler 2003; Eschholz 2003). Typically, cultivation is studied in reference to television viewing as a whole, which has been shown to have a direct and persistent relationship with fear of crime (e.g., Barille 1984; Morgan 1983; Weaver and Wakshlag 1986). This is especially true for subgroups that are frequently depicted as victims in the media and, thus, might more readily identify with television victims rather than perpetrators. These groups of people may have higher fear levels than other heavy viewers. For example, although Whites, women, and the elderly are actually the segments of the population that are least likely to be victimized, they often report the highest levels of fear (Gerbner, Gross, Morgan, and Signorielli 1980; Liska and Baccaglini 1990).

The fear and anxiety that appears to be related to television viewing has implications for public attitudes toward criminal justice policy. For example, Garofalo (1981) found that viewing crime news was associated with greater public pressure for more effective policing. Reith (1999) found that, for White males, viewing crime shows led to more aggression toward criminal perpetrators and less aggression toward those who defend the law. Likewise, Surette (1998) found that viewing crime coverage was associated with support for punitive crime policies, and Dowler (2003) found that heavy viewing of crime dramas was related to fear of crime, and fear of crime was associated with punitive criminal justice attitudes. Therefore, it appears that the fear that is generated by media representations may both grant more leniency to law enforcement, and potentially lead to more public pressure for effective policing.

NEW MEDIA

Finally, there is a third narrative this chapter examines. While many questions in media research are as old as the major traditional media, there have been remarkable and fast-paced innovations in recent decades that have led to a drastic change in accessibility of the media and of the nature of mass communication. Digital technologies and social media have created fast message exchange networks that allow people to share information and respond to it, virtually in real time (see chapter 15). Law enforcement has thus become a profession that is permanently in the public eye. This section will explore the extent to which new media might provide both challenges and opportunities for law enforcement officers.

One way that new media technologies are affecting criminal justice is that they make it easier or possible to commit particular kinds of crime or aggression. Cybercrimes, or crime that involves Internet-enabled technologies, have become a major national security concern all over the world (see chapter 21). These concerns have led to the establishment of cross-national organizations to encourage innovation in combating cybercrime such as the European Cybercrime Center and the Interpol Global Complex for Innovation (Wall and Williams 2013). Cybercrime includes computer network break-ins, financial extortion, credit card fraud, software piracy, and distribution of child pornography, among other things (Loader and Thomas 2013). In some cases, the Internet provides a new, and sometimes *easier*, way to commit crimes, such as credit card fraud, and it can also create entirely new crimes such as hacking into large computer networks and stealing data.

Aside from dealing with cybercrime, Internet-enabled technologies present new challenges for police officers in that they offer new ways for the public to surveil them on the job. There are few Americans today that do not own a smartphone, or some Internet-enabled device with which they can share content quickly and widely. Consequently, police and first responders have had to learn to deal with ubiquitous cameras. The ability of citizens to record police behavior has, arguably, undermined the ability of the police to control the media narrative and perception of the institution and has uncovered many cases of misconduct and use of force incidents in recent times. These incidents have garnered widespread attention and, for many, called police culture into question. While many of these incidents have been dismissed as individualized behavior, that becomes increasingly harder to defend as the number of incidents shared with the public rises (see chapter 1).

However, police are also increasingly leveraging new media for public relations and operational purposes (Lee and McGovern 2013; Leishman and Mason 2012). Social media in particular are used to investigate crimes and alert the public of safety concerns (Kim, Oglesby-Neal, and Mohr 2017). This immediate and widespread access to the community can accelerate crime investigations and offer new ways to track criminals, as well as new ways to keep the public informed.

Social media can also be used by law enforcement to maintain a positive image and increase public confidence. In some cases, social media (and reality television) can allow police to bypass traditional media and shape their own image (Lee and McGovern 2013). In addition to humanizing police work, social media can help police provide more transparency for their communities in order to restore police–community relationships (Lieberman, Koetzle, and Sakiyama 2013; Mayes 2017). Thus, social media can be an avenue by which police may strengthen their image within the communities they serve and subsequently boost perceptions of police legitimacy.

CONCLUSIONS

There is a tendency to see the media as "out there," as an external force that disrupts reality. Much academic research does not contradict that view: Most social sciences developed their foundational theories when the mass media were either not very ubiquitous yet or were seen as trivial because their content was deemed to be trivial. The overview in this chapter of ways in which media use touches upon the world of law enforcement, however, shows why that view of the media is not the right perspective. The media are part of our world. As such, they inform how the public sees the police but also how members of the law enforcement community see the public. Lawmakers and other decision makers are also part of that interlocking network, as are victims and lawbreakers (on how the media shaped expectations of first-time prisoners, see Van den Bulck and Vandebosch 2003).

There are a number of takeaways from this observation. As long as there are media, there will be a fascination for lawbreakers and law enforcement. This fascination will be fed by reality and will, in turn, affect reality, either by affecting behaviors of players in the network or by affecting beliefs, judgments, and other views. Finding out what the sequence of cause and effect is may, therefore, be less fruitful than acknowledging the interrelatedness of the various elements. Michael Slater's (2007) concept of "reinforcing spirals" may be the best description of what goes on. Slater describes media effects as a multidirectional process, where media use can change behavior and beliefs, which in turn can change media exposure. In a continuous, accumulative process, both media effects and selection of media can therefore nudge a media user in a particular direction, gradually changing and reinforcing beliefs or behaviors.

Whether citizens or members of the law enforcement community feel the media present an accurate and fair image of reality or not, all involved have to realize that these images and their consequences are part of the world of law enforcement. Instead of treating them as an unwanted distraction, they should be studied as a part of reality that only changes if it is superseded by something that offers the same gratification of needs as the current system and something additional. Any affordance the media offers today is unlikely to go away. Police officers have slowly learned that citizens with mobile phone cameras can record their every move, just as many of those citizens have developed the reflex to switch on those cameras whenever a law enforcement action takes place. It is the new normal. Acknowledging that reality should probably be a part of planning and management designs throughout the network we have just described.

REFERENCES

Allen, Jessica, Sonia Livingstone, and Robert Reiner. 1998. "True Lies: Changing Images of Crime in British Postwar Cinema." *European Journal of Communication* 13 (1): 53–75.

Anderson, Craig A., Leonard Berkowitz, Edward Donnerstein, L. Rowell Huesmann, James D. Johnson, Daniel Linz, Neil M. Malamuth, and Ellen Wartella. 2003. "The Influence of Media Violence on Youth." *Psychological Science in the Public Interest* 4 (3): 81–110.

Anderson, Craig A., and Nicholas L. Carnagey. 2014. "The Role of Theory in the Study of Media Violence: The General Aggression Model." In *Media Violence and Children: A Complete Guide for Parents and Professionals* (second edition), edited by Douglas A. Gentile, 103–33. Westport: Praeger.

Barille, Leo 1984. "Television and Attitudes about Crime: Do Heavy Views Distort Criminality and Support Retributive Justice?" In *Justice and the Media: Issues and Research*, edited by Douglas A. Gentile, 141–58. Springfield: Charles C. Thomas.

Beckett, Kathrine 1999. *Making Crime Pay: Law and Order in Contemporary American Politics*. Oxford: Oxford University Press.

Bennett, W. Lance. 2016. *News: The Politics of Illusion*. University of Chicago Press.

Bottomley, A. Keith, and Ken Pease. 1986. *Crime and Punishment: Interpreting the Data*. Milton Keynes: Open University Press.

Britto, Sarah, Tycy Hughes, Kurt Saltzman, and Colin Stroh. 2007. "Does 'Special' Mean Young, White and Female? Deconstructing the Meaning of 'Special' in Law and Order: Special Victims Unit." *Journal of Criminal Justice and Popular Culture* 14 (1): 39–57.

Brown, N. J. 2001. "A Comparison of Fictional Television Crime and Crime Index Statistics." *Communication Research Reports* 18 (2): 192–99.

Bureau of Justice Statistics. 2011. "FAQ: How Many Persons Have Contact with the Police in a Given Year?" US Department of Justice, Office of Justice Programs. Retrieved from https://www.bjs.gov/index.cfm?ty=qa&iid=371 .

Callanan, Valerie J., and Jared S. Rosenberger. 2011. "Media and Public Perceptions of the Police: Examining the Impact of Race and Personal Experience." *Policing and Society* 21 (2): 167–89.

Cavender, Gray, and Sarah Deutsch. 2007. "CSI and Moral Authority: The Police and Science." *Crime, Media, Culture* 3 (1): 67–81.

Cavender, Gray, and Mark Fishman. 1998. "Television Reality Crime Programs: Context and History." In M. Fishman and G. Cavender, *Entertaining Crime: Television Reality Programs*, edited by Mark Fishman and Gray Cavender, 3–15. New York: Aldine De Gruyter.

Chiricos, Ted, Sarah Eschholz, and Marc Gertz. 1997. "Crime, News and Fear of Crime: Toward an Identification of Audience Effects." *Social Problems* 44 (3): 342–56.

Christensen, Jon, Janet Schmidt, and Joel Henderson. 1982. "The Selling of the Police: Media, Ideology, and Crime Control." *Contemporary Crises* 6 (3): 227–239.

Culver, John H. 1978. "Television the Police." *Policy Studies Journal* 7 (1): 500.

Deutsch, Sarah Keturah, and Gray Cavender. 2008. "CSI and Forensic Realism." *Journal of Criminal Justice and Popular Culture* 15(1): 34–53.

Diakopoulos, Nicholas, and Michael Koliska. 2017. "Algorithmic Transparency in the News Media." *Digital Journalism* 5 (7): 809–28.

Dirikx, Astrid, Jan Van den Bulck, and Stephan Parmentier. 2012. "The Police as Societal Moral Agents: 'Procedural Justice' and the Analysis of Police Fiction." *Journal of Broadcasting and Electronic Media* 56 (1): 38–54.

Dixon, Travis L., Cristina L. Azocar, and Michael Casas. 2003. "The Portrayal of Race and Crime on Television Network News." *Journal of Broadcasting & Electronic Media* 47 (4): 498–523.

Donovan, Kathleen M., and Charles F. Klahm IV. (2015). "The Role of Entertainment Media in Perceptions of Police Use of Force." *Criminal Justice and Behavior* 42 (12): 1261–81.

Dorling, Danny. 2004. "Prime Suspect: Murder in Britain." In *Beyond Criminology*, edited by Paddy Hillyard, C. Pantazis, S. Tombs, and D. Gordon, 178–91. London: Pluto.

Dowler, Kenneth. 2003. "Media Consumption and Public Attitudes toward Crime and Justice: The Relationship between Fear of Crime, Punitive Attitudes, and Perceived Police Effectiveness." *Journal of Criminal Justice and Popular Culture* 10 (2): 109–26.

Dowler, Kenneth, and Valerie Zawilski. 2007. "Public Perceptions of Police Misconduct and Discrimination: Examining the Impact of Media Consumption." *Journal of Criminal Justice* 35 (2): 193–203.

Druckman, James N. 2005. "Media Matter: How Newspapers and Television News Cover Campaigns and Influence Voters." *Political Communication* 22 (4): 463–81.

Dryer, Trevor D. 2007. "All the News That's Fit to Print: The *New York Times*, Yellow Journalism, and the Criminal Trial 1898–1902." *Nevada Law Journal* 8 (2): 541–70.

Ericson, Richard V., Patricia M. Baranek, and Janet B. Chan. 1991. *Representing Order: Crime, Law, and Justice in the News Media*. Milton Keynes: Open University Press.

Ericson, Richard V., Patricia M. Baranek, and Janet Chan. 1987. *Visualizing Deviance*. Toronto: University of Toronto Press.

Eschholz, Sarah. 2003. "Crime on Television-Issues in Criminal Justice." *Journal of the Institute of Justice and Internal Studies* 1 (2): 9–18.

Eschholz, Sarah, Matthew Mallard, and Stacey Flynn. 2004. "Images of Prime Time Justice: A Content Analysis of *NYPD Blue* and *Law & Order*." *Journal of Criminal Justice and Popular Culture* 10 (3): 161–80.

Estep, Rhoda, and Patrick T. MacDonald. 1984. "How Prime-Time Crime Evolved on TV, 1976–1983." *Journalism Quarterly* 60 (2): 293–300

Fishman, Marc. 1981. "Police News: Constructing an Image of Crime." *Urban Life* 9 (4): 371–94.

Fishman, Marc, and Gray Cavender. 1998. *Entertaining Crime: Television Reality Programs*. New York: Aldine De Gruyter.

Garofalo, James. 1981. "Crime and the Mass Media: A Selective Review of Research." *Journal of Research in Crime and Delinquency* 18 (2): 319–50.

Gekoski, Anna, Jacqueline M. Gray, and Joanna R. Adler. 2012. "What Makes a Homicide Newsworthy? UK National Tabloid Newspaper Journalists Tell All." *British Journal of Criminology* 52 (6): 1212–32.

Gerbner, George, Larry Gross, Michael Morgan, and Nancy Signorielli. 1980. "The Mainstreaming of America: Violence Profile No. 11." *Journal of Communication* 30 (3): 10–29.

Gilliam Jr., Franklin D., and Shanto Iyengar. 2000. "Prime Suspects: The Influence of Local Television News on the Viewing Public." *American Journal of Political Science* 44 (3): 560–73.

Greer, Chris. 2003. *Sex, Crime and the Media*. Cullompton: Willan.

Greer, Chris, and Robert Reiner. 2015. "Mediated Mayhem: Media, Crime and Criminal Justice." In *The Oxford Handbook of Criminology* (fifth edition), edited by Mike Maguire, Rod Morgan, and Robert Reiner, 245–78. Oxford: Oxford University Press.

Huston, Aletha C., Edward Donnerstein, Halford Fairchild, Norma D. Feshbach, Phyllis A. Katz, John P. Murray, Eli A. Rubinstein, Brian L. Wilcox, and Diana M. Zuckerman. 1992. *Big World, Small Screen: The Role of Television in American Society*. Lincoln: University of Nebraska Press.

Intravia, Jonathan, Kevin T. Wolff, and Alex R. Piquero. 2018. "Investigating the Effects of Media Consumption on Attitudes towards Police Legitimacy." *Deviant Behavior* 39 (8): 963–80.

Iyengar, Shanto. 1991. *Is Anyone Responsible? How Television Frames Political Issues*. Chicago: University of Chicago Press.

Kim, KiDeuk, Ashlin Oglesby-Neal, and Edward Mohr. 2017. "2016 Law Enforcement Use of Social Media." Urban Institute. Retrieved from http://www.urban.org/research/publication/2016-law-enforcement-use-social-mediasurvey/view/fullreport .

King, Peter. 2009. "Making Crime News: Newspapers, Violent Crime and the Selective Reporting of Old Bailey Trials in the Late Eighteenth Century." *Crime, History and Societies* 13 (1): 91–116.

Kooistra, Paul G., John S. Mahoney, and Saundra D. Westervelt. 1998. "The World According to Cops." In *Entertaining Crime: Television Reality Programs*, edited by March Fishman and Gray Cavender, 141–18. New York: Aldine de Gruyter.

Kort-Butler, Lisa A., Kelley J. Sittner Hartshorn. 2011. "Watching the Detectives: Crime Programing, Fear of Crime, and Attitudes about the Criminal Justice System." *The Sociological Quarterly* 52 (1): 36–55.

Lasley, James R. 1994. "The Impact of the Rodney King Incident on Citizen Attitudes toward Police." *Policing and Society* 3 (4): 245–55.

Lawrence, Regina G. 2000. *The Politics of Force: Media and the Construction of Police Brutality*. Berkeley: University of California Press.

Lee, Murray, and Alyce McGovern. 2013. *Policing and Media: Public Relations, Simulations and Communications*. New York: Routledge.

Leishman, Frank, and Paul Mason. 2012. *Policing and the Media*. New York: Routledge.

Lichter, S. Robert, Linda S. Lichter, and Stanley Rothman. 1994. *Prime Time: How TV Portrays American Culture*. Washington DC: Regnery.

Lieberman, Joel D., Deborah Koetzle, and Mari Sakiyama. 2013. "Police Departments' Use of Facebook: Patterns and Policy Issues." *Police Quarterly* 16 (4): 438–62

Liska, Allen, and William Baccaglini. 1990. "Feeling Safe by Comparison: Crime in the Newspapers." *Social Problems* 37 (3): 360–74.

Loader, Brian D., and Douglas Thomas, eds. 2013. *Cybercrime: Security and Surveillance in the Information Age*. New York: Routledge.

Marsh, Harry L. 1991. "A Comparative Analysis of Crime Coverage in Newspapers in the United States and Other Countries from 1960–1989: A Review of the Literature." *Journal of Criminal Justice* 19 (1): 67–79.

Martin, Greg. 2018. *Crime, Media and Culture*. New York: Routledge.

Mason, Paul, ed. 2003. *Criminal Visions*. New York: Routledge.

Mayes, Lauren. 2017. *Law Enforcement in the Age of Social Media: Examining the Organizational Image Construction of Police on Twitter and Facebook*. Unpublished doctoral dissertation, Temple University.

Mazerolle, Lorraine, Emma Antrobus, Sarah Bennett, and Tom R. Tyler. 2013. "Shaping Citizen Perceptions of Police Legitimacy: A Randomized Field Trial of Procedural Justice." *Criminology* 51 (1): 33–63.

McLaughlin, Elliot C. (2015). "We're Not Seeing More Police Shootings, Just More News Coverage." CNN, April, 21 (Update). Retrieved from: https://www.cnn.com/2015/04/20/us/police-brutality-video-social-media-attitudes/index.html .

Morgan, Michael. 1983. "Symbolic Victimization and Real-World Fear." *Human Communication Research* 9 (2): 146–57.

Morgan, Michael. 2012. *George Gerbner: A Critical Introduction to Media and Communication*. New York: Peter Lang.

Oliver, Mary B. 1994. "Portrayals of Crime, Race and Aggression in 'Reality-Based' Police Shows: A Content Analysis." *Journal of Broadcasting and Electronic Media* 38 (2): 179–92.

Perlmutter, David D. 2000. *Policing the Media: Street Cops and Public Perceptions of Law Enforcement*. Thousand Oaks: Sage.

Perrin, Andrew, and Maeve Duggan. 2015. "Americans' Internet Access: 2000–2015." Pew Research Center. Retrieved from https://www.pewresearch.org/internet/2015/06/26/americans-internet-access-2000-2015/ .

Phillips, Nickie, and Natasha Frost. 2010. "Crime in Prime Time." In *Race, Crime and the Media*, edited by Robert L. Bing, III, 121–40. New York: McGraw-Hill.

Podlas, Kimberlianne. 2006. "The CSI Effect: Exposing the Media Myth." *Fordham Intellectual Property Media and Entertainment Law Journal* 16 (2): 429.

Potter, W. James. 2014. "A Critical Analysis of Cultivation Theory." *Journal of Communication* 64 (6): 1015–36.

Prior, Markus. 2005. "News vs. Entertainment: How Increasing Media Choice Widens Gaps in Political Knowledge and Turnout." *American Journal of Political Science* 49 (3): 577–92.

Reiner, Robert. 2007. "Media Made Criminality: The Representation of Crime in the Mass Media." In *The Oxford Handbook of Criminology* (fourth edition), edited by Mike Maguire, Rod Morgan, and Robert Reiner, 302–40. Oxford: Oxford University Press.

Reiner, Robert, Sonia Livingstone, and Jessica Allen. 2000. "No More Happy Endings? The Media and Popular Concern about Crime since the Second World War." In *Crime, Risk and Insecurity*, edited by Tim Hope and Richard Sparks, 107–25. London: Routledge.

Reiner, Robert, Sonia Livingstone, and Jessica Allen. 2003. "Casino Culture: Media and Crime." In *Crime, Risk and Justice*, edited by Paul Mason, 175–94. New York: Routledge.

Reiner, Robert, Sonia Livingstone, and Jessica Allen. 2012. "From Law and Order to Lynch Mobs: Crime News since the Second World War." In *Criminal Visions*, edited by Paul Mason, 25–44. New York: Routledge.

Reith, Margaret. 1999. "Viewing of Crime Drama and Authoritarian Aggression: An Investigation of the Relationship between Crime Viewing, Fear and Aggression." *Journal of Broadcasting and Electronic Media* 43 (2): 211–21.

Rhineberger-Dunn, Gayle, Nicole Rader, and Kevin Donald Williams. 2008. "Constructing Juvenile Delinquency Through Crime Drama: An Analysis of Law and Order." *Journal of Criminal Justice and Popular Culture* 15 (1): 94–116.

Roberts, Julian, and Anthony Doob. 1990. "News Media Influences on Public Views of Sentencing." *Law and Human Behavior* 14 (5): 451–68.

Romer, Daniel, Kathleen H. Jamieson, and Nicole J. De Coteau. 1998. "The Treatment of Persons of Color in Local Television News: Ethnic Blame Discourse or Realistic Group Conflict?" *Communication Research* 25 (3): 286–305.

Sacco, Vincent F. 1995. "Media Constructions of Crime." *Annals of the American Academy of Political and Social Science* 539: 141–54.

Schweitzer, Nicholas J., and Michael J. Saks. 2007. "The CSI Effect: Popular Fiction about Forensic Science Affects the Public's Expectations about Real Forensic Science." *Jurimetrics* 47 (1): 357–64.

Signorielli, Nancy, Michael Morgan, and James Shanahan. 2019. "The Violence Profile: Five Decades of Cultural Indicators Research." *Mass Communication and Society* 22 (1): 1–28.

Skogan, Wesley G., and Michael G. Maxfield. 1981. *Coping with Crime*. Beverly Hills: Sage.

Slater, Michael D. 2007. "Reinforcing Spirals: The Mutual Influence of Media Selectivity and Media Effects and Their Impact on Individual Behavior and Social Identity." *Communication Theory* 17 (3): 281–303.

Starr, Paul. 2012. An Unexpected Crisis: The News Media in Postindustrial Democracies. *The International Journal of Press/Politics* 17 (2): 234–42.

Surette, Ray. 1998. *Media, Crime, and Criminal Justice: Images and Realities* (second edition). New York: Wadsworth.

Surette, Ray. 2007. *Media, Crime, and Criminal Justice: Images, Realities and Policies.* New York: Wadsworth.

Tyler, Tom R. 1990. *Why People Obey the Law: Procedural Justice, Legitimacy, and Compliance.* New Haven: Yale University Press.

Tyler, Tom R. 2004. "Enhancing Police Legitimacy." *The Annals of the American Academy of Political Science* 593 (1): 84–99.

Umanailo, M. Chairul Basrun, Imam Fachruddin, Deviana Mayasari, Rudy Kurniawan, Dewien N. Agustin . . . Trinovianto G. R. Hallatu. 2019. "Cybercrime Case as Impact Development of Communication Technology That Troubling Society." *International Journal of Science & Technology Research* 8 (9): 1224–28.

Van den Bulck, Jan. 2002. "Fictional Cops: Who Are They, and What Are They Teaching Us?" In *Law Enforcement, Communication and Community*, edited by Howard Giles, 107–27. Amsterdam: John Benjamins.

Van den Bulck, Jan, and Heidi Vandebosch. 2003. "When the Viewer Goes to Prison: Learning Fact from Watching Fiction. A Qualitative Cultivation Study." *Poetics* 31 (2): 103–16.

Wall, David S., and Matthew L. Williams. 2013. "Policing Cybercrime: Networked and Social Media Technologies and the Challenges for Policing." *Policing and Society* 23 (4): 409–12.

Weaver, James, and Jacob Wakshlag. 1986. "Perceived Vulnerability to Crime, Criminal Experience and Television Viewing." *Journal of Broadcasting and Electronic Media* 30 (2): 141–58.

Weitzer, Ronald. 2002. "Incidents of Police Misconduct and Public Opinion." *Journal of Criminal Justice* 30 (5): 397–408.

White, David M. 1950. "The Gate Keeper: A Case Study in the Selection of News." *Journalism Quarterly* 27 (4): 383–90.

Williams, Christine, and Jane Fedorowicz. 2019. "Does Social Media Promote the Public's Perception of the Police: Survey Results on Trust Cultivation." In *Proceedings of the 52nd Hawaii International Conference on System Sciences*, edited by Tung X. Bui, 3109–18. Honolulu: Hawaii International Conference on System Sciences. Retrieved from http://hdl.handle.net/10125/59747.

Zillman, Dolf, and Jacob Wakshlag. 1985. "Fear of Victimization and the Appeal of Crime Drama." In *Selective Exposure to Communication*, edited by Dolf Zillman and Jennings Bryant, 141–56. New York: Routledge.

CHAPTER 15

Social Media and Intergroup Encounters with "Cops"

Biased Samples, Echo Chambers, and Research Opportunities

Joseph B. Walther

In May of 2020, seemingly the whole world witnessed video replays of the death of George Floyd at the hands of a Minneapolis, Minnesota, police officer. Amid the subsequent demonstrations, news coverage occasionally depicted police officer joining protesters, "taking a knee in solidarity, reading the names of police brutality victims out loud or quietly crying alongside protesters. But the protests have also revealed widespread incidents of police aggression, documented with the same tool that captured Mr. Floyd's death under the knee of a white police officer in Minneapolis: video" (*New York Times*, June 5, 2020).[1] What is the effect of watching video of interactions between law enforcement officers and civilians?

Ubiquitous recording devices and social media have the potential to amplify and exacerbate stereotypical impressions of law enforcement at unprecedented levels of magnitude. While a single observer fortuitously had a video camcorder when he saw the beating of Rodney King by Los Angeles police officers in 1991, cameras and recording devices seem to be everywhere now. They include civilians' ever-ready smartphones, surveillance cameras, and even cameras put in place by law enforcement like dash cams and body cams as well (Kowalyk 2019).

Although the sharing and rebroadcast of ubiquitous cameras' pervasive recordings may be enough to affect civilians' impressions, these elements are only half of the story when it comes to how social media perpetuate stereotypes of police (see chapter 14). The presentation of recordings on social media such as YouTube, Facebook, or other sites involves certain underlying algorithms that select which videos to serve to viewers based on certain characteristics of the videos and the viewers' watching history (Sunstein 2009). Thus social media do not simply collect and store obscure and isolated recordings until they are searched, as if in a library. Social media embed them in interconnected, endless groupings of related presentations; that is, if you watch one video depicting police misconduct, social media are likely to present to you another, similar video next. Moreover, the recordings that garner the greatest attention depict police conduct that is the most outrageous—rude, duplicitous, or aggressive. With the boost to their repetition and exposure that algorithms provide, it is likely that the most disturbing and questionably typical vignettes have disproportionate effects on civilian viewers' stereotyped perceptions of law enforcement through social media. Because social media viewers identify with the peer civilians interacting with cops in these videos, intergroup perceptions are certain to develop.

Because many social media users are unaware of the application of selection algorithms, viewers may be likely to think that a series of videos displayed in succession by social media depicting law enforcement officers' offensive interactions with civilians captures a random and representative selection of all such videos that may exist (see McNamee 2019). Selection algorithms, and their potential to bias the presentation of information, create what is called an "echo chamber," which has the potential to affect users' perceptions of reality. Echo chambers may arise in social media regarding any topic or social stereotype (Carr 2017). The serial display of related videos makes social media different from broadcast media of the past in which an isolated news story, TV show, or movie offered single portrayals of law enforcement officers, for better or worse (Donovan and Klahm 2015). The seriation, repetition, and multiple exposures to negative stereotypes in cop videos on social media provide negative instances of vicarious intergroup contact (Vezzali, Hewstone, Capozza, Giovannini, and Wölfer 2014). They provide surrogate interactions with cops that viewers experience as if they were their own experience, which affects their intergroup perceptions and, potentially, their future contact with police, in possibly harmful ways.

This chapter focuses on the sources and potential effects of videos presented through YouTube that focus on interactions between law enforcement officers and civilians. It discusses how and why social media platforms capture and preserve viewers' attention through algorithmic selection of related videos. It presents an informal analysis of the types of portrayals of law enforcement that are common in such videos, and why a comprehensive survey of these portrayals is beyond the capacity of a single viewer or analyst. The chapter then elaborates on the various sources of police-related videos and raises questions of whether sources differ with respect to their impact on viewers' perceptions. It concludes by suggesting research questions and research methods with the potential to advance understanding of the effects of social media videos on perceptions of police and on any stereotyped role in society, including basic issues on the effects of stereotype change and the potential for big data to assess echo chamber effects.

OLD MEDIA, NEW MEDIA

Media may be the primary source for most people's views of police. According to Choi and Giles (2012, 266), "Few Americans have much direct contact with law enforcement officials, and it is almost entirely through media representations that they create and develop their impressions of police officers." Depictions of law enforcement officers, like other groups depicted in media, have always been subject to stereotyping (Mastro 2009). Those of us of a certain age who hear the phrase "Just the facts, ma'am" recall the TV image of no-nonsense, stoic, clean-cut detective Joe Friday. These images remain a part of the public's stereotypes, even though we knew they were fiction.

Newer TV shows portray police officers in ostensibly real, not fictional terms (see, again, chapter 14). *Cops*, for instance, ran for thirty-two years, and *Live PD* ran for four, until both were cancelled in 2020. *Cops* and *Live PD* were part of the nonfiction genre of reality television and may be more believable than the fictional portrayals of the past. *Cops*, although unscripted, was obviously edited, and segments were selected by directors and producers for the audience. *Live PD* claimed to show spontaneous, naturally occurring encounters between law enforcement and civilians, although the off-screen coercion of suspects is a matter of record (Taberski 2019).[2] While there is a considerable range of positive and negative portrayals of the police in traditional media (Perlmutter 2000; Van den Bulck 2002), these two "reality shows," in particular, "glorified police" (Sperling 2020), depicting cops in the United States, Britain, Hong Kong, and elsewhere as "crime-solving heroes" having to endure tedium, resistance, deception, and stupidity, while serving the public's interests.

Digital devices and social media have changed the landscape profoundly. The impressions that viewers garner from social media videos cannot be dismissed as the fantastic imaginings of screenwriters, editors, or producers. And many are far from flattering.

THE TWIN EVILS OF SOCIAL MEDIA: ATTENTION HACKING AND ECHO CHAMBERS

The perpetuation and selection of certain depictions of police, in social media presentations, is no accident. They are the products of a common profit-maximization strategy, attention hacking, and its by-product, echo chambers. Attention hacking refers to strategies that social media platforms use to keep viewers looking at their sites as frequently and for as long as possible (Abi-Heila 2018). They do this to maximize viewers' exposure to the advertisements on their web pages that social media companies sell. The more people watch social media, the more ads they see, and the more revenue social media companies accrue.

One of the most effective ways that YouTube hacks users' attention is by recommending additional videos that a user might wish to see. That is, when a YouTube user searches for and selects a video to watch, YouTube populates the user's screen with additional videos. Those selections appear based on computational formulas, or algorithms, that have determined that a viewer who looks at one particular video is likely to be interested in looking at other specific videos as well. According to the *New York Times* (Roose and Conger 2019), the algorithm is responsible for more than 70 percent of overall time spent on YouTube, and it has been a major engine for the platform's growth. But it has also drawn accusations of leading users down rabbit holes filled with extreme and divisive content in an attempt to keep them watching and drive up the site's usage.

Algorithmic selection of social media content such as videos includes a variety of factors into its selections and recommendations. The precise combinations of factors are trade secrets, but among them, the databases that "tag" the properties of any given content may include its sensationalistic value (which makes content more likely to be watched), as well as other individual characteristics. Additionally, the algorithms take into consideration social network characteristics: content that an individuals' online friends watched or liked, as well as content watched and liked by other people who simply share a users' demographic and viewing patterns, even though they may be entirely unknown to the individual (Cappella 2017). Figure 15.1 shows one investigator's depiction of how Facebook's algorithms select what individuals see in their newsfeeds (Rose-Stockwell n.d.).

While attention-hacking alone may have a pernicious influence on users, of greater influence may be attention-hacking's evil twin, the so-called echo chamber. An echo chamber is the presentation of content that repeats a similar ideological point of view to the exclusion of alternative points of view, leading an individual to see only a certain portrayal of groups or a particular side of an issue. People may experience something like an echo chamber if they watch only conservative TV news or liberal TV news, but TV viewers know they can change the channel when they want to (and they do; Dubois and Blank 2018). In social media, when people get a skewed presentation, the echo chamber, hypothetically, creates an impression that that representation is all there is to see. Users generally may not realize that the portrayals they observe are skewed or that they were chosen for them to see. As a result, individuals get shown ideologically similar content (news, comments, and videos) again and again, and may infer (falsely) that

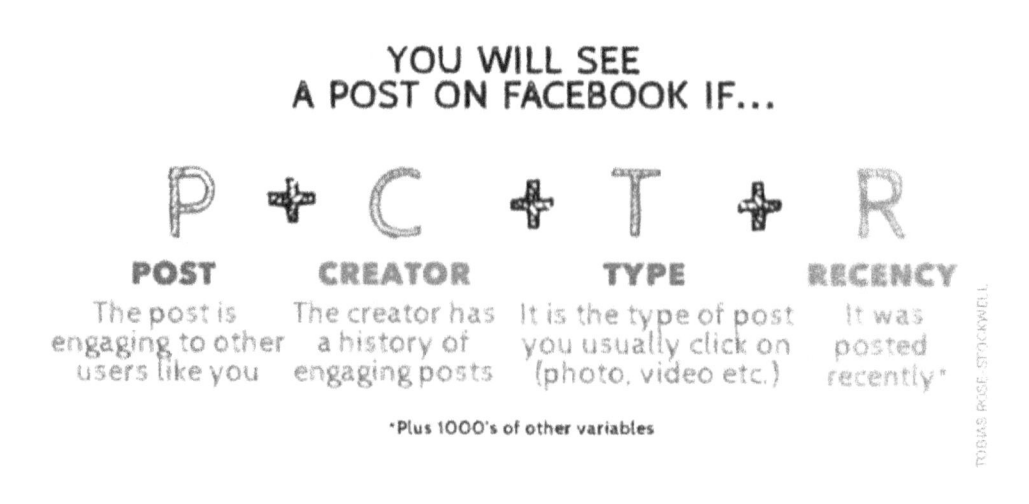

FIGURE 15.1. Characteristics Leading Messages to Appear on Facebook

the biased content represents society (McNamee 2019). In this way, echo chambers fed by consistently skewed portrayals of cops enhance both the intergroup distinctiveness, and relative deplorability, of cops to viewers (see Tajfel and Turner 1979).

It is easy to observe the top-level manifestation of algorithmic selection of videos on YouTube. Certain features are evident whether an individual views YouTube videos on a desktop computer or a smartphone app. In addition to the primary video a viewer sees on a YouTube page, YouTube also indicates what video is "Up next," a photo and title of which also appear on the page. In this way, YouTube recommends to viewers another video courtesy of its algorithm, which has been built to predict their enjoyment and retention on the site—without the users having to search for another video on their own. Moreover, YouTube also offers an autoplay feature. When activated, YouTube will continue showing the "Up next" videos in succession, one after another, continuously without interruption.

As an illustration, figure 15.2 shows three sequentially presented pages from a viewing of YouTube on a smartphone. The far-left panel shows a topmost, larger view of a video titled "Houston Police Harassment and Double standards, etc. etc. Speed much?" Halfway down that very screen, to the left, appear the words "Up next," adjacent to which appears the switch to enable autoplay. The video that appears as "Up next" is titled "Return To Naval Station Mayport." Looking at the middle screen, "Return to Naval Station Mayport" is now the topmost video, having risen in succession. The next "Up next" video is titled "Video raises question was this man stopped 'for jogging . . .,'" which, in turn, rises in succession on the third (right-hand) screen. This capacity exemplifies the topography of the echo chamber exceedingly well and more explicitly than most social media platforms make apparent.

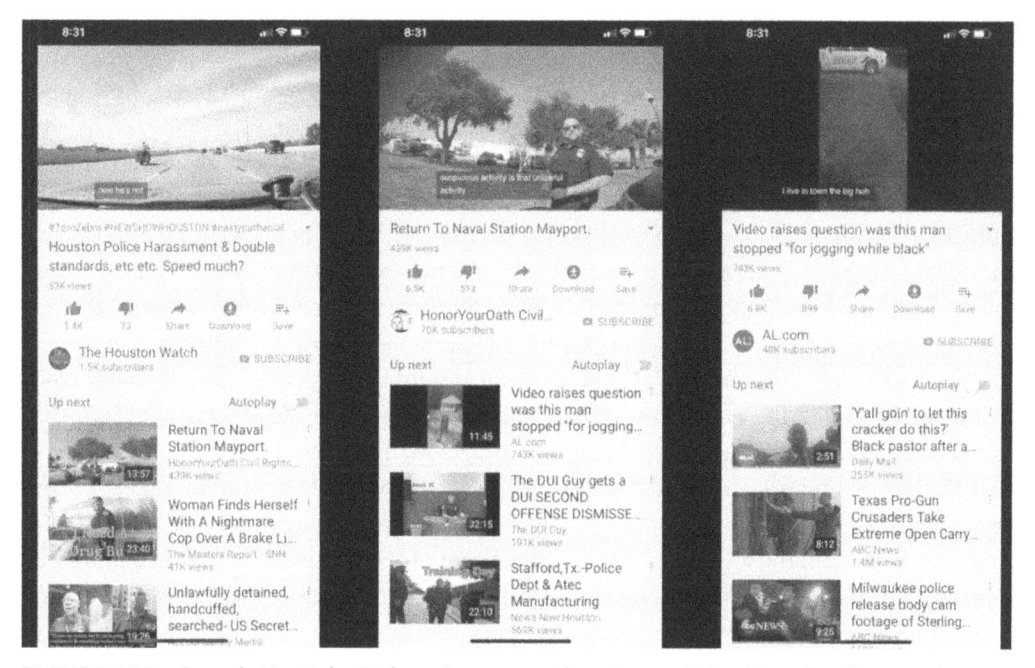

FIGURE 15.2. Sample YouTube Videos Sequence Showing an Echo Chamber Progression

Although the echo chambers hypothesis is reasonable and important, research supporting its existence is not entirely unambiguous. Most research showing a relationship between extreme views and repeated exposure to ideological social media content is correlational. It is not clear whether exposure to biased content leads to extremism or whether extremists select biased content. A recently articulated model of attitudes and media and some initial tests (not involving social media) suggest there is a combination of these pathways; people who hold certain moral views seek media content that is compatible with those views (see Abrams and Giles 2007). If media content often repeats those themes, further shifts in individuals' attitudes can occur (Tamborini and Weber 2020). Although echo chambers have the potential to bias individuals' reception and interpretation of news events, a number of empirical studies find that most individuals tend not to rely on social media for the majority of their news consumption (Dubois and Blank 2018; Flaxman, Goel, and Rao 2016; Fletcher and Nielsen 2017). However, some viewers' interest in watching depictions of police officers may not be the same as the general population's interest in current events, politics, and news. Individuals who are interested in depictions of police may have different motivations or ideologies that bring them to this very particularized type of content, where the echo chamber may have a stronger impact than on news in general.

The impact of videos may come not only from their succession and aggregation in echo chambers, however. The sources of these videos also differ, and the differences among sources may also affect the degree to which videos impact viewers' impressions of the police officers.

TYPES OF VIDEO CONTENT AND LIMITATIONS IN THEIR DISCOVERY

YouTube's algorithms tailor the selection of videos it presents to each individual viewer's previous viewing selections and patterns; and no two YouTube viewers see the same succession of videos. That phenomenon calls for a big disclaimer when it comes to any single researcher's ability to provide generalizable descriptions about the overall nature or frequency of depictions of police officers on YouTube. No single analyst can randomly sample the corpus of police videos, and no sample is unbiased. While readers are invited to conduct their own inspection of the types of behavior or general themes law enforcement officers appear to personify in these videos, replicability is also subject to algorithmically influenced bias: Perceptions among viewers are likely to differ from one another, due to their own exposure to different series and collections of videos that the algorithms determine for each respective person. Therefore, the following general description of themes and incidents in YouTube police videos, as interpreted by the author of this chapter, must be taken as suggestive and not definitive or exhaustive. The degree to which, in the aggregate, law enforcement officers appear competent, ignorant, benevolent, malevolent, polite, profane, respectful, or excessive may differ from one individual YouTube viewer to the next.

Despite the variations in what videos different individuals are likely to see, some types of videos are more likely to be presented than others. Because negative and sensational depictions tend to be more arousing than positive and peaceful ones, they are shared more, watched more, and therefore become more likely to be featured in any individual's video lineup (Amoore 2020; Horwitz and Seetharaman 2020). With these disclaimers, here is one description of the types of portrayals in which law enforcement officers appear, based on several months' viewing of hundreds of videos.

Police as Ignorant

Many videos portray police officers as ignorant, particularly with respect to law, procedures, or derivations of Constitutional rights. It may be the case that an officer appears to be ill-informed regarding civil liberties, or an officer does not know the specific laws or codes with which the officer is charging a civilian. These depictions range from simple naivety to what appears to be outright duplicity.

Police as Dishonest

In some cases, officers threaten to apply ambiguous criminal charges in order to assert control. Threatening to charge an individual with obstruction of justice or obstructing an investigation appears frequently in these videos when a civilian declines either to produce identification, to back away a certain distance, to answer questions, and so forth. In other cases, officers appear to be making up laws and regulations ad hoc, and if civilians protest, the officers may simply invite the civilians to defend themselves in court. Videos can reveal significant discrepancies between the recordings of events and how they are described to have occurred in police reports. Field sobriety tests with negative results, where drivers are nevertheless arrested for drunk driving, are not uncommon among the videos. Rare videos capture police discussing among themselves what charges they can concoct and how they will corroborate one another. Even more rare are videos that find officers planting evidence.

Police as Abusers of Power

Many videos depict law enforcement officers intimidating civilians. Officers shout at civilians, curse, issue orders, and interrupt, in addition to detaining individuals in ways that appear arbitrary. Naturally, these episodes are presented as though from the point of view of a neutral observer, leaving viewers to judge for themselves how justifiable these exercises in control may be. Likewise, many episodes portray officers' instigation of excessive force, and as mentioned above, the video-recorded events are sometimes shown to contradict police reports that claim that the civilian initiated aggression against the police officer. In some cases officers appear to be making up laws and regulations ad hoc. Such episodes may be counter-normative, but their dramatic appeal to viewers' sense of outrage leads to repetition and greater prominence in social media's algorithmic ecosphere.

Lest readers conclude that these interpretations and characterizations are one-sided, it is worth noting that the videos one sees on YouTube are generally one-sided. They can hardly be representative of a random sample of day-to-day police interactions with civilians. They are not "ride-alongs" portraying the normal day of the average officer.

"Self-broadcast creates an important historical record and serves as a powerful tool to document systemic abuse," observed a *New York Times* technology reporter (Ovide 2020), who added "BUT, unfortunately . . . when you lose the (news media) gatekeepers, you can also lose context of any event or fact, making it easy for anyone to interpret it to fit their worldview." Civilians initiate recordings when they apprehend that something is amiss, and they save them when indeed things go badly; or they create videos when they initiate actions that are intended to provoke police officers' dramatic responses. Dash cam and body cam footage is culled when it is known to have recorded a controversial encounter. Recordings are deliberately and selectively uploaded to social media because they are dramatic and not ordinary. In this way, they contribute to the portrayal of a civilian ingroup as being subject to threat from the police outgroup, potentially enhancing the ingroup's solidarity (Veenstra and Haslam 2000; see chapter 1). Although different viewers may indeed interpret the videos differently, the motivations of their contributors and the algorithmic favoritism with which they are displayed should make it no surprise that they tend to depict the worst of the worst in cop videos on social media.

Police as Racists

Many YouTube videos portray the seemingly unwarranted harassment of minority members by police. Less often are direct comparisons between police encounters with White and Black civilians over the same issue, although at times these are staged (see Second Amendment Audits, below on page 238). More often individuals of color are pulled over while driving, or interrogated while walking, for no clear reason beyond an officer's whim (see chapter 5). Often officers can be heard explaining the detention of a Black civilian saying that some crime was reported in the vicinity, and the civilian matches a partial description from that other scene. These videos often appear with some variation of the title "Driving While Black" or "Walking While Black," reflecting the feeling of the victims that, although they have done nothing suspicious, they are being treated as if their very identity made them as guilty of crimes as people who are "Driving While Intoxicated."

A rather perplexing variation of this theme appears in videos in which police officers attempt to question a person of color, explaining that they are responding to a call about a suspicious person in a neighborhood matching the description of the civilian. A viewer may sense that a call probably was made to police but was motivated by racism on the part of the caller, since the civilian does not seem to do anything suspicious in the scene. The officer then faces a conundrum when the civilian claims to live there, or work there, or is merely passing through. Some officers seem embarrassed to have inconvenienced the civilian, and apologize, while more often, officers attempt to rationalize their interdiction. They may escalate the confrontation, assert control, and exacerbate the racial problem.

SOURCES OF VIDEOS AND THEIR POTENTIAL IMPACT

Videos on YouTube depicting police encounters come from a variety of sources, or types of origination. We may hypothesize that the sources and contexts from which these videos come are liable to arouse different assumptions about their veracity and representativeness, rendering potentially different magnitudes of effects on social media viewers' perceptions of police.

Recordings Captured by Law Enforcement

As mentioned above, police and sheriff's departments increasingly use dash cam recordings to document motorists' behavior and to record interactions during traffic stops. Cameras, mounted in police vehicles, point forward, capturing the other vehicle and, to some extent, its driver. Officers often wear microphones that transmit audio recordings of police/civilian dialogue to the recording system.

Many officers are equipped with body cams, which provide similar functions as dash cams, although they provide a narrower field of vision. Although they record voices well, they are less likely to capture the physical movements of police officers than they are to display behaviors of civilians.

There seems to be a wide variety in how videos recorded by law enforcement come into the possession of civilians and, therefrom, onto social media platforms. The processes for procurement of videos from the law enforcement agencies seem to vary by jurisdiction. Most assuredly they can be subpoenaed as evidence for trial or obtained through Freedom of Information requests.[3]

Because these videos are owned by law enforcement, it stands to reason that civilians and social media consumers may invest them with different levels of credibility, depending on whether their portrayal of police and civilians tend to be more favorable to one entity or another. For instance, a video captured and released by police that depicts an instance of police misconduct seems not to be in a police department's self-serving interest. Such a video may therefore be more likely to be seen as authentic and realistic. A police video that depicts police officers behaving positively may seem self-selected or unrepresentative to those who hold police in low esteem. Although speculative, these are researchable suggestions.

Recordings Captured by Civilians

Individuals frequently record their own interactions with law enforcement personnel, quite commonly during traffic stops or pedestrian encounters. Individuals use cell phones mounted in their cars or held in their hands. These videos tend to have poor stability and visual qualities, as is to be expected when a camera operator holding a cell phone also has to retrieve a driver's license, vehicle registration, and other documents. These complications lead to very low-quality recordings and difficult viewing, but in so doing they add to the spontaneity and verisimilitude of the images (see Van Der Heide, Johnson, and Vang 2013). Because these encounters seem spontaneous and realistic—especially when an officer is unaware that a recording is occurring—they are likely to be highly credible and convincing to social media viewers. Police who swear, aggress, appear arbitrary or uninformed, or otherwise appear to mistreat civilians in these recordings may deleteriously affect viewers' perceptions of law enforcement.

While many such recorded encounters are spontaneous, there is a substantial number of videos on YouTube depicting deliberately maneuvered encounters between civilians and law enforcement officers. Many of these recordings depict individuals asserting various rights in a manner that arouse police officers' concerns. For instance, in the United States, where it is legal for civilians to carry firearms openly, individuals appear with menacing-looking rifles walking down suburban sidewalks, testing law enforcement's response and recording it. The videos often show armed civilians being questioned, commanded to lie on the ground, treated with profanity, sometimes held at gunpoint, forcibly disarmed, or assaulted by one or many anxious law enforcement officers at a time. These individuals often assert that they are within their rights to carry their weapon; they explain that they have no intention other than to exercise their rights or to invoke their right not to answer questions. Seldom do videos depict calm conversations with law enforcement personnel. It is not uncommon to see videos that compare how gun-carrying civilians are treated differently by police if the civilians are Black or White.

Another variation involves civilian protagonists videotaping police department buildings, military base entrances, or police encounters with third parties, anticipating that they will be questioned by law enforcement about their purposes. It is typical for these individuals to assert that they have a constitutionally protected right to take pictures in public; since they are committing no crime, they are not required by law to produce identification when police (seemingly inevitably) request (or demand) it. It seems clear in many of these videos that the protagonists are baiting or daring police to harass, abuse, and/or arrest them. In many cases, police are depicted proclaiming that photography of property owned by government or of police themselves is not allowed without permission, sometimes threatening arrest, or, rarely, confiscating cameras.

These types of encounters appear to be sanctioned by a number of officially or loosely organized groups who undertake to provide demonstrations of spontaneous police misconduct, under the guise of providing some kind of public service. Associations or movements such as Cop Watch, First Amendment Audit, and Second Amendment Audit promote and propagate such recorded encounters. They sometimes assert that they expect their efforts to influence law enforcement organizations to train officers in the subtleties of the protections they assert, and ultimately to curb police misconduct.

In light of these characteristics, it is difficult to predict how much of an impact deliberately maneuvered user-generated videos have on social media viewers. Many seem contrived. If police officers behave unprofessionally, the degree to which they seem provoked may counteract the potential negativity of their own conduct. If they lose control, however, not much sympathy may be afforded them.

One final variation of civilian-generated video occurs when a third party records a police encounter, unbeknownst to any of the primary parties. For example, a high school student's video recording of a school resource officer assaulting a different, belligerent student in class went viral in 2015. These kinds of recordings seem honest, real, and credible, and we can hypothesize that they are more likely than staged conflicts to have some impact on perceptions of law enforcement officers.

SURVEILLANCE CAMERAS

An additional variation on the source of police/civilian encounters is when episodes are recorded by surveillance cameras of some kind. Whether they are set up for security purposes inside or outside of buildings, or are positioned for traffic monitoring, cameras that produce recordings that are not made by police or by civilians may offer the most perceived objectivity and credibility.

QUESTIONS OF EFFECTS

A number of research questions arise from this description of the nature of YouTube videos depicting police interactions with civilians, curated by algorithmic echo chambers. These questions do not pertain only to viewers' impressions of cops. They have the potential also to inform knowledge about how this new medium affects perception of any number of intergroup stereotypes groups that are propagated by slanted portrayals on social media.

What are the effects of watching videos of law enforcement officers interacting with civilians? Social media research shows that viewers adopt the perspective of figures they see online who resemble themselves, and they internalize what happens to those figures as they interact online with outgroup individuals (Dai and Walther 2018). Based on social identification and self-categorization, individuals who see someone like themselves verbally bullied by a celebrity or politician online reflect more negative attitudes toward the bully than those who experience less social identification with their online surrogate. At a larger scale, the echo chamber hypothesis suggests that the repeated, biased representations of a group or event affect viewers' perceptions of reality. If this is so, and if YouTube videos of cops are predominantly negative, research suggests (Vezzali et al. 2014) that perceptions of cops should become more negative as a result of watching some number of these videos. It remains to be seen, however, whether perceptions of officers' potential ignorance, dishonesty, abuse of power, racism, or other respective characteristics are equally as amenable to influence as a result of exposure to these media, or whether some dimensions are more robust to change than others.

We have already raised the question: Do different sources of videos differentially impact, or moderate, viewers' perceptions of police? Are there differences due to whether a video emanates from dash cams or body cams versus spontaneous civilian smartphone recordings or the deliberate confrontations by "cop watchers," or the neutral eye of a surveillance camera?

For whom do these effects occur? Recent critiques and new approaches to mass media research (Valkenburg and Peter 2013) caution against the assumption that we can learn about the effects of media portrayals using typical experimental research methods. Media experiments typically involve a random selection of human subjects, randomly assigned to watch different media depictions. But some media messages are not typically consumed by a random swath of people. A danger in accepting the echo chambers hypothesis for the general population may be that only individuals with preexisting ideological biases consume certain types of media messages in the first place: "Moral beliefs shape media exposure, and these beliefs are influenced as a result," conclude Huskey et al. (2018, 315). In other words, people who already hate cops may watch cop videos—or watch them a lot. Those individuals' attitudes toward police may already be extreme, and more videos reinforce but do not change their perceptions. While a more mainstream, neutral audience might be more susceptible to the influence of algorithmically aggregated YouTube videos, they may be less likely to expose themselves to the videos in the first place. Whether people who stumble onto this genre of videos, or seek one local or viral story and then succumb to the lure of the algorithm, will be an important qualification to the echo chamber effect on any subject.

Is there an echo chamber after all? In other words, does algorithmic cultivation and presentation of cop videos differ than a random selection of videos with police in them? Although an individual may be unable to make such assessments due to the way that social media platforms try to customize the presentation of videos for each individual, big data may provide answers. Researchers are able to request access to YouTube's database using the company's "application program interface," or API ("YouTube Data API Overview" n.d.). By limiting a search for data to certain keywords, they can download a vast amount of data with many analyzable characteristics. In other words, by downloading big data concerning YouTube videos about "cops" and "police," a researcher should be able to describe the central tendencies and distributions of keywords, title words, number of viewings, and other information, sufficient to develop an unbiased profile of what is actually out there online. If algorithmically curated videos do in fact differ from random samples, further human subjects research might determine whether the echo chamber has a real effect: Does watching video views automatically selected by the echo chamber algorithm have different effects on viewers' perceptions of the police than occurs from watching a similar number of police videos that are self-selected by individual viewers?

Do the comments people post on videos influence the impact of the videos? The web pages that comprise YouTube show not only the videos themselves but also the written comments of other users. User-generated comments on social media range from wistful to combative. The comments accompanying police videos often give explicit articulation to the sentiments that the videos implicitly suggest. They pass judgment, condemn, and call for retribution, sometimes violently. Research shows that YouTube's user-generated comments have a strong effect on subsequent users' evaluations of the videos, and depending on the reader's level of identification with the writers of those comments, their attitudes, and perceptions about the subject of the videos as well (Walther et al. 2010).

A final question has to do with how, precisely, intergroup perceptions evolve and change as a result of exposure to YouTube video echo chambers. Does this most unusual form of vicarious contact, in which exposures to ingroup/outgroup interactions are serial, related, and algorithmically biased, change one's perceptions with regard to *all* cops, the *average* cop, or is it one's estimate of the *proportion* of cops that are undesirable that changes? Previous research on outgroup stereotype change suggests it may be the latter (Hamburger 1994). In other words, an individual may previously believe that nine out of ten law enforcement officers are professional, knowledgeable, and benevolent, although one out of ten should not be on the job. Does exposure to the negative YouTube videos change that individual's perception of the distribution, to eight good ones out of ten, or seven out of ten? And as these distributions change, how do individuals apprehend their own odds of being treated professionally and fairly in their own singular encounter when they see flashing lights in their own rearview mirror? As other chapters in this volume describe, the quality of a police/civilian interaction is determined in part by the apprehensions that a civilian brings to an encounter as well as those concerning the officer (see chapters 5–9 and 11).

CONCLUSIONS

As in many other aspects of social life, the Internet and social media have the potential to exert profound effects. Many aspects of this are for the good: Half the respondents in a survey of North American adults agreed that YouTube is very important in "figuring out how to do things they haven't done before" (Pew Research Center 2018). But 28 percent of the respondents also use the platform for "Just passing the time," and within that space, the potential for attraction to conflicts, conspiracies, and echo chambers awaits.

YouTube is not the only social media platform capitalizing on sensationalistic content and creating echo chambers with implications for intergroup perceptions. As Evans (2017) describes,

> Facebook has become a feedback loop which can and does, despite its best intentions, become a vicious spiral. At Facebook's scale, behavioral targeting doesn't just *reflect* our behavior, it actually *influences* it. . . . The more you engage with a particular kind of post, the more you will see its ilk. So far so good! It's just showing you what you've demonstrated you're interested in. What's wrong with that? The answer is twofold. First, this eventually constructs a small "in-group" cluster of Facebook friends and topics that dominate your feed; and as you grow accustomed to interacting with them, this causes your behavior to change, and you interact with them even more, reinforcing their in-group status. . . . Second, and substantially worse, because "engagement" is the metric, Facebook inevitably selects for the shocking and the outrageous.

Likewise with regard to Instagram, for which Cotter (2019, 896) notes not only the impact of algorithms, but how some users learn to "game the system" through "conscious, instrumental interactions" with the platform's algorithms in order to achieve disproportionate influence for themselves and their views.

Sergeant Joe Friday, the 1960s fictional TV cop, was likeable. "The whole world is watching," was the chant of Vietnam War protestors, aware of the presence of TV coverage, as Chicago police beat and arrested them outside of the August 1968 Democratic National Convention.[4] In those days, the available viewing of television recordings such as these lasted one night a week or only as long as a news cycle, after which the public had no additional access. Nowadays, there is no shortage of video to fuel social media's fires: According to the *Police Chief* magazine (Kowalyk 2019, 27), "Police officers have never been more accountable than they are today. Their actions are often recorded on smartphones or CCTV cameras. Split-second decisions can be cross-examined for weeks in a court of law" and in the court of public opinion as well. "The whole world is watching" became a part of society's consciousness. How modern, ubiquitous, algorithmically fed, ever-available recordings have the potential to affect intergroup stereotypes and social attitudes—about racial groups, political parties, or law enforcement officers, leading to perceptual as well as behavioral consequences—warrants great social awareness, concerns over public safety, and continued, critical research.

NOTES

1. "Bystanders captured video of George Floyd, a 46-year-old African-American man . . . being handcuffed and pinned to the ground by . . . a white police officer . . . using his knee to pin Mr. Floyd by his neck," who died. "The next day, the video was widely shared on social media" (Taylor 2020), leading to tens of thousands of people protesting in at least 140 cities across America, curfews, and the deaths of protestors, police, and innocent bystanders (Robertson, Rojas, and Taylor 2020).

2. *Live PD* acknowledged after the fact that it did not air, and destroyed its recording, of the death of a Black man with congestive heart failure who resisted apprehension and was eventually tased repeatedly by Texas sheriff deputies during a traffic stop, initiated because the driver did not dim his headlights in the face of oncoming traffic (Osborn 2020).

3. "Since 1967, the (US) Freedom of Information Act (FOIA) has provided the public the right to request access to records from any federal agency. . . . Federal agencies are required to disclose any information requested under the FOIA unless it falls under one of nine exemptions which protect interests such as personal privacy, national security, and law enforcement" (US Department of Justice, n.d.). This provision also applies to state and local government agencies.

4. https://en.wikipedia.org/wiki/The_whole_world_is_watching.

REFERENCES

Abi-Heila, Georges. 2018. "Attention Hacking Is the Epidemic of Our Generation . . ." *Medium*. December 17. Retrieved from https://uxdesign.cc/attention-hacking-is-the-epidemic-of-our-generation-e212e111c675 .

Abrams, J., and Giles, H. 2007. "Ethnic Identity Gratifications Selection and Avoidance by African Americans: A Group Vitality and Social Identity Gratifications Perspective." *Media Psychology* 9 (1): 115–35.

Amoore, Louise. 2020. *Cloud Ethics: Algorithms and the Attributes of Ourselves and Others*. Durham: Duke University Press.

Cappella, Joseph N. 2017. "Vectors into the Future of Mass and Interpersonal Communication Research: Big Data, Social Media, and Computational Social Science." *Human Communication Research* 43 (4): 545–58.

Carr, Caleb T. 2017. "Social Media in Intergroup Communication." In *The Oxford Encyclopedia of Intergroup Communication*, edited by Howard Giles and Jake Harwood, 349–67. Oxford: Oxford University Press.

Choi, Charles W., and Howard Giles. 2012. "Intergroup Messages in Policing the Community." In *The Handbook of Intergroup Communication*, edited by Howard Giles, 264–77. New York: Routledge.

Cotter, Kelley. 2019. "Playing the Visibility Game: How Digital Influencers and Algorithms Negotiate Influence on Instagram." *New Media & Society* 21 (4): 895–913.

Dai, Yue, and Joseph B. Walther. 2018. "Vicariously Experiencing Parasocial Intimacy with Public Figures through Observations of Interactions on Social Media." *Human Communication Research* 44 (3): 322–42.

Donovan, Kathleen M., and Charles F. Klahm IV. 2015. "The Role of Entertainment Media in Perceptions of Police Use of Force." *Criminal Justice and Behavior* 42 (12): 1261–81.

Dubois, Elizabeth, and Grant Blank. 2018. "The Echo Chamber Is Overstated: The Moderating Effect of Political Interest and Diverse Media." *Information, Communication & Society* 21 (5): 729–45.

Evans, Jon. 2017. "Facebook Is Broken." *TechCrunch*. June 4. Retrieved from https://techcrunch.com/2017/06/04/when-you-look-into-the-news-feed-the-news-feed-looks-into-you/ .

Flaxman, Seth, Sharad Goel, and Justin M. Rao. 2016. "Filter Bubbles, Echo Chambers, and Online News Consumption." *Public Opinion Quarterly* 80 (S1): 298–320.

Fletcher, Richard, and Rasmus Kleis Nielsen. 2017. "Are News Audiences Increasingly Fragmented? A Cross-National Comparative Analysis of Cross-Platform News Audience Fragmentation and Duplication." *Journal of Communication* 67 (4): 476–98.

Hamburger, Yair. 1994. "The Contact Hypothesis Reconsidered: Effects of the Atypical Outgroup Member on the Outgroup Stereotype." *Basic and Applied Social Psychology* 15 (3): 339–58.

Horwitz, Jeff, and Deepa Seetharaman. 2020. "Facebook Executives Shut Down Efforts to Make the Site Less Divisive." *The Wall Street Journal*. May 26. Retrieved from https://www.wsj.com/articles/facebook-knows-it-encourages-division-top-executives-nixed-solutions-11590507499 .

Huskey, Richard, Nicholas Bowman, Allison Eden, Matthew Grizzard, Lindsay Hahn, Robert Lewis, Nicholas Matthews, Ron Tamborini, Joseph B. Walther, and René Weber. 2018. "Things We Know about Media and Morality." *Nature Human Behavior* 2: 315.

Kowalyk, Apollo. 2019. "Better Days Ahead: Artificial Intelligence, Machine Learning, and the Quest for the Holy Grail of Analytics." *Police Chief* 86 (4): 26–30.

Mastro, Dana. (2009). "Effects of Racial and Ethnic Stereotyping." In *Media Effects: Advances in Theory and Research* (3rd ed.), edited by Jennings Bryant and Mary Beth Oliver, 325–341. New York: Routledge.

McNamee, Roger. 2019. *Zucked: Waking Up to the Facebook Catastrophe*. New York: Penguin.

New York Times. 2020. "Protests Over Police Violence Unveil More Police Violence." Live Updates on George Floyd Protests. June 5. Retrieved from https://www.nytimes.com/2020/06/05/us/george-floyd-protests.html .

Osborn, Claire. 2020. "'Live PD' Says Video of In-Custody Death of Javier Ambler Has Been Destroyed." Austin American *Statesman*. June 9. Retrieved from https://www.statesman.com/news/20200609/lsquolive-pdrsquo-says-video-of-in-custody-death-of-javier-ambler-has-been-destroyed .

Ovide, Shira. 2020. "On Tech: Protests Captured Unfiltered." *New York Times OnTech Newsletter*. June 2. Retrieved from https://www.nytimes.com/2020/06/02/technology/protests-twitter.html .

Perlmutter, David D. 2000. *Policing the Media: Street Cops and Public Perceptions of Law Enforcement*. Thousand Oaks: Sage.

Pew Research Center. 2018. "Many Turn to YouTube for Children's Content, News, How-To Lessons." *Pew Research Center: Internet, Science & Tech* (blog). November 7. Retrieved from https://www.pewinternet.org/2018/11/07/many-turn-to-youtube-for-childrens-content-news-how-to-lessons/ .

Robertson, Campbell, Rick Rojas, and Kate Taylor. 2020. "After George Floyd's Death, Toll Rises in Protests across Country." *New York Times*. June 2. Retrieved from https://www.nytimes.com/2020/06/01/us/george-floyd-unrest-toll.html .

Roose, Kevin, and Kate Conger. 2019. "YouTube to Remove Thousands of Videos Pushing Extreme Views." *New York Times*. June 5. Retrieved from https://www.nytimes.com/2019/06/05/business/youtube-remove-extremist-videos.html .

Rose-Stockwell, Tobias. n.d. "This Is How Your Fear and Outrage Are Being Sold for Profit." Quartz. Retrieved from https://qz.com/1039910/how-facebooks-news-feed-algorithm-sells-our-fear-and-outrage-for-profit/ .

Sperling, Nicole. 2020. "'Cops,' Long-Running Reality Show that Glorified Police, Is Canceled." *New York Times*, June 9. Retrieved from https://www.nytimes.com/2020/06/09/business/media/cops-canceled-paramount-tv-show.html .

Sunstein, Cass R. 2009. *Republic.com 2.0*. Princeton: Princeton University Press.

Taberski, Dan. 2019. "Anything You Say Can and Will Be Used . . . on Television." *This American Life* [podcast], 675. Retrieved from https://www.thisamericanlife.org/675/im-on-tv/act-one-7 .

Tajfel, Henri, and John C. Turner. 1979. "An Integrative Theory of Intergroup Conflict." In *The Social Psychology of Intergroup Relations*, edited by William G. Austin and Stephen Worchel, 33–47. Monterey: Brooks/Cole.

Tamborini, Ron, and René Weber. 2020. "Advancing the Model of Intuitive Morality Exemplars." In *Communication Science and Biology*, edited by Kory Floyd and René Weber, 456–69. New York: Routledge.

Taylor, Derrick. 2020. "George Floyd Protests: A Timeline." *New York Times*. May 31. Retrieved from https://www.nytimes.com/article/george-floyd-protests-timeline.html .

US Department of Justice. n.d. "What Is FOIA?" May 8. Retrieved from https://www.foia.gov/about.html .

Valkenburg, Patti M., and Jochen Peter. 2013. "The Differential Susceptibility to Media Effects Model: Differential Susceptibility to Media Effects Model." *Journal of Communication* 63 (2): 221–43.

Van den Bulck, Jan J. M. 2002. "Fictional Cops: Who Are They, and What Are They Teaching Us?" In *Law Enforcement, Communication, and Community*, edited by Howard Giles, 107–128. Amsterdam: Johns Benjamins.

Van Der Heide, Brandon, Benjamin K. Johnson, and Mao H. Vang. 2013. "The Effects of Product Photographs and Reputation Systems on Consumer Behavior and Product Cost on eBay." *Computers in Human Behavior* 29 (3): 570–76.

Veenstra, Kristine, and S. Alexander Haslam. 2000. "Willingness to Participate in Industrial Protest: Exploring Social Identification in Context." *British Journal of Social Psychology* 39 (4): 153–72.

Vezzali, Loris, Miles Hewstone, Dora Capozza, Dino Giovannini, and Ralf Wölfer. 2014. "Improving Intergroup Relations with Extended and Vicarious Forms of Indirect Contact." *European Review of Social Psychology*, 25 (1): 314–89.

Walther, Joseph B., David DeAndrea, Jinsuk Kim, and James C. Anthony. 2010. "The Influence of Online Comments on Perceptions of Antimarijuana Public Service Announcements on YouTube." *Human Communication Research* 36 (4): 469–92.

"YouTube Data API Overview." n.d. Google Developers. Retrieved from https://developers.google.com/youtube/v3/getting-started .

CHAPTER 16

Newsworthiness of Police

Changes in Print Media Coverage of Police Post-Ferguson

David H. F. Tyler and Edward R. Maguire

On August 9, 2014, Michael Brown, an eighteen-year old African American man, was shot and killed by police officer Darren Wilson in Ferguson, Missouri. While an investigation into Michael Brown's death exonerated the officer (US Department of Justice 2015a), a separate US Department of Justice investigation revealed a pattern of institutional racism throughout the Ferguson Police Department (US Department of Justice 2015b). Brown's death at the hands of a White police officer sparked protests and riots in and around Ferguson, which later spread across the United States.

Events in and around Ferguson following the death of Michael Brown helped bolster the growth of the #BlackLivesMatter movement, which had emerged to advocate for Black Americans after the death of Trayvon Martin about two and a half years earlier. Across the United States, people took to the streets to protest police use of force against Black people. Millions more engaged in activism using social media (for an intergroup communication perspective, see Carr 2018). Protests focused primarily on perceived disparities in the way police treat citizens of color, particularly the notion that Black people are disproportionately subjected to police use of force relative to other racial or ethnic groups (Durose, Smith, and Langan 2007; Hyland, Langton, and Davis 2015; Nowacki 2015; Smith and Holmes 2014; see chapter 5). While most protests were peaceful, some devolved into violence and rioting against police (Buchanan et al. 2015; Snyder 2016).

In the aftermath of these chaotic events, many observers claimed that the news media became more critical of the police (Fabian 2015; Frankel 2015; Mac Donald 2016).

Some hypothesize that incidents like the death of Michael Brown led to an increase in negative media coverage of police officers (Mac Donald 2015). Critics argued that a so-called "Ferguson Effect" emerged, whereby increased media coverage and more negative portrayals of police therein drove police to back off from discretionary enforcement activities. This phenomenon, now known as "de-policing," is thought by some to be responsible for a new national crime wave (Mac Donald 2015, 2016). Increased media coverage of the police is a key element of the causal logic underlying the Ferguson Effect. Yet, little is known about how events in and around Ferguson influenced either the volume or the content of media coverage of the police.

The news media plays a significant role in the construction of social problems through the nature and volume of news coverage (Barak 1994; Dowler 2002; McCombs and Shaw 1972; Sacco 1995). Media decisions about which people, institutions, topics, and events are newsworthy can exert a potent influence on public perceptions of these phenomena (Ha 2013; Haigh 2014; Haigh, Bruce, and Craig 2008; Luther and Radovic 2014). The news media helps to shape the boundaries of public discourse on issues by highlighting certain aspects of reality while downplaying or ignoring others (Ibrahim 2010). Media choices about which issues to highlight can have profound effects on intergroup dynamics, such as those involving police and racial and ethnic minorities (Mastro and Seate 2012; Stewart, Pitts, and Osborne 2011). A significant body of research in sociology, journalism, and mass communication has sought to understand the factors that influence newsworthiness (Chermak 1995; Clayman and Reisner 1998; Shoemaker 2006; Shoemaker, Danielian, and Brendlinger 1991). Drawing on the multidisciplinary literature on newsworthiness, this chapter examines the influence of Michael Brown's death and subsequent events in and around Ferguson in August 2014 on the volume of news coverage about police. We also examine the influence of three other controversial deaths—Tamir Rice, Freddie Gray, and Sandra Bland—on newsworthiness of police. Our findings contribute to recent academic and policy debates on public scrutiny of policing in the United States, including the Ferguson Effect.

US POLICING IN THE POST-FERGUSON ERA

In the aftermath of events in and around Ferguson, police in the United States experienced the most significant legitimacy crisis since the riots following the Rodney King incident in 1992 (Jones 2015). The shooting death of Michael Brown served as an "environmental jolt," catapulting police into the national spotlight and raising significant questions about police use of force, particularly against minorities.[1] Since the events in Ferguson, an ongoing parade of videos showing police using deadly force against minorities under questionable circumstances has emerged in both the conventional news media and in social media (Pyrooz, Decker, Wolfe, and Shjarback 2016; Wolfe and Nix 2016). Widespread public scrutiny of the police following these incidents led some to conclude that the nation was experiencing a "war on cops" (Mac Donald 2016; Sutton 2015).

Critics, pundits, and politicians all claim that in the aftermath of events in Ferguson, the nation experienced a crime wave (Mac Donald 2015, 2016; Tracinski 2016; Trump 2016). This "Ferguson Effect" is thought to have emerged because increased public scrutiny of police led officers to become less proactive (that is, "de-policed") which, in turn, led to an increase in crime (Mac Donald 2015, 2016). Although the principal hypothesis emerging from the Ferguson Effect debate is that de-policing resulted in more crime, the Ferguson Effect implies several different hypotheses.[2] Debate over the Ferguson Effect has inspired a rapidly emerging body of research that seeks to test some of these hypotheses. For instance, several studies have sought to determine whether de-policing is occurring within police agencies (e.g., Morgan and Pally 2016; Oliver 2017; Shjarback, Pyrooz, Wolfe, and Decker 2017). Other research has sought to illuminate the links between negative publicity and police officers' attitudes and behaviors (Nix and Wolfe 2017; Wolfe and Nix 2016). The most vigorous debate about the Ferguson Effect has focused on its effects on crime. Proponents argue that spikes in homicides and shootings in many large US cities after the death of Michael Brown are consistent with the idea of a Ferguson Effect (Mac Donald 2016). Certain politicians and law enforcement officials have claimed that a crime wave swept the nation post-Ferguson (Clarke 2016a, 2016b; Trump 2016). The validity of these claims is still being debated. The growing academic literature on these claims suggests that there are good reasons to question their veracity (Pyrooz et al. 2016; Rosenfeld 2015, 2016; Rosenfeld, Gaston, Spivak, and Irazola 2017).

Although research has begun to test certain hypotheses associated with the Ferguson Effect, much remains to be learned. For instance, the causal logic underlying the Ferguson Effect assumes that police are now under greater scrutiny from the media (see chapters 14 and 15). Implicit in this assumption are two hypotheses: that the *volume* of media coverage of police has increased, and that the *content* of this coverage is now more negative. However, these hypotheses have not yet been tested empirically. The public debate over media coverage of police is long on speculation and short on evidence, relying heavily on anecdotes and untested assumptions (Canterbury 2016; DeMarche 2015; Hattem 2015; Mac Donald 2015, 2016). Longitudinal research on media coverage of the police before and after the shooting of Michael Brown could illuminate some of the key causal mechanisms thought to be fueling the Ferguson Effect. One useful way of framing research on the role of the media in the causal relationships underlying the Ferguson Effect is around the concept of "newsworthiness" from the study of communication and mass media.

NEWSWORTHINESS

Newsworthiness has been referred to as "one of the most elusive concepts" in research on mass communication (Shoemaker, Danielian, and Brendlinger 1991, 781). In general, the idea of newsworthiness refers to the degree to which particular topics, institutions, persons, or events (hereafter referred to as "events" for the sake of simplicity) are of sufficient interest to warrant news coverage (Chermak 1995, 1998). The literature suggests that multiple characteristics of events play a key role in the extent to which they will become newsworthy. We discuss three such characteristics here: the extent to which events deviate from existing societal norms; how actors associated with events fit into existing stereotypes and narratives; and the social significance of events (Chermak 1995, 1998; Tuchman 1978). These characteristics are not mutually exclusive and tend to overlap in practice.

The first characteristic thought to influence judgments about newsworthiness is the extent to which an event deviates from existing social norms. Because crime constitutes a significant violation of social norms, it tends to be newsworthy. Certain types of serious crime, like public corruption cases or particularly gruesome homicides, are generally considered more newsworthy than less serious crimes, such as traffic violations or shoplifting (see chapter 17). Certain victims, such as children or the elderly, also tend to be considered more newsworthy, due to well-established social norms against victimizing those who are most vulnerable (Chermak 1995, 1998; Chermak and Gruenewald 2006). Police use of deadly force against unarmed minorities is considered newsworthy, in part, because it represents a significant violation of social justice norms.

The second characteristic thought to influence newsworthiness assessments is the extent to which an event fits into established stereotypes and narratives. Such determinations enable journalists to use readymade scripts and connect events for their readers (Gilliam and Iyengar 2000; Oliver and Meyers 1999). Journalists might refer to separate events in drawing inferences about broader national narratives. For instance, journalists have routinely connected the deaths of Eric Garner, Michael Brown, Tamir Rice, Walter Scott, Freddie Gray, Laquan McDonald, and George Floyd as part of a broader narrative about the treatment of minorities by the police and the failure of the criminal justice system to hold police accountable for their actions (see the introduction and this book's conclusion). Media organizations limit the bounds of discourse on particular topics by selecting stories that already fit existing narratives while ignoring other potential stories that may conflict with these narratives (Ibrahim 2010).

The third characteristic thought to influence perceptions of newsworthiness is the social significance of an event. Journalists play a key role in the social construction of reality for media consumers. In choosing to run a particular story, media outlets make a judgment about its social significance. Shoemaker and Cohen (2006, 8) define social significance as "that which has relevance for the social system—whether the social system is as large as the world or as small as a neighborhood." Social significance has been shown to have political, economic, cultural, and public dimensions (Shoemaker and Cohen 2006; Shoemaker et al. 1991). According to this perspective, stories that focus on themes that are politically, economically, culturally, or publicly significant will be more newsworthy. Stories containing themes that resonate across two or more of these dimensions will be even more newsworthy.

Taken together, the literature on newsworthiness suggests that socially significant events that deviate from social norms, and that fit into a broader narrative will be viewed as more newsworthy than events that do not have these characteristics (Shoemaker et al. 1991). By these standards, there are compelling reasons to expect that police treatment of minorities, and particularly the use of deadly force against minorities, would be considered highly newsworthy.

DID POLICE BECOME MORE NEWSWORTHY POST-FERGUSON?

We conducted analyses to determine whether police became more newsworthy post-Ferguson. The number of stories about an event is often used as an indicator of its newsworthiness (Dyck, Volchkova, and Zingales 2008; Lundman 2003). Using a statistical technique known as interrupted time series analysis, we examined whether the shooting of Michael Brown and subsequent events in and around Ferguson in August 2014 led to significant changes in the frequency of news stories about the police in the *New York Times*. We also examined the effects of three other controversial deaths (those of Tamir Rice, Freddie Gray, and Sandra Bland) on police newsworthiness. Note that our analysis focuses only on the *volume* of news stories about the police, not about the *content* of these stories.

The data used in our analyses are based on a review of news stories appearing in the *New York Times*.[3] Using LexisNexis, we searched all articles published in the *New York Times* between December 30, 2012, and July 3, 2016, that were not written by the foreign desk, the editorial desk, or the *New York Times* blog.[4] In order to obtain stories that focused primarily on police, the search was limited to articles in which the term "police" appeared more than five times. Using these selection procedures, we identified a total of 4,290 news articles about the police.[5] We then constructed a database containing the total number of news articles about police per week.

Our analysis focuses specifically on the impact of events in and around Ferguson following the death of Michael Brown. We have 183 weeks of data in total, including 84 weeks prior to Brown's death, and 99 weeks after his death (Brown was killed on the last day of the 84th week in the series). Figure 16.1 illustrates the weekly number of stories about police in the *New York Times* during this period. The vertical line at week 85 represents Brown's death, and it demarcates the pre- and post-Ferguson periods. Figure 16.1 provides strong visual evidence in favor of a Ferguson Effect on the number of news stories about the police.

During the pre-Ferguson period from weeks 1 through 84 (December 30, 2012, through August 9, 2014), the mean weekly number of articles pertaining to police was 17.6 (with a median of 17). During the post-Ferguson period from weeks 85 through 183 (August 10, 2014, through July 3, 2016), the mean weekly number of articles pertaining to police was 28.4 (with a median of 28). This represents a 61.4 percent increase in the mean number of stories per week and a 64.7 percent increase in the median number of stories per week. The difference in the mean number of fatal shootings before and after the death of Brown is statistically significant.[6] This preliminary analysis suggests that the shooting death of Michael Brown, and subsequent events in and around Ferguson, exerted a significant influence on the frequency of news stories about police published in the *New York Times*. However, this preliminary analysis does not account for some of the complexities associated with the analysis of time series data. Therefore, we rely on time series analysis techniques to conduct further analyses of the weekly newspaper data.[7,8]

When testing the effects of an incident or intervention using time series analysis, two key characteristics of these effects are their onset and duration. *Onset* is generally

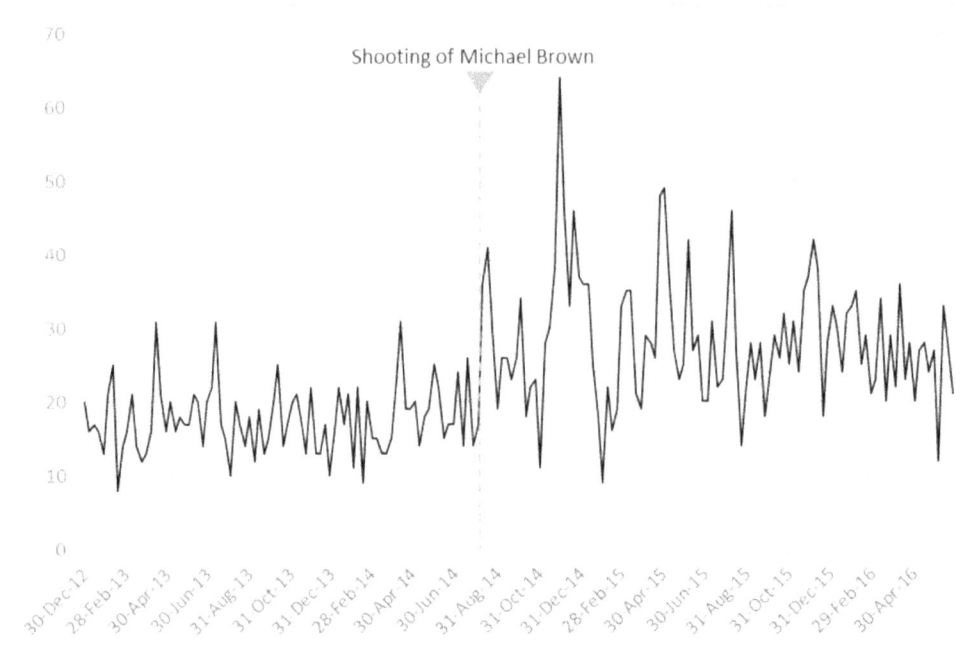

FIGURE 16.1. Police Related Articles in the *New York Times* (December 30, 2012 – July 3, 2016)

thought of as being either abrupt (occurring immediately after the incident) or gradual (unfolding slowly during the period following the incident). *Duration* is generally thought of as being permanent (lasting through the end of the time series) or temporary (reverting back to zero over time) (McCleary and Hay 1980; McDowell et al. 1980). With regard to onset, the prevailing logic is that the Ferguson Effect, if it exists, would likely have occurred abruptly. For instance, scholars have described events in Ferguson as an "environmental jolt" or a "sudden shock," both of which imply a sudden onset (Maguire, Nix, and Campbell 2016; Pyrooz et al. 2016). With regard to duration, we do not have any a priori expectation about whether the effect is either temporary or permanent, thus we tested for both possibilities. Our analysis revealed that the shooting death of Michael Brown and subsequent events in Ferguson exerted a statistically significant positive effect on the mean weekly number of stories pertaining to police in the *New York Times*. Further, our analysis revealed that the effect was not temporary; the changes we observed were permanent changes within the period examined here.[9]

Testing the Effects of Other Controversial Deaths

Our findings so far reveal that news coverage of the police in the *New York Times* expanded significantly after the death of Michael Brown in August 2014. This finding validates one of the underlying assumptions of the Ferguson Effect: that Brown's death resulted in greater media coverage of the police. However, the death of Michael Brown was not the only instance during the time series when a minority was killed by police or died in police custody under questionable circumstances. To account for the possibility that other controversial police-involved deaths may have influenced the newsworthiness of police, we tested for the effects of three additional deaths: Tamir Rice, Freddie Gray, and Sandra Bland. Tamir Rice was a twelve-year old boy who was shot and killed by police in Cleveland while carrying a toy gun on November 22, 2014. Freddie Gray was a twenty-five-year-old man who died on April 19, 2015, as a result of injuries sustained a week earlier while being transported in a Baltimore police van following his arrest for possession of an illegal knife. Sandra Bland, a twenty-eight-year old African American woman, was found hanging in her jail cell in Waller County, Texas, on July 13, 2015, following a controversial stop by police for a minor traffic infraction (Lowrey-Kinberg and Buker 2017).

Our results reveal that newspaper coverage of police following the deaths of Tamir Rice, Freddie Gray, and Sandra Bland did not generate any permanent changes (that persist throughout the entire period) in the weekly number of news stories about police. However, our findings did show that two of the three deaths (Freddie Gray and Tamir Rice) had significant short-term "pulse" effects during the week after the incident. Overall, our results indicate that Michael Brown's death generated a significant permanent change in the number of news articles about the police. These effects remained robust even when we included variables representing other controversial minority deaths associated with the police. We also observed a substantial increase in news stories about police in the week after Tamir Rice's death and the week after Freddie Gray's death. The week following the death of Tamir Rice saw thirty additional articles about police beyond the increase observed from the death of Michael Brown. The week following the death of Freddie Gray saw fifteen more articles than expected. The findings indicate that the deaths of both Tamir Rice and Freddie Gray had temporary impacts on the series in the week *after* each event. No such effect was found the week of or the week following the death of Sandra Bland.

These results suggest that the frequency of news stories about police post-Ferguson experienced an abrupt permanent change following the death of Michael Brown, with significant short-term pulse effects in the weeks following the deaths of Tamir Rice and Freddie Gray. The changes associated with these two deaths each lasted a single week and did not affect the overall trend. We now turn to a discussion of these findings and suggest possible avenues for future theory development and research.

DISCUSSION

The findings we just presented add to a growing body of knowledge about the social changes that emerged (or did not emerge) in the United States following the shooting death of Michael Brown in August 2014. While most researchers and social commentators have taken for granted that "the news media pump out a seemingly constant stream of stories" about the police (Mac Donald 2015), we are not aware of any previous research that has empirically tested changes in the volume of media coverage of police post-Ferguson.

Prior to the death of Michael Brown, the *New York Times* featured about 17.5 articles about police each week. Our findings reveal that that the average number of articles per week increased by about 10.5 following the death of Michael Brown. This serves as evidence in favor of one link in the causal chain implicit in the so-called Ferguson Effect: Police became more newsworthy post-Ferguson. At the same time, our findings reveal that although different incidents may share certain similarities, some generate more national attention than others. The death of Michael Brown in Ferguson had a significantly greater effect on the newsworthiness of police than the other three deaths we examined. The death of Sandra Bland did not have a significant effect on the newsworthiness of police. The deaths of Tamir Rice and Freddie Gray produced temporary increases, but neither incident influenced the long-term trend.

The newsworthiness literature is useful for making sense of these differential effects. The shooting death of Michael Brown by a Ferguson police officer represented a seminal event in the United States for several reasons. The incident fed into decades of racial tension within the community, and events in Ferguson following Brown's death were reminiscent of the rioting, destruction, and police oppression seen in Los Angeles after the beating of Rodney King (Nazaryan 2017). Within a month of Michael Brown's death, the US Department of Justice had opened an investigation into the Ferguson Police Department, which uncovered decades of systematic targeting of minorities within the city (US Department of Justice 2015b). The protests, riots, and investigations served as the launching pad for a national dialogue on policing minorities and the police abuse of authority, thereby increasing the perceived newsworthiness of US police post-Ferguson.

Events like the deaths of Tamir Rice and Freddie Gray fit the emerging narrative and, therefore. generated temporary increases in police newsworthiness. Our findings show that the impact of those two events decayed after a single week, leaving no lasting effect on the overall series. This pattern may suggest the possibility of a saturation effect whereby additional events did not generate as much attention. The initial event (the death of Michael Brown) served as an environmental jolt that shocked the long-term trend, while additional events provided only brief deviations from this "new normal." Since neither case offered a new perspective on the ongoing narrative, they did not have a lasting effect on the volume of news articles about the police. Further, it is possible that practical constraints, such as a limited capacity for articles within the newspaper, may have also reduced the staying power of additional events post-Ferguson.

Meanwhile, the death of Sandra Bland did not generate any significant deviation from the ongoing news coverage of police. While tragic, her death likely did not produce substantial media attention for several reasons. First, the facts of the case did not fit the ongoing narrative: police in urban communities killing unarmed African American men. Bland was found hanging in a small sheriff's office in the middle of Texas and her death was ruled a suicide (Barned-Smith and Binkovitz 2015). The deaths of Tamir Rice and Freddie Gray may have been seen as resulting more directly from the actions of police. Sandra Bland was clearly mistreated by police during her traffic stop and arrest, but evidence suggests that she took her own life, therefore, her death may have been seen as resulting only *indirectly* from the actions of police. Second, while the traffic stop of Bland was caught on camera, her death was not captured on video (Barned-Smith and Binkovitz 2015). Newspapers and television broadcasts rely heavily on photos and videos to cement their narratives (Chermak 1995; Van Brunschot, Sydie, and Krull 2000). Without photographs or videos, the death of Sandra Bland may have been considered less newsworthy than the other events we examined. In addition, theory and research on intersectionality would suggest that Bland, as a Black woman, might receive less media coverage than others because she may be perceived as ranking lower in the social hierarchy (e.g., Barak 1994; Brennan, Chesney-Lind, Vandenberg, and Wulf-Ludden 2011; Chermak 1995; Cho, Crenshaw, and McCall 2013).

Our findings contribute to the growing body of knowledge on newsworthiness. Our finding of a "Ferguson Effect" on the newsworthiness of police in the *New York Times* is consistent with previous research which suggests that stories fitting into broader narratives that are highly salient or resonant are generally viewed as more newsworthy than stories not fitting into such narratives (Gilliam and Iyengar 2000; Ibrahim 2010). This interpretation, if valid, suggests that in the post-Ferguson era, stories about police may have been selected because they fit an ongoing script. Our findings provide preliminary support for the first link in the causal chain underlying the supposed Ferguson Effect: that media coverage of police expanded dramatically in the post-Ferguson era (Mac Donald 2015). While several of the major claims associated with the Ferguson Effect are viewed by many scholars as suspect—such as the emergence of a new national crime wave, a national movement toward de-policing, and police officers facing increased safety risks—certain portions of its underlying logic may still be valid (e.g., Maguire, Nix, and Campbell 2016; Nix and Wolfe 2017; Pyrooz et al. 2016; Rosenfeld 2015; Wolfe and Nix 2016). Events in Ferguson do appear to have generated a sustained impact on the newsworthiness of police within one influential media outlet (*New York Times*).

While the increased media coverage of police has fundamental implications for American policing, it also has broader social implications. Mass media serves an integral role in shaping and maintaining public discourse (Chermak 1995; Ibrahim 2010; McCombs and Shaw 1972). To the extent that the allocation of newspaper space is a zero-sum game, increased coverage of police-related issues likely means decreased coverage of other issues. In this way, the media helps sets the agenda for political leaders and national dialogue and policy debate (McCombs and Shaw 1972). For instance, events in and around Ferguson after the death of Michael Brown are often described as the beginning of a new civil rights or social justice movement in the United States (Demby 2014). The news media play a crucial role in the framing and agenda-setting that feeds the growth of social movements (Gamson and Wolfsfeld 1993).

The present study provides a number of useful findings upon which to base future research, but it is not without limitations. First, it relied on data from a single newspaper, an approach that provides certain benefits, but also limits the generalizability of our findings. On one hand, the *New York Times* is often considered a "newspaper of record" in the United States (Haigh, Bruce, and Craig 2008). On the other hand, research has found that it is biased on certain issues and may have a more liberal orientation than certain other media outlets (Groseclose and Milvo 2005; Zelizer, Park, and Gudelunas 2002). In addition, the use of a national daily newspaper like the *New York Times* does not allow us to tap into local or regional variation in news coverage of the police. Other local, regional, or national media outlets—including radio and television stations—may have behaved very differently post-Ferguson than the *New York Times*. Research shows that the agenda-setting functions of local and national media can differ considerably for certain issues (Hester and Gibson 2007). Furthermore, the methodology used here did not provide us access to the internal organizational dynamics at the *New York Times* that might have influenced news coverage of police.

Future studies should seek to examine the newsworthiness of influential events across multiple media outlets. One intriguing possibility is research that examines regional differences in media coverage following major events. Such research could examine multiple media genres, including both conventional media and social media. While coverage of police in conventional media sources is a useful indicator of newsworthiness, much of the conversation surrounding the Ferguson Effect focused on social media as well. The present study does not tap into key social media outlets, such as Twitter, that have become important conduits of public discourse (Hermida 2010; see chapter 14).

The present study focused only on the volume of media coverage of police, not the valence of this coverage. Thus, although we know that events in Ferguson generated a substantial impact on the volume of media coverage, we do not know whether this coverage was more positive or more negative post-Ferguson. While one of the implicit causal links underlying the Ferguson Effect is that police are now the object of more news coverage than previously, another key link is that this coverage is increasingly negative. Our methods allowed us to examine the former, but not the latter. Thus, we are unable to draw inferences about the valence of media coverage of police post-Ferguson. Empirical research on this question is sorely needed.

Finally, during the period analyzed in this study, the death of Michael Brown and subsequent events in Ferguson, Missouri, dominated the headlines and triggered a wave of protests about police use of force, treatment of minorities, and militarization. The death of George Floyd in Minneapolis in May 2020 occurred following our data collection. George Floyd's death under the knee of a Minneapolis police officer triggered a wave of protests and riots throughout the world that likely exceeded the intensity of what occurred following Michael Brown's death (see this book's conclusion). Media coverage of Floyd's death, and the social movement it fueled, presents new opportunities for exploring the newsworthiness of police and the events that influence it.

CONCLUSIONS

The analysis reported here is a useful first step in understanding changes in public discourse post-Ferguson. Our findings indicate that news coverage of police in the *New York Times* increased by almost 60 percent following the death of Michael Brown. We also found there were significant temporary increases in coverage in the week following the deaths of Tamir Rice and of Freddie Gray, but not in the week following the death of Sandra Bland. These latter three incidents did not influence the long-term trend in news coverage of the police. These findings contribute to a growing body of knowledge on the intersection of criminal justice and the media, provide a glimpse into the causal mechanisms behind the so-called Ferguson Effect, offer insights into the staying power of the current legitimacy crisis in American policing, and suggest possible ramifications of increased media scrutiny of police. As this chapter goes to press, US police are experiencing a new wave of intense scrutiny with regard to racial bias and use of force. The time is ripe for careful analysis of how the media portrays these issues, and how media coverage shapes public discourse and debate (for an intergroup perspective, see Lin and Haridakis 2018).

NOTES

1. In organizational theory, an environmental jolt is "a sudden and unprecedented event" with significant implications for the stability and health of organizations (Meyer 1982). We conceptualize the shooting death of Michael Brown as an environmental jolt with significant implications for police agencies throughout the nation (Maguire, Nix, and Campbell 2016).

2. Other hypotheses also arise in debates over the Ferguson Effect. For instance, some argue that increased scrutiny of police is leading officers to second-guess themselves when deciding whether to use force in potentially dangerous situations (Clarke 2016a; Mac Donald 2015). Research has shown that the number of people fatally shot by US police did not change post-Ferguson (Campbell, Nix, and Maguire 2018), but it is not yet clear whether police are using non-fatal force less than before. A related hypothesis is that because of the "war on cops," officers are now at greater risk of injury or death (Clarke 2016b; Comey 2015; Emanuel 2015). Recent research casts doubt on this proposition (Maguire, Nix, and Campbell 2016; Shjarback and Maguire 2019).

3. We selected the *New York Times* for several reasons. As a "newspaper of record" (Haigh, Bruce, and Craig 2008), the *New York Times* influences both public opinion and the agendas of other media outlets (Ha 2013; Haigh 2014; Luther and Radovic 2014). It has also served as a representative measure of American news coverage in cross-national studies (Haigh 2014). While some work indicates that the agenda-setting impact of newspapers has changed with the rise of online forums (Althaus and Tewksbury 2002), and newspaper readerships have declined (Pew Research 2016), the *New York Times* and other major daily newspapers still serve as a primary source from which other news outlets derive their own content. The *New York Times* has also been accused of having certain biases (Groseclose and Milvo 2005; Zelizer, Park, and Gudelunas 2002). Thus, future research should examine how the findings reported here compare to studies drawing on data from other news sources.

4. Articles written by the foreign desk were excluded because this analysis is concerned with domestic coverage of US police. Moreover, since our focus is on news coverage, we also chose to exclude editorials and blog entries.

5. Here we focus on the *volume* of news stories about police. We do not examine whether these stories are positive, neutral, or negative. While some critiques of media coverage of police have focused on *negative* portrayals of police (Clarke 2016a, 2016b; Comey 2016; Mac Donald 2015, 2016), our principal interest in this study is on newsworthiness. Therefore, we examine changes in the overall volume of media coverage of police.

6. A t-test comparing the number of fatal shootings before and after the death of Brown revealed a statistically significant difference ($t = -10.05$, $df = 181$, $p < .000$).

7. Ordinary linear regression models are inadequate for analyzing time series data due to the potential for temporal dependence in the residuals. Social scientists often rely on the Box-Jenkins approach for estimating interrupted time series models, which involves the use of autoregressive integrated moving average (ARIMA) models (Box and Jenkins 1976; McDowall et al. 1980). McDowall and colleagues (1980, 15) refer to ARIMA as "a model of the stochastic process which generated the observed time series." By controlling for the noise component of an interrupted time series though the use of an ARIMA model, researchers can assess the impact of an intervention on the realization of the process (McDowall et al. 1980).

8. A Breusch-Godfrey LM test revealed that there was serial correlation in the residuals of the pre-intervention series. A significant portmanteau Q-test indicated that the pre-intervention series differed from white noise. An augmented Dickey-Fuller test for unit root indicated that the series was stationary. Visual inspection of the autocorrelation plot suggested that an AR (1) model is most appropriate for this series. Based on these diagnostics, we selected an ARIMA (1,0,0)

specification. This specification indicates the need for a first-order autoregressive component in the model. We also confirmed this model specification using the auto.arima function available in the Forecast package in R. This function selects the most appropriate ARIMA model using information criteria like the AIC and the BIC (Hyndman and Khandakar 2008). Based on these criteria, the auto.arima function selected the ARIMA (1,0,0) specification.

9. Because the number of news articles is a count variable, we also estimated the effect of Michael Brown's death using an autoregressive Poisson model that allows for over-dispersion (Katsouyanni et al. 1996; Schwartz et al. 1996). Consistent with findings from the initial ARIMA model, the pre-post variable had a significant positive effect on the number of news articles about police in the *New York Times* ($B = 0.48$, $SE = .04$, $t = 10.75$, $p < 0.000$). Thus, we conclude that this finding is robust across multiple estimation procedures.

REFERENCES

Althaus, Scott L., and David Tewksbury. 2002. "Agenda Setting and the 'New' News." *Communication Research* 29 (2): 180–207.

Barak, Gregg. 1994. "Between the Waves: Mass-Mediated Themes of Crime and Justice." *Social Justice* 21 (3): 133–47.

Barned-Smith, St. John, and Leah Binkovitz. 2015. "Trooper Who Pulled Over Bland Placed on Administrative Duty." *The Houston Chronicle*, July 17, 2015.

Box, George E. P., and Gwilym M. Jenkins. 1976. *Time Series Analysis: Forecasting and Control*. San Francisco: Holden Day.

Brennan, Pauline K., Meda Chesney-Lind, Abby L. Vandenberg, and Timbre Wulf-Ludden. 2011. "The Saved and the Damned: Racialized Media Constructions of Female Drug Offenders." *Radical Criminology* 5: 46–98.

Buchanan, Larry, Ford Fessenden, K. K. Rebecca Lai, Haeyoun Park, Alicia Parlapiano, Archie Tse, . . . Karen Yourish. 2015. "What Happened in Ferguson?" *The New York Times*, August 10.

Campbell, Bradley A., Justin Nix, and Edward R. Maguire. 2018. "Is the Number of Citizens Fatally Shot by Police Increasing in the Post-Ferguson Era?" *Crime & Delinquency* 64 (3): 398–420.

Canterbury, Chuck. 2016. Letter from National FOP President Canterbury to President Obama, February 12, 2016. Retrieved from http://lawofficer.com/news/fop-makes-plea-to-president-obama/.

Carr, Caleb. 2018. "Social Media and Intergroup Communication." In *The Oxford Encyclopedia of Intergroup Communication*, edited by Howard Giles and Jake Harwood, Vol. 2, 349–67. New York: Oxford University Press.

Chermak, Stephen M. 1995. *Victims in the News: Crime and the American News Media*. Boulder: Westview Press.

Chermak, Stephen M. 1998. "Predicting Crime Story Salience: The Effects of Crime, Victim, and Defendant Characteristics." *Journal of Criminal Justice* 26 (1): 61–70.

Chermak, Stephen M., and Jeff Gruenewald. 2006. "The Media's Coverage of Domestic Terrorism." *Justice Quarterly* 23 (4): 428–61.

Cho, Sumi, Kimberlé W. Crenshaw, and Leslie McCall. 2013. "Toward a Field of Intersectionality Studies: Theory, Application, and Praxis." *Journal of Women in Culture and Society* 38 (4): 785–81.

Clarke, David. 2016a. News interview with Fox News. Fox News, July 8, 2016. Retrieved from http://www.realclearpolitics.com/video/2016/07/08/sheriff_david_clarke_war_has_been_declared_on_cops.html.

Clarke, David. 2016b. "Sheriff David Clarke: My Biggest Fear about the War on Police Is Being Realized." *The Hill*, October 12. Retrieved from http://thehill.com/blogs/pundits-blog/crime/300632-sheriff-david-clarke-my-biggest-fear-about-the-war-on-police-is.

Clayman, Steven E., and Ann Reisner. 1998. "Gatekeeping in Action: Editorial Conferences and Assessments of Newsworthiness." *American Sociological Review* 63 (2): 178–99.

Comey, James B. 2015. "Law Enforcement and the Communities We Serve" [Lecture]. Retrieved from https://www.youtube.com/watch?v=KvE9j2vTpSg.

Comey, James B. 2016. "F.B.I. Director Says 'Viral Video Effect' Blunts Police Work." *The New York Times*, May 11, 2016.

DeMarche, Edmund. 2015. "Police Face Recruiting Shortage Due to War on Cops." *New York Post*, September 7.

Demby, Gene. 2014. "The Birth of a New Civil Rights Movement." *Politico Magazine*, December 31.

Dowler, Kenneth. 2002. "Media Influence on Citizen Attitudes toward Police Effectiveness." *Policing and Society* 12 (3): 227–38.

Durose, Matthew R., Erica L. Smith, and Patrick A. Langan. 2007. *Contacts between Police and the Public, 2005.* Washington DC: Bureau of Justice Statistics.

Dyck, Alexander, Natalya Volchkova, and Luigi Zingales. 2008. "The Corporate Governance Role of the Media: Evidence from Russia." *The Journal of Finance* 63 (3): 1093–1135.

Emanuel, Rahm. 2015. "Here's the 'Fetal' Police Quote Causing Grief for Chicago Mayor Rahm Emanuel." *The Washington Post*, October 14, 2015.

Fabian, Jordan. 2015. "Obama, FBI Director Spar over the 'Ferguson Effect' on Police." *The Hill*, November 1. Retrieved from https://thehill.com/news/administration/258737-obama-fbi-director-spar-over-the-ferguson-effect-on-police .

Frankel, Todd C. 2015. "DEA Chief Joins FBI Chief in Giving Credence to 'Ferguson Effect.'" *The Washington Post*, November 4.

Gamson, William A., and Gadi Wolfsfeld. 1993. "Movements and Media as Interacting Systems." *Annals of the American Academy of Political and Social Science* 528: 114–25.

Gilliam Jr., Franklin D., and Shanto Iyengar. 2000. "Prime Suspects: The Influence of Local Television News on the Viewing Public." *American Journal of Political Science* 44 (3): 560–73.

Groseclose, Tim, and Jeffrey Milvo. 2005. "A Measure of Media Bias." *The Quarterly Journal of Economics* 120 (4): 1191–1237.

Ha, Jaesik. 2013. "Coverage of Guantanamo Bay Less Negative for Obama." *Newspaper Research Journal* 34 (1): 22–35.

Haigh, Michel M. 2014. "Afghanistan War Coverage More Negative over Time." *Newspaper Research Journal* 35 (3): 38–51.

Haigh, Michel M., Michael Bruce, and Elizabeth Craig. 2008. "Mad Cow Coverage More Positive in Midwest Papers." *Newspaper Research Journal* 29 (1): 50–56.

Hattem, Julian. 2015. "Killings of Police Officers on the Rise." *The Hill*, May 11. Retrieved from https://thehill.com/policy/national-security/241594-fbi-officer-killings-on-the-rise .

Hermida, Alfred. 2010. "Twittering the News: The Emergence of Ambient Journalism." *Journalism Practice* 4 (3): 297–308.

Hester, Joe Bob, and Rhonda Gibson. 2007. "The Agenda-Setting Function of National versus Local Media: A Time-Series Analysis for the Issue of Same-Sex Marriage." *Mass Communication and Society* 10 (3): 299–317.

Hyland, Shelley, Lynn Langton, and Elizabeth Davis. 2015. *Police Use of Nonfatal Force, 2002–2011.* Washington DC: Bureau of Justice Statistics.

Hyndman, Rob J., and Yeasmin Khandakar. 2008. "Automatic Time Series Forecasting: The Forecast Package for R." *Journal of Statistical Software* 27 (3): 1–22.

Ibrahim, Dina. 2010. "The Framing of Islam on Network News Following the September 11th Attacks." *The International Communication Gazette* 72 (1): 111–25

Jones, Jeffrey M. 2015. "In US, Confidence in Police Lowest in 22 Years." *Gallup*, June 19. Retrieved from http://www.gallup.com/poll/183704/confidence-police-lowest-years.aspx .

Katsouyanni, K., J. Schwartz, C. Spix, G. Touloumi, D. Zmirou, A. Zanobetti, and . . . H.R. Anderson. 1996. "Short-Term Effects of Air Pollution on Health: A European Approach Using Epidemiological Time Series Data: The APHEA Protocol." *Journal of Epidemiology and Community Health* 50 (Suppl 1): S12–18.

Lin, Mei-chen, and Paul Haridakis. 2018. "Media Use in a Political Context: An Intergroup Communication Perspective." In *The Oxford Encyclopedia of Intergroup Communication*, Vol. 2, 111–28. New York: Oxford University Press.

Lowrey-Kinberg, Belén V., and Grace S. Buker. 2017. "'I'm Giving You a Lawful Order': Dialogic Legitimacy in the Sandra Bland Traffic Stop." *Law and Society Review* 51 (2): 379–412.

Lundman, Richard J. 2003. "The Newsworthiness and Selection Bias in News about Murder: Comparative and Relative Effects of Novelty and Race and Gender Typifications on Newspaper Coverage of Homicide." *Sociological Forum* 18: 357–86.

Luther, Caroline A., and Ivanka Radovic. 2014. "Newspapers Frame Julian Assange Differently." *Newspaper Research Journal* 35 (1): 64–81.

Mac Donald, Heather. 2015. "The New Nationwide Crime Wave: The Consequences of the 'Ferguson Effect' Are Already Appearing. The Main Victims of Growing Violence Will Be the Inner-City Poor." *The Wall Street Journal*, May 29.

Mac Donald, Heather. 2016. *The War on Cops: How the New Attack on Law and Order Makes Everyone Less Safe*. New York: Encounter Books.

Maguire, Edward R., Justin Nix, and Bradley Campbell. 2016. "A War on Cops? The Effects of Ferguson on the Number of U.S. Police Officers Murdered in the Line of Duty." *Justice Quarterly* 34 (5): 739–58.

Mastro, Dana, and Anita Atwell Seate. 2012. "Group-Membership in Race-Related Media Processes and Effects." In *The Handbook of Intergroup Communication*, edited by Howard Giles, 357–69. New York: Routledge.

McCleary, Richard, and Richard A. Hay, Jr. 1980. *Applied Time Series Analysis for the Social Sciences*. Beverly Hills: Sage.

McCombs, Maxwell E., and Donald L. Shaw. 1972. "The Agenda-Setting Function of Mass Media. *Public Opinion Quarterly* 36 (2): 176–87.

McDowall, David, Richard McCleary, Errol E. Meidinger, and Richard A. Hay, Jr. 1980. *Interrupted Time Series Analysis*. Newbury Park: Sage

Meyer, Alan D. 1982. "Adapting to Environmental Jolts." *Administrative Science Quarterly* 27 (4): 515–37.

Morgan, Stephen L., and Joel A. Pally. 2016. *Ferguson, Gray, and Davis: An Analysis of Recorded Crime Incidents and Arrests in Baltimore City, March 2010 through December 2015*. A report written for the 21st Century Cities Initiative at Johns Hopkins University. Retrieved from http://socweb.soc.jhu.edu/faculty/morgan/papers/MorganPally2016.pdf .

Nazaryan, Alexander. 2017. "From Los Angeles to Ferguson: 25 years after Rodney King Riots, 'There's a South Central in every State.'" *Newsweek*, April 28.

Nix, Justin, and Scott E. Wolfe. 2017. "The Impact of Negative Publicity on Police Self-Legitimacy." *Justice Quarterly* 34 (1): 84–108.

Nowacki, Jeffrey S. 2015. "Organizational-Level Police Discretion: An Application for Police Use of Lethal Force." *Crime and Delinquency* 61 (5): 643–68.

Oliver, Pamela E., and Daniel J. Myers. 1999. "How Events Enter the Public Sphere: Conflict, Location, and Sponsorship in Local Newspaper Coverage of Public Events." *American Journal of Sociology* 105 (1): 38–87.

Oliver, Willard M. (2017). "Depolicing: Rhetoric or Reality?" *Criminal Justice Policy Review* 28 (5): 437–61.

Pew Research Center. 2016. *State of the News Media, 2016*. Washington, DC: Pew Research Center. Retrieved from https://assets.pewresearch.org/wp-content/uploads/sites/13/2016/06/30143308/state-of-the-news-media-report-2016-final.pdf .

President's Task Force on 21st Century Policing. 2015. *Report of the President's Task Force on 21st Century Policing, Final Report*. Retrieved from http://www.theiacp.org/TaskForceReport .

Pyrooz, David C., Scott H. Decker, Scott E. Wolfe, and John A. Shjarback. 2016. "Was There a Ferguson Effect on Crime Rates in Large U.S. Cities?" *Journal of Criminal Justice* 46:1–8.

Rosenfeld, Richard. 2015. "Was There A 'Ferguson Effect' on Crime in St. Louis?" Retrieved from https://www.sentencingproject.org/publications/was-there-a-ferguson-effect-on-crime-in-st-louis/ .

Rosenfeld, Richard. 2016. *Documenting and Explaining the 2015 Homicide Rise: Research Directions*. Washington DC: National Institute of Justice.

Rosenfeld, Richard, Shytierra Gaston, Howard Spivak, and Seri Irazola. 2017. *Assessing and Responding to the Recent Homicide Rise in the United States*. Washington DC: National Institute of Justice.

Sacco, Vincent F. 1995. "Media Constructions of Crime." *Annals of the American Academy of Political and Social Science* 539: 141–54.

Schwartz, J., C. Spix, G. Touloumi, L. Bacharova, T. Barumamdzadeh, A. le Tertre, . . . and J. P. Schouten. 1996. "Methodological Issues in Studies of Air Pollution and Daily Counts of Deaths or Hospital Admissions." *Journal of Epidemiology and Community Health* 50 (Suppl. 1): S3–11.

Shjarback, John A., and Edward R. Maguire. 2019. "Extending Research on the 'War on Cops': The Effects of Ferguson on Nonfatal Assaults against U.S. Police Officers." *Crime & Delinquency*. Advance Online: doi.org/10.1177/0011128719890266 .

Shjarback, John A., David C. Pyrooz, Scott E. Wolfe, and Scott H. Decker. 2017. "De-Policing and Crime in the Wake of Ferguson: Racialized Changes in the Quantity and Quality of Policing among Missouri Police Departments." *Journal of Criminal Justice* 50: 42–52.

Shoemaker, Pamela J. 2006. "News and Newsworthiness: A Commentary." *Communications* 31 (1): 105–11.

Shoemaker, Pamela J., and Akiba A. Cohen. 2006. *News around the World: Content, Practitioners, and the Public*. New York: Routledge.

Shoemaker, Pamela J., Lucig H. Danielian, and Nancy Brendlinger. 1991. "Deviant Acts, Risky Business, and U.S. Interests: The Newsworthiness of World Events. *Journalism Quarterly* 68 (4): 781–95.

Smith, Brad W., and Malcolm D. Holmes. 2014. "Police Use of Excessive Force in Minority Communities: A Test of the Minority Threat, Place, and Community Accountability Hypotheses." *Social Problems* 61 (1): 83–104.

Snyder, Ron. 2016. "One Year Later: Looking Back at the Baltimore Riots." *WBALTV*. April 28. Retrieved from http://www.wbaltv.com/news/one-year-later-looking-back-at-the-Baltimore-riots/39044540 .

Stewart, Craig O., Margaret J. Pitts, and Helena Osborne. 2011. "Mediated Intergroup Conflict: The Discursive Construction of 'Illegal Immigrants' in a Regional U.S. Newspaper." *Journal of Language and Social Psychology* 30 (1): 8–27.

Sutton, Randy. 2015. "The Dangers of De-Policing: Will Cops Just Stand Down?" *New York Post*, May 5, 2015.

Tracinski, Robert. 2016. "Sheriff Clarke Is Right: There's a War on Cops." *The Federalist,* July 16.

Trump, Donald J. 2016. "Donald Trump Remarks on Veterans' Issues." *C-SPAN,* July 11. Retrieved from https://www.c-span.org/video/?412560-1/donald-trump-delivers-remarks-veterans-issues .

Tuchman, Gaye. 1978. *Making News: A Study in the Construction of Reality*. New York: Free Press.

US Department of Justice. 2015a. *Department of Justice Report regarding the Criminal Investigation into the Shooting Death of Michael Brown by Ferguson, Missouri Police Officer Darren Wilson*. Washington DC: US Department of Justice.

US Department of Justice. 2015b. *Investigation of the Ferguson Police Department*. Washington DC: US Department of Justice.

Van Brunschot, Erin G., Rosalind A. Sydie, and Catherine Krull. 2000. "Images of Prostitution: The Prostitute and Print Media." *Women & Criminal Justice* 10 (4): 47–72.

Wolfe, Scott E., and Justin Nix. 2016. "The Alleged 'Ferguson Effect' and Police Willingness to Engage in Community Partnership." *Law and Human Behavior* 40 (1): 1–10.

Zelizer, Barbie, David Park, and David Gudelunas. 2002. "How Bias Shapes the News: Challenging the *New York Times* as a Newspaper of Record on the Middle East. *Journalism* 3 (3): 283–307.

SECTION IV

COMMUNICATION DYNAMICS *RELATED TO* SPECIFIC TYPES OF CRIMES AND INCIDENTS

CHAPTER 17

Language in Traffic Stop Interactions

Patterns in Language Use and Recommendations for Fostering Trust and Compliance

Belén Lowrey-Kinberg

Traffic stops are one of the most common interactions between police and members of the public. In the United States, over 20 million traffic stops take place annually (Pierson et al. 2020). Although the vast majority of these are carried out without incident, several recent traffic stops are noteworthy for having taken an unfortunate turn, including the shooting in Odessa, Texas (Law, Mansoor, and Aguilera 2019), and Sandra Bland's traffic stop (Lowrey-Kinberg and Buker 2017). These events are a reminder that there is a potential for these encounters to result in injury and loss of life for both citizens and officers (e.g., Shapiro 2019; Torres and Nathanson 2019).[1] Moreover, even should a traffic stop proceed without incident, attitudes toward police are likely formed by repeated interactions, as opposed to any singular encounter (Lowrey, Maguire, and Bennett 2016). Traffic stops are one common way that members of the public engage with police in face-to-face interaction and, as such, may be particularly influential in civilian evaluations of police legitimacy.

Traffic stops differ from everyday talk in several important respects. First, traffic stops are inherently institutional events, as officers are acting on behalf of the police institution (Gallois, Weatherall, and Giles 2016; Shon 2005). Second, there is a large power differential between officer and citizen because officers can direct citizen actions (e.g., place them under arrest) and place sanctions upon them (e.g., give a ticket). Thus, traffic stops are not normal, everyday encounters—they are governed by rules that would not apply or be relevant in other interpersonal situations. Any evaluation of communication within traffic stops must be viewed within this context, as there is an inherent power dynamic that makes egalitarian communication between officer and citizen impossible (Shon 2005).

Despite the prevalence of traffic stops and their potential to influence public perceptions of police, there is relatively little research examining how police officers communicate during these interactions. The existing research primarily highlights the language that officers use when speaking with members of the public in traffic stops. However, a separate body of literature, primarily centered around procedural justice theory (Mazerolle, Bennett, Davis, Sargeant, and Manning 2013; see chapters 8 and 22) provides insight as to the communication strategies officers might employ to gain compliance and promote police legitimacy in traffic stops. This chapter first provides an overview of studies describing how police officers speak during traffic stops followed by a review of the research that makes recommendations as to which communication strategies officers *should* implement. Finally, future directions of research in traffic stop discourse are outlined.

HOW DO OFFICERS SPEAK IN TRAFFIC STOPS?

Until recently, researchers analyzing language or communication patterns in traffic stop interactions relied on either coding observations during ride-alongs (e.g., Jonathan-Zamir, Mastrofski, and Moyal 2013) or assessing the dialogue present in police–citizen interactions recorded for reality television shows (e.g., Shon 2003; Vandermay, Houlihan, Klein, Lewinski, and Buchanan 2008). The proliferation of body cameras, however, has opened new avenues of research. Although not without its own methodological shortcomings, the analysis of body cameras footage has allowed researchers to access a wider array of interactions than previously possible and to examine these in greater depth.[2]

Access to body camera and dash camera data has provided researchers with a window into how a typical traffic stops unfolds linguistically. In most cases, officers' language use appears to follow predictable patterns as a traffic stop progresses from opening to resolution. The traffic stop is initiated by the officer hailing the driver, typically with lights and sirens. In everyday talk, conversational openings may include greetings, an introduction or statement of identification, or a question about the other person's well-being (Gallois et al. 2016). Traffic stops start this way as well. However, traffic stop openings are typically very short. For example, an officer may begin by asking "Howz it goin'?" and then directly launch into the reason for the stop, or skip the opening all together (Gallois et al. 2016). People also tend to react in predictable ways when presented with having committed a violation by either (1) acquiescing, (2) denying, or (3) giving an "account"—a justification for the traffic violation (Smith 2010).

Once the officer has made a decision on the outcome of the stop (such as issuing a ticket), delivering this decision may be a particularly sensitive moment, as the driver might be embarrassed or threatened by what the officer has to say. Officers use a range of linguistic strategies to deliver their decisions. One set of strategies emphasizes social solidarity and similarity between the officer and the driver (Giles, Willemyns, Gallois, and Anderson 2007). For example, officers might use an informal term of address (e.g., "man") that suggests both individuals are in the same social group. Another common strategy involves phonological slurring, or the blurring of word boundaries (e.g., "gonna" or "gotcha"), or the deletion of sound to create an informal atmosphere (e.g., "k" instead of "okay"). Finally a separate form of building rapport with drivers can take place through the use of explanations and reframing decisions as a favor to the driver, for example, "All I did was no insurance even though you got cracked [sic] windshield, no registration, you're suspended third degree, so there's a lot of reasons you shouldn't be driving" (Lowrey-Kinberg 2017, 40).

A second category of strategies used by officers highlights the social distance between the officer and the driver as a way of conveying a classically "respectful" message. These strategies can include hedging, distancing, and honorific address forms. Hedging consists of softening the impact of an utterance by using a word such as "sort of" or "I guess" (Lowrey-Kinberg 2017, 25). This strategy often accompanies requests and commands, for example "*I'd just* get a hard copy in your car *it'll just* make it easier if *you know* for *any sorta*, if you ever get stopped again or or [sic] anything like that" (Lowrey-Kinberg 2017, 25). Another strategy used by officers is distancing: softening the blow of a sanction by shifting the blame away from the driver and entirely avoiding the words *ticket* or *warning* (e.g., "I didn't writecha for the expired plates just the no insurance," 30). Finally, just as some officers use address forms that emphasize social solidarity (described above), others may choose address forms that highlight social distance, such as "ma'am" and "sir" (Lowrey-Kinberg 2017). The range of strategies that officers use in traffic stops demonstrates that these are sensitive interactions requiring the careful navigation of perceived threats to the citizen.

Violent encounters may have their own communicative patterns with officers exhibiting increasingly erratic commands as the violent confrontation approaches (although note that the data in this study was not limited to traffic stop encounters):

> It appears to be the case that when officers are in an encounter with a citizen that could potentially result in a violent event, they . . . move toward a more inconsistent, variable pattern within the context of the dialogue. The more the officer appears to lose control of the situation, the more he or she seems to lose control of his or her communication skills. (Vandermay et al. 2008, 150)

If this pattern holds across a larger array of interactions, it provides one clear area where officers might benefit from communication training.

Moreover, there is evidence that communication patterns in traffic stops vary by driver race (see chapter 5). In a study examining over twenty-eight thousand traffic stops from the Oakland Police Department, Hetey, Monin, Maitreyi, and Eberhardt (2016) found that officers were more likely to be formal with White drivers (e.g., "sir") in comparison to Black drivers, with whom they were more likely to be informal (e.g., "man" instead of "sir"). These informal language choices in interactions with Black drivers may reflect unconscious biases toward them (Hetey et al. 2016).

In subsequent research, officer respect was measured by both independent participant ratings and the software program Linguistic Inquiry and Word Count (LIWC). This program examines individual words in a text, matches them to their linguistic category (e.g., articles, adjectives, emotions, and cognitive processes, among others). The program then computes the percentage of the text that each category comprises (see Tausczik and Pennebaker 2010). On average, officers spoke less respectfully to Black drivers than to White drivers. Respect in the interaction was both rated by human participants and separately operationalized using linguistic politeness theory (e.g., Brown and Levinson 1987). This trend held even considering the severity of the offense, outcome of the interaction (e.g., ticket versus no ticket), location of the stop, and officer race (Voight et al. 2017).

In a similar vein, several studies based on communication accommodation theory (CAT) have found differences between how officers speak with White and minority drivers. CAT is premised on the idea that communication style reflects social identity (Gasiorek, Giles, and Soliz 2015). Convergence in language takes the form of, for example, being approachable, courteous, and listening (Dixon, Schell, Giles, and Drogos 2008). The level of language convergence between two individuals reflects social similarity and can help foster greater solidarity between them.

In examining the degree of communicative convergence between officers and drivers in traffic stops, there is evidence that driver race, ethnicity, and accent play a role in officers' degree of accommodation. Dixon et al. (2008) examined 313 randomly sampled traffic stop videos from Cincinnati, Ohio, and examined officers' degree of accommodation. They found that race played a key role. Black drivers were more likely to be subject to extensive policing, including longer stops and those with searches (for a full description of extensive policing, see Dixon et al. 2008, 539–40). There was also a negative relationship between extensive policing and communication quality, such that a longer stop was more likely to be less accommodative. Conversely, officers were more likely to be apologetic and polite to White drivers than Black drivers. Further, when officers and drivers were the same race, the communication quality was more positive. In a similar study, Giles, Linz, Bonilla, and Gomez (2012) found that officers accommodated less to Hispanic drivers than non-Hispanic drivers. While Hispanic ethnicity itself did not predict whether a driver experienced extensive policing during a stop, those drivers with a heavier Spanish accent were more likely to experience extensive policing.

Giles, Choi, and Dixon (2010) theorize that officers may react in a nonaccommodating way to nonaccommodation by the citizen. This may partially explain tensions in interracial stops. White citizens will likely be accommodating to the officer and the officer will likely accommodate back. In contrast, Black citizens, may have had numerous negative direct and vicarious experiences with police in the past. The history of police and race relations in the United States may also influence a Black citizen's perceptions of the reasons for the stop. Thus, Black citizens will likely nonaccommodate from the start of the interaction. In response, White officers may similarly nonaccommodate, and the cycle continues. In a case study (discussed in greater depth below), Lowrey-Kinberg and Buker (2017) reach a similar conclusion as to the dialogic relationship between officer and citizen language (see also Bottoms and Tankebe 2012; Jackson, Hough, Bradford, and Kuha 2014).

Having set the groundwork for how officers *do* speak in traffic stops, this chapter now turns to what the research can tell us about best practices in fostering trust and gaining cooperation and compliance through language choices.

LESSONS FROM TRAFFIC STOP LANGUAGE STUDIES

The public has a clear idea of how they would prefer to be treated by officers in traffic stops.[3] According to one survey, people prefer when officers introduce themselves, give a reason for the stop, and are friendly and professional (Johnson 2004). These preferences are closely tied to a large body of literature within criminal justice scholarship (e.g., Mazerolle et al. 2013) and communication scholarship (e.g., Choi, Khadavy, Raddawi, and Giles 2019) that shows that how an officer speaks with a citizen influences their evaluation of the encounter and their subsequent trust in the officer and compliance with requests.

A series of experiments based on the principles of procedural justice provide some specific recommendations. Procedural justice theory posits that speaking with people respectfully, treating them fairly, and allowing them to voice questions and concerns will lead to increased police legitimacy in the eyes of the public (see chapter 8). This increase in legitimacy leads to increased cooperation and compliance with police. Procedural justice is widely regarded as a promising method of fostering trust, cooperation, and compliance with police (President's Task Force 2015).

In the first field experiment testing procedural justice theory, Mazerolle, Antrobus, Bennett, and Tyler (2013) tested two traffic stop "scripts" with Australian police officers conducting random breath tests. One group was instructed to use a standard set of messages, while the other was instructed to treat citizens according to the principles of procedural justice—fairly, respectfully, and giving them the opportunity to ask questions. A similar study was conducted in Turkey by Sahin (2014). Both studies tell a similar story: procedurally just traffic stops lead to more positive evaluations of police.[4]

A separate set of experiments tests the principles of procedural justice in a laboratory-style setting. In this set of studies participants in an online survey were randomly selected to view one short, scripted traffic stop. Depending on the condition that participants were placed into, they either viewed a standard traffic stop, or a traffic stop that was designed by the researchers to test various hypotheses. The researchers tested the relative effects of procedural justice and overaccommodation on perceptions of police (Lowrey-Kinberg 2018; Lowrey et al. 2016), of a positive and a negative traffic stop encounter (Maguire, Lowrey, and Johnson 2017), and whether the effects of procedural justice vary by race of the respondent and driver in the video (Johnson, Wilson, Maguire, and Lowrey-Kinberg 2017). Broadly speaking, procedurally just interactions in this simulated environment demonstrated positive effects on evaluations of the officers in the treatment videos. However, overaccommodation—excessively deferential or friendly language (Gasiorek 2016)—did not result in positive evaluations of officers in comparison to procedural justice (Lowrey-Kinberg 2018; Lowrey et al. 2016). Further, Johnson et al. (2017) uncovered a complex relationship between race of the respondent and perceptions, which included that the effects of procedural justice were less pronounced for Black respondents as compared to White respondents.

While officers should be trained and encouraged to engage in procedurally just policing, the acknowledgment of citizens' concerns, in particular, appears to strongly impact citizen perceptions of police. In one linguistic analysis, the researchers concluded that interactions in which officers did not attend to citizen questions and concerns (even if these were matters of public safety) were more likely to result in the use of force by the officer. Conversely, when officers "responded to or simply acknowledged civilian actions, civilians were much more likely to cooperate" (Precoda 2013, 13–14). Although this analysis was based on a reasonably large dataset (seventy-two police–citizen interactions from three agencies), further research examining a wider range of interactions and outcomes is needed.

A case study of Sandra Bland's traffic stop—an incident that garnered national attention for its rapid escalation and tragic conclusion—comes to a similar conclusion (Lowrey-Kinberg and Buker 2017).[5] One of the noteworthy elements of Bland's traffic stop was her consistent use of "Why"-prefaced questions (e.g., "Why do I have to put out my cigarette?," "Why won't you tell me that part?," "Why am I being arrested?," 391). Her persistent questioning demonstrates that Bland did not view Encinia's actions as legitimate. In this case, Encinia's dismissiveness of Bland's requests for an explanation was one critical component to the devolution of the encounter. This case study suggests that, while all components of procedural justice deserve attention, attending to the public's questions may be particularly important in establishing trust and compliance.

CHALLENGES AND FUTURE RESEARCH

Increasing numbers of police departments are taking advantage of body camera technology and implementing it in day-to-day policing. Data shows that as of 2016, almost half of US police departments use body cameras, and they are even more commonly used in larger departments (Hyland 2018). This increased use of body cameras, not just for violent incidents but in daily police interactions, has the potential to provide researchers with a wealth of data on both the traffic stop discourse as a whole, as well as individual, high-profile incidents. The implementation of body-worn cameras is accompanied by several concerns, both from the officer's perspective and from an administrative angle. Officers may feel that their every move is being supervised, and strict policies may hinder officers' abilities to protect the privacy of victims and witnesses (Velebit n.d.). From an administrative perspective, providing researchers with body camera data can present challenges that can make departments hesitant to share data. Anonymizing body camera footage can be time-consuming and costly, startup and storage costs are high, and there remain numerous privacy concerns regarding body camera use (Kotowski 2016; President's Task Force 2015). Nevertheless, given the wealth of information contained in body camera footage, researchers and police departments should work together to overcome these challenges.

There remain many unanswered questions regarding traffic stop language. To the author's knowledge there is no research examining the intersection of officers' language choices during traffic stops and the characteristics of the officer. For example, some studies examine how female police officers are viewed by the public (e.g., Breci 1997; Leger 1997) or the language they use (e.g., McElhinny 1993; Paoline and Terrill 2005; Sterling and Owen, 1982). Yet, whether male and female officers use the same language strategies in traffic stops, and whether the same language strategies are perceived differently when uttered by male versus female officers has yet to be examined (see also chapter 6). Examining how language strategies vary according to other officer variables, such as years of experience, may also provide insight into best practices.

Additionally, while Giles and colleagues have examined communication accommodation in a large number of cultures (see, for example, Hajek et al. 2006, 2008), most procedural justice research focuses on the United States and other Western countries. There is, however, a growing recognition within procedural justice scholarship that *what* is considered procedurally just and *by whom* may vary by context and culture (e.g., Barak 2016; Tankebe 2009). Refining procedural justice theory to account for cultural variation opens several fruitful avenues for future research.

Methodologically speaking, researchers should employ novel research designs and methods in exploring these questions. Experimental designs, both those in the field and in a laboratory-type setting, can be adapted to test a wide range of hypotheses. Moreover, while qualitative analysis of body camera data is useful in uncovering patterns in language use, quantitative methods have the potential to provide insight into large amounts of traffic stop language data. While using LIWC may be one option, this software program is not without its drawbacks. Panger (2016), for example, raises concerns about LIWC's applicability to short segments of text and its validity in detecting emotional content.

Other recent work points to the potential for more sophisticated automated analytical methods to provide insights into language use. For example, using the data from the Oakland Police Department, Prabhakaran et al. (2018) developed an automated method of detecting "institutional dialog acts" (467). These are common speech acts in the traffic stop setting, such as offering help or giving a reason for an action. The ability to automatically identify these speech acts in a set of body camera footage is a valuable methodological development.

Of particular note are patterns in the variation of respect used by officers when speaking with drivers of different races. Future research should attempt to replicate the study discussed above in other police jurisdictions, particularly in locations that do not have the same history of strained race relations and scandals as the Oakland Police Department (Moughty 2011). The Oakland Police Department has undergone a series of scandals, including obtaining warrants using false information (Lee 2010), sexual misconduct allegations (Queally 2016a), and a period of rapid turnover in leadership (Queally 2016b).

CONCLUSIONS

Many of the studies presented above make use of data available through relatively new police body camera technology to provide a view into what unfolds during traffic stops. This body of research shows that traffic-stop openings, citizen responses, officers' delivery of decisions, and even violent interactions follow communicative and linguistic patterns. Further, these patterns may be at least partially influenced by the race and ethnicity of the driver.

Taken together, several concrete lessons can be taken from this research. First, procedurally just and accommodative policing leads to more positive evaluations of an officer in a traffic stop. As such, officers should be trained and encouraged to be respectful and fair to drivers as well as give drivers the chance to ask questions. Using these communicative strategies in even a short interaction has positive effects for evaluations of the officer and the stop. It may be particularly important for officers to take the time to address any worries that a person may have, rather than rushing through explanations or ignoring these concerns altogether. Even a short acknowledgment of citizen concern may be helpful in promoting trust, cooperation, and compliance. Further, although citizens may generally prefer shorter traffic stop interactions (see Dixon et al. 2008), research shows that incorporating the key messages of procedural justice does not make a traffic stop too long to be evaluated positively by citizens (e.g., Lowrey et al. 2016; Maguire et al. 2017).

Ultimately, the goal of the research reviewed in this chapter is to understand the strategies used by officers when speaking in one of the most common police-citizen interactional settings: the traffic stop. One of the challenges facing researchers is how to translate findings from studies like these into better police practices. Beyond the common call for more police communication training, there is a need for researchers to identify specific strategies that officers should use when speaking with citizens in traffic stops. While there have been some tangible recommendations, delivering practical strategies is critical in this area of research.

NOTES

1. In this chapter, the term "citizen" is used broadly to refer to all non-sworn community members.
2. It is worth noting that, methodologically, body camera data presents several challenges. Police departments may be hesitant to share this data due to privacy concerns, and there is a possibility that officers and the public speak differently knowing they are being recorded.
3. It is important to note, of course, that traffic stops take place for a range of reasons and may vary significantly in threat to the officer conducting the stop.
4. Note that a similar study in Scotland (MacQueen and Bradford 2015) found that the procedural justice condition did not result in positive evaluations of the police. This study was subject to several methodological limitations that might have led to the divergent results.
5. While the traffic stop itself is dramatic and ended in Bland's arrest for assaulting a public servant, the remainder of the story is more tragic still, as Bland committed suicide in jail (Lowrey-Kinberg and Buker 2017).

REFERENCES

Barak, Maya. 2016. *A Reciprocal Approach to Legal Consciousness and (Procedural) Justice: Central American Experiences in Immigration Court*. Unpublished doctoral dissertation. Washington DC: American University.

Bottoms, Anthony, and Justice Tankebe. 2012. "Beyond Procedural Justice: A Dialogic Approach to Legitimacy in Criminal Justice." *Journal of Criminal Law and Criminology* 102 (1): 119–70.

Bottoms, Anthony, and Justice Tankebe. 2017. "Police Legitimacy and the Authority of the State." In *Criminal Law and the Authority of the State*, edited by Antje du Bois-Pedain, Magnus Ulväng, and Petter Asp, 47–88. Oxford: Hart Publishing.

Breci, Michael G. 1997. "Female Officers on Patrol: Public Perceptions in the 1990s." *Journal of Crime and Justice* 20 (2): 153–65.

Choi, Charles W., Gholam H. Khadavy, Rana Raddawi, and Howard Giles. 2019. "Perceptions of Police-Civilian Encounters: Communication and Intergroup Parameters in the USA and the United Arab Emirates." *Journal of International and Intercultural Communication* 12 (1): 82–104.

Dixon, Travis L., Terry L. Schell, Howard Giles, and Kristin L. Drogos. 2008. "The Influence of Race in Police–Civilian Interactions: A Content Analysis of Videotaped Interactions Taken during Cincinnati Police Traffic Stops." *Journal of Communication* 58 (3): 530–49.

Gallois, Cindy, Ann Weatherall, and Howard Giles. 2016. "CAT and Talk in Action." In *Communication Accommodation Theory: Negotiating Personal Relationships and Social Identities across Contexts*, edited by Howard Giles, 105–22. Cambridge: Cambridge University Press.

Gasiorek, Jessica. 2016. "The 'Dark Side' of CAT: Nonaccommodation." In *Communication Accommodation Theory: Negotiating Personal Relationships and Social Identities across Contexts*, edited by Howard Giles, 85–104. Cambridge: Cambridge University Press.

Gasiorek, Jessica, Howard Giles, and Jordan Soliz. 2015. "Accommodating New Vistas." *Language and Communication* 41 (March): 1–5.

Giles, Howard, Charles W. Choi, and Travis L. Dixon. 2010. "Police-Civilian Encounters." In *The Dynamics of Intergroup Communication*, edited by Howard Giles, Scott Reid, and Jake Harwood, 65–76. New York: Peter Lang.

Giles, Howard, Daniel Linz, Doug Bonilla, and Michelle Leah Gomez. 2012. "Police Stops of and Interactions with Latino and White (Non-Latino) Drivers: Extensive Policing and Communication Accommodation." *Communication Monographs* 79 (4): 407–27.

Giles, Howard, Michael Willemyns, Cindy Gallois, and Michelle C. Anderson. 2007. "Accommodating a New Frontier: The Context of Law Enforcement." In *Social Communication*, edited by Klaus Fiedler, 129–62. New York: Psychology Press.

Hajek, Christopher, Valerie Barker, Howard Giles, Sinfree Makoni, Loretta Pecchioni, Joha Louw-Potgieter, and Paul Meyer. 2006. "Communicative Dynamics of Police-Civilian Encounters: South African and American Interethnic Data." *Journal of Intercultural Communication Research*, 35 (3): 161–82.

Hajek, Christopher, Howard Giles, Valerie Barker, Mei-Chen Lin, Yan Bing Zhang, and Mary Lee Hummert. 2008. "Expressed Trust and Compliance in Police-Civilian Encounters: The Role of Communication Accommodation in Chinese and American Settings." *Chinese Journal of Communication* 1 (2): 168–80.

Hetey, Rebecca C., Benoît Monin, Amrita Maitreyi, and Jennifer L. Eberhardt. 2016. "Data for Change: A Statistical Analysis of Police Stops, Searches, Handcuffings, and Arrests in Oakland, Calif., 2013–14." Stanford University SPARQ: Social Psychological Answers to Real-World Questions.

Hyland, Shelley S. 2018. *Body-Worn Cameras in Law Enforcement Agencies*. Washington DC: Department of Justice Bureau of Justice Statistics.

Jackson, Jonathan, Mike Hough, Ben Bradford, and Jouni Kuha. 2014. "Empirical Legitimacy as Two Connected Psychological States." In *Improving Legitimacy of Criminal Justice in Emerging Democracies*, edited by Gorazd Meško and Justice Tankebe, 137–60. London: Springer.

Johnson, Devon, David Wilson, Edward R. Maguire, and Belén Lowrey-Kinberg. 2017. "Race, Police Citizen Interactions, and Perceptions of Police: Experimental Results on the Impact of Procedural (In)justice." *Justice Quarterly* 34 (7): 1184–212.

Johnson, Richard. 2004. "Citizen Expectations of Police Traffic Stop Behavior." *Policing: An International Journal of Police Strategies and Management* 27 (4): 487–97.

Jonathan-Zamir, Tal, Stephen D. Mastrofski, and Shomron Moyal. 2013. "Measuring Procedural Justice in Police-Citizen Encounters." *Justice Quarterly* 5 (32): 845–71.

Kotowski, Jason. 2016. "Money, Storage, Primary Obstacles in Police Body Camera Implementation." *Emergency Management*, March 8. Retrieved from https://www.govtech.com/em/safety/Police-Body-Cam-Installation.html .

Law, Tara, Sanya Mansoor, and Jasmine Aguilera. 2019. "7 People Killed, 22 Injured in Odessa-Mass Shooting: Here's What We Know So Far." *TIME Magazine*. Retrieved from https://time.com/5666249/mass-shooting-midland-odessa-texas-police/ .

Lee, Henry K. 2010. "Oakland Settles Warrant Suits for $6.5 Million." SFGate. Retrieved from https://www.sfgate.com/bayarea/article/Oakland-settles-warrant-suits-for-6-5-million-3181055.php .

Leger, Kristen. 1997. "Public Perceptions of Female Police Officers on Patrol." *American Journal of Criminal Justice* 21 (2): 231–49.

Lowrey, Belén V., Edward R. Maguire, and Richard R. Bennett. 2016. "Testing the Effects of Procedural Justice and Overaccommodation in Traffic Stops: A Randomized Experiment." *Criminal Justice and Behavior* 43 (10): 1430–49.

Lowrey-Kinberg, Belén V. 2017. *Improving Police-Citizen Interactions: Novel Approaches to the Intersection of Procedural Justice and Language*. Unpublished doctoral dissertation. Washington DC: American University.

Lowrey-Kinberg, Belén. 2018. "Procedural Justice, Overaccommodation, and Police Authority and Professionalism: Results from a Randomized Experiment." *Police Practice and Research* 19 (2): 111–24.

Lowrey-Kinberg Belén, and Grace S. Buker. 2017. "'I'm Giving you a Lawful Order': Dialogic Legitimacy in the Sandra Bland Traffic Stop." *Law and Society Review* 51 (2): 379–412.

MacQueen, Sarah, and Ben Bradford. 2015. "Enhancing Public Trust and Police Legitimacy During Road Traffic Encounters: Results from a Randomized Controlled Trial in Scotland." *Journal of Experimental Criminology* 11 (3): 419–44.

Maguire, Edward R., Belén V. Lowrey, and Devon Johnson. 2017. "Evaluating the Relative Impact of Positive and Negative Encounters with Police: A Randomized Experiment." *Journal of Experimental Criminology* 13 (3): 367–91.

Mazerolle, Lorraine, Emma Antrobus, Sarah Bennett, and Tom R. Tyler. 2013. "Shaping Citizen Perceptions of Police Legitimacy: A Randomized Field Trial of Procedural Justice." *Criminology* 51 (1): 33–63.

Mazerolle, Lorraine, Sarah Bennett, Jacqueline Davis, Elise Sargeant, and Matthew Manning. 2013. "Procedural Justice and Police Legitimacy: A Systematic Review of the Research Evidence." *Journal of Experimental Criminology* 9 (3): 245–74.

McElhinny, Bonnie Sue. 1993. *We All Wear the Blue: Language, Gender, and Police Work*. Unpublished doctoral dissertation. Serra Mall: Stanford University.

Moughty, Sarah. 2011. *The Oakland Police Department's Troubled History*. PBS Frontline. Retrieved from https://www.pbs.org/wgbh/frontline/article/the-oakland-police-departments-troubled-history/ .

Panger, Galen. 2016. "Reassessing the Facebook Experiment: Critical Thinking about the Validity of Big Data Research." *Information, Communication and Society* 19 (8): 1108–26.

Paoline, Eugene A., and William Terrill. 2005. "Women Police Officers and the Use of Coercion." *Women and Criminal Justice* 15 (3–4): 97–119.

Pierson, Emma, Camelia Simoiu, Jan Overgoor, Sam Corbett-Davies, Daniel Jenson, Amy Shoemaker, Vignesh Ramachandran, Phoebe Barghouty, Cheryl Phillips, Ravi Shro, and Sharad Goel. 2020. "A Large-Scale Analysis of Racial Disparities in Police Stops across the United States." *Nature Human Behavior*, May. Retrieved from https://doi.org/10.1038/s41562-020-0858-1 .

Prabhakaran, Vindokumar, Camila Griffiths, Hang Su, Prateek Verma, Nelson Morgan, Jennifer Eberhardt, and Dan Jurafsky. 2018. "Detecting Institutional Dialog Acts in Police Traffic Stops." *Transactions of the Association for Computational Linguistics* 6: 467–81.

Precoda, Kristin. 2013. "Key Findings for Interpersonal Skills." Retrieved from https://apps.dtic.mil/dtic/tr/fulltext/u2/a605475.pdf .

President's Task Force on 21st Century Policing. 2015. *Final Report of the President's Task Force on 21st Century Policing*. Washington DC: Office of Community Oriented Policing Services.

Queally, James. 2016a. "After a Sex Scandal Rocked Oakland Police, Officials Are Trying to Figure Out How to Restore Public Trust." *Los Angeles Times*. Retrieved from https://www.latimes.com/local/lanow/la-me-ln-oakland-sex-scandal-20160613-snap-story.html .

Queally, James. 2016b. "Oakland Loses Third Police Chief in Nine Days, Will Operate under Civilian Control." *Los Angeles Times*. Retrieved from https://www.latimes.com/local/lanow/la-me-ln-oakland-chief-figueroa-out-20160617-snap-story.html .

Sahin, Nusret M. 2014. *Legitimacy, Procedural Justice and Police-Citizen Encounters: A Randomized Controlled Trial of the Impact of Procedural Justice on Citizen Perceptions of the Police during Traffic Stops in Turkey*. Unpublished doctoral dissertation. Newark: Rutgers University.

Shapiro, Emily. 2019. "Officer Shot in the Head at Traffic Stop in Critical Condition." ABC News. Retrieved from https://abcnews.go.com/US/officer-critical-condition-shot-traffic-stop-police/story?id=66605963 .

Shon, Phillip Chong Ho. 2003. "Bringing the Spoken Words Back In: Conversationalizing (Postmodernizing) Police-Citizen Encounter Research." *Critical Criminology* 11 (2): 151–72.

Shon, Phillip Chong Ho. 2005. "'I'd Grab the SOB by His Hair and Yank Him Out the Window': The Fraternal Order of Warnings and Threats in Police–Citizen Encounters." *Discourse and Society* 16 (6): 829–45.

Smith, Wendy B. 2010. "Footing, Resistance and Control: Negotiating a Traffic Citation." *Critical Inquiry in Language Studies* 7 (2–3): 173–86.

Sterling, Bruce S., and John W. Owen. 1982. "Perception of Demanding versus Reasoning Male and Female Police Officers." *Personality and Social Psychology Bulletin* 8 (2): 336–40.

Tankebe, Justice. 2009. "Public Cooperation with the Police in Ghana: Does Procedural Fairness Matter?" *Criminology* 47 (4): 1265–93.

Tausczik, Yla R., and James W. Pennebaker. 2010. "The Psychological Meaning of Words: LIWC and Computerized Text Analysis Methods." *Journal of Language and Social Psychology* 29 (1): 24–54.

Torres, Ella, and Marc Nathanson. 2019. "Man Charged in 'Cold Blooded' Fatal Shooting of Texas Police Officer during Traffic Stop." ABC News, September 27. Retrieved from https://abcnews.go.com/US/texas-officer-dies-cold-blooded-manner-traffic-stop/story?id=65914013 .

Vandermay, Julie, Daniel D. Houlihan, Liesa A. Klein, William Lewinski, and Jeffrey Buchanan. 2008. "Command Sequence in Police Encounters: Searching for a Linguistic Fingerprint." *Law Enforcement Executive Forum* 8 (3): 141–51.

Velebit, Vuk. n.d. "Pros and Cons of Body-Worn Cameras." *Pointpulse*. Retrieved from https://pointpulse.net/magazine/pros-and-cons-of-police-body-worn-cameras/ .

Voigt, Rob, Nicholas P. Camp, Vinodkumar Prabhakaran, William L. Hamilton, Rebecca C. Hetey, Camilla M. Griffiths, David Jurgens, Dan Jurafsky, and Jennifer L. Eberhardt. 2017. "Language from Police Body Camera Footage Shows Racial Disparities in Officer Respect." *Proceedings of the National Academy of Sciences* 114: 6521–26.

CHAPTER 18

Understanding the Communication Dynamics Inherent to Police Hostage and Crisis Negotiation

Amy R. Grubb

This chapter synopsizes the current literature in relation to the communication dynamics that are inherent to police hostage and crisis negotiation (hereafter, "negotiation"). While negotiation as an entity has existed as a police tool since the 1970s (Schlossberg 1974), hostage and crisis negotiators (hereafter "negotiators") are constantly having to adapt and evolve in line with the ever-changing terrain of crisis scenarios that are encountered. Police negotiators are essentially expert communicators who utilize various communicative tools and techniques to de-escalate and resolve hostage or crisis scenarios.

The research literature reveals a variety of communication dynamics that are deemed to be effective when applied within crisis negotiation contexts, including both linguistic and behavioral patterns within the dialogue used by negotiators when communicating with subjects. These communication dynamics fall into three domains. Firstly, linguistic analysis (using linguistic/language style matching [LSM] and conversation analysis [CA]) of live negotiation scenario dialogue has revealed linguistic patterns within verbal communication that facilitate the resolution of incidents, suggesting that the language utilized by negotiators can specifically play a role in whether incidents are resolved successfully or not. Secondly, a repertoire of effective verbal communication tactics or strategies has been developed, that allows negotiators to select the most appropriate communicative tool from their metaphorical toolbox at any given time. And thirdly, academics/practitioners have developed models of negotiation based on the behavioral styles of verbal communication that are associated with successful de-escalation of crisis situations that can be used to guide operational negotiator practice. The current book chapter will describe these three different approaches and critically evaluate the usefulness of each approach to operational negotiator practice, while considering the ongoing evolution of negotiation in modern society.

THE EVOLUTION OF POLICE HOSTAGE AND CRISIS NEGOTIATION

Negotiation is one tactical option that is available to police incident commanders when responding to critical incidents (including varying forms of hostage-taking or crisis incidents). Negotiation is an important aspect of relational and family life (Abrahams 1996; Greenhalgh and Chapman 1998; Wilmot and Hocker 2018) and equally forms a core part of modern-day policing, with negotiators serving a vital role in the resolution of critical incidents. The role of the negotiator is incredibly important, with their input often playing a role in whether individuals live or die. The concept of negotiation as a specialist police discipline and method for responding to critical incidents has existed since the 1970s, with the New York Police Department (NYPD) setting up the first specialized negotiation unit (Schlossberg 1974). This development was catalyzed by several high-profile international hostage-taking events that were handled poorly by law enforcement and resulted in the deaths of multiple hostages (i.e., the Munich Massacre at the 1972 Olympic Games; see Grubb 2010).

The Munich Massacre, in particular, highlighted the distinct lack of protocol or procedure to deal with hostage-taking situations in a controlled way that resulted in limited death/harm to hostages. In the wake of this tragedy, international law enforcement agencies began to criticize the lack of effective crisis management techniques for hostage situations and began to explore new techniques which could be employed within such situations (Soskis and Van Zandt 1986). The implementation of a "negotiate first" policy when dealing with hostage-taking situations and perpetrators barricaded without hostages (Bolz 1979) led to the development of specialized hostage negotiation teams that include a designated negotiator, tactical assault team (TAC), command structure, and support personnel (Fuselier 1981). Here, the primary aim is for peaceful resolution, and the guiding operational principle is to minimize or eliminate the loss of life (McMains and Mullins 2001).

Such teams now exist on an international scale, with many larger police forces/departments containing a hostage and crisis negotiation team/unit in some guise. While the initial impetus for negotiator teams was to counteract terrorist hostage-taking events, negotiators have now become absorbed into the police response to a variety of critical incidents (see Grubb, Brown, Hall, and Bowen 2019) and are used widely by incident commanders to de-escalate and resolve incidents peacefully without the need to resort to force/tactical intervention (Grubb 2010). Negotiation as an entity has been widely praised as "one of law enforcement's most effective tools" (Regini 2002, 1), and the concept of "containment and negotiation" has been described as "one of the most effective, inexpensive and lifesaving innovations in modern police work" (Hare 1997, 152), with both anecdotal and empirical evidence attesting to the efficacy of negotiation as a police tool (Flood 2003; McMains and Mullins 2001; Rogan, Hammer, and Van Zandt 1997).

COMMUNICATION DYNAMICS INHERENT TO SUCCESSFUL POLICE NEGOTIATION

The discipline of police negotiation has evolved dramatically since its conception in the early 1970s, with various models, tools, and techniques being developed by negotiators themselves, psychologists, communication scholars, and academicians to inform the way negotiators operate in theater (Grubb 2010; Grubb, Brown, Hall, and Bowen 2020). By extrapolating findings from the broader organizational communication literature (Coleman, Marcus, and Deutsch 2014; Putnam and Roloff 1992), communication theory as a means of understanding conflict resolution processes can also extend to the world of police negotiation. Communication accommodation theory (CAT), for example, has been applied to a variety of applied contexts (Soliz and Giles 2014), including that of law enforcement (Giles, Willemyns, Gallois, and Anderson 2007) and police–civilian interactions (Giles 2002; Gnisci, Giles, and Soliz 2016). Broadly speaking, findings suggest that police officers who are willing to accommodate their behavior by listening and demonstrating perspective taking promote feelings of public trust (Tyler and Huo 2002), which then leads to increased civilian's willingness to cooperate with law enforcement (Giles et al. 2007). The concept of interpersonal accommodation viewed via the theoretical lens of CAT, therefore, has relevance to the efficacy of the interaction between the two interlocutors (negotiator/law-enforcement—subject/civilian) within a crisis negotiation scenario. Indeed, some of the more recent linguistic/language style matching (LSM) research within this arena has followed in the footsteps of CAT by promoting sympathetically aligned principles.

Negotiation has, in fact, emerged as an interdisciplinary field "with psychologists, linguists, and law enforcement professionals working together to understand and optimize crisis negotiation practice" (Sikveland, Kevoe-Feldman, and Stokoe 2019, 3). Negotiators are essentially expert communicators who are trained to utilize various communicative tools and techniques to de-escalate and resolve critical incidents. As such, it is commonsensical to assume that language use and context is likely to play a role in the outcome of negotiator-subject dyadic interactions and dialogue. The extant research literature reveals a variety of communication dynamics that are deemed to be effective when applied within hostage/crisis negotiation contexts, including both linguistic and behavioral patterns within the dialogue used by negotiators when communicating with subjects and the identification of communication patterns and predictors of success within negotiator-subject dyadic interactions.

Linguistic Patterns within Verbal Communication That Facilitate Negotiation Success

There is a steadily increasing body of work and associated corpus of literature that has focused on understanding negotiation practice from a linguistic perspective, whereby the type and style of language utilized by negotiators and subjects has been analyzed in order to identify what works (i.e., is effective) when trying to resolve hostage or crisis incidents (Giebels and Taylor 2009, 2010; Rogan 2011; Rogan and Hammer 1995; Taylor 2002a, 2002b; Taylor and Donald 2003; Taylor and Thomas 2008). Generic studies focusing on the concept of synchronicity between verbal and non-verbal cues have found that greater convergence in both of these aspects of communication results in the development of a greater level of rapport and effective bonding between interlocutors that then leads to greater communication coordination and perception of shared meanings (Garrod and Pickering 2004). Similarly, when looking at dyadic interaction specifically, convergence of vocabulary results in a reduction in perceived interpersonal differences, enhanced perceived attractiveness, enhanced communication coordination, coordination of perceived shared meaning, and a greater sense of liking and social approval (Garrod and Pickering 2004). Considering that one of the key directives of negotiation is to develop rapport with the subject and to build trust and credibility to enable the negotiator to exert influence over the subject (as directed by the Behavioral Change Stairway Model [BCSM]; developed by the Crisis Negotiation Unit of the Federal Bureau of Investigations [FBI]) (Vecchi, Van Hasselt, and Romano 2005), the concept of verbal synchronicity has relevance to the dialogue utilized within hostage/crisis negotiation contexts.

In line with this concept, Taylor and Thomas's (2008) study utilized transcripts of audio-recorded live crisis negotiation scenarios and demonstrated that greater levels of verbal synchronicity (in the form LSM) were associated with successfully negotiated outcomes compared to unsuccessful outcomes. They concluded that "in comparison to unsuccessful negotiations, the dialogue of successful negotiations involved greater coordination of turn taking, reciprocation of positive affect, a focus on the present rather than the past, and a focus on alternatives rather than on competition." Unsuccessful negotiations, however, were characterized by dramatic fluctuations in LSM and an inability "to maintain the constant levels of rapport and coordination that occurred in successful negotiations" (Taylor and Thomas 2008, 263). When viewing these findings through the lens of CAT, successful negotiations demonstrated greater levels of linguistic/paralinguistic *convergence* between the interlocutors and unsuccessful negotiations demonstrated greater levels of linguistic/paralinguistic *divergence* (Giles and Ogay 2007).

Similar work conducted by Randall Rogan in the United States also explored the concept of LSM within crisis negotiation scenarios, with a specific emphasis on how LSM is operationalized within suicidal versus surrender outcome cases. Rogan's (2011) findings demonstrated that there were differences in the LSM observed within surrender versus suicide outcomes. However, he reported a higher aggregate level of LSM within suicide outcomes than surrender outcomes, a finding which is somewhat contradictory to Taylor and Thomas's (2008) findings, whereby successfully negotiated cases (i.e., aligned to the "surrender" outcome in Rogan's work) demonstrated higher levels of conversational LSM. Rogan suggests that this finding may be the result of an attempt by negotiators to strive to connect/establish rapport with the suicidal subject (Mohandie 2010), and perhaps this occurs at an increasing level due to an increased perceived suicidal risk on the part of the negotiator. Rogan's findings also demonstrated differences in the patterns of LSM displayed over time segments for the suicide versus surrender outcome cases, with distinct patterns being observed in terms of LSM over time. Surrender cases showed a steady increase in LSM over the initial three time segments and then a consistent decrease in LSM through to the final (sixth) time segment (i.e., a positive curvilinear trend), whereas suicide cases were characterized by a negative linear correlation up to segment three and then fluctuation in LSM in the final time segments.

While fluctuation or instability in terms of LSM was associated with unsuccessful outcomes consistently across both Rogan's (2011) and Taylor and Thomas's (2008) work, the findings suggest that the concept of LSM as applied to hostage/crisis negotiation is nuanced, and it may not be as simplistic as suggesting that LSM needs to remain high at all points during a negotiation to predict successful outcome.

There are only a small number of additional studies that have focused on negotiation from a linguistic perspective and utilized real cases of negotiator-subject dialogue. These studies include Rubin's (2016) master's thesis on the use of tag questions in crisis negotiations. A tag question is a "syntactic device which serves to hedge the strength of the speech act in which it occurs" (Holmes 1986, 2). An example of a tag question is "It's hard when they aren't there with you, isn't it?" Rubin's work identified that tag questions (specifically facilitative and softening tag questions) can act as valuable discursive tools within crisis negotiations, where both the subject and negotiator perceive the negotiator to be the most powerful interlocutor; however, tag questions were less effective in instances where the subject perceived themselves to be more powerful than the negotiator. Such findings suggest that the use of specific linguistic tactics/strategies are context dependent, to some extent, with *certain* verbal strategies facilitating negotiation success in *certain* circumstances, implying that it is not as clear cut as a "one size fits all" approach.

More recently, academics have explored negotiation using a CA approach, with work by Garcia (2017), Sikveland et al. (2019), and Stokoe and Sikveland (2019) starting to provide illuminating insights into the importance of language within crisis negotiation contexts. "CA is a generic approach to the analysis of social interaction that was first developed in the study of ordinary conversation but which has since been applied to a wide spectrum of other forms of talk-in-interaction" (Goodwin and Heritage 1990, 284). CA is based in an ethnomethodological tradition and refers to the study of talk-in-interaction, or talk as the site of social action (Braun and Clark 2013). CA is used to analyze naturally occurring spontaneous talk and adopts a highly structured method whereby each turn of talk is analyzed sequentially at a micro-level. The process operates on the basis that "each turn of talk is responsive to prior turns, that is, that any specific piece of talk cannot be understood without reference to the construction and delivery of talk which precedes it" (Braun and Clark 2013, 196). Application of the CA approach is thought to fill some of the gaps within the extant literature by focusing on naturally occurring data (i.e., transcripts of live negotiator deployments) and exploring the interactional procedures involved in crisis negotiations (Garcia 2017) via nuanced analysis of the spontaneous unfolding of talk occurring between the subject and the negotiator.

Work by Sikveland et al. (2019) has identified the relevance of appropriately delivered communicative challenges by negotiators to resistant responses provided by subjects during crisis negotiations involving suicidal subjects. Their findings demonstrate that negotiators (and emergency 911 dispatchers) can successfully overcome subject resistance by challenging the reasoning within the interlocutor's resistant responses, which results in positive shifts within the suicidal subject's behavior. The authors highlight the importance of the challenges presented by negotiators as being "based on the reality, terms and reasoning put forward by the PiCs [Person(s) in Crisis] themselves" (Sikveland et al. 2019), with the negative examples reviewed within their sample demonstrating how "less logically and interactionally founded arguments were treated as refutable by the PiC" (15) and therefore did not have the desired effect of creating a positive turning point within the negotiation. Sikveland et al.'s (2019) findings contradict the previously supported notion that negotiators should avoid challenging the PiC (James 2007; Vecchi et al. 2005), and instead suggest that the use of challenging can be both appropriate and beneficial within crisis negotiations, as long it is performed productively by building on both the logic and reasoning presented by the PiC themselves.

Stokoe and Sikveland's (2019) study also provides insight into a previously unchartered territory within the negotiation process, in the form of the communicative strategies utilized by the secondary negotiator within the negotiator cell, that is, the team of negotiators that are involved in communication with the subject. A full cell typically consists of a team leader and four negotiators, but most incidents do not require the deployment of a full cell (National Policing Improvement Agency 2011) and typically involve two negotiators working in a primary and secondary (supporting) negotiator capacity. Stokoe and Sikveland's (2019) findings identified successful suggestions that resulted in progress being achieved by the primary negotiator, and unsuccessful language activity used by the secondary negotiator, which resulted in a disruption of flow of the negotiation and alignment between the primary negotiator and PiC. These findings highlight the importance of the secondary negotiator's role and the potential impact of their actions/language/behavior on the negotiation outcome, a concept that has not been academically explored to date. The suggestion is, therefore, that in contrast to the previously held notion of the secondary negotiator playing a (primarily) support role to the primary negotiator (McMains and Mullins 2014; Schlossberg 1980), their actions can in fact have an impact on whether a negotiation progresses successfully or not.

Stokoe and Sikveland's (2019) findings imply that while secondary negotiator suggestions can appear in two formats—(1) interventions made where the primary negotiator is the main recipient; and (2) suggested candidate turns (i.e., suggestions about the way a statement should be delivered or any next actions that should be taken) for the primary negotiator to animate/pass on to the PiC—it is the latter of these two formats that is riskier in terms of successful outcomes. The way the primary and secondary negotiators work together, and the language used throughout the negotiation process in conjunction with the way the suggested interventions are interpreted by the primary negotiator and then animated to the PiC has an impact on the progressivity of the negotiation. As such, the findings suggest that although secondary negotiators typically do not have direct communication with the PiC, their role is more influential than previously thought. Stokoe and Sikveland's (2019) study provides an almost microscopic analysis of the language utilized within crisis negotiations, adopting an empirical sociolinguistic approach to the understanding of effective negotiation practice. This work provides a new (and welcomed) direction for developing a deeper understanding of how negotiators can be trained to use language more effectively, with the findings already being used to train negotiators both in the UK and internationally.

The aforementioned research provides insight into the relevance of linguistics to the potential success of crisis negotiations and highlights the importance of not only *what* negotiators say during a negotiation, but *how* they say it. The adoption of LSM and CA approaches into the negotiation research literature allows negotiation practices to be analyzed on both an empirical basis (using real-life recorded negotiation dialogue) and on a microscopic basis whereby the nuances of language patterns can be identified. These findings have applications for practice by informing the training of negotiators, however, it is worth considering how easily such complex linguistic findings can be converted into user-friendly heuristics when negotiators are confronted by a pressurized environmental context *in theater*.

Effective Verbal Communication Strategies, Stratagems, and Tactics Used within Negotiation

The second approach focuses on the identification of verbal communication patterns and predictors of success within negotiator-subject dyadic interactions. Many of these strategies/stratagems have been identified on the basis of speaking to and or/observing negotiators *in situ* and others have been identified as the result of direct empirical/academic enquiry. Exemplars of these patterns include the following:

1. general communication strategies in hostage negotiation (Greenstone 2005; McMains and Mullins 1996; Miller 2005; Slatkin 2010);
2. Miller's (2005) verbal communication tactics;
3. Slatkin's (2002, 2010) stratagems;
4. Giebels's (2002 as cited in Giebels and Noelanders 2004) "Table of Ten" social influence strategies;
5. Cialdini's (2007) weapons of influence;
6. the use of active listening skills (ALS; Lanceley 1999); and
7. the specific negotiation strategies identified within Grubb's (2016) D.I.A.M.O.N.D. model of hostage and crisis negotiation (Grubb et al. 2020).

Various authors have put forward generic recommendations for communicating with hostage takers (Greenstone 2005; McMains and Mullins 1996; Miller 2005; Slatkin 2010), which include strategies such as:

1. minimizing background distractions;
2. opening dialogue with an introduction and statement of purpose;
3. asking what the hostage taker likes to be called (to build rapport);
4. speaking slowly and calmly;
5. adapting dialogue to the hostage taker's vocabulary and cognitive level;

6. encouraging venting, but de-escalating ranting;
7. asking for clarification;
8. focusing the conversation on the hostage taker, not the hostages;
9. being supportive and encouraging about the outcome; and
10. avoiding unproductive verbal strategies (such as arguing with the hostage taker).

Slatkin (2002, 250) identifies a number of verbal stratagems that are conceptualized as "the calculated and practiced techniques, means and methods of advancing the dialogue" toward successful resolution of the hostage/crisis situation. A stratagem is typically perceived as a tactic that can be used to gain an upper hand within a given scenario and may involve the use of deception; whereas a strategy tends to refer to a conventional plan of action used to obtain an overall aim. While tricks, schemes, and deceptions would appear not to have a place within crisis negotiations, Slatkin (2010, 55) suggests that "stratagems can have a legitimate place in crisis negotiations as subtle verbal techniques employed by a N[egotiator] to advance the negotiations and promote a resolution to the dangerous crisis at hand."

Slatkin (2002) refers explicitly to six stratagems that constitute verbal maneuvers that can be taught to negotiators and developed to become an effective part of their repertoire. The first stratagem is referred to as "structuring a success," by which the negotiator attempts to acquiesce to a hostage taker's demand early on within the negotiation, particularly when the demand is inconsequential (i.e., provision of cigarettes). By doing this, it communicates to the subject that negotiations work and h/she can achieve some of the things h/she wants, and equally establishes a debt that the negotiator can leverage/capitalize on later in the negotiation. The second stratagem involves creating the "illusion of choice" by generating a question that seems to offer a choice between two options, but the end result is essentially the same and benefits the negotiator equally (i.e., "Do you want to come out now or in five minutes?"). This stratagem works on the basis that subjects are more likely to acquiesce when they perceive that they are in control and are choosing the eventual outcome. The third stratagem, called "the yes set," involves asking subjects a set of simple questions that are likely to be answered as "yes" before asking a critical question, with the momentum predicting that the answer to the critical question (e.g., Can you release one of the hostages?) is also likely to be in the affirmative. The fourth stratagem, "ventilating," promotes the subject's voicing of grievances and allows the subject to discharge emotional tension (i.e., ventilate) and de-escalate any intense emotions, moving them closer toward a rational position of problem-solving. The fifth stratagem, "deflecting," enables negotiators to acknowledge demands (and therefore the subject) but deflect the demand by redirecting the request in a way that partially meets the subject's needs but does not allow for acquiescence of a demand that may not be beneficial to the negotiator. The last stratagem, "using imagery," involves the negotiator painting a mental image to enhance the emotional meaning for the subject, while also implanting a suggested desired action. The use of such imagery may subliminally or subconsciously encourage the subject to enact the suggested behavior. Slatkin has since expanded this list to include a total of twenty-six influence stratagems that can be utilized by negotiators to promote successful resolution of incidents (see Slatkin 2010).

The Table of Ten (ToT; Giebels 2002 as cited in Giebels and Noelanders 2004) was developed on the basis of interviews with European negotiators (and later empirically validated by analysis of dialogue taken from Dutch and Belgian crisis negotiation incidents). The ToT represents a framework of social influence tactics that can be used by negotiators to positively influence a subject's behavior (or to dissuade a subject from continuing with their current course of behavior). The ToT differentiates between relational tactics (i.e., those related to the sender and his or her relationship with the other party) and content tactics (i.e., those related to the content of the message and the information being conveyed to the other party). These relational/content tactics are underpinned by various principles of influence that have previously been identified as playing a role in influencing behavior within a variety of contexts. As such, the ToT presents a set of theoretically informed and psychologically reinforced tactics that have been validated within both negotiation and non-negotiation contexts, further attesting to their credibility. The ToT strategies are listed in table 18.1, with 1–3 being categorized as "relational" strategies and 4–10 being categorized as "content" strategies. Giebels, Ufkes, and van Erp (2014) present more detailed examples of how each of these interpersonal influencing strategies can be used within a negotiation context (e.g., the strategy of *being credible* can be implemented by showing expertise or proving that you are reliable, thereby tapping into the principle of authority as a method of influencing behavior).

Work by Ellen Giebels and her colleagues has established the clinical utility of these strategies as applied within crisis negotiation contexts, with studies highlighting that different strategies appear to be more/less effective in different circumstances. Giebels and Noelanders (2004), for example, identified that both siege and kidnap and extortion (K & E) cases were dominated by the use of *being kind*, *direct pressure*, and *rational persuasion*; however, they also identified differences between the two categories of negotiation deployment, with K & E cases being characterized by greater use of aggressive strategies (such as *intimidation*) and sieges being characterized by greater use of *emotional appeals* and *being credible*.

Further research indicates that different strategies have greater application (and *ergo*, impact on peaceful outcome) at different stages within the negotiation process. Kamphuis, Giebels, and Noelanders (2006), for example, found that negotiators used

TABLE 18.1. The Table of Ten (Giebels 2002 as cited in Giebels and Noelanders 2004)

Strategy	Underpinning Principle
1. Being kind	Sympathy
2. Being equal	Similarity
3. Being credible	Authority
4. Emotional appeal	Self-image
5. Intimidation	Deterrence/fear
6. Imposing a restriction	Scarcity
7. Direct pressure	Power of repetition
8. Legitimizing	Legitimacy
9. Exchanging	Reciprocity
10. Rational persuasion	Cognitive consistency

the *being equal* strategy more often during the initial and problem-solving phases within the relatively more effective negotiations. They also identified that certain strategies were more/less effective depending on whether the case was expressive (i.e., driven by emotional needs) or instrumental (i.e., driven by a desire to achieve certain goals/substantive demands), with *legitimizing* being associated with success in expressive cases but negatively associated with success in instrumental cases. These findings indicate that the utilization of these strategies (as selected by the negotiator from their "metaphorical toolbox") is not as straightforward as it would initially appear. The negotiator needs to know *which* strategy to employ, at *which* time during each individually contextually framed negotiation scenario for the strategy to be effective in achieving the aim of positive behavioral influence and peaceful resolution.

Robert Cialdini's work as an experimental social psychologist has highlighted six underpinning principles that are often used within various settings to influence behavior:

1. reciprocation (i.e., the principle of give and take; people are obligated to return favors, so if someone does something to help you, you are more likely to do something to help them in return);
2. commitment and consistency (i.e., people feel obliged to honor promises/justify decisions they have made; there is a desire to appear [and be] consistent with actions we have already taken);
3. social proof (i.e., people take cues from other people when they are not sure how to act; people will judge behavior as appropriate/correct when they see other people behaving in this way);
4. liking (i.e., people are more likely to trust/help people they like);
5. authority (i.e., people are more likely to obey/acquiesce to a person in authority); and
6. scarcity (i.e., people desire things that are perceived as less available; Cialdini 2007).

These principles have been applied to the discipline of police negotiation, whereby negotiators have been trained to use these "weapons of influence" to positively alter the subject's behavior in a manner that encourages peaceful resolution of the incident. Anecdotally, negotiators have attested to the effective utilization of these principles of influence, however, some of these weapons are more applicable/generalizable to crisis negotiation settings than others (Grubb 2016; Grubb et al. 2020); for example, the use of positive police actions/concessions (cigarettes) can be used to demonstrate *reciprocity*; the use of a demand made by an authority figure (police officer) can be used to demonstrate *authority*. For a full discussion of the applications of these techniques within police negotiations, see Mullins (2002). Although these principles have theoretically been applied to a police negotiation context, there is no published empirical literature that specifically validates the effective utilization of these weapons of influence, apart from the self-reported utilization of certain weapons within Grubb's work cited above. Further research that empirically validates the use of these techniques within live negotiations dialogue would, therefore, be beneficial to the extant literature base.

The use of active listening skills (ALS) is by far the most well-documented technique within the police negotiation literature. *Active listening* is described as the "foundation of all negotiation" regardless of the type of negotiation scenario (Vecchi 2009, 12) and is conceptualized as a range of multipurpose tools that can be applied to a variety of communicative contexts, including that of hostage and crisis negotiations (Miller 2005; Royce 2005). Exemplar ALS techniques include the use of the following:

1. emotion labeling (i.e., identifying the perceived emotion being felt by the subject);
2. paraphrasing (i.e., rephrasing/summarizing the subject's statement in your own words);
3. reflecting or mirroring (i.e., repeating the subject's last [or key] word/phrase in the form of a question);
4. minimal encouragers (i.e., conversational speech fillers that demonstrate you are listening and encourage the subject to continue talking, such as "uh-huh," "oh," "and," or "really");
5. silences and pauses (i.e., silence can encourage the subject to talk by filling in the gaps or a pause can be used to emphasize a point you have made);
6. "I" messages (i.e., framing questions/statements in the form of "I" as opposed to "you" can help to avoid statements appearing accusatory for the subject and can help to personalize the negotiator to the subject. A common model is for the negotiator to use "I feel . . . when you . . . because"); and
7. open-ended questions (i.e., asking questions that require more than a yes/no answer, which encourages the subject to talk/disclose (Miller 2005).

ALS appear consistently throughout existing models of negotiation with the emphasis being on enabling the subject to feel heard by the negotiator, which is more likely to encourage the development of rapport that can then be used to influence the subject's behavior in a positive manner (Vecchi 2009). In particular, ALS skills underpin the Behavioral Change Stairway Model (BCSM; Vecchi et al. 2005), and the later-adapted Behavioral Influence Stairway Model (BISM; Vecchi 2009), models which form the driving force for many hostage and crisis negotiation training curriculums internationally, and equally appears as a key underpinning mechanism within the D.I.A.M.O.N.D. model developed in England (Grubb 2016; Grubb et al. 2020). ALS has consistently been identified as a vital component within the successful resolution of critical incidents, with multiple authors advocating for the importance of ALS within negotiation contexts.

The D.I.A.M.O.N.D. model (Grubb 2016; Grubb et al. 2020) also presents a number of specific self-reported negotiation strategies that can be adopted as necessary by negotiators when deployed to hostage/crisis incidents *in theater*, based on empirical research conducted with police negotiators in England. The following strategies were identified, and are listed in order of *most* to *least* frequently corroborated:

1. establish why the subject is in the situation;
2. honesty;
3. identification of hooks and triggers;

4. matching of the negotiator and subject;
5. adapt strategy in line with situation or subject;
6. use of concessions and positive police actions;
7. perseverance or persistence;
8. use of time as a tactic or "playing it long";
9. disassociation from the police;
10. generate options available to subject and encourage problem-solving;
11. identify commonalities or common ground; and
12. encourage dialogue and allow subject to vent.

Models of Negotiation

Numerous models have been developed to aid our understanding of the negotiation process and subsequently used as training or operational support tools. While initially, bargaining (i.e., business) negotiation models (such as Fisher, Ury, and Patton's [1991] "principled negotiation model," Ury's [1991] "getting past no model of negotiation," and Donohue, Ramesh, Kaufmann, and Smith's [1991] "crisis bargaining model of negotiation") were developed and applied to a crisis negotiation context, more context-specific models of negotiation have since been developed and form a more substantial role in terms of informing negotiator practice in today's society (for more detailed description/analysis of these models, see Grubb 2010, 2016, and Grubb et al. 2020). The context-specific models in existence vary in focus, scope, and complexity and can broadly be categorized into (1) expressive models of negotiation, and (2) communicative or discourse models of negotiation (see table 18.2).

The first category includes Call's (2003, 2008) interpretation of crisis negotiation, McMains and Mullins's (2001) stages of a crisis model, the STEPS model (Kelln and McMurtry 2007), the four-phase model of hostage negotiation (Madrigal, Bowman, and McClain 2009), the BCSM (Vecchi et al. 2005), and the BISM (Vecchi 2009). These models were developed with a contextual backdrop of the behavioral and emotional parameters involved in hostage or crisis scenarios, and, as such, tend to identify the need to address crisis (i.e., distributive) needs in addition to addressing normative (i.e., integrative) needs. The assertion is that crisis (i.e., typically relational) issues need to be addressed prior to attempting to deal with substantive needs or specific demands, suggesting that forming a relationship between the negotiator and subject is a precursor to being able to deal with more substantive issues and engage in rational problem-solving. The models also highlight the importance of de-escalating subject emotional arousal and moving subjects out of conflict or crisis emotional states in order to successfully resolve the incident. Broadly speaking, these models take a therapeutic approach, with the emphasis being on crisis intervention, de-escalating emotion, and building relationships between the two parties, as a means to successfully facilitating positive behavioral change within the subject.

The second category includes the S.A.F.E. model (Hammer 2007) and the cylindrical model of crisis communications (Taylor 2002a), both of which are grounded in communication theory and constructs. These models imply that linguistic cues can be used by negotiators and subjects to make sense of the interaction occurring between the two

TABLE 18.2. Table Synopsizing Existing Models of Hostage and Crisis Negotiation

Model	Key Principles	Country of Origin
EXPRESSIVE MODELS		
Call's (2003, 2008) Interpretation of Crisis Negotiation	• Takes a staging approach to crisis negotiations from a forensic psychology perspective. • Outlines five procedural stages or strategic steps that need to be worked through in order to resolve incidents, while also emphasizing certain communicative aspects that are pertinent to success (i.e., the use of active listening to develop a relationship between the negotiator and subject): (1) Intelligence gathering; (2) Introduction and relationship development; (3) Problem clarification and relationship development; (4) Problem-solving; and (5) Resolution.	USA
McMains and Mullins's (2001) Stages of a Crisis Model	• Takes a staging approach to crisis negotiations from a law enforcement and corrections context. • Identifies four central, distinct stages that characterize crisis incidents: (1) Pre-crisis; (2) Crisis or defusing; (3) Accommodation or negotiation; and (4) Resolution or surrender. • This is an expressive model, that is stage-focused, whereby resolution of the incident centers around the management and de-escalation of emotions. • Negotiation begins at the crisis stage, whereby the negotiator's role is to defuse the situation by reducing emotional excitement, arousal, and distress, so that more appropriate, nonviolent solutions can be considered and problem-solving can be engaged in during the accommodation stage. The resolution stage involves both parties committing to a specific course of action in order for surrender to occur.	USA
The Structured Tactical Engagement Process (STEPs) Model (Kelln and McMurtry 2007)	• Provides a framework for understanding and influencing a barricaded subject's behavior to reach a peaceful resolution by utilizing principles from the Transtheoretical Stages of Change Model (Prochaska and DiClemente 1986). • Proposes that a crisis situation has to go through four stages in order to reach successful resolution: precontemplation (step 0), contemplation (step 1), preparation (step 2), and action (step 3); with the final stage	Canada

(continued)

TABLE 18.2. (continued)

Model	Key Principles	Country of Origin
	resulting in behavioral change that leads to peaceful resolution of the crisis incident. • A variety of skills or techniques can be utilized to help guide subjects through the stages (i.e., development of rapport, affirmation of need for peaceful resolution, problem-solving, instilling motivation and confidence in subject, and remaining supportive and directive during action or surrender phase). • This model is theoretically informed as opposed to being based on empirical investigation or research.	
The Four Phase Model of Hostage Negotiation (Madrigal et al. 2009)	• Focuses on the communication of the negotiator as opposed to communication/psychological state of the subject. • Developed based on previous research and observations from actual hostage negotiations, as opposed to being directly informed by empirical data. • Suggests there are four key phases that provide a framework for successful Hostage Negotiation: (1) Establishing initial dialogue – before active listening can be used to develop a rapport, the negotiator must first establish dialogue with the subject. This may involve superficial conversation or calming and de-escalatory statements; (2) Building rapport – negotiator uses active listening techniques, demonstrations of empathy and positive regard in order to build a personal relationship with the subject based on trust and free exchange of personal information; (3) Influencing – primary goal of the negotiator is to influence the subject to release hostages or victims and surrender peacefully; and (4) Surrender – primary goal of the negotiator is to provide the subject with instructions on how to go about the surrender process so that he or she can remain safe.	USA
The Behavioral Change Stairway Model (BCSM; Vecchi et al. 2005)	• The negotiation process consists of five stages achieved sequentially and cumulatively: (1) Active listening skills; (2) Empathy; (3) Rapport; (4) Influence; and (5) Behavioral change. • Emphasis is on establishing relationship between negotiator and subject so that the negotiator can positively influence subject's behavior to resolve situation peacefully.	USA

Model	Key Principles	Country of Origin
The Behavioral Influence Stairway Model (BISM; Vecchi 2009)	• The negotiation process consists of three stages achieved sequentially and cumulatively while being supported by active listening skills: (1) Empathy; (2) Rapport; and (3) Influence. • Active listening is conceptualized as a continuous underpinning process that occurs throughout the entirety of the negotiation in order to enhance the relationship development between negotiator and subject.	USA
The D.I.A.M.O.N.D. Model of Hostage and Crisis Negotiation (Grubb 2016; Grubb et al. 2020)	• Combined procedural/staging and communicative model of negotiation and wider critical incident management process. • Identifies three key stages within the negotiation process: (1) Initial Negotiator Deployment Tasks, (2) The Negotiation Process and Incident Resolution, and (3) Post-Incident Protocol. • The D.IA.M.O.N.D. acronym is used to highlight key procedural aspects within the model and streamline the overall theoretical model in a manner that promotes clinical utility for negotiators in theater: (1) **D**eployment; (2) **I**nformation and intelligence gathering; (3) **A**ssessment of risk and threat; (4) **M**ethods of communication; (5) **O**pen dialogue with subject; (6) **N**egotiator toolbox and repertoire, and (7) **D**ebriefing procedures. • Identifies two underpinning procedural mechanisms within the model: (1) Formal record keeping [written/electronic/audio], and (2) Defensible decision-making and accountability. • Identifies one underpinning mechanism within Stage 2 of the model: Rapport building and development of the quasi-therapeutic alliance. • Identifies 12 specific strategies that form part of the negotiator toolbox/repertoire and can be used by negotiators to resolve incidents.	England
DISCOURSE OR COMMUNICATIONAL MODELS		
The S.A.F.E. Model (Hammer 2007)	• Stipulates that three core interactive processes are essential for negotiation: (1) identifying the subject's emotional frame of reference (e.g., anger, sadness, jealousy) via communication; (2) matching the response style of the subject, and (3) attending to the negotiator's need for a peaceful resolution.	USA

(continued)

TABLE 18.2. (*continued*)

Model	Key Principles	Country of Origin
	• Negotiators must identify the predominant frame that reflects the perspective of the subject's communication, with four potential frames used to guide communication between the two parties: (1) **S**ubstantive demands (i.e., bargaining and problem-solving); (2) **A**ttunement (i.e., trust or distrust toward the negotiator); (3) **F**ace (i.e., sensitivity to how she or he is perceived); and (4) **E**motion (i.e., emotional state). Negotiators should match their communication style to the most relevant frame represented by the subject by addressing their specific wants or needs. Once needs have been met, the negotiator will have more ability to exert influence over the subject, allowing the situation to be peacefully resolved.	
The Cylindrical Model of Crisis Communications (Taylor 2002a)	• Proposes there are three general levels of interaction behavior during negotiations ranging from avoidance to distributive to integrative. Negotiators aim to move subjects through these levels progressively to move subjects away from non-active participation (avoidant) interaction through to a degree of cooperation, which may be based on self-interest (distributive) through to eventual normative and cooperative communication (integrative) that will result in reconciliation of the parties' respective divergent interests. • Proposes the existence of three different motivational emphases within negotiation behavior, and classifies these as instrumental, relational, and identity themes. The first theme refers to behavior that is linked to the subject's instrumental needs, which can be described as tangible commodities or wants. The second theme refers to behavior that is linked to the relationship or affiliation between the negotiator and the subject; and the third theme refers to the negotiating parties' concern for self-preservation or "face." • The last aspect of the model suggests that these interactions are further influenced by the intensity of the communication, with the increased use of intense behaviors having a detrimental effect on negotiation outcome.	England (utilizing data from police departments in USA)

interlocutors. In the case of the S.A.F.E. model, linguistic cues can be used by negotiators to establish and identify the subject's emotional frame of reference and match their interaction accordingly; whereas the cylindrical model is a three-dimensional model that delineates communication behavior on three levels (i.e., the interaction, motivation, and behaviors of negotiators and subjects within the negotiation process; Taylor 2002a). Both models focus on the communicative process that occurs between the negotiator and subject, with linguistics being used to identify how an interaction may change throughout the course of a negotiation and how negotiators can tailor their communicative approach and behavior in a manner that is most likely to promote successful resolution.

The majority of the aforementioned models were developed in the United States and, as such, academics have questioned the cross-cultural applicability of these models to a non-US-centric context. The author's own doctoral work was instigated in response to this critique and led to the development of the Anglo-centric D.I.A.M.O.N.D. model of hostage and crisis negotiation (see Grubb 2016; Grubb et al. 2020). This model differs from previous ones by combining both procedural and communicative elements performed by negotiators (and their wider police critical incident management colleagues) in order to successfully resolve a critical incident. As such, the model provides a more nuanced analysis of the entire process involved in the effective management of a hostage or crisis incident, as opposed to focusing solely on the aspect of communication between the negotiator and subject which has historically dominated the literature. The author's findings demonstrated that the process of negotiation takes place sequentially in three stages, with the core aspects being conceptualized using the D.I.A.M.O.N.D. mnemonic:

1. *D*eployment;
2. *I*nformation and intelligence gathering;
3. *A*ssessment of risk and threat;
4. *M*ethods of communication;
5. *O*pen dialogue with subject;
6. *N*egotiator toolbox and repertoire; and
7. *D*ebriefing procedures.

In addition to this, the model identifies a "negotiator toolbox and repertoire" containing a set of communicative styles and negotiation strategies that can be used to successfully de-escalate hostage or crisis incidents, and a number of underpinning mechanisms that represent "best practice" when responding to critical incidents (see table 18.2). The author suggests that this model has clinical utility in various forms. Firstly, it provides a blueprint of procedural critical incident management which can be used to inform training and continuing professional development of new or existing negotiators, aided by the mnemonic D.I.A.M.O.N.D. acronym that helps to break the process down into manageable chronological tasks in theater. Secondly, the negotiator toolbox and repertoire category developed within the second stage of the model highlights a number of successful specific negotiation strategies that can be used to guide negotiator practice when attempting to de-escalate hostage or crisis incidents. Lastly, the model identifies several underpinning mechanisms that are vital to the negotiation process and can be used to inform negotiator training and guide negotiators in the field (Grubb et al. 2020).

CONCLUSIONS

There is an ever-accumulating body of literature relating to the discipline of police negotiation and attempting to understand the underpinning communication dynamics that are inherent to its success. The varied approaches, as discussed above, present different perspectives and foci, with some adopting a micro-level approach to the language utilized by negotiators *in situ*, others taking a macro-level "model" approach to the staging, phases, and processes involved in the management of critical incidents, and yet others identifying a set of techniques that can be selected from the negotiator's "toolbox" and applied as necessary. Police trainers and negotiators alike can clearly learn from the application of theory and knowledge from varied disciplines, including the psychology of effective communication, influence/persuasion, compliance-gaining, behavior change, and psychotherapeutic interaction. While the literature base provides a picture of broadly "what works" in terms of negotiation success and best practices, there is still some distance to travel before a fully empirically validated set of guidance can be developed from a cross-cultural perspective.

The majority of the extant models (and verbal communication strategies) have been developed on the basis of anecdotal/practical experience (with a US-centric emphasis), as opposed to on the basis of empirical research per se, and further research is required to validate the identified models/strategies in theater (by cross-referencing the findings using live negotiation dialogue). The work conducted by Ellen Giebels and Paul Taylor attempts to derive a more empirical basis to effective communication within negotiation contexts and also provides insight into the dynamics that are relevant to negotiation within different cultures. Equally, the CA approach adopted by Elizabeth Stokoe and Rein Ove Sikveland is producing a micro-level understanding of the linguistics promoting success within negotiations and in conjunction with the work being conducted by the author and colleagues is helping to develop a picture of negotiation from an Anglo-centric perspective. These academic endeavors will continue to enhance the understanding around effective negotiation processes and communication techniques, thereby contributing to the ongoing development of evidence-based negotiation as a police discipline.

When considering the next steps required to drive forward the discipline and promote the practice of evidence-based police negotiation, there are a number of research activities that would serve to benefit the negotiator community. In particular, the author's own D.I.A.M.O.N.D. model would benefit from further empirical validation using live recorded negotiation dialogue to cross-reference and further validate the strategies identified within the negotiator toolbox. In addition to this, it is important to start building knowledge in relation to police negotiation from a cross-cultural/international perspective. Empirical mixed-methodological research that compares police negotiation practice across different countries and cultures is warranted to establish whether countries need specific models/protocols for responding to hostage/crisis incidents.

Additional aspects that form part of the future research agenda include development of evidence-based risk assessment protocols and use of risk modeling in relation to different types of incident. Such work is in the early stages within the United Kingdom, where the implementation of the National Negotiator Deployment Database (NNDD) has enabled opportunities for quantitative analysis to be performed using negotiator deployment data relating to subjects, incident characteristics, and negotiator actions/outcomes (see Grubb 2020). Addressing these gaps in the research literature will help to promote the idea of police negotiation as an evidence-based area of policing and will also provide a platform to enhance negotiator training and practice effectiveness, which will ultimately serve the purpose of saving more lives in the future.

REFERENCES

Abrahams, Naomi. 1996. "Negotiating Power, Identity, Family, and Community." *Gender and Society* 6 (10): 768–96.

Bolz, Frank Jr. 1979. "Hostage Confrontation and Rescue." In *Terrorism: Threat, Reality, Response*, edited by Robert Kupperman and Darrell Trent, 393–404. Stanford: Hoover Institution Press.

Braun, Virginia, and Victoria Clarke. 2013. *Successful Qualitative Research: A Practical Guide for Beginners*. London: Sage.

Call, John. 2003. "Negotiating Crises: The Evolution of Hostage/Barricade Crisis Negotiation." In *Terrorism: Strategies for Intervention*, edited by Harold Hall, 69–94. New York: Haworth Press.

Call, John. 2008. "Psychological Consultation in Hostage/Barricade Crisis Negotiation." In *Forensic Psychology and Neuropsychology for Criminal and Civil Cases*, edited by Harold Hall, 263–288. Boca Raton: CRC Press.

Cialdini, Robert. 2007. *Influence: The Psychology of Persuasion* (revised edition). New York: HarperCollins.

Coleman, Peter T., Eric C. Marcus, and Morton Deutsch. 2014. *The Handbook of Conflict Resolution: Theory and Practice* (third edition). San Francisco: Jossey-Bass.

Donohue, William, Clospet Ramesh, Gary Kaufmann, and Richard Smith. 1991. "Crisis Bargaining in Intense Conflict Situations." *International Journal of Group Tensions* 21 (2): 133–45.

Fisher, Roger, William Ury, and Bruce Patton. 1991. *Getting to Yes: Negotiating Agreement without Giving In* (second edition). New York: Penguin.

Flood, John. 2003. *Hostage Barricade Database (HOBAS)*. Quantico: FBI Academy.

Fuselier, G. Wayne. 1981. "A Practical Overview of Hostage Negotiations (Part 1)." *FBI Law Enforcement Bulletin* 50: 1–11.

Garcia, Angela Cora. 2017. "What Went Right: Interactional Strategies for Managing Crisis Negotiations during an Emergency Service Call." *The Sociological Quarterly* 58 (3): 495–518.

Garrod, Simon, and Martin J. Pickering. 2004. "Why Is Conversation So Easy?" *Trends in Cognitive Sciences* 8 (1): 8–11.

Giebels, Ellen, and Sigrid Noelanders. 2004. *Crisis Negotiations: A Multiparty Perspective*. The Hague: Universal Press.

Giebels, Ellen, and Paul J. Taylor. 2009. "Interaction Patterns in Crisis Negotiations: Persuasive Arguments and Cultural Differences." *Journal of Applied Psychology* 94 (1): 5–19.

Giebels, Ellen, and Paul J. Taylor. 2010. "Communication Predictors and Social Influence in Crisis Negotiations." In *Contemporary Theory, Research, and Practice of Crisis and Hostage Negotiation*, edited by Randall G. Rogan and Frederick J. Lanceley, 59–76. Cresskill: Hampton.

Giebels, Ellen, Elze Gooitzen Ufkes, and Kim van Erp. 2014. "Understanding High-Stakes Conflicts." In *Handbook of Conflict Management Research*, edited by Oluremi B. Ayoko, Neal M. Ashkanasy, and Karen A. Jehn, 66–78. Northampton: Edward Elgar.

Giles, Howard. ed. 2002. *Law Enforcement, Communication and Community*. Amsterdam: John Benjamins.

Giles, Howard, and Tania Ogay. 2007. "Communication Accommodation Theory." In *Explaining Communication: Contemporary Theories and Exemplars*, edited by Bryan B. Whaley and Wendy Samter, 293–310. Mahwah: Lawrence Erlbaum

Giles, Howard, Michael Willemyns, Cynthia Gallois, and Michelle C. Anderson. 2007. "Accommodating a New Frontier: The Context of Law Enforcement." In *Social Communication*, edited by Klaus Fiedler, 129–62. New York: Psychology Press.

Giles, Howard, Christopher Hajek, Valerie Barker, Mei-Chen Lin., Yan B. Zhang, Mary L. Hummert, and Michelle C. Anderson. 2007. "Accommodation and Institutional Talk: Communicative Dimensions of Police-Civilian Interactions." In *Language, Discourse and Social Psychology*, edited by Ann Weatherall, Bernadette M. Watson, and Cindy Gallois, 131–158. Basingstoke: Palgrave Macmillan.

Gnisci, Augusto, Howard Giles, and Jordan Soliz. 2016. "CAT on Trial." In *Communication Accommodation Theory: Negotiating Personal Relationships and Social Identities across Contexts*, edited by Howard Giles, 169–91. Cambridge: Cambridge University Press.

Goodwin, Charles, and John Heritage. 1990. "Conversation Analysis." *Annual Review of Anthropology* 19 (1): 283–307.

Greenhalgh, Leonard, and Deborah I. Chapman. 1998. "Negotiator Relationships: Construct Measurement, and Demonstration of their Impact on the Process and Outcomes of Negotiation." *Group Decision and Negotiation* 7 (6): 465–89.

Greenstone, James L. 2005. *The Elements of Police Hostage and Crisis Negotiations: Critical Incidents and How to Respond to Them*. New York: Haworth Press.

Grubb, Amy. 2010. "Modern-Day Hostage (Crisis) Negotiation: The Evolution of an Art Form within the Policing Arena." *Aggression and Violent Behavior* 15 (5): 341–48.

Grubb, Amy R. 2016. *A Mixed-Methodological Analysis of Police Hostage and Crisis Negotiation in the United Kingdom*. Unpublished doctoral dissertation. Coventry University, United Kingdom.

Grubb, Amy R. 2020. "Understanding the Prevalence and Situational Characteristics of Hostage and Crisis Negotiation in England: An Analysis of Pilot Data from the National Negotiator Deployment Database." *Journal of Police and Criminal Psychology* 35 (1): 98–111.

Grubb, Amy R., Sarah J. Brown, Peter Hall, and Erica Bowen. 2019. "From 'Sad People on Bridges' to 'Kidnap and Extortion': Understanding the Nature and Situational Characteristics of Hostage and Crisis Negotiator Deployments." *Journal of Negotiation and Conflict Management Research* 12 (1): 41–65.

Grubb, Amy R., Sarah J. Brown, Peter Hall, and Erica Bowen. 2020. "From Deployment to Debriefing: Introducing the D.I.A.M.O.N.D. Model of Hostage and Crisis Negotiation." *Police Practice and Research: An International Journal*. Advance Online: https://doi.10.1080/15614263.2019.1677229 .

Hammer, Mitchell R. 2007. *Saving Lives: The S.A.F.E. Model for Negotiating Hostage and Crisis Incidents*. Westport: Praeger.

Hare, Anthony. 1997. "Training Crisis Negotiators: Updating Negotiation Techniques and Training." In *Dynamic Processes of Crisis Negotiation: Theory, Research and Practice*, edited by Randall G. Rogan, Mitchell R. Hammer, and Clinton R. Van Zandt, 151–60. Westport: Praeger.

Holmes, Janet. 1986. "Functions of You Know in Women and Men's Speech." *Language and Society* 15 (1): 1–21.

James, Richard K. 2007. *Crisis Intervention Strategies*. Belmont: Thomson Brooks/Cole.

Kamphuis, Wim, Ellen Giebels, and Sigrid Noelanders. 2006. "Effective Influencing in Crisis Negotiations: The Role of Type of Incident and Incident Phase." *Nederlands Tijdschrift voor de Psychologie [Dutch Journal of Psychology]* 21: 83–100.

Kelln, Brad, and C. Meghan McMurtry. 2007. "STEPS-Structured Tactical Engagement Process: A Model for Crisis Negotiation." *Journal of Police Crisis Negotiations* 7 (2): 29–51.

Lanceley, Frederick J. 1999. *On-Scene Guide for Crisis Negotiators*. Boca Raton: CRC Press.

Madrigal, Demetrius O., Daniel R. Bowman, and Bryan U. McClain. 2009. "Introducing the Four-Phase Model of Hostage Negotiation." *Journal of Police Crisis Negotiations* 9 (2): 119–33.

McMains, Michael J., and Wayman C. Mullins. 1996. *Crisis Negotiations: Managing Critical Incidents and Situations in Law Enforcement and Corrections*. Cincinnati: Anderson.

McMains, Michael J., and Wayman C. Mullins. 2001. *Crisis Negotiations: Managing Critical Incidents and Situations in Law Enforcement and Corrections* (second edition). Cincinnati: Anderson.

McMains, Michael J., and Wayman C. Mullins. 2014. *Crisis Negotiations: Managing Critical Incidents and Situations in Law Enforcement and Corrections* (fifth edition). New York: Routledge.

Miller, Laurence. 2005. "Hostage Negotiation: Psychological Principles and Practices." *International Journal of Emergency Mental Health* 7 (4): 277–98.

Mohandie, Kris. 2010. "The Psychology of Hostage Takers, Suicidal and Barricaded Subjects." In *Contemporary Theory, Research, and Practice of Crisis and Hostage Negotiation*, edited by Randall G. Rogan and Frederick J. Lanceley, 155–176. Cresskill: Hampton.

Mullins, Wayman C. 2002. "Advanced Communication Techniques for Hostage Negotiators." *Journal of Police Crisis Negotiations* 2 (1): 63–81.

National Policing Improvement Agency. 2011. *The Use of Negotiators by Incident Commanders*. London: National Policing Improvement Agency. Retrieved from http://library.college.police.uk/docs/acpo/National-Negotiators-Briefing-Paper-Final-Locked-2011.pdf .

Putnam, Linda L., and Michael E. Roloff, eds. 1992. *Communication and Negotiation*. Newbury Park: Sage.

Prochaska, James, and Carlo DiClemente, 1986. "Toward a Comprehensive Model of Change." In *Treating Addictive Behaviors: Processes of Change*, edited by William R. Millar and Nick Heather, 3–27. New York: Plenum Press.

Regini, Chuck. 2002. "Crisis Negotiation Teams: Selection and Training." *FBI Law Enforcement Bulletin* 71: 1–5. Retrieved from https://leb.fbi.gov/file-repository/archives/nov02leb.pdf/view .

Rogan, Randall G. 2011. "Linguistic Style Matching in Crisis Negotiations: A Comparative Analysis of Suicidal and Surrender Outcomes." *Journal of Police Crisis Negotiations* 11 (1): 20–39.

Rogan, Randall G., and Mitchell R. Hammer. 1995. "Assessing Message Affect in Crisis Negotiations: An Exploratory Study." *Human Communication Research* 21 (4): 553–74.

Rogan, Randall G., Mitchell R. Hammer, and Clinton R. Van Zandt. 1997. *Dynamic Processes of Crisis Negotiation: Theory, Research and Practice*. Westport: Praeger.

Royce, Terry. 2005. "The Negotiator and the Bomber: Analyzing the Critical Role of Active Listening in Crisis Negotiations." *Negotiation Journal* 21 (1): 5–27.

Rubin, Gabriela B. 2016. *Negotiation Power through Tag Questions in Crisis Negotiations*. Unpublished master's thesis. Georgetown University, Washington DC.

Schlossberg, Harvey. 1974. *Psychologist with a Gun*. New York: Coward, McCann & Geoghegan Press.

Schlossberg, Harvey. 1980. "Values and Organization in Hostage and Crisis Negotiation Teams." *Annals of the New York Academy of Sciences* 347: 113–16.

Sikveland, Rein O., Heidi Kevoe-Feldman, and Elizabeth Stokoe. 2019. "Overcoming Suicidal Persons' Resistance Using Productive Communicative Challenges during Police Crisis Negotiations." *Applied Linguistics* 41 (4): 533–551.

Slatkin, Arthur A. 2002. "The Use of Stratagems in Crisis and Hostage Negotiation." *Law and Order* 50 (9): 250–54.

Slatkin, Arthur A. 2010. *Communication in Crisis and Hostage Negotiations* (second edition). Springfield: Charles C. Thomas.

Soliz, Jordan, and Howard Giles. 2014. "Relational and Identity Processes in Communication: A Contextual and Meta-Analytical Review of Communication Accommodation Theory." *Annals of the International Communication Association* 38: 107–44. Thousand Oaks: Sage.

Soskis, David A., and Clinton R. Van Zandt. 1986. "Hostage Negotiation: Law Enforcement's Most Effective Nonlethal Weapon." *Behavioral Sciences and the Law* 4 (4): 423–35.

Stokoe, Elizabeth, and Rein O. Sikveland. 2019. "The Backstage Work Negotiators Do When Communicating with Persons in Crisis." *Journal of Psycholinguistics* 24 (2): 185–208.

Taylor, Paul J. 2002a. "A Cylindrical Model of Communication Behavior in Crisis Negotiations." *Human Communication Research* 28 (1): 7–48.

Taylor, Paul J. 2002b. "A Partial Order Scalogram Analysis of Communication Behavior in Crisis Negotiation with the Prediction of Outcome." *International Journal of Conflict Management* 13 (1): 4–37.

Taylor, Paul J., and Ian Donald. 2003. "Foundations and Evidence for an Interaction-Based Approach to Conflict Negotiation." *International Journal of Conflict Management* 14 (3–4): 213–32.

Taylor, Paul J., and Sally Thomas. 2008. "Linguistic Style Matching and Negotiation Outcome." *Negotiation and Conflict Management Research* 1 (3): 263–81.

Tyler, Tom R., and Yuen J. Huo. (2002). *Trust in the Law: Encouraging Public Cooperation with the Police and Courts*. Thousand Oaks: Sage.

Ury, William. 1991. *Getting Past No: Negotiating with Difficult People*. New York: Bantam Books.

Van Hasselt, Vincent B., Stephen J. Romano, and Gregory M. Vecchi. 2008. "Role Playing: Applications in Hostage and Crisis Negotiation Skills Training." *Behavior Modification* 32 (2): 248–63.

Vecchi, Gregory M. 2009. "Critical Incident Response, Management, and Resolution: Structure and Interaction in Barricaded Hostage, Barricaded Crisis, and Kidnapping Situations." *Inside Homeland Security* (Summer): 7–16.

Vecchi, Gregory M., Vincent B. Van Hasselt, and Stephen J. Romano. 2005. "Crisis (Hostage) Negotiation: Current Strategies and Issues in High-Risk Conflict Resolution." *Aggression and Violent Behavior* 10 (5): 533–51.

Wilmot, William, and Joyce Hocker. 2018. *Interpersonal Conflict* (eighth edition). New York: McGraw-Hill Higher Educational.

CHAPTER 19

Improving Law Enforcement Responses to Gender-Based Violence

Domestic and International Perspectives

Caroline Bettinger-López and Tamar Ezer

Gender-based violence (GBV) is a pandemic that is globally ubiquitous, despite decades of efforts to address it through public health, criminal justice, education, and social welfare sectors (Smith et al. 2017).[1] GBV refers to harms inflicted on women, girls, and LGBT/gender-non-conforming individuals disproportionately or due to prevailing gender norms (see chapters 6 and 7). It includes intimate partner violence, sexual assault, and stalking and encompasses "physical, sexual, psychological or economic harm or suffering . . . , threats of such acts, harassment, coercion and arbitrary deprivation of liberty" (CEDAW 2017, 5).

GBV respects no boundaries—geographic, social, or economic—and the statistics are staggering:

- globally, one in three women has experienced physical and/or sexual violence at some point in her life (United Nations Statistics Division 2015);
- approximately three women die in the United States per day as a result of domestic violence, and for every woman killed, nine more are critically injured (Campbell, Glass, Sharps, Laughon, and Bloom 2007; DOJ 2015; Planty, Langton, Krebs, Berzofsky, and Smiley-McDonald 2013);

- nearly one in five women (19.1 percent) in the United States have been raped (Smith et al. 2017); and
- half of transgender people and bisexual women in the United States will experience sexual violence at some point in their lives (Blondeel et al. 2017; Human Rights Campaign 2020; OHCHR 2015).

Despite the devastating prevalence of GBV, the United Nations (UN) has reported that in most countries, less than 40 percent of women who experienced violence sought any sort of help, and of those, less than 10 percent sought help from the police (United Nations Statistics Division 2015). This reflects a profound mistrust of state systems whose frontline responders are usually law enforcement officers and whose purported mission is to protect and serve.

The reasons behind the fraught relationship between survivors and law enforcement are complex. They range from a lack of effective trainings on responding to GBV and communicating with survivors, to the use of investigation and prosecution policies and practices that do not account for the effects of trauma on victims, to a lack of accountability mechanisms for misconduct, including GBV perpetrated by law enforcement officers themselves, to biases (gender and otherwise) that are ingrained in the criminal legal system. These dynamics particularly impact survivors from marginalized or underserved communities, who often have a deep intergroup mistrust of the police (Richie 2012; see chapters 5-9).

Two 2015 studies provide more detail on these experiences (ACLU 2015; Logan and Valente 2015). One of these studies, conducted by the National Domestic Violence Hotline, found that less than 50 percent of women who had experienced intimate partner abuse had interacted with police about their abuse. Moreover, a substantial number of survivors—both those who had called the police and those who had not—were reluctant to turn to law enforcement for help:

- 1 in 4 reported that they would not call the police in future;
- more than half said calling the police would make things worse;
- two-thirds or more said they were afraid the police would not believe them or do nothing; and
- 43 percent of the participants who had called the police felt the police had discriminated against them, with 46 percent pointing to gender bias (Logan and Valente 2015).

A national survey by the ACLU and GBV experts also found discrimination to be a key concern among over nine hundred advocates. Of those surveyed, 55 percent "believed that police bias or discrimination against particular groups [i.e. women, immigrants, poor people, lesbian, gay, bisexual, transgendered (LGBTQ) individuals] or with regard to domestic violence/sexual assault claims was a problem in their community." Additionally, 69 percent of respondents believed police "sometimes" or "often" show bias toward women (ACLU 2015). Together, these surveys show the significance of gender bias in police responses to GBV, and the effects of bias on how people engage with the criminal legal system.

While law enforcement response is only one component of a comprehensive approach to GBV, it is a critical piece, particularly in the context of high-risk situations and when survivors seek to engage with the police. It is the state's responsibility to ensure that law enforcement response is effective, trauma-informed, and free from bias. While many survivors are reluctant to turn to the police, many others rely on them to interrupt violence or to provide protection from abusive partners. In fact, domestic violence calls make up the largest category (15 percent to 50 percent) of 911 calls received by police (Klein 2009). Although these calls are among the most dangerous assignments for survivors as well as responding officers (Breul and Keith 2016; Breul and Luongo 2017; Johnson 2011), improving the response to GBV is generally not a law enforcement priority. Indeed, national conversations about bias in policing have tended to focus more on race and national origin than sex or gender identity and often do not address the intersection of these issues (Ghandnoosh 2015; Goff, Robinson, King and Romero 2020; Opportunity Agenda 2018).

The issue of gender bias in policing has, however, gained greater attention in recent years. The above-mentioned studies and several books have prompted a reexamination of the role of the criminal legal system in addressing domestic violence (e.g., Goodmark 2018; Ritchie 2017). In 2011, the US Department of Justice (DOJ) began stepping up its investigations into discriminatory law enforcement responses to GBV in several cities (Bettinger-Lopez 2016; Park 2015; Tuerkheimer 2016); and, in 2015, the DOJ published a guide titled *Identifying and Preventing Gender Bias in Law Enforcement Response to Sexual Assault and Domestic Violence* (DOJ 2015).[2] The guide was created to improve responses to GBV by the eighteen thousand law enforcement agencies (LEAs) across the United States. It articulates eight principles and provides detailed examples for each:

1. recognize and address biases, assumptions, and stereotypes about victims;
2. treat all victims with respect and employ interviewing tactics that encourage a victim to participate and provide facts about the incident;
3. investigate sexual assault or domestic violence complaints thoroughly and effectively;
4. appropriately classify reports of sexual assault or domestic violence;
5. refer victims to appropriate services;
6. properly identify the assailant in domestic violence incidents;
7. hold officers who commit sexual assault or domestic violence accountable; and
8. maintain, review, and act upon data regarding sexual assault and domestic violence.

In 2016, the DOJ gave nearly $10 million in grants to police departments and experts in gender violence and policing to implement the guidance nationwide (DOJ 2016). From those grants, the International Association of Chiefs of Police (IACP) has developed a national demonstration site initiative to strengthen law enforcement response to domestic and sexual violence, involving six police departments across the United States (IACP 2016), and has revised its Model Policy on Domestic Violence and developed a toolkit, assessment tool, and other core resources to enhance agency responses to survivors and address gender bias (IACP 2018a, 2018b, 2019, 2020b). Additionally, the Police Executive Research Forum, End Violence Against Women International, Battered Women's Justice

Project, Futures Without Violence, among others received grants to provide training and technical assistance programs to improve the law enforcement response to GBV (DOJ 2016). This increased attention on gender bias in policing has provided unprecedented resources to the field.

In 2018, as the #MeToo movement surged worldwide, our Human Rights Clinic launched the COURAGE in Policing Project (COURAGE = Community Oriented and United Responses to Address Gender Violence and Equality).[3] This project works with community-based organizations, police departments, and GBV experts locally, nationally, and globally on improving law enforcement responses to GBV. The project aims to increase access to safety and justice for all survivors, with a particular focus on Black and brown women, immigrant women, disabled women, indigenous women, LGBTQI individuals, and other underserved populations. Over the past year, the COURAGE project developed and administered two surveys—one for domestic violence and sexual assault survivors and one for advocates—to better understand marginalized communities' experiences with law enforcement response to domestic violence and sexual assault in Miami-Dade County. COURAGE's quantitative and qualitative analysis conducted on an ethnically diverse group of ninety-eight survivors showed alarming rates of perceived bias due to immigration status, gender, and abuser connections with the police. In collaboration with partners, the project is currently developing additional surveys, model policies, trainings, supervision protocols, reports, online resources, and systems of accountability for law enforcement responses to GBV, including research and tools specific to the COVID-19 context.

INTERNATIONAL HUMAN RIGHTS LAW FRAMEWORK

International human rights law reinforces efforts to address gender bias in policing. We offer here a few thoughts on the synergies between international human rights law and the DOJ guidance.

First, we note that the DOJ guidance speaks to the central issue of gender bias presented in the 2011 case of *Jessica Lenahan v. United States* (IACHR 2011). There, the Inter-American Commission on Human Rights found that the Castle Rock, Colorado, police had exhibited gender bias in failing to respond meaningfully to a domestic violence victim's calls for help (resulting in the tragic deaths of her three daughters). The commission recommended that state actors in the United States

> continue adopting public policies and institutional programs aimed at restructuring the stereotypes of domestic violence victims, and . . . promote the eradication of discriminatory socio-cultural patterns that impede women and children's full protection from domestic violence acts, including programs to train public officials in all branches of the administration of justice and police, and comprehensive prevention programs. (IACHR 2011, 60)

The Commission's recommendation echoes the language of the UN Convention on the Elimination of All Forms Discrimination Against Women (CEDAW), which calls for the modification of "social and cultural pattern of conduct" to eliminate "prejudices and customary and all other practices which are based on the idea of the inferiority or the superiority of either of the sexes or on stereotyped roles for men and women" (OAS 1994; UN CEDAW 1979).

Under international human rights law, all countries have the responsibility to exercise "due diligence" in the GBV context—that is, to prevent, investigate, punish, and remedy acts of GBV. This applies whether the perpetrator is a state or non-state actor, and whether an act is committed in an official or private capacity (CEDAW 2015a, 2016; IACHR 1999, 2011). This is because GBV violates fundamental rights to equality and non-discrimination (OAS 1969; UN CEDAW 1979; UN ICCPR 1966; UN ICESCR 1966; UN UDHR 1948), life (OAS 1948, 1969; UN ICCPR 1966; UN UDHR 1948), health (OAS 1948; UN CEDAW 1979; UN ICESCR 1966), security of person (OAS 1969; UN ICCPR 1966; UN UDHR 1948), privacy (OAS 1948; UN ICCPR 1966; UN UDHR 1948), and freedom from torture and cruel, inhuman, or degrading treatment (OAS 1969; UN CAT 1984; UN ICCPR 1966). Moreover, GBV can prevent individuals from exercising further economic and political rights.

Human rights law expresses particular concern with LEAs in the GBV context. The CEDAW committee, charged with monitoring countries' compliance, calls for "mandatory, recurrent and effective capacity-building, education and training of . . . law enforcement officers . . . to adequately prevent and address gender-based violence against women" (CEDAW 2017, 14). The Inter-American Convention on the Prevention, Punishment and Eradication of Violence against Women requires states "to promote the education and training of all those involved in the administration of justice, police and other law enforcement" in order to advance "prevention, punishment and eradication of violence against women" (OAS 1994). And in *Lenahan v. U.S.*, the Commission recommended "training programs . . . and the design of model protocols and directives" for law enforcement as a means of protecting GBV victims (IACHR 2011, 60). However, without accountability, even optimal law enforcement training scenarios are insufficient alone to address the deep-seated gender and intersectional biases that exist in law enforcement.

HUMAN RIGHTS PRINCIPLES AND RESPONSES TO GBV

In the remainder of this chapter, we focus on four human rights principles that are essential to effectively respond to GBV, and that resonate with the DOJ guidance: accountability for officer-perpetrated GBV; trauma-informed interactions with survivors; effective investigation of GBV reports, and attention to intersecting forms of discrimination.

Accountability for Officer-Perpetrated GBV

Recent examinations of officer-perpetrated GBV reveal alarming statistics. Take, for example, the DOJ Civil Rights Division's pattern and practice investigation of the Puerto Rico Police Department, which found that ninety-eight officers had been arrested more than once on domestic violence charges between 2007 and 2010, and that of these, eighty-four remained active on the force, five were placed on leave, and only nine had been terminated (DOJ 2011). Moreover, the DOJ found vastly higher numbers of reported murders than forcible rapes—a phenomenon not seen in any other jurisdiction in the United States, and certainly an indication of underreporting (DOJ 2011, 57).

The new Henry A. Wallace Police Crime Public Database, based at Bowling Green State University, reveals similarly startling statistics on police officer-involved domestic violence and sexual assault. The database provides summary information that is not otherwise aggregated or publicly available for more than ten thousand criminal arrest cases of nonfederal sworn law enforcement officers (e.g., police officers, state troopers, deputy sheriffs) from the years 2005 to 2014. Of 9,088 criminal arrest cases of United States nonfederal sworn law enforcement officers between 2005 and 2013, the database showed 1,259 arrests for domestic/family violence, 405 arrests for forcible rape, 636 arrests for forcible fondling, and 209 arrests for forcible sodomy—likely just the tip of the iceberg (Goodmark 2015; Lave 2019; McLaughlin 2018; Stinson 2020). Marginalized survivors—Black and brown women, immigrant women, disabled women, poor women, and LGBTQI individuals—are disparately impacted by officer-involved gender violence because they are often not believed and have fewer resources (Goodmark 2009; Ritchie 2017).

Principle 7 of the DOJ guidance—"[h]old officers who commit sexual assault or domestic violence accountable"—echoes IACP's long-standing "zero-tolerance policy" for GBV perpetrated by police officers (IACP 2003a, 2; IACP 2003b). Police departments that turn a blind eye toward officers who perpetrate GBV send an unmistakable message to both their personnel and the community that responding to GBV is not a departmental priority. Moreover, police officers are especially dangerous when they perpetrate private acts of violence, as they have command authority, possess weapons, and have access to information (such as how to manipulate legal systems, and the location of confidential shelters), and specialized technology.

The DOJ guidance recommends that LEAs develop policies and practices that provide, at a minimum, for internal investigations of allegations of officer-involved gender violence, "irrespective of whether the officer was acting in his or her official capacity at the time." Moreover, "law enforcement agencies should refer allegations of officer misconduct involving potential criminal activity to the local prosecutor's office" (DOJ 2015, 21).

Trauma-Informed Interactions

LEAs may revictimize a GBV survivor by failing to take a trauma-informed approach. Trauma is rooted in the experience of helplessness and terror that "overwhelm[s] the ordinary systems of care that give people a sense of control, connection, and meaning" (Herman 1992, 33). An individual plummets into a primal response of fight, flight, or freeze, which can have crippling consequences, both directly after an event and for a significant time later (Herman 1992). By the time a law enforcement officer arrives at the scene of a GBV incident, a survivor has already endured a primary trauma and the police officer is likely the first official they encounter (Love-Craighead 2015). A trauma-informed approach is thus critical. According to the US Substance Abuse and Mental

Health Services Administration, a trauma-informed approach recognizes the symptoms and impact of trauma and pathways to recovery; integrates this knowledge into policies and practices; and seeks to avoid retraumatization (SAMHSA 2014).

Principle 2 of the DOJ guidance calls for communicating with and treating "all victims with respect" and "trauma-informed interviewing techniques" (DOJ 2015, 12; IACP 2020a). It recognizes that taking a trauma-informed approach is not only important for survivors but also critical to the success of GBV investigations: "A victim who is treated with respect is more likely to continue participating in an investigation and prosecution than one who feels judged or blamed for a sexual assault or domestic violence incident" (DOJ 2015, 12; see chapters 8 and 22). Moreover, "by taking affirmative steps to respect the dignity of all complainants, law enforcement officers may be able to increase the quality and quantity of the information they receive" (DOJ 2015, 12).

The DOJ guidance highlights the importance of "*how* and *when*" LEAs ask difficult questions in investigating complaints (see chapter 13). As an initial matter, investigations should respect the survivor's privacy and never be conducted in public areas. Additionally, if survivors desire, they should have the support of a victim advocate (DOJ 2015). LEAs should be communicative, nonjudgmental, and seek to establish trust, asking "neutral, open-ended questions that elicit a narrative of the events" (DOJ 2015, 13). Furthermore, certain questions are always inappropriate since they ignore the emotional impact of trauma, blame the victim, challenge credibility, or indicate that a survivor should not have reported a complaint. LEA reports from interviews should present events from the survivor's perspective and incorporate the "victim's words, spontaneous statements, and narrative as much as possible, as opposed to providing the officer's summary" (DOJ 2015, 14).

While the DOJ guidance focuses on a trauma-informed approach to interviewing, this approach should apply beyond the interviewing stage, to all interactions with survivors. A trauma-informed approach is based on a few key principles. First, it is survivor-centered (CEDAW 2017), respecting fundamental dignity and addressing survivors' safety and immediate needs (IACP 2018c). Second, it seeks to reinstate a sense of control and agency, allowing for choice and the survivor's voice to shape next steps. Third, it integrates peer support. Finally, it provides attention to culture, history, and intersecting forms of discrimination (SAMHSA 2014).

It is important to recognize that trauma does not just occur at an individual level; it can also impact communities and be passed down to future generations (Castelloe 2012; DeAngelis 2019; Hoffart and Jones 2018). This transmission of trauma may even have a genetic component, as indicated by a study of Holocaust survivors (Youssef et al. 2018). In the United States, we are still struggling with the lingering effects of slavery (Love 2016) and massive violence against Indigenous peoples (Hoffart and Jones 2018). Community and historical trauma thus overlays and impacts the interactions of survivors from marginalized communities with law enforcement (see this book's conclusion).

Effective Investigation of GBV Reports

Principle 3 of the DOJ guidance emphasizes the importance of law enforcement conducting thorough and effective investigations into GBV. This can be particularly challenging for GBV cases, as "[u]nlike many other crimes, incidents of sexual assault and domestic violence frequently occur in more private settings, with few, if any, witnesses present." The guidance exhorts LEAs to "undertake a thorough investigation of these crimes by gathering, preserving and analyzing as much evidence, particularly corroborative evidence, as quickly as they can" (DOJ 2015, 16).

To achieve this, LEAs are encouraged to "implement clear policies and training about how to conduct domestic and sexual violence investigations that are complete and bias-free" (DOJ 2015, 16). This means, at a minimum, developing guidelines on "collecting and preserving all relevant and corroborative evidence; ensuring that forensic medical exams, including 'rape kits,' are completed and analyzed in a timely manner; identifying and documenting victim injuries, both at the time of the incident and during subsequent interactions; identifying and documenting all psychological and sensory evidence; and interviewing all possible witnesses and suspects and conducting each interview separately" (DOJ 2015, 16). An effective investigation is critical for both substantive justice (seeking to uncover the truth, free from bias) and procedural justice (providing a fair and transparent process to survivors).

Attention to Intersecting Forms of Discrimination

Gender bias is further compounded by intersecting forms of discrimination, including on the basis of race, ethnicity, disability (see chapters 7–9), and immigration or economic status. As indicated by the ACLU report discussed above, marginalized survivors are disparately impacted by biased law enforcement responses because they are often not believed and have fewer resources (ACLU 2015; Crenshaw 1991; Goodmark 2009). The DOJ acknowledges that "the intersection of racial and gender stereotypes and biases can also pose unique difficulties for women and LGBT individuals of color seeking police services to address sexual assault and domestic violence incidents" (DOJ 2015, 7) but does not delve further into this.

We embrace the intersectionality framework originally developed by Black feminists to call attention to multiple forms of discrimination experienced by Black women and girls (Crenshaw 1989), who are all too often "over-policed and under-protected" (Crenshaw, Williams, Ocen, and Nanda 2015). Intersectionality recognizes identity as inseparable from a person's life experiences and the accumulation of vulnerabilities from several levels of societal marginalization (Crenshaw 1989). Intersectional discrimination both "increases the risk of violence and heightens the adverse consequences of violence when it occurs," as the CEDAW committee recognized in the context of missing and murdered Indigenous women (CEDAW 2015b, 48). Intersectionality provides a useful framework for understanding the lived experiences of survivors who identify with marginalized and underserved populations.

An intersectional approach to GBV requires the collection of disaggregated data to enable improvements and accountability (an approach echoed in Principle 8 of the DOJ guidance; CEDAW 2017). It further calls for law enforcement trainings and regulations that take into account "the diversity of women and the risks of intersecting forms of discrimination" (CEDAW 2017, 8, 14).

DOMESTIC VIOLENCE AND COVID-19

While this chapter was largely written before the trifecta of the COVID-19 pandemic, a deep economic recession, and civil unrest over systemic and overt racism, the human rights principles it highlights are now more crucial than ever. Rising numbers of sick people, growing unemployment, increased anxiety and financial stress, the large number of firearms purchased in recent months, a scarcity of community resources, and increased anxiety, financial stress, and consumption of alcohol or drugs have set the stage for an exacerbated domestic violence crisis (see Bettinger-Lopez and Bro 2020). Meanwhile, heightened scrutiny of discrimination and violence against Black people has led to calls by Black Lives Matter and others to defund the police and dismantle the criminal legal system.

Experts have characterized domestic violence in times of COVID-19 as a "ticking time bomb," or a perfect storm, and data from the United States and around the world supports this characterization (Chandra 2020; Dzhanova 2020; Gearin and Knight 2020; Godin 2020; Grierson 2020; Kingkade 2020; Ntsaluba 2020; Piquero et al. 2020; Wanqing 2020). Many pathways link pandemics such as COVID-19 and violence against women and children (particularly those from marginalized communities), including: reduced health service availability and access to first responders and justice systems; quarantines and social isolation; exposure to exploitative relationships due to changing demographics; inability of women to temporarily escape abusive partners; virus-specific sources of violence; exposure to violence and coercion in response efforts; and economic insecurity and poverty-related stress (Peterman et al. 2020).

More research must be conducted to understand the pathways that link pandemics such as COVID-19 and violence against women and children, determine the magnitude of the problem, highlight linkages with other social and economic factors, and inform intervention and response options. The Human Rights Clinic at University of Miami School of Law has initiated a project to conduct ephemeral, real-time research into governmental and nongovernmental interventions that respond to domestic violence during the COVID-19 pandemic. We have begun this inquiry with a focus on South Florida, a hard-hit urban area with a diverse population. Using survey instruments, interviews, and focus group discussions, we are evaluating how three sets of stakeholders—local domestic violence service providers (e.g., domestic violence helplines, shelters and other safe accommodations, counseling, hospitals and health care facilities, and legal service organizations), state actors (e.g., law enforcement agencies and family law and justice systems), and the private sector (e.g., corporations, universities, private nonprofits, religious organizations)—have responded to domestic and sexual violence during the COVID-19 pandemic, and how the crisis impacted these stakeholders' abilities to respond. Questions seek to identify services that are no longer available during the pandemic or are being delivered through new platforms; the stakeholders' greatest pandemic-related challenges; the stakeholders' evolving plans to resume normal operations; and how information on these topics is being shared with victims, families, and governmental and nongovernmental actors, including service providers.

Initial survey results show just how unprepared many organizations, especially those that do not have a strong community presence, have been to respond to victims during this pandemic. To address this, the Human Rights Clinic is creating an online collaboration database, which collects and codes information into a list reflecting how service providers are currently operating and allows service providers to update the list in real time. Ultimately, we hope to generate policy recommendations for how all system actors—governmental and nongovernmental, for-profit and nonprofit—should address domestic violence during this COVID-19 pandemic and, by extension, in future natural disasters and public health emergencies.

CONCLUSIONS

Amid increased calls for police accountability in the wake of the recent murders of Breonna Taylor, George Floyd, Tony McDade, and others, anti-GBV advocates and scholars are taking a hard and critical look at the reliance of the movement to end violence against women on the criminal legal system, for which law enforcement serves as the gateway. Their message: "Don't Use Domestic Violence Victims to Derail Police Reform" (Donegan 2020; Gruber and Goodmark 2020; Jeltsen 2020). These critics point to the research discussed earlier in this chapter, reflecting significant disapproval and mistrust of law enforcement by GBV survivors, especially survivors of color and those from other historically marginalized groups. In step with the movement for Black Lives Matter and other police reform agendas, these anti-GBV advocates are actively seeking new approaches that avoid the unintentional negative consequences of the criminalization of abuse—particularly in the context of the current pandemic, when intimate partners and families are stuck at home together and where carceral spaces (including prisons, jails, and detention centers) are COVID-19 hotbeds that can serve as a death sentence for detained individuals.

While criminalization of individuals who inflict GBV has historically been viewed as a proxy for justice, advocates and scholars are proposing alternative frameworks, such as "violence interruption," restorative justice, community justice, collective healing, economic justice, health and housing justice, and "police abolition" (Coker 2017; Coker and Macquoid 2015; Goodmark 2014; HAVI 2020; NCST 2020; Next City 2020; Weissman 2019). We endorse these calls for increased research and investment in non-criminal approaches to preventing and responding to GBV, and we believe they are in line with a human rights-based, "due diligence" approach (Goldshied and Liebowitz 2014).

While we must develop and embrace a long-term vision for safety, justice, and healing for survivors, we also believe that we must develop viable models to improve police response to GBV for the foreseeable future. For such a devastating and deadly problem, we must approach the problem in the here-and-now with tactical precision. That means investing in the alternative approaches outlined above, but it also means insisting on improvements to the criminal legal system that currently exists. In the COVID-19 context, for instance, it means advocating for decarceration of many detained individuals. But in the GBV realm, it means doing so only after conducting a lethality/danger assessment and notification, consultation, and safety planning with survivors whose lives could be at risk by the imminent release of a person who has caused harm to them.

Human rights principles compel many changes to the current system: an increase in research, which is woefully underfunded in the GBV space; more focus on prevention of GBV and protection of survivors that is directly informed by the voices and perspectives of survivors; increasing gender diversity of police forces (women make up just 12.6 percent of all police officers in the United States; Brooks 2020); and a focus on operationalization of the human rights principles laid out in this chapter. Moreover, efforts to operationalize these principles, including trainings, protocols, and accountability mechanisms, should be evaluated for efficacy. The American Public Health Association, for instance, highlights the absence of rigorous evaluation of trainings to tackle implicit bias (APHA 2018). A future administration should also develop a national action plan on GBV that takes a strategic and tactical approach to improving and reforming our national, state, and local responses to GBV—a plan that allows us to dream big and is accompanied by sufficient funding to realize our larger goals (Bettinger-Lopez 2019).

While the role of law enforcement will likely evolve in response to these crises, it remains an important system actor in the GBV context for the foreseeable future. It is thus critical that LEAs espouse and implement the following principles, expanding on the DOJ guidance: accountability for officer-perpetrated GBV; trauma-informed interactions with survivors; effective investigation of GBV reports; and attention to intersecting forms of discrimination. Doing so will help prevent gender and other intersectional forms of bias, thereby improving responses to GBV and contributing to a safer world for all of us.

NOTES

1. The authors would like to thank our students in the Human Rights Clinic and research assistants at the University of Miami School of Law for their research on which this analysis builds. In particular, we are grateful for the work of Fernando Bertoncello, Anabel Blanco, Alexander Englert, Gideon Levy, and Meredith Shea. We are also grateful for input and feedback from our colleagues Denisse Cordova Montes, Aviva Kurash, and Alexis Piquero.

2. Between 2011 and 2016, the DOJ initiated investigations into gender bias in police response to domestic violence and/or sexual assault in New Orleans, Puerto Rico, Missoula, Maricopa County, Newark, and Baltimore.

3. For more information on the COURAGE in Policing Project, see http://www.law.miami.edu/courage.

REFERENCES

ACLU. American Civil Liberties Union. 2015. "Responses from the Field: Sexual Assault, Domestic Violence, and Policing." American Civil Liberties Union. Retrieved from http://www.aclu.org/responsesfromthefield.

APHA. American Public Health Association, End Police Violence Collective. 2018. "Addressing Law Enforcement Violence as a Public Health Issue: The 2018 Statement." Retrieved from https://www.endingpoliceviolence.com/.

Bettinger-Lopez, Caroline. 2016. "Identifying and Preventing Gender Bias in Law Enforcement Response to Sexual and Domestic Violence." USA.gov. Retrieved from https://obamawhitehouse.archives.gov/blog/2016/10/28/identifying-and-preventing-gender-bias-law-enforcement-response-sexual-assault-and .

Bettinger-Lopez, Caroline. 2019. "Developing a National Plan of Action on Violence against Women and Gender Violence: A Human Rights Approach." In the *Politicization of Safety*, edited by Jane Stoever, 362–78. New York: New York University Press.

Bettinger-Lopez, Caroline, and Alexandra Bro. 2020. "A Double Pandemic: Domestic Violence in the Age of COVID-19." Council on Foreign Relations. Retrieved from https://www.cfr.org/in-brief/double-pandemic-domestic-violence-age-covid-19 .

Blondeel, Karel, Sofia de Vasconcelos, Claudia García-Moreno, Rob Stephenson, Marleen Temmerman, and Igor Toskin. 2017. "Violence Motivated by Perception of Sexual Orientation and Gender Identity: A Systematic Review." *Bulletin of the World Health Organization* 96 (1): 29–41.

Breul, Nick, and Mike Keith. 2016. "Deadly Calls and Fatal Encounters: Analysis of U.S. Law Enforcement Line of Duty Deaths when Officers Responded to Dispatched Calls for Service and Conducted Enforcement (2010–2014)." US Department of Justice. Retrieved from https://www.scribd.com/document/358277211/Department-of-Justice-report-on-officer-deaths .

Breul, Nick, and Desiree Luongo. 2017. "Making It Safer: A Study of Law Enforcement Fatalities between 2010–2016." US Department of Justice. Retrieved from https://cops.usdoj.gov/RIC/Publications/cops-w0858-pub.pdf .

Brooks, Rosa. 2020. "One Reason for Police Violence? Too Many Men with Badges." *Washington Post*. Retrieved from https://www.washingtonpost.com/outlook/2020/06/18/women-police-officers-violence/ .

Campbell, Jacquelyn C., Nancy Glass, Phyllis W. Sharps, Kathryn Laughon, and Tina Bloom. 2007. "Intimate Partner Homicide: Review and Implications of Research and Policy." *Trauma, Violence & Abuse* 8 (3): 246–69.

Castelloe, Molly S. 2012. "How Trauma Is Carried Across Generations." *Psychology Today*. Retrieved from https://www.psychologytoday.com/us/blog/the-me-in-we/201205/how-trauma-is-carried-across-generations .

CEDAW. United Nations Committee on the Elimination of Discrimination against Women. 2015a. *X and Y v. Georgia*, Comm. No. 24/2009, UN Doc. CEDAW/C/61/D/24/2009 .

CEDAW. United Nations Committee on the Elimination of Discrimination against Women. 2015b. "Report of the Inquiry Concerning Canada of the Committee on the Elimination of Discrimination against Women under article 8 of the Optional Protocol to the Convention on the Elimination of All Forms of Discrimination against Women." UN Doc. CEDAW/C/OP.8/CAN/1. United Nations. Retrieved from https://undocs.org/CEDAW/C/OP.8/CAN/1 .

CEDAW. United Nations Committee on the Elimination of Discrimination against Women. 2016. *M.W. v. Denmark*, Comm. No. 46/2012, U.N. Doc. CEDAW/C/63/D/46/2012 .

CEDAW. United Nations Committee on the Elimination of Discrimination against Women. 2017. "General recommendation No. 35 on gender-based violence against women, updating general recommendation No. 19." U.N. Doc. CEDAW/C/GC/35. United Nations. Retrieved from https://undocs.org/CEDAW/C/GC/35 .

Chandra, Jagriti. 2020. "Covid-19 Lockdown | Rise in Domestic Violence, Police Apathy: NCW." *The Hindu*. Retrieved from https://www.thehindu.com/news/national/covid-19-lockdown-spike-in-domestic-violence-says-ncw/article31238659.ece .

Coker, Donna K. 2017. "Crime Logic, Campus Sexual Assault, and Restorative Justice." *Texas Tech Law Review* 49: 147–210, 147.

Coker, Donna K., and Ahjané Macquoid. 2015. "Alternative U.S. Responses to Intimate Partner Violence." In *Comparative Approaches to Domestic Viol*ence, edited by Rashmi Goel and Leigh Goodmark, 169–81. New York: Oxford University Press.

Crenshaw, Kimberlé. 1989. "Demarginalizing the Intersection of Race and Sex: A Black Feminist Critique of Antidiscrimination Doctrine, Feminist Theory and Antiracist Politics." *University of Chicago Legal Forum* 140 (1): 139–67.

Crenshaw, Kimberlé. 1991. "Mapping the Margins: Intersectionality, Identity Politics, and Violence against Women of Color." *Stanford Law Review* 43 (6): 1241–99.

Crenshaw, Kimberlé Williams, Priscilla Ocen, and Jyoti Nanda. 2015. "Black Girls Matter: Pushed Out, Overpoliced, and Underprotected." African American Policy Forum and Center for Intersectionality and Social Policy Studies. Retrieved from https://www.atlanticphilanthropies.org/wp-content/uploads/2015/09/BlackGirlsMatter_Report.pdf .

DeAngelis, Tori. 2019. "The Legacy of Trauma." *Monitor on Psychology* 50 (2): 36–42.

DOJ. US Department of Justice Civil Rights Division (DOJ). 2011. "Investigation of the Puerto Rico Police Department." Retrieved from https://www.justice.gov/sites/default/files/crt/legacy/2011/09/08/prpd_letter.pdf .

DOJ. US Department of Justice (DOJ). 2015. "Identifying and Preventing Gender Bias in Law Enforcement Response to Sexual Assault and Domestic Violence." Retrieved from https://www.justice.gov/opa/file/799366/download .

DOJ. US Department of Justice (DOJ). 2016. "Department of Justice Awards $9.85 Million to Identify and Prevent Gender Bias in Policing." Retrieved from https://www.justice.gov/opa/pr/department-justice-awards-985-million-identify-and-prevent-gender-bias-policing .

Donegan, Moira. 2020. "'Who Will Protect You from Rape without Police?' Here's My Answer to that Question." *The Guardian*. Retrieved from https://www.theguardian.com/commentisfree/2020/jun/17/abolish-police-sexual-assault-violence .

Dzhanova, Yelena. 2020. "NY Domestic Violence Programs see Client Numbers Decline as Coronavirus Traps Survivors at Home." CNBC. Retrieved from https://www.cnbc.com/2020/03/31/new-york-coronavirus-domestic-violence-programs-see-decline-as-disease-spreads.html .

Gearin, Mary, and Ben Knight. 2020. "Family Violence Perpetrators Using COVID-19 as 'a Form of Abuse We Have Not Experienced Before.'" Australia Broadcasting Corporation News. Retrieved from https://www.abc.net.au/news/2020-03-29/coronavirus-family-violence-surge-in-victoria/12098546 .

Ghandnoosh, Nazgol. 2015. *Black Lives Matter: Eliminating Racial Inequity in the Criminal Justice System*. The Sentencing Project. Retrieved from https://www.sentencingproject.org/publications/black-lives-matter-eliminating-racial-inequity-in-the-criminal-justice-system/ .

Godin, Melissa. 2020. "French Government to House Domestic Abuse Victims in Hotels as Cases Rise during Coronavirus Lockdown." *Time*. Retrieved from https://time.com/5812990/france-domestic-violence-hotel-coronavirus/ .

Goff, Phillip Atiba, Rashad Robinson, Bernice King, and Anthony D. Romero. 2020. TED Talk. "The Path to Ending Systemic Racism in the U.S." Retrieved from https://www.ted.com/talks/dr_phillip_atiba_goff_rashad_robinson_dr_bernice_king_anthony_d_romero_the_path_to_ending_systemic_racism_in_the_us .

Goldscheid, Julie, and Debra J. Liebowitz. 2014. "Due Diligence and Gender Violence: Parsing Its Power and Its Perils." *Cornell International Law Journal* 48 (2): 301–46.

Goodmark, Leigh. 2009. "Reframing Domestic Violence Law and Policy: An Anti-Essentialist Proposal." *Washington University Journal of Law & Policy* 31: 39–56.

Goodmark, Leigh. 2014. "Stalled at 20: VAWA, the Criminal Justice System, and the Possibilities of Restorative Justice." University of Maryland Legal Studies Research Paper 2015-3. Retrieved from SSRN: https://ssrn.com/abstract=2575646 .

Goodmark, Leigh. 2015. "Hands Up at Home: Militarized Masculinity and Police Officers Who Commit Intimate Partner Abuse." *Brigham Young University Law Review* 2015 (5): 1183–246.

Goodmark, Leigh. 2018. *Decriminalizing Domestic Violence: A Balanced Policy Approach to Intimate Partner Violence*. Berkeley: University of California Press.

Grierson, Jamie. 2020. "Calls for Funds to House Domestic Violence Victims during Covid-19 Outbreak." *The Guardian*. Retrieved from https://www.theguardian.com/society/2020/mar/31/call-for-uk-domestic-violence-refuges-to-get-coronavirus-funding .

Gruber, Aya, and Leigh Goodmark. 2020. "Domestic Violence Is also a Virus: During the Coronavirus Crisis, We Need the Right Criminal Justice Response to the Crime." *New York Daily News*. Retrieved from https://www.nydailynews.com/opinion/ny-20200326-gydiz22wcraptezg34wvyic3ma-story.html .

HAVI. Health Alliance for Violence Intervention. 2020. Retrieved from https://www.thehavi.org.

Herman, Judith. 1992. *Trauma and Recovery: The Aftermath of Violence—from Domestic Abuse to Political Terror*. New York: Basic Books.

Hoffart, Renée, and Nicholas A. Jones. 2018. "Intimate Partner Violence and Intergenerational Trauma among Indigenous Women." *International Criminal Justice Review* 28 (1): 25–44.

Human Rights Campaign. 2020. "Sexual Assault and the LGBTQ Community." Human Rights Campaign. Retrieved from https://www.hrc.org/resources/sexual-assault-and-the-lgbt-community .

IACHR. Inter-American Commission on Human Rights. 1999. *Ana Beatriz and Celia Gonzalez Perez v. Mexico*, Case 11.565, Report No. 129/99.

IACHR. Inter-American Commission on Human Rights. 2011. *Jessica Lenahan (Gonzales) et al. v. United States*, Case 12.626, Report No. 80/11.

IACP. International Association of Chiefs of Police. 2003a. "Domestic Violence by Police Officers: Concepts and Issues Paper." Retrieved from https://www.theiacp.org/sites/default/files/all/d-e/DomesticViolencebyPolicePaper.pdf .

IACP. International Association of Chiefs of Police. 2003b. "Domestic Violence by Police Officers: Model Policy." Retrieved from https://www.theiacp.org/sites/default/files/all/d-e/DomesticViolencebyPolicePolicy.pdf .

IACP. International Association of Chiefs of Police. 2016. "Identifying and Preventing Gender Bias." Retrieved from https://www.theiacp.org/gender-bias .

IACP. International Associations of Chiefs of Police. 2018a. "Model Policy: Domestic Violence." Retrieved from https://www.theiacp.org/sites/default/files/2018-08/DomesticViolencePolicy2018.pdf .

IACP. International Associations of Chiefs of Police. 2018b. "Domestic Violence: Concepts and Issues Paper." Retrieved from https://www.theiacp.org/sites/default/files/2018-08/DomesticViolencePaper2018.pdf .

IACP. International Association of Chiefs of Police. 2018c. "Sexual Assault Incident Reports: Investigative Strategies." Retrieved from https://www.theiacp.org/resources/document/sexual-assault-incident-reports-investigative-strategies .

IACP. International Association of Chiefs of Police. 2019. "Model Policy: Domestic Violence." Retrieved from https://www.theiacp.org/sites/default/files/2019-04/Domestic%20Violence%20Policy%20-%202019.pdf .

IACP. International Association of Chiefs of Police. 2020a. "Trauma Informed Sexual Assault Investigation Training." Retrieved from https://www.theiacp.org/projects/trauma-informed-sexual-assault-investigation-training .

IACP. International Association of Chiefs of Police. 2020b. "Enhancing Community Trust: Proactive Approaches to Domestic and Sexual Violence." Retrieved from: https://www.theiacp.org/sites/default/files/2020-11/7585/Assessment%20Tools%20%26%20Resources.pdf .

Jeltsen, Melissa. 2020. "Don't Use Domestic Violence Victims to Derail Police Reform." *HuffPost*. Retrieved from https://www.huffpost.com/entry/domestic-violence-defund-police_n_5eda8fe1c5b692d897d2de13 .

Johnson, Richard R. 2011. "Predicting Officer Physical Assaults at Domestic Assault Calls." *Journal of Family Violence* 26 (3): 163–69.

Kingkade, Tyler. 2020. "Police See Rise in Domestic Violence Calls amid Coronavirus Lockdown." NBCNews. Retrieved from https://www.nbcnews.com/news/us-news/police-see-rise-domestic-violence-calls-amid-coronavirus-lockdown-n1176151 .

Klein, Andrew R. 2009. "Practical Implications of Current Domestic Violence Research: For Law Enforcement, Prosecutors, and Judges." US Department of Justice. Retrieved from https://www.ncjrs.gov/pdffiles1/nij/225722.pdf .

Lave, Tamara Rice. 2019. "Police Sexual Misconduct and Violence." In *The Cambridge Handbook of Policing in the United States*, edited by Tamara Rice Lave and Eric J. Miller, 392–431. Cambridge: Cambridge University Press.

Logan, T. K., and Roberta Valente. 2015. "Who Will Help Me? Domestic Violence Survivors Speak Out about Law Enforcement Responses." Washington DC: National Domestic Violence Hotline. Retrieved from http://www.thehotline.org/resources/law-enforcement-responses .

Love, David. 2016. "Post-Traumatic Slave Syndrome and Intergenerational Trauma: Slavery Is Like a Curse Passing through the DNA of Black People." *Atlanta Black Star*. Retrieved from https://atlantablackstar.com/2016/06/05/post-traumatic-slave-syndrome-and-intergenerational-trauma-slavery-is-like-a-curse-passing-through-the-dna-of-black-people/ .

Love-Craighead, Altovise. 2015. "Building Trust through Trauma-Informed Policing." Vera Institute of Justice. Retrieved from https://www.vera.org/blog/police-perspectives/building-trust-through-trauma-informed-policing .

Marshall Project. 2020. "Police Abolition: A Curated Collection of Links." Retrieved from https://www.themarshallproject.org/records/3382-police-abolition .

McLaughlin, Eliott C. 2018. "Police Officers in the U.S. Were Charged with More than 400 Rapes over a 9-year Period." CNN. Retrieved from https://www.cnn.com/2018/10/19/us/police-sexual-assaults-maryland-scope/index.html .

NCST. Newark Community Street Team. 2020. Retrieved from https://www.newarkcommunitystreetteam.org/?fbclid=IwAR2DQ5zgvjdPSeLrF83TcQVKpa_ha7g3f872HEdt1jQHj5vf8JZTXbbrbWQ .

Next City. 2020. "How Newark Became a Model for Community-Based Violence Reduction." Retrieved from https://nextcity.org/webinars/view/how-newark-became-a-model-for-community-based-violence-reduction .

Ntsaluba, Gcina. 2020. "Military Ombud's Office Handling Complaints against SANDF." *The Citizen*. Retrieved from https://citizen.co.za/news/covid-19/2264681/military-ombuds-office-handling-complaints-against-sandf/ .

OAS. Organization of American States. 1948. "American Declaration of the Rights and Duties of Man." Organization of American States. Retrieved from https://www.oas.org/dil/access_to_information_human_right_American_Declaration_of_the_Rights_and_Duties_of_Man.pdf .

OAS. Organization of American States. 1969. "American Convention on Human Rights." Organization of American States. Retrieved from https://www.cidh.oas.org/basicos/english/basic3.american%20convention.htm .

OAS. Organization of the American States. 1994. "Inter-American Convention on the Prevention, Punishment, and Eradication of Violence against Women." Organization of the American States. Retrieved from https://www.oas.org/en/mesecvi/convention.asp .

OHCHR. Office of the United Nations High Commissioner for Human Rights. 2015. "Discrimination and Violence against Individuals Based on their Sexual Orientation and Gender Identity." UN Doc. A/HRC/29/23. United Nations. Retrieved from https://undocs.org/en/A/HRC/29/23 .

Opportunity Agenda. 2018. "Redefining Sanctuary." Retrieved from https://www.opportunityagenda.org/sites/default/files/2018-02/2018.02.13_RedefiningSanctuaryFINAL.pdf .

Park, Sandra S. 2015. "Equal Protection for Survivors of Gender-Based Violence: From Criminalization to Law Enforcement Accountability." *University of Miami Race & Social Justice Law Review* 5 (2): 401–20.

Peterman, Amber, Alina Potts, Megan O'Donnell, Kelly Thompson, Niyati Shah, Sabine Oertelt-Prigione, and Nicole van Gelder. 2020. "Pandemics and Violence against Women and Children." Center for Global Development. Retrieved from https://www.cgdev.org/publication/pandemics-and-violence-against-women-and-children .

Piquero, Alex R., Jordan R. Riddell, Stephen A. Bishopp, Chelsey Narvey, Joan A. Reid, and Nicole Leeper Piquero. 2020. "Staying Home, Staying Safe? A Short-Term Analysis of COVID-19 on Dallas Domestic Violence. *American Journal of Criminal Justice*." Advance Online: https://www.ncbi.nlm.nih.gov/pmc/articles/PMC7293590/ .

Planty, Michael, Lynn Langton, Christopher Krebs, Marcus Berzofsky, and Hope Smiley-McDonald. 2013. "Female Victims of Sexual Violence, 1994–2010." US Department of Justice. Retrieved from https://www.bjs.gov/content/pub/pdf/fvsv9410.pdf .

Prochaska, James, and Carlo DiClemente. 1986. "Toward a Comprehensive Model of Change." In *Treating Addictive Behaviors: Processes of Change*, edited by William R. Millar and Nick Heather, 3–27. New York: Plenum Press.

Richie, Beth E. 2012. *Arrested Justice: Black Women, Violence, and America's Prison Nation*. New York: NYU Press.

Ritchie, Andrea J. 2017. *Invisible No More: Police Violence against Black Women and Women of Color*. Boston: Beacon Press.

SAMHSA. Substance Abuse and Mental Health Services Administration. 2014. "SAMHSA's Concept of Trauma and Guidance for a Trauma-Informed Approach." Rockville: Substance Abuse and Mental Health Services Administration. Retrieved from: https://ncsacw.samhsa.gov/userfiles/files/SAMHSA_Trauma.pdf .

Smith, Sharon G., Jieru Chen, Kathleen C. Basile, Leah K. Gilbert, Melissa T. Merrick, Nimesh Patel, Margie Walling, and Anurag Jain. 2017. "The National Intimate Partner and Sexual Violence Survey: 2010–2012 State Report." Atlanta: National Center for Injury Prevention and Control, Centers for Disease Control and Prevention. Retrieved from https://doi.org/10.3886/ICPSR34305.v1 .

Stinson, Philip Matthew. 2020. "The Henry A. Wallace Police Crime Database." Bowling Green State University. Retrieved from https://policecrime.bgsu.edu/ .

Tuerkheimer, Deborah. 2016. "Underenforcement as Unequal Protection." *Boston College Law Review* 57 (4): 1287–35.

UN CAT. United Nations General Assembly. 1984. "Convention against Torture and Other Cruel, Inhuman or Degrading Treatment or Punishment." Retrieved from https://www.ohchr.org/en/professionalinterest/pages/cat.aspx .

UN CEDAW. United Nations General Assembly. 1979. "Convention on the Elimination of All Forms of Discrimination against Women." Retrieved from https://www.ohchr.org/en/professionalinterest/pages/cedaw.aspx .

UN ICCPR. United Nations General Assembly. 1966. "International Covenant on Civil and Political Rights." Retrieved from https://www.ohchr.org/EN/ProfessionalInterest/Pages/CCPR.aspx .

UN ICESCR. United Nations General Assembly. 1966. "International Covenant on Economic, Social, and Cultural Rights." Retrieved from https://www.ohchr.org/en/professionalinterest/pages/cescr.aspx .

United Nations Statistics Division. 2015. "Violence against women." Retrieved from https://unstats.un.org/unsd/gender/downloads/WorldsWomen2015_chapter6_t.pdf .

UN UDHR. United Nations General Assembly. 1948. "Universal Declaration of Human Rights." UN Doc. A/810. Retrieved from https://www.un.org/en/universal-declaration-human-rights/ .

Wanqing, Zhang. 2020. "Domestic Violence Cases Surge during COVID-19 Epidemic." Sixth Tone. Retrieved from https://www.sixthtone.com/news/1005253/domestic-violence-cases-surge-during-covid-19-epidemic .

Weissman, Deborah M. 2019. "In Pursuit of Economic Justice: The Political Economy of Domestic Violence Laws and Policies." *Utah Law Review*: 0b. Retrieved from https://ssrn.com/abstract=3378825 .

Youssef, Nagy, Laura Lockwood, Shaoyong Su, Guang Hao, and Bart P. F. Rutten. 2018. "The Effects of Trauma, with or without PTSD, on the Transgenerational DNA Methylation Alterations in Human Offsprings." *Brain Sciences* 8 (5): 83. Published online: https://doi: 10.3390/brainsci8050083 .

CHAPTER 20

Direct Communication in Focused Deterrence

David M. Kennedy

"Focused deterrence" has emerged, over the last decades, as both a crime- and violence-prevention framework and a set of operational interventions (see also chapter 21). Emerging from problem-oriented policing and the mid-1990s Boston Gun Project and its associated Operation Ceasefire—now known as the group violence intervention, or GVI—focused deterrence now represents a body of deterrence and crime prevention theory (Braga and Kennedy 2012; Kennedy 1997, 1998, 2009b; Kennedy, Kleiman, and Braga 2017; Kleiman 2009; Scott 2017; Tillyer and Kennedy 2008). It represents a general action-research approach to addressing substantive problems (Braga, Weisburd, and Turchan 2018) and a portfolio of interventions to such problems. These include group-related violence (National Network for Safe Communities 2013); individual violent offenders (Papachristos, Meares, and Fagan 2012; Wallace, Papachristos, Meares, and Fagan 2016); drug markets (Kennedy 2009a, 2016); intimate partner violence (Morgan, Boxall, Dowling, and Brown 2020; Sechrist and Weil 2018); prison violence (Oberlander 2018; Warner, Pacholke, and Kujath 2014); and others.

An extensive evaluation literature supports the overall effectiveness of the framework, such as the most recent iteration of the Campbell Collaboration systematic review of twenty-four quasi-experimental evaluations of focused deterrence interventions finding that the approach "generate[s] noteworthy crime reduction impacts and should be part of a broader portfolio of crime reduction strategies available to policy makers and practitioners" (Braga et al. 2018, 208). Also, Abt and Winship's (2016) meta-analysis of forty-three reviews, including over 1,400 studies of community violence prevention programs, which concluded that "[f]ocused deterrence . . . has the largest direct impact on crime and violence, of any intervention in this report" (13).

Focused deterrence interventions rely, in general, on the consistent empirical finding that the most serious victimization and offending, particularly violent victimization and offending, are concentrated in a very small, very high-risk population. Such high-risk populations typically engage in a wide range of illegal and risky behavior; and victimization, offending, and violence dynamics in that high-risk population are frequently driven by groups and networks rather than by individuals (Lurie 2019; Matza 1967; Papachristos 2009; Papachristos, Wildeman, and Roberto 2015). Focused deterrence interventions seek to influence particular aspects of those illegal and high-risk behaviors—typically violence, and within that the most serious violence—and where group dynamics are central, to shift the theoretical and practical focus from individuals to groups.

In practice, this has meant that it is possible, for example, to sit down face to face with members of multiple groups (such as gangs and drug crews); have members of their own community speak to their commitment to safety and the pain caused by violence; offer immediate, practical supports and services; and convey a clear message from law enforcement that the next group that commits a homicide will get comprehensive attention to any legal vulnerabilities, such as drug dealing, outstanding cases, probation and parole conditions, and the like. Rapid and substantial reductions in violence are routine.

Despite the "focused deterrence" label, such interventions invariably include elements that go well beyond deterrence, and well beyond criminal justice frameworks, and include as central elements community engagement, supportive services, and—in apparent, though not actual, conflict with the "deterrence" label—the explicit intent to *reduce* criminal justice action and contact. The author has written elsewhere that they are

> informed by the realization that high-risk groups and group members experience shockingly high levels of victimization and trauma; that they and their communities have frequently been exposed to profligate and damaging policing and criminal justice practices; and that it is essential to reduce the exercise of state authority as much as possible, to build the legitimacy of the police and other authorities, and to build trust between the authorities and communities. (Kennedy 2019)

With others who have been central to developing the approach, the author has argued,

> When taking focused deterrence as a label for a now reasonably well-defined and understood body of crime-prevention theory and associated operational crime-prevention interventions (including theory and operational approaches developed by the authors, all of whom are implicated in the creation and use of the label), it should be recognized that the label fails to capture, and in fact distorts, both that theory and that practice. . . . [T]he clear connotation in ordinary language and thinking that deterrence . . . is entirely about punishment and the threat of punishment is out of alignment with both the underlying ideas and actual implementation of focused deterrence: and the common belief that deterrence is about a fundamentally hostile relationship between authorities and offenders is even further out of alignment. (Kennedy, Kleiman, and Braga 2017, 159–60)

One of the earliest signs of the departure of focused deterrence from ordinary criminal justice thinking and practice was the central role of direct, collective, face-to-face meetings between focused deterrence practitioners—including police, probation and parole officers, prosecutors, and federal agents—and gang members, drug dealers, and the like (see chapter 4). The "forums" invented as part of the original Boston Ceasefire are now generally known as "call-ins" (Crandall and Wong 2012) and along with smaller and more individualized "custom notifications" (Kennedy and Friedrich 2014) and other means of direct communication are essential to the theory and practice of focused deterrence. These meetings were originally seen as utterly bizarre. "Pity the poor soul who . . . would have predicted that hard-core street cops would be making a practice of sitting down with serious violent offenders and telling them politely to cease and desist," I wrote some ten years into the development of focused deterrence. "[J]ust try telling a grizzled street cop that the way to stop violent crime is to tell hard-core offenders exactly what your enforcement plans are" (Kennedy 2006, 155, 160).

One marker of the broad acceptance of the focused deterrence framework is the degree to which these sessions are now routine and unremarkable, and have in fact become identified with the overall approach: It is common, now, to hear such shorthand as "the call-in strategy." Call-ins, custom notifications, and the rest are in fact simply devices for direct communication. Those of us who work with frontline practitioners who get too caught up in the intricacies of the particular devices frequently remind them, "It's just talking to people." By extension, the broad acceptance of focused deterrence, and these mechanisms within it, in fact means a broad acceptance of direct communication as an integral part of the larger theory and practice of the approach.

Direct communication plays a central strategic role in focused deterrence: in creating effective deterrence; in mobilizing informal social control; in creating links to supportive interventions; and in enhancing legitimacy, both with respect to the core high-risk population and with respect to broader communities. This chapter will explore that role and those functions within the larger theory and practice of focused deterrence.

CREATING DETERRENCE

Deterrence is a radically subjective business (see, for example, Kennedy 2009b). The law and the workings of the law, and other processes that produce sanctions, are a reality, and have whatever direct impact they may have, but the anticipation of such sanctions and impact—and whatever impact that anticipation may have—are entirely a matter of the knowledge, perceptions, beliefs, and subsequent actions of those exposed to the underlying reality. A car speeding down the road is real and stepping in front of it will hurt. But if we could not see the car, or do not see the car, or do not believe the car is real, or believe we are possessed of superpowers and are immune to being hit by the car, the likelihood of stepping in front of cars will increase, and so will the harms caused by being hit by cars. Deterrence is, thus, fundamentally about *information* and *belief*. Zimring and Hawkins (1973), in their classic *Deterrence: The Legal Threat in Crime Control*, capture this neatly by observing that deterrence is a matter of both advertising and persuasion. While of absolutely central importance to deterrence, both theoretically and practically, what is not known cannot deter, and what is not believed will not deter; before focused deterrence, these dynamics received nearly no attention in practice (Kennedy 2009b). One of the earliest ideas in the Boston Gun Project was that of doing "retail deterrence," in effect, advertising and persuading directly to those at highest risk (Kennedy, Braga, and Piehl 2001).

Advertising

This "advertising" function can take a number of forms. Potential offenders will frequently not understand the law itself, so the law can be explained; for example, they are open to a rarely imposed but draconian federal sanction for illegal possession of a firearm. They may *misunderstand* the law, and believe, for example, that they are due a free pass for a first offense, when that "free pass" is a common, but in no way obligatory or inevitable, exercise of judicial discretion.[1] They may not understand changes in the almost constantly shifting statutory environment and may benefit from explanation. They may have well-informed and perfectly reasonable expectations based on their personal and vicarious experience—that gun possession does not lead to prison time, for example—and need to understand for any number of reasons the past is not prologue and that the consequences to which they are exposed have changed. In all such instances, and more like these, the simple provision of factual information can be critical.

Beyond the four corners of the law as such, actual sanction risk is heavily influenced by the practice of official discretion. There is ordinarily no way, outside of the observation of official action, for potential offenders to understand that authorities have decided to focus their energies on gun crime, or drug markets, or intimate partner violence, or gun crime in a particular neighborhood, or the drug market on a particular corner, or *this particular* domestic abuser. Offenders may be good Bayesians, but at enormous personal and social cost: Updated expectations come because they and those they know who carry guns, sell drugs on that corner, and assault their girlfriends go to jail (and in the meantime guns are carried and sometimes used, drugs sold in public, and girlfriends assaulted). Direct communication in focused deterrence takes the step—apparently commonsense, but previously almost unknown—of informing potential offenders of these changes in discretionary practice, with the goal of gaining compliance without exercising enforcement and sanction. Most central here, in most applications of focused deterrence, is the communication that violence is different, is special, is the authorities' top priority, and that violence will be met with special responses.

Central to many applications of focused deterrence is a focus on *groups*. As has been noted and is now well understood, much serious violent crime is concentrated in groups and driven by group and intergroup dynamics (for an intergroup communication perspective, see Goldman, Giles, and Hogg 2014; Woo 2018). The shift in focus to groups that has been so central to addressing homicide and gun violence is almost entirely a matter of official discretion: It has been driven by changes in practice, rather than by changes in law. Police and other criminal justice authorities have shifted to paying particular attention to group-involved violence, to tracking and addressing group dynamics, and to mobilizing resources around violent groups and group dynamics. Focused deterrence interventions have used direct communication to convey these shifts to group members: authorities now understand the centrality of groups to serious violence, are making them and it a priority, and that any and all legal vulnerabilities group members' actions may be producing may get heightened attention as a result of instances of group-involved violence. The intent here has been several—to communicate the shift to a focus on groups as such; to convey that violence will be "taxed" at a group level by attention to a range of offending; to convey that high levels of legal impunity for violence, as when homicides and shootings go unsolved, will be addressed by imposing sanctions in other ways; and to mobilize group dynamics in opposition to violence by creating collective accountability for serious violence. All of this is dependent on group members' understanding official intent and actions, an understanding focused deterrence seeks to create through clear and direct explanation.

At the individual level, focused deterrence takes steps to convey basic facts about legal sanctions. It is well established in the deterrence literature that the facts of the law are not well understood, even by those with a good deal of experience of offending and the criminal justice system (Apel 2013; Kleck and Barnes 2013; Kleck, Sever, Li, and Gertz 2005; Lochner 2007). Call-ins incorporate segments in which state and local prosecutors simply explain the law. A signal moment in the first Boston Operation Ceasefire call-in was the explanation that there was such a thing as a federal "armed career criminal" law, with an associated fifteen-year mandatory minimum sentence for possession of a firearm or ammunition, a moment that sent palpable shock waves through the room and, over the next weeks and months, the Boston street scene (Kennedy, Braga, and Piehl 2001, 37).

The "Chicago PSN" focused deterrence intervention relies on parolee forums in which the main criminal justice intervention is briefing attendees on federal firearms law (Papachristos, Meares, and Fagan 2012). Replications in New York State have added the refinement of a card showing each parolee his or her individualized exposure under the federal law based on an assessment of their criminal history.[2] Custom notifications frequently contain a "custom legal assessment" conveying in plain language the individual's personal legal exposure, usually for a small number of particular violent crimes, based on applicable law and the individual's prior record.

Finally, the deterrence literature establishes clearly that certainty and swiftness matter a great deal to effective deterrence, with the severity of sanctions trailing well behind (Beccaria 1986; Bentham 1996; Nagin 2018). Focused deterrence has used a number of devices to create radical shifts in swiftness and certainty, and conveyed those through direct communication. In GVI, through the device of call-ins composed of members of multiple groups, messages are conveyed that the first group to commit violence, and the group committing the most violence, will get focused attention. This "first group/worst group" formulation is designed to ensure that *all* groups understand at the same moment that there will be costs associated with being the next group to commit violence and with the most violent group in question, and that authorities are mobilized to and have the capacity to so act. Conveying and ensuring certainty and swiftness creates incentives both against that first act of violence and against violence overall, theoretically dampening all groups and creating a general race to the bottom.

In the focused deterrence drug market intervention, a prosecutable drug case is developed and "banked"—held for future use. Informing the dealer in question that any known future dealing will result in the activation of the banked case creates a shift from a low and unknown probability of sanction for such dealing to a high and known probability of rapid official action. Particularly dangerous intimate partner violent offenders are put on individual notice that their behavior is being scrutinized and that continued domestic abuse will result in greatly elevated legal attention to any and all criminal activity, both domestic and non-domestic, for example, heightened supervision under existing probation or parole status or prosecution for a pending but non-domestic drug or assault charge (Sechrist and Weil 2018). Older gang members have been put on notice that gun violence by juvenile gang members—acts essentially impervious to criminal justice action—will be met with a range of immediate enforcement attention to gang gambling enterprises (Braga, McDevitt, and Pierce, 2006). In all such moves within focused deterrence, what matters is both a shift in official strategy and action, and directly informing those exposed to that shift that there has been a shift, and what it means for them: in effect, that the stove is hot, and that therefore they should not touch it.

Persuasion

Focused deterrence also relies on direct communication for "persuasion"—establishing the credibility of official representations and actions. GVI call-ins are repeated, generally occur several times a year or more in a given jurisdiction, and occur partly with the express purpose of updating group members on official actions and promises that have been kept. Part of each call-in is devoted to conveying what has happened since the last call-in: "We made the following commitments with respect to the 'first group' and the 'worst group'; here is who those groups are and what they did; here is what we did in response." Those updates will be enhanced with general updates of broader actions around serious violence, such as enforcement around homicides, shootings, gun possession, and the like (see chapter 4). While such actions will often not have been specifically driven by the focused deterrence strategy, they happen; they are frequently unknown at the street level; and communicating them conveys important information. (Similar updates are given around those who have asked, and gotten, supportive services.)

Even more broadly, authorities will often share information that shows the extent to which they know about group and violence dynamics and that groups and group members are not anonymous, such as intelligence diagrams of group structures, surveillance photographs and footage, and the like. They will also describe the routine actions they are taking to address group violence: weekly interagency meetings sharing intelligence on each homicide and shooting, federal authorities working with local authorities in new ways, bordering jurisdictions newly sharing information, and the like. In the focused deterrence drug market interventions, it is routine to display the case files representing the dealers' "banked" cases and to show audio and video surveillance of the undercover drug buys supporting those cases (prosecutors will say to the call-in attendees, "raise your hand when you see yourself committing a felony"). In each instance, the intent is to convey the extent to which official representations about actions and intended actions are in fact credible.

A key step in these communications is to *convey cause and effect*. Legal authorities routinely take steps that have been driven by particular reasons and intended to achieve particular ends. They have a strong tendency to assume that those subject to those actions, and those observing them, understand that as well. The latter is of course frequently not the case. Police and prosecutors will focus drug enforcement on a group because of its violence; the group members in question, and other groups watching, will see only drug enforcement. Beyond that they may have powerful narratives of their own—without any connection to actual official intentions—that shape understandings of official actions as the product of deliberate malice (Brunson 2007; Kirk and Papachristos 2009). Such narratives may also inform understandings of the *lack* of official action, as in the belief that offending is successful only because authorities are knowledgeable, tolerant, and allowing it to succeed (Klofas 2001). Unless authorities speak to cause and effect—we did *this* because of *that*—such narratives go unaddressed.

Beyond such routine mismatches, focused deterrence interventions systematize the use of both legal and other actions—"levers" (Kennedy 1998)—that may not have any innate connections to identified prohibited acts, in order to deter those acts. Unless older gang members are told that raids on their gambling enterprises are because of the gun violence of juvenile members, they will not know. In one instance involving a group of violent juveniles—who because of their status were open to essentially no ordinary legal sanctions—authorities disrupted the area of a public park they had established as their turf by trimming trees and shrubs and installing lighting to expose their activities to public view, cut off the public power outlets they were using to power their phones and video games, had a local business password-protect the wireless router they had been using to upload provocative social media, and generally made it impossible for the group to function as it wished. Unless the underlying intent is made explicit—this happened because of the violence, and things like this will happen where there is violence—cause and effect will not be evident and deterrence will not be created. Focused deterrence therefore uses direct communication to convey that cause and effect.

Finally, focused deterrence seeks to persuade by *not lying*, explicitly or implicitly, about official intentions, actions, and capacity. A key concept within the deterrence literature is that of the "experiential effect": the tendency of more experienced offenders to have lower estimates of sanction risk (Saltzman, Paternoster, Waldo, and Chiricos 1982). They will, they have learned, get away with it. As Paternoster wrote, "Most people (young and old) have over pessimistic estimates of their ability to get away with breaking the law [. . .] but that when they participate in illegal acts they soon discover that they can commit them with relative impunity" (Paternoster 1987, 180). Since the problems focused deterrence is deployed against overwhelmingly tend to be driven by the most serious and intense offenders—since such offenders are overwhelmingly chronic across a wide range of offense types, and since they do in fact get away with almost everything they do—they are credibly skeptical toward official representations that they will be held accountable. They also invariably have long experience with police, prosecutors, judges, probation officers, and the like promising dire consequences "the next time," which are nearly invariably hollow.

Focused deterrence interventions recognize this reality and address it in a number of ways. One is through the central element of focus itself. Such interventions select very particular acts, as committed by very particular people, and explicitly eschew wider ambitions. As the author has written elsewhere about this thinking emerging during the Boston Gun Project,

> The normal frame said, don't be in gangs, don't commit crimes, don't sell drugs, don't carry weapons, don't violate your probation, don't drink and drug. Turn your life around. Go back to school, get a job. Go forth and sin no more. This cut to the chase: Don't hurt people. Say any more—don't carry guns, don't sell drugs, don't recruit kids into your gang—you couldn't back it up. There was just too much of it, and too little of us. Draw those lines in the sand, they would cross them, and it would be obvious that the cops had lied. They were used to being lied to, lying to them was *normal*: The next time you drop a hot urine I'm going to violate you, don't let me see you back in my court, young man. Our side lied *all the time*. It was like we were training them to ignore us. This was focused, limited. We started to call it "focused deterrence": focused on one problem, focused on the core offenders. (Kennedy 2011, 54)

An explicit tenet of focused deterrence from the outset has, therefore, been *never write a check you can't cash*. Police and other authorities are often given to exaggerated statements about how much they know, what they can do, what they will do, what consequences will follow on bad behavior, and the like; the late George Kelling, a particularly astute observer of police behavior, called such chest-beating "woofing." Breaking authorities of such woofing is an important part of establishing credibility with both offenders and the larger community. The resulting realism can be startlingly direct and refreshing. A criminal justice principal in a Chicago Project Safe Neighborhoods parolee call-in bluntly told attendees, Look, if you need to get into it with someone, don't use a gun, hit them with a shoe or something—that way you won't see me.[3] In one of the early Boston Ceasefire call-ins, a prominent black minister said, "You're not getting rich. You're living at home. You've got no bank account. You're driving hoopties. Don't you get it? The noise brings heat. All this noise is *bad for business*. You think real gangsters behave like this? If you're going to be gangsters, at least be *good* gangsters" (Kennedy 2011).

MOBILIZING INFORMAL SOCIAL CONTROL

As has been noted, "focused deterrence" is not at all entirely about deterrence. A core intent is to mobilize informal social control to do as much of the work of violence and crime prevention as possible. As the author has written elsewhere,

> The most important things that influence whether someone obeys the law or commits a crime are whether he thinks doing so is right or wrong; whether those he cares about and respects thinks it is right or wrong; and whether the

community he belongs to thinks it is right or wrong. Even most offenders, even very serious ones, obey the law most of the time; in the highest-crime communities, most people obey the law most of the time. Los Angeles, for example, estimates that there are 400 organized gangs with at least 65,000 gang members in the city. In 2009, there were estimated to be 141 gang homicides in Los Angeles. That means that 64,859 gang members (assuming one gang member per homicide), and at least 259 gangs, did not kill anybody that year. It is common to say of gang members, and high-crime communities, things like "guns have become the preferred method of dispute resolution," but such statements are simply not true: if they were true, there would be nobody left standing. Far more often than not, good sense prevails.

That good sense is mostly self-imposed. The ability of the criminal justice system to impose punishment—what scholars call "formal social control"—is the least important influence on a person's decision to commit or not commit a crime. The police are not present at every potential crime scene, most crimes that are committed are never reported, most crimes that are reported are never cleared by an arrest, and most arrests do not result in meaningful sanctions. What matters the most is the judgments of individuals, peer groups, families, and communities that to do crime, or this crime, is wrong for various reasons. Most people do not have to think about criminal justice consequences when they are tempted to shoot someone: they believe that shooting people is wrong. If they are tempted personally, they know that their friends, families and communities think that shooting people is wrong, and they care about what their friends, families and communities think. Scholars call this "informal social control," and divide it into "internal"—conscience, shame, and the like—and "external"—peers, loved ones, families, and community. Common sense, ordinary experience, and a vast amount of research show that informal social control is far more potent, overall, than formal. (Kennedy 2010)

Central to focused deterrence thinking and practice around changing behavior through informal social control is that those at highest risk for the most part *already* have, and are embedded in, value systems that stand in opposition to the most serious violence and crime. At the level of individuals at highest risk, literatures on, for example, gangs and gang offending show clearly that many gang members do not want to be gang members, do not support or enjoy violence, do not make conscious decisions to join gangs but "drift" into association, are pressured into violence by both friends and enemies, are governed by a "street code" that imposes standards to which they do not personally subscribe, and have sometimes elaborate techniques to avoid violence (Anderson 2000; Garot 2010; MacCoun and Reuter 1992; Matza 1964; Pitts 2008; Wilkinson 2003; Wilkinson and Fagan 1996). Research shows that those involved in gun violence in fact hold strongly mainstream values: They believe in the law and obeying the law, while emphatically not trusting the police (Meares and Papachristos 2009; Papachristos, Meares, and Fagan 2012). A research tradition on "techniques of neutralization" describes the mobilization of mainstream values to justify violence and crime, as by locating violence within established notions of self-defense, and shows for example "that only a small percentage of adolescents generally approve of violence or express indifference to violence" (Agnew 1994, 555; see also Brookman 2013; Sykes and Matza 1957).

At the community level, research shows clearly that "high crime" neighborhoods are in fact not tolerant of crime and violence, and are in fact notably less tolerant than safer neighborhoods (Fontaine, Esthappan, La Vigne, and Jannetta 2019; Sampson and Bartusch 1998). A "legal cynicism" literature differentiates between such intolerance and an associated mistrust of police and legal authorities; more recently, a "legal estrangement" literature depicts an even more profound alienation (Bell 2017). Related literatures such as those on "self-help" make the same essential point: that the presence and perpetration of violence and crime should not be taken as, and in fact do not indicate, a normative acceptance, and that such violence and crime is often an unwanted response to the failure—or worse—of police and other authorities to provide safety and address problems (Black 1983; Wilkinson, Beaty, and Lurry 2009). Anderson (1994), for example, locates the "code of the street" in "a cultural adaptation to a profound lack of faith in the police and the judicial system."

With its frequent focus on groups and group dynamics, focused deterrence highlights the ways in which group processes can produce outcomes at odds with individual underlying dispositions. A particularly useful idea here is that of "pluralistic ignorance," well developed in social psychology: the condition of members of a group believing that everyone in the group believes something that no member in fact believes (Matza 1964; Miller and McFarland 1987; Miller and Prentice 1994; Prentice and Miller 1996). It is routine for group members to express support for, and act according to, ideas such as "street code" norms that they clearly personally eschew: Jail and prison are no big thing, as they do everything they can to avoid getting arrested; disrespect requires a violent response, while they are extremely creative in avoiding violence; and violence is justified because they are "street soldiers" defending their neighborhood, while saying in private that they were raised better than that. Garot writes of his ethnographic research in Los Angeles gang circles:

> I could count on every young man to tell me that anyone who walked away from a fight would be punked for life. I could also count on most young man to tell me of a time when he walked away from a fight. (Garot 2007, 330)

All these considerations point to the fact that norms against violence and other serious offending are present in both affected communities and among those at highest risk for violent offending and victimization. It is not necessary, this suggests, to change values and norms as it is to assist existing and positive values and norms to surface and prevail (see Woo, Giles, Hogg, and Goldman 2015). Focused deterrence theory and practice have proceeded by asking who has standing among those at highest risk, and can therefore influence their thinking and behavior, and by bringing those figures into direct communication (an orientation very similar to the more recent formulation in community violence prevention of the idea of "credible messengers").[4] Such figures include, most prominently, mothers who have lost their children to homicide, who have extraordinary and palpable standing; older and wiser "original gangster" ex-offenders;

those already doing frontline violence prevention work in the community; others who by virtue of their particular experience and character are seen as authentic (e.g., the proprietors of the urban funeral homes who process homicide victims and deal with their families); some (but emphatically not all) faith leaders; and the like. Core themes and messages have been developed (see Wood and Giles 2014). These include the following:

- *There is no justification for the violence.* Violence is wrong, inexcusable, and cannot and will not be tolerated.
- *The community needs the violence to stop.* The harm and pain caused by violence is intolerable and the community as a whole stands against it.
- *You are valuable and important to us.* You matter and the larger community wants you safe, alive, out of jail and prison, and successful in your life.
- *The ideas of the street code are wrong.* Notions that disrespect requires violence, that jail and prison are inevitable, and that death at an early age is to be expected are incorrect and destructive.
- *We will do everything we can to help you.* You deserve and will be provided with support.
- *The community has powerful aspirations and you are and should be part of them.* Beyond stopping violence, the community wants to thrive and for you to be part of that and to contribute to it.

Focused deterrence theory and practice have developed a particular elaboration around informal social control in the idea of the "influential." First framed as part of the drug market intervention, an "influential" is a person identified as being in an existing, close, and positive relationship with an identified offender or person at high risk (Kennedy 2009b). They can be brought into call-ins, custom notifications, and the larger interventions; supported in their relationship with the person in question; and in turn work to prevent future offending and encourage and support positive outcomes. Influentials are often easily identified by consulting probation and parole authorities, reviewing jail and prison visitation logs and call records, consulting community sources, and sometimes simply by asking the person identified as high risk (Kennedy 2010).

Creating Links to Support

Focused deterrence interventions include, as a core element, organizing and providing to group-involved and otherwise high-risk populations what has come to be called "support and outreach": affirmative and effective opportunities to establish relationships with individuals and organizations who can help them, and that help themselves. Call-ins, custom notifications, relationships with and through "influentials," and the like are important mechanisms to communicate that commitment and particular concrete elements and options.

A key development over the course of this work has been the realization that traditional "social service" formulations of what should be provided badly miss the mark. Mainstream ideas that those at highest risk automatically need school and work—and particularly the enticing but deeply mistaken idea that "nothing stops a bullet like a job"[5] are grievously out of alignment with the reality that those at highest risk frequently are young; still actively offending; not necessarily interested in stopping (while almost invariably wanting to avoid violence); deeply traumatized by extraordinary levels of victimization and exposure to violence; leading lives of extreme disorganization and chaos; lacking fundamentals of food, clothing, and shelter; at high risk of additional violent victimization; have extensive criminal records and often outstanding cases, active probation or parole conditions, outstanding warrants, unpaid fines and fees, child support obligations, and the like; and are neither interested in or suited for existing "service" structures and options. Take-up of traditional "services" in focused deterrence (and other) interventions was minimal, largely did not work for those who tried, and showed no association with violence reduction (Engel, Tillyer, and Corsaro 2013).

It has thus been critical to develop new frameworks that address those real conditions and needs, and in fact—rather than simply in phrase—meet those at highest risk "where they are." Those new frameworks have been developed and are being tested and refined in practice, with a focus on affirmative and sustained outreach, protection from risk and harm, addressing trauma and immediate practical needs, supporting new relationships, and where possible building bridges to more traditional programs and opportunities (National Network for Safe Communities 2017; see also Matthay et al. 2019). Focused deterrence call-ins, custom notifications, and the like encourage service providers to articulate clearly what is available and how to get it. Doing so effectively has meant being honest about the failure of previous frameworks; the frequent experience that traditional service providers have been unhelpful and often disrespectful and worse; exactly what is being offered (avoiding professional jargon such as "needs assessments" and "referrals" in favor of "we can put you up in a hotel room if someone is trying to shoot you" and "we can put food on your table if your little brother is hungry"); and sustained, deliberate follow-up.

Enhancing Legitimacy

Finally, direct communication within focused deterrence is an opportunity to enhance legitimacy. "Legitimacy" is a formal idea in social science, connoting the perceived standing of formal authorities to govern behavior. As Tyler writes, in express connection to police legitimacy and crime control,

> a key value that people hold is their widespread support for the legitimacy of the police—the belief that the police are entitled to call upon the public to follow the law and help combat crime and that members of the public have an obligation to engage in cooperative behaviors. When people feel that an authority is legitimate, they authorize that authority to determine what their behavior will be within a given set of situations. Such an authorization of an authority "seem[s] to carry automatic justification. . . . Behaviorally, authorization obviates the necessity of making judgments or choices. Not only do normal moral principles become inoperative, but—particularly when the actions are explicitly ordered—a different type of morality, linked to duty to obey superior orders, tends to take over." People, in other words, feel responsible for following the directives of legitimate authorities. (Tyler 2004, 86–87)

A large body of literature underscores the point that, particularly in "high crime" communities, as legitimacy goes down, crime goes up, and vice versa (Desmond, Papachristos, and Kirk 2016; Eisner and Nivette 2013; Kane 2005; Tyler 2014). And as has been noted, such communities frequently do not see police and other authorities as legitimate, and high-risk group members and others even less so. Such beliefs and perceptions are driven by histories of abuse under color of law, over-policing, under-policing, mass incarceration, the failure and/or inability to control violence, the failure and/or inability to solve serious crimes and hold offenders accountable, police violence, abusive and indiscriminate strategies such as "zero tolerance" policing, and the like (Kennedy and Ben-Menachem 2019).

Focused deterrence strategies have been attentive from the beginning to these issues. While often seen as enforcement-focused and enforcement-heavy—the burden, in part, of the ordinary connotations of "deterrence"—the approach is in fact

> informed by the realization that high-risk groups and group members experience shockingly high levels of victimization and trauma; that they and their communities have frequently been exposed to profligate and damaging policing and criminal justice practices; and that it is essential to reduce the exercise of state authority as much as possible, to build the legitimacy of the police and other authorities, and to build trust between the authorities and communities. (Kennedy 2019)

From the very first Operation Ceasefire call-in, focused deterrence has centered the failures and harms of traditional policing and criminal justice practice. We haven't kept you safe, the police said in that room, but it's going to be different now:

> You know what happens when someone kills a cop, they said. We don't stop with the shooter; we go after everybody involved, we never back off, we never stop. That's what we're going to do if you guys hurt somebody. That's what we're going to do if somebody hurts *you*. Hurting you is like hurting a cop. It's all off limits now. It's over, today. (Kennedy 2011, 65–66)

Zina Jacque, one of Operation Ceasefire's key community partners, said in a call-in shortly thereafter,

> We blew it, big-time, ten years ago. We're guilty, you're pissed. You're afraid to go home without a gun. But it's a new day. We're going to reinstitute the social contract. We're going to make the streets safe again. We're here to say two things. One is, we're sorry. But sorry is never enough. The second thing is, we're going to fix it. (Kennedy 2011, 68)

The drug market intervention was framed around the failure of traditional drug enforcement and the harms thus done to minority communities plagued both by overt (open-air) drug markets and relentless, ineffective policing and prosecution, and the connection in community experience to historical harms done to minorities under color of law. It expressly included a "police/community reconciliation" process and opened its first implementation in High Point, North Carolina, with a frank admission of harm and apology to the community by the chief of police. The innovation of the "banked case" was intended in part both to avoid arresting and incarcerating young Black men and to demonstrate that commitment to the community (Kennedy 2009b). Call-ins and other forms of focused direct communication have been framed to recognize and communicate that "law enforcement has been part of the problem and would like to change," with the intent of enhancing legitimacy and building trust (Kennedy 2010, 8).

Both the design and the content of such direct communication have been informed by the procedural justice literature (see chapters 8 and 17). Procedural justice focuses on the impact on legitimacy of the quality of interactions between authorities and the public; it emphasizes elements of respect, transparency, impartiality, legitimacy of motive, and opportunities for "voice" or opportunities to be heard (Blader and Tyler 2003). Those tenets have shaped call-ins and other focused deterrence direct communication techniques, for example, by shaping messaging, shifting the early tendency to hold call-ins in courtrooms to what Meares calls "places of civic importance" such as libraries and community colleges intended to emphasize community norms and standards (Wallace et al. 2016), reformatting seating arrangements from head-on "us and them" to "in the round," building in opportunities to mingle afterward and ask and answer questions, ending with meals served to attendees by police officers, and so on. As the author and colleagues have written elsewhere,

> Those involved in Ceasefire/GVI interventions have been floored by the difference in practice when law enforcement officials say, on the one hand, "I know who you are, I know what you're doing, and if you kill somebody I'll come at you with everything I've got," and those who say, on the other, "I care about you, I care about your families, I know what we've been doing has not been keeping you safe, and I will do everything in my power to keep you alive, unhurt, and out of jail." One can feel the difference in the room, which is more than enough to drive evolving practice while the formal research record develops. (Kennedy, Kleiman, and Braga 2017, 169)

The most recent, and the most ambitious, attempt to address legitimacy within focused deterrence has been large-scale police/community reconciliation engagement (see chapter 13 and Mentel 2012). Evolving from the smaller and more targeted element of the drug market intervention, this current work seeks to engage police departments and to some extent other criminal agencies more broadly with larger segments of the community, with deeper and more explicit attention to historical and current harms, and with more extensive connections to repairing those harms and to changes in policy and practice. Informed by international experiences with reconciliation and transitional justice and developed in part through the work of the US Department of Justice–funded National Initiative for Building Community Trust and Justice, such reconciliation processes include frank admissions of harm by police leadership; sustained engagement between police leadership and rank-and-file officers with representatives of harmed populations and members of the public; mechanisms to capture and promulgate key community and police experiences and narratives; formal records and recognition of the historical facts of harm; and links from the reconciliation process to efforts to repair and prevent harm (La Vigne et al. 2019).

Police leadership involved in this work has been extraordinarily frank and direct in their engagement with communities (see chapter 2). Cameron McClay, chief in Pittsburgh, Pennsylvania—one of the National Initiative sites—said,

> The reality of U.S. policing is that our enforcement efforts have a disparate impact on communities of color. This is a statistical fact. You know, as well as I, the social factors driving this reality. The gross disparity in wealth and opportunity is evident in our city. Frustration and disorder are certain to follow. The predominant patterns of our city's increased violence involves black victims as well as actors. If we are to address this violence, we must work together with our communities of color. We, the Pittsburgh Bureau of Police, need to acknowledge how this reality feels to those impacted communities. Crime and disorder take us to the disadvantaged communities, which are predominantly those of color. The disparities in police arrest and incarceration rates that follow are not by design, but they can feel that way to some people in those communities. I know, because I have been there too. My own street drug enforcement efforts were well-intended, but had an impact I would not have consciously chosen. In retrospect, we should have been far more engaged with those in the communities where we were doing our high-impact, zero tolerance type policing; to obtain the consent of those we were policing. (Kennedy and Ben-Menachem 2019, 573)

"This needs to be said," Stockton, California—another National Initiative site—Chief Eric Jones told a Black church congregation. "There was a time when police used to be dispatched to keep lynchings 'civil.' That's a fact of our history that we need to acknowledge" (Friedrich 2019).

Evaluation of the National Initiative found small but statistically significant improvements in public perceptions of legitimacy but could not differentiate between the reconciliation work and other elements of the interventions (La Vigne et al. 2019). The intent of the reconciliation work within focused deterrence, however, is to reduce violence directly through increasing voluntary compliance with the law, and indirectly through mobilizing informal social control and strengthening working relationships with the public and authorities. Stockton, which both made the strongest commitment to reconciliation of the National Initiative cities and incorporated it into existing focused deterrence work, saw striking improvements. Between 2017 and 2018, the last year of full implementation of the National Initiative, the city saw a 40 percent drop in homicide; a 34 percent reduction in non-fatal shootings, an 80 percent reduction in officer-involved shootings, and two markers of increased public confidence in the police: an increase in calls for service, and an increase in homicide clearance from 40 percent to 67 percent (Friedrich 2019). These are precisely the sorts of movement enhancements in legitimacy are intended to produce, making reconciliation a primary interest within the evolving focused deterrence portfolio.

CONCLUSIONS

This chapter has addressed the theoretical and practical grounding for the idea that communication is an essential element in deterrence and in getting deterrence right. It has argued that the idea is literally hundreds of years old, but it has been almost entirely ignored in practice; that it has particular salience in the evolving "focused deterrence" approach to violence prevention and crime control; that direct communication can fundamentally enhance the credibility of authorities; that it can mobilize informal social control as a powerful strategic intervention; that it can convey a commitment to and opportunities for support, opportunity, and care; and that it can influence critical legitimacy dynamics.

There is a formal evaluation literature supporting these ideas. Most centrally, direct communication is an element in all focused deterrence interventions and thus implicated in the impact found in the overall body of research on the approach. Some focused deterrence interventions, such as the "Chicago PSN" gun violence strategy, are nearly or completely communication interventions: They employ little or no follow-up after the call-in, so the call-in effectively *is* the strategy. Evaluations show substantial impact, up to 50 percent reductions in violent crime at the individual level (Clark-Moorman, Rydberg, and McGarrell 2019; Papachristos et al. 2007; Wallace et al. 2016). A randomized trial showed that probationers and parolees attending a similar call-in showed significant reductions in arrest (Hamilton, Rosenfeld, and Levin 2018). Other research shows direct effects from focused deterrence communications on offender perception and behavior. A randomized trial of parolees called into the Chicago sessions found increased perceptions of both sanction risk and the legitimacy and procedural fairness of police (Trinkner 2019). A randomized trial of "prolific offenders" given custom notifications by police officers found reductions in offending both for those notified and for other offenders associated with them, indicating both direct and indirect, "cascade" information effects (Ariel, Englefield, and Denley 2019). Finally, and perhaps most congruent with the simple and direct ideas of the original Boston Operation Ceasefire, an evaluation of a partial renewal of that intervention found that Boston gangs simply visited by the police and told to stop what they were doing showed nearly 30 percent reductions in violent offending (Braga et al. 2013).

It has, however, become the conventional wisdom among those doing focused deterrence work that the approach simply cannot be understood until a call-in or the like has been witnessed: No amount of exposure to theory, practice, the evaluation literature, and the like can convey what happens when all the pieces come together in the face-to-face engagements this article has addressed. It is thus worth quoting *in extenso* one written account of such a call-in. Michael Blass, a career law enforcement official then with the Ohio attorney general, attended a call-in in Cincinnati in 2007. Later that day, he wrote the following:

> I saw something profound today.
> I saw the same players and actors, those nameless, faceless people who make up the good guys and the bad guys and the ordinary guys in any community.

They are all different from one another, but they are mirror images of the players and actors in communities all across this nation. They have roles to play, these good guys, bad guys, and ordinary guys . . . and the roles are uniform and consistent throughout America's communities. But today those roles were played in a different script.

I saw something profound today.

I watched the confused faces of those we commonly call the bad guys—angry young men, almost exclusively African American, as they filed into a room full of criminal justice professionals, social service providers, and community members. I saw, with exceptional clarity, the fear in their eyes, the apprehension on their faces, soon replaced with seemingly awkward attempts to project confidence, indifference, in some cases, perhaps, hostility. But I saw angry, street-savvy young men who were caught off-guard and struggling to find a comfort zone in what must surely have felt to them like an artificial environment. As they settled into their seats, they attempted to coax from within themselves a more comfortable demeanor while their genuine discomfort collectively and silently resounded across the room. These angry young men, used to being in control in the incredibly brutal environment of the mean streets, were noticeably off-balance and unsure of themselves.

That was profound.

I watched as the first speaker, Dr. Victor Garcia, stood and addressed the group.

He was the first to deliver this simple message: "The violence—the killing and the shooting—must stop." He provided startling statistics that supported his claim that black men killing black men has the potential to destroy the black race. He spoke of his personal experiences as a trauma surgeon saving, and losing, the lives of young men and women who are victims of violence. He told the angry young men that he loved them, that they have value to their community, and that they are better than their violent actions imply. It was clear that he wanted more for these familiar strangers than they seemed to want for themselves. I saw a few angry faces soften, almost imperceptibly.

That was profoundly interesting.

I watched as law enforcement, prosecutors, social service providers, and community members addressed the angry young men, most of whom were attentive if for no other reason than to satisfy their curiosity. The speakers talked about consequences resulting from remaining in a violent lifestyle, but they spoke just as eloquently and passionately—perhaps more so—about how to exit the cycle of violence. They offered assistance and expressed feelings of personal faith, community hope, and love for the angry young men.

I saw the faces of a few young men appear slightly less angry. I saw a few young men choke back tears. I saw in the eyes of a couple of young men the tears of a painful existence—the tears that come from the realization that reality and truth have just intersected within one's consciousness; perhaps tears reflecting a recognition that they could dare to be hopeful about their future.

I saw one young man raise his shackled hands above his head and exclaim "I never knew there was this much love out there . . . seriously, I never knew it." I saw several young men openly express a desire for respite from the pressures of their violent lifestyle. With a shrug of his shoulder, feigning nonchalance, one of the most angry young men said, "I'd like to change because I'm getting older and I'd like to get away from the violence." Nobody argued for the status quo. Not one young man tried to justify violence, or argue that change was impossible, futile, or that their situation was hopeless.

That is profoundly surprising.

I watched mothers bravely balance their own personal anger and grief on the scales of hope as they tearfully and painfully explained how their sons were murdered and how these murders have affected them, their families, and their communities. I heard mothers describe their experience of emotional survival in the company of the misery that comes with a parent outliving a child. I saw a few young men swallow hard and look away—but they couldn't stop listening and couldn't find a suitable distraction to escape the brutality of the truth these women spoke. I saw mothers speak through tears, and I saw young men hang their heads, stare at the ceiling, or simply sit with eyes transfixed on these fearless and charitable women as their words cut mercilessly through the room.

That is profoundly different.

I watched the faces of the law enforcement officers assigned to accompany the young men. I saw a subtle yet measurable change on their faces as well. Over the course of a couple of hours, their facial expressions changed from those of cynicism or polite boredom to attention and curiosity. In a couple of instances, I saw those public servants struggle to control their emotions, just as I was. I suspect that those law enforcement officers, like me, have had their moments of living the lives of angry young men, too, albeit from a different vantage point than those they were there to protect or guard. Too much anger leads to many harmful emotions, the most common among the protectors probably being best described as hopeless exhaustion.

Regardless of our politics or our propensity for honest introspection, somewhere within us we all seek unity and healing. Long ago, we grew weary of living through the experiences of angry young men dying at our feet. I believe I saw recognition in the expressions of those law enforcement officers that maybe there are solutions to what we may have considered insolvable problems. Perhaps the seeds of change were planted in the fertile soil of public service today.

That is profoundly refreshing.

I saw former gang members, convicted murderers, drug dealers—those reformed men and women who now reach out to others as their penance for what they've taken in a previous, unrepentant life—speak passionately and eloquently, pleading with the young men to take the help being offered. I saw some of these former criminals weep for the soon-to-be lost young men and maybe in some way for themselves and then be embraced by society's elite, both literally and figuratively. The young men saw that, too, and I suspect the significance of that solitary, sincere, and meaningful demonstration of community was not lost on them. And I saw the change that is coming.

It is profound change.

I walked away from this experience transformed from an observer to a participant, born of a renewed sense of hope and the warmth of a newly sparked inner fire. I believe again—I believe that there is hope for the hopeless, healing for the angry, and justice for the community. I believe that lives are being changed and will be changed. I believe that we—the community in its purest form and finest sense—will prevail, through the certain challenges and general messiness that human interactions create, through the inevitable setbacks, and the new obstacles that success itself will bring. We will prevail; we will be stronger, wiser, and more united as a community and, perhaps, eventually, as a people. (National Network for Safe Communities 2013, Appendix D)

We began this chapter with the observation that the formal mechanisms of direct communication within focused deterrence are "just talking to people." We can end it with the observation that there is nothing simple, or trivial, or—sometimes tragically—even routine about people talking to people. Focused deterrence is built on important and fundamental truths, ones that have—as this article demonstrates—scientific grounding, but much more than that social and moral grounding. Violence is special, specially harmful and specially unacceptable; people deserve to be safe; they deserve to live free and successful lives; they have worth, no matter what they may have done or not done; they deserve help; they deserve respect; they deserve to be heard; they care about each other, and influence each other both for good and for ill. Accountability matters; the state should protect and not do harm. Direct communication within focused deterrence is technique, but it is more centrally human engagement around these truths—sometimes profoundly so. Science can capture some of the outcomes of that engagement, as the evaluation literature of focused deterrence does. It cannot, at least so far, capture its moral salience or its raw human power. It is these that matter the most, in the work and in the world.

NOTES

1. In his work in New York State, the author found that high-risk youth routinely thought that they had a statutory "YO" pass for first offenses, a mistaken belief based on the frequently exercised but discretionary option for authorities to apply a "youthful offender" provision of state law.
2. Chauncey Parker, personal communication.
3. Andrew Papachristos, personal communication.
4. See, for example, the Credible Messenger Justice Center, at https://cmjcenter.org .
5. The creator of the slogan, Los Angeles' Father Greg Boyle, has since disavowed it, recognizing that work and work programs do not address the extraordinary needs of those most exposed to violence. See, for example, John Schmid, "What Stops a Bullet? Milwaukee Can Learn from L.A. Program That Has Turned to Trauma Care," *Milwaukee Journal-Sentinal*, June 18, 2018. Retrieved from https://www.jsonline.com/story/news/2018/06/18/what-stops-bullet-milwaukee-can-look-innovative-l-jobs-program/702143002/ .

REFERENCES

Abt, Thomas, and Christopher Winship. 2016. "What Works in Reducing Community Violence: A Meta-Review and Field Study for the Northern Triangle." Washington, DC: USAID. https://www.usaid.gov/sites/default/files/USAID-2016-What-Works-in-Reducing-Community-Violence-Final-Report.pdf .

Agnew, Robert. 1994. "The Techniques of Neutralization and Violence." *Criminology* 32 (4): 555–80.

Anderson, Elijah. 1994. "The Code of the Streets." *Atlantic Monthly*, May. Retrieved from http://historia.ihnca.edu.ni/ccss/dmdocuments/Bibliografia/CCSS2007/tema4/adicional/Anderson_Code_of_the_streets_1_.pdf .

Anderson, Elijah. 2000. *Code of the Street: Decency, Violence, and the Moral Life of the Inner City*. New York: WW Norton.

Apel, Robert. 2013. "Sanctions, Perceptions, and Crime: Implications for Criminal Deterrence." *Journal of Quantitative Criminology* 29 (1): 67–101.

Ariel, Barak, Ashley Englefield, and John Denley. 2019. "I Heard It through the Grapevine: A Randomized Controlled Trial on the Direct and Vicarious Effects of Preventative Specific Deterrence Initiatives in Criminal Networks." *Journal of Criminal Law and Criminology* 109 (4): 819. Advance Online: https://scholarlycommons.law.northwestern.edu/jclc/vol109/iss4/3 .

Beccaria, Cesare. 1986. *On Crime and Punishments*. Translated by David Young. Indianapolis: Hackett.

Bell, Monica. 2017. "Police Reform and the Dismantling of Legal Estrangement." *The Yale Law Journal* 126 (7): 2054–150.

Bentham, Jeremy. 1996. *The Collected Works of Jeremy Bentham: An Introduction to the Principles of Morals and Legislation*. Oxford: Clarendon.

Black, Donald. 1983. "Crime as Social Control." *American Sociological Review* 48 (1): 34–45.

Blader, Steven L., and Tom R. Tyler. 2003. "A Four-Component Model of Procedural Justice: Defining the Meaning of a 'Fair' Process." *Personality and Social Psychology Bulletin* 29 (6): 747–58.

Braga, Anthony A., Robert Apel, Brandon C. Welsh, and David L. Weisburd. 2013. "The Spillover Effects of Focused Deterrence on Gang Violence." *Evaluation Review* 37 (3–4): 314–42.

Braga, Anthony A., and David M. Kennedy. 2012. "Linking Situational Crime Prevention and Focused Deterrence Strategies." In *The Reasoning Criminologist: Essays in Honor of Ronald V. Clarke*, edited by Nick Tilley and Graham Farrell, 51–65. London: Taylor & Francis.

Braga, Anthony A., Jack McDevitt, and Glenn L. Pierce. 2006. "Understanding and Preventing Gang Violence: Problem Analysis and Response Development in Lowell, Massachusetts." *Police Quarterly* 9 (1): 20–46.

Braga, Anthony A., David Weisburd, and Brandon Turchan. 2018. "Focused Deterrence Strategies and Crime Control." *Criminology & Public Policy* 17 (1): 205–50.

Brookman, Fiona. 2013. "Accounting for Homicide and Sub-lethal Violence." In *In Their Own Words: Criminals on Crime. An Anthology* (sixth edition), edited by Paul F. Cromwell, 175–92. New York: Oxford University Press.

Brunson, Rod K. 2007. "'Police Don't Like Black People': African-American Young Men's Accumulated Police Experiences." *Criminology & Public Policy* 6 (1): 71–101.

Clark-Moorman, Kyleigh, Jason Rydberg, and Edmund F. McGarrell. 2019. "Impact Evaluation of a Parolee-Based Focused Deterrence Program on Community-Level Violence." *Criminal Justice Policy Review* 30 (9): 1408–30.

Crandall, Vaughn, and Sue-Lin Wong. 2012. *Practice Brief: Call-In Preparation and Execution. Group Violence Reduction Strategy*. Washington, DC: Community Oriented Policing Services.

Desmond, Matthew, Andrew V. Papachristos, and David S. Kirk. 2016. "Police Violence and Citizen Crime Reporting in the Black Community." *American Sociological Review* 81 (5): 857–76.

Eisner, Manuel, and Amy Nivette. 2013. "Does Low Legitimacy Cause Crime? A Review of the Evidence." In *Legitimacy and Criminal Justice: An International Exploration*, edited by Justice Tankebe and Alison Liebling, 308–25. Oxford: Oxford University Press.

Engel, Robin S., Marie Skubak Tillyer, and Nicholas Corsaro. 2013. "Reducing Gang Violence Using Focused Deterrence: Evaluating the Cincinnati Initiative to Reduce Violence (CIRV)." *Justice Quarterly* 30 (3): 403–39.

Fontaine, Jocelyn, Sino Esthappan, Nancy La Vigne, and Jesse Jannetta. 2019. "Views of the Police and Neighborhood Conditions: Evidence of Change in Six Cities Participating in the National Initiative for Building Community Trust and Justice." Washington, DC: Urban Institute. Retrieved from https://www.urban.org/sites/default/files/publication/100706/2019.11.11_ni_community_survey_brief_final_0.pdf .

Friedrich, Michael. 2019. "A Police Department's Difficult Assignment: Atonement." *Bloomberg CityLab*, October 23. Retrieved from https://www.bloomberg.com/news/articles/2019-10-23/what-police-community-reconciliation-can-look-like .

Fullilove, Mindy Thompson, Gina Arias, Moises Nunez, Ericka Phillips, Peter McFarlane, Rodrick Wallace, and Robert E. Fullilove III. 2003. "What Did Ian Tell God? School Violence in East New York." In *Deadly Lessons: Understanding Lethal School Violence*, edited by Mark Harrison Moore, Carol V. Petrie, and Anthony A. Braga, 198–246. Washington, DC: National Academies Press.

Garot, Robert. 2007. "Inner-City Teens and Face-Work: Avoiding Violence and Maintaining Honor." In *A Cultural Approach to Interpersonal Communication: Essential Readings*, edited by Leila Monaghan, Jane E. Goodman, and Jennifer Meta Robinson, 324–46. Oxford: Blackwell.

Garot, Robert. 2010. *Who You Claim: Performing Gang Identity in School and on the Streets*. New York: New York University Press.

Goldman, Liran, Howard Giles, and Michael A. Hogg. 2014. "Going to Extremes: The Forces behind Gang Membership." *Group Processes and Intergroup Relations* 17 (6): 813–32.

Hamilton, Benjamin, Richard Rosenfeld, and Aaron Levin. 2018. "Opting Out of Treatment: Self-Selection Bias in a Randomized Controlled Study of a Focused Deterrence Notification Meeting." *Journal of Experimental Criminology* 14 (1): 1–17.

Kane, Robert J. 2005. "Compromised Police Legitimacy as a Predictor of Violent Crime in Structurally Disadvantaged Communities." *Criminology* 43 (2): 469–98.

Kennedy, David M. 1997. "Pulling Levers: Chronic Offenders, High-Crime Settings, and a Theory of Prevention." *Valparaiso University Law Review* 31: 449–484.

Kennedy, David M. 1998. "Pulling Levers: Getting Deterrence Right." *National Institute of Justice Journal* 236 (2). Retrieved from https://www.ncjrs.gov/pdffiles/jr000236.pdf .

Kennedy, David M. 2006. "Old Wine in New Bottles: Policing and the Lessons of Pulling Levers." In *Police Innovation: Contrasting Perspectives*, edited by David Weisburd and Anthony A. Braga, 155–70. New York: Cambridge University Press.

Kennedy, David M. 2009a. "Drugs, Race and Common Ground: Reflections on the High Point Intervention." *National Institute of Justice Journal* 262: 12–17.

Kennedy, David M. 2009b. *Deterrence and Crime Prevention: Reconsidering the Prospect of Sanction*. New York: Routledge.

Kennedy, David M. 2010. *Practice Brief: Norms, Narratives and Community Engagement for Crime Prevention*. New York: Center for Crime Prevention and Control, John Jay College of Criminal Justice. Retrieved from https://nnscommunities.org/wp-content/uploads/2017/10/Haas__practice_brief_finalwinter2010.pdf .

Kennedy, David M. 2011. *Don't Shoot: One Man, a Street Fellowship, and the End of Violence in Inner-City America*. New York: Bloomsbury.

Kennedy, David M. 2016. "Using the Drug Market Intervention Strategy to Address the Heroin Epidemic." *United States Attorneys' Bulletin* 64 (5): 19–24.

Kennedy, David M. 2019. "Response to "What Works with Gangs: A Breakthrough." *Criminology & Public Policy* 18 (1): e1–4.

Kennedy, David, and Jonathan Ben-Menachem. 2019. "Moving Toward an American Police–Community Reconciliation Framework." In *The Cambridge Handbook of Policing in the United States*, edited by Tamara Rice Lave and Eric J. Miller, 563–80. Cambridge: Cambridge University Press.

Kennedy, David M., Anthony A. Braga, and Anne Morrison Piehl. 2001. *Reducing Gun Violence: The Boston Gun Project's Operation Ceasefire*. Washington, DC: National Institute of Justice.

Kennedy, David M., and Michael A. Friedrich. 2014. *Custom Notifications: Individualized Communication in the Group Violence Intervention*. Washington, DC: Office of Community Oriented Policing Services.

Kennedy, David M., Mark A. R. Kleiman, and Anthony A. Braga. 2017. "Beyond Deterrence: Strategies of Focus and Fairness." In *Handbook of Crime Prevention and Community Safety* (second edition), edited by Nick Tilley and Aiden Sidebottom, 157–82. New York: Routledge.

Kirk, David, and Andrew V. Papachristos. 2009. "Cultural Mechanisms and the Persistence of Neighborhood Violence." *American Journal of Sociology* 116 (4): 1190–233.

Kleck, Gary, Brion Sever, Spencer Li, and Marc Gertz. 2005. "The Missing Link in General Deterrence Research." *Criminology* 43 (3): 623–60.

Kleck, Gary, and J. C. Barnes. 2013. "Deterrence and Macro-Level Perceptions of Punishment Risks: Is There a 'Collective Wisdom'?" *Crime & Delinquency* 59 (7): 1006–35.

Kleiman, Mark. 2009. *When Brute Force Fails: How to Have Less Crime and Less Punishment*. Princeton: Princeton University Press.

Klofas, John. 2001. "Guns, Disputes, and Drug Sales: Focus Groups at Monroe Correctional Facility." *Rochester SACSI Research* Working Paper, No. 2001-08, Rochester Institute of Technology. Retrieved from https://www.rit.edu/liberalarts/sites/rit.edu.liberalarts/files/documents/our-work/2001-08.pdf .

La Vigne, Nancy, Jesse Jannetta, Jocelyn Fontaine, Daniel S. Lawrence, and Sino Esthappan. 2019. "The National Initiative for Building Community Trust and Justice: Key Process and Outcome Evaluation Findings." Washington, DC: Urban Institute. Retrieved from https://www.urban.org/sites/default/files/publication/100704/national_initiative_for_building_community_trust_and_justice_3.pdf .

Lochner, Lance. 2007. "Individual Perceptions of the Criminal Justice System." *American Economic Review* 97 (1): 444–60.

Lurie, Stephen. 2019. "There's No Such Thing as a Dangerous Neighborhood." *Bloomberg Citylab*, February 25. Retrieved from https://www.bloomberg.com/news/articles/2019-02-25/beyond-broken-windows-what-really-drives-urban-crime .

MacCoun, Robert, and Peter Reuter. 1992. "Are the Wages of Sin $30 an Hour? Economic Aspects of Street-Level Drug Dealing." *Crime & Delinquency* 38 (4): 477–91.

Matthay, Ellicott C., Kriszta Farkas, Kara E. Rudolph, Scott Zimmerman, Melissa Barragan, Dana E. Goin, and Jennifer Ahern. 2019. "Firearm and Nonfirearm Violence after Operation Peacemaker Fellowship in Richmond, California, 1996–2016." *American Journal of Public Health* 109 (11): 1605–11.

Matza, David. 1967. *Delinquency and Drift*. New York: John Wiley & Sons.

Meares, Tracey L., and Andrew V. Papachristos. 2009. "Policing Gun Crime without Guns." Retrieved from https://ssrn.com/abstract=1326932 .

Mentel, Zoe. 2012. *Racial Reconciliation, Truth Telling, and Police Legitimacy*. Washington, DC: Office of Community Oriented Policing Services. Retrieved from https://nccpsafety.org/assets/files/library/Racial_Reconciliation__Police_Legitimacy.pdf .

Miller, Dale T., and Cathy McFarland. 1987. "Pluralistic Ignorance: When Similarity Is Interpreted as Dissimilarity." *Journal of Personality and Social Psychology* 53 (2): 298–305.

Miller, Dale T., and Deborah A. Prentice. 1994. "Collective Errors and Errors about the Collective." *Personality and Social Psychology Bulletin* 20 (5): 541–50.

Morgan, Anthony, Hayley Boxall, Christopher Dowling, and Rick Brown. 2020. "Policing Repeat Domestic Violence: Would Focused Deterrence Work in Australia?" *Trends & Issues in Crime and Criminal Justice* 593 (March): 1–20.

Nagin, Daniel S. 2018. "Deterrent Effects of the Certainty and Severity of Punishment." In *Deterrence, Choice, and Crime: Contemporary Perspectives*, edited by Daniel S. Nagin, Francis T. Cullen, and Cheryl Lero Jonson, 157–85. New York: Routledge.

National Network for Safe Communities. 2013. *Group Violence Intervention: An Implementation Guide*. Washington, DC: US Department of Justice, Office of Community Oriented Policing Services.

National Network for Safe Communities. 2017. *Implementing Support and Outreach in Community Violence Prevention*. New York: John Jay College of Criminal Justice. Retrieved from https://

www.nnscommunities.org/wp-content/uploads/2017/10/Support_and_Outreach_White_Paper.pdf .

Oberlander, Derek F. 2018. "How Focused Deterrence Principles Can Reduce Violence in Correctional Facilities." *Corrections Today* 80 (4): 22–101.

Papachristos, Andrew V. 2009. "Murder by Structure: Dominance Relations and the Social Structure of Gang Homicide." *American Journal of Sociology* 115 (1): 74–128.

Papachristos, Andrew V., Tracey L. Meares, and Jeffrey Fagan. 2007. "Attention Felons: Evaluating Project Safe Neighborhoods in Chicago." *Journal of Empirical Legal Studies* 4 (2): 223–72.

Papachristos, Andrew V., Tracey L. Meares, and Jeffrey Fagan. 2012. "Why Do Criminals Obey the Law? The Influence of Legitimacy and Social Networks on Active Gun Offenders." *Journal of Criminal Law and Criminology* 102 (2): 397–440.

Papachristos, Andrew V., Christopher Wildeman, and Elizabeth Roberto. 2015. "Tragic, but Not Random: The Social Contagion of Nonfatal Gunshot Injuries." *Social Science & Medicine* 125 (January): 139–50.

Paternoster, Raymond. 1987. "The Deterrent Effect of the Perceived Certainty and Severity of Punishment: A Review of the Evidence and Issues." *Justice Quarterly*, 4 (2): 173–217.

Pitts, John. 2008. *Reluctant Gangsters: The Changing Face of Youth Crime*. Portland: Taylor & Francis.

Prentice, Deborah A., and Dale T. Miller. 1996. "Pluralistic Ignorance and the Perpetuation of Social Norms by Unwitting Actors." In *Advances in Experimental Social Psychology*, edited by Mark P. Zanna, Vol. 28, 161–209. San Diego: Academic Press.

Saltzman, Linda, Raymond Paternoster, Gordon P. Waldo, and Theodore G. Chiricos. 1982. "Deterrent and Experiential Effects: The Problem of Causal Order in Perceptual Deterrence Research." *Journal of Research in Crime and Delinquency* 19 (2): 172–89.

Sampson, Robert J., and Dawn Jeglum Bartusch. 1998. "Legal Cynicism and (Subcultural?) Tolerance of Deviance: The Neighborhood Context of Racial Differences." *Law & Society Review* 32 (4): 777–804.

Scott, Michael S. 2017. *Focused Deterrence of High-Risk Individuals*. Washington, DC: Center for Problem-Oriented Policing.

Sechrist, Stacy M., and John D. Weil. 2018. "Assessing the Impact of a Focused Deterrence Strategy to Combat Intimate Partner Domestic Violence." *Violence Against Women* 24 (3): 243–65.

Sykes, Gresham M., and David Matza. 1957. "Techniques of Neutralization: A Theory of Delinquency." *American Sociological Review* 22 (6): 664–70.

Tillyer, Marie Skubak, and David M. Kennedy. 2008. "Locating Focused Deterrence Approaches within a Situational Crime Prevention Framework." *Crime Prevention and Community Safety* 10 (2): 75–84.

Trinkner, Rick. 2019. "Addressing the 'Black Box' of Focused Deterrence: An Examination of the Mechanisms of Change in Chicago's Project Safe Neighborhoods." *Journal of Experimental Criminology* 15 (4): 673–83.

Tyler, Tom R. 2004. "Enhancing Police Legitimacy." *The Annals of the American Academy of Political and Social Science* 593 (1): 84–99.

Tyler, Tom R., Jeffrey Fagan, and Amanda Geller. 2014. "Street Stops and Police Legitimacy: Teachable Moments in Young Urban Men's Legal Socialization." *Journal of Empirical Legal Studies* 11 (4): 751–85.

Wallace, Danielle, Andrew V. Papachristos, Tracey Meares, and Jeffrey Fagan. 2016. "Desistance and Legitimacy: The Impact of Offender Notification Meetings on Recidivism among High Risk Offenders." *Justice Quarterly* 33 (7): 1237–64.

Warner, Bernie, Dan Pacholke, and Carly Kujath. 2014. "Operation Place Safety: First Year in Review." Washington State Department of Corrections. Retrieved from https://www.doc.wa.gov/docs/publications/reports/200-SR002.pdf .

Wilkinson, Deanna Lyn. 2003. *Guns, Violence, and Identity among African American and Latino Youth*. El Paso: LFB Scholarly Publishing.

Wilkinson, Deanna L., Chauncey C. Beaty, and Regina M. Lurry. 2009. "Youth Violence—Crime or Self-Help? Marginalized Urban Males' Perspectives on the Limited Efficacy of the Criminal Justice System to Stop Youth Violence." *The Annals of the American Academy of Political and Social Science* 623 (1): 25–38.

Wilkinson, Deanna L., and Jeffrey Fagan. 1996. "The Role of Firearms in Violence 'Scripts': The Dynamics of Gun Events among Adolescent Males." *Law and Contemporary Problems* 59 (1): 55–89.

Woo, DaJung, Howard Giles, Michael A. Hogg, and Liran Goldman, L. 2015. "Social Psychology of Gangs: An Intergroup Communication Perspective." In *Handbook of Gangs,* edited by Scott H. Decker and David C. Pyrooz, 136–56. New York: Wiley-Blackwell.

Woo, DaJung. 2018. "Gangs and Intergroup Communication." In *The Oxford Encyclopedia of Intergroup Communication*, edited by Howard Giles and Jake Harwood, Vol. 1, 409–22. New York: Oxford University Press.

Wood, Julia, and Howard Giles, eds. 2014. "Gangs: Group and Intergroup Dimensions" [Special Issue]. *Group Processes and Intergroup Relations* 17 (6): 701–832.

Zimring, Franklin, and Gordon Hawkins. 1973. *Deterrence: The Legal Threat in Crime Control*. Chicago: University of Chicago Press.

CHAPTER 21

Policing Hate Crimes and Terrorism in the Digital Age

Brian Blakemore

From a policing perspective, hate, extremism, and terrorism have similar characteristics and are part of a continuum of inappropriate responses to messages of fear, social threat, and uncertainty (Allport 1954; Belavadi 2018) in the sense that the perpetrators are usually unknown to the law enforcement agencies; the victims and the perpetrators are dispersed throughout society; and such crimes (that are perceived to be on the rise) are the subject of a strong ongoing media focus. The need to understand intergroup hate as a mobilizing factor (see Reicher 2010) and to fully define these crimes as communicated and polarizing *messages* (see Myers and Stohl 2010) is important in order to support victims and police these crimes. After examining different definitions of hate crime, this chapter will examine the extremist agenda and modus operandi, with a view to understanding them *as* intergroup communication (Orehek 2012). The balance between free speech and privacy, versus the need to prevent and tackle offensive, subversive, and terrorist material are all explored as are the barriers victims face in reporting this crime. The ever-increasing time spent communicating on and living via the Internet and social media has wide ramifications for policing such crimes (Waltman 2018a; see chapters 15 and 17) as well as the hate agenda. This relatively new living space places new responsibilities, demands, and capabilities on law enforcement and the protection of the public. There is a need for all agencies and the public to build strong inclusive communities and a culture that proactively challenges expressions of prejudice and extremism. The police must listen to and gain the trust of all sections of society (see chapters 8 and 17).

THE GROUNDWORK OF DEFINITIONS CROSS-NATIONALLY

When considering what constitutes an unlawful expression of hate or extremism, the situation is complicated, as it curtails the right to free speech. Different countries have different legislation around these communication issues. Human Rights including "Freedom of Speech" are established in an international treaty (International Covenant on Civil and Political Rights); however, this covenant also stresses the "duties and responsibilities" attached to these rights and both elements should be fairly balanced within all legislation. The treaty specifically enables laws that prohibit advocating hatred based upon nationality, race, or religion that incites discrimination, aggression, or violence (UKFCO 2014). This treaty requires both these aspects, prejudice against a specified group and inciting such actions, to be present; it does not prohibit speech that is provocative or offensive.

Geert Wilders, an outspoken leader of a far-right Dutch political party, was found not guilty of hate speech, despite making derogatory comments about Muslims; comparing the Koran to Hitler's "Mein Kampf," and demanding cessation of further Muslim immigration in Holland. These comments were deemed to be protected speech as his comments were directed against the Muslim religion not against individuals or a group of people and did not incite violence (Jolly 2011). Hate speech is illegal within the United Kingdom. However, expression of dislike, ridicule, insult, or abuse of religions and beliefs is allowable, as the UK hate crime legislation aims to protect individuals not beliefs. If the hate speech is deemed to be an incitement to criminal action or a threatening behavior, then it is illegal. Hate speech is the expression of extremism and includes labels as rhetorical mechanisms and discrimination (see Kashima, Fielder, and Freytag 2008). Likewise, Waltman (2018a) argues that hate speech aims to dehumanize and make illegitimate the outgroup members' identity values and beliefs. It describes them as threats to the ingroup's way of life, which can lead to calls for the elimination of the outgroup (see chapter 1).

Hate crime is a wider concept than hate speech and describes illegal acts that target a victim for an aspect of their identity. As in the United States, the Crown Prosecution Service in England and Wales (CPS 2018) states that race, religion, sexual orientation, gender identity, and disability are protected characteristics for hate crime. There are two main features required in such legislation in both of these countries. Firstly, that the act was a criminal offense in its own right; secondly, that the act must have in part been committed and motivated out of prejudice toward the victim because of their protected characteristic. In the United Kingdom (UK), these acts are not defined but "use the everyday understanding of the word which includes ill-will, spite, contempt, prejudice, unfriendliness, antagonism, resentment and dislike" (CPS 2018, 1). In the United States, the law varies by state, but hate crime includes such communicative acts as threats, harassment, or physical harm (USLegal.com 2019). The purpose of hate crime legislation is to impose additional penalties where the perpetrator committing the offense was motivated by the victim's actual or perceived protected characteristic. In the UK, there have been calls to include age as a protected characteristic. This confuses the criminal's rational choice of easy prey, recognizing that the young and old may be vulnerable, with an irrational prejudice (see Bytheway 1995). Thus, the definition is complex, subjective, and potentially confusing, especially when making cross-jurisdiction comparisons.

International Comparison of Communicating Hate Crimes

The specific type of hate crime is usually defined in terms of the prejudice that motivated the offender. Table 21.1 shows the relative and absolute levels of hate crime recorded between 2016 and 2019 within the United States, and England and Wales (E&W). As for most crimes, the recorded figure is understood to be significantly lower than that experienced by victims, some of whom may experience and report more than one crime and can also report incidents that are not recorded as a crime. Most hate crimes are perceived to be driven by one prejudice, yet some are found to have been motivated by multiple prejudices. These two countries report the statistics in different formats: In the United States, the number of offenses is shown; whereas in E&W, it is the number of motivating prejudices, which is higher by around 5 percent.

Another major notable difference shown in table 21.1 is the scale of reporting, with over twelve times more hate crime, mostly "acts intended or likely to stir up racial or religious hatred—Use of words or behavior or display or written material" (Home Office 2018, 1), being reported in E&W than in the United States; even though the latter has a population over six times the former. Interestingly, in E&W, the reporting rate of hate crime (53 percent) appears to be higher than the average for all crimes (40 percent), and this trend has been apparent for the last ten years. Racial prejudice is the main motivation for hate crime in both countries, with this being more pronounced within E&W. In the United States, religion is the second most common motivation, 58 percent of this is anti-Jewish, followed by 15 percent anti-Muslim (see chapter 8); both the ranking and the amount these religions are targeted is very different in E&W being 18 percent and 47 percent, respectively. Sexual orientation is ranked third in the United States and second in E&W (see chapter 7; but with a considerably lower relative frequency in the latter), with hate crimes motivated by disability being considerably higher within E&W than within the United States (FBI 2018; Home Office 2019).

Given that these offenses are a communication of intergroup hate, driven by fear, why are the extremist groups and their self-defined outgroups different in different countries? This may reflect different issues, content, and emphasis in the national and local media in these countries. Also, different extremist groups may be more or less active in expressing their particular aims in different jurisdictions (see Belavadi 2018). There may be historical differences; the different cultures in these countries have developed dissimilar levels of social categorization that focuses hate onto different targets. The comparison of international differences is an area that has not been studied in any detail. However, one common threat that drives extremism is globalization. Bartlett, Birdwell, and Littler (2011) found that in Europe "Populist" movements that are critical of globalization are anti-establishment and support workers' rights (conventional left-wing politics), but are also very concerned with protecting national culture and opposition to immigration (conventional far right policy), which have rapidly gained supporters.

While globalization is also an issue within the United States, the narrative has not necessarily encompassed all these factors. Furthermore, foreign policy may generate feelings of injustice that can lead to radicalization. For example, Baroness Manningham-Buller, a former controller of the British security service, stated that the British

TABLE 21.1. A Comparison of the Levels of Hate Crime Recorded between the United States and the UK

Motivation	USA 2016	USA 2017	USA 2018	England and Wales 2016–17	England and Wales 2017–18	England and Wales 2018–19
Race / Ethnicity / Ancestry	58.9 % 4,229 offenses	59.4% 4,832 offenses	59.5% 4,954 offenses	74.1% 62,685 biases	71.2 % 71,264 biases	70.1 % 78,991 biases
Religion	21.1% 1,538 offenses	20.7% 1,679 offenses	18.6 % 1,550 offenses	7.0 % 5,949 biases	8.3 % 8,339 biases	7.6 % 8,556 biases
Sexual Orientation	16.7% 1,218 offenses	16.9% 1,303 offenses	16.5 % 1,404 offenses	10.8 % 9,157 biases	11.6 % 11,592 biases	12.9% 14,491 biases
Gender-Identity including Transgender	1.7 % 130 offenses	1.6 % 131 offenses	2.2 % 184 offenses	1.5 % 1,248 biases	1.6 % 1,703 biases	2.1 % 2,333 biases
Disability	1% 76 offenses	1.6 % 128 offenses	2.1 % 177 offenses	6.6 % 5,558 biases	7.2 % 7,221 biases	7.3 % 8,256 biases
Gender	0.5 % 36 offenses	0.6 % 53 offenses	0.7 % 58 offenses	In above categories	In above categories	In above categories
Multiple Prejudices	94 offenses	311 offenses	169 offenses	In above categories	In above categories	In above categories
Offenses	7,321	8,437	8,496	80,393	94,121	103,379
Prejudices	—	—	—	84,597	100,119	112,637

Source: FBI Hate crime statistics by calendar year (2018) and Home Office (2019) for all police forces in England and Wales, which cover notifiable offenses only, for period April to March.

involvement in the war in Iraq in 2003 may well have resulted in increased radicalization, extremism, support for Al Qaeda, and terrorism within the UK from British subjects (BBC News 2010): this demonstrates the importance of a making foreign policy sympathetic to home policy regarding community cohesion and encouraging support from all sections of that nation's society. Thus, the political agenda and how it is communicated may be an important factor in the level of extremist activity in a country.

SOCIAL CATEGORIZATION, EXCLUSION, AND HATE

Anderson (1983) defined an "imagined political community" as one held together by their shared worldviews and philosophy, in which a member may never actually physically meet or even really know many of this community (see identity fusion theory, Fredman et al. 2015). The Internet facilitates not only in locating such common views but also forges and co-creates a "national narrative" that espouses them, together with the coordination of collective, communicative action on behalf of these groups (Dutton 2013). Anderson (1983) also proposed that there are three "actions" necessary to create such communities: establishing threats against boundaries; demonstrating political legitimation and emotional power; and eroding other (previous) imaginings.

The boundaries are whatever differentiates the community from the outgroup, so it could be a physical or political border, a racial, religious, or any other perceived difference between the ingroup and the outgroup. The threat is whatever puts this community at risk (see integrated threat theory, Croucher 2018; Risk, Mania, and Gaertner 2006). For example, globalization and immigration are often seen as threats to national identity, existing culture, and way of life by supporters of right popularist groups (e.g., Croucher 2013). Political legitimation arises when the government or a political party makes the aims part of the national agenda within politics; this, in turn, releases emotional power from being within an official national ingroup. Following the decline of colonial empires, historians, politicians, and states have reinterpreted history and created a different narrative of reality, effectively the erosion of other (previous) imaginings, the third element in this model.

Waltman (2015, 206) espouses a similar analysis of hate and extremism within a framework of "homology of exclusion" that comprises three themes: the superiority of the ingroup, based upon their worldview and norms being the correct reality; the inferior views and values of the outgroup threaten the purity and existence of the ingroup (see above); and the ingroup is exclusively allowed to imagine and work toward the removal of the outgroup and their heretical immoral beliefs and actions. Waltman (2015) expands upon this in terms of the views of white supremacists who draw upon their religion and cultural history to describe themselves as warriors fighting for their beliefs, with another second example being ISIS, in their attempt to form their own caliphate and destroy all nonbelievers (Kafirs). Such extreme views do not allow for any form of compromise, as this is seen as heresy and the beginning of the erosion of the purity and sanctity of the ingroup's ideals. Waltman also cites right-wing Americans who support the freedom to carry guns and see any form of gun control as one of many onslaughts on their individual freedoms. Indeed, the right wing are defined by their belief in the individual being paramount and society and the state having less importance.

In a study of two extreme right-wing groups—Britain First and Reclaim Australia—Nouri and Lorenzo-Dus (2019) found that, over a period of four months, they published 318,000 messages comprising 4.7 million words mainly using Facebook and, to a much lesser extent, Twitter. These groups organized rallies and protests, so some followers would meet in reality via such activities, although they were primarily online groups. Their analysis found both had common communication structures—using their own key words, building their arguments on "topical events," and making clear distinct differences between ingroups and outgroups. Reclaim Australia's language was far more aggressive, including swear words and relatively more derogatory phrasings.

The use of topical events to raise the temperature and tempo of ingroups' actions—and activating their social identities in social media (see Carr, Varney, and Blesse 2016)—can be linked with the reported increase in hate crime following terrorist activities. Sudden spikes in hate crimes and hate incidents following a related high-profile incident, is a recognized phenomenon with anti-groups becoming more active when their perceived enemy is active or newsworthy (Blakemore 2016). Nouri and Lorenzo-Dus (2019) found Britain First proposed policies and expressed outrage, thereby conforming to the political legitimation and emotional power aspects of the Anderson model (1983). They also found that the groups praised their own ingroup morality to further bond and contrast the boundaries between themselves and outgroups (see Ellemers and van den Bos 2012). However, they found rather than eroding previous imaginings, the discourse focused on contrasting the goodness in themselves with the badness of outgroups, which is at odds with Anderson's model. Furthermore, they found that threats and boundary establishment was the main thrust of these groups' communications, which aligns well with Waltman's (2015) model. To summarize, the aim of the extremist group is to alienate, weaken, and destroy the outgroup. The form that extremist acts take and the effect they have on the victims of hate crime is considered in the following section.

BARRIERS TO REPORTING HATE CRIME AND IMPROVING SUPPORT FOR VICTIMS

Cuerden (2019) collected 209 hate crime victim responses (via telephone interviews in Wales); this study revealed no association between the particular hate crime reported and the way a victim felt at the time of choosing to communicate a crime. The victims reported mainly assault occasioning bodily harm (48 percent), harassment (29 percent), and public order issues (16 percent), along with other offenses (7 percent). Cuerden (2019) suggested that "the more violent the offence the more likely a victim is to report it" (204) (see also Corcoran, Lader, and Smith 2015). Cuerden (2019) also found that victims who do report, generally report hate crime on the first occasion, especially so with assault occasioning bodily harm and public order offenses. However, victims of harassment and various other offenses have a slightly higher tendency to report the matter following suffering prolonged hate abuse.

Hate victims may experience internal and external barriers to reporting and communicating about the matter. The former barriers are factors that lie within the victim's mind, whereas the latter barriers are associated with culture, society, and the effectiveness of the services available to support them. Cuerden's (2019) respondents stated that they experienced more external barriers than internal barriers when reporting hate crime, and these were as follows:

- the police; officers' attitude; lack of trust in the police; poor previous performance and support from officers;
- society in general in that hate crime is not taken seriously; and
- that there is insufficient information and support available to aid them to communicate about the matter.

It is arguable that these factors together have caused hate crime to become almost *normalized* as perceived by victims (Wong, Christmann, Meadows, Albertson, and Senior 2013). Thus, they may feel that to report the matter is a waste of time, that nothing positive happens when it is reported, the matter continues despite it being reported, and, lastly, that any resolution takes far too long. Many of these external barriers fall within the remit of the police as, for example, in the case of gay hate crime victims reporting they perceived poor responses and treatment (Herek, Gillis, and Cogan 1999). While these data are twenty years old, and efforts have been made to recruit more gay and transpersons since then (Colvin 2012), training manuals have been prepared to facilitate better and more accommodative communication by law enforcement with these communities (Perry and Franey 2017). Such victims have communicated that besides improved service from police, they would like to see more encouragement to report; accessible reporting centers for them to feel safe when communicating about their victimhood; and instant punishments, harsher sentences, and effective prosecutions (Cuerden 2019). This may reflect the need for justice to be seen to be done or to remove the fear of making the situation worse if the victim reports (an internal barrier) as found by Wong and Christmann (2008).

Key decision points may occur in the process of reporting of, and communicating about, a hate crime (McDevitt, Balboni, Bennett, Weiss, Orchowsky, and Walbot 2000) and these include the following. First, the victim needs to recognize that a crime has been committed and realize that it may be a hate crime. Second, the police need to acknowledge and recognize that a bias or prejudice may have contributed to the motivation to commit the crime, and then document and record it as a hate crime. Many of these steps may be influenced by better education, better communication, and better relationships as the potential here is rife for the maintenance of intergroup barriers between law enforcement and victims. To facilitate the communication of hate crime within E&W, the government has introduced and supports third-party organizations as reporting agencies. In this way, victims can report directly to the police by telephone or online through "True Vision," the third-party reporting website; victims may also report directly to Victim Support Cymru, within Wales. However, third-party reporting centers may only be effective in raising awareness of the issue in settings where opportunities to report such incidents already exist (Torfaen People First 2012), such as day opportunity centers, community education establishments, or services focused upon protection of vulnerable adults. The community, in general, has limited knowledge that these communicative centers actually exist.

Cuerden and Blakemore (2019) found that the police and other service providers, such as, for example, the National Health Service, housing associations, probation services, the Race Equality Council, and Citizens Advice, had very different perceptions of the barriers to reporting. They focused on three barriers—some already attested to above—in the following order of importance: the victims' fear that reporting would make things worse and give rise to repercussions; society not taking the problem seriously and giving little or no support; and the victims' feelings of shame, vulnerability, embarrassment, stigma, and self-blame (Lyons 2006). This focus is mainly on internal barriers within the victims' minds and evidences communication failure by many public service providers in not demonstrating an ability to communicate about a common understanding of the situation.

Necessarily, of course, victims of hate crime must expect that meaningful action will be taken, that they will be safe, and that the action will resolve their predicament. Lessened compassion fatigue by police (Grant, Lavery, and Decarlo 2019) and other service providers, better support, and communicative efficiency and effectiveness in dealing with the issue are all important factors to increase victim's reporting rates and resolution of the situation. Some victims lack awareness of what constitutes a hate crime and may not disclose sufficient details for the police to view it as such (Chakraborti, Garland, and Hardy 2014). Unfortunately, the police are not always able to identify accurately when a hate crime has occurred; this may be due to such factors as high levels of demand and reductions in police numbers; not realizing the importance to the victim and society of such crimes; and compassion fatigue. To counter these weaknesses police culture and police training are important factors needing constant improvement (Wickes, Pickering, Mason, Maher, and McCulloch 2016).

GOVERNMENT STRATEGIES TO COUNTER THE HATE AGENDA

In the UK, the government's counter-terrorism strategy known as Contest has four strands: pursue, prevent, protect, and prepare. The *prevent* strategy aims "to stop people becoming terrorists or supporting terrorism" (Home Office 2011a, 9). This strand of proactive policing is focused on dealing with the threats of extremist propaganda and preventing the recruitment of extremist members (for understanding the communication of radicalization and recruitment in the digital age, see Archetti 2015). The strategy has three objectives:

- respond to the ideological challenge of terrorism and the threat we face from those who promote it;
- prevent people from being drawn into terrorism and ensure that they are given appropriate advice and support; and

- work with sectors and institutions where there are risks of radicalization which we need to address. (Home Office 2011b)

More recently, section 26 of the Counter-Terrorism and Security Act 2015, has placed a legal duty on specific authorities who must help prevent people from being drawn into terrorism (Home Office 2015). This introduces a local emphasis to act among educational institutions, health services, and youth offending services; social workers; and housing and voluntary groups. Hence, teachers, for example, have a duty to look for any signs of radicalization, both violent and nonviolent, and to report the suspect to the police. The Channel board (within the *prevent* strand) would then assess the nature and extent of the risk and provide appropriate support at an early stage to such a vulnerable child. Criticisms of this strategy include the erosion of human rights; defining what constitutes extremism, especially nonviolent extremism; the potential to create a perceived bias against Islam; and the moral difficulty in naming and labeling vulnerable children. The main problem in identifying and dealing with a child developing an unacceptable ideological position, as opposed to nonviolent extremist radicalization, is that there is no specific route found in the development profile of terrorists.

The British Security Service found that extremists and terrorists were widely distributed within their communities and that they could not be profiled based upon nationality and demographics. They were mostly British citizens, not immigrants or foreign nationals; many were not regularly practicing their religion; they were not disproportionately suffering from mental illness or pathological personality traits; and many had steady relationships and families (Travis 2008). This contests the "conveyor belt" theory of radicalization that supposes that individuals who are disillusioned and aggrieved with society become simultaneously more religious and extreme, and this, in turn, leads to extremism, violence, and terror.

Displaying anti-British values is one part of the UK definition of radicalization, thus students may be reported for displaying typical rebellious youth attitudes and behavior. Given that free thought, free speech ,and a right to privacy are also human rights in democratic countries, should teachers report any student for voicing their opinion? Furthermore, if students feel they cannot debate sensitive issues in schools and universities, this may drive such discussion underground, thereby making the students more vulnerable to radicalization. Instead teachers need to encourage debate in schools about issues in society and how different religions view these issues. The pupils need to develop an appreciation of, respect for, and tolerance of the views of others (Kundnani 2009).

This is supported by Sunstein (2009) who states the way to combat extremism and group polarization is information exchange via debate. This scholar argues that social networks can operate as polarization machines helping to confirm and amplify people's antecedent views. Mass communication via the Internet produces cascade effects, where large groups of people agree to a polarized view—even if that view is false—convinced by the number and status of other people holding that view. To counter such cascades, he suggests setting up public debate composed of a number of heterogeneous and articulate people, with reasonable views, to facilitate polarized groups arguing out issues in a rigorous and factual process. Sunstein suggests that governments should organize such debate. However, each individual within society must also contribute to countering the intolerance and lies espoused by extremist and terrorist hate groups and individuals as part of their daily discourse.

ONLINE EXTREMISM AND TERRORISM

Historically, the creators and providers of the Internet have supported a philosophy of unlimited access, anonymity, and total freedom of speech online, with Berners-Lee (2010) capturing well this sentiment. Community involvement, such as the wiki movement and especially Wikileaks and digital popularism, has flourished within this freedom (Blakemore 2016). The development of society and policing in the physical world started with tribes, then into larger communities that self-policed. Following industrialization, large cities arose, facilitating more diverse crime and the anonymity of criminals, which required the formation of separate police forces. Initially, the World Wide Web was small and limited in scope but, after twenty years, the scale of the Internet dwarfs that of the largest city and has more recently become recognized as a virtual wild west (Blakemore 2012) for crime, terror, and state-sponsored cyber war. Recent public opinion, including Berners-Lee (2019), and national governments have decided regulation and enforcement are needed.

The Internet and social media can be used to help police in various communicative ways: (1) victims can report crime directly or via other perceived more friendly and understanding organizations; (2) the police may give prompt and inclusive communication as part of neighborhood watch; raise general awareness especially when a critical incident is occurring, such as a terrorist attack; organize community action to solve a problem or support those in need, for example, cleaning up local areas and giving support for victims in the UK following the 2011 London riots (Procter, Crump, Karlstedt, Voss, and Cantijoch 2013); and (3) citizens may send footage of incidents recorded on their smart devices. However, there can be problems too; victims may prefer face-to-face interaction with a known officer, unfounded rumors may spread rapidly, and broadcasting community situations can inform and possibly stimulate vigilante groups (Huey, Nhan, and Broll 2012). Most importantly, the question of respecting the freedoms expected in a modern democracy, such as privacy and anonymity, may conflict with surveillance on the Internet. In the United States, police working with private data mining companies have monitored specific social media sites used by Black and Muslim rights organizations (Perez 2018). This raises a moral question, on whether a "noble cause" justifies an unethical means to an end. When such activities become public, they cause deep mistrust between these mistreated groups and the police.

The Internet has given virtually free and unlimited space for anyone to communicate and express their views, including their discourse of hatred (Meleagrou-Hitchens, Alexander, and Kaderbhai 2017) together with the creation and maintenance of like-minded social networks (Chatfield, Reddick, and Brajawidagda 2015). This coupled with a lack of comprehensive legislation and authority to limit online content has allowed political discourse to be based on "deep fake news" accompanied by hate speech. According to Waltman (2018b), political campaigns now intentionally use this approach to divide Americans into ingroups and outgroups that, arguably, contribute to making such discourse in the United States increasingly susceptible to mainstreaming hate. President Trump was vocal in the need for a wall to prevent illegal immigration and crime emanating from Mexico in the 2016 presidential election. During and subsequent to his election, increased bomb threats against both the Jewish community and other ethnic minorities were recorded (Potok 2017; Torok 2017). The trend to support political groups highly concerned with both the loss of their cultural and social identities and stopping immigration was also made clear in the European Parliament elections in 2014 and again in 2019 (see communicative elements of identity negotiation theory, Ting-Toomey 2005). In these elections, mainly right-wing and anti-European integration groups tripled their parliamentary representation. The so-called dynamic model of mobilization (McAdam, Tarrow, and Tilly 2001) notes that successful organizations modify their collective actions to accommodate changes or developments based on their shared knowledge by and between key members of their social networks (for discussion of the role of networks in intergroup communication, see Stohl, Giles, and Maass 2016). Online groups have a simple and direct way of sharing knowledge, and key members tend to be active on the web pages informing all members of the need to adapt. Hence, online groups are well positioned to mobilize at least some of their members into action (Blakemore 2016).

Controlling Internet content using human censors is difficult; the amount of material added every hour is so large that until sufficiently intelligent algorithms can check and censor it, the human resources needed are not sustainable. Recent state legislation and reviews in Europe are moving in the direction of attempting to control Internet content. In Germany, the Netzwerkdurchsetzungsgesetz Law, introduced at the beginning of 2018, requires the removal of illegal material within twenty-four hours of being notified about such material (BBC News 2018). Within the UK, the use of social media to indoctrinate and recruit into extremist and terrorist activities has been established over many years. In 2020, the UK government reviewed what controls should be imposed upon Internet providers, including making them responsible and liable for the content they allow on their sites (as is the case for publishers of hard copy). However, governments must balance individual freedoms against security needs: The Patriot Act after 9/11 in the United States and the Counter Terrorism Act 2000 in the UK are examples where, arguably, overreaction led to removing privacy and extending custody times, respectively. The UK government is working with the IT sector to develop algorithms and software that will detect extremist content with the required level of accuracy (UK Home Office 2018; see chapter 15). This is the only practical resource to monitor and remove this content, which is akin to seeking a needle in a haystack.

However, existing commercial algorithms used by social media platforms may make fake news more likely to become widely distributed. In this regard, Meserole (2018) describes how two different descriptions of a terrorist attack in Canada were quickly put onto Twitter by a reporter, one stating the attacker was Middle Eastern and angry, the other as being white. The former was retweeted 1,400 times in the following five hours, whereas the latter was hardly retweeted at all. Social media algorithms prioritize content that "engages," that is, that which has been cascaded more beforehand. Thus, inflammatory comments and items that fit current worldviews are prioritized and will be published more widely and more rapidly, even if incorrect. One social media platform, WhatsApp, has taken steps to limit the cascade of fake news and misinformation and in practice mass communication of any sort. This platform restricted its forwarding function to no more than five contacts in 2018. This reduced forwarded cascades by 25 percent over two years. In 2020, WhatsApp restricted the forwarding function on any message that has previously been forwarded five times, to only one new contact, resulting in an immediate 70 percent reduction in forwarded messages (England 2020). WhatsApp defends this curtailment by emphasizing it is a platform for personal not mass communication.

TOWARD COUNTERING THE HATE AGENDA

The recent increase in police budgets in some regions of the world (Knowles 2018) is in and of itself not sufficient to contain and combat terrorism and extremism. There are also complex social consequences to both under- and over-policing ethnic communities (Hawkins 2011), one of which could, ironically, be an increase in local radicalization. Education and honest debate are tools available *within society* to counter the intolerance and lies espoused by extremist and terrorist hate groups and individuals. Furthermore, Waltman (2018b) suggests that hate speech is becoming normalized within US media and that society may stop recognizing it for what it is. Thus, educators and concerned citizens using social media can form the frontline in the battle to resist this assault on tolerance and logical discourse. Educators and all public figures must expose and talk to the aims, fallacies, and lies used by extremists and counter such hatred with honest, logical, and rational debate.

Society must also demonstrate that it communicatively supports those targeted by extremists or terrorists. Vigils and demonstrations of support following such incidents often occur spontaneously, driven by a sense of community-oriented values. The phenomena of online counter *extremist* extremism have also arisen, including the use of direct argument and of sarcastic humor on social media to create a counterargument ("counter-imaginings" in Anderson's model). For example, Tweets such #MuslimApologies, ironically, apologized for all the benefits Muslims had made: "Sorry for Algebra, cameras, universities, hospitals, oh and coffee too" (BBC News 2014, 1). This is a bottom-up community force that potentially can be used to counter online radicalization. This approach follows that favored by Sunstein (2009) to produce meaningful public debate as opposed to the cascade of fake news and false argument. However, this type of action is somewhat reactive, and a more proactive demonstration of cohesiveness and support is also needed. A proactive approach should be on the expressed agenda of all public and community organizations, which should attempt to reach out and form strong bonds and encourage understanding and unbiased debate on contentious matters, across all diverse sections within society (see chapter 12 for a discussion of community resilience).

In a study of proactive policing within the UK, Innes and Roberts (2011) found that the full involvement and resources of the community were not being tapped into. The police may ask the community what their problems and priorities are, but then the police and local council interpreted and implemented their solutions (called horizontal coproduction). The police must not only listen to the problems in a community but also allow that community to fully contribute to defining and implementing the solution; it should be a two-way communicative street. The apportioning of resources between reactive and preventative policing is a major, ongoing strategic question for police services tackling hate crime. Not unrelatedly, how can security services, police forces, and community-safety organizations prevent hateful and violent extremism, given the heterogeneity of extremist's backgrounds and the variety of routes to extremism and terrorism? These organizations need to recognize this variation and develop both proactive campaigns and communicatively reactive responses that are both tailored and targeted. Nonetheless, challenges continually remain given the persistent dilemma to balance trust and human rights against security concerns (for a particular failure to maintain this balance, see Awan and Blakemore 2013).

CONCLUSIONS

There has been much research across the disciplines that argued terrorism and extremism are messages (e.g., Matusitz 2013; Tuman 2017). For instance, Decker and Rainey in a convention paper in 1980 stated, "Terrorism has become not merely a political act, but a carefully designed and rhetorically sophisticated attempt at communication." Counterterrorism has also been articulated in terms of its communicative actions and processes (e.g., Crelinsten 2002; Güler 2012; Sparks, Kreps, Botan, and Rown 2005). In this chapter on policing hate crime, we have examined different definitions and forms of it, barriers to reporting it, ingredients of its inherent agenda, its prevalence in digital media, and ways of reducing it. In line with the title and thrust of this *Handbook*, effective policing of crimes, while benefiting from intergroup communication analyses, needs to be embedded more broadly in an understanding of how society can contribute to the proliferation of felonies, such as various hate crimes, as well as a reduction in them.

Indeed, to counter extremism, truly integrated communities are needed, with encouragement and freedom to openly communicate about contentious issues and allow the building of relationships between different groups holding different belief systems. It must also allow all to maintain their identity and prevent any fear of their group identity being under threat. All public service providers must implement proactive and inclusive communication strategies to underpin such relationships. Educators and public speakers must show the fallacies and lies within hate speech and promote discussion that is inclusive and does not allow for the creation of outgroups, superior groups, hate myths, and mystiques. The apparent increase in hate crimes (see Williams, Burnap, Javed, Liu, and Ozalp 2020), generally thought to be mainly driven by a higher reporting rate, suggests that government policies may be encouraging victims to report such crimes. However, further understanding of victims' needs and their barriers to reporting is needed by all support and policing services.

Community policing that generates open, full two-way communication within coproduction of solutions to the community's disparate problems, coupled with both national and foreign policy to support a cosmopolitan view, is required (see chapter 10). Government law makers and law enforcers must maintain a balanced approach to introducing laws that curtail existing freedoms, policing the Internet without abusing human rights and drifting into an electronic police state; and policing communities without alienating groups especially avoiding over- and under-policing communities based upon class, politics, race, religion, or any other point of difference.

REFERENCES

Allport, Gordon. W. 1954. *The Nature of Prejudice*. Reading: Addison Wesley.
Anderson, Benedict. 1983. *Imagined Communities: Reflections on the Origin and Spread of Nationalism*. London: Verso.
Archetti, Cristina. 2015. "Terrorism, Communication and New Media: Explaining Radicalization in the Digital Age." *Perspectives on Terrorism* 9 (1): 49–59.
Awan, Imran, and Brian Blakemore. 2013. *Extremism, Counter-Terrorism and Policing*. Farnham: Ashgate.
Bartlett, Jamie, Jonathan, Birdwell, and Mark Littler. 2011. "The New Face of Digital Populism." Demos. Retrieved from http://www.demos.co.uk/project/the-new-face-of-digital-populism/ .
BBC News. 2010. "Iraq Inquiry: Ex-MI5 Boss Says War Raised Terror Threat." Retrieved from http://www.bbc.co.uk/news/uk-politics-10693001 .
BBC News. 2014. "Sorry for Algebra, and More #MuslimApologies." Retrieved from http://www.bbc.co.uk/news/blogs-trending-29362370 .
BBC News. 2018. "Germany Starts Enforcing Hate Speech Law." Retrieved from https://www.bbc.co.uk/news/technology-42510868 .
Belavadi, Sucharita. 2018. "Uncertainty and Extremism." In *The Oxford Encyclopedia of Intergroup Communication*, edited by Howard Giles and Jake Harwood, Vol. 2, 434–47. New York: Oxford University Press.
Berners-Lee, Tim. 2010. "Long Live the Web." *Scientific American* 303 (5): 56–61.
Berners-Lee, Tim. 2019. "How to Save the World-Wide-Web." *The (London) Sun*. Retrieved from https://www.thesun.co.uk/news/8622762/tim-berners-lee-how-to-save-the-world-wide-web/ .
Blakemore, Brian. 2012. "Cyberspace, Cyber Crime and Cyber Terrorism." In *Policing Cyber Hate, Cyber Threat and Cyber Terror,* edited by Imran Awan and Brian Blakemore, 21–38. Farnham: Ashgate.
Blakemore, Brian. 2016. "Online Hate and Political Activist Groups." In *Islamophobia in Cyberspace: Hate Crimes Go Viral*, edited by Imran Awan, 63–84, Abingdon: Routledge.
Bytheway, Bill. 1995. *Ageism. (Rethinking Ageing)*. Buckingham: Open University Press.
Carr, Caleb, Eric J. Varney, and J. Ryan Blesse. 2016. "Social Media and Intergroup Communication: Collapsing and Expanding Group Contexts." In *Advances in Intergroup Communication*, edited by Howard Giles and Anne Maass, 155–73. New York: Peter Lang.
Chakraborti, Neil, Jon Garland, and Stevie-Jade Hardy. 2014. "The Leicester Hate Crime Project: Findings and Conclusions." Retrieved from http://www2.le.ac.uk/departments/criminology/hate/documents/fc-full-report .
Chatfield, Akemi Takeoka, Christopher G. Reddick, and Uuf Brajawidagda. 2015. "Tweeting Propaganda, Radicalization and Recruitment: Islamic State Supporters Multi-Sided Twitter Networks." Proceedings of the 16th Annual International Conference on Digital Government Research, May, 239–49: Retrieved from https://doi.org/10.1145/2757401.2757408 .
Colvin, Roddick A. 2012. *Gay and Lesbian Cops: Diversity and Effective Policing*. Boulder: Lynn Rienner.
Corcoran, Hannah, Deborah Lader, and Kevin Smith. 2015. *Hate Crime, England and Wales, 2014/15*. Statistical Bulletin 05/15. London: Home Office.
CPS. 2018. "Hate Crime." Crown Prosecution Service England and Wales. Retrieved from http://www.cps.gov.uk/hate-crime .
Crelinsten, Ronald D. 2002. "Analyzing Terrorism and Counter-terrorism: A Communication Model." *Terrorism and Political Violence* 14 (2): 77–122.

Croucher, Stephen M. 2013. "Integrated Threat Theory and Acceptance of Immigrant Assimilation: An Analysis of Muslim Immigration in Western Europe." *Communication Monographs* 80 (1): 46–62.

Croucher, Stephen M. 2018. "Integrated Threat Theory." In *The Oxford Encyclopedia of Intergroup Communication*, edited by Howard Giles and Jake Harwood, Vol. 1, 627–35. New York: Oxford University Press.

Cuerden, Gareth, and Brian Blakemore. 2019. "Barriers to Reporting Hate Crime: A Welsh Perspective." *The Police Journal: Theory, Practice and Principles.* Advance Online: https://doi.org/10.1177/0032258X19855113 .

Cuerden, Gareth J. 2019. "Identifying the 'Tipping Point' to Reporting Hate Crime and Removing Barriers to Hate Crime Reporting in Wales: A Victim Led Approach." Unpublished PhD dissertation. Sydney: University of South Wales.

Decker, Warren, and Daniel Rainey. 1980. "Terrorism as Communication." Proceedings of the 66th Annual Meeting of the Speech Communication Association. New York. Retrieved from https://eric.ed.gov/?id=ED196091 .

Dutton, William H., ed. 2013. *The Oxford Handbook of Internet Studies.* Oxford: Oxford University Press.

Ellemers, Naomi, and Kees van den Bos. 2012. "Morality in Groups: On the Social-Regularity Functions of Right and Wrong." *Social and Personality Psychology Compass* 61 (12): 878–89.

England, Rachael. 2020. "WhatsApp Says Its Forwarding Limits Are Slowing the Spread of Fake News." Endgadget. Retrieved from https://www.engadget.com/whats-apps-new-forwarding-limits-are-slowing-the-spread-of-fake-news-105500893.html .

FBI. 2018. "Hate Crime Statistics 2018 Victims." Retrieved from https://ucr.fbi.gov/hate-crime/2018/tables/table-1 .

Fredman, Leah A., Michael D. Buhrmester, Angel Homez, William T Fraser, Sanaz Talaifar, Skylar M. Brannon, and William B. Swann, Jr. 2015. "Identity Fusion, Extreme Pro-Group Behavior, and the Path to Defusion." *Social and Personality Compass* 9 (9): 468–80.

Grant, Heath Blair, Cathryn F. Lavery, and John Decarlo. 2019. "An Exploratory Study of Police Officers: Low Compassion Satisfaction and Compassion Fatigue." *Frontiers in Psychology* 9: 2793. Advance Online: https:// doi:10.3389/fpsyg.2018.02793 .

Guardian. 2019. "Election Results across Europe." Retrieved from https://www.theguardian.com/world/ng-interactive/2019/may/26/eu-election-results-2019-across-europe .

Güler, Riza. 2012. "The Role and Place of Strategic Communication in Countering Terrorism." *Savunma Bilimleri Dergisi: The Journal of Defense Sciences* 11 (2): 1–31.

Hawkins, Darnell, F. 2011. Things Fall Apart: Revisiting Race and Ethnic Differences in Criminal Violence amidst a Crime Drop. *Race and Justice* 1 (1): 3–48.

Herek, Gregory, M. J. Roy Gillis, and Jeanine C. Cogan 1999. "Psychological Sequelae of Hate Crime Victimization among Lesbian, Gay and Bisexual Adults." *Journal of Consulting and Clinical Psychology* 67 (6): 945–51.

Home Office. 2011a. "CONTEST: The United Kingdom's Strategy for Countering Terrorism." London: HM Government. Retrieved from https://www.gov.uk/government/uploads/system/uploads/attachment_data/file/97994/c ontest-summary.pdf .

Home Office. 2011b. "Prevent Strategy." London: HM Government. Retrieved from https://www.gov.uk/government/uploads/system/uploads/attachment_data/file/97976/prevent-strategy-review.pdf .

Home Office. 2015. "Counter-Terrorism and Security Act." London: HM Government. Retrieved from http://www.gov.uk/government/collections/counter-terrorism-and-security-bill .

Home Office. 2018. "Hate Crime and Wales 2017 to 2018 Statistics on Hate Crimes and Racial Incidents Recorded by the Police." Retrieved from http://www.gov.uk/government/statistics/hate-crime-england-and-wales-2017-to-2018 .

Home Office. 2019. "Hate Crime England and Wales 2018 to 2019, Statistics on Hate Crimes and Racial Incidents Recorded by the Police." Retrieved from http://www.gov.uk/government/statistics/hate-crime-england-and-wales-2018-to-2019 .

Huey, Laura, Johnny Nhan, and Ryan Broll. 2012. "Uppity Civilians and Cyber-Vigilantes: The Role of the General Public in Policing Cyber-Crime." *Criminology and Criminal Justice* 13 (1): 81–97.

Innes, Martin, and Colin Roberts. 2011. "Field Studies on the Co-Production of Social Control." A Backing Paper for the UPSI ESRC Expert Seminar, Universities' Police Science Institute, Cardiff University 17th/18th March 2011. Retrieved from http://www.upsi.org.uk%252Fresources%252Fsignalcrimesin60secs.pdf .

Jolly, David. 2011. "The Netherlands: Anti-Muslim Speech Is Found Offensive but Legal." *New York Times* 24 June: A6(L).

Kashima, Yoshihisa, Klaus Fiedler, and Peter Freytag. 2008. *Stereotype Dynamics: Language-based Approaches to the Formation, Maintenance, and Transformation of Stereotypes*. Abingdon: Taylor & Francis.

Knowles, Michael. 2018. "£1 Billion Boost for Policing as Tories Finally Confront Crisis on the Frontline." *London Express* December 14: 8–9.

Kundnani, Arun. 2009. "Spooked! How Not to Prevent Violent Extremism." London: Institute of Race Relations. Retrieved from https://irr.org.uk/app/uploads/2016/12/spooked.pdf .

Lyons, Christopher L. 2006. "Stigma or Sympathy? Attributions of Fault to Hate Crime Victims and Offenders." *Social Psychology Quarterly* 69 (1): 39–59.

Matusitz, Jonathan. 2013. *Terrorism and Communication: A Critical Introduction*. Sage: Thousand Oaks.

McAdam, Doug, Sidney Tarrow, and Charles Tilly. 2001. *Dynamics of Contention*. Cambridge: Cambridge University Press.

McDevitt, Jack, Jennifer Balboni, Susan Bennett, Joan Weiss, Stan Orchowsky, and Lisa Walbot. 2000. *Improving the Accuracy of Bias Crime Statistics Nationally*. Washington, DC: US Department of Justice.

Meleagrou-Hitchens, Alexander, Audrey Alexander, and Nick Kaderbhai. 2017. "The Impact of Digital Communications Technology on Radicalization and Recruitment." *International Affairs* 93 (5): 1233–49.

Meserole, Chris. 2018. "How Misinformation Spreads on Social Media—And What to Do About It." Retrieved from https://www.lawfareblog.com/how-misinformation-spreads-on-social-media-and-what-to-do-about-it .

Myers, Paul D., and Michael Stohl. 2010. "Terrorism, Identity, and Group Boundaries." In *The Dynamics of Intergroup Communication*, edited by Howard Giles, Scott Reid, and Jake Harwood, 141–53. New York: Peter Lang.

Nouri, Lella, and Nuria Lorenzo-Dus. 2019. "Investigating Reclaim Australia and Britain First's Use of Social Media: Developing a New Model of Imagined Political Communities." *Journal of Deradicalization* 18: Spring, 1–31.

Orehek, Edward. 2012. "Terrorism as Intergroup Communication." In *The Handbook of Communication*, edited by Howard Giles, 141–52. New York: Routledge.

Perez, Chris. 2018. "Boston Cops Used Social Media to Spy on Black, Muslim Protesters: ACLU." *New York Post* February 7. Retrieved from https://nypost.com/2018/02/07/boston-cops-used-social-media-to-spy-on-black-muslim-protesters-aclu/ .

Perry, Joanna, and Paul Franey. 2017. *Policing Hate Crime against LGBI Persons: Training for a Professional Police Response*. Strasbourg: Council of Europe.

Potok, Mark. 2017. "The Trump Effect: The Campaign Language of the Man Who Would Become President Sparks Hate Violence, Bullying, Before and After the Election." *Intelligence Report* 162 (Spring). Montgomery, Alabama: Southern Poverty Law Center. Retrieved from https://www.splcenter.org/fighting-hate/intelligence-report/2017/trump-effect .

Procter, Robert, Jeremy Crump, Susanne Karlstedt, Alex Voss, and Marta Cantijoch. 2013. "Reading the Riots: What Were the Police Doing on Twitter?" *Policing and Society* 23 (4): 413–36.

Reicher, Stephen. 2010. "The Mobilizing of Intergroup Hatred." In *the Dynamics of Intergroup Communication*, edited by Howard Giles, Scott Reid, and Jake Harwood, 167–77. New York: Peter Lang.

Risk, Blake M., E. W. Mania, and Samuel L. Gaertner. 2006. "Intergroup Threat and Outgroup Attitudes: A Meta-Analytical Review." *Personality and Social Psychology Review* 10 (4): 336–53.

Sparks, Lisa, Gary L. Kreps, Carl Botan, and Katherine E. Rowan. 2005. "Responding to Terrorism: Translating Communication Research into Practice." *Communication Research Reports* 22 (1): 1–5.

Stohl, Cynthia, Howard Giles, and Anne Maass. 2016. "Social Networks and Intergroup Communication." In *Advances in Intergroup Communication*, edited by Howard Giles and Anne Maass, 317–39. New York: Peter Lang.

Sunstein, Cass, R. 2009. *Going to Extremes: How Like Minds Unite and Divide*. Oxford: Oxford University Press.

Ting-Toomey, Stella. 2005. "Identity Negotiation Theory: Crossing Cultural Boundaries." In *Theorizing about Intercultural Communication*, edited by William B. Gudykunst, 211–33. Thousand Oaks: Sage.

Torfaen People First. 2012. "Researching Effectiveness of Third Party Reporting Centers." Retrieved from http://www.gov.wales/ .

Torok, Ryan. 2017. "Rabbis Denounce Trump Tweets at Interfaith Events." *Jewish Journal*. Retrieved from http://jewishjournal.com/news/los_angeles/228345/rabbis-denounce-trump-tweets-interfaith-event/ .

Travis, Alan. 2008. "MI5 Report Challenges Views on Terrorism in Britain." *Guardian*. Retrieved from http://www.guardian.co.uk/uk/2008/aug/20/uksecurity.terrorism1 .

Tuman, Joseph S. 2017. *Communicating Terror: The Rhetorical Dimensions of Terrorism*. Thousand Oaks: Sage.

UK Home Office. 2018. "New Technology Revealed to Help Fight Terrorist Content Online." Retrieved from https://www.gov.uk/news/new-technology-revealed-to-help-fight-terrorist-activity-online .

UKFCO. 2014. "Hate Speech, Freedom of Expression and Freedom of Religion: A Dialogue." Retrieved from https://www.gov.uk/government/publications/hate-speech-freedom-of-expression-and-freedom-of-religion-a-dialogue .

USLegal.com. 2019. "Hate Crime Law and Legal Definition." Retrieved from https://definitions.uslegal.com/h/hate-crime/ .

Waltman, Michael. 2015. *Hate on the Right: Right-Wing Political Groups and Hate Speech*. New York: Peter Lang.

Waltman, Michael S. 2018a, "Understanding Hate Speech." In *The Oxford Encyclopedia of Intergroup Communication*, edited by Howard Giles and Jake Harwood, 461–83. New York: Oxford University Press.

Waltman, Michael S. 2018b. "The Normalizing of Hate Speech and How Communication Educators Should Respond." *Communication Education* 67 (2): 259–65.

Wickes, Rebecca L., Sharon Pickering, Gail Mason, Jane M. Maher, and Jude McCulloch. 2016. "From Hate to Prejudice: Does the New Terminology of Prejudice Motivated Crime Change Perceptions and Reporting Actions?" *British Journal of Criminology* 56 (2): 239–55.

Williams, Matthew L., Pete Burnap, Amir Javed, Han Liu, and Sefa Ozalp. 2020. "Hate in the Machine: Anti-Black and Anti-Muslim Social Media Posts as Predictors of Offline Racially and Religiously Aggravated Crime." *The British Journal of Criminology* 60 (1): 93–117.

Wong, Kevin, and Kris Christmann. 2008. "The Role of Victim Decision-Making in Reporting of Hate Crimes." *Safer Communities* 7 (2): 19–35.

Wong, Kevin, Kris Christmann, Linda Meadows, Kate Albertson, and Paul Senior. 2013. *Hate Crime in Suffolk: Understanding Prevalence and Support Needs*. Sheffield: Sheffield Hallam University Press.

CHAPTER 22

Crowd Theory, Communication, and Policing

Clifford Stott, Matthew Radburn, and Leanne Savigar-Shaw

On June 9, 2019, an estimated one million people took to the streets of the Admiralty district in Hong Kong to peacefully protest against a proposed new extradition law between the Special Administrative Region (SAR) and Mainland China. The bill was highly controversial, even among Hong Kong's "pro-establishment" community, and was scheduled to pass through the SAR's Legislative Council (LegCo) just a few days later. After the demonstration had concluded, a smaller group of a few hundred more "radical" protesters came into conflict with police, as they sought to occupy the streets around the LegCo complex and disrupt the reading of the bill. Despite the scale of the protest, Chief Executive Carrie Lam pressed on to try to secure the new legislation. As a result, on June 12, a second demonstration once again descended on Admiralty. Such was the scale of the protest that by late morning the streets surrounding the LegCo complex were entirely filled by protestors. With legislators unable to get into the building, the reading of the bill was suspended. Following some confrontations, and with little warning, later that day the police dispersed the entire crowd from the area using tear gas, baton charges, and energy projectiles.

The aggressive and heavy-handed nature of the policing of the protest on June 12 attracted international criticism. As Purbrick (2019, 470) notes,

> The Police proceeded to attempt to clear the entire crowd, which numbered at least several tens of thousands, stretching around the government complex and back into Admiralty and Central Districts. In doing so the Police engaged with the rear of the protest crowd that was peaceful and not attempting to storm the Legislative Council. Amnesty International published a report detailing 14 instances of excessive use of force by the Hong Kong Police and found that "the use of force by police in the largely peaceful protest that took place on 12 June violated international human rights law and standards."

Yet, the policing of the crowd on June 12 was important not just because it violated basic human rights; it is also significant because it transformed the protest movement in Hong Kong. For example, "five demands" subsequently emerged as a core driver for the almost daily protests and violent confrontations between police and protestors that developed across the SAR over the subsequent five months. Three of these were related directly to a sense of injustice about the policing of events on June 12. In this sense, the protests in Hong Kong expose the intimate relationships that often exists between how crowds behave and how they are policed.

Drawing upon this central theme, the following chapter will set out the case for how and why crowd psychology is centrally important in helping to understand and improve the policing of crowd events. The chapter will begin by exploring the origins of "classical" crowd psychology in the late nineteenth century. It exposes how this body of crowd theories is problematic because, while flawed and rejected from the social sciences, their concepts and ideas are still regularly deployed in contemporary political rhetoric, and often serve counterproductively as the conceptual basis for police strategy and tactics, of the kind witnessed in Hong Kong. The chapter will then outline a body of contemporary research underpinning the development of the elaborated social identity model of crowd behavior (ESIM) and the subsequent emphasis upon the role of intergroup dynamics in the origins, spread, and escalation of riots. The chapter concludes by exploring the impact and potential practical implications of the ESIM for crowd policing and outlines a program of ESIM based research on the de-escalatory potential of effective intergroup communication between crowd participants and police.

CLASSICAL CROWD PSYCHOLOGY

Immediately following the emergence of widespread confrontations between protesters and police in Hong Kong, authorities in China and the SAR began to attribute the levels of violence to agitators exploiting "mob psychology" in order to bring chaos and a breakdown of law and order. As examples, on June 13 the newspaper *China Daily* published an article headlined "Stay Vigilant to Rise of Mob Rule." The article was a translated speech from Judith Yu, a Hong Kong member of the National Committee of the Chinese People's Political Consultative Conference, effectively an upper advisory body to the Chinese government. In the article, Yu warned that the "revolt against the fugitive law, the radical opposition and secessionist forces are not simply launching a movement of populism, but rather a combination of mobocracy and separatism" (Yu 2019). Twelve days later the chief news editor of the *South China Morning Post* published a YouTube video condemning the behavior of a "belligerent" and "howling mob" that had surrounded a police station. Contrasting these protests with otherwise peaceful marchers on June 12, he went on to assert that "the take-over of roads and government buildings, which seems to have become the new norm now, is not people power—it's mob rule in motion" (*South China Morning Post* 2019). Indeed, on August 9, 2019, the *Hong Kong Economic Journal* published an article that quoted New People's Party chairwoman Regina Ip and National People's Congress deputy Ip Kwok-him as asserting that a powerful "mastermind" was manipulating the protestors "who were totally willing to follow instructions they are given during protests" and as such "the current unrest will only end after the mastermind is caught" (EJ Insight 2019).

These arguments are just contemporary examples of the use of a form of crowd psychology that actually emerged in Europe in the late nineteenth century in the wake of the Franco Prussian war (McClelland 1989; Stott and Drury 2016). At this time, a highly influential French academic, Hippolyte Taine, began writing a fourteen-volume historical treatise as an attempt to analyze what he saw as his nation's catastrophic demise. The first volume, *The Ancient Regime*, was published in 1876. Within it, he set out a powerful social and political theory at the heart of which resided an analysis of the crowd and its underlying psychology. Taine drew heavily on Hobbesian and Darwinian ideas to both pathologize and reify the crowd as an aberration. Drawing on Hobbes, he conceptualized the elites of France as deserving of their social and political power because they had imposed a social order on the primal barbarism inherent in the masses, suppressing the "war on war"–like state he assumed was the natural state of all humanity. As such, Taine understood the hierarchical social order of early to mid-nineteenth century France as a triumph of evolution that had been smashed apart by the revolutionary crowd.

In his treatise, Taine (1876) set out a mechanism through which a pathology of the crowd had taken hold in contemporary France and underpinned the nation's "decline." He argued that these aberrant crowds were populated by the "lower orders," who when gathered together were subject to a "vibration of the nervous mechanism" (221). The result of this was a "deranged mind prey to hallucination and delirium" (36–37). Consequently, crowd participants would be subject to "feverishness" (52) through which ideas and behaviors would spread unconstrained, like a disease, through "contagion." As Taine put it, these lower orders were "accustomed to the open air," and if left standing "for a quarter of an hour, generalized expressions find their way into his [sic] mind only as sound. He becomes drowsy unless a powerful vibrating voice contagiously arouses in him the instincts of flesh and blood, the personal cravings, the secret enmities which, restrained by outward discipline, are always ready to be set free" (240). For Taine, this mechanism, universal to all crowds, functioned essentially to inhibit conscious control and, as a result, crowd behavior was unavoidably irrational, meaningless, open to casual social influence and was inherently pathological.

The *Ancient Regime* was extremely important because it provided the first pseudo-scientific gloss on a version of crowd psychology that is, as we have seen above, still evident in political discourse today. Moreover, there is an almost identical narrative at work in Philip Zimbardo's (1970) "de-individuation" theory, still a staple of social psychology textbooks over a century later, despite a recent plethora of contrary evidence (e.g., Reicher and Haslam 2006). Nonetheless, a key problem with classical theory is its lack of explanatory power; it simply cannot and does not adequately account for how crowds behave. For this reason, classical theory has been widely rejected by historians who have long recognized that the theoretical approach fails to account for the complexity of the historical data of which they purported to be an "explanation" (Stott and Drury 2016). Moreover, social psychologists have been aware for some time that the bulk of scientific research actually contradicts the core assumptions of the theory (Postmes and Spears 1998).

The resilience of classical theory in contemporary discourse is perhaps because from the outset it has never been politically neutral, despite its pretense otherwise. For Taine, the philosophies of the Enlightenment, and the political ideas of equality and egalitarianism they led to, were a toxin. They implanted reason in the brains of the masses, whose minds he saw as incapable of dealing with such complexities. As he put it, the "glowing expressions of Rousseau and his successors . . . blaze up like burning coals discharging clouds of smoke and intoxicating vapor" (Taine 1876, 326). The ideological "poison" he argued had broken down the naturally evolved hierarchical political structures that he, like Hobbes, believed maintained "civilized" behavior. As a result, "men began to live again like beasts" (Taine 1876, 208; see Barrows 1981; McClelland 1989). In this way, his theory led seamlessly into a strategy for remedying this malaise. If the crowd was an aberrant intrusion, then a restoration of hierarchical social relations and reactionary social control was a requirement, a barrier to resist the pathology inherent in the nature of masses. Indeed, Taine was clear that such were the dangers of these revolutionary forces, manifest in the form of the crowd, that it was necessary to be "despotic if need be against their despotism" (Taine 1876, 242). It is perhaps no surprise that Taine's ideas were widely adopted by the far right in France and fed seamlessly through Gustave LeBon (1895) and race science into the political ideologies underpinning the rise of Italian fascism and German National Socialism during the 1920s and 1930s (McClelland 1970, 1989).

Taine's work subsequently formed the basis of an intellectual project with very dubious heritage and consequence, which developed, in part, through the challenge of attributing criminal responsibility to those detained by the authorities in the context of violent and "disorderly" crowds. This criminological perspective had its origins in a debate primarily between a French magistrate, Gabriel Tarde, and an Italian sociologist and Lombrosian criminologist, Scipio Sighele. At the time of this discussion, Tarde was developing a more general social theory based around laws of imitation and was heavily influenced by then-dominant ideas on hypnosis being put forward by Ambroise-Auguste Liébeault. For Tarde, the crowd was an environment whereby ordinary (i.e., "non-hysterical") people could come under the sway of hypnotic suggestion and thus be readily drawn into violent and criminal behavior. However, for Sighele, those committing crimes in the crowd did so because of physical anomalies. In line with Lombrosian theories of criminality more generally, those committing crimes in crowds represented primitive or subhuman types that led them to be predisposed to act in ways contrary to the rules and expectations of modern "civilized" society (McClelland 1989).

These two positions of the *pathology of convergence* versus the *convergence of the pathological* are what remains with us, where they are merged into the coherent "agitator" model of the kind deployed by the authorities in Hong Kong and elsewhere. On the one hand, crowds are seen as places where ordinary people are easily drawn into an irrational "mob psychology." On the other, "agitators" can exploit "mobs" and steer them toward otherwise meaningless violence that, unless suppressed, leaves society open to the existential threat of "mob rule." This theoretical perspective is not simply problematic because it is outdated and lacks explanatory power. Rather, it is also because it has been widely adopted *by police forces* as the conceptual basis for their strategic and tactical approach to managing crowds. Moreover, where this understanding is in place there is also strong evidence of an increase in police officers support for, and use of, tactics that rely upon indiscriminate force against crowds as a whole. This research suggests that a convergence of these factors of "police knowledge" then interacts with the practical constraints of operational policing (e.g., equipment, training, command, and control) in a way that increases the likelihood that the police will use indiscriminate and disproportionate force against whole crowds, even when it is only a minority that are judged to be posing any threat to public order (Drury, Stott, and Farsides 2003; Stott and Drury 2000; Stott and Reicher 1998).

Taken together, it is reasonable to assume that classical theory survives because it is overwhelmingly ideological and political, more so than it is scientific and valid (Barrows 1981; Nye 1975; Reicher 1982; Stott and Drury 2016; Turner et al. 1987). This is perhaps unsurprising in that it serves several ideological functions. First, it was never developed as some neutral scientific attempt to understand the crowd. It was primarily an attempt to pathologize and control it, indeed "classical theory" is better understood as a project seeking to develop a technology of social control. In so doing, classical theory stripped crowd action of meaning and as such denies any role of the state or the police in the production of violence. Second, if people in crowds are "mindless," reason rationality and communication are seen as an anathema for dealing with them. If crowds have a natural tendency toward "disorder," then remaining in tight control of them through deterrence and coercion becomes a key strategic priority for the authorities. Third, as crowds are constructed as a pathology "infecting" the otherwise "healthy" social order, violent suppression of crowds is legitimized as a means of protecting civilization from the inherent pathology of the "mob." Nonetheless, its widespread use as a rationale for understanding and interacting with crowds remains ubiquitous, particularly among powerful groups such as the police, governments, and media.

THE SOCIAL IDENTITY APPROACH

While classical crowd psychology saw its zenith in the work of Le Bon (1895), and remains deeply entrenched in political and police discourse, it has been superseded in social scientific circles. Taking its place in social psychology is a model of crowds that has its basis in a theory of the self-concept initially proposed by social identity theory (SIT; Tajfel and Turner 1979) and later more comprehensively developed through self categorization theory (SCT; Turner, Hogg, Oakes, Reicher, and Wetherell 1987; see chapters 1 and 6). These separate theories are often used in combination to form what is now referred to as the social identity approach or SIA (Jetten, Mols, and Selvanathan, 2020). The SIA assumes that as well as having an idiosyncratic personal identity (i.e., an identity as a unique individual), people also have a range of different "social identities" that can become more or less psychologically salient, depending upon the surrounding social context. For example, while at work it may make sense to define oneself as a university professor or police officer in contrast to a student or protestor; when at home it may be far more relevant to see oneself as a father, mother, son, or daughter. Each can be equally "true" about who we might be but their respective relevance to self-definition is entirely dependent upon the social contexts we are encountering at the time. In other words, while one can define oneself in terms of an idiosyncratic "personality," one can equally define oneself and *communicate* in terms of a range of social identities such as occupation, gender, nationality, ethnic origins, political views, sporting affiliations, sexuality, and so on (Giles and Harwood 2018; Giles and Maass 2016). While each of these identities are equally defining of who one is, they are characteristics that are irreducible to individuality. They are to all intents and purposes sociologically, historically, and shared senses of who one is. At the same time these social identities proscribe how one should behave within that given context, so they are not just shared senses of who we are but also of how we should relate to others. Social identity is, therefore, the psychological conduit through which humans engage with the group level realities that surround us within our everyday social encounters.

Correspondingly, collective action can be understood as any other form of group action, behavior that becomes possible when a particular social identity is made salient and shared among participants within a crowd. Therefore, being in a crowd does not entail a loss of identity, leading to unregulated behavior and casual social influence as classical theory suggests. Rather, crowds facilitate shifts in the focus of self-definition among participants away from their individual attributes to more shared and contextually defined properties of the psychological group. For example, consider a football stadium where people in a single physical crowd can define themselves in terms of their shared psychological affiliations with the "home" and "visiting" teams (see Giles and Stohl 2016). As one team scores a goal, the spontaneous collective behaviors that emerge within the stadium are different depending on which team participants identify with (Neville and Reicher 2011). The extent to which people define themselves in terms of shared identity is largely dependent upon the extent to which it makes sense of or "fits" with the social context. For example, it would be odd for people at a football game to define themselves in terms of their professional identities, unless they are police officers or stewards gainfully employed at that time to support safety and security at the event. Given that the salience of an identity is intimately linked to the social context, the salience, form, and content of social identity can change. It is widely recognized that a shared "common fate" is a core driver for the emergence of shared identities in crowd situations (Drury 2018). Thus, if a disaster develops in the context of a football stadium, as it did at Hillsborough stadium in 1989, previously opposed groups can unite into new shared identities and social relations come to be (re)defined less in terms of competitive opposition and more in terms of collaborative cooperation, helping, justice, and governance (Scraton 2016).

As and where people share a social identity, there will be an increased tendency among them to adhere to the perspectives, values, beliefs, and norms of that social group as it is relevant to the specific context. The ideological dimensions of the shared identity (e.g., what it means to be a protestor against government legislation) determine and constrain what can and does become influential in the crowd. Social identities, therefore, limit and enable the spread of ideas and behaviors to those who share this common self-categorization. In other words, people in crowds do not suffer "mindless contagion" where any idea from "agitators" can spread uncontrolled like an infectious disease. Rather, the ideas and behaviors that become influential are those that make sense to people because they are in line with the beliefs that define their identity as it relates to the specific social context at that time. The extent to which others are seen to share the same identity also gives crowd participants some basis for judging whether they are able to act in particular ways. This sense of collective empowerment is primarily because the shared identity signifies that others in the crowd are likely to support particular actions as they are seen as similar to self (Drury and Reicher 2000). Salient social identities, therefore, orientate crowd members toward meaningful forms of collective action and intergroup interaction in any given context. This is construed both in terms of what behavior is seen by them and others as appropriate or legitimate but also in terms of what behavior they feel is collectively possible given the power relationships within that context.

Intergroup Dynamics and Social Change

From its original proposition onward, the social identity approach to crowds, unlike the "classical" account, has been underpinned by substantial empirical evidence. This body of data began through analysis of one of the major inner-city disturbances in England in the 1980s (Reicher 1987). However, since its initial proposition, Reicher's social identity model of crowd behavior (SIM) has been elaborated and gained further empirical support through studies of student "rioting" during a protest against the removal of grants (Reicher 1996), demonstrators "rioting" during a protest against the implementation of a tax (Drury and Reicher 1999; Stott and Drury 2000), a series of protests around the extension of a motorway in London (Drury and Reicher 2000, 2005), "rioting" among football fans (Stott and Reicher 1998; Stott et al. 2001, 2011) and more recently has been extended to explain data related to the spread of the August 2011 riots in the United Kingdom (UK; Ball et al. 2019; Drury et al. 2020; Stott, Drury, and Reicher, 2016; Stott et al. 2018).

This elaborated social identity model of crowd behavior or ESIM, in contrast to the SIM, highlights the centrality of intergroup interaction in setting the context for, then shaping and reshaping, a crowd's social identity. As such, the ESIM recognizes the importance of dynamic interactions during crowd events in shaping and then reshaping the nature of the collective behavior that occurs, particularly in terms of the emergence, escalation, and spread of "rioting." For example, in August 2011, riots began in Tottenham in North London and spread throughout England across the next four days. It is evident that political and economic geography provided a critically important structural context of inequality for these riots (Drury et al. 2019). It is equally evident that highly intense campaigns of stop and search[1] by police in the areas where rioting occurred were also a key element that fed widely shared experiences of police illegitimacy among sections of the population in the areas where rioting occurred (Drury et al. 2019, 2020; Newburn 2016; Newburn et al. 2018). However, these structural factors are not sufficient to explain the precise patterning to the rioting that emerged.

The riots flowed in the wake of the fatal shooting by police of a young mixed-heritage man named Mark Duggan. However, rioting did not develop for two days after he was shot. Stott et al. (2016) argue that far from being a "flashpoint" to ignite dry "tinder," it was failures in police dialogue and communication with the local community and family during this time that culminated in attacks on police property just outside a police station in nearby Tottenham some two days later. The police reacted to these attacks by trying to disperse a crowd that until that time had been peacefully protesting outside the police station about the shooting of Mr. Duggan. Stott et al. (2016) argue that the forceful and indiscriminate nature of police intervention into this crowd added to the experiences of police illegitimacy among those involved. These intergroup interactions in the early stages of rioting led directly to a change in the nature of the crowd's social identity which was critical in shaping how, where, and why the rioting began to escalate.

Stott et al. (2018) go on to show that as the riot intensified in Tottenham, it also began to spread across the surrounding borough of Haringey and, as it did, it changed in form. The question of how this evident patterning of collective behavior changed and how "disorder" spread to different targets and locations had been relatively neglected in previous social identity research, despite its theoretical and practical importance (Reicher 1987). This limitation was partially addressed through this second study utilizing a triangulated analysis of multiple sources of data (including police reports, media accounts, and videos) that confirmed a shifting from collective attacks on police targets in one location during the early stages to widespread looting of retail outlets in other areas during the latter. A thematic analysis of interview accounts from participants involved in the riot suggested that, after the initial police intervention and escalation, the police became disempowered relative to the intensity of the collective violence that had developed. During this period, lasting for around two hours, it was apparent that other people began to converge into the area, many of them youths who had long-standing antagonistic intergroup rivalries, given the fierce, sometimes fatal, hostilities that exist between youths in different "postcode" areas of London (see chapter 21).

Given the high levels of stop and search in the months leading up to the riots, many of these youths had shared historical experiences of disempowerment and humiliation at the hands of the police. Thus, arriving into a context of visible police disempowerment was unique for many of them, and it appears to have been a social context that enabled these previously antagonistic groups to coalesce, through their realization of a shared anti-police identity. This process appears to have occurred just at a time where the police were themselves being reinforced. The police's subsequent inability to defeat the increasingly powerful rioters then formed the basis of further collective action and empowerment, whereby protagonists both within and beyond the riot began to recognize their own agency and capability to spread the riot to different locations and targets, such as retail parks nearby (Ball et al. 2019; Drury et al. 2020; Stott et al. 2018).

POLICING CROWDS

As we set out above, a central position of the ESIM is a rejection of the assumption that collective "disorder" is meaningless for those involved. Rather, it explains collective violence as the outcome of complex social psychological processes and intergroup dynamics of which "police knowledge," strategies, and tactics are ubiquitously a component part. A central advantage of the ESIM is that it can and does begin to expose a set of theoretical concepts and principles through which the likelihood of collective conflict can be reduced, in particular by changing the nature of the policing of crowds (Reicher et al. 2004, 2007; Stott 2009). In turn, if public order policing is oriented toward managing these group level dynamics, it can and does increase police capacity to minimize the potential for collective confrontations to emerge and escalate. A major step toward developing such "new wave" approaches to public order policing first developed in relation to the UEFA European Football Championships in Portugal in 2004. Here a program of UK government–funded collaboration prior to the tournament saw one of Portugal's two national police forces, the Polícia de Segurança Pública or PSP, develop their policing model based upon the social identity approach (Stott and Pearson 2007).

The PSP's use-of-force policy for the tournament went against the dominant police orthodoxy because it was oriented strategically toward facilitating fans' legitimate behaviors and based tactically upon communication, rather than deterrence through early displays of police capability for coercive force. More specifically, where crowds were gathered, there was often no obvious sign of "riot police." Instead, small numbers of police in normal uniform were deployed in crowded areas working in pairs and small groups. The role of these officers was to interact and *communicate* with fans. Their task was to be deliberately accessible and friendly (e.g., providing directions and advice about places to eat and drink) and, in so doing, actively construct a social context whereby crowd participants would be more likely to see their intergroup relationships with the police as legitimate, socially valuable, and accommodative. Simultaneously, small teams of plain-clothed officers operated, subtly but not covertly, within these crowds constantly monitoring for activity likely to provoke confrontation (e.g., groups or individuals acting in openly hostile ways). These "low profile" and communication-based deployments allowed the PSP to assess both the presence and, perhaps more importantly, the absence of any emergent threats and "test" their intelligence against what was actually materializing on the ground. This helped them to avoid unnecessary deployment of their "riot units." As and where problems emerged, the PSP did deploy larger groups of police. However, because of the earlier interactions, these escalations in police profile tended to be more "information" led and proportionate, rather than ill-informed and targeted indiscriminately against anyone who just happened to present.

European Football had, until that time, a long and sour history of violent confrontations involving fans and police. However, during this tournament in all of the major towns and cities hosting matches, there were no major incidents of collective confrontation. Correspondingly, the visibility of paramilitary style police was almost zero throughout the tournament. These contrastingly low levels of disorder compared with other tournaments corresponded with evidence of widespread perceptions of police legitimacy among fans and higher levels of "self-regulation" that helped prevent major "disorder," despite the presence of known and self-defined "hooligans" (Schreiber and Stott 2012; Stott et al. 2007, 2008). This major inroad into shaping the policing of crowds, based on the social identity approach, was a powerful example of how successful public order outcomes did not lie in police capabilities to utilize force, so much as they did in their capacity for communication and dialogue (see also Maguire, Khade, and Mora 2020). Moreover, research also suggested that these communication-based approaches worked in part because they created common bonds of social identification between crowd participants and the police, bonds that emerge during the crowd event itself as an outcome of the perceived legitimacy of police tactics.

Police Communication and the Maintenance of "Public Order"

The example of Euro2004 is now one of many that point toward the importance of police communication in crowd management contexts. Instead of a focus on police capacity to react to situations where conflict has developed with use of overwhelming force (i.e., riot control), the emphasis is, instead, on the capacity to engage with crowd participants through communication prior to conflict developing (i.e., public order management). The evidence increasingly points toward the conclusion that the latter is more effective than the former in managing crowd dynamics in ways that assist the police in preventing widespread confrontation. This is not just evidence in some abstract form, because the SIA has also gone on to influence crowd policing in Sweden, Denmark, Queensland in Australia, and the UK, as just four examples. In each case, police have developed specific units designed to promote effective and ongoing communication between police and crowd participants and as a result have seen their capacity to avoid confrontation increase (e.g., Stott et al. 2019). For example, following the death of a member of the public, Ian Tomlinson, the UK's main policing oversight authority, conducted a systematic and comprehensive analysis of the national approach to crowd management. The inquiry exposed some fundamental issues related to poor police capacity for police communication during public order operations. As a result, new units of police liaison officers have been established to develop effective pathways of communication between crowd participants and police. There is now substantial evidence that such units contribute directly to the avoidance of police coercion and conflict (Stott and Gorringe 2013).

Such communication-based approaches to crowd policing are important not just because they are consistent with scientific understanding. They are also a powerful example of the entrenchment of fundamental principles of democratic and human rights–based approaches. On the one hand, modern policing is itself an outcome of the realization that reactionary state repression of public protest is unsustainable in a society that aspires to be democratic in its orientation. Nine principles attributed to the UK's home secretary Sir Robert Peel in 1829 laid the foundation of what Reith (1956) suggests is an approach to the prevention of crime and disorder built upon public approval and cooperation, primarily among those communities who were themselves involved in the very "disorder" the police service was designed to "control." Through this, the police effectively were merely "citizens" in uniform, policing of the public, by the public for the public (Stott and Gorringe 2013). On the other hand, to be "democratic" a nation's policing approach has to respect specific rights such as freedom of peaceful assembly, expression, and consciousness. Considered together, these issues mean that police must develop and deploy communication-based tactics so that they can be deployed, if it is reasonable to do so, prior to any police use of force. Failure to deploy these alternatives renders any use of force disproportionate and, if such rights are protected under the law, therefore unlawful.

CROWD THEORY AND PROCEDURAL JUSTICE

The "Peelian" emphasis on building consensual rather than coercive police–public interactions resonates strongly with a preeminent criminological theory of police–community relations, procedural justice theory (PJT; Tyler 1990; see chapter 8). PJT emphasizes the importance of police communication and dialogue as a means of enhancing public perceptions of police legitimacy and securing public compliance and cooperation (Sunshine and Tyler 2003a; see chapters 8 and 17). Accordingly, there is a great deal of synergy between PJT and the ESIM (Stott, Hoggett, and Pearson 2011). However, police–crowd relations pose important challenges to PJT both conceptually and empirically (Radburn et al. 2018; Radburn and Stott 2019; Radburn et al. under submission), and it is argued that PJT can advance by drawing on the theoretical insights of the social identity approach to crowd psychology and its application to exploring and explaining crowd action (Radburn and Stott 2019).

For example, one key challenge that crowds pose to PJT is that the theory is premised on the idea that police–public interactions are dyadic. However, we know anecdotally, as well as from research evidence, that police–crowd interactions are typically experienced by participants as *intergroup* encounters (e.g., a pro-fascist demonstration meeting a crowd of anti-fascist and separated from each other by police lines). Accordingly, as we have seen, the ESIM emphasizes the importance of building an adequate theoretical understanding of the *group-level* dynamics of these interactions (Reicher et al. 2004) in order to implement more effective communication-based policing practices (Stott and Pearson 2007). In other words, what this suggests is that the intergroup context of crowd situations is a crucial determinant of how people involved in them will respond to police behavior and communications (Radburn et al. 2018; Urbanska et al. 2019). This is a point that is largely neglected in the wider PJT literature that has, instead, predominantly focused on *interpersonal* relations.

Moreover, while the identity-based models of procedural justice forefront the importance of group processes and psychology, the underlying conceptualization of the groups that are thought to be important to people in their interactions with police officers has been largely limited to superordinate categories such as community or national identity or a citizen's sense of themselves as law-abiding. Since the police are positioned in PJT as morally prototypical group authorities (Sunshine and Tyler 2003b), the way in which police officers treat members of the public (e.g., the extent to which an officer gives the citizen a "voice" or "say" in their decision making) is viewed as important since it indicates their relative inclusion or exclusion in these important social categories. Therefore, as leading proponents of PJT suggest, "the framework views authorities and the individuals they have power over as part of one group" and, thus, the value of procedurally fair police communication strategies lies in the "information it conveys about people's relationship to the community and with authorities" (O'Brien, Tyler, and Meares 2019, 2). However, in contrast, what police–crowd encounters show us is that police officers and "citizens" may not uncomplicatedly view themselves as members of the same social categories (e.g., "community," national identity). Indeed, as we have seen, those who took part in the August 2011 English "riots" tended to define themselves and others as oppositional to the police, certainly not viewing them as prototypical representatives of their community.

While studies of the August 2011 English riots clearly demonstrate the importance of a group-level analysis and an intergroup focus, this work also shows that the group psychology of the "rioters" was largely embedded in everyday (ostensibly interpersonal) policing practices such as the (mis)use of stop and search. Given that PJT is the primary theoretical model for such "routine" police-public encounters, the overriding challenge is how the theory can draw on the lessons of the social identity approach to help advance an understanding of this group psychology and how situationally defined groups and group-level communication strategies are important in day-to-day encounters between citizens and police officers (c.f. O'Brien et al. 2019). Taken together, these insights suggest that contemporary crowd theory is useful not just in debunking the "mad mob" accounts of the likes of Le Bon, Taine, and Zimbardo. It also provides fruitful avenues of theoretical and empirical development in respect to our understanding of police-public interactions more generally. More specifically, it forefronts the impact that group-level police communication strategies may have on promoting public perceptions of police legitimacy and empowering consensual relationships between the police and "those being policed" (see chapter 1).[2]

CONCLUSIONS

This chapter has first sought to demonstrate the relationships that exist between crowd theory and matters of "crowd control" and to do so in ways that drew parallels to how such issues play themselves out in contemporary times as they did in the late nineteenth century. In short, crowd theory is central to the ways in which societies understand and respond to crowd events. However, we have also shown that different versions of crowd theory can be at work. On the one hand, there is a "classical" model of "mob psychology," which decontextualizes, reifies, and pathologizes crowd action. At the same time, it provides a theory that attributes the causes of violent protests to the activities of violent agitators who insidiously exploit the irrationality of the crowd to foment social disorder as a means to achieving their end of destabilizing the state. While such perspectives bear little relationship to historical fact, they nonetheless survive as a basis for understanding and policing "riots."

On the other, the ESIM places crowd action back into its structural and micro-sociological context. In so doing, it recognizes the meaningful and symbolic nature of crowd action, driven as it is by an underlying social shared collective self-definition. According to this approach, collective violence is often an outcome of policing practice, particularly where such action involves the indiscriminate use of force against crowds. Where such actions take place, they tend to change the nature of the underlying social identity enabling collective action in the crowd such that collective violence comes to be seen as both appropriate and possible social action. Far from merely a criticism of those that deploy classical theory, the ESIM actually acts as a tool for helping to understand that human rights–based communication and dialogue-oriented approaches to the exercise of power are effective at helping avoid the kinds of dynamics we now know to be at work in driving some crowds unintentionally toward conflict.

The dynamics of identity, legitimacy, and power that the ESIM helps elucidate not only represent a clear advance over classical crowd theories but also serve to offer new insights and challenges to a contemporary criminological account of police–public relations, procedural justice theory. In so doing, our argument is that the interdisciplinary empirical study of crowds and the development of crowd theory should not be seen as a peripheral debate but one that is at the center of the social sciences (Reicher 2011), for it allows us to engage with fundamental theoretical issues and at the same time work toward empowering democratic modes of policing, oriented toward communication and dialogue.

NOTES

1. In the UK, "stop and search" is a street-based search that would be referred to as "stop and frisk" in the United States.
2. See https://gtr.ukri.org/projects?ref=ES%2FR011397%2F1 .

REFERENCES

Ball, Roger, Clifford Stott, John Drury, Fergus Neville, Stephen Reicher, and Sanjeedah Choudhury. 2019. "Who Controls the City? A Micro-Historical Case Study of the Spread of Rioting across North London in August 2011." *City*. doi:10.1080/13604813.2019.1685283 .

Barrows, Susanna. 1981. *Visions of the Crowd in Late Nineteenth Century France*. Yale: Yale University Press.

Drury, John. 2018. "The Role of Social Identity Processes in Mass Emergency Behavior: An Integrative Review." *European Journal of Social Psychology* 29 (1): 38–81.

Drury, John, and Stephen Reicher. 1999. "The Intergroup Dynamics of Collective Empowerment: Substantiating the Social Identity Model of Crowd Behavior." *Group Processes and Intergroup Relations* 2 (4): 381–402.

Drury, John, and Stephen Reicher. 2000. "Collective Action and Psychological Change: The Emergence of New Social Identities." *British Journal of Social Psychology* 39 (4): 579–604.

Drury, John, and Stephen Reicher. 2005. "Explaining Enduring Empowerment: A Comparative Study of Collective Action and Psychological Outcomes." *European Journal of Social Psychology* 35 (1): 35–58.

Drury, John, Roger Ball, Fergus Neville, Stephen Reicher, and Clifford Stott. 2019. "Re-reading the 2011 Riots: ESRC beyond Contagion Interim Report." Retrieved from http://sro.sussex.ac.uk/id/eprint/82292/ .

Drury, John, Clifford Stott, Roger Ball, Stephen Reicher, Fergus Neville, Linda Bell, Mikey Biddlestone, Sanjeedah Choudhury, Max Lovell, and Ryan Caoimhe. 2020. "A Social Identity Model of Riot Diffusion: From Injustice to Empowerment in the 2011 London Riots." *European Journal of Social Psychology* 50 (3): 646–61.

Drury, John, Clifford Stott, and Tom Farsides. 2003. "The Role of Police Perceptions and Practices in the Development of 'Public Disorder.'" *Journal of Applied Social Psychology* 33 (7): 1480–500.

EJ Insight. 2019. "Two ExCo Members say 'Mastermind' behind Recent Protests." August 9. Retrieved from http://www.ejinsight.com/20190809-two-exco-members-say-mastermind-behind-recent-protests .

Giles, Howard, and Jake Harwood, J., eds. 2018. *The Oxford Encyclopedia of Intergroup Communication*, Vols. 1 and 2. New York: Oxford University Press.

Giles, Howard, and Anne Maass, eds. 2016. *Advances in Intergroup Communication*. New York: Peter Lang.

Giles, Howard, and Michael Stohl. 2016. "Sport as Intergroup Communication." In *Defining Sport Communication*, edited by Andrew Billings, 150–64. New York: Routledge.

Jetten, Jolanda, Frank Mols, and Hema Preya Selvanathan. 2020. "How Economic Inequality Fuels the Rise and Persistence of the Yellow Vest Movement." *International Review of Social Psychology* 33, (1). Advance Online: https://doi.org/10.5334/irsp.356 .

Le Bon, Gustave. 1926 [1895]. *The Crowd: A Study of the Popular Mind*. London: Allen & Unwin.

Maguire, Edward, Natasha Khade, and Victor Mora. 2020. "Improve the Policing of Crowds." In *Transforming the Police: Thirteen Key Reforms*, edited by Charles Katz and Edward Maguire, 235–48. Long Grover, IL: Waveland Press.

McClelland, John S. (ed.). 1970. *The French Right: From De Maistre to Maurras*. London: Jonathan Cape.

McClelland, John S. 1989. *The Crowd and the Mob: From Plato to Canetti*. London: Unwin Hyman.

Neville, Fergus, and Stephen Reicher. 2011. "The Experience of Collective Participation: Shared Identity, Relatedness and Emotionality." *Contemporary Social Science* 6 (3): 377–96.

Newburn, Tim. 2016. "The 2011 England Riots in European Context: A Framework for Understanding the 'Life-Cycle' of Riots." *European Journal of Criminology* 13 (5): 540–55.

Newburn, Tim, Rebekah Diski, Kerris Cooper, Rachel Deacon, Alex Burch, and Maggie Grant. 2018. "'The Biggest Gang'? Police and People in the 2011 England Riots." *Policing and Society* 28 (2): 205–22.

Nye, Robert A. 1975. *The Origins of Crowd Psychology*. Beverly Hills: Sage.

O'Brien, Thomas C., Tom R. Tyler, and Tracey L. Meares. 2019. "Building Popular Legitimacy with Reconciliatory Gestures and Participation: A Community-Level Model of Authority." *Regulation and Governance*. doi:10.1111/rego.12264 .

Postmes, Tom, and Russell Spears. 1998. "Deindividuation and Anti-normative Behavior: A Meta-analysis." *Psychological Bulletin* 123 (3): 238–59.

Purbrick, Martin. 2019. "A Report of the 2019 Hong Kong Protests." *Asian Affairs* 50 (4): 465–87.

Radburn, Matthew, and Clifford Stott. 2019. "The Social Psychological Processes of 'Procedural Justice': Concepts, Critiques and Opportunities." *Criminology and Criminal Justice* 19 (4): 421–38.

Radburn, Matthew, Clifford Stott, Ben Bradford, and Mark Robinson. 2018. "When Is Policing Fair? Groups, Identity and Judgements of the Procedural Justice of Coercive Crowd Policing." *Policing and Society* 28 (6): 647–64.

Radburn, Matthew, Leanne Savigar, Clifford Stott, Deborah Tallent, and Arabella Kyprianides. Under submission. "How do Police Officers Talk about Their Encounters with 'the Public'? Group Interaction, Procedural Justice, and Officer Constructions of Police Identity." *Criminology and Criminal Justice*.

Reicher, Stephen. 1982. "The Determination of Collective Behavior." In *Social Identity and Intergroup Relations*, edited by Henri Tajfel, 41–84. Cambridge: Cambridge University Press.

Reicher, Stephen. 1987. "Crowd Behavior as Social Action." In *Rediscovering the Social Group*, edited by John C Turner, Michael Hogg, Penelope Oakes, Stephen Reicher, and Margaret S. Wetherell, 171–202. Oxford: Blackwell.

Reicher, Stephen. 1996. "'The Battle of Westminster': Developing the Social Identity Model of Crowd Behavior in Order to Explain the Initiation and Development of Collective Conflict." *European Journal of Social Psychology* 26 (1): 115–34.

Reicher, Stephen. 2011. "Mass Action and Mundane Reality: An Argument for Putting Crowd Analysis at the Centre of the Social Sciences." *Contemporary Social Science* 6 (3): 433–49.

Reicher, Stephen, and Alexander S. Haslam. 2006. "Rethinking the Psychology of Tyranny: The BBC Prison Study." *British Journal of Social Psychology* 45 (1): 1–40.

Reicher, Stephen, Clifford Stott, Patrick Cronin, and Otto Adang. 2004. "An Integrated Approach to Crowd Psychology and Public Order Policing." *Policing: An International Journal of Police Strategies and Management* 27 (4): 558–72.

Reicher, Stephen, Clifford Stott, John Drury, Otto Adang, Patrick Cronin, and Andrew Livingstone. 2007. "Knowledge-based Public Order Policing: Principles and Practice." *Policing: A Journal of Policy and Practice* 1 (4): 403–15.

Reith, Charles. 1956. *A New Study of Police History.* London: Oliver & Boyd.

Schreiber, Martina, and Clifford Stott. 2012. "Policing International Football Tournaments and the Cross-Cultural Relevance of the Social Identity Approach to Crowd Behavior." *Police Practice and Research* 13 (5): 407–20.

Scraton, Phil. 2016. *Hillsborough: The Truth.* New York: Random House.

South China Morning Post. 2019. "People Power or Mob Rule: Hong Kong's Young Protesters Blur the Line." Retrieved from https://www.youtube.com/watch?v=w6UJNw6hcjs .

Stott, Clifford. 2009. "*Crowd Psychology and Public Order Policing: An Overview of Scientific Theory and Evidence.*" Submission to the HMIC Policing of Public Protest Review Team. Liverpool: University of Liverpool.

Stott, Clifford, Otto Adang, Andrew Livingstone, and Martina Schreiber. 2007. "Variability in the Collective Behavior of England Fans at Euro2004: 'Hooliganism,' Public Order Policing and Social Change." *European Journal of Social Psychology* 37 (1): 75–100.

Stott, Clifford, Roger Ball, John Drury, Fergus Neville, Stephen Reicher, Andrea Boardman, and Sanjeedah Choudhury. 2018. "The Evolving Normative Dimensions of 'Riot': Towards an Elaborated Social Identity Explanation." *European Journal of Social Psychology* 48 (6): 834–49.

Stott, Clifford, and John Drury. 2000. "Crowds, Context and Identity: Dynamic Categorization Processes in the 'Poll Tax Riot.'" *Human Relations* 53 (2): 247–73.

Stott, Clifford, and John Drury. 2016. "The Inter-group Dynamics of Empowerment: A Social Identity Model." In *Transforming Politics*, edited by Sasha Roseneil, 32–45. London: Palgrave Macmillan.

Stott, Clifford, John Drury, and Stephen Reicher. 2016. "On the Role of a Social Identity Analysis in Articulating Structure and Collective Action: The 2011 Riots in Tottenham and Hackney." *British Journal of Criminology* 57 (4): 964–81.

Stott, Clifford, and Hugo Gorringe. 2013. "From Sir Robert Peel to PLTs: Adapting to Liaison Based Public Order Policing in England and Wales." In *The Future of Policing*, edited by Jennifer M. Brown, 239–51. London: Routledge.

Stott, Clifford, Jonas Havelund, and Neil Williams. 2019. "Policing Football Crowds in Sweden." *Nordic Journal of Criminology* 20 (1): 35–53.

Stott, Clifford, James Hoggett, and Geoff Pearson. 2011. "'Keeping the Peace' Social Identity, Procedural Justice and the Policing of Football Crowds." *The British Journal of Criminology* 52 (2): 381–99.

Stott, Clifford, Paul Hutchison, and John Drury. 2001. "'Hooligans' Abroad? Inter-group Dynamics, Social Identity and Participation in Collective 'Disorder' at the 1998 World Cup Finals." *British Journal of Social Psychology* 40 (3): 359–84.

Stott, Clifford, Andrew Livingstone, and James Hoggett. 2008. "Policing Football Crowds in England and Wales: A Model of 'Good Practice.'" *Policing and Society* 18 (3): 258–81.

Stott, Clifford, and Geoff Pearson. 2007. *Football 'Hooliganism': Policing and the War on the 'English Disease.'* London: Pennant Books.

Stott, Clifford, and Stephen Reicher. 1998. "How Conflict Escalates: The Inter-group Dynamics of Collective Football Crowd Violence." *Sociology* 32 (2): 353–77.

Sunshine, Jason, and Tom R. Tyler. 2003a. "The Role of Procedural Justice and Legitimacy in Public Support for Policing." *Law and Society Review* 37(3): 513–48.

Sunshine, Jason, and Tom R. Tyler. 2003b. "Moral Solidarity, Identification with the Community, and the Importance of Procedural Justice: The Police as Prototypical Representatives of a Group's Moral Values." *Social Psychology Quarterly* 66 (2): 153–65.

Taine, Hippolyte. 1876. *The Ancient Regime: The Origins of Contemporary France* (Vol. 1). John Durand, Trans. London: Daldy, Ibister & Co.

Tajfel, Henri, and John C. Turner. 1979. "An Integrative Theory of Intergroup Conflict." In *The Social Psychology of Intergroup Relations*, edited by William G. Austin and Stephen Worchel, 33–47. Monterey: Brooks Cole.

Turner, John C., Michael Hogg, Penelope Oakes, Stephen Reicher, and Margaret Wetherell. 1987. *Rediscovering the Social Group.* Oxford: Blackwell.

Tyler, Tom R. 1990. *Why People Obey the Law.* New Haven: Yale University Press.

Urbanska, Karolina, Samuel Pehrson, and Rhiannon N. Turner. 2019. "Authority Fairness for All? Intergroup Status and Expectations of Procedural Justice and Resource Distribution." *Journal of Social and Political Psychology* 7 (2): 766–89.

Yu, Judith. 2019. "Stay Vigilant to Rise of Module Rule, Separatism." *China Daily*, December 12. Retrieved from http://www.chinadaily.com.cn/hkedition/2019-06/13/content_37480087.htm .

Zimbardo, Phillip G. 1970. "The Human Choice: Individuation, Reason, and Order Versus Deindividuation, Impulse, and Chaos." In *Nebraska Symposium on Motivation 1969*, edited by William J. Arnold and David Levine, 237–307, Lincoln: University of Nebraska Press.

Conclusion

New Directions in Policing and Intergroup Communication

Howard Giles, Shawn L. Hill, Edward R. Maguire, and Daniel Angus

The chapters in this book have made a compelling case for the critical roles of communication in handling many different issues in policing, including crowd management, traffic stops, criminal investigations, and a variety of specific types of crimes and crises. In tandem, we have seen how communication within the police organization is crucial for effective recruitment, retention, and supervision as well as establishing relationships with other agencies and institutions. The authors' contributions make it clear that the success or failure of policing in society depends heavily on the nature and quality of communication by its practitioners.

All of these processes—many of which are intergroup in nature—are impacted by messages played out in various genres including the news media, social media, and fictional accounts of policing. In this conclusion, we attempt to pull out many of the abiding constructs evident in the previous chapters—and the relationships between them—using automated text analysis methods. Thereafter, we propose a heuristic, working model of significant relationships operating between communities and policing that is related to all the specified chapters in this volume. The components and the links between them in this model are illustrated by discussing a series of protest incidents between police and the public in Minneapolis (May–June 2020) in response to the killing of George Floyd, an event that received global attention. We end with some major communicative challenges we will face going forward that are suggested by this intergroup strife and beyond.

THEMES EMERGING IN THIS COLLECTION

Recently, and with a view to quickly capturing the essence of key themes in the field of intergroup communication, we provided a word cloud analysis of the titles of papers presented at the 1st International Symposium of Intergroup Communication in Thessaloniki, Greece, in 2017 (Keblusek, Giles, Maass, and Gardikiotis 2018). From this, four clusters emerged relating to: theories of identity expression and negotiation; the verbal and nonlinguistic features of communicating those expressions; the language and cultures in which they were studied; and the settings and contexts in which the intergroup phenomena operate. Inspired by the usefulness of this approach, we performed a word cloud analysis on the texts of all the conclusion sections of the chapters in this book (see figure 23.1). We are mindful of the limitations of such rudimentary visualizations (Harris 2011; Relihan 2020), such as a reliance on simple word counts rather than more complex word frequency and co-occurrence statistics. At the same time, we find them useful as a simplistic tool for capturing themes present in the cumulative text of each chapters' conclusion.

FIGURE 23.1. A Word Cloud Analysis of the Conclusion Sections to the Handbook Chapters.

From this analysis, we can see our authors' juxtapositioning of police, policing, and officers on the one hand, and community, communities, and citizens on the other. Clearly, and perhaps not surprisingly given the focus of this volume, communication, communications, relationships, and the media are central in this equation, as is research and the notions of time and change. Also prominent are the social constructs of enforcement, justice, trust, perceptions, intergroup, and resilience. It is interesting to note—with social groups such as women, Muslims, and LGBTQ highlighted—what processes are either *not* apparent or absent in this image (and hence the chapter conclusions), such as biases, prejudice, discrimination, and stereotyping.

As a means of gaining more sophisticated insight into the relationships between these and other constructs, we submitted these same textual data to Leximancer, which has been used in a number of intergroup settings, particularly communication accommodation in health-related settings (see Baker, Gallois, Driedger, and Santesso 2011; Gallois, Cretchley, and Watson 2012). Leximancer is a text-mining tool for detecting concepts in textual data and developing concept maps. Concepts in the Leximancer-sense are statistically meaningful groups of words (called bag-of-words) generated from the input data using word occurrence and co-occurrence information. This technique has the advantage that the layout of concept names can then represent interconceptual similarity as can be seen from the Leximancer Concept Network (visualized using the Gephi graph layout tool) in figure 23.2.

It is not surprising that the top ranked concepts in the Leximancer concept network are guides to the entire collection. Other themes identified (moving in a clockwise direction from the nine o'clock position) focus on the role of social media, issues relating to

FIGURE 23.2. A Leximancer Concept Network Analysis of the Conclusion Sections of the Handbook Chapters.

violence, organizational-level change, the role of gender, and interactional practices (and closely related, although in its own cluster, the specific dynamics of police interaction). Noteworthy, but perhaps not surprising, is the centrality of the concept "intergroup," particularly in linking concepts on interaction dynamics, gender, and social processes to police and public institutions.

A HEURISTIC MODEL OF POLICING, COMMUNICATION, AND SOCIETY

Choi and Giles (2012) crafted what was essentially the first schematic model to attend to communication and police encounters with the public. The chapters in this current book explore a far wider and more complex range of communication processes and settings than what was available at the time this model was introduced. For example, the model did not address communication issues internal to police organizations; but with the rapid ascent of research on organizational justice in policing (see chapters 2 and 3), these issues clearly deserve attention. Therefore, we elaborate on the Choi and Giles model (see figure 23.3 with components letter-labeled) with the goal of providing a more holistic (yet parsimonious) framework for understanding policing, communication, and society. A key element of this goal is to develop a model that modestly and coherently integrates the chapters herein. Positive–negative valence is visually depicted as signaling potentially contrastive effects associated with each link.

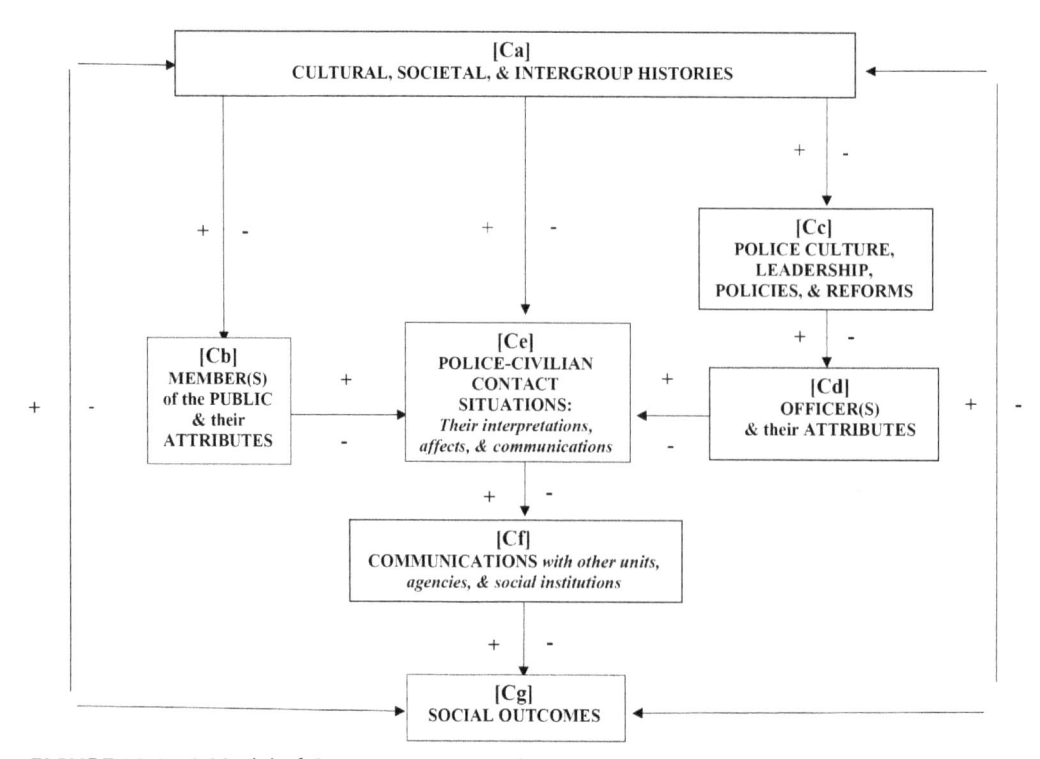

FIGURE 23.3. A Model of Communication, Policing, and Society

At the top of the model is an amalgam component that refers to distinctive cultural and societal values, including media activities that reflect them. This component critically includes the objective and subjectively perceived social histories (e.g., of slavery, lynchings, civil rights movements, disasters, and so forth) as well as past and recent policing incidents that have gained significant attention. Changes over the decades in racial equality and police reform have been considered glacial by some. Of course, many perspectives disagree, and certain communities demand more transparency and influence in how they are policed. Nonetheless, this (top central) contextual conglomerate [Ca] can shape and enable three entities. First [Cb], members of the public's attributes are highlighted, including their gender, age, ethnicity schemas, values, and personalities. Also relevant are people's social networks and social identities, attitudes toward and expectations of police, public bystanders, and their community resilience (see chapters 6–9, and 13). Second [Cc], police culture (and allied professional associations and unions) is featured, including recruitment and retention procedures, leadership and management practices and their media communiques, community- and reform-orientations (see chapters 1, 2, and 10). These, in turn [Cd], mold officers' attributes, including their gender and ethnicity schemas, personalities, worldviews, communication skills, resilience, well-being, and intergroup biases.

All these components (see figure 23.3) impinge upon the ingredients of contact between police and the public [Ce], be they traffic stops, domestic violence, suicide attempts, hostage negotiations, or other types of encounters. Contact situations is pluralized as it can be a specific contained incident and/or its subsequent aftermath (which can be prolonged, as evident in the 2020 Minneapolis case study below). Processually, this component embraces how these situations are interpreted and with what kinds of experiences and expressed affect and communication patterns. These may include accommodation or nonaccommodation, de-escalation, use of procedural justice principles, and the exercise of various levels of force. This [Cf] can necessitate, or not, mutual aid from other internal units, such as SWAT and detectives and, arguably, affiliated external units and institutions, such as other first responders (fire, medics), coroners' offices, social workers, medical and mental health professionals, district attorneys, the National Guard, mayors, governors, and journalists and the news media (see chapter 4, 9, and 19). These forces together have a wide range of longer-term social (and intergroup) outcomes [Cg], such as officer indictments, police complaints and legal procedures, certain communities' willingness (or not) to report crime, community support, and collaborative dialogue on the one hand, and aggravated public mistrust on the other (see chapter 13). These forces also have career implications for officers, as well as effects on officer health and wellness.

Transactionally, all these forces feedback to [Ca], and continually refashion societal and cultural values and practices, and the very nature of the evolving intergroup history associated with police-public relations. Figure 23.4 signifies where we believe the preceding chapters' analyses fit appropriately within our model. As can be seen, chapters can be located in more than one conceptual space, while it is acknowledged that some chapters—and for a variety of reasons including the breadth of their coverage—could be positioned elsewhere, too.

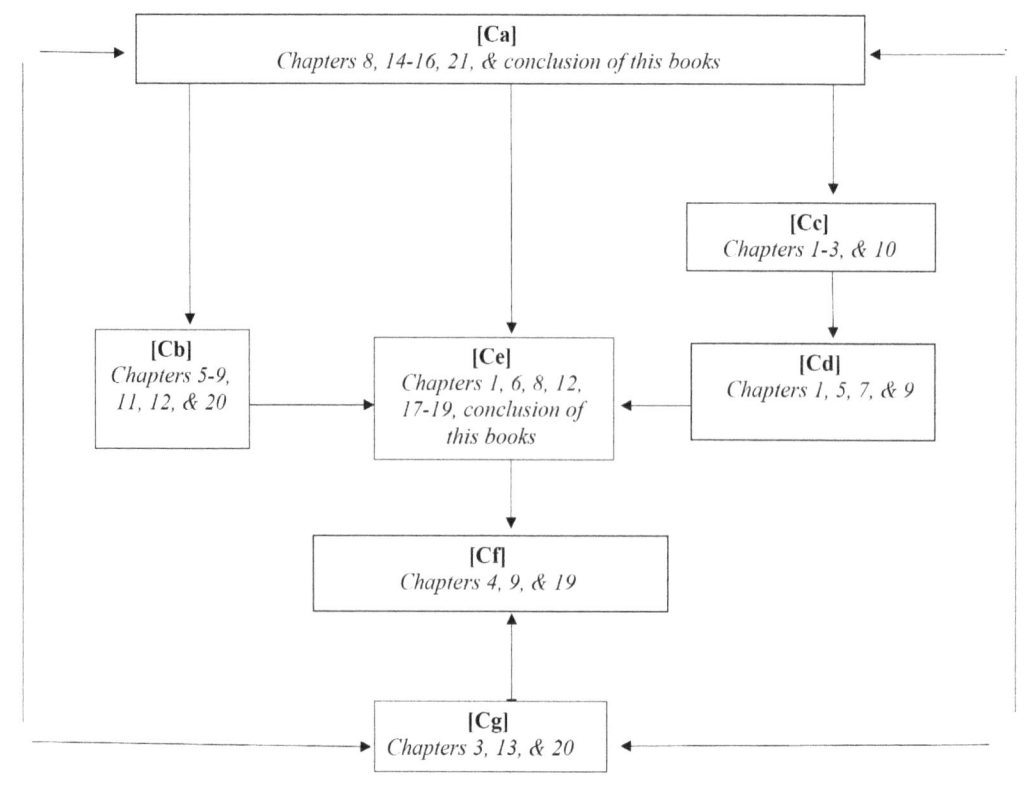

```
                    ┌─────────────────────────────────────────────┐
           ────────▶│                    [Ca]                     │◀────────
                    │  Chapters 8, 14-16, 21, & conclusion of this books │
                    └─────────────────────────────────────────────┘
                         │                    │
                         │                    │
                         │                    ▼
                         │              ┌──────────────┐
                         │              │    [Cc]      │
                         │              │ Chapters 1-3, & 10 │
                         │              └──────────────┘
                         │                    │
                         ▼                    ▼
            ┌──────────────┐    ┌──────────────┐    ┌──────────────┐
            │    [Cb]      │    │    [Ce]      │    │    [Cd]      │
            │ Chapters 5-9,│───▶│ Chapters 1, 6, 8, 12,│◀───│ Chapters 1, 5, 7, & 9 │
            │  11, 12, & 20│    │ 17-19, conclusion of │    │              │
            │              │    │  this books  │    │              │
            └──────────────┘    └──────────────┘    └──────────────┘
                                       │
                                       ▼
                                ┌──────────────┐
                                │    [Cf]      │
                                │ Chapters 4, 9, & 19 │
                                └──────────────┘
                                       ▲
                                       │
                                ┌──────────────┐
                    ───────────▶│    [Cg]      │◀───────────
                                │ Chapters 3, 13, & 20 │
                                └──────────────┘
```

FIGURE 23.4. The Model of Communication, Policing and Society with Illustrative Chapters

For us, the value of this working and developing heuristic is that, arguably, it provides a bird's eye view of the many, albeit not all, interlocking factors that make up policing and perceptions of it in a society. This more or less all-inclusive structure, thereby, encourages the perspective that interventions, education, and reforms regarding any single component of the model necessitate examining the need for change at most other levels, too, if success is to ensue. Robust evaluative assessments over time are necessary, of course, to determine the latter. Taking a conservative, cautious approach to the network of causal links implied in figure 23.3, the model in its entirety is, admittedly, beyond total empirical scrutiny. The next phase of theorizing—which should be international, cross-cultural, and multidisciplinary—should be to specify the conditions necessary, and reasons for, the links between the components of the model as well as defining their boundary conditions (such as, for example, temporal aspects of [Ce] in different locales and across varying incidents and intergroup encounters).

To contextualize our framework in real time, with real events, and real people, we examine the dynamics of a recent dramatic incident that occurred in Minneapolis in May 2020, and which resulted in protests and riots lasting much longer than either the Watts riots in 1965 or the Rodney King riots in 1992 (see, for example, Hazen 1992; Horne 1997). This was the death of a forty-six-year-old black man named George Floyd, who was arrested by three white officers and one Asian American officer for possession of a counterfeit $20 bill and resisting arrest. As manifested by videos from an array of public bystanders, Mr. Floyd was killed, while handcuffed, by one of the officers kneeling on his neck—and another kneeling on his back—for about eight minutes. Other officers stood by and failed to intervene as Mr. Floyd was killed. This viral event, which showed Floyd uttering that he could not breathe sixteen times (while also asking for his deceased mother), triggered worldwide anger and outrage regarding police use of force. It was followed by concentrated global media coverage of hundreds of thousands of people protesting and rioting across the United States for well over a week (see also Horace and Harris 2018; Nelson 2000; Pegues 2017).

The unfolding of this incident and its numerous consequences are exceedingly complex and occurred over a prolonged period of time. We cannot do full justice below to any analytical untangling of all the sequencing of its communicative and intergroup dynamics. But we draw on important features of this incident and its aftermath to illustrate the relationships within and between the components of the model in figure 23.3, some of which, understandably, are more directly relevant to understanding this particular situation than others. Information about this incident and its aftermath is derived, in part, from mainstream media sources. At the time this chapter was written, an authoritative, well-documented account of these events was not yet available (such as the results of a federal investigation or an after-action report written by a neutral party). Given the literature on media bias, we acknowledge the possibility of bias in some of the media sources used in this section (Clark, Bland, and Livingston 2017; Dukes and Gaither 2017). As more evidence becomes available, it will be possible to corroborate these details more carefully.

The Model Applied to a Real Event: The Police Killing of George Floyd[1]

[Ca] SOCIETY AND EVOLVING INTERGROUP HISTORIES:

While "intergroup histories" appeared in the earlier Choi and Giles (2012) model, it was given short shrift there. We consider it more extensively here as a fundamental construct in this book's tripartite title and one vividly playing out during the course of this incident.

- Many media commentators and the public viewed this incident as the last straw. They alleged that since the demonstrations following the Rodney King incident in 1991 (see, for example, Martin 2005), no real reforms had been enacted nationally to address racial injustice involving the police.
- Just a couple of months before this incident, Ahmaud Arbery, a twenty-five-year-old black man who was out for a jog in a Georgia neighborhood, was chased by three white men, one of whom shot and killed him. Local authorities released the suspects after determining that the shooting constituted an act of self-defense. Under great pressure, state authorities took on the case and arrested the suspects two months later.
- Activists, scholars, and celebrities (e.g., Jane Fonda and Spike Lee) argued that the United States had a history of violating black people's civil rights in the context of white privilege going back four hundred years.

- Increased attention during the aftermath was given recalling past events as "Juneteenth," which goes back to 1866 and commemorates the ending of slavery.
- Increased attention was also given to "Black Wall Street," an event in Tulsa that caused the death of over three hundred Black people and the destruction of their neighborhoods in 1921.
- The aftermath of Floyd's death also essentially resurrected memories of "Windrush Day" in Britain, an annual event that marks the arrival of Afro-Caribbean people in 1948.
- Relatedly, others pointed to the historical disadvantage people of color faced in terms of health care and economic well-being. For instance, COVID-19 has exerted a disproportionate toll on racial and ethnic minorities. George Floyd's death occurred during the COVID-19 pandemic. Unemployment rates soared due to business closures during the pandemic, affecting minorities more heavily than others. The cumulative effect of these multiple sources of racial inequity and injustice arising at the same time is not yet well studied, but it is likely that the co-occurrence of these factors fueled the massive wave of protests and riots that took place in the summer of 2020 following Mr. Floyd's death.

[Cb] MEMBERS OF THE PUBLIC'S ATTRIBUTES:

- George Floyd was raised in the Third Ward of Houston, Texas, where his large, media-covered, and emotionally moving funeral was held. Stephen Jackson, his long-time friend and former NBA player, speaking at a rally celebrating the victim, characterized him as "a gentle giant. He was a protector, a provider. He wanted everybody to be happy and have a good time. That was his thing."
- A number of bystanders witnessed the police use of force against Mr. Floyd and begged the officers to release him.
- The next day, this incident led large numbers of people to protest in major cities across the country and around the world. The crowds were diverse in terms of visible characteristics like age and race. Some events were peaceful, and others evolved into riots, with property destruction, theft, and violence. Video footage of the incidents revealed people experiencing a variety of emotions, including anger and sadness. As conflict arose between police and protesters, there were also many instances of crowds that behaved in a defiant and rebellious manner. Many reported feeling fear, as in "Am I the next?," but also exclaimed intergroup sentiments, such as "These are *our* streets!" The intergroup composition of protesters was also diverse in terms of their being, in the main, peaceful participants, but present with other various infiltrating groups, such as outside agitators, anarchists, opportunists (and possibly White supremacists and Antifa). Often, and while coordinated, the latter interweaved into the crowd. This prompted community leaders, self-appointed or elected, to be heard urging protesters to be wary of outside looters and to keep their own message of the movement focused, vocal, and clear. Not unrelatedly, a self-described Ku Klux Klan leader was arrested for allegedly driving his car into a group of Black Lives Matters protesters gathered in Virginia (see BBC News 2020).

[Cc] **POLICE CULTURE, LEADERSHIP, AND POLICIES:**

- Leaders of the Minneapolis Police Department declared that there were clear policies in place dictating appropriate use of force to be used by officers. The officers' actions suggest their organizational culture influenced their actions despite their policy.

[Cd] **OFFICERS' ATTRIBUTES:**

- As said above, three of four officers were White (with another being of Hmong descent and only four days on the job), with the "neck-kneeling" officer Derek Chauvin reportedly having a history of involvement in at least eighteen prior complaints. Chauvin, together with the three officers working with him, was fired two days after the incident (Andone, Silverman, and Alonso 2020).
- Subsequently, Chauvin was arrested for third degree murder and manslaughter, a charge that inflamed the victim's family who felt it should have been first-degree murder. Later, the other three officers were arrested for their complicity and charged with aiding and abetting murder, and Chauvin's charge amended to second-degree murder.
- Albeit rarely commented on by media journalists, many of the officers working the demonstrations were themselves members of the Black community.

[Ce] **CONTACT SITUATIONS (IN THE STREETS) AND THE EMERGENT AFTERMATH:**

- The viral video footage of Mr. Floyd's death led hundreds of thousands of people across the nation to demonstrate and chant slogans against the police and calling for racial justice.
- Nationwide, the behavior of the protesters in the streets varied, with some remaining peaceful and others choosing more destructive or violent tactics. Some protesters set alight police cruisers; lit fires; shut down freeways; threw frozen plastic water bottles, bricks, and other projectiles at the police; engaged in looting and burning of buildings (including a small fire at a historic church in Washington, DC, and the burning of a police precinct in Minneapolis).[2] Thousands across the nation engaged in civil disobedience, some admitting (given COVID-19) they were participating while knowingly risking their personal health, and were arrested for curfew (and other) violations; at least thirty-seven cities across the nation were under curfew, and 2,700 people were arrested in Los Angeles County alone over four days. In some cities, police chose not to arrest peaceful protesters for curfew violations or ignoring orders to disperse.
- Many events across the nation portrayed the police and allied agencies as acting unnecessarily aggressively; some commentators went so far as to claim "the police are rioting" (DeBoule 2020). One incident that went viral was a Kansas City officer arresting and pepper-spraying a member of the public who was merely yelling at him (and other officers). Another viral video showed a Philadelphia police inspector hitting a student in the head with a metal baton, sending the student to

the hospital (Ly 2020). A crowd of about a hundred officers there gathered outside their local union headquarters in support of one of their own and applauded him. The most potent of these incidents was the now infamous occasion when US president Donald Trump allegedly orchestrated the removal of peaceful protesters from Lafayette Park with officers and agents using batons, chemical agents, and kinetic impact munitions, This was allegedly so that the president could participate in a brief photo opportunity at a nearby church. In one of many acts of solidarity with the #BlackLivesMatter movement, Washington, DC, mayor Muriel Bowser quickly renamed the street across from the White House where this incident occurred "Black Lives Matter Plaza."

- Looting in several cities, particularly at night, led to extensive graffiti, some of which, with epithets, categorized *all* police officers as "bad" and even called for their deaths.
- Looters reportedly moved strategically into side alleys and streets using scouts and social media to orchestrate their movements, thereby avoiding confrontations with law enforcement as well as in some cases feeding opportunities for vandalism.
- Nonetheless, some protesters often protected not only stores from looters but also lone officers physically under threat from members of the public.
- A few officers working these demonstrations were summarily dismissed by their chiefs for excessive use of force. The Los Angeles Police Department is investigating no less than fifty-six allegations of misconduct by officers during protests in the wake of George Floyd's death. Of those investigations, twenty-eight involve alleged use of force.
- One evening in Washington, DC, a Black Hawk helicopter was seen flying low trying to disperse the crowd, which caused a public outcry against the use of military force.
- Nonetheless, many police chiefs, police associations, and unions quickly and openly condemned the actions that led to the death of George Floyd.
- With an aim of promoting positive relationships (intergroup contact), officers from many police agencies (e.g., Coral Gables and Atlanta) and police chiefs and sheriffs (e.g., New York City and Flint, Michigan) knelt alongside protesters in solidarity. This aligns with social psychological work on superordinate identities as in, for example, "We're all in this together as Americans" (Khan and Samarina 2007). It also aligns with the common ingroup identity theory, which suggests that intergroup biases can be reduced if different groups conceive of themselves as having shared experiences or being part of the same group (Dovidio, Gaertner, Ufkes, Saguy, and Pearson 2016; Gaertner and Dovidio 2012; see chapter 1). Houston Police Chief Art Acevedo also offered unprecedented security for the victim's funeral and even offered a police escort to the funeral entourage in his city.
- Minneapolis Police chief Medaria Arradondo threw down his baton and hugged protesters and spoke in a TV interview with members of the Floyd family, apologizing and expressing regret and support for them. He also removed his hat a number of times for respect of the family. In many ways, this is communication accommodation (see Giles 2016)—acts that have been discussed throughout this book—at its most profound level.

[Cf] OTHER UNITS AND AGENCIES:

- Many police departments requested mutual aid from other nearby agencies, and the National Guard was drafted in some of these instances. In Washington, DC, the Trump administration called on officers from a number of different federal agencies, many of whom showed up in riot gear without badges, agency identifiers, or personal identifiers. Put differently, heavily armed agents lined the streets of Washington, DC, without any indication of who they were or what agency they worked for. Anecdotal observations by some contended that certain external agencies tended to be more aggressive on occasion than the local agencies. These concerns are reminiscent of a larger debate about how to calibrate the use of mutual aid when handling crowd events (Maguire and Oakley 2020).
- At one point, a CNN news crew was arrested and detained without providing an explanation; the Minneapolis mayor saw this on television and apologized to CNN. On another occasion, a TV crew was told to comply with curfew rules even though they insisted that they were essential workers legally excluded from such legal requirements. These incidents raise constitutional issues associated with the First Amendment's freedom of the press provision.
- When addressing the issue of whether Chauvin's accomplices were going to be indicted, a Minneapolis district attorney erroneously claimed there were video data suggesting the officers' actions were lawful. This statement, for which he later publicly apologized, was yet another message that ignited public fury.
- Another message that detonated public outrage was when President Trump said on live television that he might send in the military "to dominate the streets" if governors could not control the civil disturbances in their own states. This suggestion of using the military against American citizens was resoundingly criticized in the media by both current and former secretaries of defense and other military leaders who historically have refrained from speaking out on political matters.

[Cg] SOCIAL OUTCOMES

- Campaign Zero, a well-known police reform nonprofit, argues that its ten recommended policy solutions will reduce police use of force and hold police accountable (see https://www.joincampaignzero.org/#vision). Although Campaign Zero makes bold claims about these "data driven" solutions, many of them are not evidence-based. The US Congress, only two weeks following the Floyd killing, tabled a police reform bill. A couple of days later, the International Association of Chiefs of Police (IACP) announced their own policy framework for "Improved Community-Police Engagement."
- Disney reported that it was donating $5 million to nonprofit organizations that advance social justice. Michael Jordan's Foundation also donated $5 million for nonprofit social justice agencies, the first $2 million going immediately to the National Association for the Advancement of Colored People (NAACP), while Bank of America pledged $1 billion over four years to minority communities to restore economic and racial equality.

- The mural of George Floyd painted in the vicinity of his demise, where large numbers of Minneapolis citizens gathered to meditate, pay tribute, and celebrate his life, will likely remain a historic visual symbol of his role in American life for many years to come. Other vividly impressive murals have appeared elsewhere in the country, such as a street near the White House, and in downtown Santa Barbara, California.
- The California governor announced that restrictions were going to be placed on certain neck restraints and chokeholds. The New York Assembly passed the Eric Garner Anti-Chokehold Act that makes the use of a chokehold by a police officer a felony. It creates a new crime called aggravated strangulation and carries a maximum sentence of fifteen years.
- The Floyd incident also led to the resurrection of previous controversial police-related deaths. One such case involved Breonna Taylor, a twenty-six-year-old emergency medical technician shot by Louisville police, who allegedly broke into her apartment on March 13, 2020. Subsequently, Louisville's city council unanimously voted to ban "no knock" warrants and required officers to activate their body cameras upon entry; this was called Breonna's Law. Another such case had occurred on March 28, 2019, in Williamson County, Texas, where a forty-year-old Black man was pleading with deputies that he had a heart condition and could not breathe. He was repeatedly tased following a pursuit that began when the man had not dimmed his headlights to an oncoming police cruiser. This case never made national headlines until after Floyd's death. On March 3, 2020, medical examiners ruled Manuel Ellis's death a homicide and said the Black man died from a lack of oxygen due to physical restraint by police officers in Tacoma, Washington. Certain police-involved deaths, like George Floyd's in 2020 and Michael Brown's in 2014, become highly newsworthy. Such incidents not only serve to raise awareness about racial justice issues, they also help to shine a light on incidents that, for whatever reason, were not previously deemed as newsworthy (see chapter 16).
- The National Football League's commissioner announced that he had been wrong, seasons ago, to decry players kneeling while the national anthem was being played at the start of game. Taking a knee was intended to call attention to police misconduct and racial injustice. The National Association for Stock Car Auto Racing (NASCAR) drivers also threw their support behind the protesters after a noose was discovered in the garage of African American driver Bubba Wallace. Indeed, a CNN poll showed that 84 percent of Americans supported the peaceful protests thirteen days into the demonstrations, with 65 percent evaluating police practices as harmful (Sparks 2020).
- Large-scale demonstrations in major cities across the globe emerged many times in light of the Floyd killing. In a protest supporting the US Black Lives Matter movement, a prominent statue of a slave trader, Edward Colston, which was erected in 1895, was pulled down by protesters in Bristol, UK. Google maps locates it now in the Avon River.
- Two weeks into the aftermath, House Democrats unveiled a legislative blueprint for reforming policing policies.[3]
- Widespread cries to "defund the police" were proclaimed, even printed in large letters on a street near the White House. While this has received mixed support

and at best is ambiguously conceived, the Minneapolis City Council did support an intention toward such actions by means of a veto-proof 9 to 13 majority. The movement to defund the police has various strands, from outright abolition of police to reassigning certain social problems to other agencies or professions, such as social workers or clinicians. Some politicians have interpreted the defunding movement as a means to transfer funds away from certain aspects of police work that critics view as inappropriate (such as assigning resource officers to schools or responding to mental health crises).

FEEDBACK FROM [Cg] TO [Ca] AND THEN FLUIDLY IMPACTING OTHER COMPONENTS:

- In a seemingly unrelated incident the same week, the mayor of Louisville fired his police chief (who was about to retire that month anyway) following an incident in which police shot a man but body camera footage was unavailable from three officers present at the incident. Undoubtedly, this action was spurred by the social and outcomes described in [Cg] that feed back into [Ca] and then trickled down to [Ce]; and all this much in contrast to any traditional code of police silence (see chapter 1).
- Similarly, the public's learning of other Black deaths due to restraint holds and other violent actions (as above) will necessarily also feed back into revising society's understandings of the extent of police misconduct.

Research and Practical Challenges Arising from This Case Study

In sum, and returning to our model of figure 23.3, we have seen how historical messages passed down for generations, and even intergroup events witnessed by the public and police in more recent times, can affect how an encounter between them plays out as well as the course of its aftermath. Intergroup messaging is ubiquitous throughout. We also saw that both sides—along with other agencies and social institutions—can act and communicate in accommodative *as well as* nonaccommodative ways. Put another way, recent events have really brought out some of the best and some of the worst of all participating sides. Whether this event is a tipping point, as has been declared by so many, that brings more awareness and breaks cycles of inequality and racism will become clear in due course. In this regard, former president Barack Obama argued that "there is a mindset that's taking place, a greater recognition that we can do better." Furthermore, he proposed that each mayor should review their local police procedures regularly and report on them; some have agreed to do that.

The task of reform is, however, Herculean as indicated thirteen days into the protests in Buffalo. A seventy-five-year-old man was suddenly pushed to the ground by an officer, fell quickly, and remained motionless with blood visibly seeping from his head onto the ground. Later in the hospital he was suspected of having brain damage and was unable to walk. The officer who committed this act and another walked past without aiding him. The victim was taken to the hospital in a stable but serious condition. These two officers were suspended without pay, but fifty-seven of their colleagues resigned from a special operations unit in solidarity with their disciplined colleagues.

Furthermore, these officers were charged with felony assault and applauded when leaving the courthouse by some of their colleagues. These incidents, and others, occurring *at that particular point in time* highlight the intergroup nature of the police–citizen relationship and the influence of ingroup solidarity.

Longitudinal research is needed not only to monitor any changes (or not) emerging in police reforms but, especially, the social consequences of these for different intergroup entities of both the public and law enforcement agencies. Charges of racism are, of course, not confined to the United States as this has been endemic to many European nations for a very long time (e.g., Cole 1997; MacEwen 1995; MacMaster 2001). Hence, it will be interesting to see what kinds of changes, if any, emerge across that continent in terms of tackling institutional racism and police reforms. Not unrelatedly, an unpredictably large number of three thousand protesters attended a memorial for George Floyd outside the US Embassy in Madrid. Clearly, *international* collaborations to conduct such longitudinal studies more globally would be invaluable.

Our hope in these uncertain times is that mechanisms can be put in place which proactively and creatively generate an armory of harmonious solutions to these intergroup tensions (see Mckesson 2019; McPherson 2018; Watson 2016) and that go well beyond mere conversations and enhance societal processes in a favorable way (for hope theory, see Snyder 2002). The fact that large and different social communities and races have been united in taking joint action to work on racism is very encouraging; as were the continual words of love and justice rather than words of hate and revenge at Floyd's funeral service. Furthermore, the proposed bill in Congress[4] and the policy guidelines from the IACP (both mentioned above) as well as actions of police chiefs are significant and swift signals that these institutions and leaders recognize the need for change. Consequently, we will have to wait and see in what ways police organizations modify their selection procedures and training academies and programs (see chapter 3). How all this, in turn, affects the next generation's desire to be recruited and retained in law enforcement as an appealing and respected profession could be another social outcome on the horizon.

Nonetheless, how totally unexpected—but perhaps inevitable—future events such as members of the public seeing and benefiting from courageous first responders saving lives in mass shootings could have significant and salutary effects in transforming the current social climate. Indeed, the support that law enforcement provides the community (e.g., Police Activities League) is rarely dramatic enough fodder for news reporting and its lack thereof probably plays some part in some members of the public (as seen by protesters' placards) believing that *all* cops are racist and abusive (e.g., ACAB, "All Cops Are Bastards"). This speaks to the fact that the community also has profound biases that need to be socially as well as educationally addressed (see Giles, Willemyns, Gallois, and Anderson 2007).

While the focus has, understandably, been on targeting police reform given the death of George Floyd and similar events, the implications are far wider in terms of tackling systemic, institutional racism (e.g., ethnic disparities in housing, employment, health care, wealth, and criminal justice). Often, police reform is provided as a solution to societal ills in a social vacuum. Furthermore, the victims of social and institutional discrimination go far beyond ethnic minorities to other marginalized communities, for example, people with disabilities, older folk, and those with different sexual orientations and identities, such as Black transwomen who have increasingly been the victims of violence (for the important notion of so-called "intersectionality," see chapters 7 and 19; also Crenshaw 1991).

That said, cultural shifts were beginning to be evident in the unifying number of White protesters with Black and other members of the public calling for reforms; NASCAR drivers' requests that no Confederate flags be waved at their sporting events; the pulling down of long-standing statues of slave owners in and beyond the United States; the pleas for the stripping of Confederate generals' names associated with military bases as well as their statues; the acknowledgement of some that certain TV shows (e.g., cop shows; see chapter 15) and classic movies (e.g., *Gone with the Wind*) are inherently racist; and the restoration of affirmative action for academic institutions (e.g., University of California). The question is this: What number and nature of these changes over time need to be visibly in place to quell protesters' (and others') anger, fear, and anxieties so that people can proclaim "justice" now prevails?

Arguably, there are more *questions* raised by incidents such as the Floyd case and their aftermath than ready-made answers. These questions might propel communication and policing research toward being part of the societal solution:

- What forms of communication, besides physical street protest, can propel changes regarding policing excessive use of force: letters, emails, and social media posts to mayors, police chiefs, governors, and other key officials? There must be an alternative for people to take action that has some real impact without getting in close physical proximity to potential COVID-19 carriers; a phenomenon that could be called protest "suicide by COVID-19."[5]
- How should protesters most effectively communicate their message of disapproval of police brutality? Is marching together with placards sufficient; if so, where and for how long? Toward what benefit should protesters engage officers, when, how, and why?
- To what extent do current policing practices stimulate self-policing within crowds so that moderate protesters help to prevent more radical protesters from engaging in property damage, violence, and looting behaviors? What types of communication-based reforms can police implement to encourage self-policing and other pro-social behaviors within crowds (see chapter 22)?
- Do Black and White protesters feel integrated in a common cause and set of values? And how do they communicate this to each other, if at all? Does the communicative presence of racial and ethnic minority officers (and women) have any beneficial effects on calming and de-escalating the protests?
- Are public messages from police chiefs and police associations condemning police brutality, and expressing empathy for victims and their families, effective forms of communication? How are such messages perceived by those involved in protesting police brutality and racial injustice?
- Given the serious concerns being expressed by Black Lives Matter protesters and their allies, what steps can police leaders take to build trust and establish legitimacy among people who allege that police engage in racially discriminatory behavior?

- Given mounting evidence of significant morale deficits among police officers, what steps can communities take to support, empower, and reward dedicated police officers who engage in fair, judicious, empathetic, and skilled policing?

OTHER MAJOR CHALLENGES

The previous conjecture segues into the title of this last section. One opening avenue here is to acknowledge an admission we made in the prologue of this book, namely, that not all topics, social groups, and crimes could be accommodated in one volume and, indeed, too few have communication research associated with them as yet. Relatedly, and appearing below, is a selected sample of topics that might benefit from methodologically diverse research from intergroup communication and other theoretical stances (for example, uncertainty management theories, see Hogg and Belvadi 2018).

First, little is known about communication dynamics in policing outside of the developed industrial democracies where most police research takes place. Understanding these dynamics within developing nations, emerging democracies, and other settings would be a useful contribution (see Pino and Wiatrowski 2016). For instance, we know that police play a fundamental role in both facilitating and undermining democratic governance, but little is known about the extent to which communication dynamics play a role in generating these powerful effects.

Second, international collaboration between law enforcement agencies represents a robust communication challenge. These agencies are often geographically distant from one another; have different governmental and organizational mandates; have different regional, national, organizational, and operational cultures; and often speak different languages. All these challenges make it difficult for these agencies to come together in the fight against terrorism and organized criminal elements worldwide (Sellar 2020). To what extent are these efforts hindered or facilitated by communication issues and how can such issues be most effectively addressed?

Third, much remains to be learned about policing homeless people of different generations (Dollar and Zimmers 1998; Gately 2019) and opioid (and other) substance abusers (Smith 2019; see chapter 9). These populations attract a significant proportion of calls for service from law enforcement as the number of homeless people and addicts have continued to increase in size in major cities during the last decade, particularly on the West Coast (https://www.hud.gov/press/press_releases_media_advisories/HUD_No_19_177). As such, this topic is inevitably likely to command a considerable amount of attention in the upcoming years, particularly as it relates policing policies, practices, and interventions (see Hipple 2016; Hipple, Schaefer, Hipple, and Ballew 2016), and in crisis situations like a global pandemic.

Fourth, as we were finalizing this book, the world was suddenly forced to deal with COVID-19, a global pandemic with massive implications for policing and society. We regret that we were unable to include a chapter on this timely issue, but we recognize the likelihood that epidemics and pandemics will likely continue to be salient issues. As COVID-19 spread globally, the world saw numerous examples of communication issues involving the police. As governments and public health authorities released mandates, the duty for enforcing those mandates often fell on the police. Suddenly, police agencies that had invested heavily in building legitimacy in the eyes of the public found themselves enforcing curfews, social distancing and stay-at-home orders, and public health guidelines recommending or requiring the public to wear face masks. How police chose to respond to the communication challenges inherent in their pandemic response had fundamental effects on public trust and police legitimacy. Understanding these communication issues at a deeper level will be important for police and those who study them.

Fifth, scholars have long recognized that police are one part of a network of institutions for addressing community problems. Some of these networks are vertical, such as in the local, provincial/state, and national law enforcement and intelligence response to terrorism and organized crime. Some of these are horizontal, such as in the law enforcement and public health response to emotionally disturbed people and those with addiction problems (Gilson 2020). Certain police officers or officials serve as boundary-spanners in these interorganizational relationships, with responsibility for communicating on behalf of their organization with other organizations in the network. For example, a police officer who serves on a multiagency task force serves as the linchpin for his or her organization to communicate with the boundary-spanners from the other organizations in the network. Little is known about these interorganizational communication dynamics in the various networks of organizations in which police agencies are enmeshed. Furthermore, it would be interesting to know when mutual aid for police departments is successful (as in the Minneapolis protests around the country), when and why it might falter, and what communicative improvements need to be put in place to benefit the collaborative efforts.

CONCLUSIONS

Communication matters. It is perhaps the most important tool a police officer will use in their career. Communication can resolve conflict or have the potential for devastating effects to relationships. Understanding the processes surrounding how we communicate is integral to successful police–citizen interactions. Additionally, acknowledging the intergroup anxieties forged in the history shared by police and marginalized groups can help police become better prepared to succeed in an intergroup setting. We suggest that most, if not all, police–citizen interactions are intergroup in nature, and many of these forces can, in their own ways, work within the profession.

Research in communication accommodation theory (CAT) and intergroup communication (see chapter 1) suggests that people tend to *converge* communicatively toward people with whom they identify. That is, they accommodate the interlocutor's communication style, which leads to improved communication effectiveness. Or, *divergence* can occur; that is, people use communication to put social distance between themselves and their perceived outgroups (often subconsciously). This can be the case when intergroup bias exists, and people discriminate against outgroups. Considering that police hold a complex place in society where they are authorized to coerce the public with physical force in order to protect civil peace and, at the same time, have to negotiate and manage challenging communicative issues and dilemmas within their organizations, we suggest that research in the field of communication, especially intergroup communication, be embraced and expanded.

The chapters in this volume address many of the issues that challenge police and the public in today's society. Most of these challenges involve communicating between different groups. The "us versus them" mentality between police and the public is perhaps the most salient of these intergroup relationships; and as many of these chapters suggest, this mentality remains an obstacle to community policing efforts. This book provides a foundation to begin identifying and understanding policing problems in a variety of intergroup contexts.

NOTES

1. Much of the description of events was obtained through news outlets and the editors' experience.
2. This effect, originally posited after the Kitty Genovese murder in 1964, claims that the more bystanders there are around someone in distress, the less likely it is that someone will do something to help (Darley and Latané 1968).
3. Relatedly, Giles (2012, 10) wrote that "although rarely highlighted in the study of intergroup communication, the strength of a group can often be a function of the distinctiveness of its geographic and cultural homes. . . .The distinctiveness of a structure . . . can be a source of considerable pride." Not unrelated, protestors in Seattle took control of six blocks, an area called CHAZ (Capitol Hill Autonomous Zone, and later CHOP); there protesters temporarily commandeered a police precinct.
4. This bill includes reforms making it easier to sue police officers for misconduct in civil court and to prosecute them for criminal behavior. It would prohibit the use of chokeholds and certain no-knock warrants by police nationwide and give the Justice Department civil rights division subpoena power to investigate local police departments.

The bill also mandates the use of body cameras, bans the transfer of certain military equipment to police departments, and creates a national database disclosing the names of officers with a pattern of abuse. It would make lynching a federal crime. Even if passed, the bill would need to go before the Senate. In tandem, the French interior minister has declared that the use of chokeholds will be discontinued in police training.

5. Labeled to us in a personal communication, by one of our contributors, Joseph Walther.

REFERENCES

Andone, Dakin, Hollie Silverman, and Melissa Alonso. 2020. "The Minneapolis Police Officer Who Knelt on George Floyd's Neck had 18 Previous Complaints against Him, Police Department Says." CNN. May 29. Retrieved from https://www.cnn.com/2020/05/28/us/minneapolis-officer-complaints-george-floyd/index.html .

Baker, Susan C., Cindy Gallois, S. Michelle Driedger, and Nancy Santesso. 2011. "Communication Accommodation and Managing Musculoskeletal Disorders: Doctors' and Patients' Perspectives." *Health Communication* 26 (4): 379–88.

BBC News. 2020. "KKK 'Leader' Charged for Attack on Black Lives Matter Protesters." June 9. Retrieved from https://www.bbc.com/news/world-us-canada-52973398 .

Choi, Charles W., and Howard Giles. 2012. "Intergroup Messages in Policing the Community." In *The Handbook of Intergroup Communication*, edited by Howard Giles, 264–77. New York: Routledge.

Clark, Meredith D., Dorothy Bland, and Jo Ann Livingston. 2017. "Lessons from #McKinney: Social Media and the Interactive Construction of Police Brutality." *Journal of Social Media in Society* 6 (1): 284–313.

Cole, Jeffrey. 1997. *The New Racism in Europe: A Sicilian Ethnography*. Cambridge: Cambridge University Press.

Crenshaw, Kimberlé. 1991. "Mapping the Margins: Intersectionality, Identity Politics, and Violence against Women of Color." *Stanford Law Review* 43 (6): 1241–99.

Darley, John M., and Bibb Latané. 1968. "Bystander Intervention in Emergencies: Diffusion of Responsibility." *Journal of Personality and Social Psychology* 8 (4): 377–83.

DeBoule, Jamelle. 2020. "The Police Are Rioting. We Need to Talk about It." *New York Times*, Sunday Review, June 5. Opinion. Retrieved from https://www.nytimes.com/2020/06/05/opinion/sunday/police-riots.html .

Dollar, Natalie, and Brooke G. Zimmers. 1998. "Social Identity and Communicative Boundaries: An Analysis of Youth and Young Adult Street Speakers in a U.S. American Community." *Communication Research* 25 (6): 596–617.

Dovidio, John F., Samuel L. Gaertner, Elze Gooitzen Ufkes, Tamar Saguy, and Adam R. Pearson. 2016. "Included but Invisible? Subtle Bias, Common Identity, and the Darker Side of 'We.'" *Social Issues and Policy Review* 10 (1): 6–46.

Dukes, Kristin N., and Sarah E. Gaither. 2017. "Black Racial Stereotypes and Victim Blaming: Implications for Media Coverage and Criminal Proceedings in Cases of Police Violence against Racial and Ethnic Minorities." *Journal of Social Issues* 73 (4): 789–807.

Gaertner, Samuel L., and John F. Dovidio, J. F. (2012). "The Common Ingroup Identity Model." In *Handbook of Theories of Social Psychology*, edited Paul A. M. Van Lange, Ari W. Kruglanski, and E. Tory Higgins, 439–57. Thousand Oaks: Sage.

Gallois, Cynthia, Julia Cretchley, and Bernadette M. Watson. 2012. "Approaches and Methods in Intergroup Communication." In *The Handbook of Intergroup Communication*, edited by Howard Giles, Vol. 1, 31–43. New York: Routledge.

Gately, Tim. 2019. "Homelessness in Suburban Communities." *Police Chief* 86 (7): 50–55.

Giles, Howard. 2012. "Principles of Intergroup Communication." In *The Handbook of Intergroup Communication*, edited by Howard Giles, 3–16. New York: Routledge.

Giles, Howard, ed., 2016. *Communication Accommodation Theory: Negotiating Personal Relationships and Social Identities across Contexts*. Cambridge: Cambridge University Press.

Giles, Howard, Michael Willemyns, Cindy Gallois, and Michelle C. Anderson. 2007. "Accommodating a New Frontier: The Context of Law Enforcement." In *Social Communication*, edited by Klaus Fiedler, 129–62. New York: Psychology Press.

Gilson, Thomas. 2020. "Death Investigations." *Police Chief* 87 (2): 28–33.

Harris, Jacob. 2011. "Word Clouds Considered Harmful." NiemLab. Retrieved from https://www.niemanlab.org/2011/10/word-clouds-considered-harmful/ .

Hazen, Don. 1992. *Inside the L.A. Riots: What Really Happened and Why It Will Happen Again*. New York: Institute of Alternative Journalism.

Hipple, Natalie, K. 2016. "Policing and Homelessness: Using Partnerships to Address a Cross System Issue." *Policing: A Journal of Policy and Practice* 11 (2): 14–28.

Hipple, Natalie K., Sarah J. M. Shaefer, Robert F. Hipple, Jr., and Alfarena T. Ballew. 2016. "Can We Prevent Deaths of Homeless Persons? Police-Led Public Health Approach to Prevent Homeless Deaths." *Journal of Social Distress and Homelessness* 25 (2): 78–85.

Hogg, Michael, A., and Sucharita Belvadi. 2018. "Uncertainty Management Theories." In *The Oxford Encyclopedia of Intergroup Communication*, edited by Howard Giles and Jake Harwood, Vol. 2, 447–61. New York: Oxford University Press.

Horace, Maurice, and Ron Harris. 2018. *The Black and the Blue*. Brentwood: Hachette.

Horne, Gerald. 1997. *Fire This Time: The Watts Uprising and the 1960s*. Brentwood: Hachette.

Hortensius, Ruud, and Beatrice de Gelder. 2018. "From Empathy to Apathy: The Bystander Effect Revisited." *Current Directions in Psychological Science* 27 (4): 249–56.

Hua, Zhu. 2020. "Making a Stance: Social Action for Language and Intercultural Communication Research." *Language and Intercultural Communication* 20 (2): 206–12.

Keblusek, Lauren, Howard Giles, Anne Maass, and Antonis Gardikiotis. 2018. "Intersections of Intergroup Communication Research." *Atlantic Journal of Communication* 26 (2): 75–85.

Khan, Saera R., and Viktoriya Samarina. 2007. "Realistic Group Conflict Theory." In *The Encyclopedia of Social Psychology*, edited by Roy F. Baumeister and Kathleen D. Vohs, 725–26. Thousand Oaks: Sage.

Ladegaard, Hans J., and Alison Phipps. 2020. "Intercultural Research and Social Activism." *Language and Intercultural Communication* 20 (2): 67–80.

Ly, Laura. 2020. "After Reviewing Video, Prosecutors Charge Police Inspector Instead of Protester." CNN. June 9. Retrieved from https://www.cnn.com/2020/06/06/us/philly-student-protester/index.html .

MacEwen, Martin. 1995. *Tackling Racism in Europe: An Examination of Anti-Discrimination Law in Practice*. New York: Bloomsbury.

MacMaster, Neil. 2001. *Racism in Europe*. New York: Red Globe Press.

Maguire, Edward R., and Megan Oakley. 2020. *Policing Protests: Lessons from the Occupy Movement, Ferguson, and Beyond—A Guide for Police*. New York: Harry Frank Guggenheim Foundation.

Martin, Brian. 2005. "The Beating of Rodney King: The Dynamics of Backfire." *Critical Criminology* 13 (3): 307–26.

Mckesson, LeRay. 2019. *On the Other Side of Freedom: The Case for Hope*. New York: Penguin Random House.

McPherson, Miles 2018. *The Third Option: Hope for a Racially Divided Nation*. New York: Simon & Schuster.

Nelson, Jill (ed.). 2000. *Police Brutality Matters: An Anthology*. New York: Norton.

Pegues, Jeff. 2017. *Black and Blue: Inside the Divide between the Police and Black America*. Lanham: Rowman & Littlefield.

Petrosino, Anthony, Sarah Guckenburg, and Trevor Fronius. 2012. "Policing Schools' Strategies: A Review of the Evaluation Evidence." *Journal of MultiDisciplinary Evaluation* 8 (17): 80–101.

Philpot, Richard, Lasse S., Levine, Mark Bernasco, Wim Lindegaard, and Marie Rosenkrantz. 2020. "Would I Be Helped? Cross-National CCTV Footage Shows that Intervention if the Norm in Public Conflicts." *American Psychologist* 76 (1): 66–75.

Pines, Rachyl, and Howard Giles. 2018. "Dance as Intergroup Communication. In *The Oxford Encyclopedia of Intergroup Communication*, edited by Howard Giles and Jake Harwood, Vol. 1, 263–78. New York: Oxford University Press.

Pino, Nathan W., and Michael D. Wiatrowski. 2016. *Democratic Policing in Transitional and Developing Countries*. New York: Routledge.

Reicher, Steve D. 1984. "The St. Pauls' Riot: An Explanation of the Limits of Crowd Action in Terms of a Social Identity Model." *European Journal of Social Psychology* 14 (1): 1–21.

Relihan, Robert. 2020. "Use Word Clouds Cautiously." Retrieved from https://www.crresearch.com/blog/market-research-use-of-word-clouds-vs-data-journalism .

Sellar, John M. 2020. "Expanding the Armory in the Fight against Organized Crime." *Police Chief* 87 (2): 42–47.

Smith, John T. T. 2019. "Drug Abuse Response Team Achieves Community-Wide Change." *Police Chief* 86 (7): 44–48.

Snyder, Charles R. 2002. "Hope Theory: Rainbows in the Mind." *Psychological Inquiry* 13 (4): 249–75.

Sparks, Grace. 2020. "Polls Show Widespread Support of Black Lives Matters Protests and Varied Views on How to Reform Police." CNN. June 18. Retrieved from https://www.cnn.com/2020/06/18/politics/protests-polling-support-movement-policies-kaiser-quinnipiac/index.html .

Watson, Benjamin. 2016. *Under Our Skin: Getting Real about Race. Getting Free from the Fears and Frustrations that Divide Us*. Carol Stream: Tyndale House.

Index

abstraction level, 176–78, *177*
accommodativeness, 380; accommodative chase and, 25; African Americans and, 77–78; measures of, 29n3; nonaccommodation and, 26, 27, 28, 266, 383; public perception on, 26, 77–78; racial disparity and, 77–78; in traffic stops, 77–78, 266
accountability, 381; for GBV, officer-perpetrated, 301–2, 306; OPA and, 206; transparency and, 201
Acevedo, Art, 380
Acker, Joann, 96
ACLU. *See* American Civil Liberties Union
active listening skills (ALS), 285
actors, 173–74, *174*
Adams, J. S., 36
advertising, 22, 316–18
African Americans: accommodativeness and, 77–78; discrimination against, 3; Juneteenth and, 378; in Los Angeles, 83; media depictions of, 79–80; opinions, of police, 18; racialized treatment in tone and searches of, 81–83, *82*; the "talk" and, 76–77; traffic stops and, 76–78, 81–83, 84–85; Windrush Day and, 378. *See also* racial disparities; racial injustice; racial violence
agenda setting, 8, 253
aggression, 220–21
agitators, 358–61
Albuquerque Police Department, 143, 164
algorithms, 230, 231–34, 241, 347–48
Allport, Gordon, 95
ALS. *See* active listening skills
alternative policing model, 180–82. *See also* community policing
American Civil Liberties Union (ACLU), 298
The Ancient Regime (Taine), 357–58
Antifa, 378
anxieties, 203; fear and, 220–21; intergroup, 95; of marginalized communities, 18
appearance, 2–3, 11n2

Arbery, Ahmaud, 377
Ardern, Jacinda, 132
ARIMA. *See* autoregressive integrated moving average models
Arradondo, Medaria, 380
asymmetric communication, 157–58, *158*
Atlanta Police Department, 113, 116
ATP. *See* attitudes toward police
attention hacking, 230, 231–34
attitudes toward police (ATP), 25–26
Australia, 124, 126–32, 267
authority-subordinate relations, 36–39, 285
autoregressive integrated moving average (ARIMA) models, 255nn7–8, 256n9

Babin, Leif, 40–41
Baton Rouge shooting, 4
Battered Women's Justice Project, 299–300
battlefield missions, 40–41
BCSM. *See* Behavioral Change Stairway Model
behavior: crowd theory and, 10, 359–61; focused deterrence and, 321–22; in hostage negotiation, 284–85; management and, 38–39; mediation and, 202–3, 205; organizational justice and, 37–38; social identity and, 19–20, 22, 359–61
Behavioral Change Stairway Model (BCSM), 286, *288*
Behavioral Influence Stairway Model (BISM), 286, *289*
beliefs: SIT and, 360–61; terrorism and, 341–42
bias, 387–88; category of criminal activity and, 84; cognitive association, race, and policing, 78–79; explicit, 78; first- and second-, 93; gender, 93–99, 300–301; heteronormativity and, 109–10; implicit, 78–79, 80; linguistic intergroup, 20, 94; in management, 40; prosecutorial misconduct and, 64; race and, 76–79; social media and, 239–40; stereotypes and, 78–79, 94; traffic stops and, 76–78; of women, 93, 95–99
Bies, Robert J., 37

BISM. *See* Behavioral Influence Stairway Model
BJA-CCP. *See* Bureau of Justice Assistance Comprehensive Communities Program
Black Lives Matter (BLM), 378, 380, 382; Brown, Ferguson, and, 3, 245; Dallas shooting and, 4; growth of, 245; rights and, 305; social media and, 216
Bland, Sandra, 246, 251, 252–53, 254, 268, 270n5
BLM. *See* Black Lives Matter
blue code of silence, 20
BLUE H.E.L.P., 147
body cameras, 146, 229, 237, 264, 268, 388n4
Border Patrol agents, 39
Boston Gun Project, 313, 316, 320
Boston Operation Ceasefire, 145, 313, 317, 320, 325, 328
Bowser, Muriel, 380
Breusch-Godfrey LM test, 255n8
Brewer, Marilynn B., 96–97
Britain First, 342
British Security Service, 345
Brown, Michael: ARIMA model and, 256n9; environmental jolt after shooting of, 250, 252, 255n1; examining shooting of, 249–54; racial injustice and killing of, 3–4, 8, 178, 216, 245–46, 249–54, 255n1. *See also* Ferguson, Missouri; "Ferguson Effect"
buildings, 187, 238, 356, 379
bullying, 239
Bureau of Justice Assistance Comprehensive Communities Program (BJA-CCP), 145
Bureau of Justice Statistics, 3
burning, 379
bystanders, 63, 242n1, 375, 376–77, 378, 388n2

call-ins, 315, 317, 324–26, 328
Call's Interpretation of Crisis Negotiation, 286, *287*
cameras: body, 146, 229, 237, 264, 268, 388n4; dash, 77, 146, 209, 230, 237, 264; surveillance, 239; videos and, 229–30, 236–42, 242n1
Campaign Zero, 381
Campbell Collaboration, 313
Capitol Hill Autonomous Zone (CHAZ) (CHOP), 388n3
career expectations, 51–52
carrying, of firearms, 238, 317
caseload management, 63
CAT. *See* communication accommodation theory
cause and effect, 319

CEDAW. *See* Elimination of All Forms Discrimination Against Women
censorship, internet, 347
Cervera, Jim, 4
change: communication and, 41–42; government intervention and, 2; in police culture, 20, 23; in policy, 41–42; societal, 2, 75, 117, 153–54, 361–62
chanting, 3
Charlotte Mecklenburg Police Department (CMPD), 57–58, 64–68
Chauvin, Derek, 379, 381
CHAZ. *See* Capitol Hill Autonomous Zone
Chicago Police Department, 143, 160, 241
Chicago Project Safe Neighborhoods, 317, 320, 328
China, 355–57
choice, illusion of, 282
chokeholds, 248, 382, 388n4
CHOP. *See* Capitol Hill Autonomous Zone
Christchurch massacre, 132
CIIM. *See* common ingroup identity model
Cincinnati Police Department, 328–29
CIT. *See* crisis intervention
Civilian Review Authority, 207
civil libertarians, 154
Civil Rights Act, 1964, 93
civil unrest: Brown and, 3–4; crowd theory and, 10, 355–59; disorder and, 215; Floyd and, 18, 377–86; LGBTQ+ communities and, 107–8; during 1960s, 153–54; racial injustice and, 3–4, 229, 242n1, 245, 376–86; rights and, 153–54; rioting and, 361–62, 365–66, 376–87; violence and, 379–80
classical crowd psychology, 356–59
clearance rates, 58, 60–64, 68
Clinton, Bill, 155–56
clothing, 2–3, 11n2
CMPD. *See* Charlotte Mecklenburg Police Department
CNN, 381
Cochran, Sam, 138
cognitive association, 78–79, 94
Colquitt, Jason, 36, 37
command and control, 136–37
commonality condition, 129–30
common ingroup identity model (CIIM), 95
communication: asymmetric, 157–58, *158*; change and, 41–42; in community policing, 153–66; community resilience and, 190–91; crisis, 135–49; culture relating to, 161; failures, 208–9; in focused deterrence, 313–31; formal, 162–63; heuristic model of, 10, *374*, 374–87, *376*; interpersonal, 24, 175, 365;

management and, 35–43; nonverbal, 29n4, 91, 204–5; in police culture, 18–19; in police recruitment, 49–50, 53–54; purpose of, 175–76, *176*; subjectivity of, 24; symmetric, 157–59, *158*; worldviews and, 19–25. *See also* interagency communication; intergroup communication; strategic communication; *specific topics*

communication accommodation theory (CAT): on hostage negotiation, 277–78; interagency communication and, 61–62; interpersonal communication and, 24; language use and, 266; LGBTQ+ communities and, 111; mediation and, 203–4; procedural justice and, 204; research in, 387–88; social identity and, 111; traffic stops and, 76–77, 203–4; in us versus them mentality, 24, 28–29

community, 10; attributes, 191, 196–97; competence, 191; fear, 62; focused deterrence and, 322–27; gangs and, 322–23; imagined political community, 341–42; internet and, 341, 346–47; local knowledge in, 190; local networks in, 190; narrative, 191; racial injustice and, 327; social service and, 323–24; trust and, 325–27

community policing: case studies, 160–61; communication in, 153–66; community resilience and, 195; cooperation and, 84; crisis intervention and, 136–37; culture relating to, 161; emergence and growth of, 155–57, 166n2; external communication reform in, 157–62; in heuristic model, 10, *374*, 374–87, *376*; history of, 153–57; intergroup communication in, 7–8, 84–85; internal communication reform in, 162–65; language use and, 158; in marginalized communities, 161, 373–74; models, 125–26; Muslim communities and, 124, 127–32; neutrality in, 126, 130–31; Office of Community Oriented Policing Services and, 137; partnership arrangements, 125–26; police training for, 137; professional policing compared to, 22; public perception in, 8; public relations and, 157–60, *158*; research evidence on, 159–66; respect in, 126, 129, 130; themes in, 371–74, *374*; three dimensions of, 156; trust in, 158

community relations units, 155

community resilience: communication and, 190–91; community based policing and, 195; crisis intervention and, 188, 191–93, 196; defining, 188; four components of, 190–91; information sources and, 190, 191–93; in marginal communities, 194; models, 188–90, *189*; police-community relations and, 193–98; police engagement with community attributes and, 196–97; policing and, 187–88, 191–98, *192*; public perceptions and, 193–94; rights, values, and, 194; strategic communication and, 195–96; trust and, 194–95

community trust, 62

complaints: categories of, 205–6; expectations and, 202–3, 210; language use and, 204–5; mediation and, 201–10; rights and, 204–5; traditional complaint process, 204–6

compliance, 176

Confederate flags, 385

Confederate generals, 385

confidence levels, in police, 18

consensus building, 182

consortiums, 59

contact situations, 379–80

contemporary policing, 177–79

Contest counter-terrorism strategy, 344–45

contraband, 83

convergence, 28

convergence pathology, 358–59

cooperation, 84

cop culture. *See* police culture

coproduction model, 196

Cops, 231

COPS. *See* Office of Community Oriented Policing Services

Cop Watch, 238

Counter-Terrorism and Security Act, 2015, 345

counterterrorism policing, 124–25, 127–32

COURAGE in Policing Project, 300

COVID-19, 5, 305–7, 378, 385, 386–87

Cozzarelli Prize, 27

credibility, 283–84

crime: barriers to reporting of, 303, 342–44; cyber, 221–22; drug use and, 317–19, 325–27; fear of, 215; fictional, 217–19, 231, 241–42; in high-crime neighborhoods, 322–23, 325; journalism, 213–16; normalization of, 343; partnerships affecting crime control, 145–46; prevention, 176; programs affecting crime control, 145–46; rates, during 1960s-1970s, 154; scenes, 61, 63; Violent Crime Control Act and, 137, 141, 146. *See also specific crimes*

Crime Stoppers, 62

criminal justice: agencies, 38–43; crime journalism and, 214; crowd theory and, 358–59; focused deterrence and, 314–20, 324–27; "free pass" in, 316, 331n1; interagency communication in, 57–68;

LGBTQ+ and system of, 109–10, 113–14; organizational justice in, 36, 38–39
criminal task forces, 58–59
Criminal Trial Model, 204–5
crisis intervention (CIT): benefits of, 141–42; communication and, 135–49; community policing and, 136–37; community resilience and, 188, 191–93, 196; Cylindrical Model of Crisis Communications in, *290*; data on crisis intervention model, 141–45; disaster processes and, 188, 191, 196; historical perspective on, 136–41; impact on officers, 147–48; law enforcement partnerships for, 138, 145–48; in Memphis Model, 136, 138–41; mental health and, 135–36, 139–40, 144–45; models on, 138–45; police training for, 138–39, 142–44; programs focused on communication affecting crime control, 145–46; research findings, 136, 139–41; teams, 142–45; technology for, 146–47, 149; use of force and, 139–40; us versus them mentality and, 136–37. *See also* hostage negotiations
crowd management techniques, 147
crowd theory: agitators in, 358–61; behavior and, 10, 359–61; civil unrest and, 10, 355–59; classical crowd psychology and, 356–59; convergence pathology and, 358–59; criminal justice and, 358–59; de-individuation theory and, 357; disorder and, 215, 358; ESIM and, 356, 361, 362–67; maintaining "public order" and police communication in, 364; mob psychology and, 358–59; policing crowds and, 10, 355–56, 362–67; procedural justice and, 365–66; social identity and, 359–62; societal change and, 361–62; violence in, 357–59
Crown Prosecution Service, England and Wales, 338
"CSI effect," 218–19
cultivation, 80, 219–20
cultural norms: intergroup fusion and, 20; in police culture, 21–22; social norms and, 201–4, 248
culture: communication relating to, 161; community policing relating to, 161; in gangs, 4, 322–23; organizational, 23, 92, 109–10, 163–65, 180, 182; police training relating to, 161. *See also* police culture
Cunningham, Terrence, 3–4
custom notifications, 315, 324
cyber crime, 221–22
Cylindrical Model of Crisis Communications, *290*

DA. *See* district attorney
Dallas Police Department, 143–44
dash cams, 77, 146, 209, 229, 237, 264
data sharing, 175, 381
deadly force encounters, 23, 177–78. *See also* shootings
deep fake news, 346–48
de-escalation, 9; in police training, 19, 138–41, 143–44
deflecting, 283
"defunding" the police, 18, 382–83
de-individuation theory, 357
demonstrations. *See* civil unrest
Department of Justice (DOJ), 140–41, 155–56, 252; Brown and, 245; GBV and, 299, 301–2, 303–4, 307n2; on trauma, 303
de-policing, 23, 245–47, 255n2
detectives, 58, 61, 64–65
deterrence: creating, 315–20; focused, 9–10, 313–31; retail, 316; theory, 9–10
Deterrence (Zimring and Hawkins), 315–16
D.I.A.M.O.N.D. model, 282, 285–86, *289*, 291–92
Dickey-Fuller test, 255n8
direct experiences, 76
disaster processes, 188, 191, 196
discretion, 23, 316–17
discrimination: against African Americans, 3; GBV and intersecting forms of, 298, 304; in interagency communication, 59; SIT and, 20, 80–81; of women, 92, 93, 95–96. *See also* bias; racial injustice
dishonesty, 235
Disney, 381
disorder, 215, 358. *See also* civil unrest
distancing, 265
distributive justice, 36
district attorney (DA), 64, 65
divergence, 28
diversion, 138–40
diversity, 98
DOJ. *See* Department of Justice
domestic abuse, 9, 297–301; COVID-19 pandemic and, 305–7; LGBTQ+, 108. *See also* gender-based violence
drivers, 83, 85, 203, 235, 382, 385. *See also* traffic stops
drug use, 76, 386; crime and, 317–19, 325–27
Duggan, Mark, 361–62
Dupont, Randolph, 138
duration, 249–50

echo chamber, 8, 230, 231–34, *233*, 239–40
economic development, 191

elaborated social identity model (ESIM), 356, 361, 362–67
elections, 347
Elimination of All Forms Discrimination Against Women (CEDAW), 300–301
Ellis, Manuel, 382
emergency calls, 176
emotional appeals, 284
empowerment, 8
End Violence Against Women International, 299–300
entertainment media, 79, 217–20, 231, 242n2, 385
environmental jolt, 246, 250, 252, 255n1
Equal Employment Opportunity Act, 93
equity theory, 36
Eric Garner Anti-Chokehold Act, 382, 388n4
ESIM. *See* elaborated social identity model
Euro2004, 364
Europe, 110, 124, 214, 221, 276, 293, 372; CEDAW and, 300–301; crowds in, 361–65; internet in, 347. *See also* United Kingdom
exclusion, 126, 341–42
expectancy violation theory, 202–3
expectations, 202–3, 210
experiential effect, 319
explicit bias, 78
external communication reform, 157–62
extortion, 284
Extreme Ownership (Willink and Babin), 40–41
extremism, 10, 338–41; online, 341, 346–48; outgroups and, 341–42; radicalization and, 345–46; rights and, 345; social media and, 342, 346–48. *See also* hate crimes; terrorism

Facebook, 232, 232–33, 241, 342
facial cues, 29n4
fairness: heuristic, 37–38; justice and, 35; management and, 35–36, 38–40; in police training, 26, 43; procedural, 24, 26, 154
fake news, 346–48
fascism, 358
Fayetteville, Arkansas, 4
Fayetteville Police Department, North Carolina, 43
FBI. *See* Federal Bureau of Investigation
fear: community, 62; of crime, 215; mean world syndrome and, 220–21
Federal Bureau of Investigation (FBI), 58, 179
feedback loop, 241
Ferguson, Missouri: BLM and, 3, 245; policing after, 3–4, 245–47; racial injustice and Brown, 3–4, 8, 178, 216, 245–46, 249–54, 255n1

"Ferguson Effect," 8, 39; de-policing and, 245–47, 255n2; media and, 245–47, 249–55; newsworthiness and, 249–55; social media and, 254
fictional depictions, of law enforcement, 217–19, 231, 241–42
1st International Symposium of Intergroup Communication in Thessaloniki, Greece, 372
First Amendment Audit, 238
first responders, 61
Floyd, George: civil unrest after killing of, 18, 377–86; community action taken after, 381–86; examining death of, 249–54; as heuristic case study, 377–86; media and, 377–87; mural of, 382; racial injustice and, 18, 178, 229, 242n1, 248, 306, 371, 376–86; social outcomes after killing of, 381–83; video of, 229, 242n1, 376–77
focused deterrence, 9–10; with advertising, 316–18; behavior and, 321–22; community and, 322–27; conveying cause and effect in, 319; creating, 315–20; criminal justice and, 314–20, 324–27; direct communication in, 313–31; emergence of, 313–14; enhancing legitimacy of, 324–27; evaluation of, 313, 328–31; frameworks, 313–15; for group-involved violence, 316–23, 328–31; mobilizing social control and, 320–27; with persuasion, 318–20; practitioners, 315; "problem-oriented policing" and, 313; procedural justice and, 326–27; support links for, 323–24; voice and, 326
FOIA. *See* Freedom of Information Act
football, 360, 361, 363, 382
foreign policy, 339–40
formal communication, 162–63; formal complaints and, 204–6
formal social control, 321
Four Phase Model of Hostage Negotiation, 286, *288*
Franco Prussian war, 357
Freedom of Information Act, 1967 (FOIA), 242n3
"free pass," 316, 331n1
free speech, 10, 337–38, 347
free will, 8, 183
frisks, 81, 367n1
Futures Without Violence, 299–300

gangs, 145; community and, 322–23; culture in, 4, 322–23; entry and "drift" into, 321; group-involved violence and, 9–10, 316–23, 328–31

Garner, Eric, 3, 248
gender: ATP and, 25; bias, 93–99, 300–301; cognitive association and, 94; conceptual and measurement considerations on, 92–93; improving intergroup relations, 94–95; intergroup communication and, 91–99; narrative and, 98; norms, 96; police-community relations and, 94–95, 268–69; police culture and, 92–93; police identity and, 7; policing and, 91–99; SIA and, 91, 93–94; SIT and, 93–94; social categorization and linguistic intergroup bias, 94, 98; tensions, 7; theoretical overview of, 93–95; use of force and, 97; in "us versus them" mentality, 92; women in policing and, 91–93, 95–99
gender-based violence (GBV): accountability, for officer-perpetrated, 301–2, 306; CEDAW and, 300–301; discrimination forms intersecting with, 298, 304; DOJ and, 299, 301–2, 303–4, 307n2; domestic abuse and, 9, 108, 297–301, 305–6; effective investigation of, 303–4; global perspectives on, 297–300; Henry A. Wallace Police Crime Public Database on, 302; human rights principles and responses to, 301–4; international human rights and, 297–301; in LGBTQ+ communities, 108, 298; marginal communities and, 300, 304; #MeToo movement and, 300; statistics and rates of, 297–99; trauma-informed interactions and, 302–3
Genovese, Kitty, 388n2
Germany, 347, 358
GIS mapping, 146
globalization, 339–40
goals, 40, 155, 158, 162–63, 206
Goldstein, Herman, 155
governance, 179, 191
government: change and intervention by, 2; in China, 355–57; politics and, 179; strategies countering hate crime and terrorism, 344–46
Gray, Freddie, 246, 248, 251, 252, 254
group identity, 19–20, 22; group boundaries and, 94; membership and, 1, 2–3, 25, 93–94; models, 95; outgroup negativity or denigration, 93, 94, 98; SIT and, 76, 80–81, 359–60. See also social identity
group-involved violence, 9–10, 316–23, 328–31
group subcultures, 60–61. See also police culture
group verbal communication, 175
group violence intervention (GVI), 313, 318, 326

guardians, police as, 21
gun laws, 238, 317
GVI. See group violence intervention

handbooks, 1, 11n1, 23, 126
harassment, 93, 96, 233, 300, 342–44
hate crimes, 387; barriers to reporting of, 342–44; countering hate agenda, 348–50; definitions of, 337–38; in digital age, 337–50; exclusion and, 341–42; free speech and, 10, 337–38; government strategies countering, 344–46; harassment and, 342–44; international comparisons of, 338–41, *340*, 344–45, 348–49; law and, 124–25, 347, 349–50; LGBTQ+ communities and, 107–8, 111–12, 339; motivations for, 339, *340*; against Muslim communities, 338, 339; as normalized, 343; online extremism and, 341, 346–48; politics and, 338–40; social categorization and, 341–42; victim support and, 342–44
health: COVID-19 and, 5, 305–7, 378, 385, 386–87; crisis, 135; services for, 344. See also mental health
hedging, 265
helicopter, 380
Henry A. Wallace Police Crime Public Database, 302
heteronormativity, 107–10
heuristic model, 37–38; contact situations and emergent aftermath in, 379–80; feedback in, 383; framework, 374–77; killing of Floyd, as heuristic case study, 377–86; members of public's attributes in, 379; officer attributes in, 379; other unit and agencies in, 381; of policing, communication, and society, 10, *374*, 374–87, *376*; research and practical challenges in, 383–86; social outcomes in, 381–83; society and evolving intergroup histories in, 377–78
heuristic processing, 78
hierarchy, 92, 95
high-crime neighborhoods, 322–23, 325
Hispanic communities, 81, *82*, 83, 85, 114–15, 266. See also racial injustice
history: of alternative policing model, 180–82; of community policing, 153–57; contemporary policing, 178–79; evolving intergroup histories, in heuristic model, 377–78; intergroup, 18, 25; narrative and, 9; policing, 153–57, 178–79; of standard policing model, 178–80; of use of force, 154
Hobbes, Thomas, 357–58
Holocaust, 19
"home-grown" terrorism, 123

homeless population, 7, 140, 142, 386
homicide, 318; challenges to communication within context of investigations, 60–61; clearance rates, 58, 60–61, 62–64, 68; early stages of investigating, 61; effective communication within context of investigations, 60; first responders to, 61; interagency communication and, 57–58, 60–68; witnesses, 61–62, 63
Homicide Team Roundtable, 66
homophobia, 107–12, 115–17
homosexuality. *See* LGBTQ+ communities
Hong Kong, 355–57
Hoover, J. Edgar, 179
hostage negotiations, 9; ALS and, 285; authority-subordinate relations in, 285; in BCSM, 286, *288*; behavior in, 284–85; in BISM, 286, *289*; CAT on, 277–78; communication dynamics inherent to success in, 277–78; Cylindrical Model of Crisis Communications in, *290*; in D.I.A.M.O.N.D. model, 282, 285–86, *289*, 291–92; effective verbal strategies, stratagems, and tactics used within, 281–92; evolution of, 276; Four Phase Model of, 286, *288*; in Interpretation of Crisis Negotiation, 286, *287*; language use in, 278–81, 292–93; metaphorical toolbox in, 277–78; models of, 281–82, 286, *287–90*, 291–92; NNDD and, 293; power relations in, 285; reasoning in, 280; in S.A.F.E. model, *289–90*, 291; Stages of Crisis Model, 286, *287*; in STEPs Model, 286, *287–88*; Table of Ten Influence Strategies for, *283*, 283–84; TAC and, 276; trust in, 278–79; verbal communication and, 278–93
Houston Police Department, 84, 143, 233, 380
human rights. *See* rights
Human Rights Clinic, 305–6, 307n1

IACP. *See* International Association of Chiefs of Police
ICAT. *See* Integrating Communication, Assessment, and Tactics
ICMA. *See* International City-County Management Association
Identifying and Preventing Gender Bias in Law Enforcement Response to Sexual Assault and Domestic Violence (DOJ), 299
identity, 1; national, 341, 365; police, 7. *See also* group identity; social identity
ideological contrast, 21
IGC. *See* intergroup communication
illusion of choice stratagem, 282
imagery, 283

imagined political community, 341–42
immigrants, 24, 347
implicit bias, 78–79, 80
incarceration, 139–40, 146
Indianapolis Police Department, 143–44
inequality regime framework, 96
influence, 284–85, 323
informal addresses, 265
informal social control, 321
informational justice, 37
information managers, 61
information sources: community resilience and, 190, 191–93; FOIA and, 242n3; from police officers, 191–93; social media as, 216, 242n3
ingroup solidarity, 61
instrumental voice, 130
integrated threat theory, 95
Integrating Communication, Assessment, and Tactics (ICAT), 143
interactional justice, 37
interagency communication, 6; best practices, 62–64; CAT and, 61–62; CMPD Roundtable process, as case study for, 64–66; conflicts in, 59–60; in criminal justice, 57–68; discrimination in, 59; in group subcultures, 60; homicide and, 57–58, 60–68; importance of, 57–62, 68; intergroup communication and, 59–60; OIS impacts on, 66–67; prosecutors and, 57–58, 64, 66–68; in Roundtable process, 57–58, 64–68; trust in, 61–62, 63; in us versus them mentality, 59
Inter-American Convention on the Prevention, Punishment and Eradication of Violence against Women, 301
intergroup anxiety, 95
intergroup communication (IGC): ATP and, 25–26; in community policing, 7–8, 84–85; defining group interactions versus personal interactions, 173, 183n1; dynamics and, 5–6; gender and, 91–99; group membership and, 1, 2–3, 25, 93–94; interagency communication and, 59–60; intergroup contact and communication in the field, 26–28; intergroup dynamics and societal change, 361–62; intergroup tensions and, 3–9; language use in, 23–24, 25; within law enforcement environment, 59–60; mediation and, 8; mistrust and consequences of racial disparities in, 84–86; policing through, 1–11; prejudice and, 7–8, 94–95; Principles of Intergroup Communication, 24–25; race and, 27; racial injustice and, 6–7; reform, 156–57; social identity and, 1, 5, 19–20, 23–25, 28–29;

INDEX • 397

use of force and, 1–2, 3; in us versus them mentality, 17–29. *See also specific topics*
intergroup fusion, 20
intergroup histories, 18, 25
intergroup relations, 18, 19–25, 202–3, 229–42
intergroup theory development, 23–24
internal affairs, 8
internal communication reform, 162–65
internal investigations, 42, 66–67
International Association of Chiefs of Police (IACP), 3–4, 299, 381, 384
International City-County Management Association (ICMA), 48
international hate crimes, 338–41, *340*, 344–45
international human rights, 297–301
international news, 213–14
internet, 337; censorship, 347; community and, 341, 346–47; cyber crime and, 221–22; in Europe, 347; free speech and, 10, 347; law and, 347; online extremism, 341, 346–48; public perception on, 346; victims and, 346; wiki movement and, 346. *See also* social media
interpersonal communication, 24, 175, 365
interpersonal justice, 37
Interpretation of Crisis Negotiation, 286, *287*
interrupted time series analysis, 249–54
intersectionality, 106–7, 298, 304
Ip Kwok-him, 356–57
Iraq war, 339, 341
Islamophobia, 7, 123, 132

Jackson, Stephen, 378
Jessica Lenahan v. United States (2011), 300
job satisfaction, 35–39
journalism, 8; narrative and, 248; news coverage and, 213–16, 246, 248, 255n3, 381; *New York Times* and, 249–54, *250*, 255n3
Juneteenth, 378
justice. *See* fairness; procedural justice

Kanter, Rosabeth Moss, 95–96
kidnapping, 284
King, Rodney, 177–78, 229, 246, 252, 376, 377
Ku Klux Klan, 378

Lam, Carrie, 355
language style matching (LSM), 277, 278–79
language use, 9; bias and, 20, 94; CAT and, 266; community policing and, 158; complaints and, 204–5; in contemporary policing, 177–78; in hostage negotiations, 278–81, 292–93; in intergroup communication, 23–24, 25; LGBTQ+ communities and, 109–12, 115; limits of data on, 115; LIWC and, 266, 269; officer speak in, 264–67; social identity and, 266; tactical communications and, 177–78; in traffic stops, 263–70; transcriptions and, 27, 29n4
LAPD. *See* Los Angeles Police Department
Latino communities, 81, *82*, 83, 85, 114–15, 266
law: GBV and international human rights law framework, 300–301; gun, 238, 317; hate crime and, 124–25, 347, 349–50; internet and, 347; mediation and, 206–9; policy and, 24, 381–85; rights and, 235; sexuality and, 106–7; terrorism and, 124–25
Law and Order (television show), 218
law enforcement councils (LECs), 58–59
law enforcement partnerships, 125–26, 138, 145–48, 156. *See also* interagency communication
Lawrence v. Texas (2003), 107
lawsuits, 8, 106–7, 208–9, 300, 301
leadership, 157, 327
LeBon, Gustave, 358, 359
LECs. *See* law enforcement councils
LegCo complex, 355–56
legitimacy: political, 341; as social science, 324–27
Lenahan v. U.S. (1994), 301
level of abstraction, 176–78, *177*
Lewis, James, 4
Leximancer Concept Network, *373*, 373–74
LGBTQ+ communities: case studies on, 112–14; CAT and, 111; civil unrest and, 107–8; criminal justice system and, 109–10, 113–14; documenting perceptions of, 112–15; domestic abuse and GBV in, 108, 298; hate crimes and, 107–8, 111–12, 339; heteronormativity and, 106–10; homophobia and, 107–12, 115–17; intersectionality and, 106–7; language use and, 109–12, 115; LGBTQ Policing Scale, 115; liaisons, 113, 116; *Masterpiece Cakeshop v. Colorado Civil Rights Commission* and, 106; microaggressions against, 112; *Obergefell v. Hodges* and, 106; organizational culture and, 109–10; police misconduct and, 108, 112–13; policing and, 105–17; Pride festivals, 113, 114, 116; procedural justice for, 113–15; public perception and, 110–15; rights, 108; stereotypes of, 109; transgender and cisgender identities, 113–14; trust by, 105, 111, 116
Liébeault, Ambroise-Auguste, 358
Lind, Edgar A., 37, 38
linear regression models, 255n7
line-level police officers, 157

Linguistic Inquiry and Word Count (LIWC), 266, 269
linguistic intergroup bias, 20, 94
listening, 285
litigation and mediation, 208–9
Liu, Wenjian, 4
Live PD, 231, 242n2
LIWC. *See* Linguistic Inquiry and Word Count
local networks, 190
Lombrosian theories, 358
London Metropolitan Police, 110
looting, 380
Los Angeles Police Department (LAPD), 83, 144, 160, 380
LSM. *See* language style matching
lying, 319–20
lynching, 194, 327, 388n4

management, 6; authority-subordinate relations and, 36–39; behavior and, 38–39; bias in, 40; caseload, 63; communication and, 35–43; crowd, 147; fairness and, 35–36, 38–40; "Ferguson Effect" in, 39; job satisfaction and, 35–39; managerial philosophy and, 40–41; organizational justice in, 35–43; trust and, 38; women, in supervisory roles, 92
marginalized communities, 3–4; anxieties of, 18; ATP and, 25–26; community policing in, 161, 373–74; community resilience in, 194; COVID-19 and, 378; GBV and, 300, 304; politics and, 347; sexual abuse of, 302; use of force in, 154
Martin, Trayvon, 245
mass media communications, 175, 192
Masterpiece Cakeshop v. Colorado Civil Rights Commission (2018), 106
McDade, Tony, 306
McDonald, Laquan, 248
mean world syndrome, 220–21
media: African American depictions in, 79–80; content and effects of, 79–80; cultivation and traditional media effects, 80, 219–20; emerging and new, 80–84, 221–22; entertainment, 79, 217–20, 231, 242n2, 385; on Ferguson, Missouri, 8, 216; "Ferguson Effect" and, 245–47, 249–55; fictional depictions of law enforcement, 217–19, 231, 241–42; Floyd and, 377–87; mass media communications and, 175, 192; mean world syndrome and, 220–21; news coverage of law enforcement, 213–16; newsworthiness and, 245–56; police-community relations, and SMSM, 80–84, 85; on police misconduct, 79–80, 154; public perception

and, 8, 78–84, 213–23; public relations and, 222; on racial injustice, 75, 78–84, 245–56; research on, 220–23; television shows, 218–21, 231, 242n2; trust, mistrust, and, 79–84. *See also* social media
mediation: behavior and, 202–3, 205; CAT and, 203–4; complaints and, 201–10; complaints process and, 204–6; intergroup communication and, 8; law and, 206–9; litigation and, 208–9; mistrust and, 209–10; power relations and, 204, 209; process distinctions, 208–9; process of, 206–8; social norms and, 201–4
medium, 174–75, *175*
Memphis Model, 136, 138–41
Men and Women in Corporations (Kanter), 95–96
mental health, 7; crisis intervention and, 135–36, 139–40, 144–45; help, for police officers, 147–48; NAMI and, 138–39, 144–45; PTSD and, 140, 147; victim support for, 344. *See also* trauma
Mental Health Inventory, 114
mentorship, 53
metaphorical toolbox, 277–78
#MeToo movement, 300
Michael Jordan's Foundation, 381
microaggressions, 112
MIDM. *See* mutual intergroup differentiation model
mindfulness, 86
mindsets, 136
Minneapolis Police Department, 207, 376–86
misgendering, 111–12
mistrust. *See* trust
Moag, J. F., 37
mob psychology, 358–59
Morrison, Scott, 124
movements, 238, 339. *See also specific movements*
Munich Massacre, 276
Muslim communities: Christchurch massacre of, 132; community policing and, 124, 127–32; effective communication between police and, 125–27; hate crimes against, 338, 339; increasing securitization of, 124–25, 130–31; Islamophobia and, 7, 123, 132; neutrality and, 130–31; policing, 123–32; procedural justice for, 123–32; respect for, 129; terrorism and, 123, 124–25, 127–32; trust by, 124–25, 127–28; us versus them mentality and, 123–24; voice for, 129–30; women in, 131; youth in, 131
mutual intergroup differentiation model (MIDM), 95

NAACP. *See* National Association for the Advancement of Colored People
NAMI. *See* National Alliance for the Mentally Ill
narrative: community, 191; gender and, 98; history and, 9; journalism and, 248; news and, 248; public perception and, 213
NASCAR drivers, 382, 385
National Academy of Sciences, 27
National Advisory Commission on Civil Disorders, 154
National Alliance for the Mentally Ill (NAMI), 138–39, 144–45
National Alliance to End Homelessness, 142
national anthem, 382
National Association for the Advancement of Colored People (NAACP), 381
National Committee of the Chinese People's Political Consultative Conference, 356–57
National Domestic Violence Hotline, 298
National Football League, 382
National Guard, 380, 381
National Health Service, 344
national identity, 341, 365
National Initiative for Building Community Trust and Justice, 326–27
nationalism, 358
National Negotiator Deployment Database (NNDD), 293
National Weather Services, 192
natural hazards, 188, 192–93, 196
Navy SEALs, 40–41
negotiations: hostage, 9, 275–93; influence and, 284–85
networks, 163, 175, 190–91, 347, 387
neutrality, 126, 130–31
New People's Party, 356–57
Newport, Rhode Island, 107
news: ARIMA models on, 255nn7–8, 256n9; coverage, of law enforcement, 213–16; coverage measures, 255n3; fake and deep fake, 346–48; "Ferguson Effect" and newsworthiness, 249–55; international, 213–14; journalism and coverage of, 213–16, 246, 248, *250*, 255n3, 381; media and newsworthiness, 245–56; narrative and, 248; newsworthiness characteristics, 247–48; from *New York Times*, 249–54, *250*, 255n3; public perceptions on, 248; on racial injustice, 245–56; sensationalism and, 215, 232, 234–35; social norms and, 248; stereotypes and, 248; volume, 255n5
New York City Police Department (NYPD), 78, 83, 108, 144, 276
New York Times news, 249–54, *250*, 255n3

911 calls, 176
Nix, Justin, 39
NNDDS. *See* National Negotiator Deployment Database
nonaccommodation, 26, 27, 28, 266, 383. *See also* accommodativeness
noninstrumental voice, 130
nonverbal communication, 29n4, 91, 204–5
normalization, of crime, 343
not sustained complaints, 205–6
NYPD. *See* New York City Police Department

Oakland Police Department, 269
Obama, Barack, 383
Obergefell v. Hodges (2015), 106
occupational culture, 163
Office of Community Oriented Policing Services (COPS), 137, 155–56, 209
Office of Police Accountability (OPA), 206
officer-involved shootings (OIS), 66–67. *See also* shootings
official source of information, 191–93
OIS. *See* officer-involved shootings
online extremism, 341, 346–48
onset, 249–50
OPA. *See* Office of Police Accountability
optimal distinctiveness theory, 96–97
organizational adaptation, 156, 162–63, 178
organizational culture, 23, 92, 163–65, 180, 182; LGBTQ+ communities and, 109–10; worldview and, 109
organizational justice: behavior and, 37–38; in criminal justice, 36, 38–39; defining, 36–38; in internal investigations, 42; in management, 35–43; in managerial philosophy, 40–41; in police agencies, 39–43; in police training, 42–43; policy change and, 41–42
organizational mission, 179–82
organizational reform, 23, 162–65, 178–83
organizational theory, 159, 162–63, 166n3
outgroups: extremism and, 341–42; negativity or denigration, 93, 94, 98

pandemic, 5, 305–7, 378, 385, 386–87
parole, 317–18, 323–24
partnership arrangements, 125–26, 138, 145–48, 156
paternalistic condition, 129–30
pathology of convergence, 358–59
Patrol officers, 40
Patterns and Practices Assessment of Law Enforcement Agencies' Delivery of Police Services, 141

peacekeeping, 179
pedestrian stops, 81–83
Peel, Robert, 110, 364, 365
Perceptions of Police Scale, 114
PERF. *See* Police Executive Research Forum
person-focused policing, 194–95
persuasion, 318–20
Pew Research Center, 77–78
Philadelphia Police Department, 143
Phoenix Rainbows Festival, 114
PJT. *See* procedural justice theory
place-based policing, 194–95
pluralistic ignorance, 322
Poisson model, 256n9
polarization, 337, 345–46
Police Chief magazine, 241–42
police-community-partner communications, 174
police-community relations: community relations units, 155; community resilience and, 193–98; gender and, 94–95, 268–69; media, SMSM, and, 80–84, 85; police-public communications and, 174; public relations and, 157–60, *158*, 166nn3–4, 222; reform, 156–57; traffic stops and, 263–64; women and, 97–99
police culture: blue code of silence and, 20; change in, 20, 23; communication in, 18–19; cultural norms in, 21–22; Floyd and changes in, 379; gender and, 92–93; hierarchy in, 92, 95; intergroup fusion and, 20; organizational culture in, 23, 92; police working personality and, 17; Principles of Intergroup Communication and, 24–25; socialization in, 21–23, 92; street cop culture, 23; us versus them communication and, 17–29; warrior ethos in, 21–22; women and, 92, 95–96, 97
police depictions: as dishonest, 235; fictional, 217–19, 231, 241–42; as ignorant, 235; news coverage and, 213–16; as power abusers, 235–36; as racists, 235–36; on social media, 234–36; stereotypes and, 230
Police Executive Research Forum (PERF), 67, 137, 143–45, 299
police identity, 7
police misconduct: blue code of silence and, 20; categories of, 205–6; civil unrest over, 3–4, 229, 242n1, 245, 376–86; complaints and mediation of, 201–10; GBV, officer-perpetrated, 301–2, 306; internal affairs and, 8; LGBTQ+ communities and, 108, 112–13; media on, 79–80, 154; Oakland Police Department scandals of, 269; police versus public perception on, 78; prosecutorial bias and misconduct, 64
police officers: ambushing, 4; attributes of, in heuristic model, 379; fictional depictions of, 217–19, 231, 241–42; as guardians, 21; information sources from, 191–93; justifying actions of, 176; line-level, 157; police-police communications, 174; as power abusers, 235–36; shooting of, 4; suicides of, 4–5, 147; violence against police officers, 4; vulnerabilities of, 4–5, 36; working personality, 17; worldviews of, 19, 21, 28–29. *See also specific topics*
police-public communications, 174
police recruitment, 21; candidate expectations, 51–52; candidate hiring process, 50; candidate qualifications, 49–52; candidate shortages, 47; candidate status and pushing forward, 52; challenge, 48–49; communication in, 49–50, 53–54; "crisis" in, 47; irony of, 52–53; listening to candidates, 51–52; mentorship and, 53; mission of, 49–50; recruiter qualities and training, 51; research on, 52–54; what agencies are looking for, 47–48; workforce development and, 49–50
police resources, securing, 176, 180, 182
police training: for community policing, 137; for crisis intervention, 138–39, 142–44; culture relating to, 161; de-escalation in, 19, 138–41, 143–44; by external organizations, 42; fairness in, 26, 43; graduation from, 22; mindfulness in, 86; organizational justice in, 42–43; requirements, 42–43; social interaction training, 26, 27–28; us versus them mentality and, 21–22
Polícia de Segurança Pública (PSP), 363
policing: case study, 377–86; challenges, addressing, 383–88; crowds, 10, 355–56, 362–67; history, 153–57, 178–79; through intergroup communication, 1–11; new directions in, 372–88; philosophy, 98; research and practical challenges, 383–86. *See also specific topics*
Policing Outcomes Scale, 114
Policing Qualities Scale, 114
policy: globalization and, 339–40; law and, 24, 381–85; organizational justice and change in, 41–42
political legitimacy, 341
politics, 2–3, 179; elections and, 347; hate crimes and, 338–40; imagined political community and, 341–42; immigration and, 347; marginalized communities and, 347;

right-wing groups and, 342; social science and, 357–59
populist movements, 339
Portugal, 363
positive policing, 5
post traumatic stress disorder (PTSD), 140, 147
power: police, as power abusers, 235–36; voice and, 183
power relations: in hostage negotiations, 285; mediation and, 204, 209; in traffic stops, 263–67
"pre-booking" diversion, 139–40
pre-intervention series, 255n8
prejudice, 7–8, 94–95. *See also* bias
Pride festivals, 113, 114, 116
Principles of Intergroup Communication, 24–25
privacy, 108, 147, 268, 270n2, 337, 345–46
probation, 323–24
"problem-oriented policing," 155, 313
problem-solving, 156, 161, 195–96
procedural justice, 36–37; CAT and, 204; crowd theory and, 365–66; fairness and, 24, 26, 154; focused deterrence and, 326–27; for LGBTQ+ communities, 113–15; for Muslim communities, 123–32; respect and, 267; in traffic stops, 267–68
procedural justice theory (PJT), 24, 267, 365–66
professional policing, 22, 137, 148
prolific offenders, 328–31
prosecutors, 57–58, 64, 66–68
protests. *See* civil unrest
PSP. *See* Polícia de Segurança Pública
psychiatric triage, 140
psychology, crowd, 356–59
PTSD. *See* post traumatic stress disorder
public health, 5
public perception, 2–3; on accommodativeness, 26, 77–78; ATP and, 25–26; in community policing, 8; community resilience and, 193–94; confidence levels, in police, 18, 84; expectations and, 202–3, 210; Hoover and, 179; on internet, 346; LGBTQ+ communities and, 110–15; media and, 8, 78–84, 213–23; narrative and, 213; on newsworthiness, 248; Perceptions of Police Scale of, 114; on racial injustice, 75, 77–85; social media and, 229–42; of traffic stops, 84–85, 264, 267; of women officers, 268–69
public relations, 157–60, *158*, 166nn3–4, 222. *See also* police-community relations
public's attributes, 379
public trust, 62

purpose, 22, 175–76
purpose, of communication, 175–76, *176*

Al-Qaeda, 341
Q-test, 255n8

race: bias and, 76–79; cognitive association, bias, and policing, 78–79; intergroup communication and, 27
racial disparities, 6–7; accommodativeness and, 77–78; COVID-19 and, 378; intergroup consequences of mistrust and, 84–86; in Los Angeles, 83; in respect, 266; in searches, 81, *82*, 83; traffic stops and, 77–78, 265; in use of force, *82*, 83–84, 97
racial injustice: Brown and, 3–4, 8, 178, 216, 245–46, 249–54, 255n1; civil unrest and, 3–4, 229, 242n1, 245, 376–86; community and, 327; Duggan and, 362–63; Floyd and, 18, 178, 229, 242n1, 248, 306, 371, 376–86; Gray and, 246, 248, 251, 252, 254; inequality regimes and, 96; intergroup communication and, 6–7; King, R., and, 177–78, 229, 246, 252, 376, 377; Martin and, 245; media on, 75, 78–84, 245–56; news on, 245–56; in pedestrian stops, 81–83; police, depicted as racists, 236; public perception on, 75, 77–85; racialized treatment in tone and searches, 81–83, *82*; Rice and, 246, 248, 251, 252, 254; shootings and, 3–4, 8, 77–78, 84; societal change and, 75; Taylor and, 306, 382; in traffic stops, 27, 76–78, 80–83, *82*, 265–66; trust and, 77–86; use of force and, 18, 83–84
racial violence, 2; category of criminal activity relating to, 84; controversial deaths and effects of, 250–55. *See also* "Ferguson Effect"
radicalization, 345–46
Ramos, Rafael, 4
rapport, 142, 265
RCPI. *See* Regional Community Policing Institutes
Reagan era, 76
realistic threats, 95
reciprocity, 285
Regional Community Policing Institutes (RCPI), 137
relentlessness, 180
resonance, 80
respect, 142; in community policing, 126, 129, 130; condition, 129–30; for Muslim communities, 129; procedural justice and, 267; racial disparities in, 266; in traffic stops, 266
retail deterrence, 316

retention, 48–49
Rice, Tamir, 246, 248, 251, 252, 254
rights: ACLU and, 298; BLM and, 305; to carry firearms, 238; civil unrest and, 153–54; community resilience, values, and, 194; complaints and, 204–5; extremism and, 345; free speech and, 10, 337–38; GBV and human rights principles and responses, 301–4; international human, 297–301; law and, 235; for LGBTQ+ communities, 108; for women, 93
right-wing groups, 342
rioting, 361–62, 365–66, 376–87. *See also* civil unrest
Roosevelt, Franklin D., 107
Roundtable process, 57–58, 64–68

S.A.F.E. model, *289–90*, 291
safety, 8, 136–41, 176–77, 182, 193–98
SAR. *See* Special Administrative Region
Scott, Walter, 248
SCT. *See* self-categorization theory
searches, 81, *82*, 83, 367n1
Seattle Police Department, 160, 206
Second Amendment Audit, 238
self-categorization theory (SCT), 93–94
sensationalism, 215, 232, 234–35
September 11, 2001, 124
sexism, 96. *See also* women
sexual abuse and harassment, 93, 96, 300–302
sexuality, 106–7
sexual orientation, 7. *See also* LGBTQ+ communities
shock: environmental jolt and, 246, 250, 252, 255n1; sensationalism and, 215, 232, 234–35
shootings: of Arbery, 377; Baton Rouge, 4; of Brown, 3–4, 8, 178, 216, 245–46, 249–54, 255n1; category of criminal activities relating to, 84; controversial deaths and effects of, 250–55; Dallas shooting and, 4; deadly force encounters and, 23, 177–78; of Duggan, 362–63; incident rates, 4; OIS, 66–67; of police officers, 4; racial injustice and, 3–4, 8, 77–78, 84; rates of, 255n2, 255n6; of Taylor, 306, 382
"Shoot Team," 66
SIA. *See* social identity approach
siege, 284
Sighele, Scipio, 358
SIM. *See* social identity model
SIT. *See* social identity theory
slavery, 18, 194, 303, 378
smartphones, 146, 222, 233

SMSM. *See* socially mediated stereotyping model
sobriety tests, 235
social categorization, 94, 98, 341–42, 359–60
social control, mobilizing, 320–27
social distancing, 76
social dominance theory, 95
social identity: behavior and, 19–20, 22, 359–61; CAT and, 111; crowd theory and, 359–62; ESIM and, 356, 361, 362–67; intergroup communication and, 1, 5, 19–20, 23–25, 28–29; language use and, 266; overlapping, 5; social categorization, hate, and, 341–42; social science and, 357–58; values and, 19–20
social identity approach (SIA), 91, 93–94, 359–60
social identity model (SIM), 361–62
social identity theory (SIT), 19–20; beliefs and, 360–61; gender and, 93–94; group identity and, 76, 80–81, 359–60
social interaction training, 26, 27–28
socialism, 358
socialization, 21–23, 92
socially mediated stereotyping model (SMSM), 80–84, 85
social media, 193; algorithms, 230, 231–34, 241; attention hacking and echo chamber of, 8, 230, 231–34, *233*, 239–40; bias and, 239–40; BLM and, 216; in China, 356–57; effects of and research questions on, 239–42; extremism and, 342, 346–48; Facebook and, *232*, 232–33, 241, 342; "Ferguson Effect" and, 254; as information source, 216, 242n3; intergroup relations and, 229–42; old and new, 231; police depictions on, 234–36; public perception and, 229–42; stereotypes and, 230; technology and, 147; Twitter and, 342, 347, 348; types of video content and limitations in their discovery, 234–36; videos and, 229–30, 234–42; WhatsApp and, 348; YouTube and, 8, 230, 231–34, *233*, 240, 241
social norms, 201–4, 248
social science, 19–20, 324–27, 357–59
social service, 323–24
societal change, 2, 75, 117, 153–54, 361–62
sodomy, 107
Special Administrative Region (SAR), 355–57
special weapons and tactics (SWAT), 140
sports, 360, 361, 363, 381, 382
Stages of Crisis Model, 286, *287*
standard policing model, 178–81
Stephan, Walter G., 95

STEPs. *See* Structured Tactical Engagement Process Model
stereotypes, 8; bias and, 78–79, 94; emergence of, 19; of LGBTQ+ communities, 109; negative, 95; news and, 248; police depictions and, 230; in SMSM, 80–84, 85; social media and, 230; of women, 93
Stonewall Inn raid, 108
strategic communication: by abstraction level, 176–78, *177*; actors in, 173–74, *174*; for alternative policing model, 180–82; community resilience and, 195–96; conceptual map of, 173–78; defining, 178; free will and, 183; by medium, 174–75, *175*; by purpose, 175–76, *176*; for standard policing model, 178–80; tactical communications and, 177–78; voice and, 183
Strategic Communications Practices (Stephens, Greenberg, and Hill), 178
street code, 322
street cop culture, 23
street-level bureaucracy, 157
Structured Tactical Engagement Process (STEPs) Model, 287
structuring success stratagem, 282
subordinates, 36–39, 285
success, structuring stratagem, 282
suicides, 4–5, 147
Supreme Court, 106–7, 154, 300
surveillance cameras and videos, 239
suspects, 61–62
sustained complaints, 205–6
SWAT. *See* special weapons and tactics
symbolic communications, 175
symbolic threats, 95
symmetric communication, 157–59, *158*

Table of Ten (ToT) Influence Strategies, *283*, 283–84
tactical assault team (TAC), 276
tactical communications, 177–78
tag questions, 279
Taine, Hippolyte, 357–58
Tajfel, Henri, 19–20, 23
the "talk," 76–77
Tarde, Gabriel, 358
Taylor, Breonna, 306, 382
team policing, 137, 155
technology: for crisis intervention, 146–47, 149; cyber crime and, 221–22; GIS mapping and, 146; LIWC and, 266, 269; mass media communications and, 175, 192; smartphones and, 146, 222, 233. *See also* cameras; internet; social media

television shows, 218–21, 231, 242n2
terrorism, 7, 10, 387; beliefs and, 341–42; countering hate and, 348–50; counterterrorism policing and, 124–25, 127–32; in digital age, 337, 340–41, 344–50; government strategies countering, 344–46; "home-grown," 123; law and, 124–25; Muslim communities and, 123, 124–25, 127–32; online extremism and, 341, 346–48; Al-Qaeda and, 341; radicalization and, 345–46; of September 11, 2001, 124
theater crisis skits, 281, 286
thin blue line, 22, 28
third-party recorded videos, 238
311 calls, 176
tip lines, 62
tokenism, 93, 95–96
Tomlinson, Ian, 364
tone, racialized, 81–83, *82*
ToT strategies. *See* Table of Ten Influence Strategies
traffic stops, 26–27, 202; accommodativeness in, 77–78, 266; African Americans and, 76–78, 81–83, 84–85; bias and, 76–78; of Bland, 268, 270n5; body cameras and, 264, 268; CAT and, 76–77, 203–4; drivers and, 83, 85, 203, 235; language use in, 263–70; pedestrian stops and, 81–83; police-community relations and, 263–64; power relations in, 263–67; procedural justice in, 267–68; public perception of, 84–85, 264, 267; racial disparity and, 77–78, 265; racial injustice in, 27, 76–78, 80–83, *82*, 265–66; research and lessons, from language studies, 267–70; respect in, 266; routine, 76–78, 85–86; "scripts" for, 267; violent encounters in, 265
transcriptions, 27, 29n4
transgender and cisgender identities, 113–14. *See also* LGBTQ+ communities
transparency, 201
trauma, 9–10, 302–3, 344
True Vision reporting website, 343–44
Trump, Donald, 347, 380, 381
trust, 9; ATP and, 26; community and, 325–27; in community policing, 158; community resilience and, 194–95; in hostage negotiation, 278–79; in interagency communication, 61–62, 63; intergroup consequences of mistrust and racial disparities, 84–86; by LGBTQ+ communities, 105, 111, 116; management and, 38; media, mistrust, and, 79–84; mediation and mistrust, 209–10; by Muslim communities, 124–25, 127–28; public, 62;

racial injustice and, 77–86; trustworthiness, 38, 127–28
Tucson Police Department, Arizona, 43
turbulence, environmental, 159
turnover, 47, 53, 269
Twitter, 342, 347, 348

unemployment, 378
unfounded complaints, 205–6
United Kingdom, 110, 293; Britain First in, 342; British Security Service in, 345; crowds in, 361–62; hate crime in, 338–39, *340*, 344–45, 348–49; internet in, 347; rioting in, 361–62, 365; Victim Support Cymru in, 343; Windrush Day in, 378
use of force: crisis intervention and, 139–40; gender and, 97; history of, 154; in marginalized communities, 154; news coverage on, 216; racial disparities in, *82*, 83–84, 97; racial injustice and, 18, 83–84; reports of, 3. *See also* racial injustice; shootings
us versus them mentality, 5, 388; CAT and, 24, 28–29; communication and police culture, 17–29; conclusions on, 28–29; crisis intervention and, 136–37; gender in, 92; interagency communication in, 59; intergroup communication in, 17–29; intergroup relations, communication, and worldviews, 18, 19–25; Muslim communities and, 123–24; "police" and "community" terms in, 18; police training and, 21–22; policing and, 25–29; research in, 28; socialization and, 21–23

values: organizational culture and, 164, 180, 182; rights, community resilience, and, 194; social identity and, 19–20
Van den Bos, Kees, 38–39
ventilating, 283
verbal communication, 204–5, 264, 266–67; group, 175; hostage negotiations and, 278–93; interpersonal, 175. *See also* language use
vicarious experiences, 76, 79–80
victimization, 220–21
victims: blaming of, 303, 344; internet and, 346; support, for hate crimes, 342–44; vulnerabilities of, 342–44
Victim Support Cymru, 343
videos: cameras and, 229–30, 236–42, 242n1; by civilians, 229–30, 237–38, 242n1; of Floyd's arrest, 229, 242n1, 376–77; impact of, 236–39; by law enforcement, 237; on racial injustice, 236; social media and, 229–30, 234–42; surveillance, 239; third-party recorded, 238; types of video content and their limitations, 234–36; viral, 75, 238, 376–77, 379–80; worst of the worst documentation, 236
Vietnam War, 153–54, 241
vigils, 348
violence: civil unrest and, 379–80; in crowd theory, 357–59; domestic abuse and, 9, 108, 297–301, 305–6; group-involved, 9–10, 316–23, 328–31; gun, 145, 316; GVI and, 313, 318, 326; traffic stops and, 265. *See also* racial injustice; racial violence; shootings; terrorism
Violent Crime Control Act, 1994, 137, 141, 146, 155–56
viral videos, 75, 238, 376–77, 379–80
vocal cues, 29n4
voice: focused deterrence and, 326; instrumental and noninstrumental, 130; for Muslim communities, 129–30; power and, 183; strategic communication and, 183
Voigt, et al., 27
Vollmer, August, 179
vulnerabilities: of police officers, 4–5, 36; of victims, 342–44

Wallace, Bubba, 382
war: Franco Prussian, 357; Iraq, 339, 341; Vietnam, 153–54, 241; World War II, 19
War on Cops, 4, 23, 246–47, 255n2
War on Drugs, 76
Warren, Earl, 154
warrior ethos, 21–22
Washington, DC, 381
Watts riots, 376
weapons of influence, 284–85
WhatsApp, 348
white supremacists, 378
wiki movement, 346
Wilders, Geert, 338
Willink, Jocko, 40–41
Wilson, Darren, 3
Wilson, O. W., 179
Windrush Day, 378
witnesses, 61–62, 63, 304
Wolfe, Scott E., 39
women: bias of, 93, 95–99; conceptual and measurement considerations of, 92–93; discrimination of, 92, 93, 95–96; domestic abuse and, 9, 108, 297–301, 305–6; harassment of, 93, 96, 300, 302; inequality regimes and, 96; integrated threat theory and, 95; measures of, 93, 96–97; in Muslim communities, 131; optimal distinctiveness theory and, 96–97; police-community

relations and, 97–99; police culture and, 92, 95–96, 97; in policing, 91–93, 95–99, 268–69; public perceptions of women police, 268–69; rights for, 93; sexism and, 96; social dominance theory and, 95; status of, in policing, 92–93; stereotypes of, 93; in supervisory roles, 92; tokenism and, 95–96. *See also* gender; gender-based violence

woofing, 320

word cloud, 372, *372*

workforce development, 49–50

World Trade Center attacks, 124

worldviews: communication and, 19–25; GBV, in global perspective, 297–300; organizational culture and, 109; of police, 19, 21, 28–29; in us versus them mentality, 18, 19–25

World War II, 19

youth, 131

youthful offender (YO), 331n1

YouTube, 8, 230, 231–34, *233*, 240, 241

Zimbardo, Philip, 357

About the Contributors

Daniel Angus is associate professor of digital communication in the School of Communication, Queensland University of Technology. His research focuses on the development of computational analysis methods for communication data, with a specific focus on interaction data. His novel computational methods have improved our understanding of the nature of communication in medical consultations, conversations in aged care settings, television broadcast, social media, and news reporting. Daniel presently leads the Computational Communication and Culture program within the QUT Digital Media Research Centre. He contributes regularly to media and industry on the impact of technology on society.

Caroline Bettinger-López is a professor of law and director of the Human Rights Clinic at the University of Miami School of Law, and an Adjunct Senior Fellow at the Council on Foreign Relations. From 2015 to 2017, she worked in the Obama administration as the White House advisor on violence against women to Vice President Joe Biden. She was lead counsel on *Jessica Lenahan (Gonzales) v. United States*, the first international human rights case brought by a domestic violence victim against the United States. Recently, she initiated the COURAGE (Community Oriented and United Responses to Address Gender Violence and Equality) in Policing Project.

Brian Blakemore ran police sciences courses at the University of South Wales (UK) from inception in 2003 until 2013, becoming associate head of the School of Health Sport and Professional Practice with responsibilities for subject areas of policing and security; health and social care / social work; exercise health and well-being; and public health. He recently retired from university life with the exception of supervising postgraduate research in policing. Brian's research areas include cartographies of neighborhoods; mapping perceptions of crime; engaging Muslim communities in researching the impact of counterterrorism; the engagement process between the police and adults with learning difficulties; and extremism, counterterrorism, and policing.

Scott E. Branton is graduate teaching assistant in the Department of Communication and Graduate Fellow with the Disaster and Community Crisis Center at the University of Missouri. His research draws on post-structural and post-humanist theories to explore the socio-material practices of workplace diversity and difference. Specifically, his research focuses on how these socio-material organizing and disorganizing practices communicatively produce and reproduce social ordering in work and organizations.

Chandrika C. Collins is graduate teaching assistant in the Department of Communication and Graduate Fellow with the Disaster and Community Crisis Center at the University of Missouri. She has spent over ten years helping communities rebuild post-disaster—natural or human-caused—working on the ground in the United States and the Middle East. As an advocate for solutions, her current research lies at the intersections of crisis communication, conflict resolution, and police–citizen encounters.

Travis Dixon is professor of communication at the University of Illinois at Urbana-Champaign. He is an internationally recognized expert whose research focuses on the effects of mediated stereotypes and citizen–police interactions. Much of Dr. Dixon's work has been focused on racial stereotyping in television news. His more recent investigations examine the content and effects of stereotypes and counter-stereotypes in major news events, online news, and musical contexts.

Tamar Ezer is the associate director and lecturer in law with the Human Rights Clinic at the University of Miami School of Law. Previously, Tamar taught at Yale Law School and the Georgetown University Law Center. As deputy director of the Law and Health Initiative of the Open Society Public Health Program, she pursued legal advocacy to advance health and human rights in Eastern and Southern Africa, Eastern Europe, and Central Asia. Additionally, she clerked at the Southern District of New York and Supreme Court of Israel. Tamar graduated from Stanford University and Harvard Law School.

Howard Giles is distinguished research professor of communication at the University of California, Santa Barbara. He is founding editor of the *Journal of Language and Social Psychology* and the *Journal of Asian Pacific Communication* and past president of the International Communication Association and the International Association of Language and Social Psychology. His research interests encompass interpersonal and intergroup communication processes in intergenerational, police–citizen, and other intergroup settings, and he is coeditor of the two-volume *The Oxford Encyclopedia of Intergroup Communication* (2018). His research on communication and attitudes toward law enforcement spans over a dozen nations from Mongolia to Bulgaria to Russia. Currently, he is also director of volunteer services at the Santa Barbara Police Department, where, for fifteen years, he was a former reserve officer (and 24/7 member of the Crisis Negotiation Response Team as well as a police chaplain), and the recipient of thirteen outstanding service awards (including one at the State level).

Amy R. Grubb is a chartered psychologist, HCPC registered forensic psychologist, chartered scientist, and Associate Fellow of the British Psychological Society. Currently, she is head of the Department of Violence Prevention, Trauma, and Criminology within the School of Psychology at the University of Worcester. Her main research interests focus on the application of psychology within police settings, with an emphasis on hostage and crisis negotiation. She has experience working with a number of police forces nationally, in both a training and consultancy/advisory capacity.

Shawn L. Hill is a lieutenant with the Santa Barbara Police Department (SBPD) and adjunct faculty at Santa Barbara City College in the justice studies program. He earned a bachelor's degree in English literature from Old Dominion University, and a master's degree in criminal justice from Arizona State University. Lt. Hill currently serves on the community policing committee of the International Association of Chiefs of Police, served as a member of the Bureau of Justice Assistance Executive Session on Police Leadership, and is a National Police Foundation Policing Fellow. He has written curricula for courses certified by the California Peace Officers Standards and Training (POST), grounded in intergroup contact theory, during which police officers and college students work collaboratively through critical thinking exercises to broaden their perspectives. He currently oversees the development, implementation, and evaluation of department processes and initiatives related to police accountability.

J. Brian Houston is chair and associate professor in the Department of Communication and director of the Disaster and Community Crisis Center at the University of Missouri. His research is interdisciplinary and focuses on communication at all phases of disasters and community crises. His work examines the mental, behavioral, and public health effects and political consequences of these events.

David M. Kennedy is a professor of criminal justice at John Jay College of Criminal Justice in New York City and the director of the National Network for Safe Communities at John Jay. Kennedy was a principal in the groundbreaking Boston Gun Project in the mid-1990s, which pioneered a high-level action-research approach to public safety and in which Kennedy developed the "focused deterrence" intervention framework. He and the National Network support cities implementing strategic interventions to reduce violence, minimize arrest and incarceration, enhance police legitimacy, and strengthen relationships between law enforcement and communities. These interventions have been proven effective in a variety of settings, have amassed a robust evaluation record, and are widely employed nationally and internationally.

Joseph B. Kuhns is professor of criminal justice and criminology at the University of North Carolina at Charlotte. He has managed and implemented numerous research and evaluation projects that focused on officer-involved shooting investigations; homicide unit effectiveness; arbitrary profiling; use of deadly force by and against the police; and health, safety, and wellness programming, among others. His coedited book about police use of force, firearms, and non-lethal weapons in various countries was recognized with a Choice Award in 2010. Dr. Kuhns continues to collaborate with local departments, national associations, and federal agencies to improve policing practices, identify emerging law enforcement priorities, and enhance officer and community safety.

Belén Lowrey-Kinberg is an assistant professor in the Department of Sociology and Criminal Justice at St. Francis College. She received her PhD from the Department of

Justice, Law, and Criminology at American University in Washington, DC. She has been involved with several large-scale projects, including the President's Task Force on 21st Century Policing, COPS Office Law Enforcement Review Project, and the Prosecutorial Charging Practices Project funded by the Deason Criminal Justice Reform Center. Her research focuses on the application of linguistics to the criminal justice system, including procedural justice, police–citizen interactions, and wrongful convictions.

Edward R. Maguire is a professor of criminology and criminal justice at Arizona State University. He received his PhD in criminal justice from the State University of New York at Albany in 1997. Professor Maguire's research focuses primarily on policing and violence. He has served as principal investigator on nearly $10 million in externally funded research in the United States and abroad. His violence portfolio has focused on homicide, gang and gun violence, human trafficking, and violence in crowds. His policing portfolio has focused on a variety of topics, including police innovation; procedural justice and legitimacy; police response to gangs; criminal investigation; police response to mass demonstrations; and policing the COVID-19 pandemic. In addition to his US research, Professor Maguire has worked extensively in developing countries and is now carrying out research in Native American communities. He currently serves as the senior researcher for law enforcement on the CrimeSolutions.gov initiative and as chair of the research advisory board for the Police Executive Research Forum.

Bernard K. Melekian is currently the assistant county executive officer over public safety and criminal justice for Santa Barbara County, California. He has over forty-five years of law enforcement experience. He has served as the chief of police for the city of Pasadena California (1996–2009), director of the Office of Community Oriented Policing Services (2009–2013), and undersheriff for the Santa Barbra County Sheriff's Office (2015–2018). He holds a doctorate in policy, planning, and development from the University of Southern California. His doctoral dissertation was on *Values-Based Discipline: The Key to Organizational Transformation within Law Enforcement Agencies.*

Shannon Messer earned her MS in criminal justice from the University of North Carolina at Charlotte, where she also worked as a research assistant from 2016 to 2019. During that time, she contributed to several projects including a study of deadly force against the police and a study assessing the impact of burglary offending and victimization. She is currently a Grant Manager for the Safety + Justice Challenge grant awarded to Mecklenburg County. The grant aims to adopt and implement best practices for reducing jail populations, while maintaining public safety and working toward eliminating racial and ethnic disparities in the criminal justice system.

Kristina Murphy is a professor of criminology and an Australian Research Council Future Fellow. She is currently based at the Griffith Criminology Institute at Griffith University, Australia. She was awarded her PhD in psychology from the Australian National University in 2002, after which she held several academic appointments at the Australian National University, Deakin University, and Griffith University in Australia.

Murphy's research explores the importance of procedural justice in the context of policing immigrant, ethnic minority, and Muslim communities in Australia; specifically, how procedural justice policing can improve police–community relations. She has received more than $4 million in grants and consultancies to support her research.

Matea Mustafaj is a doctoral student and a Rackham Merit Fellow at the University of Michigan. She received her bachelor of science from the University of Michigan in neuroscience, psychology, and philosophy. She studies the cognitive processing of narratives and the social impacts of entertainment media including its impact on consumers' perceptions of groups of people, and the world more generally. Mustafaj is also interested in the differential interpretation and selection of entertainment media across subgroups.

Stephen Owen is a professor of criminal justice at Radford University (Radford, Virginia), where he has been recognized as a recipient of the Distinguished Creative Scholar Award. Dr. Owen holds a bachelor of science in criminal justice from Southeast Missouri State University and a master of arts and doctor of philosophy in political science from the University of Missouri – St. Louis. Dr. Owen's areas of research include criminal justice education, LGBTQ+ issues in criminal justice, criminal justice policy issues, and emergency management.

Cara E. Rabe-Hemp is the associate dean in the College of Applied Sciences and Technology at Illinois State University. She received her PhD in criminal justice from the University of Illinois at Chicago in 2005 and her research is focused in policing. Specifically, she is interested in how diversity in policing affects police behavior, as well as opportunities in the field. Her recent publications have appeared in *Women and Criminal Justice, Police Quarterly, Feminist Criminology, Journal of Criminal Justice,* and *Policing: An International Journal of Police Strategies and Management*. Rabe-Hemp is the author of *Thriving in an All Boys Club: Women Police and Their Fight for Equality* and coeditor of *Women Policing across the Globe: Shared Challenges and Successes in the Integration of Women Police Worldwide* and *Corruption, Accountability and Discretion*.

Matthew Radburn is a postdoctoral Research Fellow at Keele University working on a range of policing and security related projects as part of the academic team within the Keele Policing Academic Collaboration (KPAC). This includes the ESRC funded project "From Coercion to Consent: Social Identity, Legitimacy, and a Process Model of Police Procedural Justice (CONSIL)." He is also currently the lead Research Fellow on Strand 3 of the UKRI funded project "Facilitating the Public Response to COVID-19 by Harnessing Group Processes," which aims to build upon understandings of psychological group processes to address how to develop and sustain shared identity and social solidarity during pandemics.

Leanne Savigar-Shaw is a lecturer in policing at Staffordshire University. She is currently involved in ethnographic research concerning police–public interaction, procedural justice and fairness within policing. Her research interests also include road safety, driver education and, in particular, mobile phone use by drivers.

Charlie Scheer is an associate professor of criminal justice at the University of Southern Mississippi. His research specializations are in police workforce management, police training, and police legitimacy. His research has been published in *Police Quarterly*, *Policing: An International Journal*, *Sheriff & Deputy*, *Justice Research and Policy*, and *Law Enforcement Executive Forum*. He has provided briefings and testimony at academic and professional conferences such as the Presidential Commission on Law Enforcement and Administration of Justice, International Association of Chiefs of Police (IACP) Annual Conference, and Police Executive Research Forum (PERF) Conference on Recruitment and Retention. He also is a sworn sheriff's deputy.

Amie M. Schuck is an associate professor in the Criminology, Law and Justice Department at the University of Illinois at Chicago. She received her PhD from the University at Albany and her research interests lie in the areas of policing, community engagement, and planned change management. Her work has been published in *American Journal of Community Psychology*, *Journal of Quantitative Criminology*, *Journal of Research in Crime and Delinquency*, and *Police Quarterly*.

Michael S. Scott is clinical professor at Arizona State University's School of Criminology and Criminal Justice and director of the Center for Problem-Oriented Policing. He was formerly clinical professor at the University of Wisconsin Law School; police chief in Lauderhill, Florida; special assistant to the police chief in St. Louis; director of police administration in Fort Pierce, Florida; a senior researcher at the Police Executive Research Forum; legal assistant to the police commissioner in New York City; and a police officer in Madison, Wisconsin. Scott has a JD from Harvard Law School and a BA from the University of Wisconsin–Madison.

Ellen Scrivner is a national expert on criminal justice policy as well as public safety and policing. Among her many executive leadership positions, she was appointed by President Obama as deputy director of the National Institute of Justice and director of the High Intensity Drug Trafficking Areas program in the Office of National Drug Control Policy. Recipient of the 2010 Academy of Criminal Justice Sciences' O.W. Wilson Award, she was past president of the American Psychological Division 18 (Psychologists in Public Service) and, currently, serves as an Executive Fellow at the National Police Foundation, Washington DC.

Marisa A. Smith is currently a PhD candidate in the Department of Communication at the University of Illinois, Urbana-Champaign. Her research investigates news disseminated in digital environments and examines the sociopolitical influence of these messages. In fall 2020, she will join the College of Communication Arts and Sciences at Michigan State University as an assistant professor in the Department of Advertising, Public Relations and the School of Journalism.

Darrel W. Stephens has over fifty years' experience in policing—starting in 1968 in Kansas City, Missouri. He served as a chief in four cities, retiring from Charlotte-Mecklenburg after nine years in 2008, serving also as executive director of the Major Cities Chiefs Association and the Police Executive Research Forum. He was one of two technical advisors to the President's Task Force on 21st Century Policing, has written extensively on a wide range of policing issues throughout his career, and is the cofounder and a faculty member of the MCCA Police Executive Leadership Institute.

Clifford Stott is a professor of social psychology and dean for research in the Faculty of Natural Sciences at Keele University. His interdisciplinary research uses the social identity approach to understand the social psychological dynamics of police encounters with the public. He has particular expertise in the area of policing crowd events and has advised governments and police forces internationally in this regard. During the COVID-19 pandemic, he chaired a subgroup advising the UK government on security and policing.

David H. F. Tyler recently received his PhD in criminology and criminal justice from Arizona State University. His research applies quantitative methodologies to examine the intersection of group dynamics and policing. His work broadly focuses on two areas: unpacking the role of internal fairness in shaping police officer identification with department values and goals; and second, exploring the relationships between police and crowd behavior during mass demonstrations and protests.

Kristopher R. Weeks is currently a doctoral candidate in communication at the University of Illinois at Urbana–Champaign. In Fall 2020, he will serve as an assistant professor of communication at East Stroudsburg University. He primarily investigates the intersections of minority media representations, interracial violence, audience affect, and audience perceptions of criminal justice. He also integrates conflict management scholarship into microaggression training programs intended for higher education classrooms and administrations.

Jeremy M. Wilson is a criminal justice professor at Michigan State University, where he founded and directed the Center for Anti-Counterfeiting and Product Protection and the program on Police Consolidation and Shared Services. Formerly, he was a behavioral scientist at RAND, where he developed the Center on Quality Policing and the Police Recruitment and Retention Clearinghouse. As a scholar, educator, trainer, advisor, and consultant, Dr. Wilson has collaborated with police agencies, communities, task forces, multinational corporations, professional associations, governments, and other public and private entities throughout the world. His current research focuses on police organizations and brand protection.

Jan Van den Bulck is professor of media psychology at the Department of Communication and Media, and director of the Quantitative Methods in the Social Sciences Program at the University of Michigan. He is interested in unintended effects of entertainment media and in the methodological issues involved in studying them. Much of his research deals with perceptions of crime and law enforcement, the influence of media on trust in authorities, and fear of violence. In recent years, he has also studied the relationship (and competition) between media use and sleep.

Joseph B. Walther is the Mark and Susan Bertelsen Presidential Chair in Technology and Society, a Distinguished Professor of Communication, and director of the Center for Information Technology and Society at the University of California, Santa Barbara. He is a Fulbright Scholar, a Fellow of the International Communication Association, and a Distinguished Scholar in the National Communication Association. His research focuses on the impact of interpersonal and intergroup dynamics in the attitudes and behaviors people develop via mediated interaction, in personal relationships, groups, educational settings, and inter-ethnic conflict.

Scott Wolfe is an associate professor in the School of Criminal Justice at Michigan State University. He earned his PhD in criminology and criminal justice from Arizona State University. Wolfe's research focuses on organizational justice, policing, police training, officer safety, and criminology. His work has appeared in *Justice Quarterly*, *Journal of Research in Crime and Delinquency*, and *Law and Human Behavior*.

Milton Keynes UK
Ingram Content Group UK Ltd.
UKHW030658280424
441763UK00035B/102